The Editors

Since 1991, HENRY LOUIS GATES JR. has been the W. E. B. Du Bois Professor of the Humanities and chair of the Department of Afro-American studies at Harvard University. He has been the co-editor of such collections as *Encarta Africana* and *The Norton Anthology of African American Literature*. Professor Gates edited the forty-volume *Schomburg Library of Nineteenth-Century Black Women Writers*, the thirty-volume *African American Women Writers 1910–1940*, and was the series editor for the complete works of Zora Neale Hurston. He is the author of *The Signifying Monkey*, which received the American Book Award, *Figures in Black*, *Thirteen Ways of Looking at a Black Man*, *Colored People*, a memoir, and other books. A winner of the MacArthur Prize and a staff writer for *The New Yorker*, he lives in Cambridge, Massachusetts.

TERRI HUME OLIVER is a doctoral candidate in the Department of English and American Literature and Language at Harvard University. She also serves as Graduate and Undergraduate Coordinator in the Afro-American Studies Department. The title of her dissertation is *The Ends of Childhood: An American Rhetoric of Minority*. Ms. Oliver has published the essay "Prison, Perversion, and Pimps: The White Temptress in *The Autobiography of Malcolm* X and Iceberg Slim's *Pimp*," which appears in the collection *White Women in Racialized Spaces*. She has published reference entries on Cynthia Ozick, Susan Cheever, and Robert Beck, and was a research assistant for *The Norton Anthology of African American Literature*.

A NORTON CRITICAL EDITION

W. E. B. Du Bois

THE SOULS OF BLACK FOLK

AUTHORITATIVE TEXT

CONTEXTS

CRITICISM

Edited by

HENRY LOUIS GATES JR.   TERRI HUME OLIVER

HARVARD UNIVERSITY   HARVARD UNIVERSITY

W • W • NORTON & COMPANY • *New York* • *London*

The text of this book is composed in Electra
with the display set in Bernhard Modern.
Composition by PennSet, Inc.
Manufacturing by Maple-Vail Book Group

Library of Congress Cataloging-in-Publication Data
Du Bois, W. E. B. (William Edward Burghardt), 1868–1963.
   The souls of Black folk : authoritative text, contexts, criticism
/ W.E.B. Du Bois ; edited by Henry Louis Gates, Jr., Terri Hume
Oliver.
       p.   cm. — (A Norton critical edition)
   Includes bibliographical references (p.   ).

ISBN 0-393-97393-X (pbk.)

   1. Afro-Americans.   I. Gates, Henry Louis.   II. Oliver, Terri
Hume.   III. Title.   IV. Series.
E185.6.D797   1998b
973'.0496073 — dc21   98-31634
                                                                       CIP

W. W. Norton & Company, Inc., 500 Fifth Avenue, New York, N.Y. 10110
www.wwnorton.com
W. W. Norton & Company Ltd., Castle House, 75/76 Wells Street,
London W1T 3QT

1 2 3 4 5 6 7 8 9 0

Contents

Preface

A Century of *Souls*

Few African Americans shaped the course of African American history more centrally in the twentieth century than did William Edward Burghardt Du Bois. Indeed, if one were challenged to identify a black "Person of the Century," one would be hard-pressed to identify a candidate more compelling than Du Bois. As a scholar, a journalist, a creative writer, and a political activist, no one did more to give full voice to the American Negro than did W. E. B. Du Bois, the first African American to earn a Ph.D. from Harvard.

By the end of the nineteenth century, Du Bois had already become the living symbol of the potential in Negro intellection, the embodiment of the black scholar. He was not only the first professionally trained historian of the African and African American experience, he was also one of the founding fathers of the discipline of sociology in the American academy. Scholarship, however, seems not to have been an end in itself for Du Bois, but merely one fundamental compartment in the cabinet of wonder that contained Du Bois's remarkably diverse and fecund interests. Few human beings could do so many things so well both in the academy and outside of it.

It seems to me that Du Bois will be recalled for two signal achievements, one political, the other literary. In the political arena, many consider Du Bois the father of the Civil Rights Movement. He was the shaping force and organizational genius behind the creation of both the NAACP and its most immediate predecessor, the Niagara Movement. In the NAACP, Du Bois's vision of an activist, engaged, and systematic campaign to end *de jure* segregation—articulated in a seemingly endless stream of editorials in the *Crisis* magazine, which he edited—found an institutional form that would enable millions of like-minded Americans, black and white, to consolidate their resources and mount the struggle that eventually culminated in the passage of the Civil Rights Acts of 1964 and the Voting Rights Act of 1965. While we will remember Du Bois as an *eminence grise* of the Harlem Renaissance, as the founder of the modern Pan-African movement, as the architect of *The Encyclopedia Africana*, as a staunch opponent of nuclear weapons, and an unflinching opponent of the excesses of multinational corporate capitalism, Du Bois's most lasting political achievements were his role in creating the NAACP and shaping its direction in the first few decades of its existence, and then internationalizing the plight of the American Negro by linking the struggle for black citizenship to the decolonization movement in Africa and throughout the Third World. "The problem of the Twentieth-Century," he had predicted in 1900, "is the problem of the color-line."[1] As a major theorist of the political economy of racism, on the one hand, and as a creator of one of the most important organizations dedicated to the abolition of segregation on the other, Du Bois had no peer.

If this was Du Bois's complex political achievement, his role in the history of African American literature—his second signal achievement —was no less important. While Du Bois published sixteen major books and thousands of pivotal essays, no single text has proven to be more seminal in the shaping of the black belles-lettristic tradition in the twentieth century than *The Souls of Black Folk*.

The Souls has seen no less than one hundred nineteen editions since it first appeared in 1903. Consisting of a short story and thirteen essays, many written for occasions other than this book, *The Souls* nevertheless achieved a formal force and aesthetic unity that led his contemporary James Weldon Johnson to conclude that the essays had yielded "a greater effect upon and within the Negro race in America than any other single book published in this country since *Uncle Tom's Cabin*." Johnson was referring to the book's political impact, but a similar claim can be made for its literary impact as well, starting with Johnson's own novel *The Autobiography of an Ex-Coloured Man*, published in 1912, nine years after *The Souls*.

When I wrote earlier that no writer had done more to give full voice to the American Negro than Du Bois, I had in mind two things. The first is a subtle yet grand achievement. Despite its episodic, occasional, fragmented structure, Du Bois's curious book of essays somehow managed to place in narrative form the identity of a nation-within-a-nation, to modify Homi Bhabha's useful phrase. *The Souls* gave voice to the collective, semi-conscious state of a people-in-formation, the great African American culture still nascent only thirty-eight years "up from slavery," as Booker T. Washington put it. Cultures, of course, are always dynamic, always in process. But this was especially true of a young, semi-free African American culture at the turn-of-the-century, when the sons and daughters of slaves and former slaves were struggling to shape and define a collective identity in shared social practices at once as old as the black presence in North America, yet as fragile and vulnerable

1. See n. 1, p. 5.

as their perilous citizenship status following the Civil War, Reconstruction, and Redemption.

The sublime and compelling African American culture in 1900 was vibrant yet disparate. It was a culture born within the chaos of slavery, a richly splendid body of plots and stories now desperately in search of a master narrator, just as the vast collections of melodies, harmonies, and rhythms had searched to find their master composers in what Du Bois called "the Sorrow Songs." And it was *The Souls*, with its resonant, recurring themes, tropes, and leitmotifs, that would find the metaphors for crucial aspects of the still unconscious feelings of nameless African Americans.

This became Du Bois's second magnificent artistic achievement in *The Souls*, which followed from the first: finding metaphors to name these largely unconscious, unarticulated beliefs and feelings. The capacity to turn a phrase, to summarize or represent complex concepts and social phenomena in figurative language—to run "data into metaphor," as Robert Stepto put it—was Du Bois's greatest gift as a writer. Every literary tradition is, in part, defined by shared metaphors and images that are repeated and revised from text to text. This sort of repetition and revision makes a tradition a tradition—that is, makes a disparate body of writing into a coherent chain of signifying texts, texts that "speak" to each other over time. Even from its earliest manifestations in the eighteenth century, for example, five authors of the slave narratives (between 1772 and 1815) used the trope of the talking book in their texts, indicating that they read and revised each other. The trope of the talking book yielded pride of place to metaphors of freedom and literacy, and was predominant in African American letters until the turn of the twentieth century—that is until Du Bois published *The Souls*.

Du Bois coined two metaphors for the black condition that proved to be especially redolent to subsequent African American writers, almost as soon as the book was published. One he called "double consciousness": Du Bois wrote that "One ever feels his two-ness,—an American, a Negro; two souls, two thoughts, two unreconciled strivings; two warring ideals in one dark body, whose dogged strength alone keeps it from being torn asunder."[2] Scholars suggest that Du Bois first encountered the concept of double consciousness through his Harvard professor, William James; the term itself—most probably coined by Emerson—appeared in the title of two works in psychology in 1895 and 1896. Du Bois drew upon this concept from psychology to define the peculiarly marginal status of the African American citizen. The second was his metaphor of an enclosed black world behind a "veil": Du Bois describes

2. W. E. B. Du Bois, *The Souls of Black Folk* (New York: W. W. Norton, 1999), 11.

his childhood initiat... 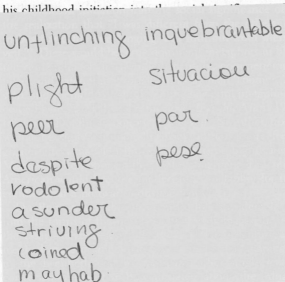 his blackness as
...or like, mayhap, ...world by a vast ...ck literature for ; with Johnson's ...Zora Neale Hur- ...of "invisibility," ...52), was a direct ...es of blackness ...quently or with ...veiled cultures. ...y of the African ...e entire human

...naginative gifts ...sfully as he did ...o that arguably ...of the tradition ...Moreover, the ..ity" of African Americans—their double-consciousness—became a signal contribution to the notion of the fragmentation of the self, a defining condition of modernism. The once audacious idea that all identities are multiple is now a commonplace. Once a problem to be solved, the multiplicities of identities is now understood to be a basic aspect of human existence. And *The Souls of Black Folk* not only played a major part in initiating this discourse, but its resonant use of metaphor enabled it to transcend even the urgent occasions for which these essays were written. While articulating so poignantly the fragmented social and psychological condition of the Negro-American citizen at the turn-of-the-century, Du Bois simultaneously spoke prophetically about a fundamental aspect of modernity itself. Delving into the particular to speak to the universal is what, of course, a classic does. Through his curiously powerful text, the particularity of the Negro became a metaphor, a universal aspect of the human condition. And because of this, *The Souls of Black Folk* continues to speak so compellingly to a new generation of readers today.

Henry Louis Gates Jr.
Cambridge, Massachusetts

3. Ibid., 10.

Introduction

W. E. B. Du Bois, Wilberforce, Green Co., Ohio

The Passing of Douglass

20 February, 1895

Then Douglass Passed—his massive form
Still quivering at unrighted Wrong;
His soul aflame, and on his lips
A tale of prophecy and waiting Work.
Low he chanted, and his hot accents,
Full[1] in rich melodious cadence
Before God's altar. Then—O, Christ!
Not as the sickening dying flame,
That fading glows into the night,
Passed our mightiest—nay, but as the watch fire,
Waving and bending in crimson glory,
Suddenly flashes to the Mountain, and leaves
A grim and horrid blackness in the world.
            Selah.[2]
Live, warm and wondrous memory, My Douglass,
    Live, all men do love thee.
            Amen!

Rise weird and weary wheeling wave, waft
My Douglass on, o'er earth and sea—
Strength of the Strong sweep round us
            Alleluiah!
Rest, dark and tired soul, My Douglass,
    Thy God Receive thee
            Amen
            and
            Amen!

1. Manuscript damaged, word only partially legible. This elegy, along with several other versions, can be found in *The Papers of W. E. B. Du Bois*, University of Massachusetts, Amherst. Microfilm, reel 88.
2. Hebrew word of unknown meaning often marking the end of a verse in the Psalms and thought to be a term indicating a pause or rest.

On February 20, 1895, only hours after delivering a rousing speech at a rally for women's rights, Frederick Douglass died of a heart attack in Washington, D.C. He had long been celebrated internationally as the most prominent African American, establishing his reputation through both his electrifying speaking presence and his three widely read autobiographies. Although W. E. B. Du Bois had never met this outstanding man, Douglass's role as "the greatest of American Negro leaders" (according to Du Bois) haunted him. Douglass was the model to be emulated, a mighty public intellectual and a courageous foe of both racism and accommodation to it. After hearing about Douglass's death, Du Bois, a new Wilberforce University[3] professor of Classics, was so grief stricken that he wrote a series of elegies to Douglass. Over and over, he struggled with the poems' tone, searching to capture the image of death and the legacy of tradition. Du Bois possessed no great skill in verse; as he admitted in 1930, "My poetry has been simply a part of my urge to express myself, and has been written quite unconscious of any accepted form."[4] In 1895 the heir apparent to Douglass's mantle of leadership was Booker T. Washington, whose policies of industrial education and accommodationism were becoming increasingly problematic to Du Bois. Spurred on by the loss of Douglass, Du Bois turned his prodigious energies to challenging Washington's influence over the ideological direction of the struggle for Negro rights. The epigraph above, written in a fair hand and signed by Du Bois, indicates Du Bois's outrage at the "unrighted Wrong" of racism in America. And, through his publication of The Souls of Black Folk, Du Bois achieves his intention to continue Douglass's "tale of prophecy and waiting Work."

When The Souls of Black Folk appeared on April 18, 1903, Du Bois had already established himself "as one of the two or three best-known Afro-Americans in the nation."[5] He had, by dint of careful preparation and enormous talent, managed to rise from the obscurity of the Massachusetts Berkshires to a position of educational and political leadership. Indeed, Du Bois's emergence as a dominant political figure in the Afro-American community is without parallel in the history of black leadership: his vehicle to prominence had been the *written* word. Even his contemporaries realized how curious this route to power was. As the Afro-American educator William H. Ferris, a Yale graduate, put the matter in The African Abroad in 1913:

> Du Bois is one of the few men in history who was hurled on the throne of leadership by the dynamic force of the written word. He is one of the few writers who leaped to the front as a leader and

3. Institution administered by the African Methodist Episcopal Church in Xenia, Ohio.
4. Letter to John Francis McDermott, June 3, 1930.
5. Introduction to W. E. B. Du Bois, *The Souls of Black Folk*, ed. Herbert Aptheker (Millwood, NY: Kraus-Thomson, 1973), 7.

became the head of a popular movement through impressing his personality upon men by means of a book.[6]

What's more, Ferris argues, Du Bois's ascendancy was inadvertent: "He had no aspiration of becoming a race leader when he wrote his 'Souls of Black Folk.' But that book had launched him upon a brilliant career."[7] Du Bois's intertwined literary and political careers, however, contradict this view of an accidental ascendancy to a leadership role within the African American community, as does his concern to pay tribute to his hero and conscious antecedent, Frederick Douglass.

The Origins of the Race Man

In order to understand what Manning Marable has called "a great ambition,"[8] it is necessary to review the atypical nature of Du Bois's origins. Born on February 23, 1868 in Great Barrington, Massachusetts, Du Bois was the only child of Mary Burghardt Du Bois and Alfred Du Bois. At the time of his birth, his mother was thirty-six years old and the youngest of ten children in a household headed by Othello Burghardt, owner of a small farm. Despite her parents disapproval, Mary, who worked as a domestic servant, married the unemployed but charming Alfred. Du Bois admits that he knew "very little of my father" and describes him in glowing romantic terms:

> He was small and beautiful of face and feature, just tinted with the sun, and his wavy hair chiefly revealing his kinship to Africa. In nature, I think, he was a dreamer—romantic, indolent, kind, unreliable. He had in him the making of a poet, an adventurer, or a Beloved Vagabond, according to the life that closed round him; and that life gave him all too little.[9]

But within a year of his son's birth, Alfred Du Bois left town and never returned. Although he was adored by his mother and surrounded by the hearty Burghardt men, the young Will, nevertheless, felt keenly the absence of a father figure who might have understood his great intellectual curiosity and his desire for refinement. Later, while a Harvard graduate student, Du Bois commented that he possessed "no line of distinguished ancestors—indeed I have often been in a quandary as to how those revered ones spent their time."[1]

Nellie McKay argues that Du Bois was primarily influenced by the women in his family; supporting her argument she quotes from *Dark-*

6. William H. Ferris, "The Souls of Black Folk: The Book in Its Era," in *Critical Essays on W. E. B. Du Bois*, ed. William L. Andrews (Boston: G. K. Hall, 1985), 128.
7. Ibid.
8. Manning Marable, *W. E. B. Du Bois: Black Radical Democrat* (Boston: Twayne Publishing, 1986), 1.
9. W. E. B. Du Bois, *The Autobiography of W. E. B. Du Bois*, ed. Herbert Aptheker (New York: International Publishers, 1968), 71.
1. Marable, 7.

water (1920) in which Du Bois states, "All the way back in these dim distances it is the mothers and mothers of mothers who seem to count, while fathers are shadowy memories."[2] Yet on his first and only visit to his paternal grandfather, Alexander Du Bois, the young W. E. B. Du Bois, fifteen years old at the time, was impressed by his grandfather's "masterful" way with women, his "breeding, "manners," and his "stilted" poetry.[3] In contrast to the practical, blue-collar Burghardts, Alexander seemed to inhabit a world of culture and controlled artistic sensibility. In fact, as McKay points out, Du Bois wanted to be buried at the Grove Street Cemetery in New Haven, the graveyard in which his grandfather was interred.[4] Although his desire to be united in death with his cultivated grandfather, who was mostly a stranger to him, may seem affecting if sentimental, it serves to illustrate Du Bois's lifelong fascination with great men. When exposed to continental literature, Du Bois's favorite author was Goethe; he recommended to Fisk undergraduates that they read Goethe in German in order to understand the full effect of his poetry.[5] Perhaps it is not surprising that Du Bois was infected by the Romantic infatuation with exceptional men who struggle against society.

Despite his lack of a male relative who shared his affinities, the young Du Bois claims to have enjoyed a happy early childhood in an environment that, if not idyllic, was remarkably free of the color line. The Burghardt family (both black and white branches) represented some of the oldest citizens of Great Barrington, having arrived in the early eighteenth century. The town's black population was relatively small; Will attended a predominantly white school and usually worshipped in the white Congregational church. Speaking of his various relatives' stories of racism in other towns, Du Bois writes:

> In this way I must have gotten indirectly a pretty clear outline of color bars which I myself did not experience. Moreover, I couldn't rationalize my own case, because I found it easy to excel most of my classmates in studies, if not in games. The secret of life and the loosing of the color bar, then, lay in excellence, in accomplishment. If others of my family, of my colored kin, had stayed in school * * * they could have risen to equal whites. On this my mother quietly insisted. There was no real discrimination on account of color—it was all a matter of ability and hard work.[6]

Du Bois graduated in 1884 with high honors, the first black graduate of his high school. He immediately went to work in order to save money

2. Nellie McKay, "W. E. B. Du Bois: The Black Woman in His Writings—Selected Fictional and Autobiographical Portraits," in *Critical Essays on W. E. B. Du Bois,* 235.
3. McKay, 235.
4. Ibid.
5. *Fisk Herald,* September 1893, pp. 5–7. The original letter was dated May 1893 and sent from the University of Berlin.
6. Du Bois, *The Autobiography,* 75.

for college. In March of 1885, Mary Sylvina Du Bois died unexpectedly, leaving her son freed of family responsibilities but totally impoverished. Into the breach stepped the white community, whose leaders urged various Congregational churches, including Du Bois's own, to donate scholarship funds. Although Du Bois had decided to attend Harvard, they deemed that Fisk University in Nashville, Tennessee, one of the great Negro academic institutions,[7] was the appropriate setting for a promising young Negro man. Unlike the rest of his family Du Bois offered no resistance to the plan, deciding to take advantage of seeing the South for the first time, and planning to attend Harvard after graduation.[8] He explained his own passivity in *Darkwater*:

> Harvard was the goal of my dreams, but my white friends hesitated and my black friends were silent. Harvard was a mighty conjureword in that hill town, and even the mill owners' sons had aimed lower.

In addition, Du Bois felt the lure of the South, the home to most black people: "I was going into the South; the South of slavery, rebellion and black folk; above all, I was going to meet colored people of my own age and education, of my own ambition."[9]

Leaving the protected environs of Great Barrington in 1885, Du Bois descended into a white South still resentful over its defeat in the Civil War and bitter over what it considered to be the excesses of Reconstruction. Although Du Bois repeated in his three autobiographies a description of the racial insult he received as a schoolboy when a white girl refused his greeting card,[1] it wasn't until Nashville that he began to understand fully the daily humiliation of being black in America:

> No one but a Negro going into the South without previous experience of color caste can have any conception of its barbarism * * * On a Nashville street, 71 years ago, I quite accidentally jostled a white woman as I passed. She was not hurt in the least * * * I raised my hat and begged her pardon. The woman was furious; why I never knew; somehow, I cannot say how, I had transgressed the interracial mores of the South * * * I only sensed scorn and hate; the kind of despising which a dog might incur.[2]

---

7. Fisk University was initially founded in 1866 as the Fisk Free Colored School in south Nashville. The founders were members of the American Missionary Association, later aided by the Freedmen's Bureau. In August 1867, the principal, John Ogden, renamed the school Fisk University.
8. Marable, 8.
9. Du Bois, W. E. B., *Darkwater*, in *The Oxford W. E. B. Du Bois Reader*, ed. Eric J. Sundquist (New York: Oxford University Press, 1996), 490.
1. In *Souls of Black Folk* (1903), *Dusk of Dawn* (1940), and *The Autobiography* (1968).
2. Du Bois, *The Autobiography*, 121.

The white population of Nashville continued to live down to Du Bois's low expectations, even after he had moved from the area. In an anonymous review of *The Souls of Black Folk*, the *Nashville American* opined, "This book is indeed dangerous for the negro [sic] to read, for it will only excite discontent and race hatred and fill his imagination with things that do not exist, or things that should not bear upon his mind." Even though the full imposition of Jim Crow laws did not take effect during his Fisk years, Du Bois was well aware of the South's true character:

> Murder, killing, and maiming Negroes, raping Negro women—in the 80's and in the southern South, this was not even news; it got no publicity, it caused no arrest; and punishment for such transgression was so unusual that the fact was telegraphed North.[3]

Clearly, his experiences in the South shaped Du Bois's urge to be involved in the politics of race and racism at the turn of the century. But at the same time he was thrilled to be in a milieu where his color and ambition were the rule not the exception. Du Bois described his classmates as "people of my own color or rather of such various and extraordinary colors, which I had only glimpsed before."[4] Furthermore, they were his own age, "young men so self-assured and who gave themselves such airs, and colored men at that." It was at Fisk, too, that he began his lifelong appreciation of young women of color—"for the first time I saw beautiful girls."[5] Du Bois records his response to these women in the Fisk dining hall: "I promptly lost my appetite, but I was deliriously happy!"[6]

While at Fisk, Du Bois spent several summers teaching at a small school roughly fifty miles outside of Nashville. The first summer he taught in rural Tennessee was only the second time since Reconstruction that public instruction was offered during the summer to these black citizens. For the first time in his life, Du Bois witnessed the overwhelming poverty and lack of opportunities facing the majority of black folk. Throughout *The Souls of Black Folk* the impact of these days in the South is as evident as Du Bois's deep outrage.

To prepare himself as a force for the race and against institutional racism, Du Bois, before graduating from Fisk in 1888, finally gained admittance and a scholarship to Harvard University. Curiously, he attributes his success at breaching the walls of Harvard to the university's desire for diversity. Speaking as a recipient of Harvard's (very limited) commitment to regional and cultural diversity, Du Bois states, "A determined effort was made in 1884 and later to make Harvard a more

---

3. Du Bois, *The Autobiography*, 122.
4. Ibid., 107.
5. Ibid.
6. Ibid.

national institution * * * In my favor were my New England elementary education, and the fact that I was studying in the South and that I was colored."[7]

Harvard accepted Du Bois as a junior undergraduate, a common practice at the time for students coming from less prestigious institutions. As Du Bois later explained, he was a Harvard man in name only: he used the university for its educational resources but his social life was essentially segregated. "I never felt myself a Harvard man as I'd felt myself a Fisk man,"[8] he wrote. Nevertheless, he excelled at Harvard, finding mentors such as William James and George Santayana (philosophy), Frank Taussig (economics) and Albert Bushnell Hart (history). Du Bois's first love was philosophy, but because he felt employment opportunities to be limited for black philosophers (and perhaps because he received a "B" from Santayana),[9] he decided on graduate work in history. Study in Europe had long been Du Bois's dream; so, in October 1892, having earned the M. A. in history at Harvard the year before, he pursued further graduate work at Friedrich Wilhelm University in Berlin, studying sociology and economics with Gustav Schmoller and Adolph Wagner, both leading exponents of planned economies. Du Bois also enrolled in a course entitled "Politics" taught by Heinrich von Treistschke, a professor Du Bois described as a "fire-eating Pan-German."[1]

Berlin was all that he had hoped for academically; Du Bois was even able to hear lectures by the great sociologist Max Weber (who would later participate in Du Bois's annual conference at Atlanta University in 1904). Du Bois wrote a thesis on agricultural economics in the South and ardently desired to pursue a Ph.D. in Berlin. Unable to do so because of residency requirements that he could not satisfy because of a lack of funds, Du Bois returned to the United States. By leaving Europe, he abandoned a student life of cultured poverty that he had greatly enjoyed. Furthermore, for the first time since early childhood, he had been able to live without constant reference to racial questions. But Du Bois's mind was never far from the issues of race. On his twenty-fifth birthday in Berlin, he wrote about his great desire to "work for the rise of the Negro people, taking for granted that their best development means the best development for the world." He then sketched out his ambitions—"to make a name in science, to make a name in literature

---

7. Du Bois, *The Autobiography*, 125.
8. "W. E. B. Du Bois—a Recorded Autobiography" (1961), Folkways Records.
9. David Levering Lewis charts Du Bois's academic progress in *W. E. B. Du Bois: Biography of a Race* (New York: Henry Holt, 1993). Lewis reports that Du Bois earned an A– in his first philosophy class with William James. In his senior year he made a B+ in James's Logic and Psychology course and a B in Santayana's Earlier French Philosophy. In pre-grade inflation Harvard, these marks were very impressive, if not outstanding. However, in his history classes, Du Bois performed brilliantly, earning an A+ from the demanding Albert Hart in Constitutional and Political History of the United States.
1. W. E. B. Du Bois, *Dusk of Dawn* (New York: Harcourt, Brace, and Co., 1940), 47.

and thus to raise my race."[2] These statements argue strongly against Ferris's view that Du Bois's ascendancy was unintentional.

His arrival in America signaled the beginning of a phenomenal career. He secured a position teaching classics at Wilberforce University in Xenia, Ohio. A year later, in 1895, he became the first person of African descent to receive a Ph.D. from Harvard. Du Bois's next eight years were exceptionally productive. In 1896 he published his doctoral dissertation, *The Suppression of the African Slave-Trade to the United States of America, 1638–1870,* as volume one of the Harvard Historical Monograph Series. Finding time for romance in Ohio, he married a student, Nina Gomer, on May 12, 1896. That autumn he left Wilberforce (which he had always disliked because of its excessive religious fervor) to undertake a sociological study of the Negro population in Philadelphia. One year later, he joined Alexander Crummell and other black scholars in founding the American Negro Academy, the first black institute of arts and letters in the world.

During the fall of 1897 Du Bois commenced a professorship of economics and history at Atlanta University, where he also became director of the "Atlanta Conferences," annual conventions that generated precise scientific research regarding the actual living conditions of Negroes in America, about whom surprisingly little sound scientific data had ever been gathered. Du Bois edited the results of these conferences and published them in a sixteen-volume monograph series between 1898 and 1914. His intention was to collect, collate, and analyze socioeconomic data about every conceivable facet of being black in America. This project was a bold, imaginative venture, one motivated by Du Bois's belief that ignorance, rather than xenophobia or economic relationships, was the primary cause of racism. Much later Du Bois would abandon this view, deciding that material relationships—economic scarcity—masked themselves in the guise of race relationships.

In 1889 the results of his research at the University of Pennsylvania were published as *The Philadelphia Negro.* Between 1897 and 1903 Du Bois, starting with an essay printed in the *Atlantic Monthly,* became one of the most widely published authors in the United States. His essays appeared in prominent publications such as *The Independent, The Nation, The Southern Workman, Harper's Weekly, The World's Work, The Outlook, The Missionary Review, The Literary Digest, Annals of the American Academy of Political and Social Sciences,* and *The Dial.* Publication in *The Dial,* a journal owned by the McClurg Company and edited by W. R. Browne and Francis Fisher Browne, proved fortuitous: Francis Fisher Browne would later serve as the editor of *The Souls of Black Folk.* By 1903, when *The Souls of Black Folk* appeared, the thirty-five-year-old Du Bois could not only count himself among

2. W. E. B. Du Bois, *Against Racism: Unpublished Essays, Papers, Addresses, 1887–1961,* ed. Herbert Aptheker (Amherst: University of Massachusetts Press, 1985), 29.

the most widely read, most broadly traveled, and most impeccably educated human beings in the world, he had also become the most widely
published black essayist in the history of African Americans. More than
any other figure at the turn of the century, Du Bois was the public
written "voice" of the Negro American intellectual, just as his model,
Frederick Douglass, had been the Negro's splendid and troubling voice
during the nineteenth century.

The Portrait of the Author as a Young Writer

As Shamoon Zamir has noted, the complex structure of *The Souls
of Black Folk* incorporates "historical, sociological, political, and cultural commentaries with autobiographical reflections and dramatizations" into a form that Zamir calls a *Bildungsbiographie*."[3] Without
engaging Zamir's central argument, his use of this term is instructive
because it suggests the central role of authorship in Du Bois's strategy
for winning prominence for himself and his political views. Writing
yourself into being as an artist is a predictable stage of development for
a young author, but the centrality of literacy to a claim of humanity is
peculiarly African American. At least since Phillis Wheatley, writers of
African descent have tried to prove, through literature, their status as
humans *qua* humans in a world that would deny them this status.
Certainly, this issue continued to be of importance during Du Bois's
day. John Spencer Bassett, reviewing *Souls*, favorably compared the
book to the racist *The Negro A Beast, or In the Image of God* and asked
the rhetorical question, "* * * a more stupid book it is impossible to
conceive; yet it is worth while to place it and its author side by side
with 'The Souls of Black Folk' and its author. Can a 'beast' write a
book like the latter?"[4]

Within these larger issues, Du Bois also was driven to write by the
urgency that he felt during the first few years after Douglass's death,
years in which Booker T. Washington seemingly had secured the mantle of leadership from Frederick Douglass. Du Bois's *Souls* arises from
the political philosophy that he had been preparing since the passing
of his only true antecedent as America's dominant black intellectual.
The figure of Douglass persisted in Du Bois's imagination, dogging his
steps as the model to be emulated, as a counter force to Booker T.
Washington's theories of laissez-faire economics and laissez-faire political accommodation.

While Frederick Douglass had first impressed the American public
with his oratory, later securing his place as a man of letters with various
versions of his autobiography, his essays, and his journalism, Du Bois's

3. Shamoon Zamir, " 'The Sorrow Songs' / 'Song of Myself': Du Bois, the Crisis of Leadership,
and Prophetic Imagination," *The Black Columbiad*, ed. Werner Sollors and Maria Diedrich
(Cambridge, MA: Harvard University Press, 1994), 145.
4. John Spencer Bassett, "Two Negro Leaders," *South Atlantic Quarterly* II (July 1903): 267–
72.

early impact was purely that of the written word. Although he had won second prize in the Boylston Competition in Oratory at Harvard, Du Bois lacked Douglass's personal magnetism. In fact, an anonymous reviewer in *The Nation* seemed amazed at the emotional power of *The Souls of Black Folk*, since he found Du Bois to be such a cold, intellectual speaker. Once dedicated to his role as writer, Du Bois certainly fulfilled it handsomely. According to Aptheker's definitive annotated bibliography of Du Bois's published works, he produced some 1,975 books, essay, and poems throughout his celebrated career.

One would assume, given this prodigious output, that Du Bois was a born writer. In this, as in most other things, Du Bois blended his natural genius with a great deal of hard work and preparation. As a teenager, Du Bois began to write for T. Thomas Fortune's New York *Globe*. Between April 10, 1883 and May 16, 1885 he published a total of twenty-four articles in this newspaper and its successor, *The Freeman*. David Levering Lewis, Du Bois's biographer, points out that Fortune was "one of the first African-American men outside his own family whom Willie Du Bois admired."[5] Du Bois may have considered the newspaperman a role model for a future career. In any event, his pieces, as well as his reporting on the African American community, are often peppered with uplifting commentary, such as his proposal that a literary society be formed. However, concerning this plan, he regretfully notes, "there was not much interest manifested."[6] At the Great Barrington High School, Du Bois co-edited the short-lived newspaper, *The Howler*. Encouraged by his early success as a volunteer correspondent to *The Globe* and *New York Age*, Du Bois also began writing for the *Springfield Republican*, "the most influential newspaper outside New York City and the largest newspaper in western Massachusetts."[7] As a special correspondent, Du Bois probably anonymously wrote three or four lost articles.[8] While at Fisk, he edited *The Fisk Herald*, a fact that he notes in his Harvard application letter of October 29, 1887.

At Harvard, Du Bois suspended his publishing career focusing instead on a compulsory course, English C, "Forensics." Du Bois would recall that this almost became his "Waterloo at Harvard"—he received the first failing grade of his life under the merciless judgment of George Kittredge, the newly arrived English medieval and Shakespeare scholar.[9] Eventually, Du Bois managed a "C" in English C, not an uncommon grade for Harvard's gentlemen scholars, but hardly encouraging to an aspiring author. Explaining his problems with writing at Harvard, Du Bois remembered that, "I was at the point in my intellectual development when the content rather than the form of my writ-

5. Lewis, *Biography of a Race* 38–39.
6. Ibid., 40.
7. Ibid., 47.
8. Ibid.
9. Ibid., 90.

ing was to me of prime importance . . . I knew the Negro problem and this was more important to me than literary form."[1] Ever the avid student, Du Bois knew what it took to succeed:

> It was the first time in my scholastic career that I had encountered such a failure. I was aghast, but I was not a fool. I did not doubt but what my instructors were fair in judging my English technically even if they did not understand the Negro problem.[2]

In his senior English, another year-long course, Du Bois's performance was improved, and he earned a "B." Although he was not required to take another composition course, Du Bois, with characteristic tenacity, took Barrett Wendell's English 12 as a first-year graduate student.[3] In his *Autobiography*, Du Bois remembers a theme he wrote for Professor Wendell, whom he calls "the great pundit of Harvard English."[4]

> Spurred by my circumstances, I have always been given to systematically planning my future * * * I determined while in high school to go to college—partly because other men did, partly because I foresaw that such discipline would best fit me for life * * * I believe, foolishly perhaps, but sincerely, that I have something to say to the world, and I have taken English 12 in order to say it well.[5]

Although Du Bois's essay predicts his later success in blending autobiographical detail with political fervor, he also produced less elegant and restrained prose for Barrett Wendell. Manning Marable reports on one such essay, "The American Girl," in which Du Bois's makes a bitter and brutal attack on white womanhood:

> When I wish to meet the American Hog in its native simplicity; when I wish to realize the world-pervading presence of the Fool; when I wish to be reminded that whatever rights some may have I have none * * * I seek the company of the American girl.[6]

Describing the American girl physically, Du Bois comments, "her face * * * is apt to be more shrewd than intelligent, arrogant than dignified, silly than pleasant."[7] His cure for "this eye-sore" is that the white woman should "emancipate herself from the rule of the Ribbon," become educated, and "lastly, go to work."[8] Wendell, as Charlene Avallone points out, was a social Darwinist who believed that opposition to abolitionists showed a "thoughtful" concern for the safety of white

1. Du Bois, *The Autobiography*, 144.
2. Du Bois, *The Autobiography*, 144
3. Lewis, *Biography of a Race*, 90.
4. Du Bois, *The Autobiography*, 144.
5. Ibid., 145.
6. Marable, 15.
7. Ibid.
8. Ibid., 16.

women exposed to the "lust of brutal savages."[9] Still, his objections to
Du Bois's excesses on this occasion seem justified. Barrett wrote, "Such
truculence as yours is thoroughly injudicious. Nothing could more certainly induce an average reader to disagree."[1]

At Harvard, Du Bois allows his anger at racism to show for the first
time in his writing. Perhaps the anger is linked to his feeling of rejection
by his beloved university; regarding his Harvard years, Du Bois pro-
nounces, "I was in Harvard, but not of it."[2] Because he had a good
voice and had been a member of Fisk University's Mozart Choir, Du
Bois auditioned for the Glee Club. Writing of this experience, Du Bois
recalls, "I ought to have known that Harvard could not afford to have
a Negro on its Glee Club traveling about the country. Quite naturally
I was rejected."[3] Furthermore, in his personal papers, Du Bois began
to attack religion for its ties to racism, and he singled out the "high
Episcopal Nicene creed" as a "rationale for racism."[4]

Despite feeding Du Bois's fury at exclusion, Harvard and its composition courses taught him to transform this rage into the well-
polished, nineteenth-century prose style that characterizes *The Souls of
Black Folk*. One of his rare moments of rage comes when he is composing his elegies to Douglass in 1895. As part of a dirge descrying
Douglass's absence, Du Bois pens the following stanza:

> I hate them—O!
> I hate them well
> I hate them, Christ!
> As I hate Hell!
> If I were God
> I'd sound the knell
> Tomorrow[5]

Never one to discard good material, Du Bois uses this stanza in a poem
published in *The Horizon* in November 1907, "The Burden of Black
Women," later retitled "The Riddle of the Sphinx" and reprinted in
Darkwater (1920). Although Du Bois utilizes the stanza above to aid
in his impassioned protest against the "White World's vermin and filth,"
especially in its vicious abuse of black women, the poem also calls for
a "Black Christ" to be born, again emphasizing Du Bois's fascination
with prophetic leadership.

9. Charlene Avallone, "What American Renaissance? The Gendered Genealogy of a Critical
   Discourse," *The Publications of the Modern Language Association of America* (October 1997):
   1111.
1. Marable, 16.
2. Du Bois, *The Autobiography*, 130.
3. Ibid., 134–35.
4. Marable, 16.
5. *Du Bois Papers*, University of Massachusetts, Amherst. Microfilm, reel 88.

The Mantle of the Great Man

In 1895, Du Bois, at the age of only twenty-seven, was well on his way to achieving the first goal he had set for himself on his twenty-fifth birthday: he had already begun to make his name in the fledgling field of sociology. His other two ambitions, "to make a name in literature and thus to raise my race," were inextricably linked to his inevitable rise in the ranks of Negro leadership, especially in the face of Booker T. Washington's seemingly indomitable position. Kelly Miller, the distinguished professor of sociology at Howard, questioned who Douglass's true heir would be:

> He [Douglass] did not aspire to be the master mechanic of the colored race. The greatest things of this world are not made with hands, but reside in truth and righteousness and love. Douglass was the moral leader and spiritual prophet of his race. Unless all the signs of the times are misleading, the time approaches, and is even now at hand, which demands a moral renaissance. Then, O for a Douglass, to arouse the conscience of the white race, to awaken the almost incomprehensible lethargy of his own people, and to call down the righteous wrath of Heaven upon injustice and wrong.[6]

For Du Bois, the idea that Booker T. Washington would inherit Douglass's mantle of leadership was intolerable.

Throughout his education, Du Bois had celebrated "great men," individual leaders, particularly leaders of "nations." Upon his graduation from high school, he had delivered an oration on the abolitionist, Wendell Phillips. At Fisk University he chose Bismark because, "he had made a nation out of a mass of bickering peoples."[7] As one of six graduating seniors chosen to speak at the Harvard Commencement ceremony in June 1890, Du Bois chose the improbable subject of Jefferson Davis in order to face "Harvard and the nation with a discussion of slavery."[8] For Du Bois, especially at this time, the idea of race and nationhood were conjoined, as is evident in his March 5, 1897 address to the American Negro Academy entitled "The Conservation of Races." In this speech, perhaps with Washington's ascendancy in mind, Du Bois warns against the abuse of leadership: "Individualism coupled with the rule of might" advances "a part of the world at the expense of the whole."[9] He would return to this theme in his seminal essay, "The Talented Tenth," published in 1903, the same year as *Souls*.

In the face of Washington's dominance, Du Bois turned to the ex-

---

6. Kelly Miller, "Frederick Douglass," in *Radicals and Conservatives*, ed. Philip Rieff (New York: Schocken Books, 1968), 234.
7. Du Bois, *The Autobiography*, 126.
8. Ibid., 146.
9. Ibid.

ample of Frederick Douglass to chart his own line of descent. At a Wilberforce memorial service for Douglass soon after his death, Du Bois delivered the main address. Unfortunately, the speech does not survive. However, the three versions of *The Passing of Douglass*, Du Bois's elegies to the spirit of Douglass, can be studied in his collected papers. The poem reprinted on the first page of this preface was obviously Du Bois's favorite; it is the only version that is signed. Within a longer, less polished elegy, Du Bois's poetic attempt to honor Douglass's legacy fills some twenty stanzas. The first and the sixth stanzas of the longer poem fervently proclaim Du Bois's reverence for Douglass's heroism:

> Then hath passed a Mighty Form
> A man majestic and a hero soul.
> He is the bronzen warrior, scarred
> and hot with blood and dust of strife

*　*　*

> Receive dark spirit this mine offering
> For thee I loved and wildly worshipped
> Blood of my blood and hero of my race
> More than all the pale cold world beside.

In this poem, Du Bois twice proclaims his status as neophyte: "New is my voice." Yet he promises Douglass that "I will, that at thy name/All earth shall bow and darken."

A familial connection existed between Douglass and Du Bois. Despite Du Bois's contention that he possessed "no line of distinguished ancestors," Alexander Du Bois, his paternal grandfather, was an activist in his own right, having helped in 1842 to form St. Luke's, a black Episcopal church, after Trinity Parish made African Americans feel unwelcome. Later, Alexander Du Bois became involved in the affairs of Frederick Douglass when he became director, on the eve of the Civil War, of the Haytian Bureau of Emigration in Boston. Frederick Douglass, in despair over the existence of the Confederate States of America, considered emigrating to Haiti with many of St. Luke's parishioners. After the news of Fort Sumter on April 12, 1861, Frederick Douglass withdrew from the proposed exodus, but Alexander Du Bois, despite reservations, set sail and reached Port-au-Prince on June 3. His initial impressions were unfavorable: "Jackasses, Negroes, mud, water, soldiers, universal filth." Not one to waste time, Alexander Du Bois left Haiti just five days later, on June 8, 1861.[1] Although it is impossible to know exactly when Du Bois discovered his grandfather's interesting history, he was bequeathed Alexander Du Bois's diaries following his death in late 1887, and Du Bois had deciphered their cryptic notations by the

---

1. Lewis, *Biography of a Race*, 45–46.

time he reached his twenty-first birthday.[2] Du Bois's willed relationship to Frederick Douglass was both ideological and familial.

The urgency that impelled Du Bois to publish at such an astonishing rate between 1895 and 1903 was undoubtedly fueled in 1901 when Booker T. Washington published *Up From Slavery: An Autobiography*. Not only had Washington launched Tuskegee into national prominence and won support of both northern and southern whites, he was now usurping Douglass's place as autobiographer and representative black man. Du Bois titled his review of *Up From Slavery* "The Evolution of Negro Leadership"[3] and analyzed the methods by which Washington, "in the eyes of the nation typifies at present more nearly than all others the work and worth of his nine million fellows."

First, Du Bois explains his own concept of leadership: "History is but the record of this group leadership; and yet how infinitely changeful is its type and history * * * All this is the social student's inspiration and despair." The review continues with the assertion that the "evolution of race leaders among American Negroes" culminated with Douglass, "a national leadership—a dynasty not to be broken." According to Du Bois, beginning about 1840 "Frederick Douglass and the moral revolt against slavery dominated Negro thought and effort until after the war." Here, Du Bois considers Washington's reign as the end of Douglass's legacy, not its continuation:

> Then came the reaction. War memories and ideals rapidly passed * * * then it was that Booker Washington's leadership began. Mr. Washington came with a clear simple program, at the psychological moment; at a time when the nation was a little ashamed of having bestowed so much sentiment on Negroes and was concentrating its energies on Dollars. The industrial training of Negro youth was not an idea originating with Mr. Washington * * * he changed it from an article of belief into a whole creed; he broadened it from a by-path into a veritable way of life.

Extending his critiques, Du Bois refers to a portion of *Up From Slavery* in which Washington describes "the absurdity of a black boy studying a French grammar in the midst of weeds and dirt. One wonders how Socrates or St. Francis of Assisi would receive this." Whatever these historical figures might have thought, Du Bois's attitude is clear: "Among the Negroes, Mr. Washington is still far from a popular leader." Du Bois places himself among blacks represented by "Dunbar, Tanner, Chesnutt, Miller, and the Grimkés" who "believe in self-assertion and ambition; and they believe in the right of suffrage for blacks on the same terms with whites."

With this and other publications, especially "The Talented Tenth,"

2. Ibid., 43.
3. Published in *The Dial* 31 (July 1901): 53–55.

Du Bois threw down the gauntlet of this deep ideological division in black leadership, which persisted until Washington's death in 1915. One can imagine the annoyance that Du Bois must have felt when his essay "The Negro As He Really Is" appeared in *The World's Work*[4] in the same issue that *Up From Slavery* was listed as eighteenth on their list of Most Popular Books.[5] *The Souls of Black Folk*, despite Du Bois's contention that the essays were "fugitive pieces," was clearly designed, as Arnold Rampersad points out, to triumph over *Up From Slavery*. This challenge was met in the Bookerite[6] press with silence, but the struggle over Douglass's legacy continued. When approached in the autumn of 1903 to write a biography for the *American Crises* series Du Bois chose Douglass. However, he received news on January 25, 1904 that Booker T. Washington had finally answered the publisher's request for a manuscript and had himself decided to write a biography of Douglass. Unable to turn down Washington, the abashed editor requested another topic from Du Bois. Even his second choice, Nat Turner, was stymied, and the publisher asked him to consider yet another alternative, the life of John Brown.

If denied the chance to write about Douglass, Du Bois could at least emulate his mentor's work in journalism. Long interested in owning a newspaper, Du Bois began printing *The Moon* on December 2, 1905. A precarious enterprise with limited readership, *The Moon* collapsed within the year. On February 16, 1961 Du Bois answered an inquiry by Paul Partington, one of his bibliographers, concerning *The Moon*:

> As to your questions, from my boyhood in Great Barrington, Massachusetts, I always had the idea of editing a magazine, and I took the name "moon" because it seemed to me that the names of the other stars had been used too often. I had no financial assistance, but supported the *Moon* out of savings from my salary of $1200 a year and income from a few lectures.[7]

When Du Bois referred to "the names of the other stars" no doubt he had in mind Douglass's newspaper, *The North Star*, which occupied a principal place in the race's journalistic constellations. It was not until the appearance of *The Crisis*, the official publication of the NAACP,

4. *The World's Work*, June 1901. Du Bois revised and expanded this essay into "Of the Black Belt" and "Of the Quest of the Golden Fleece" in *The Souls of Black Folk*.
5. As a short-lived experiment, *The World's Work*, a popular magazine roughly resembling *Life Magazine*, attempted, at least ten years before the advent of accurate best-seller lists, to quantify what people were reading. In the Book-Dealers' Report, *World's Work* relied on information from Detroit, Boston, Philadelphia, Los Angeles, San Francisco, Louisville, St. Paul, New York City, Pittsburgh, Cleveland, and St. Louis. Washington's autobiography was number eighteen on this list in June and number sixteen in July. All of the other thirty books listed in June's list were fiction except for *Up From Slavery*, indicating the profound interest in Washington's work.
6. Term used to indicate those politically allied with Booker T. Washington.
7. Paul C. Partington, *W. E. B. Du Bois: A Bibliography of His Published Writings* (Whittier, CA: Paul C. Partington Book Publisher, 1977).

that Du Bois was able to mount a significant challenge to Washington's hegemony of the press.[8] Du Bois's true advantage over Washington in the dissemination of ideas was his prodigious talent as a writer. Washington had hired writers and editors to manage his journalistic organs; Du Bois was a writer, *par excellence*.

Double-Consciousness and Tripartite Yearnings

The two most famous insights that Du Bois offers in *The Souls of Black Folk* are his accurate prediction that, for America, "the problem of the Twentieth Century is the problem of the color-line"[9] and his beautifully poignant and disturbing definition of the double-consciousness of the Negro:

> After the Egyptian and the Indian, the Greek and Roman, the Teuton and Mongolian, the Negro is a sort of seventh son, born with a veil, and gifted with second-sight in this American world, —a world which yields him no true self-consciousness, but only lets him see himself through the revelation of the other world. It is a peculiar sensation, this double-consciousness, this sense of always looking at one's self through the eyes of others, of measuring one's soul by the tape of a world that looks on in amused contempt and pity. One ever feels his two-ness,—an American, A Negro; two souls, two thoughts, two unreconciled strivings; two warring ideals in one dark body, whose dogged strength alone keeps it from being torn asunder.

Later in this Norton Critical Edition, Dickinson Bruce Jr. and Eric Sundquist consider in detail the philosophical and cultural origins of Du Bois's concept of double-consciousness. Let us here look briefly at these ideas.

In the Forethought of *Souls* Du Bois provides a metaphoric explanation for the division between the white and black world. He speaks of black life as within a veil, and he promises to step "within the Veil, raising it that you may view faintly its deeper recesses,—the meaning of its religion, the passion of its human sorrow, and the struggle of its greater souls" (5). Du Bois's veil metaphor—"and he saw himself— darkly as through a veil" (14)—is an allusion to St. Paul's famous phrase ("For now we see through a glass, darkly") in his first letter to the Corinthians[1], and Du Bois's use of it suggests, among other things, that

8. Du Bois began editing the fledgling *Crisis* in 1910. His papers contain a 1910 notice from the advertising department of the Freeman Publishing Company, touting the advantages of placing ads with *The Freeman*. Claiming to be the "OFFICIAL ORGAN" of Booker T. Washington, *The Freeman* asserted that their circulation is more than half the combined circulation of all the other Negro publications and that "the brains and culture of the Negro Race comprise our list of contributors."

9. W. E. B. Du Bois, *The Souls of Black Folk* (New York: W. W. Norton, 1999). Hereafter, citations to pages in this Norton Critical Edition will appear in the text.

1. 1 Corinthians 13.12 and Isaiah 25.7.

the African American's attempt to gain self-consciousness in a racist society will always be impaired because any reflected image coming from the gaze of white America is necessarily a distorted one, and quite probably a harmful one as well.

Werner Sollors points out that this same metaphor also functions to "separate Afro-Americans from American culture at large but also gives them a more profound vision and higher destiny."[2] Sollors discusses two allusions to the veil in the Hebrew Scriptures:

> Du Bois imaginatively adapted two biblical images of the veil as a division within the Temple [Exodus 26.33] and as the cover that the divinely inspired Moses wore when he came back from Mount Sinai and spoke to the people [Exodus 34.33–35].[3]

Thus, particularly for Du Bois, the veil offers the opportunity to see and to report to America the truth of a divided nation. Although the veil can certainly serve as a metaphor for mourning, veiled figures (particularly women in Victorian fiction) have the opportunity to pass unnoticed, to observe without being observed, and to conceal their identity. Furthermore, as one who speaks from behind the veil ("And, finally, need I add that I who speak here am bone of the bone and flesh of the flesh of them that live within the Veil?" [6]), Du Bois consciously aligns himself with Moses, drawing upon the prophetic voice. As the reader is greeted by Du Bois in the text, the author comes from behind the veil of the third person to declare both his race and his mission.

Beyond his personal ambition and his desire to challenge Washington, Du Bois's self-fashioning as the prophet of double-consciousness derives from a profound outrage at the treatment of African Americans. Du Bois was saddened and shocked by the reality of life in the Black Belt during his Fisk years, but conditions worsened in the 1890s, the "nadir" of black life, as historian Rayford W. Logan aptly put it. The ascendancy of the Ku Klux Klan, the increase in lynchings, and anti-black rioting were effectively sanctioned by the 1896 Supreme Court decision of *Plessy v. Fergeson* in which Jim Crow segregation based upon "race" became the law of the land. *Plessy v. Ferguson* was one of Du Bois's dark, silent second texts for *Souls*.

To combat *Plessy*, Du Bois employed a subtle and complex rhetorical strategy, both metaphorical and, at times, lyrical. The doubling of characters that Du Bois draws upon in "Of the Coming of John" illustrates the obsession of turn-of-the-century America with issues of race, "personality," and the tension between genetics and environment. In this short story, the only fiction within *Souls*, there is a white John and a

2. Werner Sollors, *Beyond Ethnicity: Consent and Descent in American Culture* (New York: Oxford University Press, 1986), 49.
3. Ibid.

black John, the fate of each determined by race and proximity to each other. Both are educated; both spend time in the North. But in the bloody soil of the South, the white John, attempting to take liberties with a young black girl, is murdered by the good (black) John. Perhaps predictably, the story ends with the black John waiting for the white mob to lynch him. Both of their houses are cursed; neither black nor white survives.

Tales of doubling, with the added interest of the racial divide, became a popular subject for both white and black authors by the end of the nineteenth century. As Eric Sundquist has written, *Pudd'nhead Wilson* (1894), a tale of doublings, switched babies, and passings, "embodies the erosion of promised racial equality."[4] Sundquist sees *Pudd'nhead Wilson* as the dark textual doppelgänger to the more positive *Adventures of Huckleberry Finn* (1885):

> * * * Pudd'nhead Wilson must be counted a dark double of *The Adventures of Huckleberry Finn*, Twain's nightmare measurement of both the failed vision of the masterwork and the further and seemingly irredeemable decline in the 1890s, in the prospect for African American civil rights. Judged by its capacity to represent the perversions of justice and the nearly hallucinatory structures of pseudoscientific theory that coursed through nineteenth-century intellectual, political, and legal debate about race * * * its apparently grave artistic flaws [are] the true sign of wisdom.[5]

In the African American literary tradition, doubling expresses the same concerns that Twain had, but, naturally, the literature is more passionate in its outrage. For example, Charles Chesnutt, the black fiction writer known for his humorous sketches of black southern life in works such as *The Conjure Woman* (1899), changed his style of writing from humorous to didactic in the aftermath of the 1898 Wilmington, North Carolina, riots. In *The Marrow of the Tradition* (1901), the first of his serious novels, he presents a fictional rendition of the riot. The story involves two doublings, nearly identical white and black half-sisters and their two infant sons. The mulatto child is shot in the riots the same night that his father, a heroic young physician, performs a delicate operation and saves the white child of the racist white sister. As in "Of the Coming of John," neither education nor community status can save the black son in the South.

This central theme of mourning associated with the veil is also embedded in Du Bois's "Of the Passing of the First Born." Although Burghardt Du Bois, infant son of William and Nina, succumbed to a disease (diphtheria), his father was unable, in the child's critical hours, to find

4. Eric Sundquist, *To Wake the Nations: Race in the Making of American Literature* (Cambridge, MA: Harvard University Press, 1993), 255.
5. Ibid., 226.

either a black physician to attend his dying son or a white physician in Atlanta who was willing to treat a black child. Occasionally Du Bois writes as if he is somehow beyond or above the veil, but the sad reality of his son's death and its tragic circumstance undercuts this posture.

For Du Bois, substance is also style. In *The Souls of Black Folk*, this is seen most clearly in his use of the double headings for each chapter, with the exception of the Forethought and the Afterthought that frame his text. As Rampersad claims, one of the uses for these quotations is to provide unity for the anthology:

> The first, with one exception, is a piece of verse written by an accepted author of the Western poetic heritage. The second is a few notes from one of the fourteen well-known sorrow songs, the gifts of black people to America. Taken together, the lines of verse signify the strivings of the souls of white folk toward lofty ideals; they reflect the spiritual dignity and artistic capacity of the white world. The sorrow songs deployed beneath them remind the reader of the community of soul which transcends race and color.[6]

In a perfect world, these two headings would work together as a confluence of interests. Du Bois's text can be seen, structurally, as reifying this ideal of unity in its introduction, in the twin framing device of Forethought and Afterthought, and in the division of the text into revised essays followed by new pieces.

Unfortunately, as Du Bois shows in his short story, doubling brings about conflict and tension more often than mutual understanding. As David W. Blight and Robert Gooding-Williams have shown, Du Bois's description of the following "two figures" that represent the post-war South is a "stunning metaphor about passion in the New South":

> the one, a gray-haired gentleman, whose fathers had quit themselves like men, whose sons lay in nameless graves * * * and the other, a form hovering dark and mother-like, her awful face black with the mists of centuries.[7]

Du Bois offers no resolution to or unification of the opposed figures; no one stands as a bridge or conduit to racial reconciliation.[8] Du Bois expresses the racial divide as an actual physical parting of the ways for these two archetypes: "hating, they went to their long home, and, hating, their children's children live to-day" (27). Within the warring doubleness of consciousness, Du Bois allows no hope. Rather, the figures are weighted down with their ancient hatreds.

6. Arnold Rampersad, *The Art and Imagination of W. E. B. Du Bois* (Cambridge, MA: Harvard University Press, 1976), 71.
7. W. E. B. Du Bois, *The Souls of Black Folk*, ed. and intro. David W. Blight and Robert Gooding-Williams (Boston: Bedford Books, 1997), 15.
8. Ibid.

The full burden of the inability to escape history falls on the black man. In "Of the Faith of the Fathers," Du Bois maintains that:

> From the double life every American Negro must live, as a Negro and as an American, as swept on by the current of the nineteenth while yet struggling in the eddies of the fifteenth century,—from this must arise a painful self-consciousness, an almost morbid sense of personality and a moral hesitancy which is fatal to self-confidence (127).

In twentieth-century America, Du Bois sees two major, geographically shaped "Negro groups" representing "divergent ethical tendencies, the first tending toward radicalism, the other toward hypocritical compromise." (128) In the South, Du Bois identifies the hypocrisy that is necessary for survival: "The price of culture is a Lie" (128). On the other hand, the radicalism inspired in the North leads "to excess,—radical complaint, radical remedies, bitter denunciation or angry silence" (128).

Yet, Du Bois does posit a future, as yet unrealized, that provides an escape from the soul-destroying effects of doubleness. The last paragraph in "Of the Faith of the Fathers" rejects both hypocrisy and bitter radicalness:

> But back of this still broods silently the deep religious feeling of the real Negro heart, the stirring, unguided might of powerful human souls who have lost the guiding star of the past and are seeking in the great night a new religious ideal. Some day the Awakening will come, when the pent-up vigor of ten million souls shall sweep irresistibly toward the Goal, out of the Valley of the Shadow of Death, where all that makes life worth living—Liberty, Justice, and Right—is marked "For White People Only" (129).

Ultimately, the Great Awakening, the religious movement of white America, has not yet transpired for Du Bois. Instead, he awaits an inclusive Awakening, where the "Goal" of equality will satisfy his three yearnings for Liberty, Justice, and Right.

In the formal structure of *The Souls of Black Folk*, Du Bois also employs a tripartite approach. The failure of doubleness inspires a Hegelian tripleness, what Stanley Brodwin calls the rhetorical shape of "neo-Hegelian dialectic," consisting of the tripartite structure of thesis, antithesis, and synthesis. This tripartite structure assumes several forms for literary scholars. Arnold Rampersad sees chapters one through three of *Souls* as the historical section, chapters four through nine the sociological section, and chapters ten through fourteen as the spiritual section. For Robert Stepto *Souls* consists of a stasis, immersion, ascent (or North-South-North) motif; and for Elaine Newsome, pursuit, captivity, and escape form the book's central thematic structuring principle. Despite the variety of schematic representations of the three-part structure, critics generally agree that Du Bois employs it to shape his narrative.

However, the many *internal* lists of threes, the presence of a certain neo-Hegelian dialectic within *Souls*, has been largely ignored. Writing on one of his favorite subjects, the nature and ethics of leadership, in "Of Mr. Booker T. Washington and Others," Du Bois describes the "attitude of the imprisoned group" as consisting of three parts: "a feeling of revolt and revenge; an attempt to adjust all thought and action to the will of the greater group; or, finally, a determined effort at self-realization and self-development despite environing opinion" (37). Du Bois's move to a position that synthesizes and resolves the failed double solutions of the past echoes his hope for a new Awakening.

Despite this hope for an ultimate positive resolution, Du Bois scatters lists of less inspiring triplings throughout his book, including the "Three Temptations" of Alexander Crummell:

> * * * the temptation of Hate, that stood out against the red dawn; the temptation of Despair, that darkened noonday; and the temptation of Doubt, that ever steals along with twilight (134–35).

Although Crummell triumphs over these obstacles, Du Bois clearly sees him as an exceptional man, one he compares to a martyr, worthy of the affirmation of Christ, "a dark and pierced Jew, who knows the writhings of the earthly damned" (142).

Unfortunately, in his earthly life, Crummell earns Du Bois's sorrow because "he worked alone, with so little human sympathy. His name to-day, in this broad land, means little, and comes to fifty million ears laden with no incense of memory or emulation" (141). For Du Bois, Crummell's life—by extension—demonstrates the "tragedy of the age * * * that men know so little of men" (142). In *The Souls of Black Folk*, Du Bois attempts to expose an America that thinks of itself as "one nation, under God" to the fractured consciousness of its forgotten people.

For less exceptional if famous men such as Booker T. Washington, Du Bois employs lists of threes to critique what he sees as failed leadership. Du Bois asserts that Washington asks black people to sacrifice political power, judicial insistence of civil rights, and higher education of Negro youth. Instead of the desired conciliation of the South, the return for these three sacrifices has been the triad of disenfranchisement, civil inferiority, and the loss of financial support for institutions of higher education for blacks. All of this leads, according to Du Bois, to the "triple paradox in Mr. Washington's position" (41). Not surprisingly, Du Bois has his own answer to Washington's failure of leadership in his advocacy of those men who "feel in conscience bound to ask of this nation three things":

1. The right to vote.
2. Civic equality.
3. The education of youth according to ability (42).

Here, Du Bois lists his criticisms as well as his goals in a manner reminiscent of a political manifesto.

However, in the last chapter of *Souls*, "Of the Sorrow Songs," Du Bois's outraged demands for a new Awakening of civil liberty are intermingled with his lyric praise of the power of the Sorrow Songs. In the shaping of American identity, Du Bois emphasizes the three major contributions by blacks to America, then asks:

> Your country? How came it yours? Before the Pilgrims landed we were here. Here we have brought our three gifts and mingled them with yours: a gift of story and song—soft, stirring melody in an ill-harmonized and unmelodious land; the gift of sweat and brawn to beat back the wilderness, conquer the soil, and lay the foundations of this vast economic empire two hundred years earlier than your weak hands could have done it; the third, a gift of the Spirit (162).

In the "thrice a hundred years" of the Negro presence in America, "generation after generation have pleaded with a headstrong, careless people to despise not Justice, Mercy, and Truth, lest the nation be smitten with a curse" (162). Although Du Bois had previously offered some sense of hope for a recognition of the worth of African Americans by the majority culture, it is the Sorrow Songs that he offers as a final proof of the value of "the souls" of black folk. Even within his history of the Sorrow Songs, Du Bois again employs a tripartite structure, presenting the Sorrow Songs as "a third step in the development of the slave song" in which there is a "blending of Negro music with the music heard in the foster land" (158).

Oddly enough, without the publisher's insistence, this last, unifying chapter would not have been included in *Souls*. In a letter dated January 21, 1903, his editor, Francis Fisher Browne, assures Du Bois that he has not forgotten "the little book" and that it will be issued in the spring. He further compliments Du Bois, saying that the book is "a *good* one" that "grows on one," and it should "provoke a good deal of discussion." Asking, "Is it too late to carry out your original intention of having a chapter on 'Sorrow Songs of the Negroes?' " he asserts that "it would be a capital addition to the book." Like most publishers, Browne had to nag the author to receive the completed manuscript. On February 21, Du Bois is again asked, "Will you kindly let me know if the additional chapter on the Sorrow Songs is working out?" By March 19, the proofs were finally ready, and Browne accurately predicts "that it will make an impression on the country I am certain."

Articles of Faith from an African American Prophet

Critics, in their contemplation of *The Souls of Black Folk*, almost always invoke the word "prophetic" to describe the fundamental style of the book. Shamoon Zamir, in a meditation upon Du Bois's "prophetic imagination," is careful to make the distinction between prophecy in terms of "predictive or futuristic sense" and the prophetic tradition of the artist.[9] Although Zamir is interested in Du Bois's poetic prophecy and its relation to both American Transcendentalism and European Romanticism, others, including Houston Baker, Jr., apply the term "prophetic" in a more inclusive fashion. Baker asserts that throughout *Souls* there are "passages (indeed, entire essays) that pulsate with the oracular biblical tones of the prophet."[1] Writing about "Of the Wings of Atalanta," Keith E. Byerman states, "Du Bois's stand here is that of the Old Testament prophet as a cultured gentleman."[2] Shifting the attention from the prophet to the prophecy, Arnold Rampersad has argued in "Slavery and the Literary Imagination" that among black intellectuals *Souls* "became a kind of sacred book, the central text for the interpretation of the Afro-American experience."[3] As David W. Blight and Robert Gooding-Williams note, William Ferris, as early as 1913, called *Souls* "the political Bible of the Negro race."[4]

On one level, Du Bois's construction of this work as a prophesying text can be viewed as an extension of his attack on Washington. As we have noted above, Du Bois charges Washington with transforming industrial training "from an article of belief into a whole creed." *The Souls of Black Folk* is a repudiation of accommodation and pragmatism, and its emphasis on "Souls" necessarily employs Christian religious idioms. However, Du Bois's larger project is the revelation of black life not only to other "black folk" but also to white folk, to those who have no experience within or of the Veil. In his examination of Du Bois's poetry, Arnold Rampersad points out that "religion in Du Bois's work has distinctly earthly correspondences."[5] The same holds true for his prose. Although Du Bois had lost his religiosity, at least in any conventional sense by his Harvard years, Rampersad explains the political uses of the biblical language:

> The justification for the use of religion in this way did not come from the place of religion in Du Bois's life, or in the culture of

9. Shamoon Zamir, *Dark Voices: W. E. B. Du Bois and American Thought 1888–1903* (Chicago: University of Chicago Press, 1971), 125.
1. Houston A. Baker, Jr., "The Black Man of Culture: W. E. B. Du Bois and *The Souls of Black Folk*," in *Critical Essays on W. E. B. Du Bois*, 137.
2. Keith E. Byerman, *Seizing the Word: History, Art and Self in the Work of W. E. B. Du Bois* (Athens: University of Georgia Press, 1994), 20.
3. Rampersad, "Slavery and the Literary Imagination," *Slavery and the Literary Imagination: Du Bois's "The Souls of Black Folk"* (Baltimore: Johns Hopkins University Press), 105.
4. Blight and Gooding-Williams, 21.
5. Arnold Rampersad, "W. E. B. Du Bois as a Man of Literature," in *Critical Essays on W. E. B. Du Bois*, 67.

the black folk, but from the historical role of religion in white culture.[6]

Despite his characterization of the "high Episcopal Nicene creed" as a "rationale for racism," Du Bois was not loathe to use the traditional pieties of turn-of-the-century America to express his own important message. Furthermore, despite his own ambivalence toward traditionally black churches, Du Bois, by personal experience and as a trained sociologist, was well aware of the place of the church in black life. As he writes in "Of the Faith of the Fathers," "a little investigation reveals * * * that, in the South, at least, practically every American Negro is a church member" (122). For most of both black and white America, the language of the Protestant churches, from high Episcopal to "hard-core" Baptist, comprised the vocabulary of morality, of ethical appeals to political justice and to individual behavior.

Throughout *The Souls of Black Folk*, Rampersad notes, Du Bois's narrator adopts a "patriarchal tone" encouraged by the frequent borrowing from the King James Bible.[7] Yet, Rampersad warns, the reader should not fall into the misconception that Du Bois is writing sermons: "He praised the black preacher for many things, but not for his preaching."[8] While Rampersad is correct in assuming that Du Bois had no clerical ambitions, Du Bois also had no compunctions about using religious means for secular ends. Except for the final chapter, "Of the Sorrow Songs,"—"a tale twice told and seldom written"[9]—Du Bois's religious language is basically that of mainline, white Protestant churches, especially of the Episcopal church.

Although much is made of Du Bois's Congregational church affiliation, he and his mother, for the first ten years of his life, attended the Episcopal church, a Burghardt family tradition.[1] His grandfather, Alexander Du Bois, was a founding member of a black Episcopal church. In a letter dated 1907, Du Bois identifies himself as a product of the Episcopal church: "Let me say that my family represents five generations in the Episcopal church including my little girl and perhaps other generations if I chose to count certain parts of my family which I do not count."[2] Despite his disdain of Episcopal social policy, the impact

6. Ibid.
7. Rampersad, *The Art and the Imagination of W. E. B. Du Bois*, 76.
8. Ibid.
9. Du Bois, *Souls*, 5. In the Forethought, Du Bois, in describing the text to follow, states, "All of this I have ended with a tale twice told but seldom written." Nathaniel Hawthorne, in 1837, published a set of short stories entitled *Twice-Told Tales*. The title is a self-deprecating allusion to Shakespeare's *King John* 3.4: "Life is as tedious as a twice-told tale, / Vexing the dull ear of a drowsy man."
1. Lewis, *Biography of a Race*, 48.
2. Herbert Aptheker, *The Correspondence of W. E. B. Du Bois*, vol. 1 (Amherst: University of Massachusetts Press, 1973), 131. Du Bois goes on to say that "I have however no particular affection for the Church. I think its record on the Negro problem has been simply shameful and while I am looking with interest to the work which the Church institute proposes to do yet I confess I have many misgivings."

of *The Book of Common Prayer* (1789) seems evident through the titling of the individual chapters in *Souls*. In the table of contents, archaically and passively constructed as "Herein is Written," Du Bois lists his fourteen chapters, all of which, with the exception of "The Sorrow Songs," use a prepositional phrase containing "of." This phraseology was used in various philosophical texts; both Hume's *A Treatise of Human Nature* and Burke's *Philosophical Inquiry into the Sublime* employ subheadings exclusively using "of." More significantly, the thirty-nine articles of religion that the Protestant Episcopal church in the United States adopted in 1801 are prefaced by "of" and feature inclusive pronouns. The exclusion of "The Sorrow Songs" from Du Bois's articles of faith may indicate his reception of these songs as a legacy, "the articulate message of the slave to the world." As "the sole American music" (155), the Sorrow Songs require no explication by the author of *Souls*. Rather, they function as the psalter for this faith.

In *The Souls of Black Folk*, Du Bois warns against both the "Gospel of Work and Money" and the "Gospel of Revolt and Revenge." Obviously, he is not offering a new gospel in any religious sense,[3] but, in this text, he provides a social gospel based on history, sociology, and personal experience. Although his prophecy is not divinely inspired, he uses the language of divine inspiration to become the spokesman of a movement for social equality. As Robert B. Stepto has written:

> *The Souls* is not a social scientific study or the verbal tracings of a muckraker; rather, it is a book of prophecy. In the narrative, data become metaphor, rough winds become melodious songs, swamps occasion meditations, and, through art, Du Bois may place his life and voice amid his culture's pantheon of named and nameless articulate heroes.[4]

Within this religious ideation, Du Bois also creates his own *Credo*, and, in response to the Atlanta riots of 1906, wrote his most powerful piece of poetry, *A Litany of Atlanta*. His creed, a bold challenge to the racist creed of previous generations, affirms the belief that all men differ "in no essential particular," and avows:

3. However, in his creative writings, Du Bois used a number of New Testament stories, translating them to the Negro experience in America. The following short stories were published in the *Crisis*: "Jesus Christ in Georgia," "The Gospel According to Mary Brown," "The Temptation in the Wilderness," "The Son of God," The Three Wise Men," "Pontius Pilate," "The Gospel According to St. John, Chapter 12," "The Woman," and "The Second Coming." These can be found in *Creative Writings by W. E. B. Du Bois*, ed. Herbert Aptheker (New York: Kraus-Thomas, 1985).
4. Robert B. Stepto, *From Behind the Veil: A Study of Afro-American Narrative* (Chicago: University of Illinois Press, 1979), 91.

> Especially, do I believe in the Negro Race; in the beauty of its genius, the sweetness of its soul and its strength in that meekness which shall yet inherit this turbulent earth.[5]

As well as a litany and a creed, Du Bois also published a number of "collects" (prayers), "The Prayer of the Bantu" and "The Christmas Prayers of God."[6] (In addition, one poem is named "Hymn to the Peoples.")

Yet despite Du Bois's confidence in his own ability to speak for the future and the "problem of the Twentieth century," his greatest reverence was for the "Mighty Form" of Douglass whom, in one version of his elegy, he compares to Moses:

> First of the First born—wanderer
> On paths unwandered—Seer
> That saw beyond the mountains, fields
> And folds of promised lands

A few stanzas later, Du Bois compares Douglass to the Messiah of Isaiah, "Despised and of the world rejected." In Douglass's praise, Du Bois urges Africa (Muse of the Night) to awake and sing to the fallen hero, and in an unusual imperative, bids both Christ and God to sing to Douglass. However, in the end, this is a task that Du Bois takes on himself: "God is white, God is white/But the singer and the song/They are black, they are black." In *The Souls of Black Folk*, Du Bois has left the world a document that articulated the individual black voice of the singer and the song, while simultaneously giving a face to those "black and unknown bards" of the great vernacular tradition that his book valorizes. For the first time, a collective voice of the nation-within-a-nation, which America's African people long had constructed, found its resplendent voice in the pages of this classic work that is as timely and compelling now as it was at the turn of the century.

Henry Louis Gates Jr.
Terri Oliver
Cambridge, Massachusetts

---

5. W. E. B. Du Bois, "Credo," in *W. E. B. Du Bois: A Reader*, ed. David Levering Lewis (New York: Henry Holt and Company, 1995), 105.
6. Among the papers that Du Bois left to Herbert Aptheker was a packet of prayers written between 1909 and 1910 for the students of Atlanta University, especially its grammar school and high school students. The prayers are generally short and usually include a biblical source for the prayers' inspiration. The prayers emphasize uplift; topics include cleanliness, sobriety, work habits, and promptness. Again, Du Bois utilizes religious language for social ends. The prayers are available in *Prayers for Dark People*, ed. Herbert Aptheker (Amherst: University of Massachusetts Press, 1980).

Acknowledgments

We are deeply indebted to the work of other scholars. Specifically, the 1997 Bedford Books edition of *The Souls of Black Folk* greatly expanded the historical and philosophical contextualization of the text. David W. Blight and Robert Gooding-Williams have rigorously researched and thoughtfully commented upon both the literary and sociological aspects of *Souls*.

The following editions were consulted:

Blight, David W., and Robert Gooding-Williams, eds. Notes to *The Souls of Black Folk*, by W. E. B. Du Bois. Boston: Bedford Books, 1997.

Gates, Henry Louis Jr., ed. Introduction to *The Souls of Black Folk*, by W. E. B. Du Bois. New York: Bantam, 1989.

Elbert, Monica M. Notes to *The Souls of Black Folk*, by W. E. B. Du Bois. Intro. Donald B. Gibson. New York: Penguin Books, 1989.

Huggins, Nathan I. Notes to *The Souls of Black Folk*, by W. E. B. Du Bois. Intro. John Edgar Wideman. New York: Vintage Books/The Library of America, 1990.

Note on the Text

The text of *The Souls of Black Folk* presented here is a copy of the original edition printed by A. C. McClurg and Company on April 18, 1903. Between 1903 and 1940, McClurg published twenty-four editions from the original plates, reporting to Du Bois in 1935 that the total number of sales had reached fifteen thousand. In January 1949, Du Bois bought the text plates of his book for exactly one hundred dollars. By October 1953, a Fiftieth Anniversary Jubilee Edition was published by Blue Heron Press, a printing house established by Howard Fast to provide publication for works in danger of repression by McCarthyism.

In the introduction to the Blue Heron edition, Du Bois informed his readers that he had "made less than a half-dozen alterations in word or phrase" from the original text. With the assistance of the Black Periodical Literature project, Henry Louis Gates Jr. undertook a line-by-line collation to identify changes between the two versions. Herbert Aptheker had made a similar study in 1974, and the Gates team found two more revisions to add to Aptheker's discovery of seven alterations. These nine alterations were published in the 1989 Bantam edition of *The Souls of Black Folks*.

Except for one modification that involved a school name, the changes made by Du Bois clearly indicate his desire to preclude any interpretation of his text that might lend itself to anti-Semitism. Aptheker reports that as early as 1905, Du Bois had been approached by Jacob Schiff to make such changes, and Nathan Huggins points out that in the ninth printing (December 10, 1911) Du Bois revised the phrase "A Yankee or a Jew" to read "a Yankee or his like." In his new preface to the Jubilee Edition, "Fifty Years Later," Du Bois explains his previous reluctance to alter his text:

> Several times I planned to revise the book and bring it abreast of my own thought and to answer criticism. But I hesitated and finally decided to leave the book as first printed, as a monument to what I thought and felt in 1903. I hoped in other books to set down changes of fact and reaction.
>
> In the present Jubilee Edition I have clung to this decision, and my thoughts of fifty years ago appear again as then written. Only in a few cases have I made less than a half-dozen alterations in

word or phrase and then not to change my thought as previously set down but to avoid any possible misunderstanding today of what I meant to say yesterday.

In the post–World War II era, Du Bois's concern about anti-Semitism led him to consider adding the following paragraph to the chapter "Of the Black Belt":

> In the foregoing chapter, "Jews" have been mentioned five times, and the late Jacob Schiff once complained that I gave an impression of anti-Semitism. This at the time I stoutly denied; but as I read the passage again in the light of subsequent history, I see how I laid myself open to this possible misapprehension. What, of course, I meant to condemn was the exploitation of black labor and that it was in this country and at that time in part a matter of immigrant Jews, was incidental and not essential. My inner sympathy with the Jewish people was expressed better in the last paragraph on page 227 (NCE, p. 142). But this illustrates how easily one slips into unconscious condemnation of a whole group.

Although Du Bois eventually decided not to add this paragraph, he did make the following alterations, which are listed in the table below. In the body of this text, we have also footnoted each revision.

Nine of the fourteen chapters in *Souls* are revisions of essays published between 1897 and 1902 in the following magazines and journals: *Atlantic Monthly, The World's Work, The Dial, Annals of the American Academy of Political and Social Science,* and *The New World: A Quarterly Review of Religious Ethics and Theology*. The first footnote of each chapter provides a full citation of the original article as well as identification of the opening lines of verse and musical notation.

Text	1903/NCE editions	1953 edition
1. And first we may say that this type of college, including Atlanta, Fisk, and Howard, Wilberforce, and *Lincoln*. . . .	p. 99 / p. 68	changed to: *Claflin* (p. 99).
2. *The Jew is the heir* of the slavebaron in Dougherty. . . .	p. 126 / p. 83	changed to: *Immigrants are heirs* (p. 126).
3. . . . *nearly all* failed, and *the Jew* fell heir.	p. 126 / p. 84	changed to: *most* failed and *foreigners* fell heir (p. 126).
4. This plantation, owned now by a *Russian Jew*. . . .	p. 127 / p. 84	changed to: *an immigrant* (p. 127).
5. . . . out of which only a Yankee or a Jew could squeeze more blood from debt-cursed tenants.	p. 127 / p. 84	changed to: *an immigrant* (p. 127).
6. Since then his *nephews and the poor whites and the Jews* have seized it.	p. 132 / p. 87	changed to: *poor relations and foreign immigrants* (p. 132).
7. . . . thrifty and avaricious Yankee, shrewd and unscrupulous *Jews*.	p. 169 / p. 108	changed to: *immigrants* (p. 169).
8. . . . the enterprising *Russian Jew* who sold it to him. . . .	p. 170 / p. 109	changed to: *American* (p. 170).
9. It is the same defense which *the Jews* of the Middle Age used. . . .	p. 204 / p. 128	changed to: *peasants* (p. 204).

The Text of
THE SOULS OF BLACK FOLK

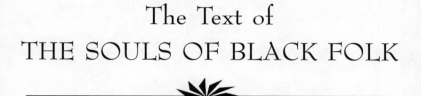

THE
Souls of Black Folk
Essays and Sketches

BY

W. E. BURGHARDT DU BOIS

CHICAGO
A. C. McCLURG & CO.
1903

TO

BURGHARDT AND YOLANDE

THE LOST AND THE FOUND

The Forethought

Herein lie buried many things which if read with patience may show the strange meaning of being black here in the dawning of the Twentieth Century. This meaning is not without interest to you, Gentle Reader; for the problem of the Twentieth Century is the problem of the color-line.[1]

I pray you, then, receive my little book in all charity, studying my words with me, forgiving mistake and foible for sake of the faith and passion that is in me, and seeking the grain of truth hidden there.

I have sought here to sketch, in vague, uncertain outline, the spiritual world in which ten thousand thousand Americans live and strive. First, in two chapters I have tried to show what Emancipation meant to them, and what was its aftermath. In a third chapter I have pointed out the slow rise of personal leadership, and criticised candidly the leader[2] who bears the chief burden of his race to-day. Then, in two other chapters I have sketched in swift outline the two worlds within and without the Veil,[3] and thus have come to the central problem of training men for life. Venturing now into deeper detail, I have in two chapters studied the struggles of the massed millions of the black peasantry, and in another have sought to make clear the present relations of the sons of master and man.

Leaving, then, the world of the white man, I have stepped within the Veil, raising it that you may view faintly its deeper recesses,—the meaning of its religion, the passion of its human sorrow, and the struggle of its greater souls. All this I have ended with a tale twice told[4] but seldom written.[5]

Some of these thoughts of mine have seen the light before in other guise. For kindly consenting to their republication here, in altered and extended form, I must thank the publishers of *The Atlantic Monthly*,

1. This statement, "the problem of the Twentieth Century is the problem of the color-line," was first made by Du Bois in his address, "To the Nations of the World," in London at the first Pan-African conference, July 1900.
2. Booker T. Washington.
3. See Exodus 34.33–35, where Moses covers his shining face after speaking to God; also Isaiah 25.7, which prophesies that the Lord will destroy "the veil that is spread over all nations."
4. Nathaniel Hawthorne (1804–1864), American author, published a set of short stories in March 1837 entitled *Twice-Told Tales*. The title was a self-deprecating allusion to Shakespeare's *King John* 3.4.108–9: "Life is as tedious as a twice-told tale, / Vexing the dull ear of a drowsy man."
5. In 1953 edition of *The Souls of Black Folk*, sentence is changed to "All this I have ended with a tale twice told but seldom written, and a chapter of song."

The World's Work, The Dial, The New World, and the *Annals of the American Academy of Political and Social Science.*

Before each chapter, as now printed, stands a bar of the Sorrow Songs,[6]—some echo of haunting melody from the only American music which welled up from black souls in the dark past. And, finally, need I add that I who speak here am bone of the bone and flesh of the flesh of them that live within the Veil?[7]

W. E. B. Du B.

ATLANTA, GA., Feb. 1, 1903.

---

6. Term used by Du Bois as synonym for spirituals. The spiritual is a religious folksong that is deeply emotional and often profoundly sad. It derives from blending African song with nineteenth-century hymn.
7. In Genesis 2.23, Adam says of the newly created Eve: "This at last is bone of my bone and flesh of my flesh; she shall be called Woman because she was taken out of Man."

Herein is Written

7

The Souls of Black Folk

I

Of Our Spiritual Strivings[1]

O water, voice of my heart, crying in the sand,
   All night long crying with a mournful cry,
As I lie and listen, and cannot understand
     The voice of my heart in my side or the voice of the sea,
O water, crying for rest, is it I, is it I?
    All night long the water is crying to me.

Unresting water, there shall never be rest
   Till the last moon droop and the last tide fail,
And the fire of the end begin to burn in the west;
     And the heart shall be weary and wonder and cry like the sea,
   All life long crying without avail,
     As the water all night long is crying to me.

ARTHUR SYMONS.

Between me and the other world there is ever an unasked question:
unasked by some through feelings of delicacy; by others through the
difficulty of rightly framing it. All, nevertheless, flutter round it. They
approach me in a half-hesitant sort of way, eye me curiously or com-
passionately, and then, instead of saying directly, How does it feel to
be a problem? they say, I know an excellent colored man in my town;
or, I fought at Mechanicsville;[2] or, Do not these Southern outrages
make your blood boil? At these I smile, or am interested, or reduce the

---

1. Revised from "Strivings of the Negro People," *Atlantic Monthly* (August 1897): 194–98. The
verses are from *The Crying of Waters* (1903) by Arthur Symons. The music quotation is from
the Negro spiritual "Nobody Knows the Trouble I've Seen."
2. Site of a Civil War battle of June 1862, near Richmond, Virginia.

boiling to a simmer, as the occasion may require. To the real question, How does it feel to be a problem? I answer seldom a word.

And yet, being a problem is a strange experience,—peculiar even for one who has never been anything else, save perhaps in babyhood and in Europe. It is in the early days of rollicking boyhood that the revelation first bursts upon one, all in a day, as it were. I remember well when the shadow swept across me. I was a little thing, away up in the hills of New England, where the dark Housatonic[3] winds between Hoosac and Taghkanic to the sea. In a wee wooden schoolhouse, something put it into the boys' and girls' heads to buy gorgeous visiting-cards—ten cents a package—and exchange. The exchange was merry, till one girl, a tall newcomer, refused my card,—refused it peremptorily, with a glance.[4] Then it dawned upon me with a certain suddenness that I was different from the others; or like, mayhap, in heart and life and longing, but shut out from their world by a vast veil. I had thereafter no desire to tear down that veil, to creep through; I held all beyond it in common contempt, and lived above it in a region of blue sky and great wandering shadows. That sky was bluest when I could beat my mates at examination-time, or beat them at a foot-race, or even beat their stringy heads. Alas, with the years all this fine contempt began to fade; for the worlds I longed for, and all their dazzling opportunities, were theirs, not mine. But they should not keep these prizes, I said; some, all, I would wrest from them. Just how I would do it I could never decide: by reading law, by healing the sick, by telling the wonderful tales that swam in my head,—some way. With other black boys the strife was not so fiercely sunny: their youth shrunk into tasteless sycophancy, or into silent hatred of the pale world about them and mocking distrust of everything white; or wasted itself in a bitter cry, Why did God make me an outcast and a stranger in mine own house?[5] The shades of the prison-house closed round about us all:[6] walls strait and stubborn to the whitest, but relentlessly narrow, tall, and unscalable to sons of night who must plod darkly on in resignation, or beat unavailing palms against the stone, or steadily, half hopelessly, watch the streak of blue above.

After the Egyptian and Indian, the Greek and Roman, the Teuton and Mongolian, the Negro is a sort of seventh son, born with a veil, and gifted with second-sight in this American world,[7]—a world which

3. River that runs through Du Bois's hometown of Great Barrington, Massachusetts.
4. In *The Autobiography of W. E. B. Du Bois* (1968) he reports that this incident took place during his high-school years.
5. An ironic rewriting of Exodus 2.22, in which Moses declares, "I have been a stranger in a strange land."
6. Reference to William Wordsworth's Ode *Intimations of Immortality from Recollections of Early Childhood.*
7. In African American folklore, seventh sons as well as those children born with a caul, a membrane that sometimes covers the head at birth, are reported to have special abilities, such as predicting the future and seeing ghosts.

what exactly is this double consciousness

yields him no true self-consciousness, but only lets him see himself through the revelation of the other world. It is a peculiar sensation, this double-consciousness,[8] this sense of always looking at one's self through the eyes of others, of measuring one's soul by the tape of a world that looks on in amused contempt and pity. One ever feels his two-ness,— an American, a Negro; two souls, two thoughts, two unreconciled strivings; two warring ideals in one dark body, whose dogged strength alone keeps it from being torn asunder. *① you are who you see yourself & and what other people see you as)*

The history of the American Negro is the history of this strife,—this longing to attain self-conscious manhood, to merge his double self into a better and truer self. In this merging he wishes neither of the older selves to be lost. He would not Africanize America, for America has too much to teach the world and Africa. He would not bleach his Negro soul in a flood of white Americanism, for he knows that Negro blood has a message for the world. He simply wishes to make it possible for a man to be both a Negro and an American, without being cursed and spit upon by his fellows, without having the doors of Opportunity closed roughly in his face.

This, then, is the end of his striving: to be a co-worker in the kingdom of culture, to escape both death and isolation, to husband and use his best powers and his latent genius. These powers of body and mind have in the past been strangely wasted, dispersed, or forgotten. The shadow of a mighty Negro past flits through the tale of Ethiopia the Shadowy and of Egypt the Sphinx. Throughout history, the powers of single black men flash here and there like falling stars, and die sometimes before the world has rightly gauged their brightness. Here in America, in the few days since Emancipation, the black man's turning hither and thither in hesitant and doubtful striving has often made his very strength to lose effectiveness, to seem like absence of power, like weakness. And yet it is not weakness,—it is the contradiction of double aims. The double-aimed struggle of the black artisan—on the one hand to escape white contempt for a nation of mere hewers of wood and drawers of water, and on the other hand to plough and nail and dig for a poverty-stricken horde—could only result in making him a poor craftsman, for he had but half a heart in either cause. By the poverty and ignorance of his people, the Negro minister or doctor was tempted toward quackery and demagogy; and by the criticism of the other world, toward ideals that made him ashamed of his lowly tasks. The would-be black *savant*[9] was confronted by the paradox that the knowledge his people needed was a twice-told tale to his white neighbors, while the knowledge which would teach the white world was Greek to his own flesh and blood.

8. See below, p. 236, Dickson D. Bruce Jr.'s essay on the origins and meaning of double-consciousness.
9. A learned scholar.

The innate love of harmony and beauty that set the ruder souls of his people a-dancing and a-singing raised but confusion and doubt in the soul of the black artist; for the beauty revealed to him was the soul-beauty of a race which his larger audience despised, and he could not articulate the message of another people. This waste of double aims, this seeking to satisfy two unreconciled ideals, has wrought sad havoc with the courage and faith and deeds of ten thousand thousand people,—has sent them often wooing false gods and invoking false means of salvation, and at times has even seemed about to make them ashamed of themselves.

Away back in the days of bondage they thought to see in one divine event the end of all doubt and disappointment; few men ever worshipped Freedom with half such unquestioning faith as did the American Negro for two centuries. To him, so far as he thought and dreamed, slavery was indeed the sum of all villainies, the cause of all sorrow, the root of all prejudice; Emancipation was the key to a promised land of sweeter beauty than ever stretched before the eyes of wearied Israelites.[1] In song and exhortation swelled one refrain—Liberty; in his tears and curses the God he implored had Freedom in his right hand. At last it came,—suddenly, fearfully, like a dream. With one wild carnival of blood and passion came the message in his own plaintive cadences:—

> "Shout, O children!
> Shout, you're free!
> For God has bought your liberty!"[2]

Years have passed away since then,—ten, twenty, forty; forty years of national life, forty years of renewal and development, and yet the swarthy spectre sits in its accustomed seat at the Nation's feast. In vain do we cry to this our vastest social problem:—

> "Take any shape but that, and my firm nerves
> Shall never tremble!"[3]

The Nation has not yet found peace from its sins; the freedman has not yet found in freedom his promised land. Whatever of good may have come in these years of change, the shadow of a deep disappointment rests upon the Negro people,—a disappointment all the more bitter because the unattained ideal was unbounded save by the simple ignorance of a lowly people.

1. Following their Egyptian captivity, the Israelites reached Canaan, the Promised Land, after forty years of wandering in the wilderness.
2. Refrain of the freedom spiritual "Shout, O Children!"
3. *Macbeth* 3.4.102–3. Du Bois symbolically represents the American character as guilty and blood-stained, like the central character of Shakespeare's tragedy.

The first decade was merely a prolongation of the vain search for freedom, the boon that seemed ever barely to elude their grasp,—like a tantalizing will-o'-the-wisp,[4] maddening and misleading the headless host. The holocaust of war, the terrors of the Ku-Klux Klan,[5] the lies of carpet-baggers,[6] the disorganization of industry, and the contradictory advice of friends and foes, left the bewildered serf with no new watchword beyond the old cry for freedom. As the time flew, however, he began to grasp a new idea. The ideal of liberty demanded for its attainment powerful means, and these the Fifteenth Amendment gave him.[7] The ballot, which before he had looked upon as a visible sign of freedom, he now regarded as the chief means of gaining and perfecting the liberty with which war had partially endowed him. And why not? Had not votes made war and emancipated millions? Had not votes enfranchised the freedmen? Was anything impossible to a power that had done all this? A million black men started with renewed zeal to vote themselves into the kingdom. So the decade flew away, the revolution of 1876 came,[8] and left the half-free serf weary, wondering, but still inspired. Slowly but steadily, in the following years, a new vision began gradually to replace the dream of political power,—a powerful movement, the rise of another ideal to guide the unguided, another pillar of fire by night after a clouded day. It was the ideal of "booklearning"; the curiosity, born of compulsory ignorance, to know and test the power of the cabalistic[9] letters of the white man, the longing to know. Here at last seemed to have been discovered the mountain path to Canaan;[1] longer than the highway of Emancipation and law, steep and rugged, but straight, leading to heights high enough to overlook life.

Up the new path the advance guard toiled, slowly, heavily, doggedly; only those who have watched and guided the faltering feet, the misty

4. A delusive or misleading goal.
5. Secret society formed in 1866 by Confederate veterans with the stated intent of protecting white, Protestant interests. It rapidly became a terrorist organization responsible for widespread violence against African Americans.
6. Northern politicians and businessmen who entered the South following the Civil War. Portrayed as carrying their belongings in cheap, fabric valises (carpetbags), they were seen as enriching themselves at the cost of a defeated Confederacy.
7. Ratified March 10, 1870; it granted voting rights to men regardless of "race, color, or previous condition of servitude." Although the amendment was a moderate measure and did not outlaw qualification tests for voters, it allowed Congress to enforce the law through federal sanctions.
8. The results of the presidential elections of 1876 were disputed by Louisiana, Florida, and South Carolina, three states that backed Democrat Samuel J. Tilden against Rutherford B. Hayes. Some Southern Democrats threatened a "revolution" of secession from the Union. Republicans, in their attempt to mollify the Democrats, significantly reduced their support of the freedmen.
9. Mystical. The cabala, or Kabbalah, is a body of esoteric Jewish doctrines dealing with the manifestations of God. Written between the third and the sixteenth centuries, these books are difficult to interpret.
1. The Promised Land. Du Bois is reinforcing his identification of African Americans with the Israelites during their years of Egyptian captivity and their forty years of wandering in the wilderness.

minds, the dull understandings, of the dark pupils of these schools know
how faithfully, how piteously, this people strove to learn. It was weary
work. The cold statistician wrote down the inches of progress here and
there, noted also where here and there a foot had slipped or some one
had fallen. To the tired climbers, the horizon was ever dark, the mists
were often cold, the Canaan was always dim and far away. If, however,
the vistas disclosed as yet no goal, no resting-place, little but flattery
and criticism, the journey at least gave leisure for reflection and self-
examination; it changed the child of Emancipation to the youth with
dawning self-consciousness, self-realization, self-respect. In those sombre forests of his striving his own soul rose before him, and he saw
himself,—darkly as through a veil;[2] and yet he saw in himself some
faint revelation of his power, of his mission. He began to have a dim
feeling that, to attain his place in the world, he must be himself, and
not another. For the first time he sought to analyze the burden he bore
upon his back, that dead-weight of social degradation partially masked
behind a half-named Negro problem. He felt his poverty; without a
cent, without a home, without land, tools, or savings, he had entered
into competition with rich, landed, skilled neighbors. To be a poor
man is hard, but to be a poor race in a land of dollars is the very bottom
of hardships. He felt the weight of his ignorance,—not simply of letters,
but of life, of business, of the humanities; the accumulated sloth and
shirking and awkwardness of decades and centuries shackled his hands
and feet. Nor was his burden all poverty and ignorance. The red stain
of bastardy, which two centuries of systematic legal defilement of Negro
women had stamped upon his race, meant not only the loss of ancient
African chastity, but also the hereditary weight of a mass of corruption
from white adulterers, threatening almost the obliteration of the Negro
home.

A people thus handicapped ought not to be asked to race with the
world, but rather allowed to give all its time and thought to its own
social problems. But alas! while sociologists gleefully count his bastards
and his prostitutes, the very soul of the toiling, sweating black man is
darkened by the shadow of a vast despair. Men call the shadow prejudice, and learnedly explain it as the natural defence of culture against
barbarism, learning against ignorance, purity against crime, the
"higher" against the "lower" races.[3] To which the Negro cries Amen!
and swears that to so much of this strange prejudice as is founded on
just homage to civilization, culture, righteousness, and progress, he
humbly bows and meekly does obeisance.[4] But before that nameless

2. 1 Corinthians 13.12: "For now we see through a glass, darkly; but then face to face: now I
   know in part; but then shall I know even as also I am known."
3. During the Enlightenment, philosophers such as Kant and Hume were convinced that certain
   races could be ranked hierarchically according to their psychological and moral characteristics
   as well as their bodily traits.
4. An attitude of deference or homage.

prejudice that leaps beyond all this he stands helpless, dismayed, and well-nigh speechless; before that personal disrespect and mockery, the ridicule and systematic humiliation, the distortion of fact and wanton license of fancy, the cynical ignoring of the better and the boisterous welcoming of the worse, the all-pervading desire to inculcate disdain for everything black, from Toussaint[5] to the devil,—before this there rises a sickening despair that would disarm and discourage any nation save that black host to whom "discouragement" is an unwritten word.

But the facing of so vast a prejudice could not but bring the inevitable self-questioning, self-disparagement, and lowering of ideals which ever accompany repression and breed in an atmosphere of contempt and hate. Whisperings and portents came borne upon the four winds: Lo! we are diseased and dying, cried the dark hosts; we cannot write, our voting is vain; what need of education, since we must always cook and serve? And the Nation echoed and enforced this self-criticism, saying: Be content to be servants, and nothing more; what need of higher culture for half-men? Away with the black man's ballot, by force or fraud,—and behold the suicide of a race! Nevertheless, out of the evil came something of good,—the more careful adjustment of education to real life, the clearer perception of the Negroes' social responsibilities, and the sobering realization of the meaning of progress.

So dawned the time of *Sturm und Drang*:[6] storm and stress to-day rocks our little boat on the mad waters of the world-sea; there is within and without the sound of conflict, the burning of body and rending of soul; inspiration strives with doubt, and faith with vain questionings. The bright ideals of the past,—physical freedom, political power, the training of brains and the training of hands,—all these in turn have waxed and waned, until even the last grows dim and overcast. Are they all wrong,—all false? No, not that, but each alone was over-simple and incomplete,—the dreams of a credulous race-childhood, or the fond imaginings of the other world which does not know and does not want to know our power. To be really true, all these ideals must be melted and welded into one. The training of the schools we need to-day more than ever,—the training of deft hands, quick eyes and ears, and above all the broader, deeper, higher culture of gifted minds and pure hearts. The power of the ballot we need in sheer self-defence,—else what shall save us from a second slavery? Freedom, too, the long-sought, we still seek,—the freedom of life and limb, the freedom to work and think, the freedom to love and aspire. Work, culture, liberty,—all these we need, not singly but together, not successively but together, each grow-

5. Toussaint L'Ouverture (1746–1803), leader of the black forces during the Haitian Revolution that overthrew French rule. After Napoleon tricked him into going willingly to France in 1800, L'Ouverture died there in 1803.
6. Literally, storm and stress (German). The term characterizes a German literary movement that valorizes emotional experience and spiritual struggle. Johann Wolfgang von Goethe, Du Bois's favorite author, was a leading figure in this movement.

ing and aiding each, and all striving toward that vaster ideal that swims before the Negro people, the ideal of human brotherhood, gained through the unifying ideal of Race; the ideal of fostering and developing the traits and talents of the Negro, not in opposition to or contempt for other races, but rather in large conformity to the greater ideals of the American Republic, in order that some day on American soil two world-races may give each to each those characteristics both so sadly lack. We the darker ones come even now not altogether empty-handed: there are to-day no truer exponents of the pure human spirit of the Declaration of Independence than the American Negroes; there is no true American music but the wild sweet melodies of the Negro slave; the American fairy tales and folk-lore are Indian and African; and, all in all, we black men seem the sole oasis of simple faith and reverence in a dusty desert of dollars and smartness. Will America be poorer if she replace her brutal dyspeptic blundering with light-hearted but determined Negro humility? or her coarse and cruel wit with loving jovial good-humor? or her vulgar music with the soul of the Sorrow Songs?

Merely a concrete test of the underlying principles of the great republic is the Negro Problem, and the spiritual striving of the freedmen's sons is the travail of souls whose burden is almost beyond the measure of their strength, but who bear it in the name of an historic race, in the name of this the land of their fathers' fathers, and in the name of human opportunity.

And now what I have briefly sketched in large outline let me on coming pages tell again in many ways, with loving emphasis and deeper detail, that men may listen to the striving in the souls of black folk.

II

Of the Dawn of Freedom[1]

Careless seems the great Avenger;
    History's lessons but record
One death-grapple in the darkness
    'Twixt old systems and the Word;
Truth forever on the scaffold,
    Wrong forever on the throne;
Yet that scaffold sways the future,
    And behind the dim unknown
Standeth God within the shadow
    Keeping watch above His own.
                LOWELL.

    The problem of the twentieth century is the problem of the color-line,—the relation of the darker to the lighter races of men in Asia and Africa, in America and the islands of the sea. It was a phase of this problem that caused the Civil War; and however much they who marched South and North in 1861 may have fixed on the technical points of union and local autonomy as a shibboleth,[2] all nevertheless knew, as we know, that the question of Negro slavery was the real cause of the conflict. Curious it was, too, how this deeper question ever forced itself to the surface despite effort and disclaimer. No sooner had Northern armies touched Southern soil than this old question, newly guised, sprang from the earth,—What shall be done with Negroes? Peremptory military commands, this way and that, could not answer the query; the Emancipation Proclamation seemed but to broaden and intensify the difficulties; and the War Amendments[3] made the Negro problems of to-day.

    It is the aim of this essay to study the period of history from 1861 to

1. Revised from "The Freedmen's Bureau," *Atlantic Monthly* (March 1901): 354–65. The verse is from James Russell Lowell's *The Present Crisis* (1844). The music quotation is from the Negro spiritual "My Lord, What a Mourning!"
2. A common saying or idea.
3. Amendments to the U.S. Constitution associated with the Civil War. The Thirteenth, ratified in 1865, abolished slavery; the Fourteenth (1866) provided "equal protection under the law"; and the Fifteenth (1870) granted the right to vote to black males.

1872 so far as it relates to the American Negro. In effect, this tale of the dawn of Freedom is an account of that government of men called the Freedmen's Bureau,[4]—one of the most singular and interesting of the attempts made by a great nation to grapple with vast problems of race and social condition.

The war has naught to do with slaves, cried Congress, the President, and the Nation; and yet no sooner had the armies, East and West, penetrated Virginia and Tennessee than fugitive slaves appeared within their lines. They came at night, when the flickering camp-fires shone like vast unsteady stars along the black horizon: old men and thin, with gray and tufted hair; women, with frightened eyes, dragging whimpering hungry children; men and girls, stalwart and gaunt,—a horde of starving vagabonds, homeless, helpless, and pitiable, in their dark distress. Two methods of treating these newcomers seemed equally logical to opposite sorts of minds. Ben Butler, in Virginia, quickly declared slave property contraband of war,[5] and put the fugitives to work; while Fremont, in Missouri, declared the slaves free under martial law.[6] Butler's action was approved, but Fremont's was hastily countermanded, and his successor, Halleck, saw things differently.[7] "Hereafter," he commanded, "no slaves should be allowed to come into your lines at all; if any come without your knowledge, when owners call for them deliver them." Such a policy was difficult to enforce; some of the black refugees declared themselves freemen, others showed that their masters had deserted them, and still others were captured with forts and plantations. Evidently, too, slaves were a source of strength to the Confederacy, and were being used as laborers and producers. "They constitute a military resource," wrote Secretary Cameron,[8] late in 1861; "and being such, that they should not be turned over to the enemy is too plain to discuss." So gradually the tone of the army chiefs changed; Congress forbade the rendition[9] of fugitives, and Butler's "contrabands" were welcomed as military laborers. This complicated rather than solved the problem, for now the scattering fugitives became a steady stream, which flowed faster as the armies marched.

Then the long-headed man with care-chiselled face who sat in the

---

4. The U.S. Bureau of Refugees, Freedmen, and Abandoned Lands established in 1865 to act primarily as a welfare agency for freed slaves. Its efforts also included establishing courts and negotiating labor relations between the ex-slaves and the Southern landowners. Despite lack of funding and personnel, the Bureau built Negro hospitals, schools, and colleges. Always controversial for its attempts to improve the rights of freedmen, it was dissolved by Congress in 1872.

5. Benjamin F. Butler (1818–1893), Massachusetts politician and Civil War general, claimed slaves within his military lines as confiscated enemy property.

6. John C. Fremont (1813–1880), Civil War general and Republican candidate for president in 1856, issued, in 1861, orders that slaves escaping to his line were free. This proclamation, issued without authority, was countermanded by Lincoln.

7. Henry H. Halleck (1815–1872), Union general who succeeded Fremont.

8. Simon L. Cameron (1799–1889), secretary of war at this time.

9. Surrender.

White House saw the inevitable, and emancipated the slaves of rebels on New Year's, 1863.[1] A month later Congress called earnestly for the Negro soldiers whom the act of July, 1862, had half grudgingly allowed to enlist. Thus the barriers were levelled and the deed was done. The stream of fugitives swelled to a flood, and anxious army officers kept inquiring: "What must be done with slaves, arriving almost daily? Are we to find food and shelter for women and children?"

It was a Pierce of Boston who pointed out the way,[2] and thus became in a sense the founder of the Freedmen's Bureau. He was a firm friend of Secretary Chase;[3] and when, in 1861, the care of slaves and abandoned lands devolved upon the Treasury officials, Pierce was specially detailed from the ranks to study the conditions. First, he cared for the refugees at Fortress Monroe; and then, after Sherman[4] had captured Hilton Head, Pierce was sent there to found his Port Royal experiment of making free workingmen out of slaves. Before his experiment was barely started, however, the problem of the fugitives had assumed such proportions that it was taken from the hands of the over-burdened Treasury Department and given to the army officials. Already centres of massed freedmen were forming at Fortress Monroe, Washington, New Orleans, Vicksburg and Corinth, Columbus, Ky., and Cairo, Ill., as well as at Port Royal. Army chaplains found here new and fruitful fields; "superintendents of contrabands" multiplied, and some attempt at systematic work was made by enlisting the able-bodied men and giving work to the others.

Then came the Freedmen's Aid societies, born of the touching appeals from Pierce and from these other centres of distress. There was the American Missionary Association, sprung from the *Amistad*,[5] and now full-grown for work; the various church organizations, the National Freedmen's Relief Association, the American Freedmen's Union, the Western Freedmen's Aid Commission,—in all fifty or more active organizations, which sent clothes, money, school-books, and teachers southward. All they did was needed, for the destitution of the freedmen was often reported as "too appalling for belief," and the situation was daily growing worse rather than better.

1. Issued by President Abraham Lincoln (1809–1865), the Emancipation Proclamation took effect on January 1, 1863 and abolished slavery in the rebel states.
2. Edward L. Pierce (1829–1897), an abolitionist from Boston, traveled to the South during the war to help the freedmen.
3. Salmon P. Chase (1808–1873), secretary of the treasury (1861–64), appointed Pierce as government agent at Port Royal, South Carolina. Chase's Point Royal experiment attempted to revive cotton production through the paid labor of freed blacks from 1862 to 1865.
4. William Tecumseh Sherman (1820–1891), Union general and supreme commander of the West, who led the "march to the sea" in 1864, capturing Atlanta and then continuing victorious to Savannah.
5. *La Amistad* was a slave ship on which Africans, led by Joseph Cinqué, mutinied off the coast of Cuba. Attempting to return to Africa, the mutineers were tricked by the sailors, who landed the ship in Connecticut instead. The slaves were imprisoned for two years, but the abolitionist defense finally won their release and their right return to Africa.

And daily, too, it seemed more plain that this was no ordinary matter of temporary relief, but a national crisis; for here loomed a labor problem of vast dimensions. Masses of Negroes stood idle, or, if they worked spasmodically, were never sure of pay; and if perchance they received pay, squandered the new thing thoughtlessly. In these and other ways were camp-life and the new liberty demoralizing the freedmen. The broader economic organization thus clearly demanded sprang up here and there as accident and local conditions determined. Here it was that Pierce's Port Royal plan of leased plantations and guided workmen pointed out the rough way. In Washington the military governor, at the urgent appeal of the superintendent, opened confiscated estates to the cultivation of the fugitives, and there in the shadow of the dome gathered black farm villages. General Dix[6] gave over estates to the freedmen of Fortress Monroe, and so on, South and West. The government and benevolent societies furnished the means of cultivation, and the Negro turned again slowly to work. The systems of control, thus started, rapidly grew, here and there, into strange little governments, like that of General Banks in Louisiana,[7] with its ninety thousand black subjects, its fifty thousand guided laborers, and its annual budget of one hundred thousand dollars and more. It made out four thousand pay-rolls a year, registered all freedmen, inquired into grievances and redressed them, laid and collected taxes, and established a system of public schools. So, too, Colonel Eaton, the superintendent of Tennessee and Arkansas,[8] ruled over one hundred thousand freedmen, leased and cultivated seven thousand acres of cotton land, and fed ten thousand paupers a year. In South Carolina was General Saxton,[9] with his deep interest in black folk. He succeeded Pierce and the Treasury officials, and sold forfeited estates, leased abandoned plantations, encouraged schools, and received from Sherman, after that terribly picturesque march to the sea, thousands of the wretched camp followers.

Three characteristic things one might have seen in Sherman's raid through Georgia, which threw the new situation in shadowy relief: the Conqueror, the Conquered, and the Negro.[1] Some see all significance in the grim front of the destroyer, and some in the bitter sufferers of the Lost Cause.[2] But to me neither soldier nor fugitive speaks with so deep a meaning as that dark human cloud that clung like remorse on the rear of those swift columns, swelling at times to half their size,

6. John A. Dix (1798–1879), Union officer directing freedmen's affairs.
7. Nathaniel P. Banks (1816–1894), Union general.
8. John Eaton, Jr. (1829–?), Union officer.
9. Rufus Saxton, Jr. (1824–1908), Union general.
1. The Conqueror refers to the Union army, led by Sherman. The Conquered were the defeated white Southerners.
2. Sentimental phrase many white Southerners used after the war to refer to the South of the Secession.

almost engulfing and choking them. In vain were they ordered back, in vain were bridges hewn from beneath their feet; on they trudged and writhed and surged, until they rolled into Savannah, a starved and naked horde of tens of thousands. There too came the characteristic military remedy: "The islands from Charleston south, the abandoned rice-fields along the rivers for thirty miles back from the sea, and the country bordering the St. John's River, Florida, are reserved and set apart for the settlement of Negroes now made free by act of war." So read the celebrated "Field-order Number Fifteen."[3]

All these experiments, orders, and systems were bound to attract and perplex the government and the nation. Directly after the Emancipation Proclamation, Representative Eliot had introduced a bill creating a Bureau of Emancipation; but it was never reported. The following June a committee of inquiry, appointed by the Secretary of War, reported in favor of a temporary bureau for the "improvement, protection, and employment of refugee freedmen," on much the same lines as were afterwards followed. Petitions came in to President Lincoln from distinguished citizens and organizations, strongly urging a comprehensive and unified plan of dealing with the freedmen, under a bureau which should be "charged with the study of plans and execution of measures for easily guiding, and in every way judiciously and humanely aiding, the passage of our emancipated and yet to be emancipated blacks from the old condition of forced labor to their new state of voluntary industry."

Some half-hearted steps were taken to accomplish this, in part, by putting the whole matter again in charge of the special Treasury agents. Laws of 1863 and 1864 directed them to take charge of and lease abandoned lands for periods not exceeding twelve months, and to "provide in such leases, or otherwise, for the employment and general welfare" of the freedmen. Most of the army officers greeted this as a welcome relief from perplexing "Negro affairs," and Secretary Fessenden, July 29, 1864, issued an excellent system of regulations, which were afterward closely followed by General Howard.[4] Under Treasury agents, large quantities of land were leased in the Mississippi Valley, and many Negroes were employed; but in August, 1864, the new regulations were suspended for reasons of "public policy," and the army was again in control.

Meanwhile Congress had turned its attention to the subject; and in

3. Issued by General Sherman in the summer of 1865 to allow freed slaves to cultivate land from Charlestown, South Carolina to Jacksonville, Florida. In the fall of that year, President Andrew Johnson countermanded the order and gave back the land to its former white owners.
4. General Oliver Otis Howard (1830–1909), commissioner of the Freedmen's Bureau in 1865. Because he conceived of the Bureau as a Christian mission, he was known as the "Christian General." After helping to found Howard University in Washington, D.C., he served as its president from 1869 to 1874. William Pitt Fessenden, secretary of the treasury (1864–65).

March the House passed a bill by a majority of two establishing a Bureau for Freedmen in the War Department. Charles Sumner,[5] who had charge of the bill in the Senate, argued that freedmen and abandoned lands ought to be under the same department, and reported a substitute for the House bill attaching the Bureau to the Treasury Department. This bill passed, but too late for action by the House. The debates wandered over the whole policy of the administration and the general question of slavery, without touching very closely the specific merits of the measure in hand. Then the national election took place; and the administration, with a vote of renewed confidence from the country, addressed itself to the matter more seriously. A conference between the two branches of Congress agreed upon a carefully drawn measure which contained the chief provisions of Sumner's bill, but made the proposed organization a department independent of both the War and the Treasury officials. The bill was conservative, giving the new department "general superintendence of all freedmen." Its purpose was to "establish regulations" for them, protect them, lease them lands, adjust their wages, and appear in civil and military courts as their "next friend." There were many limitations attached to the powers thus granted, and the organization was made permanent. Nevertheless, the Senate defeated the bill, and a new conference committee was appointed. This committee reported a new bill, February 28, which was whirled through just as the session closed, and became the act of 1865 establishing in the War Department a "Bureau of Refugees, Freedmen, and Abandoned Lands."

This last compromise was a hasty bit of legislation, vague and uncertain in outline. A Bureau was created, "to continue during the present War of Rebellion, and for one year thereafter," to which was given "the supervision and management of all abandoned lands and the control of all subjects relating to refugees and freedmen," under "such rules and regulations as may be presented by the head of the Bureau and approved by the President." A Commissioner, appointed by the President and Senate, was to control the Bureau, with an office force not exceeding ten clerks. The President might also appoint assistant commissioners in the seceded States, and to all these offices military officials might be detailed at regular pay. The Secretary of War could issue rations, clothing, and fuel to the destitute, and all abandoned property was placed in the hands of the Bureau for eventual lease and sale to ex-slaves in forty-acre parcels.[6]

Thus did the United States government definitely assume charge of the emancipated Negro as the ward of the nation. It was a tremendous

5. An abolitionist (1811–1874), leader of the Radical Republicans, and U.S. senator from Massachusetts, he was a committed advocate of Negro suffrage and civil rights.
6. The idea of parceling abandoned lands into forty-acre plots led to the misunderstanding that "forty acres and a mule" were to be allotted to every ex-slave.

undertaking. Here at a stroke of the pen was erected a government of millions of men,—and not ordinary men either, but black men emasculated by a peculiarly complete system of slavery, centuries old; and now, suddenly, violently, they come into a new birthright, at a time of war and passion, in the midst of the stricken and embittered population of their former masters. Any man might well have hesitated to assume charge of such a work, with vast responsibilities, indefinite powers, and limited resources. Probably no one but a soldier would have answered such a call promptly; and, indeed, no one but a soldier could be called, for Congress had appropriated no money for salaries and expenses.

Less than a month after the weary Emancipator passed to his rest, his successor[7] assigned Major-Gen. Oliver O. Howard to duty as Commissioner of the new Bureau. He was a Maine man, then only thirty-five years of age. He had marched with Sherman to the sea, had fought well at Gettysburg, and but the year before had been assigned to the command of the Department of Tennessee. An honest man, with too much faith in human nature, little aptitude for business and intricate detail, he had had large opportunity of becoming acquainted at first hand with much of the work before him. And of that work it has been truly said that "no approximately correct history of civilization can ever be written which does not throw out in bold relief, as one of the great landmarks of political and social progress, the organization and administration of the Freedmen's Bureau."

On May 12, 1865, Howard was appointed; and he assumed the duties of his office promptly on the 15th, and began examining the field of work. A curious mess he looked upon: little despotisms, communistic experiments, slavery, peonage,[8] business speculations, organized charity, unorganized almsgiving,—all reeling on under the guise of helping the freedmen, and all enshrined in the smoke and blood of war and the cursing and silence of angry men. On May 19 the new government— for a government it really was—issued its constitution; commissioners were to be appointed in each of the seceded States, who were to take charge of "all subjects relating to refugees and freedmen," and all relief and rations were to be given by their consent alone. The Bureau invited continued coöperation with benevolent societies, and declared: "It will be the object of all commissioners to introduce practicable systems of compensated labor," and to establish schools. Forthwith nine assistant commissioners were appointed. They were to hasten to their fields of work; seek gradually to close relief establishments, and make the destitute self-supporting; act as courts of law where there were no courts, or where Negroes were not recognized in them as free; establish the institution of marriage among ex-slaves, and keep records; see that freedmen were free to choose their employers, and help in making fair

7. Andrew Johnson (1808–1875), U.S. president (1865–69).
8. System by which debtors are bound in servitude to their creditors until their debts are paid.

contracts for them; and finally, the circular said: "Simple good faith, for which we hope on all hands for those concerned in the passing away of slavery, will especially relieve the assistant commissioners in the discharge of their duties toward the freedmen, as well as promote the general welfare."

No sooner was the work thus started, and the general system and local organization in some measure begun, than two grave difficulties appeared which changed largely the theory and outcome of Bureau work. First, there were the abandoned lands of the South. It had long been the more or less definitely expressed theory of the North that all the chief problems of Emancipation might be settled by establishing the slaves on the forfeited lands of their masters,—a sort of poetic justice, said some. But this poetry done into solemn prose meant either wholesale confiscation of private property in the South, or vast appropriations. Now Congress had not appropriated a cent, and no sooner did the proclamations of general amnesty appear than the eight hundred thousand acres of abandoned lands in the hands of the Freedmen's Bureau melted quickly away. The second difficulty lay in perfecting the local organization of the Bureau throughout the wide field of work. Making a new machine and sending out officials of duly ascertained fitness for a great work of social reform is no child's task; but this task was even harder, for a new central organization had to be fitted on a heterogeneous and confused but already existing system of relief and control of ex-slaves; and the agents available for this work must be sought for in an army still busy with war operations,—men in the very nature of the case ill fitted for delicate social work,—or among the questionable camp followers of an invading host. Thus, after a year's work, vigorously as it was pushed, the problem looked even more difficult to grasp and solve than at the beginning. Nevertheless, three things that year's work did, well worth the doing: it relieved a vast amount of physical suffering; it transported seven thousand fugitives from congested centres back to the farm; and, best of all, it inaugurated the crusade of the New England schoolma'am.[9]

The annals of this Ninth Crusade are yet to be written,—the tale of a mission that seemed to our age far more quixotic[1] than the quest of St. Louis seemed to his.[2] Behind the mists of ruin and rapine waved

---

9. This crusade, employing young teachers and missionaries known as "Gideon's Band," consisted mostly of middle-class white women who used their experience as teachers or abolitionists. The crusade also included white men who were often recent graduates of colleges or divinity schools.

1. Idealistic without regard to practicality.

2. Louis IX, King of France, led the Seventh Crusade to the Holy Land. In all, there were eight such crusades. Du Bois posits that "the crusade of the New England schoolma'am" was the "Ninth Crusade," and as ambitious as the Seventh because it attempted to bring literacy to children and to the 90 percent of the black adult population that was illiterate. By 1869 nearly 3,000 schools with 150,000 students reported to the Freedmen's Bureau.

the calico dresses of women who dared, and after the hoarse mouthings of the field guns rang the rhythm of the alphabet. Rich and poor they were, serious and curious. Bereaved now of a father, now of a brother, now of more than these, they came seeking a life work in planting New England schoolhouses among the white and black of the South. They did their work well. In that first year they taught one hundred thousand souls, and more.

Evidently, Congress must soon legislate again on the hastily organized Bureau, which had so quickly grown into wide significance and vast possibilities. An institution such as that was well-nigh as difficult to end as to begin. Early in 1866 Congress took up the matter, when Senator Trumbull, of Illinois,[3] introduced a bill to extend the Bureau and enlarge its powers. This measure received, at the hands of Congress, far more thorough discussion and attention than its predecessor. The war cloud had thinned enough to allow a clearer conception of the work of Emancipation. The champions of the bill argued that the strengthening of the Freedmen's Bureau was still a military necessity; that it was needed for the proper carrying out of the Thirteenth Amendment,[4] and was a work of sheer justice to the ex-slave, at a trifling cost to the government. The opponents of the measure declared that the war was over, and the necessity for war measures past; that the Bureau, by reason of its extraordinary powers, was clearly unconstitutional in time of peace, and was destined to irritate the South and pauperize the freedmen, at a final cost of possibly hundreds of millions. These two arguments were unanswered, and indeed unanswerable: the one that the extraordinary powers of the Bureau threatened the civil rights of all citizens; and the other that the government must have power to do what manifestly must be done, and that present abandonment of the freedmen meant their practical re-enslavement. The bill which finally passed enlarged and made permanent the Freedmen's Bureau.[5] It was promptly vetoed by President Johnson as "unconstitutional," "unnecessary," and "extrajudicial," and failed of passage over the veto. Meantime, however, the breach between Congress and the President began to broaden, and a modified form of the lost bill was finally passed over the President's second veto, July 16.

The act of 1866 gave the Freedmen's Bureau its final form,—the form by which it will be known to posterity and judged of men. It extended the existence of the Bureau to July, 1868; it authorized ad-

3. Lyman Trumbull (1813–1869), U. S. senator from Illinois, headed the move to extend the tenure and authority of the Freedmen's Bureau. Congress passed the bill over President Johnson's veto.
4. See n. 3, p. 17.
5. Andrew Johnson, Lincoln's successor, disagreed with the Republican Congress concerning Reconstruction policy. Johnson's recalcitrance concerning black rights and his insistence on states rights fueled the political furor that led to his impeachment in 1868.

ditional assistant commissioners, the retention of army officers mustered out of regular service, the sale of certain forfeited lands to freedmen on nominal terms, the sale of Confederate public property for Negro schools, and a wider field of judicial interpretation and cognizance. The government of the unreconstructed South was thus put very largely in the hands of the Freedmen's Bureau, especially as in many cases the departmental military commander was now made also assistant commissioner. It was thus that the Freedmen's Bureau became a full-fledged government of men. It made laws, executed them and interpreted them; it laid and collected taxes, defined and punished crime, maintained and used military force, and dictated such measures as it thought necessary and proper for the accomplishment of its varied ends. Naturally, all these powers were not exercised continuously nor to their fullest extent; and yet, as General Howard has said, "scarcely any subject that has to be legislated upon in civil society failed, at one time or another, to demand the action of this singular Bureau."

To understand and criticise intelligently so vast a work, one must not forget an instant the drift of things in the later sixties. Lee had surrendered, Lincoln was dead, and Johnson and Congress were at loggerheads; the Thirteenth Amendment was adopted, the Fourteenth pending, and the Fifteenth declared in force in 1870. Guerrilla raiding, the ever-present flickering after-flame of war, was spending its force against the Negroes, and all the Southern land was awakening as from some wild dream to poverty and social revolution. In a time of perfect calm, amid willing neighbors and streaming wealth, the social uplifting of four million slaves to an assured and self-sustaining place in the body politic and economic would have been a herculean task; but when to the inherent difficulties of so delicate and nice a social operation were added the spite and hate of conflict, the hell of war; when suspicion and cruelty were rife, and gaunt Hunger wept beside Bereavement,— in such a case, the work of any instrument of social regeneration was in large part foredoomed to failure. The very name of the Bureau stood for a thing in the South which for two centuries and better men had refused even to argue,—that life amid free Negroes was simply unthinkable, the maddest of experiments.

The agents that the Bureau could command varied all the way from unselfish philanthropists to narrow-minded busybodies and thieves; and even though it be true that the average was far better than the worst, it was the occasional fly that helped spoil the ointment.

Then amid all crouched the freed slave, bewildered between friend and foe. He had emerged from slavery,—not the worst slavery in the world, not a slavery that made all life unbearable, rather a slavery that had here and there something of kindliness, fidelity, and happiness,— but withal slavery, which, so far as human aspiration and desert were concerned, classed the black man and the ox together. And the Negro knew full well that, whatever their deeper convictions may have been, Southern men had fought with desperate energy to perpetuate this slavery under which the black masses, with half-articulate thought, had writhed and shivered. They welcomed freedom with a cry. They shrank from the master who still strove for their chains; they fled to the friends that had freed them, even though those friends stood ready to use them as a club for driving the recalcitrant South back into loyalty. So the cleft between the white and black South grew. Idle to say it never should have been; it was as inevitable as its results were pitiable. Curiously incongruous elements were left arrayed against each other,—the North, the government, the carpet-bagger, and the slave, here; and there, all the South that was white, whether gentleman or vagabond, honest man or rascal, lawless murderer or martyr to duty.

Thus it is doubly difficult to write of this period calmly, so intense was the feeling, so mighty the human passions that swayed and blinded men. Amid it all, two figures ever stand to typify that day to coming ages,—the one, a gray-haired gentleman, whose fathers had quit themselves like men, whose sons lay in nameless graves; who bowed to the evil of slavery because its abolition threatened untold ill to all; who stood at last, in the evening of life, a blighted, ruined form, with hate in his eyes;—and the other, a form hovering dark and mother-like, her awful face black with the mists of centuries, had aforetime quailed at that white master's command, had bent in love over the cradles of his sons and daughters, and closed in death the sunken eyes of his wife,— aye, too, at his behest had laid herself low to his lust, and borne a tawny man-child to the world, only to see her dark boy's limbs scattered to the winds by midnight marauders riding after "cursed Niggers." These were the saddest sights of that woful day; and no man clasped the hands of these two passing figures of the present-past; but, hating, they went to their long home, and, hating, their children's children live to-day.

Here, then, was the field of work for the Freedmen's Bureau; and since, with some hesitation, it was continued by the act of 1868 until 1869, let us look upon four years of its work as a whole. There were, in 1868, nine hundred Bureau officials scattered from Washington to Texas, ruling, directly and indirectly, many millions of men. The deeds of these rulers fall mainly under seven heads: the relief of physical suffering, the overseeing of the beginnings of free labor, the buying and selling of land, the establishment of schools, the paying of bounties, the administration of justice, and the financiering of all these activities.

Up to June, 1869, over half a million patients had been treated by Bureau physicians and surgeons, and sixty hospitals and asylums had been in operation. In fifty months twenty-one million free rations were distributed at a cost of over four million dollars. Next came the difficult question of labor. First, thirty thousand black men were transported from the refuges and relief stations back to the farms, back to the critical trial of a new way of working. Plain instructions went out from Washington: the laborers must be free to choose their employers, no fixed rate of wages was prescribed, and there was to be no peonage or forced labor. So far, so good; but where local agents differed *toto cœlo*[6] in capacity and character, where the *personnel* was continually changing, the outcome was necessarily varied. The largest element of success lay in the fact that the majority of the freedmen were willing, even eager, to work. So labor contracts were written,—fifty thousand in a single State,—laborers advised, wages guaranteed, and employers supplied. In truth, the organization became a vast labor bureau,—not perfect, indeed, notably defective here and there, but on the whole successful beyond the dreams of thoughtful men. The two great obstacles which confronted the officials were the tyrant and the idler,—the slaveholder who was determined to perpetuate slavery under another name; and the freedman who regarded freedom as perpetual rest,—the Devil and the Deep Sea.

In the work of establishing the Negroes as peasant proprietors, the Bureau was from the first handicapped and at last absolutely checked. Something was done, and larger things were planned; abandoned lands were leased so long as they remained in the hands of the Bureau, and a total revenue of nearly half a million dollars derived from black tenants. Some other lands to which the nation had gained title were sold on easy terms, and public lands were opened for settlement to the very few freedmen who had tools and capital. But the vision of "forty acres and a mule"[7]—the righteous and reasonable ambition to become a landholder, which the nation had all but categorically promised the freedmen—was destined in most cases to bitter disappointment. And those men of marvellous hindsight who are to-day seeking to preach the Negro back to the present peonage of the soil know well, or ought to know, that the opportunity of binding the Negro peasant willingly to the soil was lost on that day when the Commissioner of the Freedmen's Bureau had to go to South Carolina and tell the weeping freedmen, after their years of toil, that their land was not theirs, that there was a mistake—somewhere. If by 1874 the Georgia Negro alone owned three hundred and fifty thousand acres of land, it was by grace of his thrift rather than by bounty of the government.

The greatest success of the Freedmen's Bureau lay in the planting of the free school among Negroes, and the idea of free elementary education among all classes in the South. It not only called the school-mistresses through the benevolent agencies and built them school-houses, but it helped discover and support such apostles of human

6. Literally, by the whole heaven (Latin), that is, entirely, absolutely.
7. See n. 6, p. 22.

culture as Edmund Ware, Samuel Armstrong, and Erastus Cravath.[8] The opposition to Negro education in the South was at first bitter, and showed itself in ashes, insult, and blood; for the South believed an educated Negro to be a dangerous Negro. And the South was not wholly wrong; for education among all kinds of men always has had, and always will have, an element of danger and revolution, of dissatisfaction and discontent. Nevertheless, men strive to know. Perhaps some inkling of this paradox, even in the unquiet days of the Bureau, helped the bayonets allay an opposition to human training which still to-day lies smouldering in the South, but not flaming. Fisk, Atlanta, Howard, and Hampton[9] were founded in these days, and six million dollars were expended for educational work, seven hundred and fifty thousand dollars of which the freedmen themselves gave of their poverty.

Such contributions, together with the buying of land and various other enterprises, showed that the ex-slave was handling some free capital already. The chief initial source of this was labor in the army, and his pay and bounty as a soldier. Payments to Negro soldiers were at first complicated by the ignorance of the recipients, and the fact that the quotas of colored regiments from Northern States were largely filled by recruits from the South, unknown to their fellow soldiers. Consequently, payments were accompanied by such frauds that Congress, by joint resolution in 1867, put the whole matter in the hands of the Freedmen's Bureau. In two years six million dollars was thus distributed to five thousand claimants, and in the end the sum exceeded eight million dollars. Even in this system fraud was frequent; but still the work put needed capital in the hands of practical paupers, and some, at least, was well spent.

The most perplexing and least successful part of the Bureau's work lay in the exercise of its judicial functions. The regular Bureau court consisted of one representative of the employer, one of the Negro, and one of the Bureau. If the Bureau could have maintained a perfectly judicial attitude, this arrangement would have been ideal, and must in time have gained confidence; but the nature of its other activities and the character of its *personnel* prejudiced the Bureau in favor of the black litigants, and led without doubt to much injustice and annoyance. On the other hand, to leave the Negro in the hands of Southern courts was impossible. In a distracted land where slavery had hardly fallen, to

8. Erastus M. Cravath (1833–1900), clergyman, educator, and abolitionist who helped establish Fisk University, Du Bois's undergraduate school in Nashville, Tennessee, in 1866. Edmund A. Ware (1837–1885), appointed by General Howard as director of education for Georgia in 1867, founded Atlanta University in 1865. Samuel Armstrong (1839–1893), a Union officer in command of a black regiment during the Civil War, founded Hampton Institute in Virginia in 1868. Armstrong became a mentor to Booker T. Washington.
9. Black colleges established in the South after the Civil War. Hampton Institute was located at Hampton, Virginia, in 1868; Fisk University, in Nashville, Tennessee, was founded in 1866; Atlanta University was begun in 1865; and Howard University was established in 1867, in Washington, D.C.

keep the strong from wanton abuse of the weak, and the weak from gloating insolently over the half-shorn strength of the strong, was a thankless, hopeless task. The former masters of the land were peremptorily ordered about, seized, and imprisoned, and punished over and again, with scant courtesy from army officers. The former slaves were intimidated, beaten, raped, and butchered by angry and revengeful men. Bureau courts tended to become centres simply for punishing whites, while the regular civil courts tended to become solely institutions for perpetuating the slavery of blacks. Almost every law and method ingenuity could devise was employed by the legislatures to reduce the Negroes to serfdom,—to make them the slaves of the State,[1] if not of individual owners; while the Bureau officials too often were found striving to put the "bottom rail on top," and give the freedmen a power and independence which they could not yet use. It is all well enough for us of another generation to wax wise with advice to those who bore the burden in the heat of the day. It is full easy now to see that the man who lost home, fortune, and family at a stroke, and saw his land ruled by "mules and niggers," was really benefited by the passing of slavery. It is not difficult now to say to the young freedman, cheated and cuffed about, who has seen his father's head beaten to a jelly and his own mother namelessly assaulted, that the meek shall inherit the earth. Above all, nothing is more convenient than to heap on the Freedmen's Bureau all the evils of that evil day, and damn it utterly for every mistake and blunder that was made.

All this is easy, but it is neither sensible nor just. Some one had blundered, but that was long before Oliver Howard was born; there was criminal aggression and heedless neglect, but without some system of control there would have been far more than there was. Had that control been from within, the Negro would have been re-enslaved, to all intents and purposes. Coming as the control did from without, perfect men and methods would have bettered all things; and even with imperfect agents and questionable methods, the work accomplished was not undeserving of commendation.

Such was the dawn of Freedom; such was the work of the Freedmen's Bureau, which, summed up in brief, may be epitomized thus: For some fifteen million dollars, beside the sums spent before 1865, and the dole of benevolent societies, this Bureau set going a system of free labor, established a beginning of peasant proprietorship, secured the recognition of black freedmen before courts of law, and founded the free common school in the South. On the other hand, it failed to begin the establishment of good-will between ex-masters and freedmen, to guard its work wholly from paternalistic methods which discouraged self-reliance, and to carry out to any considerable extent its implied

1. The slave codes of 1865, passed by Southern state legislatures, were overturned by Congress in 1866–67.

promises to furnish the freedmen with land. Its successes were the result of hard work, supplemented by the aid of philanthropists and the eager striving of black men. Its failures were the result of bad local agents, the inherent difficulties of the work, and national neglect.

Such an institution, from its wide powers, great responsibilities, large control of moneys, and generally conspicuous position, was naturally open to repeated and bitter attack. It sustained a searching Congressional investigation at the instance of Fernando Wood[2] in 1870. Its archives and few remaining functions were with blunt discourtesy transferred from Howard's control, in his absence, to the supervision of Secretary of War Belknap[3] in 1872, on the Secretary's recommendation. Finally, in consequence of grave intimations of wrong-doing made by the Secretary and his subordinates, General Howard was court-martialed in 1874. In both of these trials the Commissioner of the Freedmen's Bureau was officially exonerated from any wilful misdoing, and his work commended. Nevertheless, many unpleasant things were brought to light,—the methods of transacting the business of the Bureau were faulty; several cases of defalcation[4] were proved, and other frauds strongly suspected; there were some business transactions which savored of dangerous speculation, if not dishonesty; and around it all lay the smirch of the Freedmen's Bank.[5]

Morally and practically, the Freedmen's Bank was part of the Freedmen's Bureau, although it had no legal connection with it. With the prestige of the government back of it, and a directing board of unusual respectability and national reputation, this banking institution had made a remarkable start in the development of that thrift among black folk which slavery had kept them from knowing. Then in one sad day came the crash,—all the hard-earned dollars of the freedmen disappeared; but that was the least of the loss,—all the faith in saving went too, and much of the faith in men; and that was a loss that a Nation which to-day sneers at Negro shiftlessness has never yet made good. Not even ten additional years of slavery could have done so much to throttle the thrift of the freedmen as the mismanagement and bankruptcy of the series of savings banks chartered by the Nation for their especial aid. Where all the blame should rest, it is hard to say; whether the Bureau and the Bank died chiefly by reason of the blows of its selfish friends or the dark machinations of its foes, perhaps even time will never reveal, for here lies unwritten history.

Of the foes without the Bureau, the bitterest were those who attacked not so much its conduct or policy under the law as the necessity for

2. Mayor of New York City who employed inflammatory pro-Southern rhetoric.
3. William W. Belknap (1829–1890), secretary of war under Ulysses S. Grant. Belknap was impeached by the House of Representatives in 1876 for accepting bribes.
4. Misuse or embezzlement of funds.
5. The Freedmen's Savings and Trust Company was incorporated by Congress in 1865, but it failed in 1874 under its final president, Frederick Douglass.

any such institution at all. Such attacks came primarily from the Border States[6] and the South; and they were summed up by Senator Davis, of Kentucky,[7] when he moved to entitle the act of 1866 a bill "to promote strife and conflict between the white and black races . . . by a grant of unconstitutional power." The argument gathered tremendous strength South and North; but its very strength was its weakness. For, argued the plain common-sense of the nation, if it is unconstitutional, unpractical, and futile for the nation to stand guardian over its helpless wards, then there is left but one alternative,—to make those wards their own guardians by arming them with the ballot. Moreover, the path of the practical politician pointed the same way; for, argued this opportunist, if we cannot peacefully reconstruct the South with white votes, we certainly can with black votes. So justice and force joined hands.

The alternative thus offered the nation was not between full and restricted Negro suffrage; else every sensible man, black and white, would easily have chosen the latter. It was rather a choice between suffrage and slavery, after endless blood and gold had flowed to sweep human bondage away. Not a single Southern legislature stood ready to admit a Negro, under any conditions, to the polls; not a single Southern legislature believed free Negro labor was possible without a system of restrictions that took all its freedom away; there was scarcely a white man in the South who did not honestly regard Emancipation as a crime, and its practical nullification as a duty. In such a situation, the granting of the ballot to the black man was a necessity, the very least a guilty nation could grant a wronged race, and the only method of compelling the South to accept the results of the war. Thus Negro suffrage ended a civil war by beginning a race feud. And some felt gratitude toward the race thus sacrificed in its swaddling clothes on the altar of national integrity; and some felt and feel only indifference and contempt.

Had political exigencies been less pressing, the opposition to government guardianship of Negroes less bitter, and the attachment to the slave system less strong, the social seer can well imagine a far better policy,—a permanent Freedmen's Bureau, with a national system of Negro schools; a carefully supervised employment and labor office; a system of impartial protection before the regular courts; and such institutions for social betterment as savings-banks, land and building associations, and social settlements. All this vast expenditure of money and brains might have formed a great school of prospective citizenship, and solved in a way we have not yet solved the most perplexing and persistent of the Negro problems.

---

6. Southern states that both shared borders with Northern states and did not secede to the Confederacy. They were Kentucky, Missouri, West Virginia, and Maryland.
7. Garrett Davis (1815–1882), Democratic senator from Kentucky, actively opposed federal intervention on behalf of freedmen.

That such an institution was unthinkable in 1870 was due in part to certain acts of the Freedmen's Bureau itself. It came to regard its work as merely temporary, and Negro suffrage as a final answer to all present perplexities. The political ambition of many of its agents and *protégés* led it far afield into questionable activities, until the South, nursing its own deep prejudices, came easily to ignore all the good deeds of the Bureau and hate its very name with perfect hatred. So the Freedmen's Bureau died, and its child was the Fifteenth Amendment.[8]

The passing of a great human institution before its work is done, like the untimely passing of a single soul, but leaves a legacy of striving for other men. The legacy of the Freedmen's Bureau is the heavy heritage of this generation. To-day, when new and vaster problems are destined to strain every fibre of the national mind and soul, would it not be well to count this legacy honestly and carefully? For this much all men know: despite compromise, war, and struggle, the Negro is not free. In the backwoods of the Gulf States, for miles and miles, he may not leave the plantation of his birth; in well-nigh the whole rural South the black farmers are peons, bound by law and custom to an economic slavery, from which the only escape is death or the penitentiary. In the most cultured sections and cities of the South the Negroes are a segregated servile caste, with restricted rights and privileges. Before the courts, both in law and custom, they stand on a different and peculiar basis. Taxation without representation is the rule of their political life. And the result of all this is, and in nature must have been, lawlessness and crime. That is the large legacy of the Freedmen's Bureau, the work it did not do because it could not.

I have seen a land right merry with the sun, where children sing, and rolling hills lie like passioned women wanton with harvest. And there in the King's Highway[9] sat and sits a figure veiled and bowed, by which the traveller's footsteps hasten as they go. On the tainted air broods fear. Three centuries' thought has been the raising and unveiling of that bowed human heart, and now behold a century new for the duty and the deed. The problem of the Twentieth Century is the problem of the color-line.

8. See n. 3, p. 17.
9. In the Hebrew Scriptures, Numbers 20.17 and 21.22 mention the main trans-Jordanian route, "The King's Highway." In these passages, the people of Israel are denied the use of this public road, thus increasing their time of wandering in the desert before reaching the Promised Land. This veiled figure of the Negro is similarly denied progress.

III

Of Mr. Booker T. Washington and Others[1]

From birth till death enslaved; in word, in deed, unmanned!

Hereditary bondsmen! Know ye not
Who would be free themselves must strike the blow?

BYRON.

 Easily the most striking thing in the history of the American Negro since 1876 is the ascendancy of Mr. Booker T. Washington. It began at the time when war memories and ideals were rapidly passing; a day of astonishing commercial development was dawning; a sense of doubt and hesitation overtook the freedmen's sons,—then it was that his leading began. Mr. Washington came, with a simple definite programme, at the psychological moment when the nation was a little ashamed of having bestowed so much sentiment on Negroes, and was concentrating its energies on Dollars. His programme of industrial education, conciliation of the South, and submission and silence as to civil and political rights, was not wholly original; the Free Negroes from 1830 up to wartime had striven to build industrial schools, and the American Missionary Association had from the first taught various trades; and Price[2] and others had sought a way of honorable alliance with the best of the Southerners. But Mr. Washington first indissolubly linked these things; he put enthusiasm, unlimited energy, and perfect faith into this programme, and changed it from a by-path into a veritable Way of Life.[3] And the tale of the methods by which he did this is a fascinating study of human life.

 It startled the nation to hear a Negro advocating such a programme after many decades of bitter complaint; it startled and won the applause

---

1. Revised from "The Evolution of Negro Leadership," *The Dial* (July 16, 1901): 53–55. The three lines of verse are from Canto 2 of Lord Byron's *Childe Harold's Pilgrimage* (1812). The music quotation is from the Negro spiritual "A Great Camp Meeting in the Promised Land."
2. Joseph C. Price (1854–1893), A. M. E. Zion minister, orator, and liberal arts advocate, founded Zion Wesley College in 1882 and Livingston College in 1885.
3. Booker Taliaferro Washington (1856–1915) published his autobiography, *Up From Slavery*, in 1901. It has been called the autobiography of an institution because much of its content concerns Washington's founding of Tuskegee Institute.

of the South, it interested and won the admiration of the North; and after a confused murmur of protest, it silenced if it did not convert the Negroes themselves.

To gain the sympathy and coöperation of the various elements comprising the white South was Mr. Washington's first task; and this, at the time Tuskegee[4] was founded, seemed, for a black man, well-nigh impossible. And yet ten years later it was done in the word spoken at Atlanta: "In all things purely social we can be as separate as the five fingers, and yet one as the hand in all things essential to mutual progress." This "Atlanta Compromise"[5] is by all odds the most notable thing in Mr. Washington's career. The South interpreted it in different ways: the radicals received it as a complete surrender of the demand for civil and political equality; the conservatives, as a generously conceived working basis for mutual understanding. So both approved it, and to-day its author is certainly the most distinguished Southerner since Jefferson Davis,[6] and the one with the largest personal following.

Next to this achievement comes Mr. Washington's work in gaining place and consideration in the North. Others less shrewd and tactful had formerly essayed to sit on these two stools and had fallen between them; but as Mr. Washington knew the heart of the South from birth and training, so by singular insight he intuitively grasped the spirit of the age which was dominating the North. And so thoroughly did he learn the speech and thought of triumphant commercialism, and the ideals of material prosperity, that the picture of a lone black boy poring over a French grammar amid the weeds and dirt of a neglected home soon seemed to him the acme of absurdities.[7] One wonders what Socrates and St. Francis of Assisi would say to this.[8]

And yet this very singleness of vision and thorough oneness with his age is a mark of the successful man. It is as though Nature must needs make men narrow in order to give them force. So Mr. Washington's cult has gained unquestioning followers, his work has wonderfully prospered, his friends are legion, and his enemies are confounded. To-day

---

4. Washington founded Tuskegee Institute in 1881 as a normal, or secondary, school in Tuskegee, Alabama. He served as president until his death, turning the Institute from two unequipped buildings into a complex of over one hundred buildings. Washington also expanded Tuskegee into a college dedicated to industrial education and the training of black schoolteachers.

5. Speech delivered in Atlanta on September 18, 1895, at the Cotton States Exposition. In this famous and controversial speech, Washington not only emphasizes economic self-development for blacks but he also accepts social segregation between the races (see p. 167 for complete text).

6. President of the Confederate States of America during the Civil War. Davis (1808–1889) was also the topic for Du Bois's commencement address, delivered when he graduated from Harvard in 1890.

7. In Up From Slavery, Washington is distressed to find that a young man living in a one-room cabin is attempting to learn French, with "filth all around him, and weeds in the yard and garden" (p. 58).

8. Italian preacher (1182–1226), founder of the Franciscan Order of monks. Socrates, Greek philosopher (469?–399 B.C.E.).

he stands as the one recognized spokesman of his ten million fellows, and one of the most notable figures in a nation of seventy millions. One hesitates, therefore, to criticise a life which, beginning with so little, has done so much. And yet the time is come when one may speak in all sincerity and utter courtesy of the mistakes and shortcomings of Mr. Washington's career, as well as of his triumphs, without being thought captious or envious, and without forgetting that it is easier to do ill than well in the world.

The criticism that has hitherto met Mr. Washington has not always been of this broad character. In the South especially has he had to walk warily to avoid the harshest judgments,—and naturally so, for he is dealing with the one subject of deepest sensitiveness to that section. Twice—once when at the Chicago celebration of the Spanish-American War he alluded to the color-prejudice that is "eating away the vitals of the South," and once when he dined with President Roosevelt[9]—has the resulting Southern criticism been violent enough to threaten seriously his popularity. In the North the feeling has several times forced itself into words, that Mr. Washington's counsels of submission overlooked certain elements of true manhood, and that his educational programme was unnecessarily narrow. Usually, however, such criticism has not found open expression, although, too, the spiritual sons of the Abolitionists have not been prepared to acknowledge that the schools founded before Tuskegee, by men of broad ideals and self-sacrificing spirit, were wholly failures or worthy of ridicule. While, then, criticism has not failed to follow Mr. Washington, yet the prevailing public opinion of the land has been but too willing to deliver the solution of a wearisome problem into his hands, and say, "If that is all you and your race ask, take it."

Among his own people, however, Mr. Washington has encountered the strongest and most lasting opposition, amounting at times to bitterness, and even to-day continuing strong and insistent even though largely silenced in outward expression by the public opinion of the nation. Some of this opposition is, of course, mere envy; the disappointment of displaced demagogues and the spite of narrow minds. But aside from this, there is among educated and thoughtful colored men in all parts of the land a feeling of deep regret, sorrow, and apprehension at the wide currency and ascendancy which some of Mr. Washington's theories have gained. These same men admire his sincerity of purpose, and are willing to forgive much to honest endeavor which is doing something worth the doing. They coöperate with Mr. Washington as far as they conscientiously can; and, indeed, it is no ordinary tribute to this man's tact and power that, steering as he must between so many diverse interests and opinions, he so largely retains the respect of all.

9. Theodore Roosevelt (1858–1919), U.S. president from 1901 to 1909. Washington dined at the White House on October 16, 1901.

But the hushing of the criticism of honest opponents is a dangerous thing. It leads some of the best of the critics to unfortunate silence and paralysis of effort, and others to burst into speech so passionately and intemperately as tc lose listeners. Honest and earnest criticism from those whose interests are most nearly touched,—criticism of writers by readers, of government by those governed, of leaders by those led,—this is the soul of democracy and the safeguard of modern society. If the best of the American Negroes receive by outer pressure a leader whom they had not recognized before, manifestly there is here a certain palpable gain. Yet there is also irreparable loss,—a loss of that peculiarly valuable education which a group receives when by search and criticism it finds and commissions its own leaders. The way in which this is done is at once the most elementary and the nicest problem of social growth. History is but the record of such group-leadership; and yet how infinitely changeful is its type and character! And of all types and kinds, what can be more instructive than the leadership of a group within a group?—that curious double movement where real progress may be negative and actual advance be relative retrogression. All this is the social student's inspiration and despair.

Now in the past the American Negro has had instructive experience in the choosing of group leaders, founding thus a peculiar dynasty which in the light of present conditions is worth while studying. When sticks and stones and beasts form the sole environment of a people, their attitude is largely one of determined opposition to and conquest of natural forces. But when to earth and brute is added an environment of men and ideas, then the attitude of the imprisoned group may take three main forms,—a feeling of revolt and revenge; an attempt to adjust all thought and action to the will of the greater group; or, finally, a determined effort at self-realization and self-development despite environing opinion. The influence of all of these attitudes at various times can be traced in the history of the American Negro, and in the evolution of his successive leaders.

Before 1750, while the fire of African freedom still burned in the veins of the slaves, there was in all leadership or attempted leadership but the one motive of revolt and revenge,—typified in the terrible Maroons, the Danish blacks, and Cato of Stono,[1] and veiling all the Americas in fear of insurrection. The liberalizing tendencies of the latter half of the eighteenth century brought, along with kindlier relations between black and white, thoughts of ultimate adjustment and assimilation. Such aspiration was especially voiced in the earnest songs of Phyllis, in the martyrdom of Attucks, the fighting of Salem and Poor, the intel-

1. Leader of a major slave rebellion that took place near the Stono River in South Carolina in 1739. Maroons was the eighteenth-century designation for escaped slaves who formed guerrilla bands in the West Indies, Central America, and South America. Danish blacks were slaves who took control of an island in the Dutch West Indies (now the Virgin Islands) in 1723.

lectual accomplishments of Banneker and Derham, and the political demands of the Cuffes.[2]

Stern financial and social stress after the war cooled much of the previous humanitarian ardor. The disappointment and impatience of the Negroes at the persistence of slavery and serfdom voiced itself in two movements. The slaves in the South, aroused undoubtedly by vague rumors of the Haytian revolt, made three fierce attempts at insurrection,—in 1800 under Gabriel in Virginia, in 1822 under Vesey in Carolina, and in 1831 again in Virginia under the terrible Nat Turner.[3] In the Free States, on the other hand, a new and curious attempt at self-development was made. In Philadelphia and New York color-prescription led to a withdrawal of Negro communicants from white churches and the formation of a peculiar socio-religious institution among the Negroes known as the African Church,[4]—an organization still living and controlling in its various branches over a million of men.

Walker's wild appeal[5] against the trend of the times showed how the world was changing after the coming of the cotton-gin. By 1830 slavery seemed hopelessly fastened on the South, and the slaves thoroughly cowed into submission. The free Negroes of the North, inspired by the mulatto immigrants from the West Indies, began to change the basis of their demands; they recognized the slavery of slaves, but insisted that they themselves were freemen, and sought assimilation and amalgamation with the nation on the same terms with other men. Thus, Forten and Purvis of Philadelphia, Shad of Wilmington, Du Bois of New Haven, Barbadoes of Boston,[6] and others, strove singly and together as men, they said, not as slaves; as "people of color," not as "Negroes." The trend of the times, however, refused them recognition save in

2. Paul Cuffe (1759–1817), black ship's captain and an early proponent of black migration to Africa. Phillis Wheatley (ca. 1753–1784), American poet, was a slave when her book of verse, *Poems on Various Subjects, Religious and Moral*, was published in London in 1773. Crispus Attucks (1723–1770) was killed in the Boston Massacre in 1770. Peter Salem (1750–1816) and Salem Poor (1747–?) were black men who fought in the American Revolution. Benjamin Banneker (1731–1806), a free black, was a mathematician, scientist, and author of a farmer's almanac. James C. Durham (ca. 1762–?), born a slave, was taught to be a physician by his owner, and bought his freedom through his knowledge of medicine.
3. American slave (1800–1831) who led a rebellion in Southampton County, Virginia, in 1831 in which sixty whites were killed. His *Confessions* exploded the myth of the contented slave, and fueled controversy on both sides of the question of abolition. Gabriel Prosser (d. 1800), executed in Richmond, Virginia. Denmark Vesey (d. 1822), executed in Charleston, South Carolina.
4. The African Methodist Episcopal Church.
5. David Walker (1785–1830) published *An Appeal to the Colored Citizens of the World* in 1829. Its radical rhetoric was probably responsible for his death under suspicious circumstances in 1830.
6. James G. Barbados (1796–1841), Bostonian and co-founder of the American Anti-Slavery Society (1833). James Forten (1766–1842), black revolutionary war veteran, philanthropist, and co-founder of the American Anti-Slavery Society. Robert Purvis (1810–1898), leading abolitionist and post–bellum civil rights activist. Shad probably refers to Abraham Shadd (1801–1882), black leader in Delaware. Alexander Du Bois (1803–1888), Du Bois's paternal grandfather.

individual and exceptional cases, considered them as one with all the despised blacks, and they soon found themselves striving to keep even the rights they formerly had of voting and working and moving as free-men. Schemes of migration and colonization arose among them; but these they refused to entertain, and they eventually turned to the Ab-olition movement as a final refuge.

Here, led by Remond, Nell, Wells-Brown, and Douglass,[7] a new period of self-assertion and self-development dawned. To be sure, ulti-mate freedom and assimilation was the ideal before the leaders, but the assertion of the manhood rights of the Negro by himself was the main reliance, and John Brown's raid[8] was the extreme of its logic. After the war and emancipation, the great form of Frederick Douglass, the greatest of American Negro leaders, still led the host. Self-assertion, especially in political lines, was the main programme, and behind Douglass came Elliot, Bruce, and Langston, and the Reconstruction politicians, and, less conspicuous but of greater social significance Al-exander Crummell and Bishop Daniel Payne.[9]

Then came the Revolution of 1876,[1] the suppression of the Negro votes, the changing and shifting of ideals, and the seeking of new lights in the great night. Douglass, in his old age, still bravely stood for the ideals of his early manhood,—ultimate assimilation *through* self-assertion, and on no other terms. For a time Price arose as a new leader, destined, it seemed, not to give up, but to re-state the old ideals in a form less repugnant to the white South. But he passed away in his prime. Then came the new leader. Nearly all the former ones had become leaders by the silent suffrage of their fellows,[2] had sought to lead their own people alone, and were usually, save Douglass, little known outside their race. But Booker T. Washington arose as essentially

7. Frederick Douglass (1818–1895), ex-slave and abolitionist. Douglass edited his own newspa-per, garnered fame from his lectures, and wrote the most famous slave narrative of the nine-teenth century, the *Narrative of the Life of Frederick Douglass, an American Slave* (1845). Charles Lenox Remond (1810–1873), black Boston abolitionist and radical in the civil rights cause. William Cooper Nell (1816–1874), author of *Colored Patriots of the American Revo-lution* (1855) and leader of the movement to integrate the Boston schools in the 1840s. William Wells Brown (1814–1884), fugitive slave and author of the novel *Clotel, or the Pres-ident's Daughter* (1853), as well as a historical text.
8. John Brown (1800–1859), white abolitionist whose exploits at Harpers Ferry, Virginia, in October 1859, helped bring on the Civil War. Brown and his small band seized a government arsenal, expecting to trigger a general slave insurrection. Instead, he was arrested, tried for treason, and hanged in November 1859.
9. Daniel Alexander Payne (1811–1893), founder of Wilberforce College and bishop of the A.M.E. Church. Robert Brown Eliot (1841–1884), elected to the U.S. Congress from South Carolina during Reconstruction. Blanche K. Bruce (1841–1898), ex-slave and first black U.S. senator. Bruce was elected as a Republican from Mississippi. John Mercer Langston (1829–1897), freed black, elected as Virginia's first black congressman. Later, he became the dean of Howard University's School of Law. Alexander Crummell (1819–1898), educated at Cam-bridge University in England, ordained in the Anglican Church, served as missionary to Liberia, and later became rector of St. Luke's Church in Washington, D.C. He was a founding member of the American Negro Academy.
1. The shifting of the Republican Party away from support of the freedmen.
2. The suffrage was "silent" because of the inability of most black people to vote.

the leader not of one race but of two,—a compromiser between the South, the North, and the Negro. Naturally the Negroes resented, at first bitterly, signs of compromise which surrendered their civil and political rights, even though this was to be exchanged for larger chances of economic development. The rich and dominating North, however, was not only weary of the race problem, but was investing largely in Southern enterprises, and welcomed any method of peaceful coöperation. Thus, by national opinion, the Negroes began to recognize Mr. Washington's leadership; and the voice of criticism was hushed.

Mr. Washington represents in Negro thought the old attitude of adjustment and submission; but adjustment at such a peculiar time as to make his programme unique. This is an age of unusual economic development, and Mr. Washington's programme naturally takes an economic cast, becoming a gospel of Work and Money to such an extent as apparently almost completely to overshadow the higher aims of life. Moreover, this is an age when the more advanced races are coming in closer contact with the less developed races, and the race-feeling is therefore intensified; and Mr. Washington's programme practically accepts the alleged inferiority of the Negro races. Again, in our own land, the reaction from the sentiment of war time has given impetus to race-prejudice against Negroes, and Mr. Washington withdraws many of the high demands of Negroes as men and American citizens. In other periods of intensified prejudice all the Negro's tendency to self-assertion has been called forth; at this period a policy of submission is advocated. In the history of nearly all other races and peoples the doctrine preached at such crises has been that manly self-respect is worth more than lands and houses, and that a people who voluntarily surrender such respect, or cease striving for it, are not worth civilizing.

In answer to this, it has been claimed that the Negro can survive only through submission. Mr. Washington distinctly asks that black people give up, at least for the present, three things,—

First, political power,

Second, insistence on civil rights,

Third, higher education of Negro youth,

—and concentrate all their energies on industrial education, the accumulation of wealth, and the conciliation of the South. This policy has been courageously and insistently advocated for over fifteen years, and has been triumphant for perhaps ten years. As a result of this tender of the palm-branch,[3] what has been the return? In these years there have occurred:

1. The disfranchisement of the Negro.

---

3. Offer of peace. Du Bois, in referring to the concessions, seems to be thinking of the olive branch, the traditional symbol of a peace offering, rather than the palm branch, which symbolizes victory.

2. The legal creation of a distinct status of civil inferiority for the Negro.

3. The steady withdrawal of aid from institutions for the higher training of the Negro.

These movements are not, to be sure, direct results of Mr. Washington's teachings; but his propaganda has, without a shadow of doubt, helped their speedier accomplishment. The question then comes: Is it possible, and probable, that nine millions of men can make effective progress in economic lines if they are deprived of political rights, made a servile caste, and allowed only the most meagre chance for developing their exceptional men? If history and reason give any distinct answer to these questions, it is an emphatic *No*. And Mr. Washington thus faces the triple paradox of his career:

1. He is striving nobly to make Negro artisans business men and property-owners; but it is utterly impossible, under modern competitive methods, for workingmen and property-owners to defend their rights and exist without the right of suffrage.

2. He insists on thrift and self-respect, but at the same time counsels a silent submission to civic inferiority such as is bound to sap the manhood of any race in the long run.

3. He advocates common-school and industrial training, and depreciates institutions of higher learning; but neither the Negro common-schools,[4] nor Tuskegee itself, could remain open a day were it not for teachers trained in Negro colleges, or trained by their graduates.

This triple paradox in Mr. Washington's position is the object of criticism by two classes of colored Americans. One class is spiritually descended from Toussaint the Savior, through Gabriel, Vesey, and Turner, and they represent the attitude of revolt and revenge; they hate the white South blindly and distrust the white race generally, and so far as they agree on definite action, think that the Negro's only hope lies in emigration beyond the borders of the United States. And yet, by the irony of fate, nothing has more effectually made this programme seem hopeless than the recent course of the United States toward weaker and darker peoples in the West Indies, Hawaii, and the Philippines,—for where in the world may we go and be safe from lying and brute force?[5]

The other class of Negroes who cannot agree with Mr. Washington has hitherto said little aloud. They deprecate the sight of scattered counsels, of internal disagreement; and especially they dislike making their just criticism of a useful and earnest man an excuse for a general discharge of venom from small-minded opponents. Nevertheless, the ques-

4. Public elementary schools.
5. After the Spanish-American War in 1898, Hawaii and the Philippines became U.S. possessions.

tions involved are so fundamental and serious that it is difficult to see how men like the Grimkes, Kelly Miller, J. W. E. Bowen,[6] and other representatives of this group, can much longer be silent. Such men feel in conscience bound to ask of this nation three things:

1. The right to vote.
2. Civic equality.
3. The education of youth according to ability.

They acknowledge Mr. Washington's invaluable service in counselling patience and courtesy in such demands; they do not ask that ignorant black men vote when ignorant whites are debarred, or that any reasonable restrictions in the suffrage should not be applied; they know that the low social level of the mass of the race is responsible for much discrimination against it, but they also know, and the nation knows, that relentless color-prejudice is more often a cause than a result of the Negro's degradation; they seek the abatement of this relic of barbarism, and not its systematic encouragement and pampering by all agencies of social power from the Associated Press to the Church of Christ. They advocate, with Mr. Washington, a broad system of Negro common schools supplemented by thorough industrial training; but they are surprised that a man of Mr. Washington's insight cannot see that no such educational system ever has rested or can rest on any other basis than that of the well-equipped college and university, and they insist that there is a demand for a few such institutions throughout the South to train the best of the Negro youth as teachers, professional men, and leaders.

This group of men honor Mr. Washington for his attitude of conciliation toward the white South; they accept the "Atlanta Compromise" in its broadest interpretation; they recognize, with him, many signs of promise, many men of high purpose and fair judgment, in this section; they know that no easy task has been laid upon a region already tottering under heavy burdens. But, nevertheless, they insist that the way to truth and right lies in straightforward honesty, not in indiscriminate flattery; in praising those of the South who do well and criticising uncompromisingly those who do ill; in taking advantage of the opportunities at hand and urging their fellows to do the same, but at the same time in remembering that only a firm adherence to their higher ideals and aspirations will ever keep those ideals within the realm of possibility. They do not expect that the free right to vote, to enjoy civic rights, and to be educated, will come in a moment; they do not expect to see the bias and prejudices of years disappear at the blast of a trum-

6. John Wesley Edward Bowen (1855–1933), Methodist minister and educator. Archibald H. Grimké (1849–1930), lawyer, author, and leader of the Washington D.C. branch of the NAACP. His brother, Francis J. Grimké (1850–1937), was an influential minister. Kelly Miller (1863–1939), mathematician and sociologist who taught at Howard University.

pet;[7] but they are absolutely certain that the way for a people to gain their reasonable rights is not by voluntarily throwing them away and insisting that they do not want them; that the way for a people to gain respect is not by continually belittling and ridiculing themselves; that, on the contrary, Negroes must insist continually, in season and out of season, that voting is necessary to modern manhood, that color discrimination is barbarism, and that black boys need education as well as white boys.

In failing thus to state plainly and unequivocally the legitimate demands of their people, even at the cost of opposing an honored leader, the thinking classes of American Negroes would shirk a heavy responsibility,—a responsibility to themselves, a responsibility to the struggling masses, a responsibility to the darker races of men whose future depends so largely on this American experiment, but especially a responsibility to this nation,—this common Fatherland. It is wrong to encourage a man or a people in evil-doing; it is wrong to aid and abet a national crime simply because it is unpopular not to do so. The growing spirit of kindliness and reconciliation between the North and South after the frightful differences of a generation ago ought to be a source of deep congratulation to all, and especially to those whose mistreatment caused the war; but if that reconciliation is to be marked by the industrial slavery and civic death of those same black men, with permanent legislation into a position of inferiority, then those black men, if they are really men, are called upon by every consideration of patriotism and loyalty to oppose such a course by all civilized methods, even though such opposition involves disagreement with Mr. Booker T. Washington. We have no right to sit silently by while the inevitable seeds are sown for a harvest of disaster to our children, black and white.[8]

First, it is the duty of black men to judge the South discriminatingly. The present generation of Southerners are not responsible for the past, and they should not be blindly hated or blamed for it. Furthermore, to no class is the indiscriminate endorsement of the recent course of the South toward Negroes more nauseating than to the best thought of the South. The South is not "solid"; it is a land in the ferment of social change, wherein forces of all kinds are fighting for supremacy; and to praise the ill the South is to-day perpetrating is just as wrong as to condemn the good. Discriminating and broad-minded criticism is what the South needs,—needs it for the sake of her own white sons and daughters, and for the insurance of robust, healthy mental and moral development.

To-day even the attitude of the Southern whites toward the blacks is

---

7. Reference to Joshua 6.15–21, in which the Israelites, following the instructions of God, miraculously flatten the walls of Jericho by blowing trumpets and shouting.
8. Hosea 8.7: "For they sow the wind, and they shall reap the whirlwind."

not, as so many assume, in all cases the same; the ignorant Southerner hates the Negro, the workingmen fear his competition, the money-makers wish to use him as a laborer, some of the educated see a menace in his upward development, while others—usually the sons of the masters—wish to help him to rise. National opinion has enabled this last class to maintain the Negro common schools, and to protect the Negro partially in property, life, and limb. Through the pressure of the money-makers, the Negro is in danger of being reduced to semi-slavery, especially in the country districts; the workingmen, and those of the educated who fear the Negro, have united to disfranchise him, and some have urged his deportation; while the passions of the ignorant are easily aroused to lynch and abuse any black man. To praise this intricate whirl of thought and prejudice is nonsense; to inveigh indiscriminately against "the South" is unjust; but to use the same breath in praising Governor Aycock, exposing Senator Morgan, arguing with Mr. Thomas Nelson Page, and denouncing Senator Ben Tillman,[9] is not only sane, but the imperative duty of thinking black men.

It would be unjust to Mr. Washington not to acknowledge that in several instances he has opposed movements in the South which were unjust to the Negro; he sent memorials to the Louisiana and Alabama constitutional conventions, he has spoken against lynching, and in other ways has openly or silently set his influence against sinister schemes and unfortunate happenings. Notwithstanding this, it is equally true to assert that on the whole the distinct impression left by Mr. Washington's propaganda is, first, that the South is justified in its present attitude toward the Negro because of the Negro's degradation; secondly, that the prime cause of the Negro's failure to rise more quickly is his wrong education in the past; and, thirdly, that his future rise depends primarily on his own efforts. Each of these propositions is a dangerous half-truth. The supplementary truths must never be lost sight of: first, slavery and race-prejudice are potent if not sufficient causes of the Negro's position; second, industrial and common-school training were necessarily slow in planting because they had to await the black teachers trained by higher institutions,—it being extremely doubtful if any essentially different development was possible, and certainly a Tuskegee was unthinkable before 1880; and, third, while it is a great truth to say that the Negro must strive and strive mightily to help himself, it is equally true that unless his striving be not simply seconded, but rather aroused and encouraged, by the initiative of the richer and wiser environing group, he cannot hope for great success.

In his failure to realize and impress this last point, Mr. Washington

9. Benjamin R. Tillman (1847–1919), white supremacist governor of South Carolina and U.S. senator. Charles Aycock (1859–1912), governor of North Carolina and a reformer. John Tyler Morgan (1824–1907), white supremacist senator from Alabama. Thomas Nelson Page (1853–1922), also a white supremacist, fiction writer, and essayist.

is especially to be criticised. His doctrine has tended to make the whites, North and South, shift the burden of the Negro problem to the Negro's shoulders and stand aside as critical and rather pessimistic spectators; when in fact the burden belongs to the nation, and the hands of none of us are clean if we bend not our energies to righting these great wrongs.

The South ought to be led, by candid and honest criticism, to assert her better self and do her full duty to the race she has cruelly wronged and is still wronging. The North—her co-partner in guilt—cannot salve her conscience by plastering it with gold. We cannot settle this problem by diplomacy and suaveness, by "policy" alone. If worse come to worst, can the moral fibre of this country survive the slow throttling and murder of nine millions of men?

The black men of America have a duty to perform, a duty stern and delicate,—a forward movement to oppose a part of the work of their greatest leader. So far as Mr. Washington preaches Thrift, Patience, and Industrial Training for the masses, we must hold up his hands and strive with him, rejoicing in his honors and glorying in the strength of this Joshua[1] called of God and of man to lead the headless host. But so far as Mr. Washington apologizes for injustice, North or South, does not rightly value the privilege and duty of voting, belittles the emasculating effects of caste distinctions, and opposes the higher training and ambition of our brighter minds,—so far as he, the South, or the Nation, does this,—we must unceasingly and firmly oppose them. By every civilized and peaceful method we must strive for the rights which the world accords to men, clinging unwaveringly to those great words which the sons of the Fathers would fain[2] forget: "We hold these truths to be self-evident: That all men are created equal; that they are endowed by their Creator with certain unalienable rights; that among these are life, liberty, and the pursuit of happiness."[3]

1. After the death of Moses, Joshua, his deputy, was called by God to lead the Israelites into the Promised Land.
2. Happily; gladly.
3. The preamble of the Declaration of Independence, 1776.

IV

Of the Meaning of Progress[1]

> Willst Du Deine Macht verkünden,
> Wähle sie die frei von Sünden,
> Steh'n in Deinem ew'gen Haus!
> Deine Geister sende aus!
> Die Unsterblichen, die Reinen,
> Die nicht fühlen, die nicht weinen!
> Nicht die zarte Jungfrau wähle,
> Nicht der Hirtin weiche Seele!
>
>   SCHILLER.

Once upon a time I taught school in the hills of Tennessee, where the broad dark vale of the Mississippi begins to roll and crumple to greet the Alleghanies. I was a Fisk student then, and all Fisk men thought that Tennessee—beyond the Veil—was theirs alone, and in vacation time they sallied forth in lusty bands to meet the county school-commissioners. Young and happy, I too went, and I shall not soon forget that summer, seventeen years ago.[2]

First, there was a Teachers' Institute at the county-seat; and there distinguished guests of the superintendent taught the teachers fractions and spelling and other mysteries,—white teachers in the morning, Negroes at night. A picnic now and then, and a supper, and the rough world was softened by laughter and song. I remember how—But I wander.

There came a day when all the teachers left the Institute and began the hunt for schools. I learn from hearsay (for my mother was mortally afraid of fire-arms) that the hunting of ducks and bears and men is wonderfully interesting, but I am sure that the man who has never

---

1. Revised from "A Negro Schoolmaster in the New South," *Atlantic Monthly* (January 1899): 99–104. The verse is from Friedrich von Schiller's *The Maid of Orleans* (1801), IV, i: "If you wish to proclaim your power, / Choose those who stand free of sins, / In your eternal house! / Send out your angels! / The immortal, the pure ones, / Who are unsentimental and do not weep! / Do not choose a delicate maiden, / Not the tender soul of the shepherdess!" (German). The music quotation is from the Negro spiritual "My Way's Cloudy."
2. Du Bois's experience in rural schoolteaching took place in Alexandria, Virginia, during the summers of 1886 and 1887.

hunted a country school has something to learn of the pleasures of the chase. I see now the white, hot roads lazily rise and fall and wind before me under the burning July sun; I feel the deep weariness of heart and limb as ten, eight, six miles stretch relentlessly ahead; I feel my heart sink heavily as I hear again and again, "Got a teacher? Yes." So I walked on and on—horses were too expensive—until I had wandered beyond railways, beyond stage lines, to a land of "varmints" and rattlesnakes, where the coming of a stranger was an event, and men lived and died in the shadow of one blue hill.

Sprinkled over hill and dale lay cabins and farmhouses, shut out from the world by the forests and the rolling hills toward the east. There I found at last a little school. Josie told me of it; she was a thin, homely girl of twenty, with a dark-brown face and thick, hard hair. I had crossed the stream at Watertown, and rested under the great willows; then I had gone to the little cabin in the lot where Josie was resting on her way to town. The gaunt farmer made me welcome, and Josie, hearing my errand, told me anxiously that they wanted a school over the hill; that but once since the war had a teacher been there; that she herself longed to learn,—and thus she ran on, talking fast and loud, with much earnestness and energy.

Next morning I crossed the tall round hill, lingered to look at the blue and yellow mountains[3] stretching toward the Carolinas, then plunged into the wood, and came out at Josie's home. It was a dull frame cottage with four rooms, perched just below the brow of the hill, amid peach-trees. The father was a quiet, simple soul, calmly ignorant, with no touch of vulgarity. The mother was different,—strong, bustling, and energetic, with a quick, restless tongue, and an ambition to live "like folks." There was a crowd of children. Two boys had gone away. There remained two growing girls; a shy midget of eight; John, tall, awkward, and eighteen; Jim, younger, quicker, and better looking; and two babies of indefinite age. Then there was Josie herself. She seemed to be the centre of the family: always busy at service, or at home, or berry-picking; a little nervous and inclined to scold, like her mother, yet faithful, too, like her father. She had about her a certain fineness, the shadow of an unconscious moral heroism that would willingly give all of life to make life broader, deeper, and fuller for her and hers. I saw much of this family afterwards, and grew to love them for their honest efforts to be decent and comfortable, and for their knowledge of their own ignorance. There was with them no affectation. The mother would scold the father for being so "easy"; Josie would roundly berate the boys for carelessness; and all knew that it was a hard thing to dig a living out of a rocky side-hill.

I secured the school. I remember the day I rode horseback out to

3. The foothills of the Appalachian mountains.

the commissioner's house with a pleasant young white fellow who wanted the white school. The road ran down the bed of a stream; the sun laughed and the water jingled, and we rode on. "Come in," said the commissioner,—"come in. Have a seat. Yes, that certificate will do. Stay to dinner. What do you want a month?" "Oh," thought I, "this is lucky"; but even then fell the awful shadow of the Veil, for they ate first, then I—alone.

The schoolhouse was a log hut, where Colonel Wheeler used to shelter his corn. It sat in a lot behind a rail fence and thorn bushes, near the sweetest of springs. There was an entrance where a door once was, and within, a massive rickety fireplace; great chinks between the logs served as windows. Furniture was scarce. A pale blackboard crouched in the corner. My desk was made of three boards, reinforced at critical points, and my chair, borrowed from the landlady, had to be returned every night. Seats for the children—these puzzled me much. I was haunted by a New England vision of neat little desks and chairs, but, alas! the reality was rough plank benches without backs, and at times without legs. They had the one virtue of making naps dangerous,—possibly fatal, for the floor was not to be trusted.

It was a hot morning late in July when the school opened. I trembled when I heard the patter of little feet down the dusty road, and saw the growing row of dark solemn faces and bright eager eyes facing me. First came Josie and her brothers and sisters. The longing to know, to be a student in the great school at Nashville, hovered like a star above this child-woman amid her work and worry, and she studied doggedly. There were the Dowells from their farm over toward Alexandria,—Fanny, with her smooth black face and wondering eyes; Martha, brown and dull; the pretty girl-wife of a brother, and the younger brood.

There were the Burkes,—two brown and yellow lads, and a tiny haughty-eyed girl. Fat Reuben's little chubby girl came, with golden face and old-gold hair, faithful and solemn. 'Thenie was on hand early,—a jolly, ugly, good-hearted girl, who slyly dipped snuff and looked after her little bow-legged brother. When her mother could spare her, 'Tildy came,—a midnight beauty, with starry eyes and tapering limbs; and her brother, correspondingly homely. And then the big boys,—the hulking Lawrences; the lazy Neills, unfathered sons of mother and daughter; Hickman, with a stoop in his shoulders; and the rest.

There they sat, nearly thirty of them, on the rough benches, their faces shading from a pale cream to a deep brown, the little feet bare and swinging, the eyes full of expectation, with here and there a twinkle of mischief, and the hands grasping Webster's blue-back spelling-book. I loved my school, and the fine faith the children had in the wisdom of their teacher was truly marvellous. We read and spelled together, wrote a little, picked flowers, sang, and listened to stories of the world beyond the hill. At times the school would dwindle away, and I would start out. I would visit Mun Eddings, who lived in two very dirty rooms, and ask why little Lugene, whose flaming face seemed ever ablaze with the dark-red hair uncombed, was absent all last week, or why I missed so often the inimitable rags of Mack and Ed. Then the father, who worked Colonel Wheeler's farm on shares,[4] would tell me how the crops needed the boys; and the thin, slovenly mother, whose face was pretty when washed, assured me that Lugene must mind the baby. "But we'll start them again next week." When the Lawrences stopped, I knew that the doubts of the old folks about book-learning had conquered again, and so, toiling up the hill, and getting as far into the cabin as possible, I put Cicero "pro Archia Poeta"[5] into the simplest English with local applications, and usually convinced them—for a week or so.

On Friday nights I often went home with some of the children,— sometimes to Doc Burke's farm. He was a great, loud, thin Black, ever working, and trying to buy the seventy-five acres of hill and dale where he lived; but people said that he would surely fail, and the "white folks would get it all." His wife was a magnificent Amazon,[6] with saffron face and shining hair, uncorseted and barefooted, and the children were strong and beautiful. They lived in a one-and-a-half-room cabin in the hollow of the farm, near the spring. The front room was full of great fat white beds, scrupulously neat; and there were bad chromos[7] on the walls, and a tired centre-table. In the tiny back kitchen I was often invited to "take out and help" myself to fried chicken and wheat biscuit, "meat" and corn pone,[8] string-beans and berries. At first I used to be a little alarmed at the approach of bedtime in the one lone bedroom, but embarrassment was very deftly avoided. First, all the children nodded and slept, and were stowed away in one great pile of goose feathers; next, the mother and the father discreetly slipped away to the kitchen while I went to bed; then, blowing out the dim light, they retired in the dark. In the morning all were up and away before I thought of awaking. Across the road, where fat Reuben lived, they all went out-doors while the teacher retired, because they did not boast the luxury of a kitchen.

I liked to stay with the Dowells, for they had four rooms and plenty of good country fare. Uncle Bird had a small, rough farm, all woods and hills, miles from the big road; but he was full of tales,—he preached

---

4. Sharecropping was the arrangement whereby a "share" of a tenant farmer's yearly "crop" went to the landowner in place of rent. Infamous for its abuses, sharecropping usually claimed 50 percent of the tenants annual yield. This practice became the usual method of agricultural employment for Southern blacks after the Civil War because they had neither land nor the means to pay cash rent.
5. Cicero's oration in which he defends the poet Archias, and, by extension, the value of art to society.
6. In Greek myth, a member of a nation of female warriors.
7. Colored print produced from a series of stone or zinc plates.
8. Corn bread made without milk or eggs.

now and then,—and with his children, berries, horses, and wheat he was happy and prosperous. Often, to keep the peace, I must go where life was less lovely; for instance, 'Tildy's mother was incorrigibly dirty, Reuben's larder was limited seriously, and herds of untamed insects wandered over the Eddingses' beds. Best of all I loved to go to Josie's, and sit on the porch, eating peaches, while the mother bustled and talked: how Josie had bought the sewing-machine; how Josie worked at service in winter, but that four dollars a month was "mighty little" wages; how Josie longed to go away to school, but that it "looked like" they never could get far enough ahead to let her; how the crops failed and the well was yet unfinished; and, finally, how "mean" some of the white folks were.

For two summers I lived in this little world; it was dull and hum-drum. The girls looked at the hill in wistful longing, and the boys fretted and haunted Alexandria. Alexandria was "town,"—a straggling, lazy village of houses, churches, and shops, and an aristocracy of Toms, Dicks, and Captains. Cuddled on the hill to the north was the village of the colored folks, who lived in three- or four-room unpainted cottages, some neat and homelike, and some dirty. The dwellings were scattered rather aimlessly, but they centred about the twin temples of the hamlet, the Methodist, and the Hard-Shell Baptist churches.[9] These, in turn, leaned gingerly on a sad-colored schoolhouse. Hither my little world wended its crooked way on Sunday to meet other worlds, and gossip, and won-der, and make the weekly sacrifice with frenzied priest at the altar of the "old-time religion."[1] Then the soft melody and mighty cadences of Negro song fluttered and thundered.

I have called my tiny community a world, and so its isolation made it; and yet there was among us but a half-awakened common conscious-ness, sprung from common joy and grief, at burial, birth, or wedding; from a common hardship in poverty, poor land, and low wages; and, above all, from the sight of the Veil that hung between us and Oppor-tunity. All this caused us to think some thoughts together; but these, when ripe for speech, were spoken in various languages. Those whose eyes twenty-five and more years before had seen "the glory of the com-ing of the Lord,"[2] saw in every present hindrance or help a dark fatalism bound to bring all things right in His own good time. The mass of those to whom slavery was a dim recollection of childhood found the world a puzzling thing: it asked little of them, and they answered with little, and yet it ridiculed their offering. Such a paradox they could not understand, and therefore sank into listless indifference, or shiftless-ness, or reckless bravado. There were, however, some—such as Josie,

9. "Hard-shell" Baptists and "foot-washing" Methodists were congregations that stressed the fun-damentalist elements of their respective denominations.
1. A popular hymn, also used in white churches, containing the refrain "Give me that old-time religion, it's good enough for me."
2. From the opening of Julia Ward Howe's "Battle Hymn of the Republic" (1861).

Jim, and Ben—to whom War, Hell, and Slavery were but childhood tales, whose young appetites had been whetted to an edge by school and story and half-awakened thought. Ill could they be content, born without and beyond the World. And their weak wings beat against their barriers,—barriers of caste, of youth, of life; at last, in dangerous moments, against everything that opposed even a whim.

The ten years that follow youth, the years when first the realization comes that life is leading somewhere,—these were the years that passed after I left my little school. When they were past, I came by chance once more to the walls of Fisk University, to the halls of the chapel of melody.[3] As I lingered there in the joy and pain of meeting old school-friends, there swept over me a sudden longing to pass again beyond the blue hill, and to see the homes and the school of other days, and to learn how life had gone with my school-children; and I went.

Josie was dead, and the gray-haired mother said simply, "We've had a heap of trouble since you've been away." I had feared for Jim. With a cultured parentage and a social caste to uphold him, he might have made a venturesome merchant or a West Point cadet. But here he was, angry with life and reckless; and when Farmer Durham charged him with stealing wheat, the old man had to ride fast to escape the stones which the furious fool hurled after him. They told Jim to run away; but he would not run, and the constable came that afternoon. It grieved Josie, and great awkward John walked nine miles every day to see his little brother through the bars of Lebanon jail. At last the two came back together in the dark night. The mother cooked supper, and Josie emptied her purse, and the boys stole away. Josie grew thin and silent, yet worked the more. The hill became steep for the quiet old father, and with the boys away there was little to do in the valley. Josie helped them to sell the old farm, and they moved nearer town. Brother Dennis, the carpenter, built a new house with six rooms; Josie toiled a year in Nashville, and brought back ninety dollars to furnish the house and change it to a home.

When the spring came, and the birds twittered, and the stream ran proud and full, little sister Lizzie, bold and thoughtless, flushed with the passion of youth, bestowed herself on the tempter, and brought home a nameless child. Josie shivered and worked on, with the vision of schooldays all fled, with a face wan and tired,—worked until, on a summer's day, some one married another; then Josie crept to her mother like a hurt child, and slept—and sleeps.

I paused to scent the breeze as I entered the valley. The Lawrences have gone,—father and son forever,—and the other son lazily digs in the earth to live. A new young widow rents out their cabin to fat Reu-

3. Jubilee Hall. The famous Fisk Jubilee Singers earned enough money through their concerts to build Jubilee Hall.

ben. Reuben is a Baptist preacher now, but I fear as lazy as ever, though his cabin has three rooms; and little Ella has grown into a bouncing woman, and is ploughing corn on the hot hillside. There are babies a-plenty, and one half-witted girl. Across the valley is a house I did not know before, and there I found, rocking one baby and expecting another, one of my schoolgirls, a daughter of Uncle Bird Dowell. She looked somewhat worried with her new duties, but soon bristled into pride over her neat cabin and the tale of her thrifty husband, the horse and cow, and the farm they were planning to buy.

My log schoolhouse was gone. In its place stood Progress; and Progress, I understand, is necessarily ugly. The crazy foundation stones still marked the former site of my poor little cabin, and not far away, on six weary boulders, perched a jaunty board house, perhaps twenty by thirty feet, with three windows and a door that locked. Some of the window-glass was broken, and part of an old iron stove lay mournfully under the house. I peeped through the window half reverently, and found things that were more familiar. The blackboard had grown by about two feet, and the seats were still without backs. The county owns the lot now, I hear, and every year there is a session of school. As I sat by the spring and looked on the Old and the New I felt glad, very glad, and yet—

After two long drinks I started on. There was the great double log-house on the corner. I remembered the broken, blighted family that used to live there. The strong, hard face of the mother, with its wilderness of hair, rose before me. She had driven her husband away, and while I taught school a strange man lived there, big and jovial, and people talked. I felt sure that Ben and 'Tildy would come to naught from such a home. But this is an odd world; for Ben is a busy farmer in Smith County, "doing well, too," they say, and he had cared for little 'Tildy until last spring, when a lover married her. A hard life the lad had led, toiling for meat, and laughed at because he was homely and crooked. There was Sam Carlon, an impudent old skinflint, who had definite notions about "niggers," and hired Ben a summer and would not pay him. Then the hungry boy gathered his sacks together, and in broad daylight went into Carlon's corn; and when the hard-fisted farmer set upon him, the angry boy flew at him like a beast. Doc Burke saved a murder and a lynching that day.

The story reminded me again of the Burkes, and an impatience seized me to know who won in the battle, Doc or the seventy-five acres. For it is a hard thing to make a farm out of nothing, even in fifteen years. So I hurried on, thinking of the Burkes. They used to have a certain magnificent barbarism about them that I liked. They were never vulgar, never immoral, but rather rough and primitive, with an unconventionality that spent itself in loud guffaws, slaps on the back, and naps in the corner. I hurried by the cottage of the misborn Neill boys. It was empty, and they were grown into fat, lazy farm-hands. I saw the home of the Hickmans, but Albert, with his stooping shoulders, had passed from the world. Then I came to the Burkes' gate and peered through; the inclosure looked rough and untrimmed, and yet there were the same fences around the old farm save to the left, where lay twenty-five other acres. And lo! the cabin in the hollow had climbed the hill and swollen to a half-finished six-room cottage.

The Burkes held a hundred acres, but they were still in debt. Indeed, the gaunt father who toiled night and day would scarcely be happy out of debt, being so used to it. Some day he must stop, for his massive frame is showing decline. The mother wore shoes, but the lion-like physique of other days was broken. The children had grown up. Rob, the image of his father, was loud and rough with laughter. Birdie, my school baby of six, had grown to a picture of maiden beauty, tall and tawny. "Edgar is gone," said the mother, with head half bowed,—"gone to work in Nashville; he and his father couldn't agree."

Little Doc, the boy born since the time of my school, took me horseback down the creek next morning toward Farmer Dowell's. The road and the stream were battling for mastery, and the stream had the better of it. We splashed and waded, and the merry boy, perched behind me, chattered and laughed. He showed me where Simon Thompson had bought a bit of ground and a home; but his daughter Lana, a plump, brown, slow girl, was not there. She had married a man and a farm twenty miles away. We wound on down the stream till we came to a gate that I did not recognize, but the boy insisted that it was "Uncle Bird's." The farm was fat with the growing crop. In that little valley was a strange stillness as I rode up; for death and marriage had stolen youth and left age and childhood there. We sat and talked that night after the chores were done. Uncle Bird was grayer, and his eyes did not see so well, but he was still jovial. We talked of the acres bought,—one hundred and twenty-five,—of the new guest-chamber added, of Martha's marrying. Then we talked of death: Fanny and Fred were gone; a shadow hung over the other daughter, and when it lifted she was to go to Nashville to school. At last we spoke of the neighbors, and as night fell, Uncle Bird told me how, on a night like that, 'Thenie came wandering back to her home over yonder, to escape the blows of her husband. And next morning she died in the home that her little bow-legged brother, working and saving, had bought for their widowed mother.

My journey was done, and behind me lay hill and dale, and Life and Death. How shall man measure Progress there where the dark-faced Josie lies? How many heartfuls of sorrow shall balance a bushel of wheat? How hard a thing is life to the lowly, and yet how human and real! And all this life and love and strife and failure,—is it the twilight of nightfall or the flush of some faint-dawning day?

Thus sadly musing, I rode to Nashville in the Jim Crow car.[4]

V

Of the Wings of Atalanta[1]

O black boy of Atlanta!
But half was spoken;
The slave's chains and the master's
Alike are broken;
The one curse of the races
Held both in tether;
They are rising—all are rising—
The black and white together.

WHITTIER.

South of the North, yet north of the South, lies the City of a Hundred Hills,[2] peering out from the shadows of the past into the promise of the future. I have seen her in the morning, when the first flush of day had half-roused her; she lay gray and still on the crimson soil of Georgia; then the blue smoke began to curl from her chimneys, the tinkle of bell and scream of whistle broke the silence, the rattle and roar of busy life slowly gathered and swelled, until the seething whirl of the city seemed a strange thing in a sleepy land.

Once, they say, even Atlanta slept dull and drowsy at the foot-hills of the Alleghanies, until the iron baptism of war awakened her with its sullen waters, aroused and maddened her, and left her listening to the sea. And the sea cried to the hills and the hills answered the sea, till the city rose like a widow and cast away her weeds, and toiled for her daily bread; toiled steadily, toiled cunningly,—perhaps with some bitterness, with a touch of *réclame*,[3]—and yet with real earnestness, and real sweat.

4. A car on a train designated for blacks only. Jim Crow laws mandated segregated seating. In practice, whites often rode in Jim Crow cars, although blacks were not allowed in the "white only" cars.
1. The verse is stanza six of John Greenleaf Whittier's *Howard at Atlanta* (1869). The music quotation is from the Negro spiritual "The Rocks and Mountains."
2. Poetic name for Atlanta, Georgia.
3. Public acclaim; a taste or flair for publicity.

It is a hard thing to live haunted by the ghost of an untrue dream; to see the wide vision of empire fade into real ashes and dirt; to feel the pang of the conquered, and yet know that with all the Bad that fell on one black day, something was vanquished that deserved to live, something killed that in justice had not dared to die; to know that with the Right that triumphed, triumphed something of Wrong, something sordid and mean, something less than the broadest and best. All this is bitter hard; and many a man and city and people have found in it excuse for sulking, and brooding, and listless waiting.

Such are not men of the sturdier make; they of Atlanta turned resolutely toward the future; and that future held aloft vistas of purple and gold:—Atlanta, Queen of the cotton kingdom; Atlanta, Gateway to the Land of the Sun; Atlanta, the new Lachesis,[4] spinner of web and woof for the world. So the city crowned her hundred hills with factories, and stored her shops with cunning handiwork, and stretched long iron ways to greet the busy Mercury[5] in his coming. And the Nation talked of her striving.

Perhaps Atlanta was not christened for the winged maiden of dull Bœotia;[6] you know the tale,—how swarthy Atalanta, tall and wild, would marry only him who out-raced her; and how the wily Hippomenes laid three apples of gold in the way.[7] She fled like a shadow, paused, startled over the first apple, but even as he stretched his hand, fled again; hovered over the second, then, slipping from his hot grasp, flew over river, vale, and hill; but as she lingered over the third, his arms fell round her, and looking on each other, the blazing passion of their love profaned the sanctuary of Love, and they were cursed. If Atlanta be not named for Atalanta, she ought to have been.

Atalanta is not the first or the last maiden whom greed of gold has led to defile the temple of Love; and not maids alone, but men in the race of life, sink from the high and generous ideals of youth to the gambler's code of the Bourse;[8] and in all our Nation's striving is not the Gospel of Work befouled by the Gospel of Pay? So common is this that one-half think it normal; so unquestioned, that we almost fear to question if the end of racing is not gold, if the aim of man is not rightly to be rich. And if this is the fault of America, how dire a danger lies before a new land and a new city, lest Atlanta, stooping for mere gold, shall find that gold accursed!

4. One of the Three Fates in Greek mythology whose measuring of the thread of life determined longevity.
5. Roman god who served as not only messenger to the other gods but also as god of commerce, travel, and thievery.
6. Province in Greece, where Thebes was located.
7. In Greek mythology, Atalanta was a maiden who agreed to marry any man who could outrun her. She was defeated by Hippomenes when he dropped three gold apples in her path, slowing her as she paused to gather them.
8. Literally, a purse (French), but here refers to the stock exchange or economic speculation.

It was no maiden's idle whim that started this hard racing; a fearful wilderness lay about the feet of that city after the War,—feudalism, poverty, the rise of the Third Estate,[9] serfdom, the re-birth of Law and Order, and above and between all, the Veil of Race. How heavy a journey for weary feet! what wings must Atalanta have to flit over all this hollow and hill, through sour wood and sullen water, and by the red waste of sun-baked clay! How fleet must Atalanta be if she will not be tempted by gold to profane the Sanctuary!

The Sanctuary of our fathers has, to be sure, few Gods,—some sneer, "all too few." There is the thrifty Mercury of New England, Pluto of the North, and Ceres of the West; and there, too, is the half-forgotten Apollo of the South,[1] under whose ægis the maiden ran,—and as she ran she forgot him, even as there in Bœotia Venus[2] was forgot. She forgot the old ideal of the Southern gentleman,—that new-world heir of the grace and courtliness of patrician, knight, and noble; forgot his honor with his foibles, his kindliness with his carelessness, and stooped to apples of gold,—to men busier and sharper, thriftier and more un-scrupulous. Golden apples are beautiful—I remember the lawless days of boyhood, when orchards in crimson and gold tempted me over fence and field[3]—and, too, the merchant who has dethroned the planter is no despicable *parvenu*.[4] Work and wealth are the mighty levers to lift this old new land; thrift and toil and saving are the highways to new hopes and new possibilities; and yet the warning is needed lest the wily Hippomenes tempt Atalanta to thinking that golden apples are the goal of racing, and not mere incidents by the way.

Atlanta must not lead the South to dream of material prosperity as the touchstone of all success; already the fatal might of this idea is beginning to spread; it is replacing the finer type of Southerner with vulgar money-getters; it is burying the sweeter beauties of Southern life beneath pretence and ostentation. For every social ill the panacea of Wealth has been urged,—wealth to overthrow the remains of the slave feudalism; wealth to raise the "cracker"[5] Third Estate; wealth to employ the black serfs, and the prospect of wealth to keep them working; wealth as the end and aim of politics, and as the legal tender for law and order;

---

9. During feudalism, the social level of the common people. The second estate was the nobility, and the first estate, the highest level of society, the clergy.

1. Du Bois is associating gods with regions of the country. Apollo, the Greek god of the sun, prophecy, music, medicine, and poetry, is "half-forgotten" because the ideals of the Old South have been destroyed by slavery and the Civil War. Mercury, identified with commerce, is seen as the god of New England. Pluto, the Greek god of the underworld and the forge, represents the industrial interests of the North. Ceres, the Roman goddess of the harvest, is associated with the agricultural strength of the West.

2. Roman goddess of love and beauty.

3. In his *Autobiography* Du Bois tells of stealing grapes from a prominent citizen's arbor with his high school friends. Judge Dewey suggested that Du Bois be sent to Reform School, but the owner of the arbor refused to press charges.

4. Someone who has suddenly risen above his or her economic class but does not possess the social background for this new status.

5. Insulting slang word for a poor white Southerner.

and, finally, instead of Truth, Beauty, and Goodness, wealth as the ideal of the Public School.

Not only is this true in the world which Atlanta typifies, but it is threatening to be true of a world beneath and beyond that world,—the Black World beyond the Veil. To-day it makes little difference to Atlanta, to the South, what the Negro thinks or dreams or wills. In the soul-life of the land he is to-day, and naturally will long remain, unthought of, half forgotten; and yet when he does come to think and will and do for himself,—and let no man dream that day will never come,—then the part he plays will not be one of sudden learning, but words and thoughts he has been taught to lisp in his race-childhood. To-day the ferment of his striving toward self-realization is to the strife of the white world like a wheel within a wheel: beyond the Veil are smaller but like problems of ideals, of leaders and the led, of serfdom, of poverty, of order and subordination, and, through all, the Veil of Race. Few know of these problems, few who know notice them; and yet there they are, awaiting student, artist, and seer,—a field for somebody sometime to discover. Hither has the temptation of Hippomenes penetrated; already in this smaller world, which now indirectly and anon directly must influence the larger for good or ill, the habit is forming of interpreting the world in dollars. The old leaders of Negro opinion, in the little groups where there is a Negro social consciousness, are being replaced by new; neither the black preacher nor the black teacher leads as he did two decades ago. Into their places are pushing the farmers and gardeners, the well-paid porters and artisans, the businessmen,—all those with property and money. And with all this change, so curiously parallel to that of the Other-world, goes too the same inevitable change in ideals. The South laments to-day the slow, steady disappearance of a certain type of Negro,—the faithful, courteous slave of other days, with his incorruptible honesty and dignified humility. He is passing away just as surely as the old type of Southern gentleman is passing, and from not dissimilar causes,—the sudden transformation of a fair far-off ideal of Freedom into the hard reality of bread-winning and the consequent deification of Bread.

In the Black World, the Preacher and Teacher embodied once the ideals of this people,—the strife for another and a juster world, the vague dream of righteousness, the mystery of knowing; but to-day the danger is that these ideals, with their simple beauty and weird inspiration, will suddenly sink to a question of cash and a lust for gold. Here stands this black young Atalanta, girding herself for the race that must be run; and if her eyes be still toward the hills and sky as in the days of old, then we may look for noble running; but what if some ruthless or wily or even thoughtless Hippomenes lay golden apples before her? What if the Negro people be wooed from a strife for righteousness, from a love of knowing, to regard dollars as the be-all and end-all of life? What if to the Mammonism[6] of America be added the rising Mammonism of the re-born South, and the Mammonism of this South be reinforced by the budding Mammonism of its half-awakened black millions? Whither, then, is the new-world quest of Goodness and Beauty and Truth gone glimmering? Must this, and that fair flower of Freedom which, despite the jeers of latter-day striplings, sprung from our fathers' blood, must that too degenerate into a dusty quest of gold,—into lawless lust with Hippomenes?

The hundred hills of Atlanta are not all crowned with factories. On one, toward the west, the setting sun throws three buildings in bold relief against the sky. The beauty of the group lies in its simple unity: —a broad lawn of green rising from the red street with mingled roses and peaches; north and south, two plain and stately halls; and in the midst, half hidden in ivy, a larger building, boldly graceful, sparingly decorated, and with one low spire. It is a restful group,—one never looks for more; it is all here, all intelligible. There I live, and there I hear from day to day the low hum of restful life. In winter's twilight, when the red sun glows, I can see the dark figures pass between the halls to the music of the night-bell. In the morning, when the sun is golden, the clang of the day-bell brings the hurry and laughter of three hundred young hearts from hall and street, and from the busy city below,—children all dark and heavy-haired,—to join their clear young voices in the music of the morning sacrifice. In a half-dozen class-rooms they gather then,—here to follow the love-song of Dido,[7] here to listen to the tale of Troy divine;[8] there to wander among the stars, there to wander among men and nations,—and elsewhere other well-worn ways of knowing this queer world. Nothing new, no time-saving devices,— simply old time-glorified methods of delving for Truth, and searching out the hidden beauties of life, and learning the good of living. The riddle of existence is the college curriculum that was laid before the Pharaohs,[9] that was taught in the groves by Plato,[1] that formed the *trivium* and *quadrivium*,[2] and is to-day laid before the freedmen's sons by Atlanta University.[3] And this course of study will not change; its methods will grow more deft and effectual, its content richer by toil of scholar and sight of seer; but the true college will ever have one goal,

6. Such intense devotion to the pursuit of riches that it exerts an evil influence.
7. In Roman mythology the founder and queen of Carthage (northern Africa). Her song is recorded in *The Aeneid.*
8. The land of Troy, whose defeat is recorded in *The Iliad.*
9. Monarchs of ancient Egypt.
1. Athenian philosopher (427–347 B.C.E.), student of Socrates, and founder of his own academy, or school of philosophy.
2. The seven liberal arts of the Middle Ages. Divided into the *trivium* (grammar, logic, and rhetoric) and the *quadrivium* (arithmetic, music, geometry, and astronomy).
3. Founded in 1865.

—not to earn meat, but to know the end and aim of that life which meat nourishes.

The vision of life that rises before these dark eyes has in it nothing mean or selfish. Not at Oxford or at Leipsic, not at Yale or Columbia,[4] is there an air of higher resolve or more unfettered striving; the determination to realize for men, both black and white, the broadest possibilities of life, to seek the better and the best, to spread with their own hands the Gospel of Sacrifice,—all this is the burden of their talk and dream. Here, amid a wide desert of caste and proscription, amid the heart-hurting slights and jars and vagaries of a deep race-dislike, lies this green oasis, where hot anger cools, and the bitterness of disappointment is sweetened by the springs and breezes of Parnassus;[5] and here men may lie and listen, and learn of a future fuller than the past, and hear the voice of Time:

"Entbehren sollst du, sollst entbehren."[6]

They made their mistakes, those who planted Fisk and Howard and Atlanta before the smoke of battle had lifted; they made their mistakes, but those mistakes were not the things at which we lately laughed somewhat uproariously. They were right when they sought to found a new educational system upon the University: where, forsooth, shall we ground knowledge save on the broadest and deepest knowledge? The roots of the tree, rather than the leaves, are the sources of its life; and from the dawn of history, from Academus to Cambridge,[7] the culture of the University has been the broad foundation-stone on which is built the kindergarten's A B C.

But these builders did make a mistake in minimizing the gravity of the problem before them; in thinking it a matter of years and decades; in therefore building quickly and laying their foundation carelessly, and lowering the standard of knowing, until they had scattered haphazard through the South some dozen poorly equipped high schools and miscalled them universities. They forgot, too, just as their successors are forgetting, the rule of inequality:—that of the million black youth, some were fitted to know and some to dig; that some had the talent and capacity of university men, and some the talent and capacity of blacksmiths; and that true training meant neither that all should be college men nor all artisans, but that the one should be made a missionary of culture to an untaught people, and the other a free workman among

4. Four excellent universities located in Oxford, England; Leipzig, Germany; New Haven, Connecticut; and New York City, respectively.
5. Mountain in Greece near Delphi, the site of the oracle of Apollo.
6. Johann Wolfgang von Goethe's Faust declares, "Renounce shalt thou, thou shalt renounce" (German). From Faust (1808).
7. Cambridge University in England, established ca. 1209, remains one of the world's most respected universities. Academus was the first school of philosophy. Founded by Plato, it was the beginning of what was to become the university system.

serfs. And to seek to make the blacksmith a scholar is almost as silly as
the more modern scheme of making the scholar a blacksmith; almost,
but not quite.

The function of the university is not simply to teach bread-winning,
or to furnish teachers for the public schools, or to be a centre of polite
society; it is, above all, to be the organ of that fine adjustment between
real life and the growing knowledge of life, an adjustment which forms
the secret of civilization. Such an institution the South of to-day sorely
needs. She has religion, earnest, bigoted:—religion that on both sides
the Veil often omits the sixth, seventh, and eighth commandments,[8]
but substitutes a dozen supplementary ones. She has, as Atlanta shows,
growing thrift and love of toil; but she lacks that broad knowledge of
what the world knows and knew of human living and doing, which she
may apply to the thousand problems of real life to-day confronting her.
The need of the South is knowledge and culture,—not in dainty limited
quantity, as before the war, but in broad busy abundance in the world
of work; and until she has this, not all the Apples of Hesperides,[9] be
they golden and bejewelled, can save her from the curse of the Bœotian
lovers.[1]

The Wings of Atalanta are the coming universities of the South. They
alone can bear the maiden past the temptation of golden fruit. They
will not guide her flying feet away from the cotton and gold; for—ah,
thoughtful Hippomenes!—do not the apples lie in the very Way of Life?
But they will guide her over and beyond them, and leave her kneeling
in the Sanctuary of Truth and Freedom and broad Humanity, virgin
and undefiled. Sadly did the Old South err in human education, de-
spising the education of the masses, and niggardly in the support of
colleges. Her ancient university foundations dwindled and withered under the foul breath of slavery; and even since the war they have fought
a failing fight for life in the tainted air of social unrest and commercial
selfishness, stunted by the death of criticism, and starving for lack of
broadly cultured men. And if this is the white South's need and danger,
how much heavier the danger and need of the freedmen's sons! how
pressing here the need of broad ideals and true culture, the conservation of soul from sordid aims and petty passions! Let us build the Southern university—William and Mary, Trinity, Georgia, Texas, Tulane,
Vanderbilt,[2] and the others—fit to live; let us build, too, the Negro

8. From the Ten Commandments (Deuteronomy 5.17–19). The sixth bans killing, the seventh
   forbids adultery, and the eighth prohibits stealing.
9. In Greek mythology, the sisters who guarded the golden apples belonging to the earth goddess,
   Hera.
1. Atalanta and Hippomenes.
2. Well-known southern schools. Trinity College, in North Carolina, was renamed Duke
   University.

universities:—Fisk, whose foundation was ever broad; Howard, at the heart of the Nation; Atlanta at Atlanta, whose ideal of scholarship has been held above the temptation of numbers. Why not here, and perhaps elsewhere, plant deeply and for all time centres of learning and living, colleges that yearly would send into the life of the South a few white men and a few black men of broad culture, catholic tolerance, and trained ability, joining their hands to other hands, and giving to this squabble of the Races a decent and dignified peace?

Patience, Humility, Manners, and Taste, common schools and kindergartens, industrial and technical schools, literature and tolerance,—all these spring from knowledge and culture, the children of the university. So must men and nations build, not otherwise, not upside down.

Teach workers to work,—a wise saying; wise when applied to German boys and American girls; wiser when said of Negro boys, for they have less knowledge of working and none to teach them. Teach thinkers to think,—a needed knowledge in a day of loose and careless logic; and they whose lot is gravest must have the carefulest training to think aright. If these things are so, how foolish to ask what is the best education for one or seven or sixty million souls! shall we teach them trades, or train them in liberal arts? Neither and both: teach the workers to work and the thinkers to think; make carpenters of carpenters, and philosophers of philosophers, and fops of fools. Nor can we pause here. We are training not isolated men but a living group of men,—nay, a group within a group. And the final product of our training must be neither a psychologist nor a brickmason, but a man. And to make men, we must have ideals, broad, pure, and inspiring ends of living,—not sordid money-getting, not apples of gold. The worker must work for the glory of his handiwork, not simply for pay; the thinker must think for truth, not for fame. And all this is gained only by human strife and longing; by ceaseless training and education; by founding Right on righteousness and Truth on the unhampered search for Truth; by founding the common school on the university, and the industrial school on the common school; and weaving thus a system, not a distortion, and bringing a birth, not an abortion.

When night falls on the City of a Hundred Hills, a wind gathers itself from the seas and comes murmuring westward. And at its bidding, the smoke of the drowsy factories sweeps down upon the mighty city and covers it like a pall, while yonder at the University the stars twinkle above Stone Hall. And they say that yon gray mist is the tunic of Atalanta pausing over her golden apples. Fly, my maiden, fly, for yonder comes Hippomenes!

read Rebou's
- Chemistry Klein
- Journal

Of the Training of Black Men[1]

Why, if the Soul can fling the Dust aside,
And naked on the Air of Heaven ride,
    Were 't not a Shame—were 't not a Shame for him
In this clay carcase crippled to abide?
                    OMAR KHAYYÁM (FITZGERALD).

From the shimmering swirl of waters where many, many thoughts ago the slave-ship first saw the square tower of Jamestown,[2] have flowed down to our day three streams of thinking: one swollen from the larger world here and over-seas, saying, the multiplying of human wants in culture-lands calls for the world-wide coöperation of men in satisfying them. Hence arises a new human unity, pulling the ends of earth nearer, and all men, black, yellow, and white. The larger humanity strives to feel in this contact of living Nations and sleeping hordes a thrill of new life in the world, crying, "If the contact of Life and Sleep be Death, shame on such Life." To be sure, behind this thought lurks the afterthought of force and dominion,—the making of brown men to delve when the temptation of beads and red calico cloys.[3]

The second thought streaming from the death-ship and the curving river is the thought of the older South,—the sincere and passionate belief that somewhere between men and cattle, God created a *tertium quid*,[4] and called it a Negro,—a clownish, simple creature, at times even lovable within its limitations, but straitly foreordained to walk within the Veil. To be sure, behind the thought lurks the afterthought,—some of them with favoring chance might become men, but in sheer self-

1. Revised from essay with the same name, *Atlantic Monthly* (September 1902): 287–97. The verse is from Edward FitzGerald's translation of *The Rubaiyat of Omar Khayyam* (1859). Khayyam was a Persian poet (fl. 1000 C.E.). The music quotation is from the Negro spiritual "March On."
2. In Virginia. The first permanent English settlement in North America, where the first slave ship arrived in 1619, only twelve years after the settlement's founding.
3. Du Bois is describing the subjugation of native peoples through the allure of beads and cloth, consumer goods traditionally used in trading with indigenous peoples. In the United States, a widely held belief is that the island of Manhattan was bought from Native Americans for similar, inexpensive goods.
4. Literally, a third something (Latin); an ambiguous state.

defence we dare not let them, and we build about them walls so high, and hang between them and the light a veil so thick, that they shall not even think of breaking through.

And last of all there trickles down that third and darker thought,— the thought of the things themselves, the confused, half-conscious mutter of men who are black and whitened, crying "Liberty, Freedom, Opportunity—vouchsafe[5] to us, O boastful World, the chance of living men!" To be sure, behind the thought lurks the afterthought,—suppose, after all, the World is right and we are less than men? Suppose this mad impulse within is all wrong, some mock mirage from the untrue?

So here we stand among thoughts of human unity, even through conquest and slavery; the inferiority of black men, even if forced by fraud; a shriek in the night for the freedom of men who themselves are not yet sure of their right to demand it. This is the tangle of thought and afterthought wherein we are called to solve the problem of training men for life.

Behind all its curiousness, so attractive alike to sage and *dilettante*,[6] lie its dim dangers, throwing across us shadows at once grotesque and awful. Plain it is to us that what the world seeks through desert and wild we have within our threshold,—a stalwart laboring force, suited to the semi-tropics; if, deaf to the voice of the Zeitgeist,[7] we refuse to use and develop these men, we risk poverty and loss. If, on the other hand, seized by the brutal afterthought, we debauch the race thus caught in our talons, selfishly sucking their blood and brains in the future as in the past, what shall save us from national decadence? Only that saner selfishness, which Education teaches men, can find the rights of all in the whirl of work.

Again, we may decry the color-prejudice of the South, yet it remains a heavy fact. Such curious kinks of the human mind exist and must be reckoned with soberly. They cannot be laughed away, nor always successfully stormed at, nor easily abolished by act of legislature. And yet they must not be encouraged by being let alone. They must be recognized as facts, but unpleasant facts; things that stand in the way of civilization and religion and common decency. They can be met in but one way,—by the breadth and broadening of human reason, by catholicity of taste and culture. And so, too, the native ambition and aspiration of men, even though they be black, backward, and ungraceful, must not lightly be dealt with. To stimulate wildly weak and untrained minds is to play with mighty fires; to flout their striving idly is to welcome a harvest of brutish crime and shameless lethargy in our very laps. The guiding of thought and the deft co-ordination of deed is at once the path of honor and humanity.

5. Grant.
6. Someone with amateurish or superficial interest in the arts or in any branch of knowledge.
7. The taste and outlook characteristic of a period or generation (German).

And so, in this great question of reconciling three vast and partially contradictory streams of thought, the one panacea of Education leaps to the lips of all:—such human training as will best use the labor of all men without enslaving or brutalizing; such training as will give us poise to encourage the prejudices that bulwark society, and to stamp out those that in sheer barbarity deafen us to the wail of prisoned souls within the Veil, and the mounting fury of shackled men.

But when we have vaguely said that Education will set this tangle straight, what have we uttered but a truism? Training for life teaches living; but what training for the profitable living together of black men and white? A hundred and fifty years ago our task would have seemed easier. Then Dr. Johnson[8] blandly assured us that education was needful solely for the embellishments of life, and was useless for ordinary vermin. To-day we have climbed to heights where we would open at least the outer courts of knowledge to all, display its treasures to many, and select the few to whom its mystery of Truth is revealed, not wholly by birth or the accidents of the stock market, but at least in part according to deftness and aim, talent and character. This programme, however, we are sorely puzzled in carrying out through that part of the land where the blight of slavery fell hardest, and where we are dealing with two backward peoples. To make here in human education that ever necessary combination of the permanent and the contingent—of the ideal and the practical in workable equilibrium—has been there, as it ever must be in every age and place, a matter of infinite experiment and frequent mistakes.

In rough approximation we may point out four varying decades of work in Southern education since the Civil War. From the close of the war until 1876, was the period of uncertain groping and temporary relief. There were army schools, mission schools, and schools of the Freedman's Bureau in chaotic disarrangement seeking system and coöperation. Then followed ten years of constructive definite effort toward the building of complete school systems in the South. Normal schools and colleges were founded for the freedmen, and teachers trained there to man the public schools. There was the inevitable tendency of war to underestimate the prejudices of the master and the ignorance of the slave, and all seemed clear sailing out of the wreckage of the storm. Meantime, starting in this decade yet especially developing from 1885 to 1895, began the industrial revolution of the South. The land saw glimpses of a new destiny and the stirring of new ideals. The educational system striving to complete itself saw new obstacles and a field of work ever broader and deeper. The Negro colleges, hurriedly founded, were inadequately equipped, illogically distributed, and of varying efficiency and grade; the normal and high schools were doing little

8. Samuel Johnson (1709–1784), English poet, essayist, and critic. He is best known for his pioneering *Dictionary of the English Language* (1755).

more than common-school work, and the common schools were training but a third of the children who ought to be in them, and training these too often poorly. At the same time the white South, by reason of its sudden conversion from the slavery ideal, by so much the more became set and strengthened in its racial prejudice, and crystallized it into harsh law and harsher custom; while the marvellous pushing forward of the poor white daily threatened to take even bread and butter from the mouths of the heavily handicapped sons of the freedmen. In the midst, then, of the larger problem of Negro education sprang up the more practical question of work, the inevitable economic quandary that faces a people in the transition from slavery to freedom, and especially those who make that change amid hate and prejudice, lawlessness and ruthless competition.

The industrial school springing to notice in this decade, but coming to full recognition in the decade beginning with 1895, was the proffered answer to this combined educational and economic crisis, and an answer of singular wisdom and timeliness. From the very first in nearly all the schools some attention had been given to training in handiwork, but now was this training first raised to a dignity that brought it in direct touch with the South's magnificent industrial development, and given an emphasis which reminded black folk that before the Temple of Knowledge swing the Gates of Toil.

Yet after all they are but gates, and when turning our eyes from the temporary and the contingent in the Negro problem to the broader question of the permanent uplifting and civilization of black men in America, we have a right to inquire, as this enthusiasm for material advancement mounts to its height, if after all the industrial school is the final and sufficient answer in the training of the Negro race; and to ask gently, but in all sincerity, the ever-recurring query of the ages, Is not life more than meat, and the body more than raiment?[9] And men ask this to-day all the more eagerly because of sinister signs in recent educational movements. The tendency is here, born of slavery and quickened to renewed life by the crazy imperialism of the day, to regard human beings as among the material resources of a land to be trained with an eye single to future dividends. Race-prejudices, which keep brown and black men in their "places," we are coming to regard as useful allies with such a theory, no matter how much they may dull the ambition and sicken the hearts of struggling human beings. And above all, we daily hear that an education that encourages aspiration, that sets the loftiest of ideals and seeks as an end culture and character rather than bread-winning, is the privilege of white men and the danger and delusion of black.

Especially has criticism been directed against the former educational

9. From Matthew 6.25.

efforts to aid the Negro. In the four periods I have mentioned, we find first, boundless, planless enthusiasm and sacrifice; then the preparation of teachers for a vast public-school system; then the launching and expansion of that school system amid increasing difficulties; and finally the training of workmen for the new and growing industries. This development has been sharply ridiculed as a logical anomaly and flat reversal of nature. Soothly[1] we have been told that first industrial and manual training should have taught the Negro to work, then simple schools should have taught him to read and write, and finally, after years, high and normal schools could have completed the system, as intelligence and wealth demanded.

That a system logically so complete was historically impossible, it needs but a little thought to prove. Progress in human affairs is more often a pull than a push, surging forward of the exceptional man, and the lifting of his duller brethren slowly and painfully to his vantage-ground. Thus it was no accident that gave birth to universities centuries before the common schools, that made fair Harvard[2] the first flower of our wilderness. So in the South: the mass of the freedmen at the end of the war lacked the intelligence so necessary to modern workingmen. They must first have the common school to teach them to read, write, and cipher; and they must have higher schools to teach teachers for the common schools. The white teachers who flocked South went to establish such a common-school system. Few held the idea of founding colleges; most of them at first would have laughed at the idea. But they faced, as all men since them have faced, that central paradox of the South,—the social separation of the races. At that time it was the sudden volcanic rupture of nearly all relations between black and white, in work and government and family life. Since then a new adjustment of relations in economic and political affairs has grown up,—an adjustment subtle and difficult to grasp, yet singularly ingenious, which leaves still that frightful chasm at the color-line across which men pass at their peril. Thus, then and now, there stand in the South two separate worlds; and separate not simply in the higher realms of social intercourse, but also in church and school, on railway and street-car, in hotels and theatres, in streets and city sections, in books and newspapers, in asylums and jails, in hospitals and graveyards. There is still enough of contact for large economic and group coöperation, but the separation is so thorough and deep that it absolutely precludes for the present between the races anything like that sympathetic and effective group-training and leadership of the one by the other, such as the American Negro and all backward peoples must have for effectual progress.

1. In truth.
2. Du Bois was the first black man to earn a doctorate from Harvard University. Harvard was founded in 1630 and is America's oldest college. Du Bois calls Harvard "fair" because "Fair Harvard" is the school song.

This the missionaries of '68 soon saw; and if effective industrial and trade schools were impracticable before the establishment of a common-school system, just as certainly no adequate common schools could be founded until there were teachers to teach them. Southern whites would not teach them; Northern whites in sufficient numbers could not be had. If the Negro was to learn, he must teach himself, and the most effective help that could be given him was the establishment of schools to train Negro teachers. This conclusion was slowly but surely reached by every student of the situation until simultaneously, in widely separated regions, without consultation or systematic plan, there arose a series of institutions designed to furnish teachers for the untaught. Above the sneers of critics at the obvious defects of this procedure must ever stand its one crushing rejoinder: in a single generation they put thirty thousand black teachers in the South; they wiped out the illiteracy of the majority of the black people of the land, and they made Tuskegee possible.

Such higher training-schools tended naturally to deepen broader development: at first they were common and grammar schools, then some became high schools. And finally, by 1900, some thirty-four had one year or more of studies of college grade. This development was reached with different degrees of speed in different institutions: Hampton is still a high school, while Fisk University started her college in 1871, and Spelman Seminary[3] about 1896. In all cases the aim was identical,— to maintain the standards of the lower training by giving teachers and leaders the best practicable training; and above all, to furnish the black world with adequate standards of human culture and lofty ideals of life. It was not enough that the teachers of teachers should be trained in technical normal methods; they must also, so far as possible, be broadminded, cultured men and women, to scatter civilization among a people whose ignorance was not simply of letters, but of life itself.

It can thus be seen that the work of education in the South began with higher institutions of training, which threw off as their foliage common schools, and later industrial schools, and at the same time strove to shoot their roots ever deeper toward college and university training. That this was an inevitable and necessary development, sooner or later, goes without saying; but there has been, and still is, a question in many minds if the natural growth was not forced, and if the higher training was not either overdone or done with cheap and unsound methods. Among white Southerners this feeling is widespread and positive. A prominent Southern journal voiced this in a recent editorial.

"The experiment that has been made to give the colored students classical training has not been satisfactory. Even though

3. Founded in 1881 as the first college in America for black women. Now called Spelman College.

many were able to pursue the course, most of them did so in a parrot-like way, learning what was taught, but not seeming to appropriate the truth and import of their instruction, and graduating without sensible aim or valuable occupation for their future. The whole scheme has proved a waste of time, efforts, and the money of the state."

While most fair-minded men would recognize this as extreme and overdrawn, still without doubt many are asking, Are there a sufficient number of Negroes ready for college training to warrant the undertaking? Are not too many students prematurely forced into this work? Does it not have the effect of dissatisfying the young Negro with his environment? And do these graduates succeed in real life? Such natural questions cannot be evaded, nor on the other hand must a Nation naturally skeptical as to Negro ability assume an unfavorable answer without careful inquiry and patient openness to conviction. We must not forget that most Americans answer all queries regarding the Negro *a priori*,[4] and that the least that human courtesy can do is to listen to evidence.

The advocates of the higher education of the Negro would be the last to deny the incompleteness and glaring defects of the present system: too many institutions have attempted to do college work, the work in some cases has not been thoroughly done, and quantity rather than quality has sometimes been sought. But all this can be said of higher education throughout the land; it is the almost inevitable incident of educational growth, and leaves the deeper question of the legitimate demand for the higher training of Negroes untouched. And this latter question can be settled in but one way,—by a first-hand study of the facts. If we leave out of view all institutions which have not actually graduated students from a course higher than that of a New England high school, even though they be called colleges; if then we take the thirty-four remaining institutions, we may clear up many misapprehensions by asking searchingly, What kind of institutions are they? what do they teach? and what sort of men do they graduate?

And first we may say that this type of college, including Atlanta, Fisk, and Howard, Wilberforce and Lincoln, Biddle, Shaw,[5] and the rest, is peculiar, almost unique. Through the shining trees that whisper before me as I write, I catch glimpses of a boulder of New England granite, covering a grave, which graduates of Atlanta University have placed there, with this inscription:

4. Without regard for empirical experience or evidence.
5. Shaw University, Raleigh, North Carolina, founded by Baptists in 1865. It was one of the first medical schools for blacks. For Fisk University, see n. 7, p. xii. For Atlanta University and Howard University, see n. 9, p. 29. Wilberforce University in Ohio, founded in 1856 by the A.M.E. Church. Lincoln University, Oxford, Pennsylvania, founded in 1854. Biddle University, Charlotte, North Carolina, founded in 1867 by the Presbyterian church to provide religious education for black men. The school changed its name in 1921 to Johnson C. Smith University.

"IN GRATEFUL MEMORY OF THEIR
FORMER TEACHER AND FRIEND
AND OF THE UNSELFISH LIFE HE
LIVED, AND THE NOBLE WORK HE
WROUGHT; THAT THEY, THEIR
CHILDREN, AND THEIR CHIL-
DREN'S CHILDREN MIGHT BE
BLESSED."[6]

This was the gift of New England to the freed Negro: not alms, but a friend; not cash, but character. It was not and is not money these seething millions want, but love and sympathy, the pulse of hearts beating with red blood;—a gift which to-day only their own kindred and race can bring to the masses, but which once saintly souls brought to their favored children in the crusade of the sixties, that finest thing in American history, and one of the few things untainted by sordid greed and cheap vainglory. The teachers in these institutions came not to keep the Negroes in their place, but to raise them out of the defilement of the places where slavery had wallowed them. The colleges they founded were social settlements; homes where the best of the sons of the freedmen came in close and sympathetic touch with the best traditions of New England. They lived and ate together, studied and worked, hoped and harkened in the dawning light. In actual formal content their curriculum was doubtless old-fashioned, but in educational power it was supreme, for it was the contact of living souls.

From such schools about two thousand Negroes have gone forth with the bachelor's degree. The number in itself is enough to put at rest the argument that too large a proportion of Negroes are receiving higher training. If the ratio to population of all Negro students throughout the land, in both college and secondary training, be counted, Commissioner Harris[7] assures us "it must be increased to five times its present average" to equal the average of the land.

Fifty years ago the ability of Negro students in any appreciable numbers to master a modern college course would have been difficult to prove. To-day it is proved by the fact that four hundred Negroes, many of whom have been reported as brilliant students, have received the bachelor's degree from Harvard, Yale, Oberlin,[8] and seventy other leading colleges. Here we have, then, nearly twenty-five hundred Negro graduates, of whom the crucial query must be made, How far did their training fit them for life? It is of course extremely difficult to collect satisfactory data on such a point,—difficult to reach the men, to get trustworthy testimony, and to gauge that testimony by any generally

6. Inscription on the memorial to Edmund A. Ware, founder of Atlanta University.
7. William Torrey Harris, U.S. commissioner of education.
8. Oberlin College, founded in 1833 in Oberlin, Ohio. Always progressive, Oberlin was the first college to institute coeducation and was one of the first to admit blacks.

acceptable criterion of success. In 1900, the Conference at Atlanta University[9] undertook to study these graduates, and published the results. First they sought to know what these graduates were doing, and succeeded in getting answers from nearly two-thirds of the living. The direct testimony was in almost all cases corroborated by the reports of the colleges where they graduated, so that in the main the reports were worthy of credence. Fifty-three per cent of these graduates were teachers,—presidents of institutions, heads of normal schools, principals of city school-systems, and the like. Seventeen per cent were clergymen; another seventeen per cent were in the professions, chiefly as physicians. Over six per cent were merchants, farmers, and artisans, and four per cent were in the government civil-service. Granting even that a considerable proportion of the third unheard from are unsuccessful, this is a record of usefulness. Personally I know many hundreds of these graduates, and have corresponded with more than a thousand; through others I have followed carefully the life-work of scores; I have taught some of them and some of the pupils whom they have taught, lived in homes which they have builded, and looked at life through their eyes. Comparing them as a class with my fellow students in New England and in Europe, I cannot hesitate in saying that nowhere have I met men and women with a broader spirit of helpfulness, with deeper devotion to their life-work, or with more consecrated determination to succeed in the face of bitter difficulties than among Negro college-bred men. They have, to be sure, their proportion of ne'er-do-weels,[1] their pedants and lettered fools, but they have a surprisingly small proportion of them; they have not that culture of manner which we instinctively associate with university men, forgetting that in reality it is the heritage from cultured homes, and that no people a generation removed from slavery can escape a certain unpleasant rawness and *gaucherie*,[2] despite the best of training.

With all their larger vision and deeper sensibility, these men have usually been conservative, careful leaders. They have seldom been agitators, have withstood the temptation to head the mob, and have worked steadily and faithfully in a thousand communities in the South. As teachers, they have given the South a commendable system of city schools and large numbers of private normal-schools and academies. Colored college-bred men have worked side by side with white college graduates at Hampton; almost from the beginning the backbone of Tuskegee's teaching force has been formed of graduates from Fisk and Atlanta. And to-day the institute is filled with college graduates, from the energetic wife of the principal[3] down to the teacher of agriculture,

9. Du Bois, while at Atlanta University, held a number of conferences. The fifth, presented in 1900, was on "The College-Bred Negro."
1. Du Bois's spelling of "ne'er-do-wells."
2. Lack of social grace (French).
3. The former Maggie Murray, the third wife of Booker T. Washington, was a classmate and intellectual rival of Du Bois's while he was at Fisk.

including nearly half of the executive council and a majority of the heads of departments. In the professions, college men are slowly but surely leavening the Negro church, are healing and preventing the devastations of disease, and beginning to furnish legal protection for the liberty and property of the toiling masses. All this is needful work. Who would do it if Negroes did not? How could Negroes do it if they were not trained carefully for it? If white people need colleges to furnish teachers, ministers, lawyers, and doctors, do black people need nothing of the sort?

If it is true that there are an appreciable number of Negro youth in the land capable by character and talent to receive that higher training, the end of which is culture, and if the two and a half thousand who have had something of this training in the past have in the main proved themselves useful to their race and generation, the question then comes, What place in the future development of the South ought the Negro college and college-bred man to occupy? That the present social separation and acute race-sensitiveness must eventually yield to the influences of culture, as the South grows civilized, is clear. But such transformation calls for singular wisdom and patience. If, while the healing of this vast sore is progressing, the races are to live for many years side by side, united in economic effort, obeying a common government, sensitive to mutual thought and feeling, yet subtly and silently separate in many matters of deeper human intimacy,—if this unusual and dangerous development is to progress amid peace and order, mutual respect and growing intelligence, it will call for social surgery at once the delicatest and nicest in modern history. It will demand broad-minded, upright men, both white and black, and in its final accomplishment American civilization will triumph. So far as white men are concerned, this fact is to-day being recognized in the South, and a happy renaissance of university education seems imminent. But the very voices that cry hail to this good work are, strange to relate, largely silent or antagonistic to the higher education of the Negro.

Strange to relate! for this is certain, no secure civilization can be built in the South with the Negro as an ignorant, turbulent proletariat. Suppose we seek to remedy this by making them laborers and nothing more: they are not fools, they have tasted of the Tree of Life, and they will not cease to think, will not cease attempting to read the riddle of the world. By taking away their best equipped teachers and leaders, by slamming the door of opportunity in the faces of their bolder and brighter minds, will you make them satisfied with their lot? or will you not rather transfer their leading from the hands of men taught to think to the hands of untrained demagogues? We ought not to forget that despite the pressure of poverty, and despite the active discouragement and even ridicule of friends, the demand for higher training steadily increases among Negro youth: there were, in the years from 1875 to

1880, 22 Negro graduates from Northern colleges; from 1885 to 1890 there were 43, and from 1895 to 1900, nearly 100 graduates. From Southern Negro colleges there were, in the same three periods, 143, 413, and over 500 graduates. Here, then, is the plain thirst for training; by refusing to give this Talented Tenth[4] the key to knowledge, can any sane man imagine that they will lightly lay aside their yearning and contentedly become hewers of wood and drawers of water?

No. The dangerously clear logic of the Negro's position will more and more loudly assert itself in that day when increasing wealth and more intricate social organization preclude the South from being, as it so largely is, simply an armed camp for intimidating black folk. Such waste of energy cannot be spared if the South is to catch up with civilization. And as the black third of the land grows in thrift and skill, unless skilfully guided in its larger philosophy, it must more and more brood over the red past and the creeping, crooked present, until it grasps a gospel of revolt and revenge and throws its new-found energies athwart the current of advance. Even to-day the masses of the Negroes see all too clearly the anomalies of their position and the moral crookedness of yours. You may marshal strong indictments against them, but their counter-cries, lacking though they be in formal logic, have burning truths within them which you may not wholly ignore, O Southern Gentlemen! If you deplore their presence here, they ask, Who brought us? When you cry, Deliver us from the vision of intermarriage, they answer that legal marriage is infinitely better than systematic concubinage and prostitution. And if in just fury you accuse their vagabonds of violating women, they also in fury quite as just may reply: The wrong which your gentlemen have done against helpless black women in defiance of your own laws is written on the foreheads of two millions of mulattoes, and written in ineffaceable blood. And finally, when you fasten crime upon this race as its peculiar trait, they answer that slavery was the arch-crime, and lynching and lawlessness its twin abortion; that color and race are not crimes, and yet they it is which in this land receives most unceasing condemnation, North, East, South, and West.

I will not say such arguments are wholly justified,—I will not insist that there is no other side to the shield; but I do say that of the nine millions of Negroes in this nation, there is scarcely one out of the cradle to whom these arguments do not daily present themselves in the guise of terrible truth. I insist that the question of the future is how best to keep these millions from brooding over the wrongs of the past and the difficulties of the present, so that all their energies may be bent toward a cheerful striving and co-operation with their white neighbors toward

4. Du Bois's concept of an educated black elite. The "Talented Tenth" assumed they had a duty to lead and inspire the rest of the race. Du Bois first uses this term in the *Atlantic Monthly* article on which this chapter is based.

a larger, juster, and fuller future. That one wise method of doing this lies in the closer knitting of the Negro to the great industrial possibilities of the South is a great truth. And this the common schools and the manual training and trade schools are working to accomplish. But these alone are not enough. The foundations of knowledge in this race, as in others, must be sunk deep in the college and university if we would build a solid, permanent structure. Internal problems of social advance must inevitably come,—problems of work and wages, of families and homes, of morals and the true valuing of the things of life; and all these and other inevitable problems of civilization the Negro must meet and solve largely for himself, by reason of his isolation; and can there be any possible solution other than by study and thought and an appeal to the rich experience of the past? Is there not, with such a group and in such a crisis, infinitely more danger to be apprehended from half-trained minds and shallow thinking than from over-education and over-refinement? Surely we have wit enough to found a Negro college so manned and equipped as to steer successfully between the *dilettante* and the fool. We shall hardly induce black men to believe that if their stomachs be full, it matters little about their brains. They already dimly perceive that the paths of peace winding between honest toil and dignified manhood call for the guidance of skilled thinkers, the loving, reverent comradeship between the black lowly and the black men emancipated by training and culture.

The function of the Negro college, then, is clear: it must maintain the standards of popular education, it must seek the social regeneration of the Negro, and it must help in the solution of problems of race contact and co-operation. And finally, beyond all this, it must develop men. Above our modern socialism, and out of the worship of the mass, must persist and evolve that higher individualism which the centres of culture protect; there must come a loftier respect for the sovereign human soul that seeks to know itself and the world about it; that seeks a freedom for expansion and self-development; that will love and hate and labor in its own way, untrammeled alike by old and new. Such souls aforetime have inspired and guided worlds, and if we be not wholly bewitched by our Rhine-gold,[5] they shall again. Herein the long-ing of black men must have respect: the rich and bitter depth of their experience, the unknown treasures of their inner life, the strange rend-ings of nature they have seen, may give the world new points of view and make their loving, living, and doing precious to all human hearts. And to themselves in these the days that try their souls, the chance to soar in the dim blue air above the smoke is to their finer spirits boon and guerdon[6] for what they lose on earth by being black.

5. In German mythology, Rhine-gold is the name for a treasure of gold guarded by Rhine river maidens.
6. A reward or requital.

I sit with Shakespeare[7] and he winces not. Across the color line I move arm in arm with Balzac and Dumas,[8] where smiling men and welcoming women glide in gilded halls. From out the caves of evening that swing between the strong-limbed earth and the tracery of the stars, I summon Aristotle and Aurelius[9] and what soul I will, and they come all graciously with no scorn nor condescension. So, wed with Truth, I dwell above the Veil. Is this the life you grudge us, O knightly America? Is this the life you long to change into the dull red hideousness of Georgia? Are you so afraid lest peering from this high Pisgah, between Philistine and Amalekite,[1] we sight the Promised Land?

VII

Of the Black Belt[1]

I am black but comely, O ye daughters of Jerusalem,
As the tents of Kedar, as the curtains of Solomon.
Look not upon me, because I am black,
Because the sun hath looked upon me:
My mother's children were angry with me;
They made me the keeper of the vineyards;
But mine own vineyard have I not kept.

THE SONG OF SOLOMON.

Out of the North the train thundered, and we woke to see the crimson soil of Georgia stretching away bare and monotonous right and left.

7. William Shakespeare (1564–1616), English dramatist and poet.
8. Alexandre Dumas (1802–1870), French playwright and novelist. Honoré de Balzac (1799–1850), French novelist.
9. Marcus Aurelius (121–180), Roman emperor and philosopher. Aristotle (384–322 B.C.E.), Greek philosopher.
1. Member of a tribe hostile to the Israelites as they traveled to the Promised Land. Pisgah is the mountain from which Moses viewed the Promised Land. Philistine is the land of the Philistines, enemies of the Israelites.
1. Chapters VII and VIII are revisions of "The Negro As He Really Is," *The World's Work* (June 1901): 848–66. The verse is from the Song of Solomon 1.5–6. The music quotation is from the Negro spiritual "Bright Sparkles in the Churchyard."

Here and there lay straggling, unlovely villages, and lean men loafed leisurely at the depots; then again came the stretch of pines and clay. Yet we did not nod, nor weary of the scene; for this is historic ground. Right across our track, three hundred and sixty years ago, wandered the cavalcade of Hernando de Soto,[2] looking for gold and the Great Sea; and he and his foot-sore captives disappeared yonder in the grim forests to the west. Here sits Atlanta, the city of a hundred hills, with something Western, something Southern, and something quite its own, in its busy life. And a little past Atlanta, to the southwest, is the land of the Cherokees,[3] and there, not far from where Sam Hose[4] was crucified, you may stand on a spot which is to-day the centre of the Negro problem, —the centre of those nine million men who are America's dark heritage from slavery and the slave-trade.

Not only is Georgia thus the geographical focus of our Negro population, but in many other respects, both now and yesterday, the Negro problems have seemed to be centered in this State. No other State in the Union can count a million Negroes among its citizens,—a population as large as the slave population of the whole Union in 1800; no other State fought so long and strenuously to gather this host of Africans. Oglethorpe[5] thought slavery against law and gospel; but the circumstances which gave Georgia its first inhabitants were not calculated to furnish citizens over-nice in their ideas about rum and slaves. Despite the prohibitions of the trustees, these Georgians, like some of their descendants, proceeded to take the law into their own hands; and so pliant were the judges, and so flagrant the smuggling, and so earnest were the prayers of Whitefield,[6] that by the middle of the eighteenth century all restrictions were swept away, and the slave-trade went merrily on for fifty years and more.

Down in Darien, where the Delegal riots[7] took place some summers ago, there used to come a strong protest against slavery from the Scotch Highlanders; and the Moravians of Ebenezea[8] did not like the system. But not till the Haytian Terror of Toussaint[9] was the trade in men even

2. Spanish explorer (1496?–1542), discoverer of the Mississippi River, and conquistador.
3. American Indian tribe once prevalent in Georgia, the Carolinas, and Tennessee.
4. Black farm worker who lived in Palmetto, Georgia. He fled from his home after being accused of murdering his employer. When captured, he was also accused of raping his employer's wife. He admitted to the murder but denied the rape. After a lynching observed by 2,000 people (1899), Hose's burned body was dismembered and his knuckles put on display in an Atlanta store window.
5. James Edward Oglethorpe (1696–1785), founder of the colony of Georgia in 1733.
6. George Whitefield (1714–1770), English minister and public speaker who defended the institution of slavery, toured Georgia preaching for lenient treatment of slaves.
7. The riots occurred on August 23, 1899, when hundreds of blacks, after hearing rumors of a lynching, blocked the removal of a black prisoner from a jail in Darien, Georgia. Twenty-five men were later convicted of insurrection and jailed.
8. The Moravians, a Protestant denomination since 1497, were victims of persecution in Europe. In America, they were known for their missionary efforts and antislavery position. Some settled in Ebeneza, near Savannah. Scotch Highlanders refers to immigrants from Scotland who settled in Georgia in the eighteenth century.
9. See n. 5, p. 15.

checked; while the national statute of 1808 did not suffice to stop it![1]
How the Africans poured in!—fifty thousand between 1790 and 1810,
and then, from Virginia and from smugglers, two thousand a year for
many years more. So the thirty thousand Negroes of Georgia in 1790
were doubled in a decade,—were over a hundred thousand in 1810,
had reached two hundred thousand in 1820, and half a million at the
time of the war. Thus like a snake the black population writhed upward.

But we must hasten on our journey. This that we pass as we leave
Atlanta is the ancient land of the Cherokees,—that brave Indian nation
which strove so long for its fatherland, until Fate and the United States
Government drove them beyond the Mississippi. If you wish to ride
with me you must come into the "Jim Crow Car."[2] There will be no
objection,—already four other white men, and a little white girl with
her nurse, are in there. Usually the races are mixed in there; but the
white coach is all white. Of course this car is not so good as the other,
but it is fairly clean and comfortable. The discomfort lies chiefly in the
hearts of those four black men yonder—and in mine.

We rumble south in quite a business-like way. The bare red clay and
pines of Northern Georgia begin to disappear, and in their place appears a rich rolling land, luxuriant, and here and there well tilled. This
is the land of the Creek Indians;[3] and a hard time the Georgians had
to seize it. The towns grow more frequent and more interesting, and
brand-new cotton mills rise on every side. Below Macon the world
grows darker; for now we approach the Black Belt,[4]—that strange land
of shadows, at which even slaves paled in the past, and whence come
now only faint and half-intelligible murmurs to the world beyond. The
"Jim Crow Car" grows larger and a shade better; three rough field-
hands and two or three white loafers accompany us, and the newsboy
still spreads his wares at one end. The sun is setting, but we can see
the great cotton country as we enter it,—the soil now dark and fertile,
now thin and gray, with fruit-trees and dilapidated buildings,—all the
way to Albany.

At Albany, in the heart of the Black Belt, we stop. Two hundred
miles south of Atlanta, two hundred miles west of the Atlantic, and one
hundred miles north of the Great Gulf lies Dougherty County, with
ten thousand Negroes and two thousand whites. The Flint River winds
down from Andersonville, and, turning suddenly at Albany, the county-
seat, hurries on to join the Chattahoochee and the sea. Andrew Jackson[5]

---

1. An act of Congress passed in 1807 to prohibit the importation of slaves beginning on January
1, 1808.
2. See n. 4, p. 54.
3. Native Americans whose tribal lands were in Georgia, Alabama, and northern Florida.
4. Designation for parts of the South where the black population was especially dense. The term
also refers to the fertile black soil. The reason for such a large black population in these
regions was the use of slaves to work this profitable land.
5. Tennessee native (1767–1845) and major general of the militia who led U.S. troops against
the Creek Indians in 1813–14. Later, he became president of the United States (1829–37).

knew the Flint well, and marched across it once to avenge the Indian Massacre at Fort Mims.[6] That was in 1814, not long before the battle of New Orleans; and by the Creek treaty that followed this campaign, all Dougherty County, and much other rich land, was ceded to Georgia. Still, settlers fought shy of this land, for the Indians were all about, and they were unpleasant neighbors in those days. The panic of 1837,[7] which Jackson bequeathed to Van Buren, turned the planters from the impoverished lands of Virginia, the Carolinas, and east Georgia, toward the West. The Indians were removed to Indian Territory, and settlers poured into these coveted lands to retrieve their broken fortunes. For a radius of a hundred miles about Albany, stretched a great fertile land, luxuriant with forests of pine, oak, ash, hickory, and poplar; hot with the sun and damp with the rich black swamp-land; and here the cornerstone of the Cotton Kingdom[8] was laid.

Albany is to-day a wide-streeted, placid, Southern town, with a broad sweep of stores and saloons, and flanking rows of homes,—whites usually to the north, and blacks to the south. Six days in the week the town looks decidedly too small for itself, and takes frequent and prolonged naps. But on Saturday suddenly the whole county disgorges itself upon the place, and a perfect flood of black peasantry pours through the streets, fills the stores, blocks the sidewalks, chokes the thoroughfares, and takes full possession of the town. They are black, sturdy, uncouth country folk, good-natured and simple, talkative to a degree, and yet far more silent and brooding than the crowds of the Rhine-pfalz, or Naples, or Cracow.[9] They drink considerable quantities of whiskey, but do not get very drunk; they talk and laugh loudly at times, but seldom quarrel or fight. They walk up and down the streets, meet and gossip with friends, stare at the shop windows, buy coffee, cheap candy, and clothes, and at dusk drive home—happy? well no, not exactly happy, but much happier than as though they had not come.

Thus Albany is a real capital,—a typical Southern county town, the centre of the life of ten thousand souls; their point of contact with the outer world, their centre of news and gossip, their market for buying and selling, borrowing and lending, their fountain of justice and law. Once upon a time we knew country life so well and city life so little, that we illustrated city life as that of a closely crowded country district. Now the world has well-nigh forgotten what the country is, and we must imagine a little city of black people scattered far and wide over three hundred lonesome square miles of land, without train or trolley,

6. On August 30, 1813, Creek Indians staged an uprising and massacred whites and blacks at Fort Mims, Alabama.
7. Economic crisis that began in 1837 with bank failures during Jackson's presidency. The resulting financial problems continued into Martin Van Buren's presidency (1837–41).
8. Term used to encapsulate the importance of cotton to the economy of the South, and the resulting wealth and power derived from it.
9. Cities in Germany, Italy, and Poland, respectively.

in the midst of cotton and corn, and wide patches of sand and gloomy soil.

It gets pretty hot in Southern Georgia in July,—a sort of dull, determined heat that seems quite independent of the sun; so it took us some days to muster courage enough to leave the porch and venture out on the long country roads, that we might see this unknown world. Finally we started. It was about ten in the morning, bright with a faint breeze, and we jogged leisurely southward in the valley of the Flint. We passed the scattered box-like cabins of the brick-yard hands, and the long tenement-row facetiously called "The Ark," and were soon in the open country, and on the confines of the great plantations of other days. There is the "Joe Fields place"; a rough old fellow was he, and had killed many a "nigger" in his day. Twelve miles his plantation used to run,—a regular barony. It is nearly all gone now; only straggling bits belong to the family, and the rest has passed to Jews and Negroes. Even the bits which are left are heavily mortgaged, and, like the rest of the land, tilled by tenants. Here is one of them now,—a tall brown man, a hard worker and a hard drinker, illiterate, but versed in farmlore, as his nodding crops declare. This distressingly new board house is his, and he has just moved out of yonder moss-grown cabin with its one square room.

From the curtains in Benton's house, down the road, a dark comely face is staring at the strangers; for passing carriages are not every-day occurrences here. Benton is an intelligent yellow man with a good-sized family, and manages a plantation blasted by the war and now the broken staff of the widow. He might be well-to-do, they say; but he carouses too much in Albany. And the half-desolate spirit of neglect born of the very soil seems to have settled on these acres. In times past there were cotton-gins and machinery here; but they have rotted away.

The whole land seems forlorn and forsaken. Here are the remnants of the vast plantations of the Sheldons, the Pellots, and the Rensons; but the souls of them are passed. The houses lie in half ruin, or have wholly disappeared; the fences have flown, and the families are wandering in the world. Strange vicissitudes have met these whilom[1] masters. Yonder stretch the wide acres of Bildad Reasor; he died in war-time, but the upstart overseer hastened to wed the widow. Then he went, and his neighbors too, and now only the black tenant remains; but the shadow-hand of the master's grand-nephew or cousin or creditor stretches out of the gray distance to collect the rack-rent[2] remorselessly, and so the land is uncared-for and poor. Only black tenants can stand such a system, and they only because they must. Ten miles we have ridden to-day and have seen no white face.

A resistless feeling of depression falls slowly upon us, despite the

1. Former.
2. Excessively or unreasonably high rent.

gaudy sunshine and the green cotton-fields. This, then, is the Cotton Kingdom,—the shadow of a marvellous dream. And where is the King? Perhaps this is he,—the sweating ploughman, tilling his eighty acres with two lean mules, and fighting a hard battle with debt. So we sit musing, until, as we turn a corner on the sandy road, there comes a fairer scene suddenly in view,—a neat cottage snugly ensconced by the road, and near it a little store. A tall bronzed man rises from the porch as we hail him, and comes out to our carriage. He is six feet in height, with a sober face that smiles gravely. He walks too straight to be a tenant,—yes, he owns two hundred and forty acres. "The land is run down since the boom-days of eighteen hundred and fifty," he explains, and cotton is low. Three black tenants live on his place, and in his little store he keeps a small stock of tobacco, snuff, soap, and soda, for the neighborhood. Here is his ginhouse with new machinery just installed. Three hundred bales of cotton went through it last year. Two children he has sent away to school. Yes, he says sadly, he is getting on, but cotton is down to four cents; I know how Debt sits staring at him.

Wherever the King may be, the parks and palaces of the Cotton Kingdom have not wholly disappeared. We plunge even now into great groves of oak and towering pine, with an undergrowth of myrtle and shrubbery. This was the "home-house" of the Thompsons,—slave-barons who drove their coach and four in the merry past. All is silence now, and ashes, and tangled weeds. The owner put his whole fortune into the rising cotton industry of the fifties, and with the falling prices of the eighties he packed up and stole away. Yonder is another grove, with unkempt lawn, great magnolias, and grass-grown paths. The Big House stands in half-ruin, its great front door staring blankly at the street, and the back part grotesquely restored for its black tenant. A shabby, well-built Negro he is, unlucky and irresolute. He digs hard to pay rent to the white girl who owns the remnant of the place. She married a policeman, and lives in Savannah.

Now and again we come to churches. Here is one now,—Shepherd's, they call it,—a great white-washed barn of a thing, perched on stilts of stone, and looking for all the world as though it were just resting here a moment and might be expected to waddle off down the road at almost any time. And yet it is the centre of a hundred cabin homes; and sometimes, of a Sunday, five hundred persons from far and near gather here and talk and eat and sing. There is a school-house near,—a very airy, empty shed; but even this is an improvement, for usually the school is held in the church. The churches vary from log-huts to those like Shepherd's, and the schools from nothing to this little house that sits demurely on the county line. It is a tiny plank-house, perhaps ten by twenty, and has within a double row of rough unplaned benches, resting mostly on legs, sometimes on boxes. Opposite the door is a square home-made desk. In one corner are the ruins of a stove, and in the other a dim blackboard. It is the cheerfulest schoolhouse I have seen in Dougherty, save in town. Back of the schoolhouse is a lodge-house two stories high and not quite finished. Societies meet there,— societies "to care for the sick and bury the dead"; and these societies grow and flourish.

We had come to the boundaries of Dougherty, and were about to turn west along the county-line, when all these sights were pointed out to us by a kindly old man, black, white-haired, and seventy. Forty-five years he had lived here, and now supports himself and his old wife by the help of the steer tethered yonder and the charity of his black neigh-bors. He shows us the farm of the Hills just across the county line in Baker,—a widow and two strapping sons, who raised ten bales (one need not add "cotton" down here) last year. There are fences and pigs and cows, and the soft-voiced, velvet-skinned young Memnon,[3] who saun-tered half-bashfully over to greet the strangers, is proud of his home. We turn now to the west along the county line. Great dismantled trunks of pines tower above the green cotton-fields, cracking their naked gnarled fingers toward the border of living forest beyond. There is little beauty in this region, only a sort of crude abandon that suggests power,—a naked grandeur, as it were. The houses are bare and straight; there are no hammocks or easy-chairs, and few flowers. So when, as here at Rawdon's, one sees a vine clinging to a little porch, and home-like windows peeping over the fences, one takes a long breath. I think I never before quite realized the place of the Fence in civilization. This is the Land of the Unfenced, where crouch on either hand scores of ugly one-room cabins, cheerless and dirty. Here lies the Negro problem in its naked dirt and penury. And here are no fences. But now and then the criss-cross rails or straight palings break into view, and then we know a touch of culture is near. Of course Harrison Gohagen,—a quiet yellow man, young, smooth-faced, and diligent,—of course he is lord of some hundred acres, and we expect to see a vision of well-kept rooms and fat beds and laughing children. For has he not fine fences? And those over yonder, why should they build fences on the rack-rented land? It will only increase their rent.

On we wind, through sand and pines and glimpses of old plantations, till there creeps into sight a cluster of buildings,—wood and brick, mills and houses, and scattered cabins. It seemed quite a village. As it came nearer and nearer, however, the aspect changed: the buildings were rotten, the bricks were falling out, the mills were silent, and the store was closed. Only in the cabins appeared now and then a bit of lazy life. I could imagine the place under some weird spell, and was half-minded to search out the princess. An old ragged black man, honest,

3. In Greek mythology, king of Ethiopia.

simple, and improvident, told us the tale. The Wizard of the North—the Capitalist—had rushed down in the seventies to woo this coy dark soil. He bought a square mile or more, and for a time the field-hands sang, the gins groaned, and the mills buzzed. Then came a change. The agent's son embezzled the funds and ran off with them. Then the agent himself disappeared. Finally the new agent stole even the books, and the company in wrath closed its business and its houses, refused to sell, and let houses and furniture and machinery rust and rot. So the Waters-Loring plantation was stilled by the spell of dishonesty, and stands like some gaunt rebuke to a scarred land.

Somehow that plantation ended our day's journey; for I could not shake off the influence of that silent scene. Back toward town we glided, past the straight and thread-like pines, past a dark tree-dotted pond where the air was heavy with a dead sweet perfume. White slender-legged curlews flitted by us, and the garnet blooms of the cotton looked gay against the green and purple stalks. A peasant girl was hoeing in the field, white-turbaned and black-limbed. All this we saw, but the spell still lay upon us.

How curious a land is this,—how full of untold story, of tragedy and laughter, and the rich legacy of human life; shadowed with a tragic past, and big with future promise! This is the Black Belt of Georgia. Dougherty County is the west end of the Black Belt, and men once called it the Egypt of the Confederacy.[4] It is full of historic interest. First there is the Swamp, to the west, where the Chickasawhatchee flows sullenly southward. The shadow of an old plantation lies at its edge, forlorn and dark. Then comes the pool; pendent gray moss and brackish waters appear, and forests filled with wild-fowl. In one place the wood is on fire, smouldering in dull red anger; but nobody minds. Then the swamp grows beautiful; a raised road, built by chained Negro convicts, dips down into it, and forms a way walled and almost covered in living green. Spreading trees spring from a prodigal luxuriance of undergrowth; great dark green shadows fade into the black background, until all is one mass of tangled semi-tropical foliage, marvellous in its weird savage splendor. Once we crossed a black silent stream, where the sad trees and writhing creepers, all glinting fiery yellow and green, seemed like some vast cathedral,—some green Milan[5] builded of wild-wood. And as I crossed, I seemed to see again that fierce tragedy of seventy years ago. Osceola,[6] the Indian-Negro chieftain, had risen in the swamps of Florida, vowing vengeance. His war-cry reached the red Creeks of Dougherty, and their war-cry rang from the Chattahoochee

4. Du Bois's use of the word "Egypt" indicates his continuing metaphor of the South as morally equivalent to the Egypt of the Hebrew Scriptures. Black folk, also enslaved, are identified with the Israelites in bondage.
5. City in northern Italy known for its art treasures, including a beautiful cathedral.
6. Seminole Indian (1800–1838) who was also part black. Many escaping slaves joined his tribe in Florida, and he led them in the Seminole War against the United States in 1835.

to the sea. Men and women and children fled and fell before them as they swept into Dougherty. In yonder shadows a dark and hideously painted warrior glided stealthily on,—another and another, until three hundred had crept into the treacherous swamp. Then the false slime closing about them called the white men from the east. Waist-deep, they fought beneath the tall trees, until the war-cry was hushed and the Indians glided back into the west. Small wonder the wood is red.

Then came the black slaves. Day after day the clank of chained feet marching from Virginia and Carolina to Georgia was heard in these rich swamp lands. Day after day the songs of the callous, the wail of the motherless, and the muttered curses of the wretched echoed from the Flint to the Chickasawhatchee, until by 1860 there had risen in West Dougherty perhaps the richest slave kingdom the modern world ever knew. A hundred and fifty barons commanded the labor of nearly six thousand negroes, held sway over farms with ninety thousand acres of tilled land, valued even in times of cheap soil at three millions of dollars. Twenty thousand bales of ginned cotton went yearly to England, New and Old; and men that came there bankrupt made money and grew rich. In a single decade the cotton output increased four-fold and the value of lands was tripled. It was the heyday of the *nouveau riche*,[7] and a life of careless extravagance reigned among the masters. Four and six bob-tailed thoroughbreds rolled their coaches to town; open hospitality and gay entertainment were the rule. Parks and groves were laid out, rich with flower and vine, and in the midst stood the low wide-halled "big house," with its porch and columns and great fireplaces.

And yet with all this there was something sordid, something forced, —a certain feverish unrest and recklessness; for was not all this show and tinsel built upon a groan? "This land was a little Hell," said a ragged, brown, and grave-faced man to me. We were seated near a roadside blacksmith-shop, and behind was the bare ruin of some master's home. "I've seen niggers drop dead in the furrow, but they were kicked aside, and the plough never stopped. And down in the guardhouse, there's where the blood ran."

With such foundations a kingdom must in time sway and fall. The masters moved to Macon and Augusta, and left only the irresponsible overseers on the land. And the result is such ruin as this, the Lloyd "home-place":—great waving oaks, a spread of lawn, myrtles and chestnuts, all ragged and wild; a solitary gate-post standing where once was a castle entrance; an old rusty anvil lying amid rotting bellows and wood in the ruins of a blacksmith shop; a wide rambling old mansion, brown and dingy, filled now with the grandchildren of the slaves who once waited on its tables; while the family of the master has dwindled to two

7. Literally, new rich (French); one who flaunts his or her recent wealth.

lone women, who live in Macon and feed hungrily off the remnants of an earldom. So we ride on, past phantom gates and falling homes, —past the once flourishing farms of the Smiths, the Gandys, and the Lagores,—and find all dilapidated and half ruined, even there where a solitary white woman, a relic of other days, sits alone in state among miles of Negroes and rides to town in her ancient coach each day.

This was indeed the Egypt of the Confederacy,—the rich granary whence potatoes and corn and cotton poured out to the famished and ragged Confederate troops as they battled for a cause lost long before 1861. Sheltered and secure, it became the place of refuge for families, wealth, and slaves. Yet even then the hard ruthless rape of the land began to tell. The red-clay sub-soil already had begun to peer above the loam. The harder the slaves were driven the more careless and fatal was their farming. Then came the revolution of war and Emancipation, the bewilderment of Reconstruction,—and now, what is the Egypt of the Confederacy, and what meaning has it for the nation's weal or woe?

It is a land of rapid contrasts and of curiously mingled hope and pain. Here sits a pretty blue-eyed quadroon[8] hiding her bare feet; she was married only last week, and yonder in the field is her dark young husband, hoeing to support her, at thirty cents a day without board. Across the way is Gatesby, brown and tall, lord of two thousand acres shrewdly won and held. There is a store conducted by his black son, a blacksmith shop, and a ginnery.[9] Five miles below here is a town owned and controlled by one white New Englander. He owns almost a Rhode Island county, with thousands of acres and hundreds of black laborers. Their cabins look better than most, and the farm, with machinery and fertilizers, is much more business-like than any in the county, although the manager drives hard bargains in wages. When now we turn and look five miles above, there on the edge of town are five houses of prostitutes,—two of blacks and three of whites; and in one of the houses of the whites a worthless black boy was harbored too openly two years ago; so he was hanged for rape. And here, too, is the high whitewashed fence of the "stockade," as the county prison is called; the white folks say it is ever full of black criminals,—the black folks say that only colored boys are sent to jail, and they not because they are guilty, but because the State needs criminals to eke out its income by their forced labor.

The Jew is the heir[1] of the slave-baron in Dougherty; and as we ride westward, by wide stretching cornfields and stubby orchards of peach and pear, we see on all sides within the circle of dark forest a Land of Canaan. Here and there are tales of projects for money-getting, born

8. A person who is one-quarter African American.
9. A cotton gin is the machine that separates the seeds, seed hulls, and other debris from the cotton fibers. A ginnery is a location where such machines are employed.
1. "The Jew is heir" changed to "Immigrants are heirs" in 1953 edition. See page xl.

in the swift days of Reconstruction,—"improvement" companies, wine companies, mills and factories; nearly all failed, and the Jew fell heir.[2] It is a beautiful land, this Dougherty, west of the Flint. The forests are wonderful, the solemn pines have disappeared, and this is the "Oakey Woods," with its wealth of hickories, beeches, oaks, and palmettos. But a pall of debt hangs over the beautiful land; the merchants are in debt to the wholesalers, the planters are in debt to the merchants, the tenants owe the planters, and laborers bow and bend beneath the burden of it all. Here and there a man has raised his head above these murky waters. We passed one fenced stock-farm, with grass and grazing cattle, that looked very homelike after endless corn and cotton. Here and there are black freeholders:[3] there is the gaunt dull-black Jackson, with his hundred acres. "I says, 'Look up! If you don't look up you can't get up,'" remarks Jackson, philosophically. And he's gotten up. Dark Carter's neat barns would do credit to New England. His master helped him to get a start, but when the black man died last fall the master's sons immediately laid claim to the estate. "And them white folks will get it, too," said my yellow gossip.

I turn from these well-tended acres with a comfortable feeling that the Negro is rising. Even then, however, the fields, as we proceed, begin to redden and the trees disappear. Rows of old cabins appear filled with renters and laborers,—cheerless, bare, and dirty, for the most part, although here and there the very age and decay makes the scene picturesque. A young black fellow greets us. He is twenty-two, and just married. Until last year he had good luck renting; then cotton fell, and the sheriff seized and sold all he had. So he moved here, where the rent is higher, the land poorer, and the owner inflexible; he rents a forty-dollar mule for twenty dollars a year. Poor lad!—a slave at twenty-two. This plantation, owned now by a Russian Jew,[4] was a part of the famous Bolton estate. After the war it was for many years worked by gangs of Negro convicts,—and black convicts then were even more plentiful than now; it was a way of making Negroes work, and the question of guilt was a minor one. Hard tales of cruelty and mistreatment of the chained freemen are told, but the county authorities were deaf until the free-labor market was nearly ruined by wholesale migration. Then they took the convicts from the plantations, but not until one of the fairest regions of the "Oakey Woods" had been ruined and ravished into a red waste, out of which only a Yankee or a Jew[5] could squeeze more blood from debt-cursed tenants.

No wonder that Luke Black, slow, dull, and discouraged, shuffles to

2. In 1953 edition, "nearly all failed, and the Jew fell heir" changed to "most failed, and foreigners fell heir."
3. One holding an estate for life.
4. "A Russian Jew" changed to "a foreigner" in 1953 edition.
5. "Only a Yankee or a Jew" changed to "Only a Yankee or an immigrant" in 1953 edition.

our carriage and talks hopelessly. Why should he strive? Every year finds
him deeper in debt. How strange that Georgia, the world-heralded refuge of poor debtors, should bind her own to sloth and misfortune as
ruthlessly as ever England did! The poor land groans with its birth-
pains, and brings forth scarcely a hundred pounds of cotton to the acre,
where fifty years ago it yielded eight times as much. Of this meagre
yield the tenant pays from a quarter to a third in rent, and most of the
rest in interest on food and supplies bought on credit. Twenty years
yonder sunken-cheeked, old black man has labored under that system,
and now, turned day-laborer, is supporting his wife and boarding himself on his wages of a dollar and a half a week, received only part of
the year.

The Bolton convict farm formerly included the neighboring plantation. Here it was that the convicts were lodged in the great log prison
still standing. A dismal place it still remains, with rows of ugly huts
filled with surly ignorant tenants. "What rent do you pay here?" I inquired. "I don't know,—what is it, Sam?" "All we make," answered
Sam. It is a depressing place,—bare, unshaded, with no charm of past
association, only a memory of forced human toil,—now, then, and before the war. They are not happy, these black men whom we meet
throughout this region. There is little of the joyous abandon and play-
fulness which we are wont to associate with the plantation Negro. At
best, the natural good-nature is edged with complaint or has changed
into sullenness and gloom. And now and then it blazes forth in veiled
but hot anger. I remember one big red-eyed black whom we met by
the roadside. Forty-five years he had labored on this farm, beginning
with nothing, and still having nothing. To be sure, he had given four
children a common-school training, and perhaps if the new fence-law
had not allowed unfenced crops in West Dougherty he might have
raised a little stock and kept ahead. As it is, he is hopelessly in debt,
disappointed, and embittered. He stopped us to inquire after the black
boy in Albany, whom it was said a policeman had shot and killed for
loud talking on the sidewalk. And then he said slowly: "Let a white
man touch me, and he dies; I don't boast this,—I don't say it around
loud, or before the children,—but I mean it. I've seen them whip my
father and my old mother in them cotton-rows till the blood ran;
by—" and we passed on.

Now Sears, whom we met next lolling under the chubby oak-trees,
was of quite different fibre. Happy?—Well, yes; he laughed and flipped
pebbles, and thought the world was as it was. He had worked here
twelve years and has nothing but a mortgaged mule. Children? Yes,
seven; but they hadn't been to school this year,—couldn't afford books
and clothes, and couldn't spare their work. There go part of them to
the fields now,—three big boys astride mules, and a strapping girl with

bare brown legs. Careless ignorance and laziness here, fierce hate and vindictiveness there;—these are the extremes of the Negro problem which we met that day, and we scarce knew which we preferred.

Here and there we meet distinct characters quite out of the ordinary. One came out of a piece of newly cleared ground, making a wide detour to avoid the snakes. He was an old, hollow-cheeked man, with a drawn and characterful brown face. He had a sort of self-contained quaintness and rough humor impossible to describe; a certain cynical earnestness that puzzled one. "The niggers were jealous of me over on the other place," he said, "and so me and the old woman begged this piece of woods, and I cleared it up myself. Made nothing for two years, but I reckon I've got a crop now." The cotton looked tall and rich, and we praised it. He curtsied low, and then bowed almost to the ground, with an imperturbable gravity that seemed almost suspicious. Then he continued, "My mule died last week,"—a calamity in this land equal to a devastating fire in town,—"but a white man loaned me another." Then he added, eyeing us, "Oh, I gets along with white folks." We turned the conversation. "Bears? deer?" he answered, "well, I should say there were," and he let fly a string of brave oaths, as he told hunting-tales of the swamp. We left him standing still in the middle of the road looking after us, and yet apparently not noticing us.

The Whistle place, which includes his bit of land, was bought soon after the war by an English syndicate, the "Dixie Cotton and Corn Company." A marvellous deal of style their factor put on, with his servants and coach-and-six; so much so that the concern soon landed in inextricable bankruptcy. Nobody lives in the old house now, but a man comes each winter out of the North and collects his high rents. I know not which are the more touching,—such old empty houses, or the homes of the masters' sons. Sad and bitter tales lie hidden back of those white doors,—tales of poverty, of struggle, of disappointment. A revolution such as that of '63[6] is a terrible thing; they that rose rich in the morning often slept in paupers' beds. Beggars and vulgar speculators rose to rule over them, and their children went astray. See yonder sad-colored house, with its cabins and fences and glad crops! It is not glad within; last month the prodigal son of the struggling father wrote home from the city for money. Money! Where was it to come from? And so the son rose in the night and killed his baby, and killed his wife, and shot himself dead. And the world passed on.

I remember wheeling around a bend in the road beside a graceful bit of forest and a singing brook. A long low house faced us, with porch and flying pillars, great oaken door, and a broad lawn shining in the evening sun. But the window-panes were gone, the pillars were worm-eaten, and the moss-grown roof was falling in. Half curiously I peered

6. The social, political, and economic upheaval that resulted from the Emancipation Proclamation, which went into effect January 1, 1863.

through the unhinged door, and saw where, on the wall across the hall, was written in once gay letters a faded "Welcome."

Quite a contrast to the southwestern part of Dougherty County is the northwest. Soberly timbered in oak and pine, it has none of that half-tropical luxuriance of the southwest. Then, too, there are fewer signs of a romantic past, and more of systematic modern land-grabbing and money-getting. White people are more in evidence here, and farmer and hired labor replace to some extent the absentee landlord and rack-rented tenant. The crops have neither the luxuriance of the richer land nor the signs of neglect so often seen, and there were fences and meadows here and there. Most of this land was poor, and beneath the notice of the slave-baron, before the war. Since then his nephews and the poor whites and the Jews[7] have seized it. The returns of the farmer are too small to allow much for wages, and yet he will not sell off small farms. There is the Negro Sanford; he has worked fourteen years as overseer on the Ladson place, and "paid out enough for fertilizers to have bought a farm," but the owner will not sell off a few acres.

Two children—a boy and a girl—are hoeing sturdily in the fields on the farm where Corliss works. He is smooth-faced and brown, and is fencing up his pigs. He used to run a successful cotton-gin, but the Cotton Seed Oil Trust has forced the price of ginning so low that he says it hardly pays him. He points out a stately old house over the way as the home of "Pa Willis." We eagerly ride over, for "Pa Willis" was the tall and powerful black Moses who led the Negroes for a generation, and led them well. He was a Baptist preacher, and when he died two thousand black people followed him to the grave; and now they preach his funeral sermon each year. His widow lives here,—a weazened, sharp-featured little woman, who curtsied quaintly as we greeted her. Further on lives Jack Delson, the most prosperous Negro farmer in the county. It is a joy to meet him,—a great broad-shouldered, handsome black man, intelligent and jovial. Six hundred and fifty acres he owns, and has eleven black tenants. A neat and tidy home nestled in a flower-garden, and a little store stands beside it.

We pass the Munson place, where a plucky white widow is renting and struggling; and the eleven hundred acres of the Sennet plantation, with its Negro overseer. Then the character of the farms begins to change. Nearly all the lands belong to Russian Jews;[8] the overseers are white, and the cabins are bare board-houses scattered here and there. The rents are high, and day-laborers and "contract" hands abound. It is a keen, hard struggle for living here, and few have time to talk. Tired with the long ride, we gladly drive into Gillonsville. It is a silent cluster

7. In 1953 edition, "nephews and the poor whites and the Jews" changed to "poor relations and foreign immigrants."
8. In an effort to avoid appearing anti-Semitic, Du Bois changed his language throughout to exclude references to Jews except in this instance. His reasons are not known although Herbert Aptheker writes that he believes it to be an oversight.

of farm-houses standing on the cross-roads, with one of its stores closed and the other kept by a Negro preacher. They tell great tales of busy times at Gillonsville before all the railroads came to Albany; now it is chiefly a memory. Riding down the street, we stop at the preacher's and seat ourselves before the door. It was one of those scenes one cannot soon forget:—a wide, low, little house, whose motherly roof reached over and sheltered a snug little porch. There we sat, after the long hot drive, drinking cool water,—the talkative little storekeeper who is my daily companion; the silent old black woman patching pantaloons and saying never a word; the ragged picture of helpless misfortune who called in just to see the preacher; and finally the neat matronly preacher's wife, plump, yellow, and intelligent. "Own land?" said the wife; "well, only this house." Then she added quietly, "We did buy seven hundred acres up yonder, and paid for it; but they cheated us out of it. Sells was the owner." "Sells!" echoed the ragged misfortune, who was leaning against the balustrade and listening, "he's a regular cheat. I worked for him thirty-seven days this spring, and he paid me in card-board checks which were to be cashed at the end of the month. But he never cashed them,—kept putting me off. Then the sheriff came and took my mule and corn and furniture—" "Furniture?" I asked; "but furniture is exempt from seizure by law." "Well, he took it just the same," said the hard-faced man.

VIII

Of the Quest of the Golden Fleece[1]

But the Brute said in his breast, "Till the mills I grind have ceased,
The riches shall be dust of dust, dry ashes be the feast!

"On the strong and cunning few
Cynic favors I will strew;
I will stuff their maw with overplus until their spirit dies;
From the patient and the low
I will take the joys they know;
They shall hunger after vanities and still an-hungered go.
Madness shall be on the people, ghastly jealousies arise;
Brother's blood shall cry on brother up the dead and empty skies."
WILLIAM VAUGHN MOODY.

Have you ever seen a cotton-field white with the harvest,—its golden fleece hovering above the black earth like a silvery cloud edged with dark green, its bold white signals waving like the foam of billows from Carolina to Texas across that Black and human Sea? I have sometimes half suspected that here the winged ram Chrysomallus left that Fleece after which Jason and his Argonauts went vaguely wandering into the shadowy East three thousand years ago; and certainly one might frame a pretty and not far-fetched analogy of witchery and dragon's teeth, and blood and armed men, between the ancient and the modern Quest of the Golden Fleece in the Black Sea.[2]

And now the golden fleece is found; not only found, but, in its birthplace, woven. For the hum of the cotton-mills is the newest and most significant thing in the New South to-day. All through the Carolinas and Georgia, away down to Mexico, rise these gaunt red buildings, bare and homely, and yet so busy and noisy withal[3] that they scarce

1. Chapters VII and VIII are revisions of "The Negro As He Really Is," *The World's Work* (June 1901): 848–66. The verse is from William Vaughn Moody's *The Brute* (1901). The music quotation is from the Negro spiritual "Children You'll Be Called On."
2. Du Bois uses the Greek myth of Jason's travels to win the Chrysomalus's Golden Fleece to emphasize the great effort that it takes to produce the contemporary golden fleece, cotton. Only though the assistance, the "witchery," of Medea are Jason and his fellows, the Argonauts, able to defeat the armed men who sprang up from dragon's teeth.
3. Besides.

seem to belong to the slow and sleepy land. Perhaps they sprang from dragons' teeth. So the Cotton Kingdom still lives; the world still bows beneath her sceptre. Even the markets that once defied the *parvenu*[4] have crept one by one across the seas, and then slowly and reluctantly, but surely, have started toward the Black Belt.

To be sure, there are those who wag their heads knowingly and tell us that the capital of the Cotton Kingdom has moved from the Black to the White Belt,—that the Negro of to-day raises not more than half of the cotton crop. Such men forget that the cotton crop has doubled, and more than doubled, since the era of slavery, and that, even granting their contention, the Negro is still supreme in a Cotton Kingdom larger than that on which the Confederacy builded its hopes. So the Negro forms to-day one of the chief figures in a great world-industry; and this, for its own sake, and in the light of historic interest, makes the field-hands of the cotton country worth studying.

We seldom study the condition of the Negro to-day honestly and carefully. It is so much easier to assume that we know it all. Or perhaps, having already reached conclusions in our own minds, we are loth to have them disturbed by facts. And yet how little we really know of these millions,—of their daily lives and longings, of their homely joys and sorrows, of their real shortcomings and the meaning of their crimes! All this we can only learn by intimate contact with the masses, and not by wholesale arguments covering millions separate in time and space, and differing widely in training and culture. To-day, then, my reader, let us turn our faces to the Black Belt of Georgia and seek simply to know the condition of the black farm-laborers of one county there.

Here in 1890 lived ten thousand Negroes and two thousand whites. The country is rich, yet the people are poor. The keynote of the Black Belt is debt; not commercial credit, but debt in the sense of continued inability on the part of the mass of the population to make income cover expense. This is the direct heritage of the South from the wasteful economies of the slave *régime*;[5] but it was emphasized and brought to a crisis by the Emancipation of the slaves. In 1860, Dougherty County had six thousand slaves, worth at least two and a half millions of dollars; its farms were estimated at three millions,—making five and a half millions of property, the value of which depended largely on the slave system, and on the speculative demand for land once marvellously rich but already partially devitalized by careless and exhaustive culture. The war then meant a financial crash; in place of the five and a half millions of 1860, there remained in 1870 only farms valued at less than two millions. With this came increased competition in cotton culture from the rich lands of Texas; a steady fall in the normal price of cotton

---

4. Someone who has suddenly risen above his or her economic class but does not possess the social background for this new status.
5. A system of management, or a government in power.

followed, from about fourteen cents a pound in 1860 until it reached four cents in 1898. Such a financial revolution was it that involved the owners of the cotton-belt in debt. And if things went ill with the master, how fared it with the man?

The plantations of Dougherty County in slavery days were not as imposing and aristocratic as those of Virginia. The Big House[6] was smaller and usually one-storied, and sat very near the slave cabins. Sometimes these cabins stretched off on either side like wings; sometimes only on one side, forming a double row, or edging the road that turned into the plantation from the main thoroughfare. The form and disposition of the laborers' cabins throughout the Black Belt is to-day the same as in slavery days. Some live in the self-same cabins, others in cabins rebuilt on the sites of the old. All are sprinkled in little groups over the face of the land, centering about some dilapidated Big House where the head-tenant or agent lives. The general character and arrangement of these dwellings remains on the whole unaltered. There were in the county, outside the corporate town of Albany, about fifteen hundred Negro families in 1898. Out of all these, only a single family occupied a house with seven rooms; only fourteen have five rooms or more. The mass live in one- and two-room homes.

The size and arrangements of a people's homes are no unfair index of their condition. If, then, we inquire more carefully into these Negro homes, we find much that is unsatisfactory. All over the face of the land is the one-room cabin,—now standing in the shadow of the Big House, now staring at the dusty road, now rising dark and sombre amid the green of the cotton-fields. It is nearly always old and bare, built of rough boards, and neither plastered nor ceiled. Light and ventilation are supplied by the single door and by the square hole in the wall with its wooden shutter. There is no glass, porch, or ornamentation without. Within is a fireplace, black and smoky, and usually unsteady with age. A bed or two, a table, a wooden chest, and a few chairs compose the furniture; while a stray show-bill or a newspaper makes up the decorations for the walls. Now and then one may find such a cabin kept scrupulously neat, with merry steaming fireplace and hospitable door; but the majority are dirty and dilapidated, smelling of eating and sleeping, poorly ventilated, and anything but homes.

Above all, the cabins are crowded. We have come to associate crowding with homes in cities almost exclusively. This is primarily because we have so little accurate knowledge of country life. Here in Dougherty County one may find families of eight and ten occupying one or two rooms, and for every ten rooms of house accommodation for the Negroes there are twenty-five persons. The worst tenement abominations of New York do not have above twenty-two persons for every ten rooms.

6. Home of the slave owner and his family.

Of course, one small, close room in a city, without a yard, is in many respects worse than the larger single country room. In other respects it is better; it has glass windows, a decent chimney, and a trustworthy floor. The single great advantage of the Negro peasant is that he may spend most of his life outside his hovel, in the open fields.

There are four chief causes of these wretched homes: First, long custom born of slavery has assigned such homes to Negroes; white laborers would be offered better accommodations, and might, for that and similar reasons, give better work. Secondly, the Negroes, used to such accommodations, do not as a rule demand better; they do not know what better houses mean. Thirdly, the landlords as a class have not yet come to realize that it is a good business investment to raise the standard of living among labor by slow and judicious methods; that a Negro laborer who demands three rooms and fifty cents a day would give more efficient work and leave a larger profit than a discouraged toiler herding his family in one room and working for thirty cents. Lastly, among such conditions of life there are few incentives to make the laborer become a better farmer. If he is ambitious, he moves to town or tries other labor; as a tenant-farmer his outlook is almost hopeless, and following it as a makeshift, he takes the house that is given him without protest.

In such homes, then, these Negro peasants live. The families are both small and large; there are many single tenants,—widows and bachelors, and remnants of broken groups. The system of labor and the size of the houses both tend to the breaking up of family groups: the grown children go away as contract hands or migrate to town, the sister goes into service; and so one finds many families with hosts of babies, and many newly married couples, but comparatively few families with half-grown and grown sons and daughters. The average size of Negro families has undoubtedly decreased since the war, primarily from economic stress. In Russia over a third of the bridegrooms and over half the brides are under twenty; the same was true of the ante-bellum Negroes. To-day, however, very few of the boys and less than a fifth of the Negro girls under twenty are married. The young men marry between the ages of twenty-five and thirty-five; the young women between twenty and thirty. Such postponement is due to the difficulty of earning sufficient to rear and support a family; and it undoubtedly leads, in the country districts, to sexual immorality. The form of this immorality, however, is very seldom that of prostitution, and less frequently that of illegitimacy than one would imagine. Rather, it takes the form of separation and desertion after a family group has been formed. The number of separated persons is thirty-five to the thousand,—a very large number. It would of course be unfair to compare this number with divorce statistics, for many of these separated women are in reality widowed,

were the truth known, and in other cases the separation is not permanent. Nevertheless, here lies the seat of greatest moral danger. There is
little or no prostitution among these Negroes, and over three-fourths of
the families, as found by house-to-house investigation, deserve to be
classed as decent people with considerable regard for female chastity.
To be sure, the ideas of the mass would not suit New England, and
there are many loose habits and notions. Yet the rate of illegitimacy is
undoubtedly lower than in Austria or Italy, and the women as a class
are modest. The plague-spot in sexual relations is easy marriage and
easy separation. This is no sudden development, nor the fruit of Emancipation. It is the plain heritage from slavery. In those days Sam, with
his master's consent, "took up" with Mary. No ceremony was necessary,
and in the busy life of the great plantations of the Black Belt it was
usually dispensed with. If now the master needed Sam's work in another
plantation or in another part of the same plantation, or if he took a
notion to sell the slave, Sam's married life with Mary was usually un-
ceremoniously broken, and then it was clearly to the master's interest
to have both of them take new mates. This widespread custom of two
centuries has not been eradicated in thirty years. To-day Sam's grandson
"takes up" with a woman without license or ceremony; they live together decently and honestly, and are, to all intents and purposes, man
and wife.[7] Sometimes these unions are never broken until death; but
in too many cases family quarrels, a roving spirit, a rival suitor, or
perhaps more frequently the hopeless battle to support a family, lead
to separation, and a broken household is the result. The Negro church
has done much to stop this practice, and now most marriage ceremonies are performed by the pastors. Nevertheless, the evil is still deep
seated, and only a general raising of the standard of living will finally
cure it.

Looking now at the county black population as a whole, it is fair to
characterize it as poor and ignorant. Perhaps ten per cent compose the
well-to-do and the best of the laborers, while at least nine per cent are
thoroughly lewd and vicious. The rest, over eighty per cent, are poor
and ignorant, fairly honest and well meaning, plodding, and to a degree
shiftless, with some but not great sexual looseness. Such class lines are
by no means fixed; they vary, one might almost say, with the price of
cotton. The degree of ignorance cannot easily be expressed. We may
say, for instance, that nearly two-thirds of them cannot read or write.
This but partially expresses the fact. They are ignorant of the world
about them, of modern economic organization, of the function of government, of individual worth and possibilities,—of nearly all those
things which slavery in self-defence had to keep them from learning.

7. This arrangement was sometimes called a common-law marriage.

Much that the white boy imbibes from his earliest social atmosphere forms the puzzling problems of the black boy's mature years. America is not another word for Opportunity to *all* her sons.

It is easy for us to lose ourselves in details in endeavoring to grasp and comprehend the real condition of a mass of human beings. We often forget that each unit in the mass is a throbbing human soul. Ignorant it may be, and poverty stricken, black and curious in limb and ways and thought; and yet it loves and hates, it toils and tires, it laughs and weeps its bitter tears, and looks in vague and awful longing at the grim horizon of its life,—all this, even as you and I. These black thousands are not in reality lazy; they are improvident and careless; they insist on breaking the monotony of toil with a glimpse at the great town-world on Saturday; they have their loafers and their rascals; but the great mass of them work continuously and faithfully for a return, and under circumstances that would call forth equal voluntary effort from few if any other modern laboring class. Over eighty-eight per cent of them—men, women, and children—are farmers. Indeed, this is almost the only industry. Most of the children get their schooling after the "crops are laid by," and very few there are that stay in school after the spring work has begun. Child-labor is to be found here in some of its worst phases, as fostering ignorance and stunting physical development. With the grown men of the county there is little variety in work: thirteen hundred are farmers, and two hundred are laborers, teamsters, etc., including twenty-four artisans, ten merchants, twenty-one preachers, and four teachers. This narrowness of life reaches its maximum among the women: thirteen hundred and fifty of these are farm laborers, one hundred are servants and washerwomen, leaving sixty-five housewives, eight teachers, and six seamstresses.

Among this people there is no leisure class. We often forget that in the United States over half the youth and adults are not in the world earning incomes, but are making homes, learning of the world, or resting after the heat of the strife. But here ninety-six per cent are toiling; no one with leisure to turn the bare and cheerless cabin into a home, no old folks to sit beside the fire and hand down traditions of the past; little of careless happy childhood and dreaming youth. The dull monotony of daily toil is broken only by the gayety of the thoughtless and the Saturday trip to town. The toil, like all farm toil, is monotonous, and here there are little machinery and few tools to relieve its burdensome drudgery. But with all this, it is work in the pure open air, and this is something in a day when fresh air is scarce.

The land on the whole is still fertile, despite long abuse. For nine or ten months in succession the crops will come if asked: garden vegetables in April, grain in May, melons in June and July, hay in August, sweet potatoes in September, and cotton from then to Christmas. And yet on two-thirds of the land there is but one crop, and that leaves the toilers in debt. Why is this?

Away down the Baysan road, where the broad flat fields are flanked by great oak forests, is a plantation; many thousands of acres it used to run, here and there, and beyond the great wood. Thirteen hundred human beings here obeyed the call of one,—were his in body, and largely in soul. One of them lives there yet,—a short, stocky man, his dull-brown face seamed and drawn, and his tightly curled hair gray-white. The crops? Just tolerable, he said; just tolerable. Getting on? No—he wasn't getting on at all. Smith of Albany "furnishes" him, and his rent is eight hundred pounds of cotton. Can't make anything at that. Why didn't he buy land? *Humph!* Takes money to buy land. And he turns away. Free! The most piteous thing amid all the black ruin of war-time, amid the broken fortunes of the masters, the blighted hopes of mothers and maidens, and the fall of an empire,—the most piteous thing amid all this was the black freedman who threw down his hoe because the world called him free. What did such a mockery of freedom mean? Not a cent of money, not an inch of land, not a mouthful of victuals,—not even ownership of the rags on his back. Free! On Saturday, once or twice a month, the old master, before the war, used to dole out bacon and meal to his Negroes. And after the first flush of freedom wore off, and his true helplessness dawned on the freedman, he came back and picked up his hoe, and old master still doled out his bacon and meal. The legal form of service was theoretically far different; in practice, task-work or "cropping" was substituted for daily toil in gangs; and the slave gradually became a metayer,[8] or tenant on shares, in name, but a laborer with indeterminate wages in fact.

Still the price of cotton fell, and gradually the landlords deserted their plantations, and the reign of the merchant began. The merchant of the Black Belt is a curious institution,—part banker, part landlord, part contractor, and part despot. His store, which used most frequently to stand at the cross-roads and become the centre of a weekly village, has now moved to town; and thither the Negro tenant follows him. The merchant keeps everything,—clothes and shoes, coffee and sugar, pork and meal, canned and dried goods, wagons and ploughs, seed and fertilizer,—and what he has not in stock he can give you an order for at the store across the way. Here, then, comes the tenant, Sam Scott, after he has contracted with some absent landlord's agent for hiring forty acres of land; he fingers his hat nervously until the merchant finishes his morning chat with Colonel Sanders, and calls out, "Well, Sam, what do you want?" Sam wants him to "furnish" him,—*i. e.*, to advance him food and clothing for the year, and perhaps seed and tools,

---

8. Another word for sharecropper.

until his crop is raised and sold. If Sam seems a favorable subject, he and the merchant go to a lawyer, and Sam executes a chattel mortgage on his mule and wagon in return for seed and a week's rations. As soon as the green cotton-leaves appear above the ground, another mortgage is given on the "crop." Every Saturday, or at longer intervals, Sam calls upon the merchant for his "rations"; a family of five usually gets about thirty pounds of fat side-pork and a couple of bushels of corn-meal a month. Besides this, clothing and shoes must be furnished; if Sam or his family is sick, there are orders on the druggist and doctor; if the mule wants shoeing, an order on the blacksmith, etc. If Sam is a hard worker and crops promise well, he is often encouraged to buy more,— sugar, extra clothes, perhaps a buggy. But he is seldom encouraged to save. When cotton rose to ten cents last fall, the shrewd merchants of Dougherty County sold a thousand buggies in one season, mostly to black men.

The security offered for such transactions—a crop and chattel mortgage—may at first seem slight. And, indeed, the merchants tell many a true tale of shiftlessness and cheating; of cotton picked at night, mules disappearing, and tenants absconding. But on the whole the merchant of the Black Belt is the most prosperous man in the section. So skilfully and so closely has he drawn the bonds of the law about the tenant, that the black man has often simply to choose between pau- perism and crime; he "waives" all homestead exemptions in his con- tract; he cannot touch his own mortgaged crop, which the laws put almost in the full control of the land-owner and of the merchant. When the crop is growing the merchant watches it like a hawk; as soon as it is ready for market he takes possession of it, sells it, pays the land-owner his rent, subtracts his bill for supplies, and if, as sometimes happens, there is anything left, he hands it over to the black serf for his Christmas celebration.

The direct result of this system is an all-cotton scheme of agriculture and the continued bankruptcy of the tenant. The currency of the Black Belt is cotton. It is a crop always salable for ready money, not usually subject to great yearly fluctuations in price, and one which the Negroes know how to raise. The landlord therefore demands his rent in cotton, and the merchant will accept mortgages on no other crop. There is no use asking the black tenant, then, to diversify his crops,—he cannot under this system. Moreover, the system is bound to bankrupt the ten- ant. I remember once meeting a little one-mule wagon on the River road. A young black fellow sat in it driving listlessly, his elbows on his knees. His dark-faced wife sat beside him, stolid, silent.

"Hello!" cried my driver,—he has a most impudent way of addressing these people, though they seem used to it,—"what have you got there?"

"Meat and meal," answered the man, stopping. The meat lay uncovered in the bottom of the wagon,—a great thin side of fat pork covered with salt; the meal was in a white bushel bag.

"What did you pay for that meat?"

"Ten cents a pound." It could have been bought for six or seven cents cash.

"And the meal?"

"Two dollars." One dollar and ten cents is the cash price in town. Here was a man paying five dollars for goods which he could have bought for three dollars cash, and raised for one dollar or one dollar and a half.

Yet it is not wholly his fault. The Negro farmer started behind,—started in debt. This was not his choosing, but the crime of this happy-go-lucky nation which goes blundering along with its Reconstruction tragedies, its Spanish war interludes and Philippine matinees, just as though God really were dead. Once in debt, it is no easy matter for a whole race to emerge.

In the year of low-priced cotton, 1898, out of three hundred tenant families one hundred and seventy-five ended their year's work in debt to the extent of fourteen thousand dollars; fifty cleared nothing, and the remaining seventy-five made a total profit of sixteen hundred dollars. The net indebtedness of the black tenant families of the whole county must have been at least sixty thousand dollars. In a more prosperous year the situation is far better; but on the average the majority of tenants end the year even, or in debt, which means that they work for board and clothes. Such an economic organization is radically wrong. Whose is the blame?

The underlying causes of this situation are complicated but discernible. And one of the chief, outside the carelessness of the nation in letting the slave start with nothing, is the widespread opinion among the merchants and employers of the Black Belt that only by the slavery of debt can the Negro be kept at work. Without doubt, some pressure was necessary at the beginning of the free-labor system to keep the listless and lazy at work; and even to-day the mass of the Negro laborers need stricter guardianship than most Northern laborers. Behind this honest and widespread opinion dishonesty and cheating of the ignorant laborers have a good chance to take refuge. And to all this must be added the obvious fact that a slave ancestry and a system of unrequited toil has not improved the efficiency or temper of the mass of black laborers. Nor is this peculiar to Sambo;[9] it has in history been just as true of John and Hans, of Jacques and Pat, of all ground-down peasantries. Such is the situation of the mass of the Negroes in the Black Belt to-day; and they are thinking about it. Crime, and a cheap and

---

9. Derogatory name for African Americans, particularly men.

dangerous socialism, are the inevitable results of this pondering. I see now that ragged black man sitting on a log, aimlessly whittling a stick. He muttered to me with the murmur of many ages, when he said: "White man sit down whole year; Nigger work day and night and make crop; Nigger hardly gits bread and meat; white man sittin' down gits all. *It's wrong.*" And what do the better classes of Negroes do to improve their situation? One of two things: if any way possible, they buy land; if not, they migrate to town. Just as centuries ago it was no easy thing for the serf to escape into the freedom of town-life, even so to-day there are hindrances laid in the way of county laborers. In considerable parts of all the Gulf States, and especially in Mississippi, Louisiana, and Arkansas, the Negroes on the plantations in the back-country districts are still held at forced labor practically without wages. Especially is this true in districts where the farmers are composed of the more ignorant class of poor whites, and the Negroes are beyond the reach of schools and intercourse with their advancing fellows. If such a peon should run away, the sheriff, elected by white suffrage, can usually be depended on to catch the fugitive, return him, and ask no questions. If he escape to another county, a charge of petty thieving, easily true, can be depended upon to secure his return. Even if some unduly officious person insist upon a trial, neighborly comity[1] will probably make his conviction sure, and then the labor due the county can easily be bought by the master. Such a system is impossible in the more civilized parts of the South, or near the large towns and cities; but in those vast stretches of land beyond the telegraph and the newspaper the spirit of the Thirteenth Amendment[2] is sadly broken. This represents the lowest economic depths of the black American peasant; and in a study of the rise and condition of the Negro freeholder we must trace his economic progress from this modern serfdom.

Even in the better-ordered country districts of the South the free movement of agricultural laborers is hindered by the migration-agent laws.[3] The "Associated Press" recently informed the world of the arrest of a young white man in Southern Georgia who represented the "Atlantic Naval Supplies Company," and who "was caught in the act of enticing hands from the turpentine farm of Mr. John Greer." The crime for which this young man was arrested is taxed five hundred dollars for each county in which the employment agent proposes to gather laborers for work outside the State. Thus the Negroes' ignorance of the labor-market outside his own vicinity is increased rather than diminished by the laws of nearly every Southern State.

Similar to such measures is the unwritten law of the back districts

1. Civility.
2. Amendment to the U.S. Constitution that abolished slavery.
3. State law restricting labor agents from encouraging black laborers to move to another state. The laws were intended to keep agricultural laborers in the same locale without other employment options.

and small towns of the South, that the character of all Negroes un-known to the mass of the community must be vouched for by some white man. This is really a revival of the old Roman idea of the patron under whose protection the new-made freedman was put. In many in-stances this system has been of great good to the Negro, and very often under the protection and guidance of the former master's family, or other white friends, the freedman progressed in wealth and morality. But the same system has in other cases resulted in the refusal of whole communities to recognize the right of a Negro to change his habitation and to be master of his own fortunes. A black stranger in Baker County, Georgia, for instance, is liable to be stopped anywhere on the public highway and made to state his business to the satisfaction of any white interrogator. If he fails to give a suitable answer, or seems too inde-pendent or "sassy," he may be arrested or summarily driven away.

Thus it is that in the country districts of the South, by written or unwritten law, peonage,[4] hindrances to the migration of labor, and a system of white patronage exists over large areas. Besides this, the chance for lawless oppression and illegal exactions is vastly greater in the country than in the city, and nearly all the more serious race dis-turbances of the last decade have arisen from disputes in the county between master and man,—as, for instance, the Sam Hose affair.[5] As a result of such a situation, there arose, first, the Black Belt; and, second, the Migration to Town. The Black Belt was not, as many assumed, a movement toward fields of labor under more genial climatic conditions; it was primarily a huddling for self-protection,—a massing of the black population for mutual defence in order to secure the peace and tran-quillity necessary to economic advance. This movement took place between Emancipation and 1880, and only partially accomplished the desired results. The rush to town since 1880 is the counter-movement of men disappointed in the economic opportunities of the Black Belt.

In Dougherty County, Georgia, one can see easily the results of this experiment in huddling for protection. Only ten per cent of the adult population was born in the county, and yet the blacks outnumber the whites four or five to one. There is undoubtedly a security to the blacks in their very numbers,—a personal freedom from arbitrary treatment, which makes hundreds of laborers cling to Dougherty in spite of low wages and economic distress. But a change is coming, and slowly but surely even here the agricultural laborers are drifting to town and leav-ing the broad acres behind. Why is this? Why do not the Negroes become land-owners, and build up the black landed peasantry, which

4. Holding a person to labor until a debt was paid. Attempts to leave without paying the debt could result in forced labor and various forms of imprisonment. This practice, along with the abuses of the sharecropping system, created a modified form of slavery.
5. See n. 4, p. 75.

has for a generation and more been the dream of philanthropist and statesman?

To the car-window sociologist, to the man who seeks to understand and know the South by devoting the few leisure hours of a holiday trip to unravelling the snarl of centuries,—to such men very often the whole trouble with the black field-hand may be summed up by Aunt Ophelia's[6] word, "Shiftless!" They have noted repeatedly scenes like one I saw last summer. We were riding along the highroad to town at the close of a long hot day. A couple of young black fellows passed us in a mule-team, with several bushels of loose corn in the ear. One was driving, listlessly bent forward, his elbows on his knees,—a happy-go-lucky, careless picture of irresponsibility. The other was fast asleep in the bottom of the wagon. As we passed we noticed an ear of corn fall from the wagon. They never saw it,—not they. A rod farther on we noted another ear on the ground; and between that creeping mule and town we counted twenty-six ears of corn. Shiftless? Yes, the personification of shiftlessness. And yet follow those boys: they are not lazy; to-morrow morning they'll be up with the sun; they work hard when they do work, and they work willingly. They have no sordid, selfish, money-getting ways, but rather a fine disdain for mere cash. They'll loaf before your face and work behind your back with good-natured honesty. They'll steal a watermelon, and hand you back your lost purse intact. Their great defect as laborers lies in their lack of incentive to work beyond the mere pleasure of physical exertion. They are careless because they have not found that it pays to be careful; they are improvident because the improvident ones of their acquaintance get on about as well as the provident. Above all, they cannot see why they should take unusual pains to make the white man's land better, or to fatten his mule, or save his corn. On the other hand, the white land-owner argues that any attempt to improve these laborers by increased responsibility, or higher wages, or better homes, or land of their own, would be sure to result in failure. He shows his Northern visitor the scarred and wretched land; the ruined mansions, the worn-out soil and mortgaged acres, and says, This is Negro freedom!

Now it happens that both master and man have just enough argument on their respective sides to make it difficult for them to understand each other. The Negro dimly personifies in the white man all his ills and misfortunes; if he is poor, it is because the white man seizes the fruit of his toil; if he is ignorant, it is because the white man gives him neither time nor facilities to learn; and, indeed, if any misfortune happens to him, it is because of some hidden machinations of "white folks." On the other hand, the masters and the masters' sons have never been able to see why the Negro, instead of settling down to be day-

6. Ophelia St. Clare is a character in Harriet Beecher Stowe's novel *Uncle Tom's Cabin* (1852).

laborers for bread and clothes, are infected with a silly desire to rise in the world, and why they are sulky, dissatisfied, and careless, where their fathers were happy and dumb and faithful. "Why, you niggers have an easier time than I do," said a puzzled Albany merchant to his black customer. "Yes," he replied, "and so does yo' hogs."

Taking, then, the dissatisfied and shiftless field-hand as a starting-point, let us inquire how the black thousands of Dougherty have struggled from him up toward their ideal, and what that ideal is. All social struggle is evidenced by the rise, first of economic, then of social classes, among a homogeneous population. To-day the following economic classes are plainly differentiated among these Negroes.

A "submerged tenth" of croppers, with a few paupers; forty per cent who are metayers and thirty-nine per cent of semi-metayers and wage-laborers. There are left five per cent of money-renters and six per cent of freeholders,—the "Upper Ten" of the land. The croppers are entirely without capital, even in the limited sense of food or money to keep them from seed-time to harvest. All they furnish is their labor; the land-owner furnishes land, stock, tools, seed, and house; and at the end of the year the laborer gets from a third to a half of the crop. Out of his share, however, comes pay and interest for food and clothing advanced him during the year. Thus we have a laborer without capital and without wages, and an employer whose capital is largely his employees' wages. It is an unsatisfactory arrangement, both for hirer and hired, and is usually in vogue on poor land with hard-pressed owners.

Above the croppers come the great mass of the black population who work the land on their own responsibility, paying rent in cotton and supported by the crop-mortgage system. After the war this system was attractive to the freedmen on account of its larger freedom and its possibilities for making a surplus. But with the carrying out of the crop-lien system, the deterioration of the land, and the slavery of debt, the position of the metayers has sunk to a dead level of practically unrewarded toil. Formerly all tenants had some capital, and often considerable; but absentee landlordism, rising rack-rent,[7] and falling cotton have stripped them well-nigh of all, and probably not over half of them to-day own their mules. The change from cropper to tenant was accomplished by fixing the rent. If, now, the rent fixed was reasonable, this was an incentive to the tenant to strive. On the other hand, if the rent was too high, or if the land deteriorated, the result was to discourage and check the efforts of the black peasantry. There is no doubt that the latter case is true; that in Dougherty County every economic advantage of the price of cotton in market and of the strivings of the tenant has been taken advantage of by the landlords and merchants, and swallowed up in rent and interest. If cotton rose in price, the rent

7. Excessively or unreasonably high rent.

rose even higher; if cotton fell, the rent remained or followed reluctantly. If a tenant worked hard and raised a large crop, his rent was raised the next year; if that year the crop failed, his corn was confiscated and his mule sold for debt. There were, of course, exceptions to this, —cases of personal kindness and forbearance; but in the vast majority of cases the rule was to extract the uttermost farthing from the mass of the black farm laborers.

The average metayer pays from twenty to thirty per cent of his crop in rent. The result of such rack-rent can only be evil,—abuse and neglect of the soil, deterioration in the character of the laborers, and a widespread sense of injustice. "Wherever the country is poor," cried Arthur Young,[8] "it is in the hands of metayers," and "their condition is more wretched than that of day-laborers." He was talking of Italy a century ago; but he might have been talking of Dougherty County to-day. And especially is that true to-day which he declares was true in France before the Revolution: "The metayers are considered as little better than menial servants, removable at pleasure, and obliged to conform in all things to the will of the landlords." On this low plane half the black population of Dougherty County—perhaps more than half the black millions of this land—are to-day struggling.

A degree above these we may place those laborers who receive money wages for their work. Some receive a house with perhaps a garden-spot; then supplies of food and clothing are advanced, and certain fixed wages are given at the end of the year, varying from thirty to sixty dollars, out of which the supplies must be paid for, with interest. About eighteen per cent of the population belong to this class of semi-metayers, while twenty-two per cent are laborers paid by the month or year, and are either "furnished" by their own savings or perhaps more usually by some merchant who takes his chances of payment. Such laborers receive from thirty-five to fifty cents a day during the working season. They are usually young unmarried persons, some being women; and when they marry they sink to the class of metayers, or, more seldom, become renters.

The renters for fixed money rentals are the first of the emerging classes, and form five per cent of the families. The sole advantage of this small class is their freedom to choose their crops, and the increased responsibility which comes through having money transactions. While some of the renters differ little in condition from the metayers, yet on the whole they are more intelligent and responsible persons, and are the ones who eventually become land-owners. Their better character and greater shrewdness enable them to gain, perhaps to demand, better terms in rents; rented farms, varying from forty to a hundred acres, bear

8. English writer (1741–1820). His *Travels in France during the Years 1787, 1788, and 1789* (1792) examines social conditions in France before the Revolution.

an average rental of about fifty-four dollars a year. The men who conduct such farms do not long remain renters; either they sink to metayers, or with a successful series of harvests rise to be land-owners.

In 1870 the tax-books of Dougherty report no Negroes as landholders. If there were any such at that time,—and there may have been a few, —their land was probably held in the name of some white patron,—a method not uncommon during slavery. In 1875 ownership of land had begun with seven hundred and fifty acres; ten years later this had increased to over sixty-five hundred acres, to nine thousand acres in 1890 and ten thousand in 1900. The total assessed property has in this same period risen from eighty thousand dollars in 1875 to two hundred and forty thousand dollars in 1900.

Two circumstances complicate this development and make it in some respects difficult to be sure of the real tendencies; they are the panic of 1893,[9] and the low price of cotton in 1898. Besides this, the system of assessing property in the country districts of Georgia is somewhat antiquated and of uncertain statistical value; there are no assessors, and each man makes a sworn return to a tax-receiver. Thus public opinion plays a large part, and the returns vary strangely from year to year. Certainly these figures show the small amount of accumulated capital among the Negroes, and the consequent large dependence of their property on temporary prosperity. They have little to tide over a few years of economic depression, and are at the mercy of the cotton-market far more than the whites. And thus the land-owners, despite their marvellous efforts, are really a transient class, continually being depleted by those who fall back into the class of renters or metayers, and augmented by newcomers from the masses. Of the one hundred land-owners in 1898, half had bought their land since 1893, a fourth between 1890 and 1893, a fifth between 1884 and 1890, and the rest between 1870 and 1884. In all, one hundred and eighty-five Negroes have owned land in this county since 1875.

If all the black land-owners who had ever held land here had kept it or left it in the hands of black men, the Negroes would have owned nearer thirty thousand acres than the fifteen thousand they now hold. And yet these fifteen thousand acres are a creditable showing,—a proof of no little weight of the worth and ability of the Negro people. If they had been given an economic start at Emancipation, if they had been in an enlightened and rich community which really desired their best good, then we might perhaps call such a result small or even insignificant. But for a few thousand poor ignorant field-hands, in the face of poverty, a falling market, and social stress, to save and capitalize two hundred thousand dollars in a generation has meant a tremendous

9. Serious economic depression following the collapse of the New York Stock Exchange. The depression negatively affected agricultural prices through most of the 1890s.

effort. The rise of a nation, the pressing forward of a social class, means a bitter struggle, a hard and soul-sickening battle with the world such as few of the more favored classes know or appreciate.

Out of the hard economic conditions of this portion of the Black Belt, only six per cent of the population have succeeded in emerging into peasant proprietorship; and these are not all firmly fixed, but grow and shrink in number with the wavering of the cotton-market. Fully ninety-four per cent have struggled for land and failed, and half of them sit in hopeless serfdom. For these there is one other avenue of escape toward which they have turned in increasing numbers, namely, migration to town. A glance at the distribution of land among the black owners curiously reveals this fact. In 1898 the holdings were as follows: Under forty acres, forty-nine families; forty to two hundred and fifty acres, seventeen families; two hundred and fifty to one thousand acres, thirteen families; one thousand or more acres, two families. Now in 1890 there were forty-four holdings, but only nine of these were under forty acres. The great increase of holdings, then, has come in the buying of small homesteads near town, where their owners really share in the town life; this is a part of the rush to town. And for every land-owner who has thus hurried away from the narrow and hard conditions of country life, how many field-hands, how many tenants, how many ruined renters, have joined that long procession? Is it not strange compensation? The sin of the country districts is visited on the town, and the social sores of city life to-day may, here in Dougherty County, and perhaps in many places near and far, look for their final healing without the city walls.

IX

Of the Sons of Master and Man[1]

Life treads on life, and heart on heart;
We press too close in church and mart
To keep a dream or grave apart.
MRS. BROWNING.

The world-old phenomenon of the contact of diverse races of men
is to have new exemplification during the new century. Indeed, the
characteristic of our age is the contact of European civilization with
the world's undeveloped peoples. Whatever we may say of the results
of such contact in the past, it certainly forms a chapter in human action
not pleasant to look back upon. War, murder, slavery, extermination,
and debauchery,—this has again and again been the result of carrying
civilization and the blessed gospel to the isles of the sea and the heathen
without the law. Nor does it altogether satisfy the conscience of the
modern world to be told complacently that all this has been right and
proper, the fated triumph of strength over weakness, of righteousness
over evil, of superiors over inferiors. It would certainly be soothing if
one could readily believe all this; and yet there are too many ugly facts
for everything to be thus easily explained away. We feel and know that
there are many delicate differences in race psychology, numberless
changes that our crude social measurements are not yet able to follow
minutely, which explain much of history and social development. At
the same time, too, we know that these considerations have never adequately explained or excused the triumph of brute force and cunning
over weakness and innocence.

It is, then, the strife of all honorable men of the twentieth century

1. Revised from "The Relation of the Negroes to the Whites in the South," an article in the
Annals of the American Academy of Political and Social Science (July–December 1901): 121–
40. The verse is from Elizabeth Barrett Browning's *A Vision of Poets* (1844). The music
quotation is from the Negro spiritual "I'm A Rolling."

to see that in the future competition of races the survival of the fittest[2] shall mean the triumph of the good, the beautiful, and the true; that we may be able to preserve for future civilization all that is really fine and noble and strong, and not continue to put a premium on greed and impudence and cruelty. To bring this hope to fruition, we are compelled daily to turn more and more to a conscientious study of the phenomena of race-contact,—to a study frank and fair, and not falsified and colored by our wishes or our fears. And we have in the South as fine a field for such a study as the world affords,—a field, to be sure, which the average American scientist deems somewhat beneath his dignity, and which the average man who is not a scientist knows all about, but nevertheless a line of study which by reason of the enormous race complications with which God seems about to punish this nation must increasingly claim our sober attention, study, and thought, we must ask, what are the actual relations of whites and blacks in the South? and we must be answered, not by apology or fault-finding, but by a plain, unvarnished tale.

In the civilized life of to-day the contact of men and their relations to each other fall in a few main lines of action and communication: there is, first, the physical proximity of homes and dwelling-places, the way in which neighborhoods group themselves, and the contiguity of neighborhoods. Secondly, and in our age chiefest, there are the economic relations,—the methods by which individuals coöperate for earning a living, for the mutual satisfaction of wants, for the production of wealth. Next, there are the political relations, the coöperation in social control, in group government, in laying and paying the burden of taxation. In the fourth place there are the less tangible but highly important forms of intellectual contact and commerce, the interchange of ideas through conversation and conference, through periodicals and libraries; and, above all, the gradual formation for each community of that curious *tertium quid*[3] which we call public opinion. Closely allied with this come the various forms of social contact in everyday life, in travel, in theatres, in house gatherings, in marrying and giving in marriage. Finally, there are the varying forms of religious enterprise, of moral teaching and benevolent endeavor. These are the principal ways in which men living in the same communities are brought into contact with each other. It is my present task, therefore, to indicate, from my point of view, how the black race in the South meet and mingle with the whites in these matters of everyday life.

First, as to physical dwelling. It is usually possible to draw in nearly every Southern community a physical color-line on the map, on the

2. Phrase used by Charles Darwin (1809–1882) to describe biological evolution. The phrase entered nineteenth-century sociological discourse to explain the disparity in social and material success among humans as a matter of the individual's innate "fitness" to compete.
3. Literally, a third something (Latin); an ambiguous state.

one side of which whites dwell and on the other Negroes. The winding and intricacy of the geographical color line varies, of course, in different communities. I know some towns where a straight line drawn through the middle of the main street separates nine-tenths of the whites from nine-tenths of the blacks. In other towns the older settlement of whites has been encircled by a broad band of blacks; in still other cases little settlements or nuclei of blacks have sprung up amid surrounding whites. Usually in cities each street has its distinctive color, and only now and then do the colors meet in close proximity. Even in the country something of this segregation is manifest in the smaller areas, and of course in the larger phenomena of the Black Belt.

All this segregation by color is largely independent of that natural clustering by social grades common to all communities. A Negro slum may be in dangerous proximity to a white residence quarter, while it is quite common to find a white slum planted in the heart of a respectable Negro district. One thing, however, seldom occurs: the best of the whites and the best of the Negroes almost never live in anything like close proximity. It thus happens that in nearly every Southern town and city, both whites and blacks see commonly the worst of each other. This is a vast change from the situation in the past, when, through the close contact of master and house-servant in the patriarchal big house, one found the best of both races in close contact and sympathy, while at the same time the squalor and dull round of toil among the field-hands was removed from the sight and hearing of the family. One can easily see how a person who saw slavery thus from his father's parlors, and sees freedom on the streets of a great city, fails to grasp or comprehend the whole of the new picture. On the other hand, the settled belief of the mass of the Negroes that the Southern white people do not have the black man's best interests at heart has been intensified in later years by this continual daily contact of the better class of blacks with the worst representatives of the white race.

Coming now to the economic relations of the races, we are on ground made familiar by study, much discussion, and no little philanthropic effort. And yet with all this there are many essential elements in the coöperation of Negroes and whites for work and wealth that are too readily overlooked or not thoroughly understood. The average American can easily conceive of a rich land awaiting development and filled with black laborers. To him the Southern problem is simply that of making efficient workingmen out of this material, by giving them the requisite technical skill and the help of invested capital. The problem, however, is by no means as simple as this, from the obvious fact that these workingmen have been trained for centuries as slaves. They exhibit, therefore, all the advantages and defects of such training; they are willing and good-natured, but not self-reliant, provident, or careful. If now the economic development of the South is to be pushed to the

verge of exploitation, as seems probable, then we have a mass of workingmen thrown into relentless competition with the workingmen of the
world, but handicapped by a training the very opposite to that of the
modern self-reliant democratic laborer. What the black laborer needs
is careful personal guidance, group leadership of men with hearts in
their bosoms, to train them to foresight, carefulness, and honesty. Nor
does it require any fine-spun theories of racial differences to prove the
necessity of such group training after the brains of the race have been
knocked out by two hundred and fifty years of assiduous education in
submission, carelessness, and stealing. After Emancipation, it was the
plain duty of some one to assume this group leadership and training of
the Negro laborer. I will not stop here to inquire whose duty it was,—
whether that of the white ex-master who had profited by unpaid toil,
or the Northern philanthropist whose persistence brought on the crisis,
or the National Government whose edict freed the bondmen; I will not
stop to ask whose duty it was, but I insist it was the duty of some one
to see that these workingmen were not left alone and unguided, without capital, without land, without skill, without economic organization,
without even the bald protection of law, order, and decency,—left in a
great land, not to settle down to slow and careful internal development,
but destined to be thrown almost immediately into relentless and sharp
competition with the best of modern workingmen under an economic
system where every participant is fighting for himself, and too often
utterly regardless of the rights or welfare of his neighbor.

For we must never forget that the economic system of the South to-
day which has succeeded the old *régime*[4] is not the same system as that
of the old industrial North, of England, or of France, with their trades-
unions, their restrictive laws, their written and unwritten commercial
customs, and their long experience. It is, rather, a copy of that England
of the early nineteenth century, before the factory acts,—the England
that wrung pity from thinkers and fired the wrath of Carlyle.[5] The rod
of empire that passed from the hands of Southern gentlemen in 1865,
partly by force, partly by their own petulance, has never returned to
them. Rather it has passed to those men who have come to take charge
of the industrial exploitation of the New South,—the sons of poor
whites fired with a new thirst for wealth and power, thrifty and avari-
cious Yankees, shrewd and unscrupulous Jews.[6] Into the hands of these
men the Southern laborers, white and black, have fallen; and this to
their sorrow. For the laborers as such there is in these new captains of
industry neither love nor hate, neither sympathy nor romance; it is a
cold question of dollars and dividends. Under such a system all labor

4. A system of management, or a government in power.
5. Thomas Carlyle (1795–1881), Scottish historian and philosopher who believed that human
   progress was due to individual "heroes."
6. In 1953 edition, "shrewd and unscrupulous Jews" changed to "unscrupulous immigrants."

is bound to suffer. Even the white laborers are not yet intelligent, thrifty, and well trained enough to maintain themselves against the powerful inroads of organized capital. The results among them, even, are long hours of toil, low wages, child labor, and lack of protection against usury and cheating. But among the black laborers all this is aggravated, first, by a race prejudice which varies from a doubt and distrust among the best element of whites to a frenzied hatred among the worst; and, secondly, it is aggravated, as I have said before, by the wretched economic heritage of the freedmen from slavery. With this training it is difficult for the freedman to learn to grasp the opportunities already opened to him, and the new opportunities are seldom given him, but go by favor to the whites.

Left by the best elements of the South with little protection or oversight, he has been made in law and custom the victim of the worst and most unscrupulous men in each community. The crop-lien system which is depopulating the fields of the South is not simply the result of shiftlessness on the part of Negroes, but is also the result of cunningly devised laws as to mortgages, liens, and misdemeanors, which can be made by conscienceless men to entrap and snare the unwary until escape is impossible, further toil a farce, and protest a crime. I have seen, in the Black Belt of Georgia, an ignorant, honest Negro buy and pay for a farm in installments three separate times, and then in the face of law and decency the enterprising Russian Jew[7] who sold it to him pocketed money and deed and left the black man landless, to labor on his own land at thirty cents a day. I have seen a black farmer fall in debt to a white storekeeper, and that storekeeper go to his farm and strip it of every single marketable article,—mules, ploughs, stored crops, tools, furniture, bedding, clocks, looking-glass,—and all this without a warrant, without process of law, without a sheriff or officer, in the face of the law for homestead exemptions, and without rendering to a single responsible person any account or reckoning. And such proceedings can happen, and will happen, in any community where a class of ignorant toilers are placed by custom and race-prejudice beyond the pale of sympathy and race-brotherhood. So long as the best elements of a community do not feel in duty bound to protect and train and care for the weaker members of their group, they leave them to be preyed upon by these swindlers and rascals.

This unfortunate economic situation does not mean the hindrance of all advance in the black South, or the absence of a class of black landlords and mechanics who, in spite of disadvantages, are accumulating property and making good citizens. But it does mean that this class is not nearly so large as a fairer economic system might easily make it, that those who survive in the competition are handicapped so

7. "The enterprising Russian Jew" changed to "the enterprising American" in 1953 edition.

as to accomplish much less than they deserve to, and that, above all, the *personnel* of the successful class is left to chance and accident, and not to any intelligent culling or reasonable methods of selection. As a remedy for this, there is but one possible procedure. We must accept some of the race prejudice in the South as a fact,—deplorable in its intensity, unfortunate in results, and dangerous for the future, but nevertheless a hard fact which only time can efface. We cannot hope, then, in this generation, or for several generations, that the mass of the whites can be brought to assume that close sympathetic and self-sacrificing leadership of the blacks which their present situation so eloquently demands. Such leadership, such social teaching and example, must come from the blacks themselves. For some time men doubted as to whether the Negro could develop such leaders; but to-day no one seriously disputes the capability of individual Negroes to assimilate the culture and common sense of modern civilization, and to pass it on, to some extent at least, to their fellows. If this is true, then here is the path out of the economic situation, and here is the imperative demand for trained Negro leaders of character and intelligence,—men of skill, men of light and leading, college-bred men,[8] black captains of industry, and missionaries of culture; men who thoroughly comprehend and know modern civilization, and can take hold of Negro communities and raise and train them by force of precept and example, deep sympathy, and the inspiration of common blood and ideals. But if such men are to be effective they must have some power,—they must be backed by the best public opinion of these communities, and able to wield for their objects and aims such weapons as the experience of the world has taught are indispensable to human progress.

Of such weapons the greatest, perhaps, in the modern world is the power of the ballot; and this brings me to a consideration of the third form of contact between whites and blacks in the South,—political activity.

In the attitude of the American mind toward Negro suffrage can be traced with unusual accuracy the prevalent conceptions of government. In the fifties we were near enough the echoes of the French Revolution to believe pretty thoroughly in universal suffrage. We argued, as we thought then rather logically, that no social class was so good, so true, and so disinterested as to be trusted wholly with the political destiny of its neighbors; that in every state the best arbiters of their own welfare are the persons directly affected; consequently that it is only by arming every hand with a ballot,—with the right to have a voice in the policy of the state,—that the greatest good to the greatest number could be attained. To be sure, there were objections to these arguments, but we thought we had answered them tersely and convincingly; if some one

8. In 1898 Du Bois delivered the commencement speech, "Careers Open to College-Bred Negroes," at Fisk University.

complained of the ignorance of voters, we answered, "Educate them." If another complained of their venality, we replied, "Disfranchise them or put them in jail." And, finally, to the men who feared demagogues and the natural perversity of some human beings we insisted that time and bitter experience would teach the most hardheaded. It was at this time that the question of Negro suffrage in the South was raised. Here was a defenceless people suddenly made free. How were they to be protected from those who did not believe in their freedom and were determined to thwart it? Not by force, said the North; not by government guardianship, said the South; then by the ballot, the sole and legitimate defence of a free people, said the Common Sense of the Nation. No one thought, at the time, that the ex-slaves could use the ballot intelligently or very effectively; but they did think that the possession of so great power by a great class in the nation would compel their fellows to educate this class to its intelligent use.

Meantime, new thoughts came to the nation: the inevitable period of moral retrogression and political trickery that ever follows in the wake of war overtook us. So flagrant became the political scandals that reputable men began to leave politics alone, and politics consequently became disreputable. Men began to pride themselves on having nothing to do with their own government, and to agree tacitly with those who regarded public office as a private perquisite. In this state of mind it became easy to wink at the suppression of the Negro vote in the South, and to advise self-respecting Negroes to leave politics entirely alone. The decent and reputable citizens of the North who neglected their own civic duties grew hilarious over the exaggerated importance with which the Negro regarded the franchise. Thus it easily happened that more and more the better class of Negroes followed the advice from abroad and the pressure from home, and took no further interest in politics, leaving to the careless and the venal of their race the exercise of their rights as voters. The black vote that still remained was not trained and educated, but further debauched by open and unblushing bribery, or force and fraud; until the Negro voter was thoroughly inoculated with the idea that politics was a method of private gain by disreputable means.

And finally, now, to-day, when we are awakening to the fact that the perpetuity of republican institutions on this continent depends on the purification of the ballot, the civic training of voters, and the raising of voting to the plane of a solemn duty which a patriotic citizen neglects to his peril and to the peril of his children's children,—in this day, when we are striving for a renaissance of civic virtue, what are we going to say to the black voter of the South? Are we going to tell him still that politics is a disreputable and useless form of human activity? Are we going to induce the best class of Negroes to take less and less interest in government, and to give up their right to take such an interest, without a protest? I am not saying a word against all legitimate efforts to purge the ballot of ignorance, pauperism, and crime. But few have pretended that the present movement for disfranchisement in the South is for such a purpose; it has been plainly and frankly declared in nearly every case that the object of the disfranchising laws is the elimination of the black man from politics.

Now, is this a minor matter which has no influence on the main question of the industrial and intellectual development of the Negro? Can we establish a mass of black laborers and artisans and landholders in the South who, by law and public opinion, have absolutely no voice in shaping the laws under which they live and work? Can the modern organization of industry, assuming as it does free democratic government and the power and ability of the laboring classes to compel respect for their welfare,—can this system be carried out in the South when half its laboring force is voiceless in the public councils and powerless in its own defence? To-day the black man of the South has almost nothing to say as to how much he shall be taxed, or how those taxes shall be expended; as to who shall execute the laws, and how they shall do it; as to who shall make the laws, and how they shall be made. It is pitiable that frantic efforts must be made at critical times to get law-makers in some States even to listen to the respectful presentation of the black man's side of a current controversy. Daily the Negro is coming more and more to look upon law and justice, not as protecting safe-guards, but as sources of humiliation and oppression. The laws are made by men who have little interest in him; they are executed by men who have absolutely no motive for treating the black people with courtesy or consideration; and, finally, the accused law-breaker is tried, not by his peers, but too often by men who would rather punish ten innocent Negroes than let one guilty one escape.

I should be the last one to deny the patent weaknesses and shortcomings of the Negro people; I should be the last to withhold sympathy from the white South in its efforts to solve its intricate social problems. I freely acknowledge that it is possible, and sometimes best, that a partially undeveloped people should be ruled by the best of their stronger and better neighbors for their own good, until such time as they can start and fight the world's battles alone. I have already pointed out how sorely in need of such economic and spiritual guidance the emancipated Negro was, and I am quite willing to admit that if the representatives of the best white Southern public opinion were the ruling and guiding powers in the South to-day the conditions indicated would be fairly well fulfilled. But the point I have insisted upon, and now emphasize again, is that the best opinion of the South to-day is not the ruling opinion. That to leave the Negro helpless and without a ballot to-day is to leave him, not to the guidance of the best, but rather to the exploitation and debauchment of the worst; that this is no truer of the

South than of the North,—of the North than of Europe: in any land, in any country under modern free competition, to lay any class of weak and despised people, be they white, black, or blue, at the political mercy of their stronger, richer, and more resourceful fellows, is a temptation which human nature seldom has withstood and seldom will withstand.

Moreover, the political status of the Negro in the South is closely connected with the question of Negro crime. There can be no doubt that crime among Negroes has sensibly increased in the last thirty years, and that there has appeared in the slums of great cities a distinct criminal class among the blacks. In explaining this unfortunate development, we must note two things: (1) that the inevitable result of Emancipation was to increase crime and criminals, and (2) that the police system of the South was primarily designed to control slaves. As to the first point, we must not forget that under a strict slave system there can scarcely be such a thing as crime. But when these variously constituted human particles are suddenly thrown broadcast on the sea of life, some swim, some sink, and some hang suspended, to be forced up or down by the chance currents of a busy hurrying world. So great an economic and social revolution as swept the South in '63[9] meant a weeding out among the Negroes of the incompetents and vicious, the beginning of a differentiation of social grades. Now a rising group of people are not lifted bodily from the ground like an inert solid mass, but rather stretch upward like a living plant with its roots still clinging in the mould. The appearance, therefore, of the Negro criminal was a phenomenon to be awaited; and while it causes anxiety, it should not occasion surprise.

Here again the hope for the future depended peculiarly on careful and delicate dealing with these criminals. Their offences at first were those of laziness, carelessness, and impulse, rather than of malignity or ungoverned viciousness. Such misdemeanors needed discriminating treatment, firm but reformatory, with no hint of injustice, and full proof of guilt. For such dealing with criminals, white or black, the South had no machinery, no adequate jails or reformatories; its police system was arranged to deal with blacks alone, and tacitly assumed that every white man was *ipso facto*[1] a member of that police. Thus grew up a double system of justice, which erred on the white side by undue leniency and the practical immunity of red-handed criminals, and erred on the black side by undue severity, injustice, and lack of discrimination. For, as I have said, the police system of the South was originally designed to keep track of all Negroes, not simply of criminals; and when the Negroes were freed and the whole South was convinced of the impossibility of free Negro labor, the first and almost universal device was to use the courts as a means of reënslaving-the blacks. It was not then a

9. The social, political, and economic upheaval that resulted from the Emancipation Proclamation, which went into effect January 1, 1863.
1. Literally, by the fact itself (Latin); by the very nature of the case.

question of crime, but rather one of color, that settled a man's conviction on almost any charge. Thus Negroes came to look upon courts as instruments of injustice and oppression, and upon those convicted in them as martyrs and victims.

When, now, the real Negro criminal appeared, and instead of petty stealing and vagrancy we began to have highway robbery, burglary, murder, and rape, there was a curious effect on both sides the color-line: the Negroes refused to believe the evidence of white witnesses or the fairness of white juries, so that the greatest deterrent to crime, the public opinion of one's own social caste, was lost, and the criminal was looked upon as crucified rather than hanged. On the other hand, the whites, used to being careless as to the guilt or innocence of accused Negroes, were swept in moments of passion beyond law, reason, and decency. Such a situation is bound to increase crime, and has increased it. To natural viciousness and vagrancy are being daily added motives of revolt and revenge which stir up all the latent savagery of both races and make peaceful attention to economic development often impossible.

But the chief problem in any community cursed with crime is not the punishment of the criminals, but the preventing of the young from being trained to crime. And here again the peculiar conditions of the South have prevented proper precautions. I have seen twelve-year-old boys working in chains on the public streets of Atlanta, directly in front of the schools, in company with old and hardened criminals; and this indiscriminate mingling of men and women and children makes the chain-gangs perfect schools of crime and debauchery. The struggle for reformatories, which has gone on in Virginia, Georgia, and other States, is the one encouraging sign of the awakening of some communities to the suicidal results of this policy.

It is the public schools, however, which can be made, outside the homes, the greatest means of training decent self-respecting citizens. We have been so hotly engaged recently in discussing trade-schools and the higher education that the pitiable plight of the public-school system in the South has almost dropped from view. Of every five dollars spent for public education in the State of Georgia, the white schools get four dollars and the Negro one dollar; and even then the white public-school system, save in the cities, is bad and cries for reform. If this is true of the whites, what of the blacks? I am becoming more and more convinced, as I look upon the system of common-school training in the South, that the national government must soon step in and aid popular education in some way. To-day it has been only by the most strenuous efforts on the part of the thinking men of the South that the Negro's share of the school fund has not been cut down to a pittance in some half-dozen States; and that movement not only is not dead, but in many communities is gaining strength. What in the name of reason does this nation expect of a people, poorly trained and hard pressed in severe economic competition, without political rights, and with ludicrously inadequate common-school facilities? What can it expect but crime and listlessness, offset here and there by the dogged struggles of the fortunate and more determined who are themselves buoyed by the hope that in due time the country will come to its senses?

I have thus far sought to make clear the physical, economic, and political relations of the Negroes and whites in the South, as I have conceived them, including, for the reasons set forth, crime and education. But after all that has been said on these more tangible matters of human contact, there still remains a part essential to a proper description of the South which it is difficult to describe or fix in terms easily understood by strangers. It is, in fine, the atmosphere of the land, the thought and feeling, the thousand and one little actions which go to make up life. In any community or nation it is these little things which are most elusive to the grasp and yet most essential to any clear conception of the group life taken as a whole. What is thus true of all communities is peculiarly true of the South, where, outside of written history and outside of printed law, there has been going on for a generation as deep a storm and stress of human souls, as intense a ferment of feeling, as intricate a writhing of spirit, as ever a people experienced. Within and without the sombre veil of color vast social forces have been at work,—efforts for human betterment, movements toward disintegration and despair, tragedies and comedies in social and economic life, and a swaying and lifting and sinking of human hearts which have made this land a land of mingled sorrow and joy, of change and excitement and unrest.

The centre of this spiritual turmoil has ever been the millions of black freedmen and their sons, whose destiny is so fatefully bound up with that of the nation. And yet the casual observer visiting the South sees at first little of this. He notes the growing frequency of dark faces as he rides along,—but otherwise the days slip lazily on, the sun shines, and this little world seems as happy and contented as other worlds he has visited. Indeed, on the question of questions—the Negro problem —he hears so little that there almost seems to be a conspiracy of silence; the morning papers seldom mention it, and then usually in a far-fetched academic way, and indeed almost every one seems to forget and ignore the darker half of the land, until the astonished visitor is inclined to ask if after all there *is* any problem here. But if he lingers long enough there comes the awakening: perhaps in a sudden whirl of passion which leaves him gasping at its bitter intensity; more likely in a gradually dawning sense of things he had not at first noticed. Slowly but surely his eyes begin to catch the shadows of the color-line: here he meets crowds of Negroes and whites; then he is suddenly aware that he cannot discover a single dark face; or again at the close of a day's wandering he may find himself in some strange assembly, where all faces are tinged brown or black, and where he has the vague, uncomfortable feeling of the stranger. He realizes at last that silently, resistlessly, the world about flows by him in two great streams: they ripple on in the same sunshine, they approach and mingle their waters in seeming carelessness,—then they divide and flow wide apart. It is done quietly; no mistakes are made, or if one occurs, the swift arm of the law and of public opinion swings down for a moment, as when the other day a black man and a white woman were arrested for talking together on Whitehall Street in Atlanta.

Now if one notices carefully one will see that between these two worlds, despite much physical contact and daily intermingling, there is almost no community of intellectual life or point of transference where the thoughts and feelings of one race can come into direct contact and sympathy with the thoughts and feelings of the other. Before and directly after the war, when all the best of the Negroes were domestic servants in the best of the white families, there were bonds of intimacy, affection, and sometimes blood relationship, between the races. They lived in the same home, shared in the family life, often attended the same church, and talked and conversed with each other. But the increasing civilization of the Negro since then has naturally meant the development of higher classes: there are increasing numbers of ministers, teachers, physicians, merchants, mechanics, and independent farmers, who by nature and training are the aristocracy and leaders of the blacks. Between them, however, and the best element of the whites, there is little or no intellectual commerce. They go to separate churches, they live in separate sections, they are strictly separated in all public gatherings, they travel separately, and they are beginning to read different papers and books. To most libraries, lectures, concerts, and museums, Negroes are either not admitted at all, or on terms peculiarly galling to the pride of the very classes who might otherwise be attracted. The daily paper chronicles the doings of the black world from afar with no great regard for accuracy; and so on, throughout the category of means for intellectual communication,—schools, conferences, efforts for social betterment, and the like,—it is usually true that the very representatives of the two races, who for mutual benefit and the welfare of the land ought to be in complete understanding and sympathy, are so far strangers that one side thinks all whites are narrow and prejudiced, and the other thinks educated Negroes dangerous and insolent. Moreover, in a land where the tyranny of public opinion and the intolerance of criticism is for obvious historical reasons so strong as in the South, such a situation is extremely difficult to correct. The white man, as well as the Negro, is bound and barred by the color-line, and many a scheme of friendliness and philanthropy, of broad-minded sympathy and generous fellowship between the two has dropped still-born because some busybody has forced the color-question to the front and brought the tremendous force of unwritten law against the innovators.

It is hardly necessary for me to add very much in regard to the social contact between the races. Nothing has come to replace that finer sympathy and love between some masters and house servants which the radical and more uncompromising drawing of the color-line in recent years has caused almost completely to disappear. In a world where it means so much to take a man by the hand and sit beside him, to look frankly into his eyes and feel his heart beating with red blood; in a world where a social cigar or a cup of tea together means more than legislative halls and magazine articles and speeches,—one can imagine the consequences of the almost utter absence of such social amenities between estranged races, whose separation extends even to parks and street-cars.

Here there can be none of that social going down to the people,— the opening of heart and hand of the best to the worst, in generous acknowledgment of a common humanity and a common destiny. On the other hand, in matters of simple almsgiving, where there can be no question of social contact, and in the succor of the aged and sick, the South, as if stirred by a feeling of its unfortunate limitations, is generous to a fault. The black beggar is never turned away without a good deal more than a crust, and a call for help for the unfortunate meets quick response. I remember, one cold winter, in Atlanta, when I refrained from contributing to a public relief fund lest Negroes should be discriminated against, I afterward inquired of a friend: "Were any black people receiving aid?" "Why," said he, "they were *all* black."

And yet this does not touch the kernel of the problem. Human advancement is not a mere question of almsgiving, but rather of sympathy and coöperation among classes who would scorn charity. And here is a land where, in the higher walks of life, in all the higher striving for the good and noble and true, the color-line comes to separate natural friends and co-workers; while at the bottom of the social group, in the saloon, the gambling-hell, and the brothel, that same line wavers and disappears.

I have sought to paint an average picture of real relations between the sons of master and man in the South. I have not glossed over matters for policy's sake, for I fear we have already gone too far in that sort of thing. On the other hand, I have sincerely sought to let no unfair exaggerations creep in. I do not doubt that in some Southern communities conditions are better than those I have indicated; while I am no less certain that in other communities they are far worse.

Nor does the paradox and danger of this situation fail to interest and perplex the best conscience of the South. Deeply religious and intensely democratic as are the mass of the whites, they feel acutely the false position in which the Negro problems place them. Such an essentially honest-hearted and generous people cannot cite the caste-levelling precepts of Christianity, or believe in equality of opportunity for all men, without coming to feel more and more with each generation that the present drawing of the color-line is a flat contradiction to their beliefs and professions. But just as often as they come to this point, the present social condition of the Negro stands as a menace and a portent before even the most open-minded: if there were nothing to charge against the Negro but his blackness or other physical peculiarities, they argue, the problem would be comparatively simple; but what can we say to his ignorance, shiftlessness, poverty, and crime? can a self-respecting group hold anything but the least possible fellowship with such persons and survive? and shall we let a mawkish sentiment sweep away the culture of our fathers or the hope of our children? The argument so put is of great strength, but it is not a whit stronger than the argument of thinking Negroes: granted, they reply, that the condition of our masses is bad; there is certainly on the one hand adequate historical cause for this, and unmistakable evidence that no small number have, in spite of tremendous disadvantages, risen to the level of American civilization. And when, by proscription and prejudice, these same Negroes are classed with and treated like the lowest of their people, simply *because* they are Negroes, such a policy not only discourages thrift and intelligence among black men, but puts a direct premium on the very things you complain of,—inefficiency and crime. Draw lines of crime, of incompetency, of vice, as tightly and uncompromisingly as you will, for these things must be proscribed; but a color-line not only does not accomplish this purpose, but thwarts it.

In the face of two such arguments, the future of the South depends on the ability of the representatives of these opposing views to see and appreciate and sympathize with each other's position,—for the Negro to realize more deeply than he does at present the need of uplifting the masses of his people, for the white people to realize more vividly than they have yet done the deadening and disastrous effect of a color-prejudice that classes Phillis Wheatley and Sam Hose[2] in the same despised class.

It is not enough for the Negroes to declare that color-prejudice is the sole cause of their social condition, nor for the white South to reply that their social condition is the main cause of prejudice. They both act as reciprocal cause and effect, and a change in neither alone will bring the desired effect. Both must change, or neither can improve to any great extent. The Negro cannot stand the present reactionary tendencies and unreasoning drawing of the color-line indefinitely without discouragement and retrogression. And the condition of the Negro is ever the excuse for further discrimination. Only by a union of intelli-

2. See n. 4, p. 75. For Phillis Wheatley, see n. 2, p. 38.

gence and sympathy across the color-line in this critical period of the
Republic shall justice and right triumph,—

> "That mind and soul according well,
> May make one music as before,
> But vaster."[3]

x

Of the Faith of the Fathers[1]

> Dim face of Beauty haunting all the world,
>   Fair face of Beauty all too fair to see,
> Where the lost stars adown the heavens are hurled,—
>   There, there alone for thee
>   May white peace be.
>
> .   .   .   .
>
> Beauty, sad face of Beauty, Mystery, Wonder,
>   What are these dreams to foolish babbling men
> Who cry with little noises 'neath the thunder
>   Of Ages ground to sand,
>   To a little sand.
>
> FIONA MACLEOD.

It was out in the country, far from home, far from my foster home,
on a dark Sunday night. The road wandered from our rambling log-
house up the stony bed of a creek, past wheat and corn, until we could
hear dimly across the fields a rhythmic cadence of song,—soft, thrilling,
powerful, that swelled and died sorrowfully in our ears. I was a country
school-teacher then, fresh from the East, and had never seen a Southern
Negro revival. To be sure, we in Berkshire were not perhaps as stiff and
formal as they in Suffolk of olden time;[2] yet we were very quiet and
subdued, and I know not what would have happened those clear Sabbath mornings had some one punctuated the sermon with a wild

3. From the prologue of Alfred, Lord Tennyson's *In Memoriam* (1850).
1. Revised from "The Religion of the American Negro," *The New World: A Quarterly Review of Religious Ethics and Theology* (December 1900): 614–25. The verse is from *Dim Face of Beauty* by Fiona MacLeod, the pen name for William Sharp. The music quotation is from the Negro spiritual "Steal Away Home."
2. Berkshire county is the location of Du Bois's home in Great Barrington, Massachusetts. Like Suffolk county in England, it was a mostly white community dominated by mainline Prot-estant churches. Du Bois describes the reserve and formality of the Great Barrington churches to underscore the emotional fervor of a black revival service.

scream, or interrupted the long prayer with a loud Amen! And so most striking to me, as I approached the village and the little plain church perched aloft, was the air of intense excitement that possessed that mass of black folk. A sort of suppressed terror hung in the air and seemed to seize us,—a pythian madness,[3] a demoniac possession, that lent terrible reality to song and word. The black and massive form of the preacher swayed and quivered as the words crowded to his lips and flew at us in singular eloquence. The people moaned and fluttered, and then the gaunt-cheeked brown woman beside me suddenly leaped straight into the air and shrieked like a lost soul, while round about came wail and groan and outcry, and a scene of human passion such as I had never conceived before.

Those who have not thus witnessed the frenzy of a Negro revival in the untouched backwoods of the South can but dimly realize the religious feeling of the slave; as described, such scenes appear grotesque and funny, but as seen they are awful. Three things characterized this religion of the slave,—the Preacher, the Music, and the Frenzy.[4] The Preacher is the most unique personality developed by the Negro on American soil. A leader, a politician, an orator, a "boss," an intriguer, an idealist,—all these he is, and ever, too, the centre of a group of men, now twenty, now a thousand in number. The combination of a certain adroitness with deep-seated earnestness, of tact with consummate ability, gave him his preëminence, and helps him maintain it. The type, of course, varies according to time and place, from the West Indies in the sixteenth century to New England in the nineteenth, and from the Mississippi bottoms to cities like New Orleans or New York.

The Music of Negro religion is that plaintive rhythmic melody, with its touching minor cadences, which, despite caricature and defilement, still remains the most original and beautiful expression of human life and longing yet born on American soil. Sprung from the African forests, where its counterpart can still be heard, it was adapted, changed, and intensified by the tragic soul-life of the slave, until, under the stress of law and whip, it became the one true expression of a people's sorrow, despair, and hope.

Finally the Frenzy or "Shouting," when the Spirit of the Lord passed by, and, seizing the devotee, made him mad with supernatural joy, was the last essential of Negro religion and the one more devoutly believed in than all the rest. It varied in expression from the silent rapt countenance or the low murmur and moan to the mad abandon of physical fervor,—the stamping, shrieking, and shouting, the rushing to and fro and wild waving of arms, the weeping and laughing, the vision and the trance. All this is nothing new in the world, but old as religion, as

3. The Pythian priestess at Delphi, the Greek temple to Apollo, would go into a trance and deliver oracles.
4. Du Bois's term for the state in which the worshiper feels possessed by the spirit of the Lord.

Delphi and Endor.[5] And so firm a hold did it have on the Negro, that many generations firmly believed that without this visible manifestation of the God there could be no true communion with the Invisible.

These were the characteristics of Negro religious life as developed up to the time of Emancipation. Since under the peculiar circumstances of the black man's environment they were the one expression of his higher life, they are of deep interest to the student of his development, both socially and psychologically. Numerous are the attractive lines of inquiry that here group themselves. What did slavery mean to the African savage? What was his attitude toward the World and Life? What seemed to him good and evil,—God and Devil? Whither went his longings and strivings, and wherefore were his heart-burnings and disappointments? Answers to such questions can come only from a study of Negro religion as a development, through its gradual changes from the heathenism of the Gold Coast to the institutional Negro church of Chicago.

Moreover, the religious growth of millions of men, even though they be slaves, cannot be without potent influence upon their contemporaries. The Methodists and Baptists of America owe much of their condition to the silent but potent influence of their millions of Negro converts. Especially is this noticeable in the South, where theology and religious philosophy are on this account a long way behind the North, and where the religion of the poor whites is a plain copy of Negro thought and methods. The mass of "gospel" hymns which has swept through American churches and well-nigh ruined our sense of song consists largely of debased imitations of Negro melodies made by ears that caught the jingle but not the music, the body but not the soul, of the Jubilee songs.[6] It is thus clear that the study of Negro religion is not only a vital part of the history of the Negro in America, but no uninteresting part of American history.

The Negro church of to-day is the social centre of Negro life in the United States, and the most characteristic expression of African character. Take a typical church in a small Virginian town: it is the "First Baptist"—a roomy brick edifice seating five hundred or more persons, tastefully finished in Georgia pine, with a carpet, a small organ, and stained-glass windows. Underneath is a large assembly room with benches. This building is the central club-house of a community of a thousand or more Negroes. Various organizations meet here,—the church proper, the Sunday-school, two or three insurance societies,

5. In 1 Samuel 28.7–14, Endor was the medium who summoned the ghost of Samuel for King Saul. In ancient Greece, the temple of Apollo at Delphi was considered the center of the world. It was also the home of the most important oracle, whose messages often influenced state policy.
6. Du Bois uses Jubilee songs to mean the more authentic, black sacred music as opposed to the simplified, gospel songs, which are derived from the spirituals. Gospel songs were also used in white churches.

women's societies, secret societies, and mass meetings of various kinds. Entertainments, suppers, and lectures are held beside the five or six regular weekly religious services. Considerable sums of money are collected and expended here, employment is found for the idle, strangers are introduced, news is disseminated and charity distributed. At the same time this social, intellectual, and economic centre is a religious centre of great power. Depravity, Sin, Redemption, Heaven, Hell, and Damnation are preached twice a Sunday with much fervor, and revivals take place every year after the crops are laid by; and few indeed of the community have the hardihood to withstand conversion. Back of this more formal religion, the Church often stands as a real conserver of morals, a strengthener of family life, and the final authority on what is Good and Right.

Thus one can see in the Negro church to-day, reproduced in microcosm, all that great world from which the Negro is cut off by color-prejudice and social condition. In the great city churches the same tendency is noticeable and in many respects emphasized. A great church like the Bethel of Philadelphia[7] has over eleven hundred members, an edifice seating fifteen hundred persons and valued at one hundred thousand dollars, an annual budget of five thousand dollars, and a government consisting of a pastor with several assisting local preachers, an executive and legislative board, financial boards and tax collectors; general church meetings for making laws; subdivided groups led by class leaders, a company of militia, and twenty-four auxiliary societies. The activity of a church like this is immense and far-reaching, and the bishops who preside over these organizations throughout the land are among the most powerful Negro rulers in the world.

Such churches are really governments of men, and consequently a little investigation reveals the curious fact that, in the South, at least, practically every American Negro is a church member. Some, to be sure, are not regularly enrolled, and a few do not habitually attend services; but, practically, a proscribed people must have a social centre, and that centre for this people is the Negro church. The census of 1890 showed nearly twenty-four thousand Negro churches in the country, with a total enrolled membership of over two and a half millions, or ten actual church members to every twenty-eight persons, and in some Southern States one in every two persons. Besides these there is the large number who, while not enrolled as members, attend and take part in many of the activities of the church. There is an organized Negro church for every sixty black families in the nation, and in some States for every forty families, owning, on an average, a thousand dollars' worth of property each, or nearly twenty-six million dollars in all.

7. The first urban, denominational black church in America, founded in 1794.

Such, then, is the large development of the Negro church since Emancipation. The question now is, What have been the successive steps of this social history and what are the present tendencies? First, we must realize that no such institution as the Negro church could rear itself without definite historical foundations. These foundations we can find if we remember that the social history of the Negro did not start in America. He was brought from a definite social environment, —the polygamous clan life[8] under the headship of the chief and the potent influence of the priest. His religion was nature-worship, with profound belief in invisible surrounding influences, good and bad, and his worship was through incantation and sacrifice. The first rude change in this life was the slave ship and the West Indian sugar-fields. The plantation organization replaced the clan and tribe, and the white master replaced the chief with far greater and more despotic powers. Forced and long-continued toil became the rule of life, the old ties of blood relationship and kinship disappeared, and instead of the family appeared a new polygamy and polyandry,[9] which, in some cases, almost reached promiscuity. It was a terrific social revolution, and yet some traces were retained of the former group life, and the chief remaining institution was the Priest or Medicine-man. He early appeared on the plantation and found his function as the healer of the sick, the interpreter of the Unknown, the comforter of the sorrowing, the supernatural avenger of wrong, and the one who rudely but picturesquely expressed the longing, disappointment, and resentment of a stolen and oppressed people. Thus, as bard, physician, judge, and priest, within the narrow limits allowed by the slave system, rose the Negro preacher, and under him the first Afro-American institution, the Negro church. This church was not at first by any means Christian nor definitely organized; rather it was an adaptation and mingling of heathen rites among the members of each plantation, and roughly designated as Voodooism.[1] Association with the masters, missionary effort and motives of expediency gave these rites an early veneer of Christianity, and after the lapse of many generations the Negro church became Christian.

Two characteristic things must be noticed in regard to this church. First, it became almost entirely Baptist and Methodist in faith; secondly, as a social institution it antedated by many decades the monogamic[2] Negro home. From the very circumstances of its beginning, the church was confined to the plantation, and consisted primarily of a series of disconnected units; although, later on, some freedom of movement was

---

8. A society that allows men and women to have more than one spouse at a time.
9. Having more than one husband at a time.
1. Religious cult characterized by a belief in fetishes, sorcery, and rituals, all combining to produce a system of magic. Voodoo has African origins and in North America was sometimes called "Hoodoo" or "conjure."
2. Having only one wife at a time.

allowed, still this geographical limitation was always important and was one cause of the spread of the decentralized and democratic Baptist faith among the slaves. At the same time, the visible rite of baptism appealed strongly to their mystic temperament. To-day the Baptist Church is still largest in membership among Negroes, and has a million and a half communicants. Next in popularity came the churches organized in connection with the white neighboring churches, chiefly Baptist and Methodist, with a few Episcopalian and others. The Methodists still form the second greatest denomination, with nearly a million members. The faith of these two leading denominations was more suited to the slave church from the prominence they gave to religious feeling and fervor. The Negro membership in other denominations has always been small and relatively unimportant, although the Episcopalians and Presbyterians are gaining among the more intelligent classes to-day, and the Catholic Church is making headway in certain sections. After Emancipation, and still earlier in the North, the Negro churches largely severed such affiliations as they had had with the white churches, either by choice or by compulsion. The Baptist churches became independent, but the Methodists were compelled early to unite for purposes of episcopal government. This gave rise to the great African Methodist Church, the greatest Negro organization in the world, to the Zion Church and the Colored Methodist,[3] and to the black conferences and churches in this and other denominations.

The second fact noted, namely, that the Negro church antedates the Negro home, leads to an explanation of much that is paradoxical in this communistic institution and in the morals of its members. But especially it leads us to regard this institution as peculiarly the expression of the inner ethical life of a people in a sense seldom true elsewhere. Let us turn, then, from the outer physical development of the church to the more important inner ethical life of the people who compose it. The Negro has already been pointed out many times as a religious animal,—a being of that deep emotional nature which turns instinctively toward the supernatural. Endowed with a rich tropical imagination and a keen, delicate appreciation of Nature, the transplanted African lived in a world animate with gods and devils, elves and witches; full of strange influences,—of Good to be implored, of Evil to be propitiated. Slavery, then, was to him the dark triumph of Evil over him. All the hateful powers of the Under-world were striving against him, and a spirit of revolt and revenge filled his heart. He called up all the resources of heathenism to aid,—exorcism and witchcraft,

---

3. The Colored Methodist Episcopal Church was founded in Jackson, Tennessee, in 1870 by former slaves who left the Methodist or Episcopal churches of their masters. The African Methodist Episcopal Church was founded in Philadelphia in 1787. The Zion Church is a faction that broke away from the African Episcopal Church and formed its own denomination, the African Methodist Episcopal Zion Church. The Zion Church differed from its parent church by a greater emphasis on evangelical activities.

the mysterious Obi[4] worship with its barbarous rites, spells, and blood-sacrifice even, now and then, of human victims. Weird midnight orgies and mystic conjurations were invoked, the witch-woman and the voodoo-priest became the centre of Negro group life, and that vein of vague superstition which characterizes the unlettered Negro even to-day was deepened and strengthened.

In spite, however, of such success as that of the fierce Maroons, the Danish blacks, and others,[5] the spirit of revolt gradually died away under the untiring energy and superior strength of the slave masters. By the middle of the eighteenth century the black slave had sunk, with hushed murmurs, to his place at the bottom of a new economic system, and was unconsciously ripe for a new philosophy of life. Nothing suited his condition then better than the doctrines of passive submission embodied in the newly learned Christianity. Slave masters early realized this, and cheerfully aided religious propaganda within certain bounds. The long system of repression and degradation of the Negro tended to emphasize the elements in his character which made him a valuable chattel: courtesy became humility, moral strength degenerated into submission, and the exquisite native appreciation of the beautiful became an infinite capacity for dumb suffering. The Negro, losing the joy of this world, eagerly seized upon the offered conceptions of the next; the avenging Spirit of the Lord enjoining patience in this world, under sorrow and tribulation until the Great Day when He should lead His dark children home,—this became his comforting dream. His preacher repeated the prophecy, and his bards sang,—

"Children, we all shall be free
When the Lord shall appear!"[6]

This deep religious fatalism, painted so beautifully in "Uncle Tom,"[7] came soon to breed, as all fatalistic faiths will, the sensualist side by side with the martyr. Under the lax moral life of the plantation, where marriage was a farce, laziness a virtue, and property a theft, a religion of resignation and submission degenerated easily, in less strenuous minds, into a philosophy of indulgence and crime. Many of the worst characteristics of the Negro masses of to-day had their seed in this period of the slave's ethical growth. Here it was that the Home was ruined under the very shadow of the Church, white and black; here habits of shiftlessness took root, and sullen hopelessness replaced hopeful strife.

With the beginning of the abolition movement and the gradual

---

4. A religious practice associated with the use of magic. Of African origin, obi began in Jamaica, where it was known as "obeah."
5. See n. 1, p. 37.
6. Lyrics from the spiritual "Children, We All Shall Be Free."
7. The very religious, pious, passive black man who is martyred for his beliefs in Uncle Tom's Cabin (1852), the influential novel by Harriet Beecher Stowe.

growth of a class of free Negroes came a change. We often neglect the
influence of the freedman before the war, because of the paucity of his
numbers and the small weight he had in the history of the nation. But
we must not forget that his chief influence was internal,—was exerted
on the black world; and that there he was the ethical and social leader.
Huddled as he was in a few centres like Philadelphia, New York, and
New Orleans, the masses of the freedmen sank into poverty and listlessness; but not all of them. The free Negro leader early arose and his
chief characteristic was intense earnestness and deep feeling on the
slavery question. Freedom became to him a real thing and not a dream.
His religion became darker and more intense, and into his ethics crept
a note of revenge, into his songs a day of reckoning close at hand. The
"Coming of the Lord" swept this side of Death, and came to be a thing
to be hoped for in this day. Through fugitive slaves and irrepressible
discussion this desire for freedom seized the black millions still in bondage, and became their one ideal of life. The black bards caught new
notes, and sometimes even dared to sing,—

> "O Freedom, O Freedom, O Freedom over me!
> Before I'll be a slave
> I'll be buried in my grave,
> And go home to my Lord
> And be free."[8]

For fifty years Negro religion thus transformed itself and identified
itself with the dream of Abolition, until that which was a radical fad in
the white North and an anarchistic plot in the white South had become
a religion to the black world. Thus, when Emancipation finally came,
it seemed to the freedman a literal Coming of the Lord. His fervid
imagination was stirred as never before, by the tramp of armies, the
blood and dust of battle, and the wail and whirl of social upheaval. He
stood dumb and motionless before the whirlwind: what had he to do
with it? Was it not the Lord's doing, and marvellous in his eyes? Joyed
and bewildered with what came, he stood awaiting new wonders till
the inevitable Age of Reaction swept over the nation and brought the
crisis of to-day.

It is difficult to explain clearly the present critical stage of Negro
religion. First, we must remember that living as the blacks do in close
contact with a great modern nation, and sharing, although imperfectly,
the soul-life of that nation, they must necessarily be affected more or
less directly by all the religious and ethical forces that are to-day moving
the United States. These questions and movements are, however, over-
shadowed and dwarfed by the (to them) all-important question of their
civil, political, and economic status. They must perpetually discuss the

8. From the spiritual "O Freedom."

"Negro Problem,"—must live, move, and have their being in it, and interpret all else in its light or darkness. With this come, too, peculiar problems of their inner life,—of the status of women, the maintenance of Home, the training of children, the accumulation of wealth, and the prevention of crime. All this must mean a time of intense ethical ferment, of religious heart-searching and intellectual unrest. From the double life every American Negro must live, as a Negro and as an American, as swept on by the current of the nineteenth while yet struggling in the eddies of the fifteenth century,—from this must arise a painful self-consciousness, an almost morbid sense of personality and a moral hesitancy which is fatal to self-confidence. The worlds within and without the Veil of Color are changing, and changing rapidly, but not at the same rate, not in the same way; and this must produce a peculiar wrenching of the soul, a peculiar sense of doubt and bewilderment. Such a double life, with double thoughts, double duties, and double social classes, must give rise to double words and double ideals, and tempt the mind to pretence or to revolt, to hypocrisy or to radicalism.

In some such doubtful words and phrases can one perhaps most clearly picture the peculiar ethical paradox that faces the Negro of today and is tingeing and changing his religious life. Feeling that his rights and his dearest ideals are being trampled upon, that the public conscience is ever more deaf to his righteous appeal, and that all the reactionary forces of prejudice, greed, and revenge are daily gaining new strength and fresh allies, the Negro faces no enviable dilemma. Conscious of his impotence, and pessimistic, he often becomes bitter and vindictive; and his religion, instead of a worship, is a complaint and a curse, a wail rather than a hope, a sneer rather than a faith. On the other hand, another type of mind, shrewder and keener and more tortuous too, sees in the very strength of the anti-Negro movement its patent weaknesses, and with Jesuitic casuistry[9] is deterred by no ethical considerations in the endeavor to turn this weakness to the black man's strength. Thus we have two great and hardly reconcilable streams of thought and ethical strivings; the danger of the one lies in anarchy, that of the other in hypocrisy. The one type of Negro stands almost ready to curse God and die, and the other is too often found a traitor to right and a coward before force; the one is wedded to ideals remote, whimsical, perhaps impossible of realization; the other forgets that life is more than meat and the body more than raiment. But, after all, is not this simply the writhing of the age translated into black,—the triumph of the Lie which to-day, with its false culture, faces the hideousness of the anarchist assassin?

9. Disparaging reference to the sophisticated reasoning used by the Roman Catholic order of the Society of Jesus. Here Du Bois uses the expression to imply cynical, intellectual argumentation.

To-day the two groups of Negroes, the one in the North, the other in the South, represent these divergent ethical tendencies, the first tending toward radicalism, the other toward hypocritical compromise. It is no idle regret with which the white South mourns the loss of the old-time Negro,—the frank, honest, simple old servant who stood for the earlier religious age of submission and humility. With all his laziness and lack of many elements of true manhood, he was at least openhearted, faithful, and sincere. To-day he is gone, but who is to blame for his going? Is it not those very persons who mourn for him? Is it not the tendency, born of Reconstruction and Reaction, to found a society on lawlessness and deception, to tamper with the moral fibre of a naturally honest and straightforward people until the whites threaten to become ungovernable tyrants and the blacks criminals and hypocrites? Deception is the natural defence of the weak against the strong, and the South used it for many years against its conquerors; to-day it must be prepared to see its black proletariat turn that same two-edged weapon against itself. And how natural this is! The death of Denmark Vesey and Nat Turner[1] proved long since to the Negro the present hopelessness of physical defence. Political defence is becoming less and less available, and economic defence is still only partially effective. But there is a patent defence at hand,—the defence of deception and flattery, of cajoling and lying. It is the same defence which the Jews[2] of the Middle Age used and which left its stamp on their character for centuries. To-day the young Negro of the South who would succeed cannot be frank and outspoken, honest and self-assertive, but rather he is daily tempted to be silent and wary, politic and sly; he must flatter and be pleasant, endure petty insults with a smile, shut his eyes to wrong; in too many cases he sees positive personal advantage in deception and lying. His real thoughts, his real aspirations, must be guarded in whispers; he must not criticise, he must not complain. Patience, humility, and adroitness must, in these growing black youth, replace impulse, manliness, and courage. With this sacrifice there is an economic opening, and perhaps peace and some prosperity. Without this there is riot, migration, or crime. Nor is this situation peculiar to the Southern United States,—is it not rather the only method by which undeveloped races have gained the right to share modern culture? The price of culture is a Lie.

On the other hand, in the North the tendency is to emphasize the radicalism of the Negro. Driven from his birthright in the South by a situation at which every fibre of his more outspoken and assertive nature revolts, he finds himself in a land where he can scarcely earn a decent living amid the harsh competition and the color discrimination. At the same time, through schools and periodicals, discussions and lectures,

1. See n. 3, p. 38.
2. "The Jews" changed to "peasants" in 1953 edition.

he is intellectually quickened and awakened. The soul, long pent up and dwarfed, suddenly expands in new-found freedom. What wonder that every tendency is to excess,—radical complaint, radical remedies, bitter denunciation or angry silence. Some sink, some rise. The criminal and the sensualist leave the church for the gambling-hell and the brothel, and fill the slums of Chicago and Baltimore; the better classes segregate themselves from the group-life of both white and black, and form an aristocracy, cultured but pessimistic, whose bitter criticism stings while it points out no way of escape. They despise the submission and subserviency of the Southern Negroes, but offer no other means by which a poor and oppressed minority can exist side by side with its masters. Feeling deeply and keenly the tendencies and opportunities of the age in which they live, their souls are bitter at the fate which drops the Veil between; and the very fact that this bitterness is natural and justifiable only serves to intensify it and make it more maddening.

Between the two extreme types of ethical attitude which I have thus sought to make clear wavers the mass of the millions of Negroes, North and South; and their religious life and activity partake of this social conflict within their ranks. Their churches are differentiating,—now into groups of cold, fashionable devotees, in no way distinguishable from similar white groups save in color of skin; now into large social and business institutions catering to the desire for information and amusement of their members, warily avoiding unpleasant questions both within and without the black world, and preaching in effect if not in word: *Dum vivimus, vivamus.*[3]

But back of this still broods silently the deep religious feeling of the real Negro heart, the stirring, unguided might of powerful human souls who have lost the guiding star of the past and are seeking in the great night a new religious ideal. Some day the Awakening will come, when the pent-up vigor of ten million souls shall sweep irresistibly toward the Goal, out of the Valley of the Shadow of Death, where all that makes life worth living—Liberty, Justice, and Right—is marked "For White People Only."

3. While we live, let us live (Latin).

XI

Of the Passing of the First-Born[1]

O sister, sister, thy first-begotten,
The hands that cling and the feet that follow,
The voice of the child's blood crying yet,
Who hath remembered me? who hath forgotten?
Thou hast forgotten, O summer swallow,
But the world shall end when I forget.

SWINBURNE.

"Unto you a child is born,"[2] sang the bit of yellow paper that fluttered into my room one brown October morning. Then the fear of fatherhood mingled wildly with the joy of creation; I wondered how it looked and how it felt,—what were its eyes, and how its hair curled and crumpled itself. And I thought in awe of her,—she who had slept with Death to tear a man-child from underneath her heart,[3] while I was unconsciously wandering. I fled to my wife and child, repeating the while to myself half wonderingly, "Wife and child? Wife and child?"—fled fast and faster than boat and steam-car, and yet must ever impatiently await them; away from the hard-voiced city, away from the flickering sea into my own Berkshire Hills that sit all sadly guarding the gates of Massachusetts.

Up the stairs I ran to the wan mother and whimpering babe, to the sanctuary on whose altar a life at my bidding had offered itself to win a life, and won. What is this tiny formless thing, this new-born wail from an unknown world,—all head and voice? I handle it curiously, and watch perplexed its winking, breathing, and sneezing. I did not love it then; it seemed a ludicrous thing to love; but her I loved, my girl-mother, she whom now I saw unfolding like the glory of the morning—the transfigured woman.

1. The verse is from Algernon Charles Swinburne's *Itylus* (1866). The music quotation is from the Negro spiritual "I Hope My Mother Will Be There."
2. Du Bois's rewriting of Isaiah 9.6: "For unto us a child is born." Isaiah is prophesying the arrival of the Messiah, later taken by Christians to be a prediction of the birth of Jesus.
3. Nina Gomer Du Bois, a student at Wilberforce, married W. E. B. Du Bois on May 12, 1896. On October 2, 1897, Nina gave birth to their son, Burghardt Gomer Du Bois, in Great Barrington, Massachusetts, where she had gone for her delivery.

Through her I came to love the wee thing, as it grew and waxed strong; as its little soul unfolded itself in twitter and cry and half-formed word, and as its eyes caught the gleam and flash of life. How beautiful he was, with his olive-tinted flesh and dark gold ringlets, his eyes of mingled blue and brown, his perfect little limbs, and the soft voluptuous roll which the blood of Africa had moulded into his features! I held him in my arms, after we had sped far away to our Southern home,—held him, and glanced at the hot red soil of Georgia and the breathless city of a hundred hills, and felt a vague unrest. Why was his hair tinted with gold? An evil omen was golden hair in my life. Why had not the brown of his eyes crushed out and killed the blue?—for brown were his father's eyes, and his father's father's. And thus in the Land of the Color-line I saw, as it fell across my baby, the shadow of the Veil.

Within the Veil was he born, said I; and there within shall he live, —a Negro and a Negro's son. Holding in that little head—ah, bitterly!—the unbowed pride of a hunted race, clinging with that tiny dimpled hand—ah, wearily!—to a hope not hopeless but unhopeful, and seeing with those bright wondering eyes that peer into my soul a land whose freedom is to us a mockery and whose liberty a lie. I saw the shadow of the Veil as it passed over my baby, I saw the cold city towering above the blood-red land. I held my face beside his little cheek, showed him the star-children and the twinkling lights as they began to flash, and stilled with an even-song the unvoiced terror of my life.

So sturdy and masterful he grew, so filled with bubbling life, so tremulous with the unspoken wisdom of a life but eighteen months distant from the All-life,—we were not far from worshipping this revelation of the divine, my wife and I. Her own life builded and moulded itself upon the child; he tinged her every dream and idealized her every effort. No hands but hers must touch and garnish those little limbs; no dress or frill must touch them that had not wearied her fingers; no voice but hers could coax him off to Dreamland, and she and he together spoke some soft and unknown tongue and in it held communion. I too mused above his little white bed; saw the strength of my own arm stretched onward through the ages through the newer strength of his; saw the dream of my black fathers stagger a step onward in the wild phantasm of the world; heard in his baby voice the voice of the Prophet that was to rise within the Veil.

And so we dreamed and loved and planned by fall and winter, and the full flush of the long Southern spring, till the hot winds rolled from the fetid Gulf, till the roses shivered and the still stern sun quivered its awful light over the hills of Atlanta. And then one night the little feet pattered wearily to the wee white bed, and the tiny hands trembled; and a warm flushed face tossed on the pillow, and we knew baby was sick. Ten days he lay there,—a swift week and three endless days, wasting, wasting away. Cheerily the mother nursed him the first days, and laughed into the little eyes that smiled again. Tenderly then she hovered round him, till the smile fled away and Fear crouched beside the little bed.

Then the day ended not, and night was a dreamless terror, and joy and sleep slipped away. I hear now that Voice at midnight calling me from dull and dreamless trance,—crying, "The Shadow of Death! The Shadow of Death!" Out into the starlight I crept, to rouse the gray physician,[4]—the Shadow of Death, the Shadow of Death. The hours trembled on; the night listened; the ghastly dawn glided like a tired thing across the lamplight. Then we two alone looked upon the child as he turned toward us with great eyes, and stretched his string-like hands,—the Shadow of Death! And we spoke no word, and turned away.

He died at eventide, when the sun lay like a brooding sorrow above the western hills, veiling its face; when the winds spoke not, and the trees, the great green trees he loved, stood motionless. I saw his breath beat quicker and quicker, pause, and then his little soul leapt like a star that travels in the night and left a world of darkness in its train. The day changed not; the same tall trees peeped in at the windows, the same green grass glinted in the setting sun. Only in the chamber of death writhed the world's most piteous thing—a childless mother.

I shirk not. I long for work. I pant for a life full of striving. I am no coward, to shrink before the rugged rush of the storm, nor even quail before the awful shadow of the Veil. But hearken, O Death! Is not this my life hard enough,—is not that dull land that stretches its sneering web about me cold enough,—is not all the world beyond these four little walls pitiless enough, but that thou must needs enter here,—thou, O Death? About my head the thundering storm beat like a heartless voice, and the crazy forest pulsed with the curses of the weak; but what cared I, within my home beside my wife and baby boy? Wast thou so jealous of one little coign[5] of happiness that thou must needs enter there,—thou, O Death?

A perfect life was his, all joy and love, with tears to make it brighter,—sweet as a summer's day beside the Housatonic.[6] The world loved him; the women kissed his curls, the men looked gravely into his wonderful eyes, and the children hovered and fluttered about him. I can see him now, changing like the sky from sparkling laughter to darkening frowns, and then to wondering thoughtfulness as he watched

4. Burghardt Du Bois contracted diphtheria, probably due to the sewage pollution of Atlanta's water system, and suffered for ten days. He died on May 24, 1899. The night before his son's death, Du Bois tried, unsuccessfully, to find one of the two or three black physicians in Atlanta. White doctors in Atlanta would not treat black patients at that time.
5. Refers to coign of vantage, a position advantageous for action or observation.
6. River that runs through Du Bois's hometown of Great Barrington.

the world. He knew no color-line, poor dear,—and the Veil, though it shadowed him, had not yet darkened half his sun. He loved the white matron, he loved his black nurse; and in his little world walked souls alone, uncolored and unclothed. I—yea, all men—are larger and purer by the infinite breadth of that one little life. She who in simple clearness of vision sees beyond the stars said when he had flown, "He will be happy There; he ever loved beautiful things." And I, far more ignorant, and blind by the web of mine own weaving, sit alone winding words and muttering, "If still he be, and he be There, and there be a There, let him be happy, O Fate!"

Blithe was the morning of his burial, with bird and song and sweet-smelling flowers. The trees whispered to the grass, but the children sat with hushed faces. And yet it seemed a ghostly unreal day,—the wraith of Life. We seemed to rumble down an unknown street behind a little white bundle of posies, with the shadow of a song in our ears. The busy city dinned about us; they did not say much, those pale-faced hurrying men and women; they did not say much,—they only glanced and said, "Niggers!"

We could not lay him in the ground there in Georgia, for the earth there is strangely red; so we bore him away to the northward, with his flowers and his little folded hands. In vain, in vain!—for where, O God! beneath thy broad blue sky shall my dark baby rest in peace,—where Reverence dwells, and Goodness, and a Freedom that is free?

All that day and all that night there sat an awful gladness in my heart,—nay, blame me not if I see the world thus darkly through the Veil,—and my soul whispers ever to me, saying, "Not dead, not dead, but escaped; not bond, but free." No bitter meanness now shall sicken his baby heart till it die a living death, no taunt shall madden his happy boyhood. Fool that I was to think or wish that this little soul should grow choked and deformed within the Veil! I might have known that yonder deep unworldly look that ever and anon floated past his eyes was peering far beyond this narrow Now. In the poise of his little curl-crowned head did there not sit all that wild pride of being which his father had hardly crushed in his own heart? For what, forsooth, shall a Negro want with pride amid the studied humiliations of fifty million fellows? Well sped, my boy, before the world had dubbed your ambition insolence, had held your ideals unattainable, and taught you to cringe and bow. Better far this nameless void that stops my life than a sea of sorrow for you.

Idle words; he might have borne his burden more bravely than we, —aye, and found it lighter too, some day; for surely, surely this is not the end. Surely there shall yet dawn some mighty morning to lift the Veil and set the prisoned free. Not for me,—I shall die in my bonds, —but for fresh young souls who have not known the night and waken to the morning; a morning when men ask of the workman, not "Is he white?" but "Can he work?" When men ask artists, not "Are they black?" but "Do they know?" Some morning this may be, long, long years to come. But now there wails, on that dark shore within the Veil, the same deep voice, *Thou shalt forego!*[7] And all have I foregone at that command, and with small complaint,—all save that fair young form that lies so coldly wed with death in the nest I had builded.

If one must have gone, why not I? Why may I not rest me from this restlessness and sleep from this wide waking? Was not the world's alembic,[8] Time, in his young hands, and is not my time waning? Are there so many workers in the vineyard that the fair promise of this little body could lightly be tossed away? The wretched of my race that line the alleys of the nation sit fatherless and unmothered; but Love sat beside his cradle, and in his ear Wisdom waited to speak. Perhaps now he knows the All-love, and needs not to be wise. Sleep, then, child,—sleep till I sleep and waken to a baby voice and the ceaseless patter of little feet—above the Veil.

XII

Of Alexander Crummell[1]

Then from the Dawn it seemed there came, but faint
As from beyond the limit of the world,
Like the last echo born of a great cry,
Sounds, as if some fair city were one voice
Around a king returning from his wars.

TENNYSON.

This is the history of a human heart,—the tale of a black boy who many long years ago began to struggle with life that he might know the world and know himself. Three temptations he met on those dark dunes that lay gray and dismal before the wonder-eyes of the child: the temp-

---

7. Du Bois's translation of Goethe's *sollst entbehren.*
8. Something that purifies, alters, or transforms.
1. The verse is from Alfred, Lord Tennyson's *The Passing of Arthur* in *Idylls of the King* (1869). The music quotation is from the Negro spiritual "Swing Low, Sweet Chariot." Alexander Crummell (1819–1898) was a clergyman, African missionary, and antislavery activist.

tation of Hate, that stood out against the red dawn; the temptation of Despair, that darkened noonday; and the temptation of Doubt, that ever steals along with twilight. Above all, you must hear of the vales he crossed,—the Valley of Humiliation and the Valley of the Shadow of Death.[2]

I saw Alexander Crummell first at a Wilberforce commencement season, amid its bustle and crush.[3] Tall, frail, and black he stood, with simple dignity and an unmistakable air of good breeding. I talked with him apart, where the storming of the lusty young orators could not harm us. I spoke to him politely, then curiously, then eagerly, as I began to feel the fineness of his character,—his calm courtesy, the sweetness of his strength, and his fair blending of the hope and truth of life. Instinctively I bowed before this man, as one bows before the prophets of the world. Some seer he seemed, that came not from the crimson Past or the gray To-come, but from the pulsing Now,—that mocking world which seemed to me at once so light and dark, so splendid and sordid. Four-score years had he wandered in this same world of mine, within the Veil.

He was born with the Missouri Compromise and lay a-dying amid the echoes of Manila and El Caney:[4] stirring times for living, times dark to look back upon, darker to look forward to. The black-faced lad that paused over his mud and marbles seventy years ago saw puzzling vistas as he looked down the world. The slave-ship still groaned across the Atlantic, faint cries burdened the Southern breeze, and the great black father whispered mad tales of cruelty into those young ears. From the low doorway the mother silently watched her boy at play, and at nightfall sought him eagerly lest the shadows bear him away to the land of slaves.[5]

So his young mind worked and winced and shaped curiously a vision of Life; and in the midst of that vision ever stood one dark figure alone,—ever with the hard, thick countenance of that bitter father, and a form that fell in vast and shapeless folds. Thus the temptation of Hate grew and shadowed the growing child,—gliding stealthily into his laughter, fading into his play, and seizing his dreams by day and night with rough, rude turbulence. So the black boy asked of sky and sun and flower the never-answered Why? and loved, as he grew, neither the world nor the world's rough ways.

2. By using a geographical language to describe a spiritual struggle, Du Bois is invoking John Bunyan's classical allegory *The Pilgrim's Progress* (1678). Du Bois treats Crummell as a model for a black pilgrim in the fallen world of American democracy.
3. See n. 9, p. 39 for a broad outline of Crummell's life.
4. Sites in the Philippines and Cuba, respectively, of U.S. victories during the Spanish-American War. The Missouri Compromise, passed by Congress in 1820 to maintain a balance of free and slave states, admitted Missouri as a slave state and Maine as a free state.
5. Boston Crummell, Alexander's father, was believed to have been born in Africa and kidnapped into slavery at the age of thirteen. Charity Hicks, Alexander's mother, was a black woman born into freedom in Long Island. She went with her son to Liberia in 1865.

Strange temptation for a child, you may think; and yet in this wide land to-day a thousand thousand dark children brood before this same temptation, and feel its cold and shuddering arms. For them, perhaps, some one will some day lift the Veil,—will come tenderly and cheerily into those sad little lives and brush the brooding hate away, just as Beriah Green[6] strode in upon the life of Alexander Crummell. And before the bluff, kind-hearted man the shadow seemed less dark. Beriah Green had a school in Oneida County, New York, with a score of mischievous boys. "I'm going to bring a black boy here to educate," said Beriah Green, as only a crank and an abolitionist would have dared to say. "Oho!" laughed the boys. "Ye-es," said his wife; and Alexander came. Once before, the black boy had sought a school, had travelled, cold and hungry, four hundred miles up into free New Hampshire, to Canaan. But the godly farmers hitched ninety yoke of oxen to the abolition schoolhouse and dragged it into the middle of the swamp. The black boy trudged away.[7]

The nineteenth was the first century of human sympathy,—the age when half wonderingly we began to descry in others that transfigured spark of divinity which we call Myself; when clodhoppers and peasants, and tramps and thieves, and millionaires and—sometimes—Negroes, became throbbing souls whose warm pulsing life touched us so nearly that we half gasped with surprise, crying, "Thou too! Hast Thou seen Sorrow and the dull waters of Hopelessness? Hast Thou known Life?" And then all helplessly we peered into those Other-worlds, and wailed, "O World of Worlds, how shall man make you one?"

So in that little Oneida school there came to those schoolboys a revelation of thought and longing beneath one black skin, of which they had not dreamed before. And to the lonely boy came a new dawn of sympathy and inspiration. The shadowy, formless thing—the temp- tation of Hate, that hovered between him and the world—grew fainter and less sinister. It did not wholly fade away, but diffused itself and lingered thick at the edges. Through it the child now first saw the blue and gold of life,—the sun-swept road that ran 'twixt heaven and earth until in one far-off wan wavering line they met and kissed. A vision of life came to the growing boy,—mystic, wonderful. He raised his head, stretched himself, breathed deep of the fresh new air. Yonder, behind the forests, he heard strange sounds; then glinting through the trees he saw, far, far away, the bronzed hosts of a nation calling,—calling faintly, calling loudly. He heard the hateful clank of their chains, he felt them

---

6. Founder of the Oneida Institute in Whitesboro, New York. Crummell matriculated in 1836 as a member of the sophomore class.

7. Crummell and his friends, Henry Highland Garnet and Thomas S. Sidney, enrolled in the Noyes Academy in Canaan, New Hampshire. Founded by abolitionists, the school was inte- grated from its inception. Angered by the integration as well as the school's abolitionist activ- ities, a mob of white men used oxen to drag the academy's main building into a swamp in 1835. After this incident, the three friends left Noyes to return to New York.

cringe and grovel, and there rose within him a protest and a prophecy. And he girded himself to walk down the world.

A voice and vision called him to be a priest,—a seer to lead the uncalled out of the house of bondage.[8] He saw the headless host turn toward him like the whirling of mad waters,—he stretched forth his hands eagerly, and then, even as he stretched them, suddenly there swept across the vision the temptation of Despair.

They were not wicked men,—the problem of life is not the problem of the wicked,—they were calm, good men, Bishops of the Apostolic Church of God, and strove toward righteousness. They said slowly, "It is all very natural—it is even commendable; but the General Theological Seminary of the Episcopal Church cannot admit a Negro." And when that thin, half-grotesque figure still haunted their doors, they put their hands kindly, half sorrowfully, on his shoulders, and said, "Now, —of course, we—we know how *you* feel about it; but you see it is impossible,—that is—well—it is premature. Sometime, we trust—sincerely trust—all such distinctions will fade away; but now the world is as it is."[9]

This was the temptation of Despair; and the young man fought it doggedly. Like some grave shadow he flitted by those halls, pleading, arguing, half angrily demanding admittance, until there came the final No; until men hustled the disturber away, marked him as foolish, unreasonable, and injudicious, a vain rebel against God's law. And then from that Vision Splendid all the glory faded slowly away, and left an earth gray and stern rolling on beneath a dark despair. Even the kind hands that stretched themselves toward him from out the depths of that dull morning seemed but parts of the purple shadows. He saw them coldly, and asked, "Why should I strive by special grace when the way of the world is closed to me?" All gently yet, the hands urged him on,—the hands of young John Jay,[1] that daring father's daring son; the hands of the good folk of Boston, that free city. And yet, with a way to the priesthood of the Church open at last before him, the cloud lingered there; and even when in old St. Paul's the venerable Bishop raised his white arms above the Negro deacon[2]—even then the burden had not lifted from that heart, for there had passed a glory from the earth.[3]

8. Du Bois presents Crummell as a new Moses.
9. In 1838, Benjamin T. Onderdonk, Episcopal bishop of New York, turned down Crummell's admission to the Episcopal General Theological Seminary.
1. Antislavery activist and politician (1817–1894). Son of abolitionist William Jay, and grandson and namesake of the first chief justice of the Supreme Court.
2. Crummell was ordained as a deacon in St. Paul's Episcopal Cathedral on May 30, 1842. In 1844, he was ordained to the Episcopal priesthood at St. Paul's Church in Philadelphia. Crummell's ordination, unlike his theological education, had followed the normal course for Episcopal clergy.
3. An allusion to William Wordsworth's Ode *Intimations of Immortality from Recollections of Early Childhood*: "That there hath past away a glory from the earth."

And yet the fire through which Alexander Crummell went did not burn in vain. Slowly and more soberly he took up again his plan of life. More critically he studied the situation. Deep down below the slavery and servitude of the Negro people he saw their fatal weaknesses, which long years of mistreatment had emphasized. The dearth of strong moral character, of unbending righteousness, he felt, was their great shortcoming, and here he would begin. He would gather the best of his people into some little Episcopal chapel and there lead, teach, and inspire them, till the leaven spread,[4] till the children grew, till the world hearkened, till—till—and then across his dream gleamed some faint after-glow of that first fair vision of youth—only an after-glow, for there had passed a glory from the earth.

One day—it was in 1842, and the springtide was struggling merrily with the May winds of New England—he stood at last in his own chapel in Providence, a priest of the Church.[5] The days sped by, and the dark young clergyman labored; he wrote his sermons carefully; he intoned his prayers with a soft, earnest voice; he haunted the streets and accosted the wayfarers; he visited the sick, and knelt beside the dying. He worked and toiled, week by week, day by day, month by month. And yet month by month the congregation dwindled, week by week the hollow walls echoed more sharply, day by day the calls came fewer and fewer, and day by day the third temptation sat clearer and still more clearly within the Veil; a temptation, as it were, bland and smiling, with just a shade of mockery in its smooth tones. First it came casually, in the cadence of a voice: "Oh, colored folks? Yes." Or perhaps more definitely: "What do you *expect*?" In voice and gesture lay the doubt—the temptation of Doubt. How he hated it, and stormed at it furiously! "Of course they are capable," he cried; "of course they can learn and strive and achieve—" and "Of course," added the temptation softly, "they do nothing of the sort." Of all the three temptations, this one struck the deepest. Hate? He had outgrown so childish a thing. Despair? He had steeled his right arm against it, and fought it with the vigor of determination. But to doubt the worth of his life-work,—to doubt the destiny and capability of the race his soul loved because it was his; to find listless squalor instead of eager endeavor; to hear his own lips whispering, "They do not care; they cannot know; they are dumb driven cattle,—why cast your pearls before swine?"[6]—this, this seemed more than man could bear; and he closed the door, and sank upon the steps of the chancel, and cast his robe upon the floor and writhed.

The evening sunbeams had set the dust to dancing in the gloomy chapel when he arose. He folded his vestments, put away the hymn-

---

4. In Mark 8.15, Jesus warns the disciples about the power of ideas when he says, "Take heed, beware of the leaven of the Pharisees and the leaven of Herod."
5. A small black congregation of Christ Church in Providence, Rhode Island.
6. Matthew 7.6.

books, and closed the great Bible. He stepped out into the twilight, looked back upon the narrow little pulpit with a weary smile, and locked the door. Then he walked briskly to the Bishop, and told the Bishop what the Bishop already knew. "I have failed," he said simply. And gaining courage by the confession, he added: "What I need is a larger constituency. There are comparatively few Negroes here, and perhaps they are not of the best. I must go where the field is wider, and try again." So the Bishop sent him to Philadelphia, with a letter to Bishop Onderdonk.[7]

Bishop Onderdonk lived at the head of six white steps,—corpulent, red-faced, and the author of several thrilling tracts on Apostolic Succession.[8] It was after dinner, and the Bishop had settled himself for a pleasant season of contemplation, when the bell must needs ring, and there must burst in upon the Bishop a letter and a thin, ungainly Negro. Bishop Onderdonk read the letter hastily and frowned. Fortunately, his mind was already clear on this point; and he cleared his brow and looked at Crummell. Then he said, slowly and impressively: "I will receive you into this diocese on one condition: no Negro priest can sit in my church convention, and no Negro church must ask for representation there."

I sometimes fancy I can see that tableau: the frail black figure, nervously twitching his hat before the massive abdomen of Bishop Onderdonk; his threadbare coat thrown against the dark woodwork of the book-cases, where Fox's "Lives of the Martyrs" nestled happily beside "The Whole Duty of Man."[9] I seem to see the wide eyes of the Negro wander past the Bishop's broadcloth to where the swinging glass doors of the cabinet glow in the sunlight. A little blue fly is trying to cross the yawning keyhole. He marches briskly up to it, peers into the chasm in a surprised sort of way, and rubs his feelers reflectively; then he essays its depths, and, finding it bottomless, draws back again. The dark-faced priest finds himself wondering if the fly too has faced its Valley of Humiliation, and if it will plunge into it,—when lo! it spreads its tiny wings and buzzes merrily across, leaving the watcher wingless and alone.

Then the full weight of his burden fell upon him. The rich walls wheeled away, and before him lay the cold rough moor winding on through life, cut in twain by one thick granite ridge,—here, the Valley of Humiliation; yonder, the Valley of the Shadow of Death. And I know

7. Bishop Henry U. Onderdonk of Philadelphia, not to be confused with his brother, Bishop Benjamin T. Onderdonk of New York, who refused Crummell's entry into the General Theological Seminary.
8. A doctrine held by certain Christian churches that Christ's apostles ordained the first bishops, who then ordained their successors, thus forging an unbroken chain of religious authority. Most Protestant churches, excepting Episcopalians, reject this doctrine.
9. A devotional text published anonymously in 1658. John Foxe (1516–1578), English clergyman. His Book of Martyrs was published in 1563.

not which be darker,—no, not I. But this I know: in yonder Vale of the Humble stand to-day a million swarthy men, who willingly would

> ". . . bear the whips and scorns of time,
> The oppressor's wrong, the proud man's contumely,
> The pangs of despised love, the law's delay,
> The insolence of office, and the spurns
> That patient merit of the unworthy takes,"[1]

all this and more would they bear did they but know that this were sacrifice and not a meaner thing. So surged the thought within that lone black breast. The Bishop cleared his throat suggestively; then, recollecting that there was really nothing to say, considerately said nothing, only sat tapping his foot impatiently. But Alexander Crummell said, slowly and heavily: "I will never enter your diocese on such terms." And saying this, he turned and passed into the Valley of the Shadow of Death. You might have noted only the physical dying, the shattered frame and hacking cough; but in that soul lay deeper death than that. He found a chapel in New York,—the church of his father;[2] he labored for it in poverty and starvation, scorned by his fellow priests. Half in despair, he wandered across the sea, a beggar with outstretched hands.[3] Englishmen clasped them,—Wilberforce and Stanley, Thirwell and Ingles, and even Froude and Macaulay; Sir Benjamin Brodie bade him rest awhile at Queen's College in Cambridge, and there he lingered, struggling for health of body and mind, until he took his degree in '53.[4] Restless still and unsatisfied, he turned toward Africa,[5] and for long years, amid the spawn of the slave-smugglers, sought a new heaven and a new earth.[6]

So the man groped for light; all this was not Life,—it was the world-wandering of a soul in search of itself, the striving of one who vainly sought his place in the world, ever haunted by the shadow of a death that is more than death,—the passing of a soul that has missed its duty. Twenty years he wandered,—twenty years and more; and yet the hard

1. From Shakespeare's *Hamlet* 3.1.72–76.
2. In 1845, Crummell became rector of the Church of the Messiah, the church his father attended.
3. In 1848, Crummell traveled to England and began his studies in Cambridge the following year.
4. Sir Benjamin Collins Brodie (1783–1862), English physiologist and surgeon; Samuel Wilberforce (1805–1873), Anglican bishop and son of abolitionist Samuel Wilberforce; Stanley may refer to Arthur Penrhyn (1815–1881), English author and clergyman; Connop Thirwell (1797–1875), historian and Anglican bishop; Ingles (probably) John Inglis, Anglican bishop of Nova Scotia; James Anthony Froude (1818–1894), English religious historian; Thomas Babington Macaulay (1800–1859), historian and political writer.
5. Crummell lived and worked in Liberia between 1853 and 1872 before returning to the United States.
6. From Revelation 21.1: "A new heaven and a new earth." This is a vision of the new Jerusalem, predicted by Isaiah, when all creation will be renewed, freed from imperfections, and transformed by the glory of God.

rasping question kept gnawing within him, "What, in God's name, am I on earth for?" In the narrow New York parish his soul seemed cramped and smothered. In the fine old air of the English University he heard the millions wailing over the sea. In the wild fever-cursed swamps of West Africa he stood helpless and alone.

You will not wonder at his weird pilgrimage,—you who in the swift whirl of living, amid its cold paradox and marvellous vision, have fronted life and asked its riddle face to face. And if you find that riddle hard to read, remember that yonder black boy finds it just a little harder; if it is difficult for you to find and face your duty, it is a shade more difficult for him; if your heart sickens in the blood and dust of battle, remember that to him the dust is thicker and the battle fiercer. No wonder the wanderers fall! No wonder we point to thief and murderer, and haunting prostitute, and the never-ending throng of unhearsed dead! The Valley of the Shadow of Death gives few of its pilgrims back to the world.

But Alexander Crummell it gave back. Out of the temptation of Hate, and burned by the fire of Despair, triumphant over Doubt, and steeled by Sacrifice against Humiliation, he turned at last home across the waters, humble and strong, gentle and determined. He bent to all the gibes and prejudices, to all hatred and discrimination, with that rare courtesy which is the armor of pure souls. He fought among his own, the low, the grasping, and the wicked, with that unbending righteousness which is the sword of the just. He never faltered, he seldom complained; he simply worked, inspiring the young, rebuking the old, helping the weak, guiding the strong.

So he grew, and brought within his wide influence all that was best of those who walk within the Veil. They who live without knew not nor dreamed of that full power within, that mighty inspiration which the dull gauze of caste decreed that most men should not know. And now that he is gone, I sweep the Veil away and cry, Lo! the soul to whose dear memory I bring this little tribute. I can see his face still, dark and heavy-lined beneath his snowy hair; lighting and shading, now with inspiration for the future, now in innocent pain at some human wickedness, now with sorrow at some hard memory from the past. The more I met Alexander Crummell, the more I felt how much that world was losing which knew so little of him. In another age he might have sat among the elders of the land in purple-bordered toga; in another country mothers might have sung him to the cradles.

He did his work,—he did it nobly and well; and yet I sorrow that here he worked alone, with so little human sympathy. His name today, in this broad land, means little, and comes to fifty million ears laden with no incense of memory or emulation. And herein lies the tragedy of the age: not that men are poor,—all men know something of poverty; not that men are wicked,—who is good? not that men are ignorant,—what is Truth? Nay, but that men know so little of men.

He sat one morning gazing toward the sea. He smiled and said, "The gate is rusty on the hinges." That night at star-rise a wind came moaning out of the west to blow the gate ajar, and then the soul I loved fled like a flame across the Seas, and in its seat sat Death.

I wonder where he is to-day? I wonder if in that dim world beyond, as he came gliding in, there rose on some wan throne a King,—a dark and pierced Jew, who knows the writhings of the earthly damned, saying, as he laid those heart-wrung talents[7] down, "Well done!" while round about the morning stars sat singing.[8]

XIII

Of the Coming of John[1]

What bring they 'neath the midnight,
   Beside the River-sea?
They bring the human heart wherein
   No nightly calm can be;
That droppeth never with the wind,
   Nor drieth with the dew;
O calm it, God; thy calm is broad
   To cover spirits too.
     The river floweth on.
       MRS. BROWNING.

Carlisle Street runs westward from the centre of Johnstown, across a great black bridge, down a hill and up again, by little shops and meat-

7. Ancient units of weight.
8. In this final paragraph Du Bois imagines Crummell in heaven, being praised by Jesus in the words of his parable of the talents, Matthew 25.14–30.
1. The verse is from Elizabeth Barrett Browning's *A Romance of the Ganges* (1838). The music quotation is from the Negro spiritual "You May Bury Me in the East," also called "I'll Hear the Trumpet Song."

markets, past single-storied homes, until suddenly it stops against a wide green lawn. It is a broad, restful place, with two large buildings outlined against the west. When at evening the winds come swelling from the east, and the great pall of the city's smoke hangs wearily above the valley, then the red west glows like a dreamland down Carlisle Street, and, at the tolling of the supper-bell, throws the passing forms of students in dark silhouette against the sky. Tall and black, they move slowly by, and seem in the sinister light to flit before the city like dim warning ghosts. Perhaps they are; for this is Wells Institute, and these black students have few dealings with the white city below.

And if you will notice, night after night, there is one dark form that ever hurries last and late toward the twinkling lights of Swain Hall,— for Jones is never on time. A long, straggling fellow he is, brown and hard-haired, who seems to be growing straight out of his clothes, and walks with a half-apologetic roll. He used perpetually to set the quiet dining-room into waves of merriment, as he stole to his place after the bell had tapped for prayers; he seemed so perfectly awkward. And yet one glance at his face made one forgive him much,—that broad, good-natured smile in which lay no bit of art or artifice, but seemed just bubbling good-nature and genuine satisfaction with the world.

He came to us from Altamaha, away down there beneath the gnarled oaks of Southeastern Georgia, where the sea croons to the sands and the sands listen till they sink half drowned beneath the waters, rising only here and there in long, low islands. The white folk of Altamaha voted John a good boy,[2]—fine plough-hand, good in the rice-fields, handy everywhere, and always good-natured and respectful. But they shook their heads when his mother wanted to send him off to school. "It'll spoil him,—ruin him," they said; and they talked as though they knew. But full half the black folk followed him proudly to the station, and carried his queer little trunk and many bundles. And there they shook and shook hands, and the girls kissed him shyly and the boys clapped him on the back. So the train came, and he pinched his little sister lovingly, and put his great arms about his mother's neck, and then was away with a puff and a roar into the great yellow world that flamed and flared about the doubtful pilgrim.[3] Up the coast they hurried, past the squares and palmettos of Savannah, through the cotton-fields and through the weary night, to Millville, and came with the morning to the noise and bustle of Johnstown.

And they that stood behind, that morning in Altamaha, and watched the train as it noisily bore playmate and brother and son away to the world, had thereafter one ever-recurring word,—"When John comes."

---

2. "Of the Coming of John" traces the transformation of an unaware young black man into a prophetic figure, specifically, John the Baptist.
3. As he did in Chapter XII, "Of Alexander Crummell," Du Bois again uses the theme of the pilgrim.

Then what parties were to be, and what speakings in the churches; what new furniture in the front room,—perhaps even a new front room; and there would be a new schoolhouse, with John as teacher; and then perhaps a big wedding; all this and more—when John comes. But the white people shook their heads.

At first he was coming at Christmas-time,—but the vacation proved too short; and then, the next summer,—but times were hard and schooling costly, and so, instead, he worked in Johnstown. And so it drifted to the next summer, and the next,—till playmates scattered, and mother grew gray, and sister went up to the Judge's kitchen to work. And still the legend lingered,—"When John comes."

Up at the Judge's they rather liked this refrain; for they too had a John—a fair-haired, smooth-faced boy, who had played many a long summer's day to its close with his darker namesake. "Yes, sir! John is at Princeton, sir,"[4] said the broad-shouldered gray-haired Judge every morning as he marched down to the post-office. "Showing the Yankees what a Southern gentleman can do," he added; and strode home again with his letters and papers. Up at the great pillared house they lingered long over the Princeton letter,—the Judge and his frail wife, his sister and growing daughters. "It'll make a man of him," said the Judge, "college is the place." And then he asked the shy little waitress, "Well, Jennie, how's your John?" and added reflectively, "Too bad, too bad your mother sent him off,—it will spoil him." And the waitress wondered.

Thus in the far-away Southern village the world lay waiting, half consciously, the coming of two young men, and dreamed in an inarticulate way of new things that would be done and new thoughts that all would think. And yet it was singular that few thought of two Johns,—for the black folk thought of one John, and he was black; and the white folk thought of another John, and he was white. And neither world thought the other world's thought, save with a vague unrest.

Up in Johnstown, at the Institute, we were long puzzled at the case of John Jones. For a long time the clay seemed unfit for any sort of moulding. He was loud and boisterous, always laughing and singing, and never able to work consecutively at anything. He did not know how to study; he had no idea of thoroughness; and with his tardiness, carelessness, and appalling good-humor, we were sore perplexed. One night we sat in faculty-meeting, worried and serious; for Jones was in trouble again. This last escapade was too much, and so we solemnly voted "that Jones, on account of repeated disorder and inattention to work, be suspended for the rest of the term."

It seemed to us that the first time life ever struck Jones as a really

4. Princeton University, the Ivy League school in Princeton, New Jersey, was founded in 1746. Wealthy southern families considered it a source of pride to send their young men to prestigious, northern universities.

serious thing was when the Dean told him he must leave school. He stared at the gray-haired man blankly, with great eyes. "Why,—why," he faltered, "but—I haven't graduated!" Then the Dean slowly and clearly explained, reminding him of the tardiness and the carelessness, of the poor lessons and neglected work, of the noise and disorder, until the fellow hung his head in confusion. Then he said quickly, "But you won't tell mammy and sister,—you won't write mammy, now will you? For if you won't I'll go out into the city and work, and come back next term and show you something." So the Dean promised faithfully, and John shouldered his little trunk, giving neither word nor look to the giggling boys, and walked down Carlisle Street to the great city, with sober eyes and a set and serious face.

Perhaps we imagined it, but someway it seemed to us that the serious look that crept over his boyish face that afternoon never left it again. When he came back to us he went to work with all his rugged strength. It was a hard struggle, for things did not come easily to him,—few crowding memories of early life and teaching came to help him on his new way; but all the world toward which he strove was of his own building, and he builded slow and hard. As the light dawned lingeringly on his new creations, he sat rapt and silent before the vision, or wandered alone over the green campus peering through and beyond the world of men into a world of thought. And the thoughts at times puzzled him sorely; he could not see just why the circle was not square, and carried it out fifty-six decimal places one midnight,—would have gone further, indeed, had not the matron rapped for lights out. He caught terrible colds lying on his back in the meadows of nights, trying to think out the solar system; he had grave doubts as to the ethics of the Fall of Rome, and strongly suspected the Germans of being thieves and rascals, despite his text-books; he pondered long over every new Greek word, and wondered why this meant that and why it couldn't mean something else, and how it must have felt to think all things in Greek. So he thought and puzzled along for himself,—pausing per-plexed where others skipped merrily, and walking steadily through the difficulties where the rest stopped and surrendered.

Thus he grew in body and soul, and with him his clothes seemed to grow and arrange themselves; coat sleeves got longer, cuffs appeared, and collars got less soiled. Now and then his boots shone, and a new dignity crept into his walk. And we who saw daily a new thoughtfulness growing in his eyes began to expect something of this plodding boy. Thus he passed out of the preparatory school into college, and we who watched him felt four more years of change, which almost transformed the tall, grave man who bowed to us commencement morning. He had left his queer thought-world and come back to a world of motion and of men. He looked now for the first time sharply about him, and wondered he had seen so little before. He grew slowly to feel almost for the first time the Veil that lay between him and the white world; he first noticed now the oppression that had not seemed oppression before, differences that erstwhile seemed natural, restraints and slights that in his boyhood days had gone unnoticed or been greeted with a laugh. He felt angry now when men did not call him "Mister," he clenched his hands at the "Jim Crow" cars, and chafed at the color-line that hemmed in him and his. A tinge of sarcasm crept into his speech, and a vague bitterness into his life; and he sat long hours wondering and planning a way around these crooked things. Daily he found himself shrinking from the choked and narrow life of his native town. And yet he always planned to go back to Altamaha,—always planned to work there. Still, more and more as the day approached he hesitated with a nameless dread; and even the day after graduation he seized with eagerness the offer of the Dean to send him North with the quartette during the summer vacation, to sing for the Institute. A breath of air before the plunge, he said to himself in half apology.

It was a bright September afternoon, and the streets of New York were brilliant with moving men. They reminded John of the sea, as he sat in the square and watched them, so changelessly changing, so bright and dark, so grave and gay. He scanned their rich and faultless clothes, the way they carried their hands, the shape of their hats; he peered into the hurrying carriages. Then, leaning back with a sigh, he said, "This is the World." The notion suddenly seized him to see where the world was going; since many of the richer and brighter seemed hurrying all one way. So when a tall, light-haired young man and a little talkative lady came by, he rose half hesitatingly and followed them. Up the street they went, past stores and gay shops, across a broad square, until with a hundred others they entered the high portal of a great building.

He was pushed toward the ticket-office with the others, and felt in his pocket for the new five-dollar bill he had hoarded. There seemed really no time for hesitation, so he drew it bravely out, passed it to the busy clerk, and received simply a ticket but no change. When at last he realized that he had paid five dollars to enter he knew not what, he stood stock-still amazed. "Be careful," said a low voice behind him; "you must not lynch the colored gentleman simply because he's in your way," and a girl looked up roguishly into the eyes of her fair-haired escort. A shade of annoyance passed over the escort's face. "You *will* not understand us at the South," he said half impatiently, as if continuing an argument. "With all your professions, one never sees in the North so cordial and intimate relations between white and black as are everyday occurrences with us. Why, I remember my closest playfellow in boyhood was a little Negro named after me, and surely no two,—*well!*" The man stopped short and flushed to the roots of his hair, for there directly beside his reserved orchestra chairs sat the Negro he had stumbled over in the hallway. He hesitated and grew pale with anger, called the usher and gave him his card, with a few peremptory words, and slowly sat down. The lady deftly changed the subject.

All this John did not see, for he sat in a half-maze minding the scene about him; the delicate beauty of the hall, the faint perfume, the moving myriad of men, the rich clothing and low hum of talking seemed all a part of a world so different from his, so strangely more beautiful than anything he had known, that he sat in dreamland, and started when, after a hush, rose high and clear the music of Lohengrin's swan.[5] The infinite beauty of the wail lingered and swept through every muscle of his frame, and put it all a-tune. He closed his eyes and grasped the elbows of the chair, touching unwittingly the lady's arm. And the lady drew away. A deep longing swelled in all his heart to rise with that clear music out of the dirt and dust of that low life that held him prisoned and befouled. If he could only live up in the free air where birds sang and setting suns had no touch of blood! Who had called him to be the slave and butt of all? And if he had called, what right had he to call when a world like this lay open before men?

Then the movement changed, and fuller, mightier harmony swelled away. He looked thoughtfully across the hall, and wondered why the beautiful gray-haired woman looked so listless, and what the little man could be whispering about. He would not like to be listless and idle, he thought, for he felt with the music the movement of power within him. If he but had some master-work, some life-service, hard,—aye, bitter hard, but without the cringing and sickening servility, without the cruel hurt that hardened his heart and soul. When at last a soft sorrow crept across the violins, there came to him the vision of a far-off home,—the great eyes of his sister, and the dark drawn face of his mother. And his heart sank below the waters, even as the sea-sand sinks by the shores of Altamaha, only to be lifted aloft again with that last ethereal wail of the swan that quivered and faded away into the sky.

It left John sitting so silent and rapt that he did not for some time notice the usher tapping him lightly on the shoulder and saying politely, "Will you step this way, please, sir?" A little surprised, he arose quickly at the last tap, and, turning to leave his seat, looked full into the face of the fair-haired young man. For the first time the young man recognized his dark boyhood playmate, and John knew that it was the Judge's son. The white John started, lifted his hand, and then froze into his chair; the black John smiled lightly, then grimly, and followed the usher down the aisle. The manager was sorry, very, very sorry,—but he explained that some mistake had been made in selling the gentleman a seat already disposed of; he would refund the money, of course,—and indeed felt the matter keenly, and so forth, and—before he had finished John was gone, walking hurriedly across the square and down the broad

5. The prelude to Richard Wagner's opera *Lohengrin* (1850). The swan represents a guide.

streets, and as he passed the park he buttoned his coat and said, "John Jones, you're a natural-born fool." Then he went to his lodgings and wrote a letter, and tore it up; he wrote another, and threw it in the fire. Then he seized a scrap of paper and wrote: "Dear Mother and Sister —I am coming—John."

"Perhaps," said John, as he settled himself on the train, "perhaps I am to blame myself in struggling against my manifest destiny[6] simply because it looks hard and unpleasant. Here is my duty to Altamaha plain before me; perhaps they'll let me help settle the Negro problems there,—perhaps they won't. 'I will go in to the King, which is not according to the law; and if I perish, I perish.' "[7] And then he mused and dreamed, and planned a life-work; and the train flew south.

Down in Altamaha, after seven long years, all the world knew John was coming. The homes were scrubbed and scoured,—above all, one; the gardens and yards had an unwonted trimness, and Jennie bought a new gingham. With some finesse and negotiation, all the dark Methodists and Presbyterians were induced to join in a monster welcome at the Baptist Church; and as the day drew near, warm discussions arose on every corner as to the exact extent and nature of John's accomplishments. It was noontide on a gray and cloudy day when he came. The black town flocked to the depot, with a little of the white at the edges,—a happy throng, with "Good-mawnings" and "Howdys" and laughing and joking and jostling. Mother sat yonder in the window watching; but sister Jennie stood on the platform, nervously fingering her dress,—tall and lithe, with soft brown skin and loving eyes peering from out a tangled wilderness of hair. John rose gloomily as the train stopped, for he was thinking of the "Jim Crow" car; he stepped to the platform, and paused: a little dingy station, a black crowd gaudy and dirty, a half-mile of dilapidated shanties along a straggling ditch of mud. An overwhelming sense of the sordidness and narrowness of it all seized him; he looked in vain for his mother, kissed coldly the tall, strange girl who called him brother, spoke a short, dry word here and there; then, lingering neither for hand-shaking nor gossip, started silently up the street, raising his hat merely to the last eager old aunty, to her openmouthed astonishment. The people were distinctly bewildered. This silent, cold man,—was this John? Where was his smile and hearty handgrasp? " 'Peared kind o' down in the mouf," said the Methodist preacher thoughtfully. "Seemed monstus stuck up," complained a Baptist sister. But the white postmaster from the edge of the crowd expressed the opinion of his folks plainly. "That damn Nigger," said he, as he shouldered the mail and arranged his tobacco, "has gone North

6. "Manifest destiny" was a phrase coined in 1845 to imply divine sanction for the United States to control the continent of North America.
7. Esther 4.16. In this Hebrew Scriptures passage, Esther decides to risk her life to save her people from persecution by Haman.

and got plum full o' fool notions; but they won't work in Altamaha."
And the crowd melted away.

The meeting of welcome at the Baptist Church was a failure. Rain
spoiled the barbecue, and thunder turned the milk in the ice-cream.
When the speaking came at night, the house was crowded to overflow-
ing. The three preachers had especially prepared themselves, but somehow John's manner seemed to throw a blanket over everything,—he
seemed so cold and preoccupied, and had so strange an air of restraint
that the Methodist brother could not warm up to his theme and elicited
not a single "Amen"; the Presbyterian prayer was but feebly responded
to, and even the Baptist preacher, though he wakened faint enthusiasm,
got so mixed up in his favorite sentence that he had to close it by
stopping fully fifteen minutes sooner than he meant. The people moved
uneasily in their seats as John rose to reply. He spoke slowly and me-
thodically. The age, he said, demanded new ideas; we were far different
from those men of the seventeenth and eighteenth centuries,—with
broader ideas of human brotherhood and destiny. Then he spoke of
the rise of charity and popular education, and particularly of the spread
of wealth and work. The question was, then, he added reflectively,
looking at the low discolored ceiling, what part the Negroes of this land
would take in the striving of the new century. He sketched in vague
outline the new Industrial School that might rise among these pines,
he spoke in detail of the charitable and philanthropic work that might
be organized, of money that might be saved for banks and business.
Finally he urged unity, and deprecated especially religious and denominational bickering. "To-day," he said, with a smile, "the world cares
little whether a man be Baptist or Methodist, or indeed a churchman
at all, so long as he is good and true. What difference does it make
whether a man be baptized in river or wash-bowl, or not at all? Let's
leave all that littleness, and look higher." Then, thinking of nothing
else, he slowly sat down. A painful hush seized that crowded mass.
Little had they understood of what he said, for he spoke an unknown
tongue,[8] save the last word about baptism; that they knew, and they sat
very still while the clock ticked. Then at last a low suppressed snarl
came from the Amen corner, and an old bent man arose, walked over
the seats, and climbed straight up into the pulpit. He was wrinkled and
black, with scant gray and tufted hair; his voice and hands shook as
with palsy; but on his face lay the intense rapt look of the religious
fanatic. He seized the Bible with his rough, huge hands; twice he raised
it inarticulate, and then fairly burst into words, with rude and awful
eloquence. He quivered, swayed, and bent; then rose aloft in perfect
majesty, till the people moaned and wept, wailed and shouted, and a

8. A reference to Acts 2.1–11. When the Holy Spirit descended upon the Apostles at Pentecost,
   they spoke in tongues (languages) that they did not know but that were interpreted by men
   from other nations. Here, however, John's meaning remains hidden.

wild shrieking arose from the corners where all the pent-up feeling of the hour gathered itself and rushed into the air.[9] John never knew clearly what the old man said; he only felt himself held up to scorn and scathing denunciation for trampling on the true Religion, and he realized with amazement that all unknowingly he had put rough, rude hands on something this little world held sacred. He arose silently, and passed out into the night. Down toward the sea he went, in the fitful starlight, half conscious of the girl who followed timidly after him. When at last he stood upon the bluff, he turned to his little sister and looked upon her sorrowfully, remembering with sudden pain how little thought he had given her. He put his arm about her and let her passion of tears spend itself on his shoulder.

Long they stood together, peering over the gray unresting water.

"John," she said, "does it make every one—unhappy when they study and learn lots of things?"

He paused and smiled. "I am afraid it does," he said.

"And, John, are you glad you studied?"

"Yes," came the answer, slowly but positively.

She watched the flickering lights upon the sea, and said thoughtfully, "I wish I was unhappy,—and—and," putting both arms about his neck, "I think I am, a little, John."

It was several days later that John walked up to the Judge's house to ask for the privilege of teaching the Negro school. The Judge himself met him at the front door, stared a little hard at him, and said brusquely, "Go 'round to the kitchen door, John, and wait." Sitting on the kitchen steps, John stared at the corn, thoroughly perplexed. What on earth had come over him? Every step he made offended some one. He had come to save his people, and before he left the depot he had hurt them. He sought to teach them at the church, and had outraged their deepest feelings. He had schooled himself to be respectful to the Judge, and then blundered into his front door. And all the time he had meant right,—and yet, and yet, somehow he found it so hard and strange to fit his old surroundings again, to find his place in the world about him. He could not remember that he used to have any difficulty in the past, when life was glad and gay. The world seemed smooth and easy then. Perhaps,—but his sister came to the kitchen door just then and said the Judge awaited him.

The Judge sat in the dining-room amid his morning's mail, and he did not ask John to sit down. He plunged squarely into the business. "You've come for the school, I suppose. Well, John, I want to speak to you plainly. You know I'm a friend to your people. I've helped you and your family, and would have done more if you had n't got the notion of going off. Now I like the colored people, and sympathize with all

9. This old man exhibits "the frenzy" that Du Bois discusses in Chapter X, "Of the Faith of the Fathers."

their reasonable aspirations; but you and I both know, John, that in this country the Negro must remain subordinate, and can never expect to be the equal of white men. In their place, your people can be honest and respectful; and God knows, I'll do what I can to help them. But when they want to reverse nature, and rule white men, and marry white women, and sit in my parlor, then, by God! we'll hold them under if we have to lynch every Nigger in the land. Now, John, the question is, are you, with your education and Northern notions, going to accept the situation and teach the darkies to be faithful servants and laborers as your fathers were,—I knew your father, John, he belonged to my brother, and he was a good Nigger. Well—well, are you going to be like him, or are you going to try to put fool ideas of rising and equality into these folks' heads, and make them discontented and unhappy?"

"I am going to accept the situation, Judge Henderson," answered John, with a brevity that did not escape the keen old man. He hesitated a moment, and then said shortly, "Very well,—we'll try you awhile. Good-morning."

It was a full month after the opening of the Negro school that the other John came home, tall, gay, and headstrong. The mother wept, the sisters sang. The whole white town was glad. A proud man was the Judge, and it was a goodly sight to see the two swinging down Main Street together. And yet all did not go smoothly between them, for the younger man could not and did not veil his contempt for the little town, and plainly had his heart set on New York. Now the one cherished ambition of the Judge was to see his son mayor of Altamaha, representative to the legislature, and—who could say?—governor of Georgia. So the argument often waxed hot between them. "Good heavens, father," the younger man would say after dinner, as he lighted a cigar and stood by the fireplace, "you surely don't expect a young fellow like me to settle down permanently in this—this God-forgotten town with nothing but mud and Negroes?" "I did," the Judge would answer laconically; and on this particular day it seemed from the gathering scowl that he was about to add something more emphatic, but neighbors had already begun to drop in to admire his son, and the conversation drifted.

"Heah that John is livenin' things up at the darky school," volunteered the postmaster, after a pause.

"What now?" asked the Judge, sharply.

"Oh, nothin' in particulah,—just his almighty air and uppish ways. B'lieve I did heah somethin' about his givin' talks on the French Revolution,[1] equality, and such like. He's what I call a dangerous Nigger."

"Have you heard him say anything out of the way?"

"Why, no,—but Sally, our girl, told my wife a lot of rot. Then, too,

---

1. The postmaster uses this allusion to the French Revolution in order to alarm the Judge, who would associate the egalitarian ideals of the French Revolution with bloody rebellion.

I don't need to heah: a Nigger what won't say 'sir' to a white man, or—"

"Who is this John?" interrupted the son.

"Why, it's little black John, Peggy's son,—your old playfellow."

The young man's face flushed angrily, and then he laughed.

"Oh," said he, "it's the darky that tried to force himself into a seat beside the lady I was escorting—"

But Judge Henderson waited to hear no more. He had been nettled all day, and now at this he rose with a half-smothered oath, took his hat and cane, and walked straight to the schoolhouse.

For John, it had been a long, hard pull to get things started in the rickety old shanty that sheltered his school. The Negroes were rent into factions for and against him, the parents were careless, the children irregular and dirty, and books, pencils, and slates largely missing. Nevertheless, he struggled hopefully on, and seemed to see at last some glimmering of dawn. The attendance was larger and the children were a shade cleaner this week. Even the booby class in reading showed a little comforting progress. So John settled himself with renewed patience this afternoon.

"Now, Mandy," he said cheerfully, "that's better; but you must n't chop your words up so: 'If—the—man—goes.' Why, your little brother even would n't tell a story that way, now would he?"

"Naw, suh, he cain't talk."

"All right; now let's try again: 'If the man—' "

"John!"

The whole school started in surprise, and the teacher half arose, as the red, angry face of the Judge appeared in the open doorway.

"John, this school is closed. You children can go home and get to work. The white people of Altamaha are not spending their money on black folks to have their heads crammed with impudence and lies. Clear out! I'll lock the door myself."

Up at the great pillared house the tall young son wandered aimlessly about after his father's abrupt departure. In the house there was little to interest him; the books were old and stale, the local newspaper flat, and the women had retired with headaches and sewing. He tried a nap, but it was too warm. So he sauntered out into the fields, complaining disconsolately, "Good Lord! how long will this imprisonment last!" He was not a bad fellow,—just a little spoiled and self-indulgent, and as headstrong as his proud father. He seemed a young man pleasant to look upon, as he sat on the great black stump at the edge of the pines idly swinging his legs and smoking. "Why, there isn't even a girl worth getting up a respectable flirtation with," he growled. Just then his eye caught a tall, willowy figure hurrying toward him on the narrow path. He looked with interest at first, and then burst into a laugh as he said, "Well, I declare, if it is n't Jennie, the little brown kitchen-maid! Why,

I never noticed before what a trim little body she is. Hello, Jennie! Why, you have n't kissed me since I came home," he said gaily. The young girl stared at him in surprise and confusion,—faltered something inarticulate, and attempted to pass. But a wilful mood had seized the young idler, and he caught at her arm. Frightened, she slipped by; and half mischievously he turned and ran after her through the tall pines.

Yonder, toward the sea, at the end of the path, came John slowly, with his head down. He had turned wearily homeward from the school-house; then, thinking to shield his mother from the blow, started to meet his sister as she came from work and break the news of his dismissal to her. "I'll go away," he said slowly; "I'll go away and find work, and send for them. I cannot live here longer." And then the fierce, buried anger surged up into his throat. He waved his arms and hurried wildly up the path.

The great brown sea lay silent. The air scarce breathed. The dying day bathed the twisted oaks and mighty pines in black and gold. There came from the wind no warning, not a whisper from the cloudless sky. There was only a black man hurrying on with an ache in his heart, seeing neither sun nor sea, but starting as from a dream at the frightened cry that woke the pines, to see his dark sister struggling in the arms of a tall and fair-haired man.

He said not a word, but, seizing a fallen limb, struck him with all the pent-up hatred of his great black arm; and the body lay white and still beneath the pines, all bathed in sunshine and in blood. John looked at it dreamily, then walked back to the house briskly, and said in a soft voice, "Mammy, I'm going away,—I'm going to be free."

She gazed at him dimly and faltered, "No'th, honey, is yo' gwine No'th agin?"

He looked out where the North Star glistened pale above the waters, and said, "Yes, mammy, I'm going—North."

Then, without another word, he went out into the narrow lane, up by the straight pines, to the same winding path, and seated himself on the great black stump, looking at the blood where the body had lain. Yonder in the gray past he had played with that dead boy, romping together under the solemn trees. The night deepened; he thought of the boys at Johnstown. He wondered how Brown had turned out, and Carey? And Jones,—Jones? Why, *he* was Jones, and he wondered what they would all say when they knew, when they knew, in that great long dining-room with its hundreds of merry eyes. Then as the sheen of the starlight stole over him, he thought of the gilded ceiling of that vast concert hall, and heard stealing toward him the faint sweet music of the swan. Hark! was it music, or the hurry and shouting of men? Yes, surely! Clear and high the faint sweet melody rose and fluttered like a living thing, so that the very earth trembled as with the tramp of horses and murmur of angry men.

He leaned back and smiled toward the sea, whence rose the strange melody, away from the dark shadows where lay the noise of horses galloping, galloping on. With an effort he roused himself, bent forward, and looked steadily down the pathway, softly humming the "Song of the Bride,"—

"Freulig geführt, ziehet dahin."[2]

Amid the trees in the dim morning twilight he watched their shadows dancing and heard their horses thundering toward him, until at last they came sweeping like a storm, and he saw in front that haggard white-haired man, whose eyes flashed red with fury. Oh, how he pitied him,—pitied him,—and wondered if he had the coiling twisted rope. Then, as the storm burst round him, he rose slowly to his feet and turned his closed eyes toward the Sea.

And the world whistled in his ears.

XIV

The Sorrow Songs[1]

I walk through the churchyard
To lay this body down;
I know moon-rise, I know star-rise;
I walk in the moonlight, I walk in the starlight;
I'll lie in the grave and stretch out my arms,
I'll go to judgment in the evening of the day,
And my soul and thy soul shall meet that day,
When I lay this body down.

NEGRO SONG.

They that walked in darkness sang songs in the olden days—Sorrow Songs—for they were weary at heart. And so before each thought that I have written in this book I have set a phrase, a haunting echo of these

2. An adaptation of the opening line of *Lohengrin's* "Wedding March." Du Bois has changed *treulich* (faithfully) to *freulig*: "Joyfully led, pass along to that place."
1. The verse is from the Negro spiritual "Lay This Body Down." The music quotation is from the Negro spiritual "Wrestlin' Jacob."

weird old songs in which the soul of the black slave spoke to men. Ever since I was a child these songs have stirred me strangely. They came out of the South unknown to me, one by one, and yet at once I knew them as of me and of mine. Then in after years when I came to Nashville I saw the great temple builded of these songs towering over the pale city. To me Jubilee Hall[2] seemed ever made of the songs themselves, and its bricks were red with the blood and dust of toil. Out of them rose for me morning, noon, and night, bursts of wonderful melody, full of the voices of my brothers and sisters, full of the voices of the past.

Little of beauty has America given the world save the rude grandeur God himself stamped on her bosom; the human spirit in this new world has expressed itself in vigor and ingenuity rather than in beauty. And so by fateful chance the Negro folk-song—the rhythmic cry of the slave—stands to-day not simply as the sole American music, but as the most beautiful expression of human experience born this side the seas. It has been neglected, it has been, and is, half despised, and above all it has been persistently mistaken and misunderstood; but notwithstanding, it still remains as the singular spiritual heritage of the nation and the greatest gift of the Negro people.

Away back in the thirties the melody of these slave songs stirred the nation, but the songs were soon half forgotten. Some, like "Near the lake where drooped the willow," passed into current airs and their source was forgotten; others were caricatured on the "minstrel" stage[3] and their memory died away. Then in war-time came the singular Port Royal experiment[4] after the capture of Hilton Head, and perhaps for the first time the North met the Southern slave face to face and heart to heart with no third witness. The Sea Islands of the Carolinas, where they met, were filled with a black folk of primitive type, touched and moulded less by the world about them than any others outside the Black Belt. Their appearance was uncouth, their language funny, but their hearts were human and their singing stirred men with a mighty power. Thomas Wentworth Higginson hastened to tell of these songs, and Miss McKim[5] and others urged upon the world their rare beauty. But the world listened only half credulously until the Fisk Jubilee Singers[6] sang

---

2. Jubilee Hall, a building at Fisk University in Nashville, was completed in 1875. The building was built with the proceeds from the Fisk Jubilee Singers' international singing tour.
3. A staged entertainment in which white performers in blackface sang and spoke in black dialect. Minstrels relied heavily on racial stereotypes.
4. See n. 2, p. 19.
5. Lucy McKim Garrison (1842–1877), daughter of an abolitionist. She collected and transcribed the lyrics of slave songs in South Carolina during the Civil War. Higginson (1823–1911) was a Union army officer who became the commander of a black regiment, The First South Carolina Volunteers. An abolitionist, he also wrote one of the first serious studies of black music, *The Spirituals*, (1867).
6. Chorus organized at Fisk University in 1867. Originally only eleven members, the group sang all kinds of music, but their fame was based on their presentation of the spirituals in stylized form.

the slave songs so deeply into the world's heart that it can never wholly forget them again.

There was once a blacksmith's son born at Cadiz, New York, who in the changes of time taught school in Ohio and helped defend Cincinnati from Kirby Smith.[7] Then he fought at Chancellorsville and Gettysburg[8] and finally served in the Freedman's Bureau at Nashville. Here he formed a Sunday-school class of black children in 1866, and sang with them and taught them to sing. And then they taught him to sing, and when once the glory of the Jubilee songs passed into the soul of George L. White,[9] he knew his life-work was to let those Negroes sing to the world as they had sung to him. So in 1871 the pilgrimage of the Fisk Jubilee Singers began. North to Cincinnati they rode,—four half-clothed black boys and five girl-women,—led by a man with a cause and a purpose. They stopped at Wilberforce, the oldest of Negro schools, where a black bishop blessed them. Then they went, fighting cold and starvation, shut out of hotels, and cheerfully sneered at, ever northward; and ever the magic of their song kept thrilling hearts, until a burst of applause in the Congregational Council at Oberlin[1] revealed them to the world. They came to New York and Henry Ward Beecher[2] dared to welcome them, even though the metropolitan dailies sneered at his "Nigger Minstrels." So their songs conquered till they sang across the land and across the sea, before Queen and Kaiser, in Scotland and Ireland, Holland and Switzerland. Seven years they sang, and brought back a hundred and fifty thousand dollars to found Fisk University.

Since their day they have been imitated—sometimes well, by the singers of Hampton and Atlanta, sometimes ill, by straggling quartettes. Caricature has sought again to spoil the quaint beauty of the music, and has filled the air with many debased melodies which vulgar ears scarce know from the real. But the true Negro folk-song still lives in the hearts of those who have heard them truly sung and in the hearts of the Negro people.

What are these songs, and what do they mean? I know little of music and can say nothing in technical phrase,[3] but I know something of men, and knowing them, I know that these songs are the articulate message of the slave to the world. They tell us in these eager days that life was joyous to the black slave, careless and happy. I can easily believe

---

7. Edmund Kirby Smith, Confederate general, led an invasion of Kentucky in 1862 that threatened Cincinnati.
8. Town in southern Pennsylvania. One of the bloodiest and most important battles of the Civil War, fought on July 3, 1863. Chancellorsville, Virginia, was the site of another battle in 1863.
9. Vocal music teacher at Fisk University. He founded the Jubilee Singers.
1. On November 15, 1871, the Fisk Jubilee Singers gained renown for their performance at a meeting of the National Council of Congregational Churches at Oberlin College.
2. Abolitionist (1813–1887) and brother of Harriet Beecher Stowe, was pastor of Plymouth Church in New York. His invitation to the Jubilee Singers to sing at his church increased their popularity.
3. Although not a musicologist, Du Bois knew more than a little about music. He was a member of Fisk's Mozart Society and sang in Handel's *Messiah*.

this of some, of many. But not all the past South, though it rose from the dead, can gainsay the heart-touching witness of these songs. They are the music of an unhappy people, of the children of disappointment; they tell of death and suffering and unvoiced longing toward a truer world, of misty wanderings and hidden ways.

The songs are indeed the siftings of centuries; the music is far more ancient than the words, and in it we can trace here and there signs of development. My grandfather's grandmother[4] was seized by an evil Dutch trader two centuries ago; and coming to the valleys of the Hudson and Housatonic, black, little, and lithe, she shivered and shrank in the harsh north winds, looked longingly at the hills, and often crooned a heathen melody[5] to the child between her knees, thus:

The child sang it to his children and they to their children's children, and so two hundred years it has travelled down to us and we sing it to our children, knowing as little as our fathers what its words may mean, but knowing well the meaning of its music.

This was primitive African music; it may be seen in larger form in the strange chant which heralds "The Coming of John":

> "You may bury me in the East,
> You may bury me in the West,
> But I'll hear the trumpet sound in that morning,"[6]

—the voice of exile.

Ten master songs, more or less, one may pluck from this forest of melody—songs of undoubted Negro origin and wide popular currency, and songs peculiarly characteristic of the slave. One of these I have just mentioned. Another whose strains begin this book is "Nobody knows

4. Tom Burghardt, Du Bois's grandfather's grandfather, was married to the ancestor Du Bois refers to here.
5. Unidentified.
6. From the Negro spiritual "You May Bury Me in the East," also called "I'll Hear the Trumpet Song."

the trouble I've seen." When, struck with a sudden poverty, the United States refused to fulfil its promises of land to the freedmen, a brigadier-general went down to the Sea Islands to carry the news. An old woman on the outskirts of the throng began singing this song; all the mass joined with her, swaying. And the soldier wept.

The third song is the cradle-song of death which all men know,—"Swing low, sweet chariot,"—whose bars begin the life story of "Alexander Crummell." Then there is the song of many waters, "Roll, Jordan, roll," a mighty chorus with minor cadences. There were many songs of the fugitive like that which opens "The Wings of Atalanta," and the more familiar "Been a-listening." The seventh is the song of the End and the Beginning—"My Lord, what a mourning! when the stars begin to fall"; a strain of this is placed before "The Dawn of Freedom." The song of groping—"My way's cloudy"—begins "The Meaning of Progress"; the ninth is the song of this chapter—"Wrestlin' Jacob, the day is a-breaking,"—a pæan of hopeful strife. The last master song is the song of songs—"Steal away,"—sprung from "The Faith of the Fathers."

There are many others of the Negro folk-songs as striking and characteristic as these, as, for instance, the three strains in the third, eighth, and ninth chapters; and others I am sure could easily make a selection on more scientific principles. There are, too, songs that seem to me a step removed from the more primitive types: there is the maze-like medley, "Bright sparkles," one phrase of which heads "The Black Belt"; the Easter carol, "Dust, dust and ashes"; the dirge, "My mother's took her flight and gone home"; and that burst of melody hovering over "The Passing of the First-Born"—"I hope my mother will be there in that beautiful world on high."

These represent a third step in the development of the slave song, of which "You may bury me in the East" is the first, and songs like "March on" (chapter six) and "Steal away" are the second. The first is African music, the second Afro-American, while the third is a blending of Negro music with the music heard in the foster land. The result is still distinctively Negro and the method of blending original, but the elements are both Negro and Caucasian. One might go further and find a fourth step in this development, where the songs of white America have been distinctively influenced by the slave songs or have incorporated whole phrases of Negro melody, as "Swanee River" and "Old Black Joe."[7] Side by side, too, with the growth has gone the debasements and imitations—the Negro "minstrel" songs, many of the "gospel" hymns, and some of the contemporary "coon" songs,[8]—a mass of music in which the novice may easily lose himself and never find the real Negro melodies.

7. Stephen Foster (1826–1864), who wrote both of these songs, was the most famous songwriter of his day.
8. Racist songs that were used in minstrel shows. They featured a character called Zip Coon.

In these songs, I have said, the slave spoke to the world. Such a message is naturally veiled and half articulate. Words and music have lost each other and new and cant phrases of a dimly understood theology have displaced the older sentiment. Once in a while we catch a strange word of an unknown tongue, as the "Mighty Myo," which figures as a river of death; more often slight words or mere doggerel are joined to music of singular sweetness. Purely secular songs are few in number, partly because many of them were turned into hymns by a change of words, partly because the frolics were seldom heard by the stranger, and the music less often caught. Of nearly all the songs, however, the music is distinctly sorrowful. The ten master songs I have mentioned tell in word and music of trouble and exile, of strife and hiding; they grope toward some unseen power and sigh for rest in the End.

The words that are left to us are not without interest, and, cleared of evident dross, they conceal much of real poetry and meaning beneath conventional theology and unmeaning rhapsody. Like all primitive folk, the slave stood near to Nature's heart. Life was a "rough and rolling sea" like the brown Atlantic of the Sea Islands; the "Wilderness" was the home of God, and the "lonesome valley" led to the way of life. "Winter'll soon be over," was the picture of life and death to a tropical imagination. The sudden wild thunder-storms of the South awed and impressed the Negroes,—at times the rumbling seemed to them "mournful," at times imperious:

> "My Lord calls me,
>   He calls me by the thunder,
>   The trumpet sounds it in my soul."[9]

The monotonous toil and exposure is painted in many words. One sees the ploughmen in the hot, moist furrow, singing:

> "Dere's no rain to wet you,
>   Dere's no sun to burn you,
>   Oh, push along, believer,
>   I want to go home."[1]

The bowed and bent old man cries, with thrice-repeated wail:

> "O Lord, keep me from sinking down,"

and he rebukes the devil of doubt who can whisper:

> "Jesus is dead and God's gone away."[2]

Yet the soul-hunger is there, the restlessness of the savage, the wail of the wanderer, and the plaint is put in one little phrase:[3]

9. From the Negro spiritual "Steal Away."
1. From the Negro spiritual "There's No Rain to Wet You."
2. From the Negro spiritual "Keep Me from Sinking Down."
3. From the Negro spiritual "My Soul Wants Something That's New."

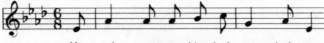

My soul wants some thing that's new, that's new

Over the inner thoughts of the slaves and their relations one with another the shadow of fear ever hung, so that we get but glimpses here and there, and also with them, eloquent omissions and silences. Mother and child are sung, but seldom father; fugitive and weary wanderer call for pity and affection, but there is little of wooing and wedding; the rocks and the mountains are well known, but home is unknown. Strange blending of love and helplessness sings through the refrain:

> "Yonder's my ole mudder,
>   Been waggin' at de hill so long;
>   'Bout time she cross over,
>   Git home bime-by."[4]

Elsewhere comes the cry of the "motherless" and the "Farewell, farewell, my only child."

Love-songs are scarce and fall into two categories—the frivolous and light, and the sad. Of deep successful love there is ominous silence, and in one of the oldest of these songs there is a depth of history and meaning:[5]

Poor Ro - sy, poor gal; Poor Ro - sy, poor gal; Ro - sy break my poor heart. Heav'n shall - a - be my home.

A black woman said of the song, "It can't be sung without a full heart and a troubled sperrit." The same voice sings here that sings in the German folk-song:

> "Jetz Geh i' an's brunele, trink' aber net."[6]

4. From the Negro spiritual "O'er the Crossing."
5. From the Negro spiritual "Poor Rosy."
6. From the German folk song "Jetzt gang I ans Brunnele," "Now I'm going to the well, but I will not drink."

Of death the Negro showed little fear, but talked of it familiarly and even fondly as simply a crossing of the waters, perhaps—who knows?—back to his ancient forests again. Later days transfigured his fatalism, and amid the dust and dirt the toiler sang:

> "Dust, dust and ashes, fly over my grave,
> But the Lord shall bear my spirit home."[7]

The things evidently borrowed from the surrounding world undergo characteristic change when they enter the mouth of the slave. Especially is this true of Bible phrases. "Weep, O captive daughter of Zion," is quaintly turned into "Zion, weep-a-low," and the wheels of Ezekiel[8] are turned every way in the mystic dreaming of the slave, till he says:

> "There's a little wheel a-turnin' in-a-my heart."[9]

As in olden time, the words of these hymns were improvised by some leading minstrel of the religious band. The circumstances of the gathering, however, the rhythm of the songs, and the limitations of allowable thought, confined the poetry for the most part to single or double lines, and they seldom were expanded to quatrains or longer tales, although there are some few examples of sustained efforts, chiefly paraphrases of the Bible. Three short series of verses have always attracted me,—the one that heads this chapter, of one line of which Thomas Wentworth Higginson has fittingly said, "Never, it seems to me, since man first lived and suffered was his infinite longing for peace uttered more plaintively." The second and third are descriptions of the Last Judgment,—the one a late improvisation, with some traces of outside influence:

> "Oh, the stars in the elements are falling,
> And the moon drips away into blood,
> And the ransomed of the Lord are returning unto God,
> Blessed be the name of the Lord."[1]

And the other earlier and homelier picture from the low coast lands:

> "Michael, haul the boat ashore,
> Then you'll hear the horn they blow,
> Then you'll hear the trumpet sound,
> Trumpet sound the world around,
> Trumpet sound for rich and poor,
> Trumpet sound the Jubilee,
> Trumpet sound for you and me."[2]

7. From the Negro spiritual "Dust and Ashes."
8. See Ezekiel 1.15–28.
9. From the Negro spiritual "There's a Little Wheel a-Turnin'."
1. From the Negro spiritual "My Lord, What a Mourning!"
2. From the Negro spiritual "Michael, Row the Boat Ashore."

Through all the sorrow of the Sorrow Songs there breathes a hope—a faith in the ultimate justice of things. The minor cadences of despair change often to triumph and calm confidence. Sometimes it is faith in life, sometimes a faith in death, sometimes assurance of boundless justice in some fair world beyond. But whichever it is, the meaning is always clear: that sometime, somewhere, men will judge men by their souls and not by their skins. Is such a hope justified? Do the Sorrow Songs sing true?

The silently growing assumption of this age is that the probation of races is past, and that the backward races of to-day are of proven inefficiency and not worth the saving. Such an assumption is the arrogance of peoples irreverent toward Time and ignorant of the deeds of men. A thousand years ago such an assumption, easily possible, would have made it difficult for the Teuton to prove his right to life. Two thousand years ago such dogmatism, readily welcome, would have scouted the idea of blond races ever leading civilization. So wofully unorganized is sociological knowledge that the meaning of progress, the meaning of "swift" and "slow" in human doing, and the limits of human perfectability, are veiled, unanswered sphinxes on the shores of science. Why should Æschylus[3] have sung two thousand years before Shakespeare was born? Why has civilization flourished in Europe, and flickered, flamed, and died in Africa? So long as the world stands meekly dumb before such questions, shall this nation proclaim its ignorance and unhallowed prejudices by denying freedom of opportunity to those who brought the Sorrow Songs to the Seats of the Mighty?

Your country? How came it yours? Before the Pilgrims[4] landed we were here. Here we have brought our three gifts and mingled them with yours: a gift of story and song—soft, stirring melody in an ill-harmonized and unmelodious land; the gift of sweat and brawn to beat back the wilderness, conquer the soil, and lay the foundations of this vast economic empire two hundred years earlier than your weak hands could have done it; the third, a gift of the Spirit. Around us the history of the land has centred for thrice a hundred years; out of the nation's heart we have called all that was best to throttle and subdue all that was worst; fire and blood, prayer and sacrifice, have billowed over this people, and they have found peace only in the altars of the God of Right. Nor has our gift of the Spirit been merely passive. Actively we have woven ourselves with the very warp and woof of this nation,—we fought their battles, shared their sorrow, mingled our blood with theirs, and generation after generation have pleaded with a headstrong, careless people to despise not Justice, Mercy, and Truth, lest the nation be smitten with a curse. Our song, our toil, our cheer, and warning have been given to this nation in blood-brotherhood. Are not these gifts

3. Ancient Greek poet and playwright (525–456 B.C.E.).
4. The pilgrims landed at Plymouth Rock, Massachusetts, in 1620. In Jamestown, Virginia, in 1619, the first Africans landed in North America. They were either slaves or indentured servants.

worth the giving? Is not this work and striving? Would America have been America without her Negro people?

Even so is the hope that sang in the songs of my fathers well sung. If somewhere in this whirl and chaos of things there dwells Eternal Good, pitiful yet masterful, then anon in His good time America shall rend the Veil and the prisoned shall go free. Free, free as the sunshine trickling down the morning into these high windows of mine, free as yonder fresh young voices welling up to me from the caverns of brick and mortar below—swelling with song, instinct with life, tremulous treble and darkening bass. My children, my little children, are singing to the sunshine, and thus they sing:[5]

5. From the Negro spiritual "Let Us Cheer the Weary Traveler."

And the traveller girds himself, and sets his face toward the Morning, and goes his way.

The After-Thought

Hear my cry, O God the Reader; vouchsafe that this my book fall not still-born into the world-wilderness. Let there spring, Gentle One, from out its leaves vigor of thought and thoughtful deed to reap the harvest wonderful. Let the ears of a guilty people tingle with truth, and seventy millions sigh for the righteousness which exalteth nations, in this drear day when human brotherhood is mockery and a snare. Thus in Thy good time may infinite reason turn the tangle straight, and these crooked marks on a fragile leaf be not indeed

THE END

CONTEXTS

Political Context

BOOKER T. WASHINGTON†

The Standard Printed Version of the
Atlanta Exposition Address

[Booker T. Washington delivered his "Atlanta Exposition Address," commonly referred to as the "Atlanta Compromise," in Atlanta, Georgia, on September 18, 1895, at the Cotton States Exposition. As well as strongly recommending industrial education for blacks, Washington asserted the accommodationist position that "the agitation of questions of social equality is the extremest folly." Du Bois would become the voice of opposition to these views; however, at the time, his response was flattering. The following brief letter from the young Wilberforce professor was written September 24, 1895:

My Dear Mr. Washington,

Let me congratulate you upon your phenomenal success at Atlanta—it was a word fitly spoken.

Sincerely Yours,
W. E. B. Du Bois

Washington published the text of his speech in his autobiography, *Up From Slavery* (1901).]

Mr. President and Gentlemen of the Board of Directors and Citizens: One-third of the population of the South is of the Negro race. No enterprise seeking the material, civil, or moral welfare of this section can disregard this element of our population and reach the highest success. I but convey to you, Mr. President and Directors, the sentiment of the masses of my race when I say that in no way have the value and manhood of the American Negro been more fittingly and generously recognized than by the managers of this magnificent Exposition at every stage of its progress. It is a recognition that will do more to cement the friendship of the two races than any occurrence since the dawn of our freedom.

Not only this, but the opportunity here afforded will awaken among us a new era of industrial progress. Ignorant and inexperienced, it is

† All notes are by the editors of this Norton Critical Edition.

not strange that in the first years of our new life we began at the top instead of at the bottom; that a seat in Congress or the state legislature was more sought than real estate or industrial skill; that the political convention or stump speaking had more attractions than starting a dairy farm or truck garden.

A ship lost at sea for many days suddenly sighted a friendly vessel. From the mast of the unfortunate vessel was seen a signal, "Water, water; we die of thirst!" The answer from the friendly vessel at once came back, "Cast down your bucket where you are." A second time the signal, "Water, water; send us water!" ran up from the distressed vessel, and was answered, "Cast down your bucket where you are." And a third and fourth signal for water was answered, "Cast down your bucket where you are." The captain of the distressed vessel, at last heeding the injunction, cast down his bucket, and it came up full of fresh, sparkling water from the mouth of the Amazon River. To those of my race who depend on bettering their condition in a foreign land or who underestimate the importance of cultivating friendly relations with the Southern white man, who is their next-door neighbour, I would say: "Cast down your bucket where you are"—cast it down in making friends in every manly way of the people of all races by whom we are surrounded.

Cast it down in agriculture, mechanics, in commerce, in domestic service, and in the professions. And in this connection it is well to bear in mind that whatever other sins the South may be called to bear, when it comes to business, pure and simple, it is in the South that the Negro is given a man's chance in the commercial world, and in nothing is this Exposition more eloquent than in emphasizing this chance. Our greatest danger is that in the great leap from slavery to freedom we may overlook the fact that the masses of us are to live by the productions of our hands, and fail to keep in mind that we shall prosper in proportion as we learn to dignify and glorify common labour, and put brains and skill into the common occupations of life; shall prosper in proportion as we learn to draw the line between the superficial and the substantial, the ornamental gewgaws of life and the useful. No race can prosper till it learns that there is as much dignity in tilling a field as in writing a poem. It is at the bottom of life we must begin, and not at the top. Nor should we permit our grievances to overshadow our opportunities.

To those of the white race who look to the incoming of those of foreign birth and strange tongue and habits for the prosperity of the South, were I permitted I would repeat what I say to my own race, "Cast down your bucket where you are." Cast it down among the eight millions of Negroes whose habits you know, whose fidelity and love you have tested in days when to have proved treacherous meant the ruin of your firesides. Cast down your bucket among these people who have, without strikes and labour wars, tilled your fields, cleared your

forests, builded your railroads and cities, and brought forth treasures
from the bowels of the earth, and helped make possible this magnificent
representation of the progress of the South. Casting down your bucket
among my people, helping and encouraging them as you are doing on
these grounds, and to education of head, hand, and heart, you will find
that they will buy your surplus land, make blossom the waste places in
your fields, and run your factories. While doing this, you can be sure
in the future, as in the past, that you and your families will be surrounded by the most patient, faithful, law-abiding, and unresentful people that the world has seen. As we have proved our loyalty to you in
the past, in nursing your children, watching by the sick-bed of your
mothers and fathers, and often following them with tear-dimmed eyes
to their graves, so in the future, in our humble way, we shall stand by
you with a devotion that no foreigner can approach, ready to lay down
our lives, if need be, in defense of yours, interlacing our industrial,
commercial, civil, and religious life with yours in a way that shall make
the interests of both races one. In all things that are purely social we
can be as separate as the fingers, yet one as the hand in all things
essential to mutual progress.

There is no defense or security for any of us except in the highest
intelligence and development of all. If anywhere there are efforts tending to curtail the fullest growth of the Negro, let these efforts be turned
into stimulating, encouraging, and making him the most useful and
intelligent citizen. Effort or means so invested will pay a thousand per
cent interest. These efforts will be twice blessed—"blessing him that
gives and him that takes."[1]

There is no escape through law of man or God from the inevitable:—

> "The laws of changeless justice bind
>   Oppressor with oppressed;
> And close as sin and suffering joined
>   We march to fate abreast."[2]

Nearly sixteen millions of hands will aid you in pulling the load
upward, or they will pull against you the load downward. We shall
constitute one-third and more of the ignorance and crime of the South,
or one-third its intelligence and progress; we shall contribute one-third
to the business and industrial prosperity of the South, or we shall prove

1. From Shakespeare's *The Merchant of Venice* 4.1: "The quality of mercy is not strained. / It
droppeth as the gentle rain from heaven / Upon the place beneath. It is twice blest / It blesseth
him that gives, and him that takes."
2. From John Greenleaf Whittier's 1862 poem *At Port Royal*, which commemorated the November 1861 capture of Port Royal by Union forces led by Commodore Dupont and General
Sherman. With Union forces in place, one of the first opportunities arose for virtual emancipation of the slave population. The middle portion of this eighteen-stanza poem, *Song of
the Negro Boatmen*, is written in dialect form.

a veritable body of death, stagnating, depressing, retarding every effort to advance the body politic.

Gentlemen of the Exposition, as we present to you our humble effort at an exhibition of our progress, you must not expect overmuch. Starting thirty years ago with ownership here and there in a few quilts and pumpkins and chickens (gathered from miscellaneous sources), remember the path that has led from these to the inventions and production of agricultural implements, buggies, steam-engines, newspapers, books, statuary, carving, paintings, the management of drug stores and banks, has not been trodden without contact with thorns and thistles. While we take pride in what we exhibit as a result of our independent efforts, we do not for a moment forget that our part in this exhibition would fall far short of your expectations but for the constant help that has come to our educational life, not only from the Southern states, but especially from Northern philanthropists, who have made their gifts a constant stream of blessing and encouragement.

The wisest among my race understand that the agitation of questions of social equality is the extremest folly, and that progress in the enjoyment of all the privileges that will come to us must be the result of severe and constant struggle rather than of artificial forcing. No race that has anything to contribute to the markets of the world is long in any degree ostracized. It is important and right that all privileges of the law be ours, but it is vastly more important that we be prepared for the exercise of these privileges. The opportunity to earn a dollar in a factory just now is worth infinitely more than the opportunity to spend a dollar in an opera-house.

In conclusion, may I repeat that nothing in thirty years has given us more hope and encouragement, and drawn us so near to you of the white race, as this opportunity offered by the Exposition; and here bending, as it were, over the altar that represents the results of the struggles of your race and mine, both starting practically empty-handed three decades ago, I pledge that in your effort to work out the great and intricate problem which God has laid at the doors of the South, you shall have at all times the patient, sympathetic help of my race; only let this be constantly in mind, that, while from representations in these buildings of the product of field, of forest, of mine, of factory, letters, and art, much good will come, yet far above and beyond material benefits will be that higher good, that, let us pray God, will come, in a blotting out of sectional differences and racial animosities and suspicions, in a determination to administer absolute justice, in a willing obedience among all classes to the mandates of law. This, coupled with our material prosperity, will bring into our beloved South a new heaven and a new earth.

W. E. B. DU BOIS

[Obituary of Booker T. Washington]

[When Booker T. Washington died in 1915, some of Du Bois's supporters were concerned that Du Bois might write a shamefully brief obituary. However his article, published in *The Crisis* in December 1915, was generous to his old rival.]

The death of Mr. Washington marks an epoch in the history of America. He was the greatest Negro leader since Frederick Douglass, and the most distinguished man, white or black, who has come out of the South since the Civil War. His fame was international and his influence far-reaching. Of the good that he accomplished there can be no doubt: he directed the attention of the Negro race in America to the pressing necessity of economic development; he emphasized technical education and he did much to pave the way for an understanding between the white and darker races.

On the other hand there can be no doubt of Mr. Washington's mistakes and short comings: he never adequately grasped the growing bond of politics and industry; he did not understand the deeper foundations of human training and his basis of better understanding between white and black was founded on caste.

We may then generously and with deep earnestness lay on the grave of Booker T. Washington testimony of our thankfulness for his undoubted help in the accumulation of Negro land and property, his establishment of Tuskegee and spreading of industrial education and his compelling of the white south to at least think of the Negro as a possible man.

On the other hand, in stern justice, we must lay on the soul of this man, a heavy responsibility for the consummation of Negro disfranchisement, the decline of the Negro college and public school and the firmer establishment of color caste in this land.

What is done is done. This is no fit time for recrimination or complaint. Gravely and with bowed head let us receive what this great figure gave of good, silently rejecting all else. Firmly and unfalteringly let the Negro race in America, in bleeding Hayti and throughout the world close ranks and march steadily on, determined as never before to work and save and endure, but never to swerve from their great goal: the right to vote, the right to know, and the right to stand as men among men throughout the world.

It is rumored that Mr. Washington's successor at Tuskegee will be Robert Russa Moton, Commandant of Cadets at Hampton. If this proves true Major Moton will enter on his new duties with the sympathy and good will of his many friends both black and white.

ALEXANDER CRUMMELL

Civilization, the Primal Need of the Race†

[Alexander Crummell, partly in response to the overwhelming popularity of Washington's plan for industrial education, organized the American Negro Academy in March 1897. As its first president Crummell gave the inaugural address, "Civilization, the Primal Need of the Race." His lecture was a call to high culture, linking civilization to the production of "letters, literature, science, philosophy* * *architecture* * *all the arts." Du Bois also appeared that March morning and gave an address, "The Conservation of Races" (see page 176), which discussed the race question in the context of American individualism. Although Du Bois's listeners were initially more confused than edified by his paper, it has since been seen as a complicated and erudite assault against racism.]

GENTLEMEN:—

There is no need, I apprehend, that I should undertake to impress you with a sense either of the need or of the importance of our assemblage here to-day. The fact of your coming here is, of itself, the clearest evidence of your warm acquiescence in the summons to this meeting, and of your cordial interest in the objects which it purposes to consider.

Nothing has surprised and gratified me so much as the anxiousness of many minds for the movement which we are on the eve of beginning. In the letters which our Secretary, Mr. Cromwell, has received, and which will be read to us, we are struck by the fact that one cultured man here and another there,—several minds in different localities,— tell him that this is just the thing they have desired, and have been looking for.

I congratulate you, therefore, gentlemen, on the opportuneness of your assemblage here. I felicitate you on the superior and lofty aims which have drawn you together. And, in behalf of your compeers, resident here in the city of Washington, I welcome you to the city and to the important deliberations to which our organization invites you.

Just here, let me call your attention to the uniqueness and specialty of this conference. It is unlike any other which has ever taken place in the history of the Negro, on the American Continent. There have been, since the landing of the first black cargo of slaves at Jamestown, Va., in 1619, numerous conventions of men of our race. There have been Religious Assemblies, Political Conferences, suffrage meetings, educa-

† All notes are by the editors of this Norton Critical Edition.

tional conventions. But *our* meeting is for a purpose which, while inclusive, in some respects, of these various concerns, is for an object
more distinct and positive than any of them.

What then, it may be asked, is the special undertaking we have before
us, in this Academy? My answer is the civilization of the Negro race
in the United States, by the scientific processes of literature, art, and
philosophy, through the agency of the cultured men of this same Negro
race. And here, let me say, that the special race problem of the Negro
in the United States is his civilization.

I doubt if there is a man in this presence who has a higher conception of Negro capacity than your speaker; and this of itself, precludes
the idea, on my part, of race disparagement. But, it seems manifest to
me that, as a race in this land, we have no art; we have no science; we
have no philosophy; we have no scholarship. Individuals we have in
each of these lines; but mere individuality cannot be recognized as the
aggregation of a family, a nation, or a race; or as the interpretation of
any of them. And until we attain the role of civilization, we cannot
stand up and hold our place in the world of culture and enlightenment.
And the forfeiture of such a place means, despite, inferiority, repulsion,
drudgery, poverty, and ultimate death! Now gentlemen, for the creation
of a complete and rounded man, you need the impress and the moulding of the highest arts. But how much more so for the realizing of a
true and lofty *race* of men. What is true of a man is deeply true of a
people. The special need in such a case is the force and application of
the highest arts; not mere mechanism; not mere machinery; not mere
handicraft; not the mere grasp on material things; not mere temporal
ambitions. These are but incidents; important indeed, but pertaining
mainly to man's material needs, and to the feeding of the body. And
the incidental in life is incapable of feeding the living soul. For "man
cannot live by bread alone, but by every word that proceedeth out of
the mouth of God."[1] And civilization is the *secondary* word of God,
given for the nourishment of humanity.

To make *men* you need civilization; and what I mean by civilization
is the action of exalted forces, both of God and man. For manhood is
the most majestic thing in God's creation; and hence the demand for
the very highest art in the shaping and moulding of human souls.

What is the great difficulty with the black race, in this era, in this
land? It is that both within their ranks, and external to themselves, by
large schools of thought interested in them, material ideas in divers
forms are made prominent, as the master-need of the race, and as the
surest way to success. Men are constantly dogmatizing theories of sense
and matter as the salvable hope of the race. Some of our leaders and
teachers boldly declare, now, that *property* is the source of power; and

---

1. From Matthew 4.4. See also Deuteronomy 8.3 and Luke 4.4.

then, that *money* is the thing which commands respect. At one time it is *official position* which is the masterful influence in the elevation of the race; at another, men are disposed to fall back upon *blood* and *lineage*, as the root (source) of power and progress.

Blind men! For they fail to see that neither property, nor money, nor station, nor office, nor lineage, are fixed factors, in so large a thing as the destiny of man; that they are not vitalizing qualities in the changeless hopes of humanity. The greatness of peoples springs from their ability to grasp the grand conceptions of being. It is the absorption of a people, of a nation, of a race, in large majestic and abiding things which lifts them up to the skies. These once apprehended, all the minor details of life follow in their proper places, and spread abroad in the details and the comfort of practicality. But until these gifts of a lofty civilization are secured, men are sure to remain low, debased and grovelling.

It was the apprehension of this great truth which led Melancthon,[2] 400 years ago, to declare—"Unless we have the scientific mind we shall surely revert again to barbarism." He was a scholar and a classic, a theologian and a philosopher. With probably the exception of Erasmus,[3] he was the most erudite man of his age. He was the greatest Grecian of his day. He was rich "with the spoils of time."[4] And so running down the annals of the ages, he discovered the majestic fact, which Coleridge has put in two simple lines:

> "We may not hope from outward things to win
> The passion and the life whose fountains are within;"[5]

which Wordsworth, in grand style, has declared,

> "By the soul only the nations shall be free."[6]

But what is this other than the utterance of Melancthon,—"Without the scientific mind, barbarism." This is the teaching of history. For 2,000 years, Europe has been governed, in all its developments, by Socrates, and Aristotle, and Plato, and Euclid. These were the great idealists; and as such, they were the great progenitors of all modern civilization, the majestic agents of God for the civil upbuilding of men and nations. For civilization is, in its origins, ideal; and hence, in the loftiest men, it bursts forth, producing letters, literature, science, philosophy, poetry, sculpture, architecture, yea, all the arts; and brings them with all their gifts, and lays them in the lap of religion, as the essential condition of their vital permanence and their continuity.

But civilization never seeks permanent abidence upon the heights of

2. Philip Melancthon (1497–1560), humanist, theologian, and friend of Martin Luther.
3. Desiderius Erasmus (1469–1536), humanist and scholar during the Renaissance.
4. From Thomas Gray (1716–1771), *Elegy Written in a Country Churchyard*.
5. From Samuel Taylor Coleridge (1772–1834), *Dejection: An Ode*.
6. From William Wordsworth (1770–1850), *September, 1802, Near Dover*.

Olympus. She is human, and seeks all human needs. And so she descends, recreating new civilizations; uplifting the crudeness of laws, giving scientific precision to morals and religion, stimulating enterprise, extending commerce, creating manufactures, expanding mechanism and mechanical inventions; producing revolutions and reforms; humanizing labor; meeting the minutest human needs, even to the manufacturing needles for the industry of seamstresses and for the commonest uses of the human fingers. All these are the fruits of civilization.

Who are to be the agents to lift up this people of ours to the grand plane of civilization? Who are to bring them up to the height of noble thought, grand civility, a chaste and elevating culture, refinement, and the impulses of irrepressible progress? It is to be done by the scholars and thinkers, who have secured the vision which penetrates the center of nature, and sweeps the circles of historic enlightenment; and who have got insight into the life of things, and learned the art by which men touch the springs of action.

For to transform and stimulate the souls of a race or a people is a work of intelligence. It is a work which demands the clear induction of worldwide facts, and the perception of their application to new circumstances. It is a work which will require the most skillful resources, and the use of the scientific spirit.

But every man in a race cannot be a philosopher: nay, but few men in any land, in any age, can grasp ideal truth. Scientific ideas however must be apprehended, else there can be no progress, no elevation.

Just here arises the need of the trained and scholarly men of a race to employ their knowledge and culture and teaching and to guide both the opinions and habits of the crude masses. The masses, nowhere are, or can be, learned or scientific. The scholar is exceptional, just the same as a great admiral like Nelson[7] is, or a grand soldier like Caesar or Napoleon. But the leader, the creative and organizing mind, is the master-need in all the societies of man. But, if they are not inspired with the notion of leadership and duty, then with all their Latin and Greek and science they are but pedants, trimmers, opportunists. For all true and lofty scholarship is weighty with the burdens and responsibilities of life and humanity.

But these reformers must not be mere scholars. They must needs be both scholars and philanthropists. For thus, indeed, has it been in all the history of men. In all the great revolutions, and in all great reforms which have transpired, scholars have been conspicuous; in the reconstruction of society, in formulating laws, in producing great emancipations, in the revival of letters, in the advancement of science, in the renaissance of art, in the destruction of gross superstitions and in the restoration of true and enlightened religion.

7. Horatio Nelson (1758–1805), English admiral, defeated the French fleet at the battle of Trafalgar (1805).

And what is the spirit with which they are to come to this work? My answer is, that *disinterestedness* must animate their motives and their acts. Whatever rivalries and dissensions may divide man in the social or political world, let generosity govern *us*. Let us emulate one another in the prompt recognition of rare genius, or uncommon talent. Let there be no tardy acknowledgement of worth in *our* world of intellect. If we are fortunate enough, to see, of a sudden, a clever mathematician of our class, a brilliant poet, a youthful, but promising scientist or philosopher, let us rush forward, and hail his coming with no hesitant admiration, with no reluctant praise.

It is only thus, gentlemen, that we can bring forth, stimulate, and uplift all the latent genius, garnered up, in the by-places and sequestered corners of this neglected Race.

It is only thus we can nullify and break down the conspiracy which would fain limit and narrow the range of Negro talent in this caste-tainted country. It is only thus, we can secure that recognition of genius and scholarship in the republic of letters, which is the rightful prerogative of every race of men. It is only thus we can spread abroad and widely disseminate that culture and enlightenment which shall permeate and leaven the entire social and domestic life of our people and so give that civilization which is the nearest ally of religion.

W. E. B. DU BOIS

The Conservation of Races†

The American Negro has always felt an intense personal interest in discussions as to the origins and destinies of races: primarily because back of most discussions of race with which he is familiar, have lurked certain assumptions as to his natural abilities, as to his political, intellectual and moral status, which he felt were wrong. He has, consequently, been led to deprecate and minimize race distinctions, to believe intensely that out of one blood God created all nations, and to speak of human brotherhood as though it were the possibility of an already dawning to-morrow.

Nevertheless, in our calmer moments we must acknowledge that human beings are divided into races; that in this country the two most extreme types of the world's races have met, and the resulting problem as to the future relations of these types is not only of intense and living interest to us, but forms an epoch in the history of mankind.

It is necessary, therefore, in planning our movements, in guiding our

---

† American Negro Academy, *Occasional Papers*, No. 2, 1897. All notes are by the editors of this Norton Critical Edition.

future development, that at times we rise above the pressing, but smaller
questions of separate schools and cars, wage-discrimination and lynch
law, to survey the whole question of race in human philosophy and to
lay, on a basis of broad knowledge and careful insight, those large lines
of policy and higher ideals which may form our guiding lines and
boundaries in the practical difficulties of every day. For it is certain
that all human striving must recognize the hard limits of natural law,
and that any striving, no matter how intense and earnest, which is
against the constitution of the world, is vain. The question, then, which
we must seriously consider is this: What is the real meaning of Race;
what has, in the past, been the law of race development, and what
lessons has the past history of race development to teach the rising
Negro people?

When we thus come to inquire into the essential difference of races
we find it hard to come at once to any definite conclusion. Many
criteria of race differences have in the past been proposed, as color,
hair, cranial measurements and language. And manifestly, in each of
these respects, human beings differ widely. . . . All these physical characteristics are patent enough, and if they agreed with each other it
would be very easy to classify mankind. Unfortunately for scientists,
however, these criteria of race are most exasperatingly intermingled.
Color does not agree with texture of hair, for many of the dark races
have straight hair; nor does color agree with the breadth of the head,
for the yellow Tartar has a broader head than the German; nor, again,
has the science of language as yet succeeded in clearing up the relative
authority of these various and contradictory criteria. The final word of
science, so far, is that we have at least two, perhaps three, great families of human beings—the whites and Negroes, possibly the yellow
race. . . .

Although the wonderful developments of human history teach that
the grosser physical differences of color, hair and bone go but a short
way toward explaining the different roles which groups of men have
played in Human Progress, yet there are differences—subtle, delicate
and elusive, though they may be—which have silently but definitely
separated men into groups. While these subtle forces have generally
followed the natural cleavage of common blood, descent and physical
peculiarities, they have at other times swept across and ignored these.
At all times, however, they have divided human beings into races,
which, while they perhaps transcend scientific definition, nevertheless,
are clearly defined to the eye of the Historian and Sociologist.

If this be true, then the history of the world is the history, not of
individuals, but of groups, not of nations, but of races, and he who
ignores or seeks to override the race idea in human history ignores and
overrides the central thought of all history. What, then, is a race? It is
a vast family of human beings, generally of common blood and lan-

guage, always of common history, traditions and impulses, who are both voluntarily and involuntarily striving together for the accomplishment of certain more or less vividly conceived ideals of life.

Turning to real history, there can be no doubt, first, as to the widespread, nay, universal, prevalence of the race idea, the race spirit, the race ideal, and as to its efficiency as the vastest and most ingenious invention for human progress. We, who have been reared and trained under the individualistic philosophy of the Declaration of Independence and the laisser-faire philosophy of Adam Smith,[1] are loath to see and loath to acknowledge this patent fact of human history. We see the Pharaohs, Caesars, Toussaints[2] and Napoleons of history and forget the vast races of which they were but epitomized expressions. We are apt to think in our American impatience, that while it may have been true in the past that closed race groups made history, that here in conglomerate America *nous avons changer tout cela*—we have changed all that, and have no need of this ancient instrument of progress. This assumption of which the Negro people are especially fond, cannot be established by a careful consideration of history.

We find upon the world's stage today eight distinctly differentiated races, in the sense in which History tells us the word must be used. They are, the Slavs of eastern Europe, the Teutons of middle Europe, the English of Great Britain and America, the Romance nations of Southern and Western Europe, the Negroes of Africa and America, the Semitic people of Western Asia and Northern Africa, the Hindoos of Central Asia and the Mongolians of Eastern Asia. There are, of course, other minor race groups, as the American Indians, the Esquimaux and the South Sea Islanders; . . .

The question now is: What is the real distinction between these nations? Is it the physical differences of blood, color and cranial measurements? Certainly we must all acknowledge that physical differences play a great part, and that, with wide exceptions and qualifications, these eight great races of to-day follow the cleavage of physical race distinctions; . . . But while race differences have followed mainly physical race lines, yet no mere physical distinctions would really define or explain the deeper differences—the cohesiveness and continuity of these groups. The deeper differences are spiritual, psychical, differences—undoubtedly based on the physical, but infinitely transcending them. The forces that bind together the Teuton nations are, then, first, their race identity and common blood; secondly, and more important, a common history, common laws and religion, similar habits of thought and a conscious striving together for certain ideals of life.

1. A philosophy that opposes government regulation of or interference in commerce. Adam Smith (1723–1790), one of the most influential political economists of Western society, believed that the general welfare was best served by permitting each person to pursue his or her own interests.
2. See n. 5, p. 15.

The whole process which has brought about these race differentiations has been a growth, and the great characteristic of this growth has been the differentiation of spiritual and mental differences between great races of mankind and the integration of physical differences.

The age of nomadic tribes of closely related individuals represents the maximum of physical differences. They were practically vast families, and there were as many groups as families. As the families came together to form cities the physical differences lessened, purity of blood was replaced by the requirement of domicile, and all who lived within the city bounds became gradually to be regarded as members of the group; i.e., there was a slight and slow breaking down of physical barriers. This, however, was accompanied by an increase of the spiritual and social differences between cities. This city became husbandmen,[3] this, merchants, another warriors, and so on. The *ideals of life* for which the different cities struggled were different. When at last cities began to coalesce into nations there was another breaking down of barriers which separated groups of men. The larger and broader differences of color, hair and physical proportions were not by any means ignored, but myriads of minor differences disappeared, and the sociological and historical races of men began to approximate the present division of races as indicated by physical researches. At the same time the spiritual and physical differences of race groups which constituted the nations became deep and decisive. . . . striving, each in its own way, to develop for civilization its particular message, its particular ideal, which shall help to guide the world nearer and nearer that perfection of human life for which we all long, that

"one far off Divine event."[4]

This has been the function of race differences up to the present time. What shall be its function in the future? Manifestly some of the great races of today—particularly the Negro race—have not as yet given to civilization the full spiritual message which they are capable of giving. I will not say that the Negro race has as yet given no message to the world, for it is still a mooted question among scientists as to just how far Egyptian civilization was Negro in its origin; if it was not wholly Negro, it was certainly very closely allied. Be that as it may, however, the fact still remains that the full, complete Negro message of the whole Negro race has not as yet been given to the world: that the messages and ideal of the yellow race have not been completed, and that the striving of the mighty Slavs has but begun. The question is, then: How shall this message be delivered; how shall these various ideals be real-

3. A person whose occupation is husbandry; a farmer.
4. From the epilogue to Alfred, Lord Tennyson's *In Memoriam* (1850), the final stanza: "That God, which ever lives and loves, / One God, one law, one element, / And one far-off divine event, / To which the whole creation moves".

ized? The answer is plain: By the development of these race groups, not as individuals, but as races. . . . We cannot reverse history; we are subject to the same natural laws as other races, and if the Negro is ever to be a factor in the world's history—if among the gaily-colored banners that deck the broad ramparts of civilization is to hang one uncompromising black, then it must be placed there by black hands, fashioned by black heads and hallowed by the travail of 200,000,000 black hearts beating in one glad song of jubilee.

For this reason, the advance guard of the Negro people—the 8,000,000 people of Negro blood in the United States of America— must soon come to realize that if they are to take their just place in the van of Pan-Negroism, then their destiny is *not* absorption by the white Americans. That if in America it is to be proven for the first time in the modern world that not only Negroes are capable of evolving individual men like Toussaint, the Saviour, but are a nation stored with wonderful possibilities of culture, then their destiny is not a servile imitation of Anglo-Saxon culture, but a stalwart originality which shall unswervingly follow Negro ideals.

It may, however, be objected here that the situation of our race in America renders this attitude impossible; that our sole hope of salvation lies in our being able to lose our race identity in the commingled blood of the nation; and that any other course would merely increase the friction of races which we call race prejudice, and against which we have so long and so earnestly fought.

Here, then, is the dilemma, and it is a puzzling one, I admit. No Negro who has given earnest thought to the situation of his people in America has failed, at some time in life, to find himself at these crossroads; has failed to ask himself at some time: What, after all, am I? Am I an American or am I a Negro? Can I be both? Or is it my duty to cease to be a Negro as soon as possible and be an American? If I strive as a Negro, am I not perpetuating the very cleft that threatens and separates Black and White America? Is not my only possible practical aim the subduction of all that is Negro in me to the American? Does my black blood place upon me any more obligation to assert my nationality than German, or Irish or Italian blood would?

It is such incessant self-questioning and the hesitation that arises from it, that is making the present period a time of vacillation and contradiction for the American Negro; combined race action is stifled, race responsibility is shirked, race enterprises languish, and the best blood, the best talent, the best energy of the Negro people cannot be marshalled to do the bidding of the race. They stand back to make room for every rascal and demagogue who chooses to cloak his selfish deviltry under the veil of race pride.

Is this right? Is it rational? Is it good policy? Have we in America a distinct mission as a race—a distinct sphere of action and an opportunity for race development, or is self-obliteration the highest end to which Negro blood dare aspire?

If we carefully consider what race prejudice really is, we find it, historically, to be nothing but the friction between different groups of people; it is the difference in aim, in feeling, in ideals of two different races; if, now, this difference exists touching territory, laws, language, or even religion, it is manifest that these people cannot live in the same territory without fatal collision; but if, on the other hand, there is substantial agreement in laws, language and religion; if there is a satisfactory adjustment of economic life, then there is no reason why, in the same country and on the same street, two or three great national ideals might not thrive and develop, that men of different races might not strive together for their race ideals as well, perhaps even better, than in isolation. Here, it seems to me, is the reading of the riddle that puzzles so many of us. We are Americans, not only by birth and by citizenship, but by our political ideals, our language, our religion. Farther than that, our Americanism does not go. At that point, we are Negroes, members of a vast historic race that from the very dawn of creation has slept, but half awakening in the dark forests of its African fatherland. We are the first fruits of this new nation, the harbinger of that black to-morrow which is yet destined to soften the whiteness of the Teutonic to-day. We are that people whose subtle sense of song has given America its only American music, its only American fairy tales, its only touch of pathos and humor amid its mad money-getting plutocracy. As such, it is our duty to conserve our physical powers, our intellectual endowments, our spiritual ideals; as a race we must strive by race organization, by race solidarity, by race unity to the realization of that broader humanity which freely recognizes differences in men, but sternly deprecates inequality in their opportunities of development.

For the accomplishment of these ends we need race organizations: Negro colleges, Negro newspapers, Negro business organizations, a Negro school of literature and art, and an intellectual clearing house, for all these products of the Negro mind, which we may call a Negro Academy. Not only is all this necessary for positive advance, it is absolutely imperative for negative defense. Let us not deceive ourselves at our situation in this country. Weighted with a heritage of moral iniquity from our past history, hard pressed in the economic world by foreign immigrants and native prejudice, hated here, despised there and pitied everywhere; our one haven of refuge is ourselves, and but one means of advance, our own belief in our great destiny, our own implicit trust in our ability and worth. There is no power under God's high heaven that can stop the advance of eight thousand thousand honest, earnest, inspired and united people. But—and here is the rub—they *must* be honest, fearlessly criticising their own faults, zealously correcting them; they must be *earnest*. No people that laughs at itself, and ridicules itself, and wishes to God it was anything but itself ever wrote its name in history; it *must* be inspired with the Divine faith of our black mothers, that out of the blood and dust of battle will march a victorious host, a mighty nation, a peculiar people, to speak to the nations of earth a Divine truth that shall make them free. And such a people must be united; not merely united for the organized theft of political spoils, not united to disgrace religion with whoremongers and ward-heelers;[5] not united merely to protest and pass resolutions, but united to stop the ravages of consumption among the Negro people, united to keep black boys from loafing, gambling and crime; united to guard the purity of black women and to reduce that vast army of black prostitutes that is today marching to hell; and united in serious organizations, to determine by careful conference and thoughtful interchange of opinion the broad lines of policy and action for the American Negro.

This is the reason for being which the American Negro Academy has. It aims at once to be the epitome and expression of the intellect of the black-blooded people of America, the exponent of the race ideals of one of the world's great races. As such, the Academy must, if successful, be

  (a). Representative in character.
  (b). Impartial in conduct.
  (c). Firm in leadership. . . .

In the field of Sociology an appalling work lies before us. First, we must unflinchingly and bravely face the truth, not with apologies, but with solemn earnestness. The Negro Academy ought to sound a note of warning that would echo in every black cabin in the land: *Unless we conquer our present vices they will conquer us*; we are diseased, we are developing criminal tendencies, and an alarmingly large percentage of our men and women are sexually impure. The Negro Academy should stand and proclaim this over the housetops, crying with Garrison: *I will not equivocate, I will not retreat a single inch, and I will be heard.*[6] The Academy should seek to gather about it the talented, unselfish men, the pure and noble-minded women, to fight an army of devils that disgraces our manhood and our womanhood. There does not stand today upon God's earth a race more capable in muscle, in intellect, in morals, than the American Negro, if he will bend his energies in the right direction; if he will

> Burst his birth's invidious bar
> And grasp the skirts of happy chance,

5. Slang for a worker in the ward organization of a political machine.
6. William Lloyd Garrison (1805–1879), American leader of the abolitionist movement, who crusaded against slavery, war, and capital punishment. The quote is from his antislavery journal *The Liberator*, which he published from 1831 until 1865.

And breast the blows of circumstance,
And grapple with his evil star.[7]

In science and morals, I have indicated two fields of work for the Academy. Finally, in practical policy, I wish to suggest the following *Academy Creed*:

1. We believe that the Negro people, as a race, have a contribution to make to civilization and humanity, which no other race can make.

2. We believe it the duty of the Americans of Negro descent, as a body, to maintain their race identity until this mission of the Negro people is accomplished, and the ideal of human brotherhood has become a practical possibility.

3. We believe that, unless modern civilization is a failure, it is entirely feasible and practicable for two races in such essential political, economic, and religious harmony as the white and colored people of America, to develop side by side in peace and mutual happiness, the peculiar contribution which each has to make to the culture of their common country.

4. As a means to this end we advocate, not such social equality between these races as would disregard human likes and dislikes, but such a social equilibrium as would, throughout all the complicated relations of life, give due and just consideration to culture, ability, and moral worth, whether they be found under white or black skins.

5. We believe that the first and greatest step toward the settlement of the present friction between the races—commonly called the Negro Problem—lies in the correction of the immorality, crime and laziness among the Negroes themselves, which still remains as a heritage from slavery. We believe that only earnest and long continued efforts on our own part can cure these social ills.

6. We believe that the second great step toward a better adjustment of the relations between the races should be a more impartial selection of ability in the economic and intellectual world, and a greater respect for personal liberty and worth, regardless of race. We believe that only earnest efforts on the part of the white people of this country will bring much needed reform in these matters.

7. On the basis of the foregoing declaration, and firmly believing in our high destiny, we, as American Negroes, are resolved to strive in every honorable way for the realization of the best and highest aims, for the development of strong manhood and pure womanhood, and for the rearing of a race ideal in America and Africa, to the glory of God and the uplifting of the Negro people.

7. From Section 64 of Alfred, Lord Tennyson's *In Memoriam* (1850) in which the actions of "some divinely gifted man" whose life began "on a simple village green" are described.

W. E. B. DU BOIS

The Niagara Movement

Address to the Country†

[Although in existence for only five years, the Niagara Movement was well known for its uncompromising, confrontational civil rights agenda. At its second annual meeting W. E. B. Du Bois presented the following "Address to the Country" in which he proclaimed, "We will not be satisfied to take one jot or tittle less than our full manhood rights."]

The men of the Niagara Movement coming from the toil of the year's hard work and pausing a moment from the earning of their daily bread turn toward the nation and again ask in the name of ten million the privilege of a hearing. In the past year the work of the Negro hater has flourished in the land. Step by step the defenders of the rights of American citizens have retreated. The work of stealing the black man's ballot has progressed and the fifty and more representatives of stolen votes still sit in the nation's capital. Discrimination in travel and public accommodation has so spread that some of our weaker brethren are actually afraid to thunder against color discrimination as such and are simply whispering for ordinary decencies.

Against this the Niagara Movement eternally protests. We will not be satisfied to take one jot or tittle less than our full manhood rights. We claim for ourselves every single right that belongs to a freeborn American, political, civil and social; and until we get these rights we will never cease to protest and assail the ears of America. The battle we wage is not for ourselves alone but for all true Americans. It is a fight for ideals, lest this, our common fatherland, false to its founding, become in truth the land of the thief and the home of the Slave—a by-word and a hissing among the nations for its sounding pretentions and pitiful accomplishment.

Never before in the modern age has a great and civilized folk threatened to adopt so cowardly a creed in the treatment of its fellow-citizens born and bred on its soil. Stripped of verbiage and subterfuge and in its naked nastiness the new American creed says: Fear to let black men even try to rise lest they become the equals of the white. And this is the land that professes to follow Jesus Christ. The blasphemy of such a course is only matched by its cowardice.

In detail our demands are clear and unequivocal. First, we would vote; with the right to vote goes everything: Freedom, manhood, the honor of your wives, the chastity of your daughters, the right to work,

† A two-page leaflet (1906). All notes are by the editors of this Norton Critical Edition.

and the chance to rise, and let no man listen to those who deny this.

We want full manhood suffrage, and we want it now, henceforth and forever.

Second. We want discrimination in public accommodation to cease. Separation in railway and street cars, based simply on race and color, is un-American, un-democratic, and silly. We protest against all such discrimination.

Third. We claim the right of freemen to walk, talk, and be with them that wish to be with us. No man has a right to choose another man's friends, and to attempt to do so is an impudent interference with the most fundamental human privilege.

Fourth. We want the laws enforced against rich as well as poor; against Capitalist as well as Laborer; against white as well as black. We are not more lawless than the white race, we are more often arrested, convicted, and mobbed. We want justice even for criminals and outlaws. We want the Constitution of the country enforced. We want Congress to take charge of Congressional elections. We want the Fourteenth amendment[1] carried out to the letter and every State disfranchised in Congress which attempts to disfranchise its rightful voters. We want the Fifteenth amendment[2] enforced and No State allowed to base its franchise simply on color.

The failure of the Republican Party in Congress at the session just closed to redeem its pledge of 1904 with reference to suffrage conditions at the South seems a plain, deliberate, and premeditated breach of promise, and stamps that party as guilty of obtaining votes under false pretense.

Fifth. We want our children educated. The school system in the country districts of the South is a disgrace and in few towns and cities are the Negro schools what they ought to be. We want the national government to step in and wipe out illiteracy in the South. Either the United States will destroy ignorance or ignorance will destroy the United States.

And when we call for education we mean real education. We believe in work. We ourselves are workers, but work is not necessarily education. Education is the development of power and ideal. We want our children trained as intelligent human beings should be, and we will fight for all time against any proposal to educate black boys and girls simply as servants and underlings, or simply for the use of other people. They have a right to know, to think, to aspire.

These are some of the chief things which we want. How shall we get them? By voting where we may vote, by persistent, unceasing agitation; by hammering at the truth, by sacrifice and work.

We do not believe in violence, neither in the despised violence of

1. See n. 3, p. 17.
2. See n. 7, p. 13.

the raid nor the lauded violence of the soldier, nor the barbarous violence of the mob, but we do believe in John Brown,[3] in that incarnate spirit of justice, that hatred of a lie, that willingness to sacrifice money, reputation, and life itself on the altar of right. And here on the scene of John Brown's martyrdom we reconsecrate ourselves, our honor, our property to the final emancipation of the race which John Brown died to make free.

Our enemies, triumphant for the present, are fighting the stars in their courses. Justice and humanity must prevail. We live to tell these dark brothers of ours—scattered in counsel, wavering and weak—that no bribe of money or notoriety, no promise of wealth or fame, is worth the surrender of a people's manhood or the loss of a man's self-respect. We refuse to surrender the leadership of this race to cowards and trucklers. We are men; we will be treated as men. On this rock we have planted our banners. We will never give up, though the trump of doom find us still fighting.

And we shall win. The past promised it, the present foretells it. Thank God for John Brown! Thank God for Garrison and Douglass! Sumner and Phillips, Nat Turner and Robert Gould Shaw,[4] and all the hallowed dead who died for freedom! Thank God for all those to-day, few though their voices be, who have not forgotten the divine brotherhood of all men white and black, rich and poor, fortunate and unfortunate.

We appeal to the young men and women of this nation, to those whose nostrils are not yet befouled by greed and snobbery and racial narrowness: Stand up for the right, prove yourselves worthy of your heritage and whether born north or south dare to treat men as men. Cannot the nation that has absorbed ten million foreigners into its political life without catastrophe absorb ten million Negro Americans into that same political life at less cost than their unjust and illegal exclusion will involve?

Courage brothers! The battle for humanity is not lost or losing. All across the skies sit signs of promise. The Slav is raising in his might, the yellow millions are tasting liberty, the black Africans are writhing toward the light, and everywhere the laborer, with ballot in his hand, is voting open the gates of Opportunity and Peace. The morning breaks over blood-stained hills. We must not falter, we may not shrink. Above are the everlasting stars.

---

3. See n. 8, p. 39.
4. Union Army Civil War hero. Shaw (1837–1863), son of a white, prominent, Boston family, led the first regiment of black troops to be raised in a free state. He was killed in battle attacking Fort Wagner, South Carolina. For Garrison, see n. 5, p. 155; for Douglass, n. 7, p. 39; for Sumner, n. 5, p. 22; for Turner, n. 3, p. 38.

Personal Context

W. E. B. DU BOIS

[Application Letter to Harvard]

[A folder in the office of the registrar at Harvard University contains the following application letter from W. E. B. Du Bois dated October 29, 1887. Written from Fisk University, it is addressed to the secretary of Harvard University. Accompanying this letter were numerous letters of recommendation—ranging from one by his high school principal to one from the president of Fisk—that were also sent by Du Bois. Although they all praise Du Bois's intellect and hard work, Herbert Aptheker notes that one six-page letter from Professor Frederick A. Chase, of the physical science department at Fisk, indicates that Du Bois might convey "the impression of being conceited."]

Dear Sir:

I am a Negro, a student of Fisk University. I shall receive the degree of A.B. from this institution next June at the age of 20. I wish to pursue at Harvard a course of study for the degree of Ph.D. in Political Science after graduation. I am poor and if I should enter your college next year would probably not be able to raise more [than] $100 or $150. If I should teach a year and then enter I could earn enough to pay my expenses for a year. I wish your advice as to what I had better do. You can see by the catalogue I shall send herewith what our course of instruction is here. I can furnish satisfactory certificates of character and scholarship from the President and Professors of Fisk, and from Western Massachusetts where I was born, and graduated from the Public Schools. I am also Editor of the Fisk Herald. As I said I wish your advice as to whether I had better teach a year or two or come immediately after graduation. I expect to take the special field of Political Economy.

I am, Sir,
Yours,
W. E. B. Du Bois

[W. E. B. DU BOIS]

From A Negro Student at Harvard at the End of the Nineteenth Century†

[The Harvard Archives owns a variant version of this memoir by W. E. B. Du Bois, and his 1968 *Autobiography* contains the same essential information. For other African American responses to the Harvard experience, see *Black at Harvard*, edited by Werner Sollors.]

* * *

Following the attitudes which I had adopted in the South, I sought no friendships among my white fellow students, nor even acquaintance-ships. Of course I wanted friends, but I could not seek them. My class was large—some three hundred students. I doubt if I knew a dozen of them. I did not seek them, and naturally they did not seek me. I made no attempt to contribute to the college periodicals since the editors were not interested in my major interests. But I did have a good singing voice and loved music, so I entered the competition for the Glee Club. I ought to have known that Harvard could not afford to have a Negro on its Glee Club travelling about the country. Quite naturally I was rejected.

I was happy at Harvard, but for unusual reasons. One of these was my acceptance of racial segregation. Had I gone from Great Barrington High School directly to Harvard, I would have sought companionship with my white fellows and been disappointed and embittered by a dis-covery of social limitations to which I had not been used. But I came by way of Fisk and the South and there I had accepted color caste and embraced eagerly the companionship of those of my own color. This was of course no final solution. Eventually, in mass assault, led by culture, we Negroes were going to break down the boundaries of race; but at present we were banded together in a great crusade, and happily so. Indeed, I suspect that the prospect of ultimate full human inter-course, without reservations and annoying distinctions, made me all too willing to consort with my own and to disdain and forget as far as was possible that outer, whiter world.

In general, I asked nothing of Harvard but the tutelage of teachers and the freedom of the laboratory and library. I was quite voluntarily and willingly outside its social life. I sought only such contacts with white teachers as lay directly in the line of my work. I joined certain clubs, like the Philosophical Club; I was a member of the Foxcroft

† Reprinted from *The Massachusetts Review: A Quarterly of Literature, the Arts and Public Affairs* (1960): 74–76, 79, 81–83. © 1960 The Massachusetts Review, Inc. All notes are by the editors of this Norton Critical Edition.

Dining Club because it was cheap. James[1] and one or two other teachers had me at their homes at meal and reception. I escorted colored girls to various gatherings, and as pretty ones as I could find to the vesper exercises, and later to the class day and commencement social functions. Naturally we attracted attention and the *Crimson* noted my girl friends. Sometimes the shadow of insult fell, as when at one reception a white woman seemed determined to mistake me for a waiter.

In general, I was encased in a completely colored world, self-sufficient and provincial, and ignoring just as far as possible the white world which conditioned it. This was self-protective coloration, with perhaps an inferiority complex, but with belief in the ability and future of black folk.

My friends and companions were drawn mainly from the colored students of Harvard and neighboring institutions, and the colored folk of Boston and surrounding towns. With them I led a happy and inspiring life. There were among them many educated and well-to-do folk, many young people studying or planning to study, many charming young women. We met and ate, danced and argued, and planned a new world.

Towards whites I was not arrogant; I was simply not obsequious, and to a white Harvard student of my day a Negro student who did not seek recognition was trying to be more than a Negro. The same Harvard man had much the same attitude toward Jews and Irishmen.

I was, however, exceptional among Negroes at Harvard in my ideas on voluntary race segregation. They for the most part saw salvation only in integration at the earliest moment and on almost any terms in white culture; I was firm in my criticism of white folk and in my dream of a self-sufficient Negro culture even in America.

This cutting of myself off from my white fellows, or being cut off, did not mean unhappiness or resentment. I was in my early manhood, unusually full of high spirits and humor. I thoroughly enjoyed life. I was conscious of understanding and power, and conceited enough still to imagine, as in high school, that they who did not know me were the losers, not I. On the other hand, I do not think that my white classmates found me personally objectionable. I was clean, not well-dressed but decently clothed. Manners I regarded as more or less superfluous and deliberately cultivated a certain brusquerie. Personal adornment I regarded as pleasant but not important. I was in Harvard, but not of it, and realized all the irony of my singing "Fair Harvard." I sang it because I liked the music, and not from any pride in the Pilgrims.

With my colored friends I carried on lively social intercourse, but

1. William James (1842–1910), American philosopher and psychologist. James originated the doctrine of pragmatism. His first major work, *The Principles of Psychology*, appeared in 1890. Among his philosophical treatises, *The Varieties of Religious Experience* (1902) became his best known. After his years at Harvard, Du Bois corresponded with James, who furnished Du Bois with a letter of introduction to his brother Henry James, the famous novelist.

necessarily one which involved little expenditure of money. I called at
their homes and ate at their tables. We danced at private parties. We
went on excursions down the Bay. Once, with a group of colored students gathered from surrounding institutions, we gave Aristophanes' *The
Birds* in a Boston colored church. The rendition was good, but not outstanding, not quite appreciated by the colored audience, but well worth
doing. Even though it worked me near to death, I was proud of it.

*   *   *

Harvard of this day was a great opportunity for a young man and a
young American Negro and I realized it. I formed habits of work rather
different from those of most of the other students. I burned no midnight
oil. I did my studying in the daytime and had my day parceled out
almost to the minute. I spent a great deal of time in the library and
did my assignments with thoroughness and with prevision of the kind
of work I wanted to do later. From the beginning my relations with
most of the teachers at Harvard were pleasant. They were on the whole
glad to receive a serious student, to whom extracurricular activities were
not of paramount importance, and one who in a general way knew
what he wanted.

*   *   *

I was repeatedly a guest in the home of William James; he was my
friend and guide to clear thinking; as a member of the Philosophical
Club I talked with Royce and Palmer;[2] I remember vividly once standing beside Mrs. Royce at a small reception. We ceased conversation for
a moment and both glanced across the room. Professor Royce was opposite talking excitedly. He was an extraordinary sight: a little body,
indifferently clothed; a big, red-thatched head and blazing blue eyes.
Mrs. Royce put my thoughts into words: "Funny-looking man, isn't
he?" I nearly fainted! Yet I knew how she worshipped him.

I sat in an upper room and read Kant's *Critique* with Santayana;
Shaler invited a Southerner, who objected to sitting beside me, to leave
his class; he said he wasn't doing very well, anyway. I became one of
Hart's[3] favorite pupils and was afterwards guided by him through my

2. George Herbert Palmer (1842–1933) instructed Du Bois in his popular class, Philosophy 4.
Strongly influenced by his New England Puritanism, Palmer published his best work, *The
Nature of Goodness*, in 1903. Josiah Royce (1855–1916), American philosopher and proponent
of Idealism. His best known works are *The World and the Individual* (1902) and *The Problem
of Christianity* (1913).
3. Albert Bushnell Hart, American historian, directed Du Bois's doctoral thesis. Although an
ardent supporter of Du Bois's scholarship, Hart asserted in *The Southern South* (1910) that
the experience of African Americans "leads to negative rather than positive conclusions as to
their intellectual and moral power." George Santayana (1863–1952), Spanish-born philosopher, wrote on aesthetics and empiricism. Du Bois took the first courses taught by Santayana
at Harvard. Nathanael Shaler, a Kentucky-born scientist, taught Du Bois in his introduction
to geology (Natural History 4). In a letter of recommendation, Shaler describes Du Bois as
"decidedly the best specimen of his race we have had in our classes."

graduate course and started on my work in Germany. Most of my courses of study went well. It was in English that I came nearest my Waterloo at Harvard. I had unwittingly arrived at Harvard in the midst of a violent controversy about poor English among students. A number of fastidious scholars like Barrett Wendell, the great pundit of Harvard English, had come to the campus about this time; moreover, New England itself was getting sensitive over Western slang and Southern drawls and general ignorance of grammar. Freshmen at this time could elect nearly all their courses except English; that was compulsory, with daily themes, theses, and tough examinations. But I was at the point in my intellectual development when the content rather than the form of my writing was to me of prime importance. Words and ideas surged in my mind and spilled out with disregard of exact accuracy in grammar, taste in word, or restraint in style. I knew the Negro problem and this was more important to me than literary form. I knew grammar fairly well, and I had a pretty wide vocabulary; but I was bitter, angry, and intemperate in my first thesis. Naturally my English instructors had no idea of, nor interest in, the way in which Southern attacks on the Negro were scratching me on the raw flesh. Tillman[4] was raging like a beast in the Senate, and literary clubs, especially those of rich and well-dressed women, engaged his services eagerly and listened avidly. Senator Morgan of Alabama had just published a scathing attack on "niggers" in a leading magazine, when my first Harvard thesis was due. I let go at him with no holds barred. My long and blazing effort came back marked "E"—not passed!

It was the first time in my scholastic career that I had encountered such a failure. I was aghast, but I was not a fool. I did not doubt but that my instructors were fair in judging my English technically even if they did not understand the Negro problem. I went to work at my English and by the end of that term had raised it to a "C." I realized that while style is subordinate to content, and that no real literature can be composed simply of meticulous and fastidious phrases, nevertheless, solid content with literary style carries a message further than poor grammar and muddled syntax. I elected the best course on the campus for English composition—English 12.

I have before me a theme which I submitted on October 3, 1890, to Barrett Wendell. I wrote: "Spurred by my circumstances, I have always been given to systematically planning my future, not indeed without many mistakes and frequent alterations, but always with what I now conceive to have been a strangely early and deep appreciation of the fact that to live is a serious thing. I determined while in high school to go to college—partly because other men did, partly because I foresaw that such discipline would best fit me for life . . . I believe,

4. See n. 9, p. 44.

foolishly perhaps, but sincerely, that I have something to say to the world, and I have taken English 12 in order to say it well." Barrett Wendell liked that last sentence. Out of fifty essays, he picked this out to read to the class.

Commencement was approaching, when, one day, I found myself at midnight on one of the swaggering streetcars that used to roll out from Boston on its way to Cambridge. It was in the spring of 1890, and quite accidentally I was sitting by a classmate who would graduate with me in June. As I dimly remember, he was a nice-looking young man; well-dressed, almost dapper, charming in manner. Probably he was rich or at least well-to-do, and doubtless belonged to an exclusive fraternity, although that did not interest me. Indeed I have even forgotten his name. But one thing I shall never forget and that was his rather regretful admission (which slipped out as we gossiped) that he had no idea as to what his life work would be, because, as he added, "There's nothing in which I am particularly interested!"

I was more than astonished—I was almost outraged to meet any human being of the mature age of twenty-one who did not have his life all planned before him, at least in general outline, and who was not supremely, if not desperately, interested in what he planned to do.

✻   ✻   ✻

W. E. B. DU BOIS

On February 23, 1893, Du Bois celebrated his twenty-fifth birthday in Berlin. In order to plan for the event, he prepared a program for his birthday eve and the day itself, and then he wrote a record of the event and the thoughts it had inspired.

[Celebrating His Twenty-fifth Birthday]†

1868–1893
Berlin, Germany, Oranienstrasse No 130A.

•   •   •

PROGRAM
for the
Celebration of my twenty-fifth birthday

•   •   •

† From W. E. B. Du Bois, *Against Racism: Unpublished Essays, Papers, Addresses, 1887–1961*, ed. Herbert Aptheker (Amherst: University of Massachusetts Press, 1985), pp. 26–29. Some of the author's footnotes have been omitted.

Birthday-eve

7–9 Music   10½–12 Letters to Grandma Mabel
9–10½ Plans   12 Sacrifice to the Zietgeist
                                             Mercy — God — work

•   •   •

Birthday

•   •   •

7–8–9½ Breakfast — old letters   6–7 Seminar
    Reflection   Parents   7–8 Supper (Greek wine, cocoa,
                 Home   Kirchen, oranges)
    Poetry   Steal Away   8–10 Year Book
    Song   Jesus Lover of my Soul   10–12 Letters to C. B. Carrington
             America   Florence
9½–11 A Wander
11–1 Art
1–3 Dinner
3–6 Coffee in Potsdam

W. E. B. Du Bois

This programme was very pleasantly carried out. I arose at eight and took coffee and oranges, read letters, thought of my parents, sang, cried, etc. (O yes, the night before I heard Schubert's beautiful Unfinished Symphony, planned my celebration and room, wrote to grandma and Mabel and had a curious . . .[1] ceremony with candle, greek wine, oil, and song and prayer. Then I dedicated my library to mother. Then I wandered up to the reading room; then to the art gallery; then to a fine dinner with Einderhof over a bottle of Rudecheimer and cigarettes. Then went to Potsdam for coffee and saw a pretty girl. Then came back to the Seminar; took a wander, supped on cocoa, wine, oranges and cake; wrote my year book and letters — and now I go to bed after one of the happiest days of my happy life.

Night — grand and wonderful. I am glad I am living. I rejoice as a strong man to run a race, and I am strong — is it egotism — is it assurance — or is [it] the silent call of the world spirit that makes me feel that I am royal and that beneath my sceptre a world of kings shall bow. The hot dark blood of that forefather — born king of men — is beating at my heart, and I know that I am either a genius or a fool. O I wonder what I am — I wonder what the world is — I wonder if Life is worth the striving — I do not know — perhaps I never shall know: but this I do know: be the Truth what it may I will seek it, on the pure assumption

---

1. One word illegible. This whole manuscript was not easy to decipher, and it is possible some words are rendered incorrectly.

that it is worth seeking and Heaven nor Hell, God nor Devil shall turn me from my purpose till I die.

I will in this second quarter century of my life, enter the dark forest of the unknown world for which I have so many years served my apprenticeship—the chart and compass the world furnishes me I have little faith in—yet, I have none better—I will seek till I find—and die. There is a grandeur in the very hopelessness of such a life—life? and is life all? If I strive, shall I live to strive again? I do not know and in spite of the wild *sehnsucht* for Eternity that makes my heart sick now and then—I shut my teeth and say I do not care. *Carpe Diem!* What is life but life, after all. Its end is its greatest and fullest self—this end is the Good. The Beautiful its attribute—its soul, and Truth its being. Not three commensurable things are these, they are three dimensions of the cube. Mayhap God is the fourth, but for that very reason incomprehensible. The greatest and fullest life is by definition beautiful, beautiful,—beautiful as a dark passionate woman, beautiful as a golden hearted school girl, beautiful as a grey haired hero. That is the dimension of *breadth*. Then comes Truth—what is, cold and indisputable: that is *height*. Now I will, so help my Soul, multiply breadth by breadth, Beauty by Truth and then Goodness, strength, shall bind them together into a solid whole.

Wherefore? I know not now. Perhaps infinite other dimensions do. This is a wretched figure and yet it roughly represents my attitude toward the world. I am striving to make my life all that life may be— and I am limiting that strife only in so far as that strife is incompatible with others of my brothers and sisters making their lives similar. The crucial question now is where that limit comes. I am too often puzzled to know. Paul put it at meat-eating, which was asinine. I have put it at the (perhaps) life-ruin of Amalie which is cruel. God knows I am sorely puzzled. I am firmly convinced that my own best development is now one and the same with the best development of the world and here I am willing to sacrifice. That sacrifice is working for the multiplication of Youth × Beauty and now comes the question how. The general proposition of working for the world's good becomes too soon sickly sentimentality. I therefore take the work that the Unknown lay in my hands and work for the rise of the Negro people, taking for granted that their best development means the best development of the world.

This night before my life's altar I reiterate, what my life . . .[3]

I remembered how when wandering in the fields I chose the realm of Mind for my territory and planned Harvard and Europe. My loves —O my loves, how many and how dear, she is the beautiful whom I worshipped, Ollie the lonely,[4] Dicky the timid, Jenny the meek, Nellie the wavery child. Then came a commencement when hundreds

3. Pages 8–10 of the original manuscript are missing.
4. The reading of this word is uncertain—perhaps "lovely" is intended.

applauded—Nell carried my diploma—and then I left for the North-west,[5] then came Harvard—scholarships, high marks, Boylston prizes when Cambridge applauded, Commencement when the Harvard applause awoke echoes in the world—then Europe where the heart of my childhood loosed from the hard iron hands of America has beat again in the great inspiring air of world culture. I only know Germany—its Rhine or memories, its München or Gemutlichkeit, its Dresden or Art, its Berlin with its music and militarism. These are the five and twenty years of my apprenticeship.

These are my plans: to make a name in science, to make a name in literature and thus to raise my race. Or perhaps to raise a visible empire in Africa thro' England, France or Germany.

I wonder what will be the outcome? Who knows?

I will go unto the king—which is not according to the law and if I perish—I PERISH.

A. RADCLYFFE DUGMORE

From The Negro As He Really Is

[The following photographs were used to illustrate W. E. B. Du Bois's article "The Negro As He Really Is," published in *The World's Work*, June 1901. For *The Souls of Black Folk*, Du Bois revised and expanded the article into "Of the Black Belt" and "Of the Quest of the Golden Fleece." The photographs were taken by Major A. Radclyffe Dugmore, a German photographer who explored the environs of Albany, Georgia, with Du Bois in preparation for this article. Because of the racist nature of the captions, it is safe to assume that Du Bois was not their author.]

---

5. Meaning Fisk University in Tennessee; note the erroneous geography.

Working by the Day in the Cotton Field

In the Cobbler's Shop

"Big House" and Negro Quarters
The house is no longer in use although the Negro quarters are.

A *Negro School near Albany, Georgia* Where children go after "crops are laid by"

Negro Woman Ploughing in a Cotton Field
A field cultivated on the rent system

A Rest in the Furrow

Women from the Country
A Saturday group in Albany, Ga.

On the Street
"They meet and gossip with their friends"

Her Week's Marketing

Learning to Shuffle Early

A Pickaninny Cake Walk

Huts near Albany, Georgia
Showing old mud and wood chimney

A typical Negro Store

At Work Making Brooms

Log Cabin Home

Women "Sowing" Guano

A Friend of George Washington
He believes that he was with Washington when the cherry tree was cut down and allowed his photograph to be taken only on condition that a copy would be sent to his old friend.

Negro Cottages Owned by the Negro who keeps the store pictured on page 208

214

W. E. B. DU BOIS

Credo†

[On October 2, 1904, on the anniversary of his son's death, Du Bois wrote his "Credo." As David Levering Lewis explains, it was meant to serve a dual purpose—as both a political manifesto and a catechism of racial pride. Published by *The Independent* on October 6, 1904, the "Credo" was enthusiastically received and soon transformed into a "hanging card" that adorned the homes of many African Americans.]

I believe in God who made of one blood all races that dwell on earth. I believe that all men, black and brown and white, are brothers, varying through Time and Opportunity, in form and gift and feature, but differing in no essential particular, and alike in soul and in the possibility of infinite development.

Especially do I believe in the Negro Race; in the beauty of its genius, the sweetness of its soul and its strength in that meekness which shall yet inherit this turbulent earth.

I believe in pride of race and lineage and self; in pride of self so deep as to scorn injustice to other selves; in pride of lineage so great as to despise no man's father; in pride of race so chivalrous as neither to offer bastardy to the weak nor beg wedlock of the strong, knowing that men may be brothers in Christ, even they be not brothers-in-law.

I believe in Service—humble reverent service, from the blackening of boots to the whitening of souls; for Work is Heaven, Idleness Hell, and Wage is the "Well done!" of the Master who summoned all them that labor and are heavy laden, making no distinction between the black sweating cotton-hands of Georgia and the First Families of Virginia, since all distinction not based on deed is devilish and not divine.

I believe in the Devil and his angels, who wantonly work to narrow the opportunity of struggling human beings, especially if they be black; who spit in the faces of the fallen, strike them that cannot strike again, believe the worst and work to prove it, hating the image which their Maker stamped on a brother's soul.

I believe in the Prince of Peace. I believe that War is Murder. I believe that armies and navies are at bottom the tinsel and braggadocio of oppression and wrong; and I believe that the wicked conquest of weaker and darker nations by nations whiter and stronger but foreshadows the death of that strength.

I believe in Liberty for all men; the space to stretch their arms and their souls; the right to breathe and the right to vote, the freedom to choose their friends, enjoy the sunshine and ride on the railroads, un-

† From *The Independent* 57 (October 6, 1904): 787.

cursed by color; thinking, dreaming, working as they will in a kingdom of God and love.

I believe in the training of children, black even as white; the leading out of little souls into the green pastures and beside the still waters, not for self or peace, but for Life lit by some large vision of beauty and goodness and truth; lest we forget, and the sons of the fathers, like Esau, for more meat barter their birthright in a mighty nation.

Finally, I believe in Patience—patience with the weakness of the Weak and the strength of the Strong, the prejudice of the ignorant and the ignorance of the Blind; patience with the tardy triumph of Joy and the mad chastening of Sorrow—patience with God.

W. E. B. DU BOIS

A Litany of Atlanta†

[A series of articles describing fictitious sexual attacks on white women by black men appeared in various Atlanta newspapers during September 1906. On September 22, riots broke out in the streets, killing ten blacks and two whites, as well as seriously wounding sixty blacks and ten whites. Hundreds of people, most of whom were black, received minor injuries, and many Negro-owned businesses were destroyed. Du Bois was in Alabama's Black Belt at the time, and he immediately took a train back to Atlanta. Fearing for the safety of family and friends, he wrote "A Litany of Atlanta" on the train. As Manning Marable points out, Du Bois's response was not merely literary; he also bought a "Winchester double-barreled shotgun and two dozen rounds of shells filled with buckshot"[1] and waited on his front porch for any possible intruders.]

O Silent God, Thou whose voice afar in mist and mystery hath left our ears a-hungered in these fearful days—
  Hear us, good Lord!

Listen to us, Thy children: our faces dark with doubt, are made a mockery in Thy sanctuary. With uplifted hands we front Thy heaven, O God, crying:
  We beseech Thee to hear us, good Lord!

We are not better than our fellows, Lord; we are but weak and human men. When our devils do deviltry, curse Thou the doer and the deed: curse them as we curse them, do to them all and more that ever they have done to innocence and weakness, to womanhood and home.
  Have mercy upon us, miserable sinners!

---

† From *The Independent* 61 (October 11, 1906): 856–58.
1. Marable, *W. E. B. Du Bois, Black Radical Democrat*, p. 60.

And yet whose is the deeper guilt? Who made these devils? Who nursed
them in crime and fed them on injustice? Who ravished and debauched their mothers and their grandmothers? Who bought and sold
their crime, and waxed fat and rich on public iniquity?

Thou knowest, good God!

Is this Thy justice, O Father, that guilt be easier than innocence, and
the innocent crucified for the guilt of the untouched guilty?

Justice, O Judge of men!

Wherefore do we pray? Is not the God of the fathers dead? Have not
seers seen in Heaven's halls Thine hearsed and lifeless form stark amidst
the black and rolling smoke of sin, where all along bow bitter forms of
endless dead?

Awake, Thou that sleepest!

Thou art not dead, but flown afar, up hills of endless light, thru blazing
corridors of suns, where worlds do swing of good and gentle men, of
women strong and free—far from the cozeage,[2] black hypocrisy and
chaste prostitution of this shameful speck of dust!

Turn again, O Lord, leave us not to perish in our sin!

From lust of body and lust of blood,
  Great God deliver us!

From lust of powers and lust of gold,
  Great God deliver us!

From the leagued lying of despot and of brute,
  Great God deliver us!

A city lay in travail, God our Lord, and from her loins sprang twin
Murder and Black Hate. Red was the midnight; clang, crack and cry
of death and fury filled the air and trembled underneath the stars when
church spires pointed silently to Thee. And all this was to sate the greed
of greedy men who hide behind the veil of vengeance!

Bend us Thine ear, O Lord!

In the pale, still morning we looked upon the deed. We stopped our
ears and held our leaping hands, but they—did not wag their heads
and leer and cry with bloody jaws: *Cease from Crime!* The word was

---

2. Fraud or trickery [*Editors*].

mockery, for thus they train a hundred crimes while we do cure one.
Turn again our captivity, O Lord!

Behold this maimed and broken thing; dear God it was an humble black man who toiled and sweat to save a bit from the pittance paid him. They told him: *Work and Rise.* He worked. Did this man sin? Nay, but some one told how someone said another did—one whom he had never seen nor known. Yet for that man's crime this man lieth maimed and murdered, his wife naked to shame, his children, to poverty and evil.
Hear us, O heavenly Father!

Doth not this justice of hell stink in Thy nostrils, O God? How long shall the mounting flood of innocent blood roar in Thine ears and pound in our hearts for vengeance? Pile the pale frenzy of blood-crazed brutes who do such deeds high on Thine altar, Jehovah Jireh, and burn it in hell forever and forever!
Forgive us, good Lord; we know not what we say!

Bewildered we are, and passion-tost, mad with the madness of a mobbed and mocked and murdered people; straining at the armposts of Thy Throne, we raise our shackled hands and charge Thee, God, by the bones of our stolen fathers, by the tears of our dead mothers by the very blood of Thy crucified Christ: *What meaneth this?* Tell us the Plan; give us the Sign!
Keep not thou silent, O God!

Sit no longer blind, Lord God, deaf to our prayer and dumb to our dumb suffering. Surely Thou too are not white, O Lord, a pale, bloodless, heartless thing?
Ah! Christ of all the Pities!

Forgive the thought! Forgive these wild, blasphemous words. Thou art still the God of our black fathers, and in Thy soul's soul sit some soft darkenings of the evening, some shadowings of the velvet night.

But whisper—speak—call, great God, for Thy silence is white terror to our hearts! The way, O God, show us the way and point us the path.

Whither? North is greed and South is blood; within, the coward, and without, the liar. Whither? To death?
Amen! Welcome dark sleep!

Whither? To life? But not this life, dear God, not this. Let the cup pass from us, tempt us not beyond our strength, for there is that clamoring

and clawing within, to whose voice we would not listen, yet shudder lest we must, and it is red, Ah! God! It is a red and awful shape.
Selah!

In yonder East trembles a star.
Vengeance is mine; I will repay, saith the Lord!

Thy will, O Lord, be done!
Kyrie Eleison![3]

Lord, we have done these pleading, wavering words.
We beseech Thee to hear us, good Lord!

We bow our heads and hearken soft to the sobbing of women and little children.
We beseech Thee to hear us, good Lord!

Our voices sink in silence and in night.
Hear us, good Lord!

In night, O God of a godless land!
Amen!

In silence, O Silent God.
Selah!

Done at Atlanta, in the Day of Death, 1906.

---

3. Greek for *Lord, Have Mercy on Us* [*Editors*].

CRITICISM

Early Criticism

DAVID LEVERING LEWIS

From W. E. B. Du Bois: Biography of a Race†

[In 1994, David Levering Lewis won the Pulitzer Prize for his remarkable work, *W. E. B. Du Bois: Biography of a Race* (1993). Among the many fine examples of Levering's detailed scholarship is his chapter on *The Souls of Black Folk*. From that section of the biography, we have excerpted his overview of the contemporary critical reception of *Souls*.]

✳   ✳   ✳

If Du Bois sincerely feared, as he suggested in "The After-Thought," that his book might fall "still-born into the world wilderness," reassurance came quickly. *The Souls of Black Folk* went into its third printing in June of its first year. By October 1903, McClurg's was selling about two hundred copies weekly of a second edition and remitting royalties to Du Bois at the rate of fifteen cents per copy. Five years after publication, 9,595 books had been sold. For a controversial work about African-Americans by an African-American, such sales were exceptional, and, by any measure, the book enjoyed an impressive run. The London firm of Constable published a British edition in the spring of 1905 and Max Weber's expectation that there would soon be a German translation was still very much alive.[1] Despite the success of the Tuskegee Machine[2] in preventing the book from being noticed in a large segment of the African-American press, the powerful AME *Christian Recorder* of Philadelphia lauded *Souls* as possessing "penetration of thought and a glow of eloquence that is almost unexampled in the literature on the Negro question." In Cincinnati, the black *Ohio*

---

† From David Levering Lewis, *W. E. B. Du Bois: Biography of a Race* (New York: Henry Holt, 1993), pp. 291–96. © 1993 by David Levering Lewis. Reprinted by permission of Henry Holt and Company, Inc.
1. Aptheker, "Introduction," *The Souls of Black Folk* (Millwood, NY: Kraus-Thomson Organization, 1973; orig. pub. 1903), p. 25; Royalty Statement, May 1, 1903; Royalty Statement, Jan. 1, 1905—both in Du Bois Papers/U. Mass.
2. Term used to designate Booker T. Washington's powerful group of friends and supporters in the areas of education, philanthropy, and the press, particularly the black press. From his Tuskegee Institute, Washington influenced the direction of funds and jobs in education [*Editors*].

Enterprise, edited by Wendell Phillips Dabney, a rascally eccentric who would become Du Bois's lifelong friend, issued a command in upper case: "SHOULD BE READ AND STUDIED BY EVERY PERSON, WHITE AND BLACK." Trotter's Boston *Guardian* concurred, as did the Detroit *Informer* and Cleveland *Gazette*.[3]

Ida B. Wells-Barnett wrote from Chicago that quite a debate had taken place over the book at a literary gathering during which the formidable white Unitarian minister, Celia Parker Woolley, announced her intention to devote her life to "help black folks with their problems." J. Douglas Wetmore, James Weldon Johnson's Atlanta University roommate and the model for the protagonist of Johnson's novel *The Autobiography of an Ex-Colored Man*, felt "compelled to write and thank [Du Bois] in the name of the Race." Not since Frederick Douglass had their people heard such a voice, Wetmore wanted him to know. A moved Francis Grimké hurried to his writing desk to tell Du Bois, "More than ever do I feel that God has raised you up at this juncture in our history, as a race, to speak to the intelligence of the country on our behalf." From the Talented Tenth of the mother continent came congratulations on Du Bois's "great work" from barrister, publisher, and recent author of *Gold Coast Native Institutions*, J. E. Casely-Hayford. The leading intellectual and politician of British West Africa, Casely-Hayford believed "this century would be likely to see the race problem solved" with more books like Du Bois's.[4]

A Cornell University English major, who had written previously seeking advice about her summer school studies, was enraptured. Jessie Fauset, a third-year student from one of Philadelphia's oldest African-American families who was headed for election to Phi Beta Kappa in an institution that had graduated a mere handful of women, thanked Du Bois "as though it has been a personal favor." She was "glad, glad" he wrote it. "We have needed someone to voice the intricacies of the blind maze of thought and action along which the modern educated colored man or woman struggles." Fauset ended on a personal note (as she would many times in the future): "It hurt you to write that book, didn't it?" for she knew so well that "the man of firm sensibilities has to suffer exquisitely, just simply because his feelings are so fine."[5] Here was an admirer with whom Du Bois decided he should become much better acquainted.

3. Aptheker, "Introduction," *SOBF*, p. 16.
4. J. E. Casely-Hayford to W. E. B. Du Bois, June 8, 1904, Du Bois Papers/U. Mass.; Francis Grimké to W. E. B. Du Bois, Oct. 16, 1903, Du Bois Papers/U. Mass.; J. Douglas Wetmore to W. E. B. Du Bois, Oct. 20, 1903, Du Bois Papers/U. Mass.; also Herbert Aptheker, ed., *The Correspondence of W. E. B. Du Bois* (Amherst: University of Mass. Press, 1973), I, p. 60; Ida B. Wells-Barnett to W. E. B. Du Bois, Mar. 30, 1903, Du Bois Papers/U. Mass.; *Correspondence*, I, pp. 55–56.
5. ". . . his feelings are so fine.": Jessie Fauset to W. E. B. Du Bois, Feb. 16, 1905, Du Bois Papers/U. Mass.; also Aptheker, *Correspondence*, I, pp. 94–95.

Like the Bookerite press, most southern white newspapers pretended not to notice *The Souls of Black Folk*, Those that did claimed, like the *Tennessee Christian Advocate*, not to know what to make of the book or the author. The Nashville *American*, however, was sure of one thing: "This book is indeed dangerous for the negro to read." The reviewer for the Houston *Chronicle* unmasked the author's terrible design and demanded the authorities indict Du Bois for "inciting rape." Southern coverage of his book was about what Du Bois would have expected, but the wide attention paid to it outside the South was sometimes just as obtuse or mean-spirited. To admit that its arguments were persuasive, that its eloquence was moving, was to risk destabilizing the entente cordiale between the North and the South, an admission that could lead to fundamental reexamination of the dogmas and policies underpinning the racial status quo. The editors of *The New York Times* took no chances. They chose a white southerner whose anonymous review conceded that *Souls* was interesting and even deserving of praise here and there. The book's fatal flaw, nonetheless, was that its author was a sophisticated northerner with only a superficial understanding of southern black people and of the history of the South. Du Bois's hidden personal agenda, the *Times* reviewer disclosed, was simply to be able to "smoke a cigar and drink a cup of tea with the white man in the South." Mrs. Elia W. Peattie harbored the same suspicion in her lengthy *Chicago Tribune* review. Having discharged her obligation to the status quo, however, Peattie allowed her professional conscience to speak about "this passionate book, incomplete and sometimes self-conscious though it is," a book compelling "profound respect. It is a real, not an imitation book."[6] Joseph Pulitzer's New York *World* agreed with Mrs. Peattie about the caliber of the writing and the searing honesty of the author.

But neither *Collier's Weekly* nor *The Outlook* faltered in their duty to uphold *Plessy v. Ferguson* and the Atlanta Compromise. *Collier's*, the muckraking weekly par excellence, dismissed concerns about the black man's soul. "With sufficient food, drink and warmth, the negro is happy, come what may." When an offended Du Bois upbraided *Collier's* editor, Richard L. Jones, for the magazine's racial stereotyping, the latter feigned hurt puzzlement, claiming "not to know just what particular article or statement has appeared in our paper to cause this offense." More serious in its concerns, *The Outlook* of May 23, 1903, reviewed *Souls* along with Washington's *The Future of the American Negro*, didactically rehearsing the latter's program of solid, slow, practical advancement and warning of the dangers of Du Bois's impatience

6. ". . . not an imitation book.": Elia W. Peattie, Chicago *Tribune*, May 22, 1903; p. 20; N.Y. *Times*, Apr. 25, 1903, pp. 19–20; Houston *Chronicle*, Aug. 15, 1903, p. 18; *Christian Advocate*, July 16, 1903, p. 16; Nashville *American*, Sept. 26, 1903, p. 17—all in Aptheker, "Introduction," *SOBF*.

and impertinence. The Atlanta professor was "half ashamed of being a negro, and he gives expression to his own bitterness of soul in the cry which he puts into the mouth of his race." The black person must learn not to "think about yourself. Do not think about your woes and wrongs. Meditate not on the 'souls of black folk,' but on 'the future of the American negro,' " it counseled.[7]

With so much calculated, critical misunderstanding, Du Bois needed to know that there were white men and women among what he called the "better classes" who were giving *Souls* a fair reading. Sending brother Henry a copy that June of the volume by "a mulatto ex-student of mine," William James complimented Du Bois that year on writing a "decidedly moving book." Robert Hunter, the well-known social worker, future author of *Socialists at Work*, and a thinker Du Bois admired, compared *Souls* to *Uncle Tom's Cabin*, while Washington Gladden was positively rhapsodic. Called the "father of the Social Gospel," and currently president of the AMA, Gladden deplored *The Outlook*'s disapproving review. "I want you all to read it," he thundered from his Sunday pulpit in Columbus, Ohio. "It will give you, I think, a deeper insight into the real human elements of the race problem than anything that has yet been written." The sometimes grumpy Albert Hart loved it. Fourteen years later, he was still insisting that his finest Ph.D. student's collection was "the only literature published by a Harvard graduate in forty years."[8]

Over the next few years, as *Souls* went through additional printings, it retained its capacity to move readers of different racial, religious, and social backgrounds. From New York's squalid Lower East Side, D. Tabak, a new American, would share with Du Bois his epiphany after a chance discovery of *Souls* "upon a book shelf in a corner of Delancy [sic] Street." The young Russian immigrant wrote of being "overpowered by a peculiar pain that was so much akin to bliss." Tabak's words fairly tumbled off the page as he confessed that he was "ashamed of being white," of now envying the "despised and abused." He found it unbearable to be a citizen of a country in which 10 percent of the population was persecuted and "denied all rights a thousand times more cruel than we Jews are in Russia."[9] In closing, Tabak thanked Du Bois

7. ". . . happy, come what may.": *Collier's Weekly*, Aug. 29, 1903, p. 6. ". . . cause this offense.": Richard L. Jones to W. E. B. Du Bois, Jan. 18, 1904, Du Bois Papers/U. Mass. ". . . 'the future of the American negro.' ": "Two Typical Leaders," *Outlook*, 74 (May 25, 1903): 214–16, Du Bois Papers/U. Mass.; also reproduced in Louis R. Harlan, ed., *B. T. Washington Papers* (Urbana: University of Illinois Press, 1972), VII, pp. 149–54, p. 153.

8. ". . . decidedly moving book.": William James to Henry James, June 6, 1903, in Henry James, ed., *The Letters of William James* (Boston: Little, Brown, 1926), 2 vols., II, p. 196. ". . . anything that has yet been written."—Gladden, quoted: Ronald C. White, Jr., and C. Howard Hopkins, *The Social Gospel: Religion and Reform in a Changing America* (New Haven: Yale University Press, 1940), p. 106. ". . . Harvard graduate in forty years.": Albert Bushnell Hart, *Books and Reading* (New York City), Oct. 1917, p. 66; in Aptheker, "Introduction," *SOBF*, p. 31 (note 25).

9. ". . . we Jews are in Russia.": D. Tabak to W. E. B. Du Bois [n.d.], Du Bois Papers/U. Mass.

for the greatly heightened sense of humanity and "sympathy to all nature's children" he had derived from *The Souls of Black Folk.*

When Professor W. D. Hooper of the University of Georgia, an old-stock American at the opposite end of the social scale from the Russian Jew, got around to reading the book in the fall of 1909 he would write immediately to tell Du Bois how profoundly moved he was—"but even the pure English was very refreshing in this day of slovenliness." Hooper was ashamed that the South had fallen from the control of its "best people." The problem was "the problem of the lower class whites," against whom, Hooper sighed, he and his kind were "utterly powerless." Having long grieved about the treatment of Du Bois's people, the professor was racked with despair that he could find no way to alleviate the situation. But upon reflection, he decided that in a small way he had been able to contribute. He begged his fellow academic to know that his own "skirts are at least clean. I have never wittingly wronged one of your race in any way." Hooper added that he had raised his son to respect black men and women. Appreciative of the moral tumult Hooper must have experienced in bringing himself to write, Du Bois would reply that he had been touched by the letter, which he had read "again and again with increasing sympathy." But with Du Bois sympathy was seldom confused with absolution. "Comrade," he admonished, "you and I can never be satisfied with sitting down before a great human problem and saying nothing can be done. We must do something. That is the reason we are here on Earth."[1]

Challenging letters like the one Du Bois received from Caroline H. Pemberton were rare. This lucid northern white woman shared her thoughts very soon after McClurg and Company released *Souls.* After praising his eloquence and insights, she gently chided Du Bois for failing to see that race hatred was a camouflage for class warfare. He did "not seem to be aware that the white laborers of the North are facing the same alternative of starvation—or submission and unceasing, unrecompensed toil." Another serious failing, she thought, was Du Bois's embrace of the culture and civilization of the white man. "What he boasts of as 'civilization' is a hideous mockery."[2] Pemberton's letter seems to have played a part in quickening Du Bois's appreciation of

---

1. ". . . here on Earth.": W. E. B. Du Bois to W. D. Hooper, Sept. 11, 1909; and W. D. Hooper to W. E. B. Du Bois, Sept. 2, 1909—both in Du Bois Papers/U. Mass. The context of Hooper's gesture was that the memory of the Bassett affair was still vivid in the South. In 1903 one of the South's leading historians, John Spencer Bassett, of Trinity College (later Duke University), founder of the *South Atlantic Quarterly*, was forced to resign his professorship and relocate in the North. Bassett's offense was that he had written an essay in the *South Atlantic Quarterly* deploring the racist excesses of certain white journalists and, in the same piece, ventured the opinion that the greatest man to be produced in the South since Robert E. Lee was Booker T. Washington. On this controversy, see Morton Philip Sosna, *In Search of the Silent South* (New York: Columbia University Press, 1977), p. 14; and, for a fuller treatment of the ramifications, Williamson, *Crucible*, pp. 261–71.
2. ". . . a hideous mockery.": Caroline H. Pemberton to W. E. B. Du Bois, Dec. 12, 1903, Du Bois Papers/U. Mass.

the possibility of solidarity across racial lines among black and white workers. The theme of class conflict was shortly to be heard, if faintly, in an article or two and an occasional speech.

Meanwhile the New York *Evening Post* and *The Nation* (both owned by Oswald Garrison Villard) had broken ranks with the pro–Booker Washington press. The unsigned review running in both publications had all the earmarks of Villard, until then counted among the Wizard's firmest supporters. Unlike Baldwin or Ogden, Villard permitted himself to doubt that the Tuskegee program was a panacea. A race whose leaders' education was largely limited to masonry and accounting Villard saw as a race unfitted for the modern world. Did it really make sense to renounce civil rights in the present on the assumption that they would be hauled up some day by cast-down buckets? Here was a "profoundly interesting and affecting book," infused with intellectual passion and unquestionable knowledge of the character and ideas of black people, said the *Evening Post* reviewer. Perhaps its criticism of Washington went too far; yet, upon reflection, the reviewer conceded that Du Bois's charges deserved "the carefullest consideration."[3]

The liberal and influential *Independent*, while also troubled by the presentation of Washington, decided that *Souls* was "the best and most logical expression of the clear facts of race hatred yet made by any student of the negro question."[4] This was a review with which Du Bois found himself in complete agreement. He knew that the triumph of *Souls* lay in its luminous presentation of the minds of thinking black folks. For the first time in the brutal, mocked, patronized, and embattled history of Negro life on the North American continent, there was now a revelation of the race's social, economic, and psychological realities and prospects of such lyricism, lucidity, and humanity as to leave its mark on a white America guilty of evasion, obfuscation, and hypocrisy.

3. ". . . the carefullest consideration.": N. Y. *Evening Post*, June 12, 1903.
4. ". . . any student of the negro question.": *The Independent*, May 28, 1903; *Dial*, May 1, 1903.

WILLIAM JAMES

[Praise for *Souls*]

[Most authors, when discussing the critical reception of *The Souls of Black Folk*, mention that William James, Du Bois's philosophy professor at Harvard University, sent the book to his brother, the famous novelist Henry James. Although William James praised *Souls*, his mention of the book is only two sentences long. His remarks are quoted in *The Letters of William James*, and read as follows.]

* * *

I am sending you a decidedly moving book by a mulatto ex-student of mine, Du Bois, professor of history at Atlanta (Georgia) negro College. Read Chapters VII to XI for local color, etc. [June 6, 1903].

* * *

[ANONYMOUS]

[Review of *Souls*]

[The following anonymous review appeared in *The Nation* on June 11, 1903. Although unsigned, this review, as David Levering Lewis points out, "had all the earmarks" of Oswald Garrison Villard, the owner of both *The Nation* and the *New York Evening Post*. Villard had previously been an ardent supporter of Booker T. Washington, but this review considers Du Bois's criticisms of industrial education worthy of "the carefullest consideration." At the same time, the reviewer distances himself from some of Du Bois's views: "It is not so clear to us as it is to Mr. Du Bois that Mr. Washington has made the base concessions here ascribed to him."]

Mr. Du Bois has written a profoundly interesting and affecting book, remarkable as a piece of literature apart from its inner significance. The negrophobist will remind us that Mr. Du Bois is not so black as he has painted himself, and will credit to the white blood in his veins the power and beauty of his book. But the fact is, that the features of Mr. Du Bois's mind are negro features to a degree that those of his face are not. They are the sensibility, the tenderness, the "avenues to God hid from men of Northern brain," which Emerson divined in the black people. The bar of music from one "Sorrow Song" or another which stands at the head of each chapter is a hint (unintended) that what follows is that strain writ large, that Mr. Du Bois's thought and expression are highly characteristic of his people, are cultivated varieties of those emotional and imaginative qualities which are the prevailing traits of the uncultivated negro mind. Hence one more argument for that higher education of the negro for which Mr. Du Bois so eloquently pleads. Such education of ten thousand negroes would be justified by one product like this.

The book will come as a surprise to some persons who have heard Mr. Du Bois speak upon his people's character and destiny, and, finding him coldly intellectual, have not been at all prepared for the emotion and the passion throbbing here in every chapter, almost every page. It is almost intolerably sad. "Bone of the bone and flesh of the flesh of them that live within the veil," the writer manifests throughout an aching sense of the wrongs done to his people, heretofore and still. But those will greatly misconceive who think that we have here merely an outburst of emotion. Back of this there is careful knowledge of past and present conditions in the South, clear insight into their meanings, a firm intellectual apprehension of their tendency, which is something to be reckoned with by every citizen who has at heart the welfare of his country, inseparable from the welfare of the colored people. The perfervid rhetoric will seem extravagant to the dull and cold, but, though it sometimes obscures what it would fain illuminate, it is the writer's individual form, it is not the substance of his protestation, which is compact of intellectual seriousness and moral truth.

The initial chapter is of a general character, setting forth the spiritual strivings of the negro—to be at once a negro and an American; "to be a co-worker in the kingdom of culture, to escape both death and isolation; to use his best powers and his latent genius," which have heretofore been so wasted, dispersed, and forgotten. A second chapter takes more definite shape, telling the story of emancipation, what it meant to the blacks, and what happened in the days of the carpet-bagger and his coadjutors in the Reconstruction period. The emphasis is on the Freedmen's Bureau, whose merits and demerits are considered in an impartial manner. There is an eloquent tribute to "the crusade of the New England schoolma'am" in the South, which in one year gave instruction to more than one hundred thousand blacks. There is a fit rebuke for the cheap nonsense, of which we hear so much, concerning the enfranchisement of the negro. There was no choice, we are very properly assured, between full and restricted suffrage; only a choice between suffrage and a new form of slavery. It is conceded that a race-feud was the inevitable consequence of the choice the North was forced to make.

But the most concrete chapter in Mr. Du Bois's book is the third, "Of Mr. Booker T. Washington and Others." Mr. Washington's ascendancy is designated as "the most striking thing in the history of the American negro since 1876." Entertained with unlimited energy, enthusiasm, and faith, his programme "startled and won the applause of the South, interested and won the admiration of the North, and, after a confused murmur of protest, it silenced if it did not convert the negroes themselves." The merits of that programme are detailed with warm appreciation, while at the same time a criticism is made upon it so thoughtfully conceived that it deserves the attention of Mr. Washington's best friends and the best friends of the negro and the white people of the South. The criticism will be resented with bitterness by those for whom Washington's attraction is the concessions they suppose him to have made, and with hardly less by many who are convinced that he has solved the race problem in a completely successful manner. There are those who seem to regard any criticism of his programme as only a less malignant form of lese-majesty than criticism of the war programme of a President. But he is strong and wise enough to welcome any honest difference from his own views and aims. The criticism is that Mr. Washington asks the negro to surrender, at least for the present, political power, insistence on civil rights, the higher education. Advocated for fifteen years, triumphant for ten, this policy has coincided with the disfranchisement of the negro, his relegation to a civil status of distinct inferiority, the impoverishment of institutions devoted to the negro's higher education. That here is not merely coincidence, but effect, is Mr. Du Bois's contention. Also, that Mr. Washington's desired ends cannot be reached without important additions to his means: the negro may not hope to be a successful business man and property owner without political rights, to be thrifty and self-respecting, while consenting to civic inferiority, to secure good common-school and industrial training without institutions of higher learning. "Tuskegee itself could not remain open a day were it not for teachers trained in negro colleges, or trained by their graduates."

It is not so clear to us as it is to Mr. Du Bois that Mr. Washington has made the base concessions here ascribed to him. We recall passages in his books and speeches and letters that point a different moral. We recall his protests sent to the disfranchising conventions in Alabama and Louisiana. It may be that of late he has become more subdued than formerly to those he has worked with, some of whom have the habit of giving his programme the color of their own exaggerated caution and timidity. Then, too, Mr. Du Bois, while acknowledging that Mr. Washington's programme is provisional, does not make this acknowledgment with sufficient emphasis. But this third chapter as a whole, and the expansion of its prominent details in the succeeding chapters, deserve the carefullest consideration. Their large intelligence and their lofty temper demand for them an appreciation as generous as the spirit in which they are conceived.

Where all is good, it is invidious to select, but the chapters "On the Training of Black Men" and "Of the Sons of Master and Man" merit, perhaps, particular attention. The pathos of the chapter called "The Passing of the First Born" is immeasurably deep. It will appeal to all who have a human heart. It tells the story of a baby's life and death, the joy his coming meant; the "awful gladness" when he died: "Not dead, but escaped; not bond, but free." Clearly the burden of Mr. Du Bois's complaint, not explicitly, but implicitly at every turn, is made more grievous by the denial of social equality to himself and his people. In the urgency of this note is there not possibly a lack of the profoundest self-respect? If Mr. Du Bois can sit with Shakespere and Plato, and they do not wince at his complexion, why should he care so much for the contempt of Col. Carter of Cartersville? Why not trample on it with a deeper pride? A society based on money values may reject such a man as scornfully as one based on the tradition of slavery, but a society based upon character and culture will always welcome him though he were blacker than the ace of spades, not as showing him a favor, but as anxious to avail itself of his ability.

JOHN SPENCER BASSETT

Two Negro Leaders†

[John Spencer Bassett, founder of the *South Atlantic Quarterly*, was one of the South's leading historians; he taught at Trinity College, which later became Duke University. In his review of *The Souls of Black Folk*, Bassett judiciously contrasts the goals of Du Bois with those of Washington. He acknowledges that "Professor DuBois is a student" while Washington "is not a notable student of books, although he has a wide knowledge of men." He believes that the greatest need in black education is industrial education, while still conceding that for "the exceptional negro* * *the door of opportunity ought to be kept open." In a fascinating footnote in his Du Bois biography, David Levering Lewis reports that Bassett (who was white) was forced to resign and move north because of an essay in which he not only deplored "the racist excesses of certain white journalists" but also proclaimed that Booker T. Washington was "the greatest man to be produced in the South since Robert E. Lee."][1]

    Two men, Booker T. Washington and William E. Burghardt DuBois, stand out as leaders of the negro race in America. Both of them are young men, teachers of negroes, and residents of the South. Both are possessed of fine minds and excellent training. Both have influence with their race and in a way are its most prominent leaders. Both are

† *The Southern Atlantic Quarterly* 2 (July 1903).
1. See n. 4, p. xvii.

thoroughly honest in their purposes, and both are contributing greatly to the progress of American negroes.

But in some respects these two men are essentially unlike. President Washington is the son of a slave woman. He is a self-made man in the truest sense. His education was gotten from an industrial school. His work in life has been to spread abroad the desire for, and the opportunity of acquiring, industrial training. He has been mostly concerned with a life of action. He is not a notable student of books, although he has a wide knowledge of men. On the other hand Professor DuBois is a student. He represents in his early life in a New England village, and in his later career, the most intellectual side of the life of the American negro. He is a graduate of Fisk University and has a doctorate of philosophy from Harvard. He has written some books of a distinctively scholarly character and his position among the students of American social conditions is very good. To the general public he is not so well known as the president of Tuskegee; but to a small public of students he is known quite as favorably. He represents the negro in his higher cultural aspect just as the other represents him in his industrial career.

Between these two men there now appears to be a striking difference of view in regard to the future of the negro race. One of them has for a long time been widely known because of his peculiar policy. His views have found acceptance in all parts of our country and with all sections of our population. The general impression has been favorable to him. But now comes from the other a book [The Souls of Black Folk] which is written from an entirely opposite point of view. Its appearance in itself is interesting; but the fact that its author is a man of known ability and honest purpose makes it distinctly worth our while to ask what there is in this book, and how its message concerns the problem to solve which it is written?

What, then, does the president of Tuskegee stand for? He stands for a progress which shall begin with the things which are and from that point move onward. He realizes that the problem is a human one, to be wrought out by human agents and in the face of all the impediments of human opposition. The negroes themselves, upon whom he must work, are very weak human beings. To develop them is a process of strengthening which must conserve a hundred weak forces. They are a child race. To give them at once the liberty of adults would debauch them. On the other hand, the white people, in whose presence this problem must be solved, have certain pronounced views of their own in regard to it. Their views may or may not be the most enlightened or the most equitable views. They may be, in fact, all that Professor DuBois would call them, a mass of prejudices; but for all this they are real views, and President Washington feels that they must be dealt with in a sensible manner. They must not be antagonized blindly.

His manner of meeting the problem is this: The most powerful force in raising a race upward is economic progress. This is the basis on which all other progress is based. The negro needs this first of all. He is, moreover, a weak race in the presence of the stronger white race. He cannot win in a fight with the white man. It behooves him to keep on the friendliest terms with this stronger race. By so doing he will bring peace between the two, and peace will give the opportunity for advance on the part of the blacks. In politics, as he very clearly sees, negroes are as nothing. It is useless to say that he ought to have the constitutional rights which the national government has granted to him. He is not now able to hold these rights, and they will not be allowed him by his opponents. It behooves him, therefore, to let politics alone—and to stress the acquisition of wealth. Of all negroes who have undertaken to advise the race President Washington is the one who leans most to the white people. Yet he has received more criticism from the whites than any other prominent negro, and it is a fine tribute to his character that he still maintains his position in regard to the relation between the races.

Professor DuBois approaches the problem from the standpoint of ethical culture. He does not, in the first place, believe in the efficacy of the gospel of material wealth. The soul is more than the body. To give up the higher life, which many negroes have longed for, and to seek for riches only would be a backward step. It would be debasement of the soul. He would not object to the acquisition of wealth; but he would object to the notion that it should be put before the development of culture. A culture[d] life for the negro is no unnatural thing to him, who is, in fact, a very cultivated man. He raises a warning against the cry for industrial education. It is not the only thing or indeed the chief thing which the negro needs. His chief want is the greatest opportunity to develop in the truest way which is open to any other citizen of America.

A word which is continually in Professor DuBois's mouth is "The Veil." By this he means the fact that a negro is everywhere made to feel that he is unlike other people, and that there is something which shuts him out of the world of other people. It is race prejudice. Ever and anon the author comes back to this idea. . . . He makes us feel what an awful thing it is to be in America a negro and at the same time to be a man of culture. . . .

To the average negro the Veil is not so dark as to his highly cultivated brother. He does not pine for the society of white people. He finds company enough of his own standard among his own race. To him race prejudice means a dark reservoir of race antagonism cropping out in frowns, in Jim Crow cars, and in suffrage amendments. However much he may feel it, it is not so much as the man of culture feels it, who at every turn finds a locked door in his face. To meet this condition Washington proposes that the negro shall accept the "Veil," and glorify the negro race until it shall be no dishonor to be black. DuBois would chafe and fret, and tear his heart out. And as for us, who are a divinely appointed superior race, how much do we do to render the burden lighter to either the one or the other?

Some good people are already regretting that "The Souls of Black Folk" has been published. The book is, in their minds, a check to the good work done by institutions like Tuskegee and Hampton. It is, too, a sign that there is disagreement between two of the most prominent leaders of the negro race. "The Souls of Black Folk" is a most respectful criticism of the views opposite to it. It deals with President Washington personally in a thoroughly considerate manner. So far as being a sign of ill-will between the author and his opponent is concerned, there can be no apprehension from the contents of the book. As to the other point, which is the main point after all, the relative merits of industrial and cultural education, that is a debatable point, and on it we need as much light as we can get.

Unquestionably the vast majority of Southern negroes need industrial training and business competency more than anything else. Perhaps ninety per cent of them come within this class. Yet the negro needs his own leaders—for who will lead him if not those of his own race. If there is any force in the argument that the white race should have higher education in order to develop its own leaders, there is the same force in a like argument as applied to the negro race. In fact, the way of the negro is hard enough in the near future. In the raw democracy of the South, which has just lost the guiding influence of the old planter class, there is not that patriarchal feeling for the dependent race which existed twenty years ago. The new citizens and the new leaders are practical men. They have shown it by legally excluding the negro from the polls. What other step they may take does not appear. The negro ought to use every moment in putting himself in a self-supporting and self-directing condition. He will have in the future a severer competition than he has ever had in the past. He will need not only a mass of self-supporting individuals, but a large number of wisely taught leaders—men of great moral weight and men of broad character. If higher education will make such leaders—and who can deny it?—he ought not for a day to think of abandoning his higher education. It may safely be said that there will never go to the negro colleges and universities enough students to lessen materially the number of negro laborers. It is a fact, too, that most negroes do not comprehend the very terminology of higher education. But the exceptional negro does exist, and every day he is more frequently encountered; for him the door of opportunity ought to be kept open. If Professor DuBois has succeeded in calling attention to the importance of this side of the problem—a side which in the popularity of industrial education was likely to be forgotten—, his book has done good.

Another matter of apprehension in regard to "The Souls of Black Folk" is that it will counteract a better understanding between the races, which, it is said, has been progressing more or less in the South recently. But has there been any such progress in recent years? While the president of Tuskegee has been advocating peace, has not State after State adopted disfranchisement? Has not this same leader been made the object of the most bitter criticism? Is there as much good feeling between blacks and whites today as twenty years ago? On the other hand, the pacific policy is a good one; first because it is right for men to live in peace with their fellows, secondly because it is useless for the negro to attempt to take vengeance upon the white man, and thirdly because it teaches the negro forbearance and self-control. The cry of Booker Washington for peace is a good cry, even though it does not secure its object. It is good because of its effects on the negro, whom it will make more patient and more self-controlled. It is good, too, because in the long run it may find willing response in the ears of a few brave Southern people who do not love the crude animalism of the passion-wrought masses.

Professor DuBois's protest is not a violent one. It is the cry of a man who suffers, rather than the reproach of a man who hates. It is a plea for soul opportunity, and it bears the evidence that its author while he was writing realized the hopelessness of it all. It deals with a most important phaze of the negro question, a phaze which must be reckoned with in the final solution of it, if we ever have any final solution of it. . . .

Within the last six months there has been handed to me a book the title of which is "The Negro a Beast, or In the Image of God." . . . A more stupid book it is impossible to conceive; yet it is worth while to place it and its author side by side with "The Souls of Black Folk" and its author. Can a "beast" write a book like the latter?

JOHN DANIELS

[Review of *Souls*]

[On September 15, 1903, John Daniels reviewed *The Souls of Black Folk* for *Alexander's Magazine*, a black periodical published in Boston. In his review, Daniels was the first critic to assert that *Souls* contained elements that makes a work "classic." *Souls* merits "the highest place" in literary history, he wrote, deserving the status of "a poem, a thing permanent."]

After a reading of Prof. Du Bois' book, "The Souls of Black Folk," one has many thoughts, many impressions. One feels the mystery and the awe of what people call "the Negro Problem." One is filled with sympathy for the Negro, and a sense of the brotherhood of man. One sees vividly the despair, the bitter misery of the Negro in his social degradation. One is exalted by the dominating spirituality of the book. And withal, one feels all the time the fine, sensitive embittered nature of the author.

This is no mere descriptive, analytic or argumentative treatment of the race question, but something which is much deeper and broader, and more ultimate; it is a poem. In motive, method, substance and effect it is a poem. Even the treatment of bare facts is refined, poetical. And since the book is a poem the sympathetic reader reads it as a poem, must so read it. He finds himself in the author's place, seeing with his eyes, feeling with his nature, influenced by his environment, his traditions. The reader does not desire to question this or that inference, to oppose this argument, or pick flaws in that course of reasoning. He does not feel inclined to take the coolly critical, argumentative attitude, for such an attitude seems petty and unworthy of the book.

If criticism may be legitimately undertaken it should concern itself with the sum total effect made upon the reader. For poems should be judged by their effect; study of metre, diction, style, ideas, is merely a study of the means of gaining the effect. Now the effect which this book makes upon the reader is that of bringing him to feel the cruelty, the hardness, the despair, the bitterness of the Negro's present plight. The tone of the book is not hopelessness; far from it; it is full of prophecy of ultimate victory. It is not pessimistic in its ultimate views. Not ultimately cynical, though it is full of passing bitterness and cynicism. It is not unrelenting and vengeful. It is simply and finally a voicing of the bitterness in the Negro's soul, the sorrow that things are as they are, which is not inconsistent with the hope of better things.

Now, the reader could wish that the motif of bitterness and complaint were subordinated to an emergent triumphal motif of overcoming, of victory. One could wish the meanness of the present irradiated by the glory of the future. The author believes in the ultimate victory; then why does he not sing a song of triumph? But, no—what are we saying? Why did Swift[1] not write panegyrics instead of satires? Why not Burns philosophy instead of heart music, why not Kipling[2] Sunday school songs instead of voicings of human fellowship? They did as they did; and as authors, should be judged by what they wrote. So the sympathetic reader feels toward Du Bois. Take his sadness and bitterness for granted, then feel it with him, its power, its justice. Judge his book not as an argument, as an anti-Washingtonian protest, but as a a poem, a spiritual, not intellectual offering, an appeal not to the head but to the heart. Give the book its highest place; not that of a polemic, a transient thing, but that of a poem, a thing permanent.

1. Jonathan Swift (1667–1745), Anglo-Irish minister, satirist, and poet [*Editors*].
2. Rudyard Kipling (1865–1936), English author, received the Nobel Prize in 1907; Robert Burns (1759–1796), Scottish poet [*Editors*].

Modern Criticism

DICKSON D. BRUCE JR.

W. E. B. Du Bois and the Idea of Double Consciousness†

As scholars have developed a greater understanding of the importance of African American literature to the American tradition, they have also developed a real appreciation for the critical place of the thought of W. E. B. Du Bois in both that literature and that tradition in the twentieth century. In particular, they have focused on the famous passage from Du Bois's 1897 *Atlantic* magazine essay, "Strivings of the Negro People"—later republished, with revisions, in *The Souls of Black Folk* (1903)—in which Du Bois spoke of an African American "double consciousness," a "two-ness" of being "an American, a Negro; two warring ideals in one dark body, whose dogged strength alone keeps it from being torn asunder."[1]

Du Bois's use of the idea of double consciousness to characterize issues of race was provocative and unanticipated; however, as has only occasionally been noted and never really pursued, the term itself had a long history by the time Du Bois published his essay in 1897. Du Bois wrote about double consciousness in a way that drew heavily on that history to create a fairly coherent pattern of connotations in both the essay and the later book. The background of meaning which the term evoked would have been familiar to many, if not most, of the educated middle- and upper-class readers of the *Atlantic*, one of the foremost popular journals of letters of the day, and should have contributed much to the understanding of Du Bois's arguments by those readers.

In using the term "double consciousness," Du Bois drew on two

---

† Published in *American Literature: A Journal of Literary History, Criticism, and Bibliography* 64.2 (June 1992): 299–309. Copyright 1992, Duke University Press. Reprinted with permission. Bracketed page numbers refer to this Norton Critical Edition.
1. W. E. B. Du Bois, "Strivings of the Negro People," *Atlantic* 80 (August 1897): 194; Du Bois, *The Souls of Black Folk* (1903; rpt., New York: Penguin, 1989), 5 [11].

main sources. One of these was essentially figurative, a product of European Romanticism and American Transcendentalism. The other, not entirely unrelated and mentioned briefly by historian Arnold Rampersad in his own analysis of Du Bois's work, was initially medical, carried forward into Du Bois's time by the emerging field of psychology. Here the term "double consciousness" was applied to cases of split personality; by the late nineteenth century, it had come into quite general use not only in professional publications but also in discussions of psychological research published for general audiences as well.[2]

The figurative sources for Du Bois's idea of double consciousness are in some ways the most telling. Although one can identify from nineteenth-century literature several possible precedents for Du Bois's use of the term—from Whittier, for example, or George Eliot—Werner Sollors has described this figurative background as Emersonian, and indeed one of the earliest such occurrences of the term may be found in Emerson's works.[3] In an 1843 essay entitled "The Transcendentalist,"[4] a piece he had delivered earlier as a lecture, Emerson employed the term "double consciousness" to refer to a problem in the life of one seeking to take a Transcendental perspective on self and world. Constantly, he wrote, the individual is pulled back from the divine by the demands of daily life. The Transcendentalist knows "moments of illumination," and this makes his situation all the more difficult, because he then sees his life, from the perspective those moments create, as too much dominated by meanness and insignificance. As Emerson wrote, "The worst feature of this double consciousness is, that the two lives, of the understanding and of the soul, which he leads, really show very little relation to each other: one prevails now, all buzz and din; the other prevails then, all infinitude and paradise; and, with the progress of life, the two discover no greater disposition to reconcile themselves." Concerned with different issues, Emerson used the term in a way that was not exactly the same as Du Bois's. But there was more

2. Arnold Rampersad, *The Art and Imagination of W. E. B. Du Bois* (1976; rpt., New York: Schocken, 1990), 74.
3. Ralph Waldo Emerson, (1803–1882), one of America's most influential authors. He was a leading figure in American transcendentalism (see note following), which stressed the mystical unity of nature. John Greenleaf Whittier, (1807–1892), American poet. Whittier was a Quaker and an influential abolitionist editor and writer. After the Civil War, he turned his attention to his very popular poetry, which depicts New England life. George Eliot, pseudonym of Mary Ann Evans, (1819–1880), major English writer known for her novels, including *Adam Bede* (1859), *Silas Marner* (1861), and *Middlemarch* (1871–72). Eliot's plots center around moral choices and personal responsibility [Editors].
4. Transcendentalism holds that there are modes of being beyond the reach of ordinary experience. The Transcendental movement flourished in New England from 1836 to 1860. Influenced by Kant and other German idealist philosophers, it proposed individual intuition as the highest source of knowledge, and emphasized God's immanence in humans and nature, individualism, self-reliance, and rejection of traditional authority [Editors].

than enough similarity to make Emerson's a useful background to what Du Bois was trying to say.[5]

In Emerson's essay, "double-consciousness" evoked a set of oppositions that had become commonplace in Transcendentalism, and, as other scholars have shown, in Romanticism generally. In the passage itself was a dichotomy between "the understanding" and "the soul," but even that referred to a more general set, all organized around a central division between world and spirit. The double consciousness plaguing the Transcendentalist summarized the downward pull of life in society—including the social forces inhibiting genuine self-realization—and the upward pull of communion with the divine; the apparent chaos of things-as-they-are and the unity of Nature comprehended by universal law; and the demanding, cold rationality of commercial society and the search for Truth, Beauty, and Goodness—especially Beauty—that ennobled the soul. Human beings, in the world, could not escape its downward pull. The worldly was an essential part of living one's life. The Transcendental double consciousness grew out of an awareness that Nature and the soul were so much more.[6]

A similar set of oppositions was an important part of Du Bois's argument in his "Strivings of the Negro People." Although in the essay Du Bois used "double consciousness" to refer to at least three different issues—including first the real power of white stereotypes in black life and thought and second the double consciousness created by the practical racism that excluded every black American from the mainstream of the society, the double consciousness of being both an American and not an American—by double consciousness Du Bois referred most importantly to an internal conflict in the African American individual between what was "African" and what was "American." It was in terms of this third sense that the figurative background to "double consciousness" gave the term its most obvious support, because for Du Bois the essence of a distinctive African consciousness was its spirituality, a spirituality based in Africa but revealed among African Americans in their folklore, their history of patient suffering, and their faith. In this sense, double consciousness related particularly to Du Bois's efforts to privilege the spiritual in relation to the materialistic, commercial world of white America. "Negro blood has a message for the world," he wrote,

5. John Greenleaf Whittier, "Among the Hills," in The Works of John Greenleaf Whittier, 7 vols. (Boston: Houghton, Mifflin, 1892), 1:274; George Eliot, "The Lifted Veil," in The Complete Works of George Eliot, 20 vols. (Boston: Colonial Press, n.d.) 20:281, 313; Werner Sollors, Beyond Ethnicity: Consent and Descent in American Culture (New York: Oxford Univ. Press, 1986), 249. See also Sollors, "Of Mules and Mares in a Land of Difference; or, Quadrupeds All?" American Quarterly 42 (1990): 182; and Ralph Waldo Emerson, "The Transcendentalist," in The Selected Writings of Ralph Waldo Emerson, ed. Brooks Atkinson (New York: Modern Library, 1940), 100.
6. Masao Miyoshi, The Divided Self: A Perspective on the Literature of the Victorians (New York: New York Univ. Press, 1969), esp. chap. 2; Karl Miller, Doubles: Studies in Literary History (New York: Oxford Univ. Press, 1985), 21. Whittier's use of the term, which occurred in 1869, very much captured this Emersonian sense.

and this message, as he had been saying since at least 1888, was of a spiritual sense and a softening influence that black people could bring to a cold and calculating world. What Sherman Paul says of Emerson's stress on the "feminine eye" one may also say of Du Bois's stress on the African soul, that it serves as an alternative to a dominant inability to "see" apart from the possibilities for action and profit, a notion Du Bois played on when, guided by his important figure of the "veil," he described the African American as gifted with a kind of "second sight."[7]

Using "double consciousness" thus placed the African spirituality Du Bois sought to celebrate in connection with a more general body of Romantic ideas and imagery. Du Bois reinforced this connection with a web of allusions and oppositions, allusions drawn from Romanticism as well as from Emersonian Transcendentalism. Some have been noted in the past; others have not. Sollors, for example, has cited the Goethean basis for Du Bois's image of the "two souls warring in one dark body," referring back to Faust's anguished cry that "Two souls, alas! reside within my breast, / And each withdraws from, and repels, its brother," a passage that Joel Porte has argued was probably a source for the ideas to which Emerson himself applied the term "double consciousness." Du Bois also contrasted what he described as a black American "hope of a higher synthesis of civilization and humanity" with an alternative search for "reception into charmed social circles of stock-jobbers, pork-packers, and earl-hunters," calling to mind not only the Emersonian distinction between the material and the ideal but also the Emersonian identification of the material with the "buzz and din" of commercial society. Whatever else Du Bois thought of the African character and of its distinctive spirituality, when he spoke of it in terms of double consciousness and embedded it in a web of readily identifiable allusions, he gave it definition in terms of a more general Romantic recognition of the human soul. Converting what had often been a racist or racialist primitivism into a Romantic primitivism, he lent much more weight to his assertion of the possibility of an African message to the world.[8]

---

7. Du Bois, "Strivings," 194, 195; Sherman Paul, *Emerson's Angle of Vision: Man and Nature in American Experience* (Cambridge: Harvard Univ. Press, 1952), 76–77; see Nathan Huggins, "W. E. B. Du Bois and Heroes," *Amerikastudien* 34 (1989): 172–73. Wilson Moses notes the "feminine aestheticism" of the tradition of a romanticized imagery of Africa on which Du Bois drew, in his article "The Poetics of Ethiopianism: W. E. B. Du Bois and Literary Black Nationalism," *American Literature* 47 (1975): 415. It was to describe a kind of "second sight," one might note, that Eliot used the term in her story with the interesting title "The Lifted Veil."

8. Johann Wolfgang Von Goethe, *Faust*, trans. Bayard Taylor (New York: Arden, n.d.), 68; Sollors, "Of Mules and Mares," 182; Joel Porte, "Emerson, Thoreau, and the Double Consciousness," *New England Quarterly* 41 (1968): 41, 50; Du Bois, "Strivings," 197; Emerson, *Selected Writings*, 100. Du Bois's stress on an African spirituality was, of course, far from new in itself, and may be tied to what George Fredrickson has labeled "Romantic racialism," originating with the abolitionists, or what Wilson Moses has described as "Ethiopianism." See George Fredrickson, *The Black Image in the White Mind: The Debate on Afro-American Character and Destiny, 1817–1914* (New York: Harper, 1971), 103; Moses, "The Poetics of Ethiopianism," 411–26 passim.

Such a conversion was a major source of the appeal of Du Bois's presentation of African spirituality as an alternative to materialism. Far from offering an eccentric "message," African American ideals offered a possible direction for American society that could be appreciated by Du Bois's readers. As such scholars as Karl Miller and Jackson Lears have stressed, in the rapidly industrializing United States of the late nineteenth century there was a real hunger, especially on the part of the middle class, for a revival of the spiritual; there was even, as Miller and Henri Ellenberger have argued, a renewed interest throughout the West in Romantic conceptions of human nature and human possibility, including that positive sense of alienation that Thomas Holt has discussed with regard to Du Bois's ideas. Double consciousness and the collection of Romantic allusions in which it was placed thus helped to give definition to the positive sense of African and African American distinctiveness Du Bois was trying to develop, and to offer in the "African" a kind of alternative to American materialism with which many in an educated readership could sympathize. It is not surprising, then, that when Du Bois gave a still fuller statement of his views in *The Souls of Black Folk* he also elaborated on the same pattern of allusions, even in his attack on the materialism of Booker Washington.[9]

Still, telling as the figurative background to double consciousness may have been, that background was supplemented in important ways by the psychological sources that gave additional meaning to Du Bois's idea of double consciousness. Despite the work of such scholars as Karl Miller and Henri Ellenberger, there remains an unexplored path between a general concern about duality as an element of European Romanticism and American Transcendentalism, and the work of those medical scientists who developed "double consciousness" as a diagnostic term, one with a well-defined technical meaning by the time Du Bois used it. Again, Arnold Rampersad has noted something of this psychological background to "double consciousness," citing its appearance in Oswald Külpe's 1893 psychology text as well as the use of the idea, if not the term, in *The Principles of Psychology*, written by Du Bois's Harvard mentor William James and published in 1890 at the very time Du Bois was at Harvard. But, in fact, as a medical term "double consciousness" already had a long history by the 1890s, having been the subject of rather extensive experimentation and debate for at least seventy-five years. One cannot really identify with certainty the first use of "double consciousness" in the medical literature. Certainly it came fairly early in the nineteenth century, even antedating Emer-

---

9. Miller, *Doubles*, especially 221; Henri F. Ellenberger, *The Discovery of the Unconscious: The History and Evolution of Dynamic Psychiatry* (New York: Basic Books, 1970), 278ff.; T. J. Jackson Lears, *No Place of Grace: Antimodernism and the Transformation of American Culture, 1880–1920* (New York: Pantheon, 1981), chap. 1; Thomas Holt, "The Political Uses of Alienation: W. E. B. Du Bois on Politics, Race, and Culture, 1903–1940," *American Quarterly* 42 (1990): 301–23; Du Bois, *Souls*, e.g., 38, 43 [40, 41].

son's application of it to Transcendentalism. Its lengthy history of development had great relevance to Du Bois's own use of "double consciousness" in "Strivings of the Negro People."[1]

In 1817, in a New York professional journal called the *Medical Repository*, an account headed "A Double Consciousness, or a Duality of Person in the same Individual" made use of the term in a way that remained fairly constant for psychology through the nineteenth century. The account was of a young woman—later identified as Mary Reynolds—who at about age nineteen fell into a deep sleep from which she awoke with no memory of who she was and with a wholly different personality. A few months later, after again falling into a deep sleep, she awoke as her old self. At the time of the 1817 account, she had periodically alternated selves for a period of about four years. As it turned out, this was to continue for about fifteen or sixteen years in total, until in her mid-thirties she permanently entered the second state. Her two lives were entirely separate; while in one, she had no knowledge or memory of the other. Such utter distinctiveness of the two selves was what made the editors of the *Medical Repository* refer to hers as a case of "double consciousness."[2]

As a result of the Mary Reynolds case, the term "double consciousness" entered into fairly extensive use. For example, Francis Wayland's influential mid-nineteenth-century textbook *Elements of Intellectual Philosophy* treated the concept of double consciousness as part of a general discussion of consciousness as such and recounted the Mary Reynolds case along with a few others by way of illustration. An 1860 article in *Harper's* also focused on the Reynolds case and on double consciousness as a medical and philosophical issue. As a medical term, then, it was hardly confined to the use of medical professionals.[3]

During the time Du Bois was formulating his ideas of African American distinctiveness, there had been renewed interest in double consciousness as a medical and theoretical issue. Most important for Du Bois was the role of his Harvard mentor William James. James stimulated this interest, not only in his *Principles*—in describing what he called "alternating selves" or "primary and secondary consciousness," he drew on a body of contemporary French work which had been widely publicized in the United States as well—but also as a result of his own experience about 1890 with a notable American case of double consciousness, that of Ansel Bourne. James's work with Bourne (whose discoverer, Richard Hodgson, did use "double consciousness" to label the case), as well as the American publication of the French studies on

1. Miller, *Doubles*, 241ff.; Ellenberger, *Discovery of the Unconscious*, 166.
2. Samuel L. Mitchell, "A Double Consciousness, or a Duality of Person in the same Individual," *Medical Repository* n.s. 3 (1817): 185–86; William S. Plumer, "Mary Reynolds: A Case of Double Consciousness," *Harper's* 20 (May 1860): 807–12.
3. Francis Wayland, *The Elements of Intellectual Philosophy* (Boston: Phillips, Sampson, 1855), 115, 423–26; Plumer, "Mary Reynolds," passim.

which James drew, occurred at the same time Du Bois's relationship with James was at its closest. Whether James and Du Bois talked about it at the time is impossible to say, but based on Du Bois's use of "double consciousness" in his *Atlantic* essay he certainly seems to have known the term's psychological background, because he used it in ways quite consistent with that background.[4]

The psychological literature of double consciousness looked directly to the issue of distinctiveness as that issue was developed in Du Bois's essay. Du Bois discussed distinctiveness within a framework provided by several implications that James and others had drawn out, providing an intellectual structure consistent with the general thrust of his argument. For one thing, the psychological idea of double consciousness further reinforced what Du Bois had emphasized as the genuinely alternative character of African American ideals. In the classic cases of double consciousness, the dual personalities were not just different from each other but were inevitably in opposition. Mary Reynolds in her first state was "sedate, sober and pensive"; in her second, "gay and cheerful, extravagantly fond of society, of fun and practical jokes." Similar contrasts were drawn in other cases. Double consciousness thus entailed a real opposition between the two consciousnesses confined within a single body.[5]

Moreover, as earlier writers had made plain, in classic cases of double consciousness, although the condition itself was clearly abnormal, it could not be said that either personality was more obviously "normal" or functional than the other. In the Reynolds case, for example, commentators noted her intellectual acuity in both states, as well as the fact that, settling permanently in her second state, she nevertheless spent her remaining years as a productive, respectable, and respected member of society. Of another influential case, that of the young French woman Fèlida X, it was emphasized that she showed both intelligence and a good sense of morality in both states, if a weaker will in her second self.

Such a background of ideas and facts made the concept of double consciousness especially useful to Du Bois, given his desire to develop a positive sense of racial distinctiveness out of a distinctively African heritage. Ideas of race and behavior were problematic in the late nineteenth century. Notions of "culture" and, especially, of anything like cultural relativism were rudimentary and not widespread at the time. "Race" itself carried biological connotations—connotations not entirely absent from Du Bois's discussion—that were troublesome, since bio-

---

4. William James, *The Principles of Psychology*, 2 vols. (1890; rpt., New York: Dover, 1950), 1:393. For an example of the French work, see Alfred Binet, "Proof of Double Consciousness in Hysterical Individuals," *Open Court* 3 (1889): 1739–41. On Bourne, see Ellenberger, *Discovery of the Unconscious*, 134–35, 177n.
5. Plumer, "Mary Reynolds," 808; J. Elliotson, "Dual Consciousness," *Cornhill* 35 (1877): 90–91.

logical notions of race served mainly to ground those beliefs concerning black inferiority which were generally accepted by whites. Thus, for good reason, black writers and intellectuals felt real ambivalence about the kinds of ideas about racial distinctiveness Du Bois was trying to portray, however positive they might appear on the surface. Indeed, Du Bois himself showed such ambivalence in other writings from this period.[6]

Because the idea of double consciousness explicitly emphasized the integrity of distinctive states in the individual who was its subject, it helped Du Bois to get around the dilemma his idea of distinctiveness so long had posed. Double consciousness allowed for a sense of distinctiveness that really did entail equality, a sense of distinctiveness that did not imply inferiority. It gave him precisely the vocabulary he needed to make the case he wanted to make. In the absence of any kind of adequate idea of cultural relativism, the idea of double consciousness allowed Du Bois to talk about an African mode of thought and what we would now call a cultural conflict between the African and the American in a way very like that made possible by a notion of relativism. Thus he could base his discussion on a body of psychological knowledge more firmly established during his time, one identifying the possibility of different but equally functional ways of dealing with the world.

None of this was to minimize for him the tragic character of African American life. One of the things his use of the concept did was to imply that if what was distinctive was not to be seen as abnormal, the condition of African Americans—given the roots of double consciousness—was. Even as the Romantic idea, with its echoes of *Sturm und Drang*, highlighted the difficulty of resolution in the war between incompatible souls, so too the psychological literature stressed its difficulty. All the accounts of double consciousness reported its sufferers' great anguish, their real unhappiness upon becoming aware of their condition, their desire to possess a single individual self.

Du Bois obviously did not break from such a treatment. For him the essence of double consciousness was its problematic character as a symptom of the difficulty that lay in the realization of any true self consciousness, of any sense of self beyond the problematic sense conveyed in the dilemma as such.

Du Bois did propose a kind of resolution, at least for that double consciousness of "African" and "American" selves. It was, he wrote, for the African American "to merge his double self into a better and truer self," losing "neither of the older selves." If the dilemma was known to the Romantics and the psychologists alike, Du Bois's rhetoric of resolution drew with special clarity on the medical background. Du Bois's

6. On Du Bois's ideas about race as a concept, see Anthony Appiah, "The Uncompleted Argument: Du Bois and the Illusion of Race," in *"Race," Writing, and Difference*, ed. Henry Louis Gates Jr. (Chicago: Univ. of Chicago Press, 1986), 27–29.

mentor William James had speculated on the possibility of a real cure for alternating consciousness involving not the victory of one over the other but a process whereby "the dissociated systems came together," resulting in a third, new Self, "different from the other two, but knowing their objects together." Francis Wayland, in his earlier text, had cited a case of just such a cure of "double consciousness," one in which a young woman's recovery was marked by "the blending together of the knowledge acquired in [her] separate conditions," a blending succeeded by a process in which the two consciousnesses "became more and more identified until the testimony of consciousness became uninterrupted and then the abnormal state vanished altogether." Mary Reynolds's settling in her second state was not a cure; she often mourned for what she had lost with her initial self. Cure came in synthesis, which Wayland and later James believed to be possible.[7]

Du Bois himself was not entirely certain about the possibility of such a synthesis. The *Atlantic* essay in particular leaves the question open, focusing more on the problem than on any possibility for its resolution. One reason for this may have been that Du Bois was attempting a rhetorical synthesis of his own, one that was not easy to accomplish, between two key senses of double consciousness—the one created by racism; the other, by conflicting perspectives on life—never really distinguishing between them himself. The key difference between the two was a question of will. The merging of African and American selves was, or at least could be, an act of will, and Du Bois so treated it. The merging of selves created by American racism was not. By treating the distinction loosely, Du Bois may have been hoping to make the latter seem more manageable, an aspect of a more general duality. But, as the *Atlantic* essay itself indicates, the resolution was one Du Bois himself had not fully worked out, and neither the Emersonian nor the psychological literature, despite the optimism of the latter, gave him much of a guide for how to do it.

One cannot know for certain how familiar Du Bois was with all the background on double consciousness either from literary or medical sources. His use of the term suggests that he was familiar with both; there is no compelling evidence that he sought to be closer to or more consistent with one or the other. Instead, when he talked about double consciousness, Du Bois was using a term that set up a variety of connotations for the educated reader, thus making an effort to give his readers a reference point on the basis of which to understand the tragedy of racism, especially for the self-conscious individual, and also to appreciate his own program for a new definition of what it meant to be black in America. The continuing influence of his work suggests the extent to which he succeeded.

7. Du Bois, "Strivings," 195; James, *Principles*, 1:399; Wayland, *Elements*, 115–16.

ROBERT GOODING-WILLIAMS

Du Bois's Counter-Sublime†

1. Introduction

Both Wilson Moses and Eric Sundquist have recently argued that "Of Alexander Crummell," the twelfth chapter of Du Bois's *The Souls of Black Folk* (hereafter *Souls*), offers little in the way of insight into Du Bois's appraisal of Crummell's thought. "Du Bois's short biography of Crummell," writes Moses, "promises much but leaves a great deal to the imagination . . . Du Bois somehow missed the opportunity . . . to analyze in detail the relationship between his ideas and those of Crummell."[1] According to Sundquist, "[Du Bois's] tribute to Crummell . . . remains a partial curiosity because it has little to say about Crummell's thought as such . . ."[2] Moses and Sundquist rightly recognize that Du Bois's response to Crummell's thought, if it is evident in Du Bois's essay on Crummell is *not* obviously and explicitly evident. Thus, "Of Alexander Crummell," the third from the last of *Souls'* chapters, differs markedly from "Of Mr. Booker T. Washington and Others," the symmetrically placed and more famous third chapter of Du Bois's book, and the only other chapter having the name of a particular individual in its title. Still, it seems to me erroneous to suggest, as Moses and Sundquist do, that in declining to engage Crummell's ideas directly—in declining, that is, to analyze and argue with them in the way in which he analyzed and argued with Washington's view—Du Bois ignores these ideas and their connection to his own thinking.

Pace Moses and Sundquist, the central thesis of this paper is that Du Bois's essay on Crummell is a masterpiece of indirection, and that Du Bois sets forth in it a substantive critique of Crummell's social philosophy.[3] My argument, more precisely, is that "Of Alexander Crummell"

---

† Reprinted from *The Massachusetts Review: A Quarterly of Literature, the Arts and Public Affairs* 35.2 (Summer 1994): 202–24. © 1994 The Massachusetts Review, Inc. Bracketed page numbers refer to this Norton Critical Edition.

1. Wilson Jeremiah Moses, *Alexander Crummell: A Study of Civilization and it Discontents* (New York: Oxford University, 1989), p. 247.

2. Eric J. Sundquist, *To Wake the Nations: Race in the Making of American Literature* (Cambridge: Harvard University Press, 1993), p. 517.

3. A question well worth addressing, that I do not address in this paper, pertains to Du Bois's decision to write about Crummell in a manner so different from the way in which he writes about Washington. Why is the engagement with Crummell's thought implicit and indirect, when Du Bois has been so careful to spell out the reasons for his opposition to Washington? In his commentary on this paper, presented in February 1993 at Harvard's Du Bois Institute, George Frederickson suggested some directions that an answer to this question might take. He noted, among other things, that while Du Bois sees Crummell as a father figure, he sees Washington as a rival, that while Du Bois believes that Crummell's celebrity is deserved (despite whatever criticism he has of Crummell), he believes that Washington's celebrity is undeserved; and that while Du Bois is quite sympathetic to Crummell's intellectualism, he repudiates Washington's materialism.

elaborates Du Bois's critical reaction to Crummell's 1885 repudiation of slave culture (in Crummell's language, "the *word* and the *thought* of slavery") and to the alienated model of racial leadership which, Du Bois implies Crummell personified.[4] Eric Sundquist insists correctly, I believe, that "[f]or Du Bois, Crummell functioned symbolically as . . . a father," and "became the mechanism for Du Bois's own ascendancy to the position of founding father of modern African American thought."[5] To this remark, I would simply add that the rhetorical path of Du Bois's ascendancy is marked out by his portrait of Crummell's life. By characterizing Crummell as a sublime father figure with respect to whom he claims for himself a superior sublimity, Du Bois attempts to re-value the culture of the slave and to produce a compelling alternative to Crummell's example of alienated leadership. In this way, he portrays himself as the founding father of modern African American thought, while re-presenting modern African American thought as thought essentially rooted in the experience of slavery.

2. *Protestant Martyrdom within the Veil*

Stanley Brodwin, in an important study of *Souls*, has observed that Du Bois tacitly refers in his chapter on Crummell to John Bunyan's *The Pilgrim's Progress*[6] Recalling Bunyan's depiction of Christian's life and journey ("Christian" is Bunyan's name for the protagonist of his allegory), Du Bois, in the very first paragraph of this chapter, represents Crummell's career as fraught with temptations (Du Bois mentions specifically the temptations of hate, despair, and doubt) and as leading Crummell, like Christian, into a "Valley of Humiliation" and a "Valley of the Shadow of Death." Du Bois's allusion here to *The Pilgrim's Progress* is significant, because it characterizes for his readers the sort of story he wishes to tell about Crummell. His "Life of Crummell," Du Bois wants to let us know, will be the history of the heart of a

---

4. For Crummell's reference to "the *word* and the *thought* of slavery," see his "The Need of New Ideas and New Aims for a New Era," the lead essay in his *Africa and America* (New York: Negro Universities Press, 1969), p. 19 (*Africa and America* was originally published by Willey and Co. of Springfield, Massachusetts, in 1891).

   In reading Du Bois's essay on Crummell as addressing the question of racial leadership, I follow the leads of Robert Stepto (see Robert Stepto, *From Behind the Veil* [Urbana: University of Illinois Press, 1979], p. 57) and Arnold Rampersad (see Arnold Rampersad, *The Art and Imagination of W. E. B. Du Bois* [New York: Schocken Books, 1990], p. 87). Recent work that, like my own, highlights the divide between Crummell and Du Bois on the value of slave culture includes that of Sundquist (*To Wake the Nations*, p. 516) and Frank M. Kirkland (see Frank M. Kirkland, "Modernity and Intellectual Life in Black," *The Philosophical Forum*, Volume XXIX, Nos. 1–3 [Fall-Spring, 1992–93], pp. 136–165). My effort in this paper complements Sundquist's and Kirkland's arguments, by attempting to show how this divide gets expressed in the form of a critique of Crummell that is present in the last three chapters of *Souls*.

5. Sundquist, p. 517.

6. See Stanley Brodwin, "The Veil Transcended: Form and Meaning in W. E. B. Du Bois' 'The Souls of Black Folk'," *Journal of Black Studies* (March 1972), p. 313.

Protestant pilgrim, a personal story of Christian faith, wandering and homeless in an alien and hostile world.[7]

Published in 1678, *The Pilgrim's Progress* is not the only early modern Protestant text Du Bois uses in framing his biography of Crummell. Dating from the same period are two other Protestant works that Du Bois names explicitly: *The Whole Duty of Man*, published in 1658, and Foxe's *Book of Martyrs*, published in 1563. *The Whole Duty of Man* is a devotional text of unknown authorship that analyzes man's duties to God and to his fellow man.[8] The *Book of Martyrs* is John Foxe's history of the Protestant church and its martyrs, as well as a source of which Bunyan seems to have relied in composing *The Pilgrim's Progress*.[9] Du Bois mentions both works in a passage in which he imagines Crummell's meeting with Bishop Onderdonk Philadelphia:

> I sometimes fancy I can see that tableau: the frail black figure, nervously twitching his hat before the massive abdomen of Bishop Onderdonk; his threadbare coat thrown against the dark woodwork of the book-cases, where Fox's "Lives of the Martyrs" nestled happily beside "The Whole Duty of Man." I seem to see the wide eyes of the Negro wander past the Bishop's broadcloth to where the swinging glass doors of the cabinet glow in the sunlight. A little blue fly is trying to cross the yawning keyhole. He marches briskly up to it, peers into the chasm in a surprised sort of way, and rubs his feelers reflectively; then he essays its depths, and, finding it bottomless, draws back again. The dark-face priest finds himself wondering if the fly too has faced its Valley of Humiliation, and if it will plunge into it,—when lo! it spreads its tiny wings and buzzes merrily across, leaving the watcher wingless and alone.
>
> Then the full weight of his burden fell upon him. The rich wall wheeled away, and before him lay the cold rough moor winding on through life, cut in twain by one thick granite ridge,—here, the Valley of Humiliation; yonder, the Valley of the Shadow of Death.[1]

7. For Bunyan's interpretation of the figure of the pilgrim as a homeless wanderer in an alien world, see Philip Edwards, "The Journey in *The Pilgrim's Progress*," in *The Pilgrim's Progress: Critical and Historical Views*, ed. Vincent Newey (Liverpool: Liverpool University Press, 1980), pp. 113–14. For two helpful discussions of the general tenets of Bunyan's Protestantism, see, in the same volume, the essays by Newey ("Bunyan and the Confines of the Mind") and Gordon Campbell ("The Theology of *The Pilgrim's Progress*"), as well as Roger Sharrock's "Introduction" to *The Pilgrim's Progress*, ed. Roger Sharrock, (Harmondsworth: Penguin, 1987).

8. See W. E. B. Du Bois, *The Souls of Black Folk* (New York: Penguin, 1989), p. 242, which gives Donald Gibson's note on Du Bois's reference to *The Whole Duty of Man*. All subsequent references to *The Souls of Black Folk* (hereafter referenced as *Souls*) will be to this edition.

9. For Bunyan's use of Foxe, see Sharrock's notes to the Penguin edition of *The Pilgrim's Progress*, pp. 394–95. I am indebted to my colleague, Margaret Hunt, for an enlightening discussion of the significance which *The Pilgrim's Progress*, *The Book of Martyrs*, and *The Whole Duty of Man* had for the militant Protestants of the early modern period.

1. Du Bois, *Souls*, p. 182 [139].

Du Bois's treatment here of Crummell's encounter with Onderdonk involves what at first seems to be bizarre meditation on the movements of a "little blue fly," as well as an ironic reference to the two Protestant texts Du Bois mentions. Du Bois's description of the fly begins with Du Bois adopting Crummell's point of view ("I seem to see the wide eyes of the Negro wander . . . to where the swinging glass doors of the cabinet glow the sunlight"), and then plays upon and develops Du Bois's earlier allusions to *The Pilgrim's Progress*. The fly, whose fate Crummell empathetically likens to his own ("The dark-face priest finds himself wondering if the fly too . . ."), seems to Crummell to face a "Valley of Humiliation" that Du Bois—not adopting the perspective of the fly—compares to a bottomless chasm. Here, Du Bois's use of Bunyan's book as a template seems straightforward, since in Bunyan's "Valley of Humiliation Christian does battle with Apollyon, a hideous monster whose name derives from *Revelations* 9.11: "And they had a King over them, which is the angel of the *bottomless pit*, whose name in the Hebrew tongue is Abaddon, but in the Greek tongue hath his name Apollyon" (emphasis mine). In Du Bois's tableau, Bishop Onderdonk and his massive abdomen monstrously preside over what a "nervously twitching" (like a fly!?) Crummell senses is the bottomless pit (or chasm) of his own "Valley of Humiliation." The comfort which Crummell begins to find here, by imaginatively attributing his plight to a fly—as if he and the fly could constitute some sort of community —is at once comic and tragic: comic because it is absurd that Crummell should seek community with a fly, and tragic, because when the fly flies away, "leaving the watcher wingless and alone," the watcher will see that he has fallen prey to an error reminiscent of the "pathetic fallacy," and so face again the pilgrim's condition of estrangement and isolation.[2]

Du Bois's ironic reference to *The Book of Martyrs* and *The Whole Duty of Man* complements his use of Bunyan. Here, the source of Du Bois's irony is his juxtaposition of Onderdonk's books, both of which esteem the religiously engaged and active life, to Onderdonk's disengaged and meditative self-satisfaction. When Crummell comes to see Onderdonk, Du Bois imagines, it is "after dinner," and just when the "corpulent, red-faced" Bishop has "settled himself for a pleasant season of contemplation."[3] Onderdonk's contentedness is such a compelling force in the setting Du Bois envisions that, in its presence, even a book of martyrs' lives seems strangely lacking in religious passion as it nestles

---

2. Strictly speaking, the pathetic fallacy concerns the ascription of human traits to inanimate nature (see M. H. Abrams, *A Glossary of Literary Terms* [New York: Holt Rinehart and Winston, 1971], pp. 121–22). Du Bois's Crummell, I am suggesting, attributes human traits, not to inanimate nature, but to an animate fly.
3. Du Bois, *Souls*, p. 182 [139].

"happily" beside a work that is itself adamant in discouraging complacency.[4] By picturing Onderdonk as a red-faced and corpulent man who has just fed his massive stomach, Du Bois cleverly recalls his readers to Foxe's depictions of the "bloody" and "fat paunched" Bishop Bonner, a persistent persecutor of Protestants who figures prominently in Foxe's narrative and who appears there as a bestial glutton that takes delight in human flesh.[5] In Du Bois's imagined "tableau," no less than in many of the tableaux which literally illustrate Foxe's book (more than 160 engravings in the editions of the 1570s and later), a Protestant martyr—in this case Alexander Crummell—finds himself set upon by a villainous and "false" Christian, a morally reprobate member of the "visible" church who knows nothing of the religious inwardness of the faithful.[6]

Portraying Crummell as a solitary pilgrim and as a persecuted martyr, Du Bois's narrative of Crummell's life is a story of doom and despair, of death and rebirth ("The Valley of the Shadow of Death gives few of its pilgrims back to the world. But Alexander Crummell it gave back"), of a wanderer who finally finds his place in the world (For Du Bois's Crummell, this place is America, not Africa) and, ultimately, of an imagined greeting from Christ, the first and prototypical Christian martyr: "I wonder where he is today? I wonder if in that dim world beyond as he came gliding in, there rose on some wan throne a King as a dark and pierced Jew, who knows the writhings of the earthly damned, saying, as he laid those heart-wrung talents down, "Well done!" while round about the morning stars singing."[7] Alluding to the biblical "parable of the talents (Matthew 25:14–30), Du Bois ends his narrative of Crummell's life by depicting a black ("dark") and persecuted ("pierced") Christ welcoming Crummell to heaven and praising him,

---

4. Consider, e.g., the following passage, taken from a 1715 edition of *The Whole Duty of Man*, printed in London by F. Leake for E. Pawlet at the Sign of the Bible in Chancery Lane, near Fleetstreet:

> . . . and the World is a vast army against us: There is no state or condition in it, nay, scarce a creature which doth not, at some time or another, fight against the Soul; The Honours of this world seek to wound us by Pride, the wealth by covetousness, the Prosperity of it tempts us to forget God, the adversities to murmur at him. Our very table becomes a snare to us, our meat draws us to gluttony, our drink to drunkenness, our company, nay, our nearest friends often bear a part in this war against us, whilst either by their example or persuasions they entice us to sin.
> 9. Consider all this and then tell me, whether a soul thus beset hath leisure to sleep (p. v).

5. For Foxe's description of Bonner as fat-paunched, see *Foxe's Book of Martyrs*, ed. and abridged by G. A. Williamson (Toronto: Little, Brown and Company, 1965), p. 420. For a general discussion of Foxe's caricatures of Bonner as a "bloody," fat, and bestial glutton see Warren W. Wooden, *John Foxe* (Boston: Twayne Publishers, 1983), pp. 56–7.
6. For Foxe's use of tableaux, see Wooden, *John Foxe*, pp. 48–50. For Foxe on the relation between religious inwardness and the distinction between the visible and the invisible church, see Wooden, *John Foxe*, pp. 28–9.
7. Du Bois, *Souls*, pp. 184–85 [142].

presumably, for the beneficence of his righteousness.[8] Having lived and worked his whole life within the Veil, Crummell receives the recognition he deserves only after he dies, explicitly from Du Bois in the tale he tells of Crummell's career ("And now that he is gone, I sweep the Veil away and cry, Lo! the son to whose dear memory I bring this little tribute") and, Du Bois speculates, from Christ himself ("Well done!").

3. Sympathy, Estrangement, and Crummell's Tragedy

Consider now the following remarks, which come near the end of Du Bois's "tribute" to Crummell:

> So he grew, and brought within his wide influence all that was best of those who walk within the Veil. They who live without knew not nor dreamed of that full power within, that mighty inspiration which the dull gauze of caste decreed that most men should not know . . .
> He did his work,—he did it nobly and well, and yet I sorrow that here he worked alone, with so little *human sympathy*. His name to-day, in this broad land, means little, and comes to fifty million ears laden with no incense of memory or emulation. And herein lies the *tragedy* of the age: not that men are poor,—all men know something of poverty; not that men are wicked,—who is good? not that men are ignorant,—what is Truth? *Nay, but that men know so little of men* (emphasis mine).[9]

Crummell was a tragic figure, says Du Bois, not because he suffered persecution, but because his life and achievements remained unknown to others. Those who lived "without [the Veil] knew not nor dreamed of that full power within," and so they could have no sympathy for what Crummell endured. The Veil of Jim Crow produces tragedy, Du Bois suggests, because it keeps men from knowing the character of each other's lives and thus from sympathizing with each other's work and striving. Du Bois's "tribute" to Crummell is his attempt to "sweep the Veil away," by revealing to the white world the character of Crummell's

8. Crummell himself seems to refer to the "parable of the talents" in at least two places. In the first instance, he alludes to a Biblical text that "shows us the satisfaction of a gracious judge, in the beneficence of the righteous" (see Alexander Crummell, *The Future of Africa* [Detroit: Negro History Press, 196?], p. 196). In a footnote to this allusion, Crummell cites Matthew 25:31, which bears no connection to his reference to a gracious judge. It is reasonable, however, to assume that Crummell meant to refer to Matthew 25:14–30, which immediately precedes the passage he does cite, and which straightforwardly admits of being construed as demonstrating the satisfaction of a gracious judge. In the second instance, Crummell seems clearly to echo Matthew's parable when he writes that "when the grace of God is given men, then there comes a fiery stimulus to human souls to make our talents, whether two, or five or ten, bring a larger value and a noble fruitage" (see Alexander Crummell, *Destiny and Race: Selected Writings 1840–1898*, ed. Wilson Jeremiah Moses [Amherst: The University of Massachusetts Press, 1992], p. 273).

9. Du Bois, *Souls*, pp. 184–85 [141–42].

life and by eliciting from that world the sympathy Crummell deserved.

In "Of the Sons of Master and Man" (chapter nine of *Souls*), Du Bois elaborates in some detail his belief that Jim Crow is inimical to interracial sympathy. Between the two worlds of black and white, he writes, "there is almost no continuity of intellectual life or point of transference where the thoughts and feelings of one race can come into direct contact and sympathy with thoughts and feelings of the other." Du Bois comments as well that "the very representatives of the two races, who for mutual benefit and the welfare of the land ought to be in complete understanding and sympathy, are so far strangers, that one side thinks all whites are narrow and prejudiced, and the other thinks educated Negroes dangerous and insolent." Time and again, he complains, the "color-question" foils schemes of "broad minded sympathy and generous fellowship" between the races, and he even sounds nostalgic when he refers to "that finer sympathy and love between some masters and house servants which the radical and uncompromising drawing of the color-line in recent years has caused almost completely to disappear." "Human advancement is not a mere question of alms-giving," Du Bois insists, "but rather of sympathy and cooperation among classes who would scorn charity." Du Bois concludes his remarks with the assertion that "only by a union of intelligence and sympathy across the color-line in this critical period of the Republic shall justice and right triumph."[1]

Read in the perspective of "Of the Sons of Master and Man," Du Bois's claim that Crummell lived and worked "with so little human sympathy" can be interpreted as identifying a single example of a general social problem. Where the Veil prevails; where, in other words, the practice of Jim Crow governs men's and women's lives, it is usually the case that black and white know little of, and have little sympathy for, each other. Du Bois's attempt, in Crummell's case, to elicit sympathy for Crummell from a white world persisting without the Veil is a concrete effort to bring "the thoughts and feelings of one race . . . into direct contact and sympathy with the thoughts and feelings of the other," and thus a form of resistance to Jim Crow.

Let me turn now to just one more passage in which Du Bois speaks of sympathy. The passage is significant, first, because it defines the concept of sympathy, and second, because it uses that concept, neither to discuss the general effects of Jim Crow nor to describe the particular tragedy of Crummell's life, but to examine Crummell's feelings as a young man for his fellow black folk living within the Veil.

> The nineteenth was the first century of human sympathy,—the age when half wonderingly we began to descry in others that transfigured spark of divinity which we call Myself; when clodhopper

1. *Ibid.* See pp. 133–153 [116–19] for the passages cited in the preceding paragraph.

and peasants, and tramps and thieves, and millionaires and—sometimes—Negroes, become throbbing souls whose warm pulsing life touched us so nearly that we half gasped with surprise, crying, "Thou too! Hast Thou seen Sorrow and the dull waters of Hopelessness? Hast Thou known Life?" And then all helplessly we peered into those Otherworlds, and wailed, "O World of Worlds, how shall man make you one?"

So in that little Oneida school there came to those schoolboys a revelation of thought and longing beneath one black skin, of which they had not dreamed before. And to the lonely boy came a new dawn of sympathy and inspiration . . . A vision of life came to the growing boy,—mystic, wonderful. He raised his head, stretched himself, breathed deep of the fresh new air. Yonder behind the forests he saw strange sounds; then glinting through the trees he saw, far, far away, the bronzed hosts of a nation calling, —calling faintly, calling loudly. He heard the fateful clank of their chains, he felt them cringe and grovel, and there rose within him a protest and a prophecy. And he girded himself to walk down the world.

A voice and a vision called him to be a priest,—a seer to lead the uncalled out of the house of bondage. He saw the headless host turn toward him like the whirling of mad waters,—he stretched forth his hands eagerly, and then, even as he stretched them, suddenly there swept across the vision the temptation of Despair.[2]

Sympathy, as Du Bois defines it, requires both knowledge and acknowledgement. To feel sympathy for another person, he suggests, is not only to know that that person personifies the same "transfigured spark of divinity" or the same "warm pulsing life" as oneself; it is likewise to be moved ("touched") by one's discovery of that sameness *to acknowledge that sameness*, and thus to say *in some way* to that person "Thou too! Hast Thou seen Sorrow and the dull waters of Hopelessness?" Sympathy, for Du Bois, is what he describes elsewhere as an "opening of heart and hand . . . in generous acknowledgement of a common humanity and a common destiny."[3] It is a movement beyond the knowledge or discovery of a shared identity to an expressed and explicit avowal of human community.

Now in the case of the young Crummell, as Du Bois characterizes him, the dawning of "sympathy and inspiration" involved a "vision of life" in which he saw "the bronze hosts of a nation calling." This vision

2. *Ibid.*, pp. 178–79 [136–37].
3. *Ibid.*, p. 150 [117]. Shamoon Zamir, in his unpublished manuscript, *W. E. B. Du Bois and the Failure of American Thought: A Study in Race and Multiplicity*, insightfully explores the connections between Du Bois's conception of sympathy and the treatment of sympathy in the writings of William James and Franz Boas.

revealed to Crummell the sorrow and the humiliation of black slaves
—"the . . . clank of their chains," their cringing and grovelling. It also
elicited in Crummell a sympathetic response, precisely to the extent
that it inspired him with a knowledge of slaves' suffering that moved
him to protest, to prophecy, and to want "to lead the uncalled out of
the house of bondage." Called to be a priest and seeing "the headless
host turn towards him," Crummell "stretched forth his hands eagerly,"
acknowledging in this way his connection to his black brethren and
declaring in his manner "Thou too! Hast Thou seen Sorrow, etc." It is
significant, here that Du Bois has Crummell avow his kinship to black
slaves by making a gesture with his hands, since, we shall see, gestures
of this sort repeatedly appear in *Souls* (both in Du Bois's chapter on
Crummell and elsewhere) as figures for a refusal of isolation and an
insistence on community that Du Bois believes are essential to expressions of sympathy.[4]

Crummell's vision-inspired sympathy is destroyed, Du Bois tells us,
by "the temptation of Despair." The young Crummell falls victim to
this temptation when he is told that " 'The General Theological Seminary of the Episcopal Church cannot admit a Negro.' "[5] Devastated by
the Church's act of racial discrimination, Crummell's life at this point
becomes but a shadow of what it once promised to be:

> And then from that Vision Splendid all the glory faded slowly away
> . . . Even the kind hands that stretched themselves toward him
> from out of the depths of that dull morning seemed but parts of
> the purple shadows. He saw them coldly and asked, "Why should
> I strive by special grace when the way of the world is closed to
> me?" All gently yet, the hands urged him on,—the hand of the
> young John Jay, that daring father's son; the hands of the good
> folk of Boston, that free city. And yet, with a way to the priesthood
> of the Church open at last before him, the cloud lingered there;
> and even when in old St. Paul's the venerable Bishop raised his
> white arms above the Negro deacon—even then the burden had
> not lifted from that heart, for there had passed a glory from the
> earth.
>   And yet the fire through which Alexander Crummell went did
> not burn in vain. Slowly and more soberly he took up again his
> plan of life. More critically he studied the situation. Deep down

4. The figure of "stretched forth" hands seems clearly to echo Psalms 68:31: "Princes shall come
out of Egypt; Ethiopia shall soon stretch out her hands to God." Ethiopianism is a recurrent
motif in African-American letters, as Wilson Jeremiah Moses shows in *The Wings of Ethiopia*
(Ames: Iowa State University Press, 1990).
5. Du Bois, *Souls*, p. 179 [137]. Here, Du Bois alludes to Crummell's meeting with Bishop
Benjamin Onderdonck, which preceded the encounter with Bishop Henry Onderdonck (Benjamin's brother) of Philadelphia, which encounter, we have seen, Du Bois describes in vivid
detail. For useful discussions of Crummell's involvement with the two Onderdoncks, see
Wilson Jeremiah Moses, *Alexander Crummell*, pp. 11–33.

below the slavery and servitude of the Negro people he saw their fatal weaknesses, which long years of mistreatment had emphasized. The dearth of strong moral character, of unbending righteousness, he felt, was their great shortcoming, and here he would begin. He would gather the best of his people into some little Episcopal chapel and there lead, teach, and inspire them, till the leaven spread, till the children grew, till the world hearkened, till—till—and then across his dream gleamed some faint after-glow of that first fair vision of youth—only an after-glow, for there had passed a glory from the earth.[6]

Embittered by the Theological Seminary's refusal to admit him, Crummell responds coolly to the "kind" hands of the "young John Jay" and the "good folk of Boston," hands that "stretched themselves toward him," even as he had "stretched forth his hands" sympathetically to suffering black slaves. Rather than *grasp* these hands, and meet sympathy with sympathy, Crummell keeps his distance, maintains his emotional isolation, and simply *sees* these hands "coldly." Du Bois reinforces our sense of Crummell's isolation, when he quotes Crummell's claim that the way of the world is closed to him. Set off against the world, Crummell feels an antagonism towards others that is utterly without sympathy and completely unresponsive to the sympathy others offer. The plight of Crummell's despair, Du Bois intimates, is that of being estranged from a human community that the sympathy of others avows.

"And yet," Du Bois insists, "the fire through which Alexander Crummell went did not burn in vain." Crummell returned to his life plan, though with a different perspective than before. Recovering some of the sympathy of which his "dark despair" had deprived him, he rededicated himself to leading, teaching and inspiring the Negro people, declaring them to be "his people," and thus acknowledging, in effect, that he and they shared a common humanity and a common destiny. Still, Du Bois argues, the vision sustaining the older Crummell's sympathy was not the "first fair vision of his youth," but "only an after-glow, for there had passed a glory from the earth." Compelled by a now dimmed-down vision of human neediness, Crummell reached out with sympathy to the deficiencies he saw in the moral character of black folk—or so Du Bois suggests. But the glory of this sympathy, Du Bois likewise suggests, was not as great as the glory of the sympathy Crummell felt as a youth. As distinct from the younger Crummell, the older Crummell *did not* extend his sympathy to the suffering that is inextricable from the experience of slavery. The product of a lesser vision, his less glorious sympathy focused on weaknesses that, "deep down *below*

6. *Souls*, p. 180 [137].

. . . *slavery and servitude*" detracted profoundly from the well being of the Negro people (emphasis mine).

By exploring the consequences of Crummell's experience with the General Theological Seminary, Du Bois complicates his conception of Crummell's estrangement. The effect of the Theological Seminary's racial discrimination, like the more general effect of the southern institution of Jim Crow, was to inhibit interracial sympathy. Reacting to the seminary's refusal to admit him, Du Bois's Crummell found it all but impossible to acknowledge his connection to the *white* community to which John Jay and the good folk of Boston had sympathetically welcomed him. Despite Jay's and others' efforts, the earlier imposition of the Veil of prejudice kept Crummell feeling estranged and set apart from a white world that had rebuffed him. So forceful was this feeling of alienation, Du Bois suggests, that its corrosive power ate its way into Crummell's relationship to other blacks, *within the Veil*. Although Crummell maintained a sympathetic connection to his black brethren, his new found sense of community excluded from its compass the trials and tribulations of the slave. A glory had passed from the earth, Du Bois seems to argue, because Crummell's rededication of himself to his people remained haunted by a bitterness that left him alienated from the lived experience of slavery, having lost sight of, and sympathy for, the cringing and groveling of a people in bondage.

The two-dimensional pattern of estrangement Du Bois sketches here is not at all unfamiliar, as it straightforwardly corresponds to the general analysis of racial alienation he originally sets forth in the first chapter of *Souls*. There, in the course of his famous discussion of "double-consciousness," Du Bois ascribes to the American Negro a self-alienation resulting from the racial alienation caused by prejudice and Jim Crow (Du Bois uses the figure of the Veil to signify both kinds of alienation). In Du Bois's view, the refusal of whites to acknowledge the common humanity of blacks entails the representation of blacks as *aliens* who exceed the proper scope of whites' sympathy (here, we may speak of white-engendered racial alienation) and produces in blacks a tendency to see themselves and/or other blacks as aliens ("It is a peculiar sensation . . . this sense of always looking at one's self through the eyes of others").[7] Crummell's experience approximates to this pattern, since it is white racial prejudice that causes him to study "more critically" the situation of black folk and to let the suffering of the black slave escape the scope of his sympathy and sense of community. For the older Crummell, as Du Bois represents him, the Negro's dearth of

---

7. *Souls*, p. 5 [11]. I provide a more detailed discussion of "double consciousness" and its connection to the themes of (failed) recognition and acknowledgement in my "Philosophy of History and Social Critique in *The Souls of Black Folk*," *Social Science Information*, 26, 1 (1987), pp. 99–114.

moral character, but not the pain and humiliation of *being* a slave, inspires the acknowledgement and cultivation of human community. In the community envisioned by the older Crummell, the slave's pain and humiliation would be strangers.

Crummell's double estrangement—from whites and from the black slave and her suffering—suggests that his tragedy was a double tragedy. For Du Bois, again, Crummell was a tragic figure because his life and achievements remained unknown to others. The "others" Du Bois had in mind, we saw, were *white* others living without the Veil. If these others knew not of Crummell's life and striving, it was because of racial alienation caused by prejudice and Jim Crow. But what now of Du Bois's suggestion that Crummell himself seemed to know "so little of men," or, at least, not to acknowlege all that he knew? Is the older Crummell's putative failure to reach out to the slave's pain any less a sign of the tragedy of the age than the failure of prejudiced whites to know Crummell, especially if one grants, as Du Bois did, that the second failure played a role in causing the first? Given this assumption, Du Bois's answer to the second question would have to be no. Crummell's tragedy, Du Bois would have admitted, extended to and conditioned his relation to the suffering in the souls of the black slaves.[8]

Du Bois's portrait of the tragic shift in Crummell's thinking—from a preoccupation with slave suffering to an emphasis on Negro moral deficiency—while it presents this shift as occurring before 1842, alludes to an argument Crummell adduces in his Harper's Ferry address of 1885, "The Need for New Ideas and New Aims for a New Era." Published eventually in 1892, this address insists that African-Americans not "dwell morbidly and absorbingly on the servile past," and urges them to "escape the 'limit and restraint' of both the *word* and the *thought* of slavery." With the advent of emancipation, says Crummell, America's blacks have entered "the new and exalted pathways of freedom," and so require new words, ideas and aims. Central among their aims, he argues, should be a mighty "moral revolution" that transforms the inner life of the Negro people: "The whole status of our condition is to be transformed and elevated. The change which is demanded is a vaster and deeper one than that of emancipation. *That* was a change . . . affecting mainly the *outer* conditions of a people . . . But outward condition does not necessarily touch the springs of life." Here, Crummell's talk of a moral change that would be "deeper" than the change

---

8. Du Bois's use of the figure of the Veil to signify a form of estrangement involving an absence of sympathy may have drawn inspiration from Nathaniel Hawthorne's short story, "The Minister's Black Veil: A Parable." Consider, for example, Hawthorne's remark that "from beneath [Mr. Hooper's] black veil, there rolled a cloud into the sunshine, an ambiguity of sin or sorrow, which enveloped the poor minister, so that love or sympathy could never reach him" (see *Hawthorne: 20 Tales* [Westvaco Corporation, 1983], p. 58). For a detailed discussion of the connection between Hawthorne's short story and Du Bois's use of the figure of the Veil, see Anita Haya Goldman, *Reconciling Race and Rights: Emerson, Liberalism, and the Constitution of Nationality*, Harvard University Ph.D. thesis, 1992.

wrought by emancipation seems to express precisely the view Du Bois attributes to Crummell when Du Bois refers to the latter's perception of moral deficiencies "deep down below . . . slavery and servitude." For the Crummell of 1885, the moral needs of black folk, though they have been *caused* by slavery, were not met by the elimination of slavery. These needs, Crummell seemed to believe, reflected a state of the soul more deeply ingrained than the pain and humiliation of *being* a slave, and thus demanded a change *deeper than emancipation per se*.[9]

In representing Crummell as a tragic figure, Du Bois remarks that the Episcopalian minister "worked alone, *with so little human sympathy*" (emphasis mine). Here, Du Bois expresses himself ambiguously, and so reinforces his earlier suggestion that Crummell withheld sympathy from others (from John Jay and, eventually, from black slaves), even as others, without the Veil, withheld sympathy from him. When, we have seen, Du Bois speaks explicitly in terms of tragedy, he depicts Crummell's estrangement as a tragedy characteristic of the times: "his name to-day, in this broad land, means little, and comes to fifty million ears laden with no incense of memory or emulation. And herein lies the tragedy of the age . . . that men know so little of men." Were Du Bois's story to end here, on a tragic note, its final message would be that loneliness, alienation, and perhaps other woes have become inescapable parameters of human existence in an era encompassing the lives of both Du Bois and Crummell. We know, however, that Du Bois's story ends not here, and so not on a tragic note, but on a comic one—comic in the sense in which the Christian plotting of human existence is almost always comic. Northrop Frye puts it this way: "Christianity . . . sees tragedy as an episode in the divine comedy, the larger scheme of redemption and resurrection. The sense of a tragedy as a prelude to comedy seems almost inseparable from anything explicitly Christian. The serenity of the final double chorus in the St. Matthew Passion would hardly be attainable if composer and audience did not know that there was more to the story."[1] A mere "episode" in his story of Crummell's life, Du Bois's tragic vision of Crummell and his age gives way ultimately, in the essay's final paragraph, to a quintessentially

9. All the quotations in the preceding paragraph come from Crummell's "New Ideas . . ." essay. See Alexander Crummell, *Africa and America*, pp. 14, 19, 34. This speech, though not widely known, is, I believe, one of the most important in the history of African-American social and political thought. As I have been arguing, Du Bois seems to allude to the speech in "Of Alexander Crummell." He alludes to it again in "Of the Coming of John." Frederick Douglass also knew the speech, as he was present in the audience when Crummell delivered it at Harper's Ferry and, apparently, voiced substantial objections when Crummell had finished (see *Africa and America*, iii–iv). For an illuminating discussion of the relation of Crummell's speech to Douglass's thought, I recommend David Blight's unpublished essay, "What Will Peace Among the Whites Bring?: Reunion and Race in the Struggle Over the Memory of the Civil War in American Culture."
1. See Northrop Frye, *Anatomy of Criticism* (Princeton: Princeton University Press, 1957), p. 215. See also Richard Sewall, *The Vision of Tragedy* (New Haven: Yale University Press, 1980), pp. 50–6.

Christian vision of Crummell in heaven, happily triumphant over human woe. Here, it seems, the divinely comic image of a resurrected and redeemed Protestant martyr displaces and ever banishes the spirit of tragedy.

Still, we must not forget that the final paragraph of "Of Alexander Crummell" begins with a speculative "I wonder . . . ," a locution that registers a certain skepticism regarding the comic ending of Du Bois's story. Du Bois "wonders about Crummell's fate, because he is not certain that lives such as Crummell's, or, for that matter, any lives, have happy endings "above the Veil."[2] Notwithstanding the image of redemption, which brings his essay on Crummell to an end, Du Bois, it appears, remains haunted by the spirit of tragedy. "Of the Coming of John," the story which follows "Of Alexander Crummell," is his attempt to give this spirit its due. Resembling in some significant ways Du Bois's portrait of Crummell, the character of John (black John) is a tragic figure but not a Protestant martyr. While the conclusion of John's story pictures him renouncing a world that has brought him nothing but loneliness and alienation, it suggests in no way that, like Du Bois's Crummell, he might find happiness beyond that world. Du Bois, in crafting the ending of this story, forgoes the speculative and "comic" finale he permits himself in "Of Alexander Crummell." To be more precise, he grants full vent to the skepticism which moved him to write "I wonder" at the end of the Crummell essay, and so lets go of the dream, perfectly typified by the image of Christ greeting Crummell in heaven, that while tragedy persists in this world happiness can be found in another one.

In the final section of this essay, I will explore the critique of Crummell's thought that is implicit in Du Bois's depiction of Crummell as a tragic figure who became alienated from slave suffering. Here, I will pay special attention to Du Bois's reasons for reprising in his own writing the "seer's" vocation to which, he claims, the young Crummell was called before being rejected by the General Theological Seminary. I will also argue that Du Bois, in reprising this vocation (mis)represents Crummell's thought as an antiquated response to modern conditions.

---

2. Compare, for example, the final lines of Du Bois's elegy "The Passing of the First Born": "Perhaps now he knows the All-love, and needs not to be wise. Sleep then child—sleep till I sleep and waken to a baby voice and the ceaseless patter of little feet—above the Veil." Du Bois's "Perhaps," with the lack of certainty it expresses, echoes his earlier lament: " 'If still he be, and he be There, and there be a There, let him be happy, O Fate!' " For a brief but insightful discussion of the anti-Christian character of Du Bois's elegy, see Arnold Rampersad, "Slavery and the Literary Imagination: Du Bois's *The Souls of Black Folk*," in *Slavery and the Literary Imagination*, ed. Deborah E. McDowell and Arnold Rampersad (Baltimore: Johns Hopkins University Press, 1989), p. 120.

4. Contra Crummell: Du Bois's Counter-Sublime

I borrow the concept of the counter-sublime from Harold Bloom, who first introduces it in *The Anxiety of Influence*. For Bloom, this concept designates one of a variety of textual strategies that later poets deploy in order to fend off the worry that their precursors have exhausted all the possibilities of poetic imagination.[3] Reacting to the sublimity of his precursor, says Bloom, the poet in pursuit of a counter-sublime "opens himself to what he believes to be a power in the parent poem that does not belong to the parent proper, but to a range of being just beyond that precursor."[4] Speaking in a more Freudian idiom, he offers the following "formula" that succinctly captures the basic idea of the counter-sublime: " 'Where my poetic father's *I* was, there *it* shall be,' or even better, 'there my *I* is, more closely mixed with *it*'."[5]

Bloom's notion of the *counter-sublime* appropriates to his theory of poetic influence a concept of the *sublime* that has been familiar to students of European aesthetics, at least since Kant. For example, says Kant, the feeling of the sublime can entail the recognition that, as a moral subject, one transcends and is superior to some natural force to which, as a physical being one could not but submit. The consciousness of being superior to a power which previously made one feel inferior is what Kant's (dynamical) sublime and Bloom's counter-sublime share in common. For Kant, the mood of the sublime can recall "man" to his supersensible moral destiny and thus to his essential superiority to some fearful object of nature before which he has felt impotent. For Bloom, the claim to a counter-sublime is a claim to have attained a poetic "might" that is somehow higher and superior than the previously intimidating poetic might of one precursor.[6]

Bloom's concept of the counter-sublime, if not the entirety of his theory of poetic influence, can be usefully brought to bear in thinking about Du Bois's representation of his relation to Crummell. In describing his first meeting with Crummell, Du Bois writes the following:

> I saw Alexander Crummell first at a Wilberforce commencement season, amidst its bustle and crush. Tall, frail and black he stood, with simple dignity and an unmistakable air of good breeding. I talked to him apart, where the storming of the lusty orators could not harm us. I spoke to him politely, then curiously, then

3. See Harold Bloom, *The Anxiety of Influence* (New York: Oxford University Press, 1973), pp. 98–112. For the interesting though not fully developed suggestion that, in the African-American literary tradition, the notion of "stylin'" or "woofing" is the counterpart to Bloom's concept of the counter-sublime, see Henry Louis Gates, Jr., *The Signifying Monkey* (New York: Oxford University Press, 1988), pp. 86–7.
4. Bloom, *The Anxiety of Influence*, p. 15.
5. *The Anxiety of Influence*, p. 110.
6. For Kant's analysis of the dynamical sublime, see Immanuel Kant, *Critique of Judgment*, trans. J.H. Bernhard (New York Hafner, 1968), pp. 99–106.

eagerly, as I began to feel the fineness of his character; his calm courtesy, the sweetness of his strength, and his fair blending of the hope and truth of life. Instinctively I bowed before this man as one bows before the prophets of the world. Some seer he seemed. . . .[7]

Here, in Du Bois's portrait, Crummell appears to be the bearer of some high and transcendent power, a man standing apart from other men—excepting, of course, Du Bois himself—and a prophet and a seer before whom it seems natural to bow. Crummell, in other words, appears as a sublime presence before whose "tall" majesty Du Bois finds himself full of reverence.

By making Crummell sublime and thus inflating the power of his presence, Du Bois sets the stage for Crummell's deflation.[8] Du Bois's comparison of Crummell to prophets and seers plays a significant role in his deflationary strategy, because it so clearly prefigures his later description of the young Crummell's experience of a "Vision Splendid": "He heard the fateful clank of their chains, he felt them cringe and grovel, and there rose within him a protest and a prophecy . . . A voice and vision called him to be a priest—a seer to lead the uncalled out of the house of bondage." As prophet and seer, Du Bois's Crummell is the personification of a vision that Du Bois himself characterizes as "mystic." Crummell's despair, we have seen, caused the glory of this vision to face "slowly away." Although Crummell later experiences an "after-glow" of this vision, he never recovers its lost glory. Though sublime he may have seemed to the young Du Bois, the Crummell Du Bois met at Wilberforce was a less inspired seer and the bearer of a less glorious vision than he would have been had he not been prone to the temptation of despair. By implying that the sublime Crummell appearing at the beginning of "Of Alexander Crummell" is a diminished version of the man he might have been, absent the racism of the General Theological Seminary, Du Bois effectively deflates his image of Crummell, and so prepares the way for his assertion of his own counter-sublime. Du Bois wishes to say, in essence: "Where Crummell's *I* was . . . there my *I* is, more closely mixed with *it*."

For Du Bois, the "it" is the glory of the "Vision Splendid." Laying claim to this glory, he suggest, would be laying claim to a sublimity that touched briefly but eluded subsequently even the sublime Crummell. Now in Du Bois's view, as I have interpreted it, the glory of Crummell's vision was the glory of his sympathy for the suffering of black slaves. It can come as no surprise, then, that I see Du Bois's claim to a counter-sublime as his purporting to possess and preserve a sympathy that Crummell lacked, or, at best, possessed only briefly. (This is

---

7. Du Bois, *Souls*, pp. 176–77 [135].

8. The counter-sublime, Bloom claims, is linked to the tropes of hyperbole and litotes. See Harold Bloom, *The Map of Misreading* (New York: Oxford University Press, 1975), p. 84.

Du Bois's version of being "more closely mixed with *it.*") Du Bois, in other words, attempts to establish his superiority to the tragic Crummell by claiming to capture and sustain in his own voice and writing a sympathy and a sense of historical community that comprehends the pain and the humiliation of the slave. No where is this clearer than in the opening paragraph of the final chapter of *Souls*, in which Du Bois, though he makes no reference to Crummell, situates his own voice in relation to the "Negro folk-song—the rhythmic cry of the slave."[9]

> They that walked in darkness sang songs in the olden days—Sorrow Songs—for they were weary at heart. And so before each thought that I have written in this book I have set a phrase, a haunting echo of these weird old songs in which the soul of the black slave spoke to men. Ever since I was a child, these songs have stirred me strangely. They came out of the South unknown to me, one by one, and yet at once I knew them as of me and mine.[1]

Here, Du Bois acknowledges what he knows, namely, that the suffering humanity of the slave is a humanity with which he identifies. His sense of community, his "of me and mine," includes the suffering of the black slave, and his book, the *Souls* itself, he presents as keeping alive, "before each thought" that he has written, the voice of that suffering. Du Bois "counters" Crummell's sublime by representing his own writing as drawing its inspiration from the sorrow songs, a rhetorical gesture by which he endeavors to realize the vocation of a "seer" who would "lead the uncalled out of the house of bondage."[2]

Writing in 1903, some forty years after *nominal* emancipation, Du Bois can continue to take seriously the vocation of the seer, because he believes *real* emancipation is a goal still to be realized. Emancipation has been proclaimed, but "the freedman," says Du Bois, "has not yet found freedom in his promised land." According to Du Bois, the Negro of the post-Reconstruction South has become the victim of a relentlessly repressive social and political order. Despite "compromise, war, and struggle," he is "not free."[3] In Du Bois's view, the post-Reconstruction Negro has fallen prey to a vicious "neo-slavery," and so still awaits genuine liberation.[4] Implicitly, then, Du Bois rejects the argument of Crummell's 1885 "New Ideas" speech, which insists that

9. Du Bois, *Souls*, p. 205 [155].
1. *Souls*, p. 204 [154–55].
2. For a closely related reading of this passage, see Dale Peterson "Justifying the Margin: The Construction of 'Soul' in Russian and African-American Texts," *Slavic Review* 51, no. 4 (Winter 1992), pp. 753–54.
3. Du Bois, *Souls*, p. 34 [33].
4. The expression "neo-slavery" I borrow from Arnold Rampersad who makes essentially the same point regarding Du Bois's view of Negro experience in the post-Reconstruction era (see Arnold Rampersad, "Slavery and the Literary Imagination: *The Souls of Black Folk*," p. 113). See also, on this point, Frank M. Kirkland, "Modernity and Intellectual Life in Black," pp. 157–58.

slavery is done with and emancipation a finished achievement. Though he no doubt approved Crummell's efforts to address the Negro's moral failings, "deep down below . . . slavery and servitude," he clearly rejected the "New Ideas" assumption that the slave experience is but a thing of the past.[5] Proceeding from Du Bois's perspective, one must infer that Crummell erred in 1885, not in his decision to attend to moral deficiencies, but in insisting that American black folk have fully completed their "exodus" from slavery.[6] As we have seen, Du Bois's portrait of Crummell explicitly echoes Crummell's 1885 speech, yet also suggests that Crummell relinquished the vocation of seer/leader-of-the-uncalled more than forty years before that speech, and so before the Emancipation Proclamation. Casting into the distant past Crummell's turn to a vocation that lacked the glory of the "Vision Splendid," Du Bois represents Crummell's thought as a curious relic of bygone days, and so obscures the conflict between his and Crummell's post-Reconstruction interpretations of the plight of the post-Reconstruction Negro. In effect, Du Bois suggests that his thought bears a relevance to modern conditions that Crummell's thought lacks.

By aligning his voice with that of the suffering slave, Du Bois elaborates further his distance from the argument of Crummell's "New Ideas" essay. If, as Du Bois says, the Negro is "not free," then Crummell's claim, that the Negro should "escape the 'limit and restraint' of both the *word* and the *thought* of slavery," loses it justification. Rejecting Crummell's claim, Du Bois reprises in his writing the seer's vocation to which Crummell was once called, not only for the reason that genuine emancipation is a goal still to be realized, but, likewise, because the words and the thoughts of the slave have retained their claim on an era (Crummell's "new" and post-emancipation era) that falls short of that goal. By representing his writing as drawing its inspiration from the sorrow songs, Du Bois avers that the words and the thoughts of these songs, which *are* the words and the thoughts of the slave, can speak significantly to and even move men who still judge men by their skins and not their souls.[7] Du Bois would "lead the uncalled out of the house of bondage," by using these words and thoughts to persuade persons without the veil to acknowledge the slave's spiritual identity. He would embrace the vocation of seer and leader by performing an inspired and, he hopes, compelling act of writing that is his "this-worldly" attempt to mark a way beyond the spirit of tragedy with which he leaves us at the end of "Of the Coming of John."

5. Du Bois himself was no less given to Victorian moralizing and in general, to complaining about the Negro's moral failings than was Crummell. See, for example, W. E. B. Du Bois, "The Conservation of Races," in *Negro Social and Political Thought*, ed. Howard Brotz (New York: Basic Books, 1966), p. 491.
6. See Crummell, *Africa and America*, p. 19.
7. Cf. Du Bois, *Souls*, p. 214 [162].

NELLIE McKAY

From W. E. B. Du Bois: The Black Women in His Writings—Selected Fictional and Autobiographical Portraits†

When the young W. E. B. Du Bois first found himself in the midst of a large company of "darkly, delicious girls . . . who sat beside [him] and actually talked to [him]," he behaved by his own admission, as uncharacteristically as he would ever do in his life again. He "gazed in tongue-tied silence or babbled in boastful dreams."[1] The year was 1885, Du Bois was seventeen years old. He had just arrived at Fisk University in Nashville, Tennessee, fresh from Massachusetts, and this was his introduction to black life in the South. Du Bois had previously had what he called "glimpses of the colored world."[2] At Rocky Point on Narragansett, two years earlier, he had attended a picnic where he witnessed "in open-mouthed astonishment the whole gorgeous color gamut of the American Negro world,"[3] and in the Congregational Church there he had heard a Hampton Quartet sing "Negro folk songs." Living in racially isolated Great Barrington, these incidents had thrilled him, but did not alter his daily life. Fisk was different; here he was an insider in a numerically dominant black community for the first time in his life. The sight of "so many people of [his] own color, or rather of such various and such extraordinary colors," overwhelmed him.[4]

Du Bois tells the story of his initial reactions to the students at Fisk in several accounts, and each time the emphasis seems to be especially on how much of an impact the sight of so many young "colored women" had on him. As a physical presence, he found the black women powerfully attractive. "At my home among my white schoolmates there were a few pretty girls," he records, but hastens to add, "either they were not entrancing or because I had known them all my life, I did not notice them." On the contrary, at Fisk, the women were the "never-to-be-forgotten marvel . . . of the most beautiful beings God ever revealed to the eyes of 17." At the supper table on his first evening at the college, in the presence of these women he lost his appetite, but

† From *Critical Essays on W. E. B. Du Bois*, ed. William L. Andrews (Boston: G. K. Hall, 1985), pp. 230–52. Bracket page numbers refer to this Norton Critical Edition.
1. W. E. B. Du Bois, *Darkwater: Voices From Behind the Veil* (New York: Harcourt, Brace & Howe, 1920), p. 14.
2. W. E. B. Du Bois, *Dusk of Dawn* (New York: Harcourt, Brace, 1940), p. 23.
3. Du Bois, *Dusk of Dawn*, p. 23.
4. W. E. B. Du Bois, *The Autobiography of W. E. B. Du Bois*, ed. Herbert Aptheker (New York: International Publishers, 1968), p. 107.

he was "deliciously happy."[5] It is safe to say that Du Bois was a black man who fell in love with black womanhood at first sight. He was also a man who deeply appreciated beauty in all of its manifestations throughout his life. "Beauty is fulfillment," he wrote. "It satisfies. It is always new and strange."[6] And he loved and admired beautiful women. It is also clear in his writings that physical beauty was but one small aspect of a very profound respect and regard that he had for women in general, and for black women in particular. When he broke his silence and ceased his youthful babblings, he wrote of "gentle" Phillis Wheatley, of Harriet Tubman, the "crude Moses," of the "sybil," Sojourner Truth, and of countless known and unknown "dusky" Cleopatras, "dark" Candaces, and "darker, fiercer Zinghases."[7]

Representations of women in his works set Du Bois apart, in significant ways, from many of his male contemporaries. As early as 1903, in *The Souls of Black Folk*, his references to women, both white and black, break with popular American images of the helpless and dependent white woman, and the ignorant and mindless black woman. The white women in this book are the New England "school marms," a courageous group who left their northern homes and families in the 1860s, '70s, and '80s, to dedicate the best years of their working lives to the education of the children of the ex-slaves. No small part of the arduous tasks of their lives was the hostility they encountered from aggrieved white Southerners who often held them in contempt and harassed them in other ways. In admiration, Du Bois wrote of them:

> Behind the mists of ruin and rapine waved the calico dresses of the women who dared, and after the hoarse mouthings of the field guns rang the rhythm of the alphabet. Rich and poor they were, serious and curious. . . . They came seeking a life work in planting New England schoolhouses among the white and black of the South. They did their work well.[8]

Portraits of black women in this volume include Josie, brave beyond the capacity of her frail body who, in the face of defeat, worked herself to death while she dreamed and labored for a better time and a different place for her poor, uneducated, back-country Tennessee family; and Jennie, "the little brown kitchen maid" who, when she learned that education made black people in the South unhappy because it made them into the kind of person that did not conform to the expectations of white Southerners, declared: "I wish I were unhappy, and—and, . . . I think I am, a little."[9] Woman as important worker, white women as

5. Du Bois, *Autobiography*, p. 107.
6. Du Bois, *Darkwater*, p. 247.
7. Du Bois, *Darkwater*, p. 166.
8. W. E. B. Du Bois, *The Souls of Black Folk* (Chicago: A. C. McClurg, 1903), p. 65 [24–25].
9. Du Bois, *The Souls of Black Folk*, p. 257 [150].

representations of the white social conscience, visionary black women in quest of a way out of black poverty and ignorance, and women with qualities that made them morally superior to their male counterparts, are the ones that are prominent in this book. Later, in two of his five novels, Du Bois put women of color at the center of the action, and in the remaining three (a trilogy), black women are responsible for directing black men who are in positions of community leadership. Beyond these fictional characters, Du Bois's support of early feminist issues, especially the Suffrage Movement, which he articulated regularly in his *Crisis* writings, and his recognition of the struggles and achievements of black women, also recorded in many of the columns of the *Crisis*, bear testimony to his estimation of women's worth and place in American society.[1]

The ideas that Du Bois expressed in his fiction and nonfiction essays, journal articles, and newspaper columns originated in his feelings toward the women who were close to him in his early years. Long before he arrived in Nashville in 1885 he had known or heard of black women in his own family who inspired in him a deep respect. These are the women who fill honored space in his autobiographical writings, and from whom he drew models for the romantic idealism that is an intrinsic quality in most of his imagined women. Many of these real-life women were forced by circumstances to make their way in life without the protection or help of men, and to a boy growing up in a fatherless home, they were not other than they should have been. Their lives exemplified the "stuff" out of which he would mold his own male life.

One of these women he revered was an ancient Bantu female forebear. He speaks of her first in *The Souls of Black Folk* (1903), later in *Darkwater* (1920), and in *The Autobiography of W. E. B. Du Bois*, a posthumous work, published in 1968.

> My Grandfather's grandmother was seized by an evil Dutch
> trader two centuries ago; and coming to the valleys of
> the Hudson and the Housatonic, black, little, and lithe,
> she shivered and shrank in the harsh north winds, looked
> longingly at the hills, and often crooned a heathen melody

1. Du Bois was a staunch supporter of women's rights in all areas of life and work. In particular, his *Crisis* writings attest to this. Under his editorship, an issue of the journal seldom appeared in which women or women's issues were not prominently featured. He spoke in favor of the Suffrage Movement, of women's work and achievements, women's writings, and on the oppression of women in a society dominated by men. He wrote stories and columns and poems about women, and singled out many women for special praise in the columns of the *Crisis*. For detailed listings of these writings on women see Irene Diggs, "Du Bois and Women—A Short Story of Black Women 1910–1934," *Current Bibliography on African Affairs*, 7 (Summer 1974), 260–63; Jean Fagan Yellin, "An Index of Literary Materials in the *Crisis*, 1910–1934," *CLA Journal*, 14 (June 1971), 452–65; and 15 (Dec. 1971), 197–234. For Du Bois on Women's Suffrage see Jean Fagan Yellin, "*The Crisis* and Women's Suffrage," *Massachusetts Review*, 14 (Spring 1973), 365–75.

to the child between her knees, thus:
Do ba-na co-ba, ge-ne me, ge-ne me!
Do ba-na co-ba, ge-ne me, ge-ne me!
Ben d' nu-li, nu-li, nu-li, nu-li, ben d'le.[2]

The song, the meaning of its words lost to time, passed down to her generations for more than two hundred years, for the meaning of the music was never lost. It was, Du Bois wrote, "the music of an unhappy people, of the children of disappointment; they [the people and their music] tell of death and suffering and unvoiced longing toward a truer world, of misty wanderings and hidden ways."[3]

Du Bois tells us the most about his family in *Darkwater* and in *The Autobiography*. With minor additions or reductions, the stories are the same from book to book. Of his great-grandmother, Violet, he tells us, there "was born a mighty family, splendidly named."[4] The splendid names included his grandfather Othello, or "Uncle Tallow." However, it was not the "strong-voiced and redolent with tobacco [Othello] who sat stiffy in a great chair beside the open fire because his hip was broken" who impressed the young boy. Cryptically, the mature Du Bois comments that Othello "was good-natured but not energetic." Instead, Du Bois lavished admiration on his grandmother, Sarah, commonly called "Aunt Sally." This grandmother had ten children, and the "energy" was in her. She was tall, thin, hawkeyed, and golden-complexioned. Her grandson believed that she must have been beautiful in her youth, but what he loved of her old age was that she was efficient and managing.[5] His mother was Aunt Sally's youngest child.

Du Bois shared a warm and close relationship with his mother, Mary Silvina, who was born in 1831 and who died in 1884. Of a dark shining bronze color, with black eyes and black hair that had "a tiny ripple," she had a heavy and kind face. He felt that she gave others the impression of "infinite patience," but that a "curious determination was concealed in her softness."[6] Earlier in her life she suffered a disappointment in love, then later, at age thirty-five, met, fell in love with, and married the handsome Alfred Du Bois of whom the clan-conscious Burghardts disapproved. He was a stranger to them and as far as they knew, he had no property, no job, and no status. They had never heard of his family in New York and Connecticut. According to his son, Alfred Du Bois must have embodied "the making of a poet, an adventurer, or a Beloved Vagabond."[7] The Mary Burghardt–Alfred Du Bois marriage

2. Du Bois, *Souls of Black Folk*, pp. 267–68 [157].
3. Du Bois, *Souls of Black Folk*, p. 267 [157].
4. Du Bois, *Autobiography*, p. 62; *Darkwater*, p. 6.
5. Du Bois, *Autobiography*, p. 64.
6. Du Bois, *Darkwater*, p. 6.
7. Du Bois, *Darkwater*, p. 7.

was short-lived and W. E. B. Du Bois never knew his father.[8] He spent his life, until he went to Fisk in 1885, living with his mother (until her death in 1884), surrounded by her close-knit family. The economic condition of the family was strained, and they lived simply, but never without necessities. While he was still a child she suffered a paralytic stroke and was lame for the rest of her life. Only many years later did Du Bois realize how great the pressures and anxieties that beset her during his growing-up years must have been, for although they were very poor, she never burdened him with the weight of her suffering. His trust and confidence in her wisdom and love enabled him to confide his childhood dreams and aspirations in her. From her he learned of the evils of alcohol (never in his life was he comfortable in a bar), the values of thrift and industry, and that "the secret of life and loosing of the color bar, then lay in excellence, in accomplishment." When she died he was glad to see her "at peace at last, for she worried all her life," but he was also relieved of the guilt of forsaking her to find his own life beyond the Berkshires.[9] In *Darkwater* he wrote that in his later years he "loved her with a fierce sense of personal loss."[1]

Aside from his mother, the women in his immediate family whom Du Bois knew and mentioned in his writings are his cousin Inez, his Aunt Minerva, and his paternal grandfather's third wife, Annie Green. Although he makes only brief mention of them, these women played important roles in his life and/or in the shaping of some of his ideas. The images he presents of them are those which he perceived to be at the heart of women's relationships to the world. He shows us the aspects and qualities of their lives with which he most sympathized or the ones he most applauded. Of Inez, his pretty, brown cousin, he wrote in anger of women's oppression in marriage. His pronouncements in 1920 were similar to ones still heard from social critics of the patriarchy. As wife and mother, Inez had been the victim of "a litter of children, poverty, a drunken, cruel companion, sickness and death." Her case addressed issues of the multiple oppression of black women who, beyond the constraints of race and class, face the common dilemma of women in Western culture. To fulfill themselves as sexual beings they must sacrifice intelligence and opportunity for self-expression through meaningful work. In a world in which men have power over women, Du Bois insists that each woman "must have a life work and economic inde-

8. It is unclear how long the marriage of Mary Burghardt and Alfred Du Bois lasted. W. E. B. Du Bois's accounts suggest that Alfred Du Bois left Great Barrington while his son was an infant, and that Alfred's unwillingness to move into the home of Mary's parents, in spite of financial pressures on the couple, may have hastened the separation between them. It appears that Alfred went to New Milford, opened a barber shop, and later became a preacher. The son claims that his father sent "urgent" letters to his wife entreating her to join him with their son. Mary, unwilling to leave her family and the only place she knew, remained in Great Barrington. In time, the letters ceased, and Alfred Du Bois faded out of their lives.
9. Du Bois, *Autobiography*, pp. 75 and 102.
1. Du Bois, *Darkwater*, p. 163.

pendence. She must have the right to knowledge. She must have the right to motherhood at her own discretion." He calls for banishment of "the beastiality of free manhood" in favor of the full liberation of womanhood, through which men will gain strength and freedom. "The uplift of women is," he wrote, "next to the problem of the color line and the peace movement, our greatest modern cause. When, now, two of these movements—woman and color—combine in one, the combination has deep meaning."[2]

Du Bois remembered his Aunt Minerva for her kindness to him in a time of need, and what she contributed to his future at that time (1884–85) was far greater than either of them imagined then. She was the person with whom he "boarded" after his mother's death, and because her charge was "nominal," he was able to save enough of his small earnings (a dollar a day) to assist with his college plans and preparations. The importance of her kindness, generosity, and loyalty to family was never lost on him. He saw her in the tradition of the Gold Coast and Ashanti groups in which "female members of the family, . . . the aunts or the sisters or the cousins or nieces" share the responsibility to guide and train the children.[3]

When Du Bois was fifteen years old he visited his paternal grandfather, Alexander Du Bois, who was then living in New Bedford. The meeting, the only time that the two ever saw each other, was engineered by Annie Green. In 1883 Green wrote to Mary Du Bois explaining that she had known and loved Alfred Du Bois, and was in sympathy with problems that had ruptured relations between Alfred and his father. She was anxious that William visit and become acquainted with his grandfather. In spite of limited resources, his mother secured the money for the trip. This was his first "excursion" away from home and it proved memorable on two accounts. Du Bois was impressed by Alexander Du Bois, noting that he was a "stern, upstanding man, unsparing but precise in his speech," who loved women in a "masterful" way and wrote "stilted" poems that were "pleading things from a soul astray." So great was his admiration for this austere, slyly sentimental grandfather, whose "manners" and "breeding" made him appear aristocratic in contrast to the black Burghardts with their "jokes" and "back-slapping," that he once recorded his wish to be buried in the same cemetery as Alexander.[4] The other outstanding feature of the trip was that on the way home he stopped in Providence, where at Rocky Mount he had his first opportunity to see a large number of black people in one group. Here, people of color from three states vacationed and the festive atmosphere, removed from poverty, made a lasting impression on him.

2. Du Bois, *Darkwater*, pp. 163–65 and 181.
3. Du Bois, *Darkwater*, p. 167.
4. Du Bois, *Dusk of Dawn*, p. 108; *Autobiography*, p. 67, 71.

Thus, Annie Green's initiative had far-reaching effects on his developing consciousness of race.

In these autobiographical portraits Du Bois indicates that in his family, women, more than men, had direct and indirect influence on his thinking and on his character. "All the way back in these dim distances it is the mothers and mothers of mothers who seem to count, while fathers are shadowy memories" emphasizes their influence.[5] These women were strong and resourceful, but they were also generous of spirit, nurturing, and sensitive, and they empowered him to cultivate both sets of qualities in himself.

Du Bois's autobiographical essay, "Of the Meaning of Progress," in *The Souls of Black Folk*, goes to the heart of the problem of race in the South in the latter part of the nineteenth century. Here he places the strength and courage of a young black woman in the foreground. During his years at Fisk he spent two summers as a teacher in the Tennessee hills, where schooltime for peasant children was wedged in between planting and harvest times and was wholly dependent on the availability and willingness of a young college man to spend his vacation teaching for very small pay. Nevertheless, many a student earned his following year's college tuition this way. Through Josie, the central figure in the piece, Du Bois learned of a school "over the hill" that needed a teacher. Only once in more than twenty years, since the end of the Civil War, had a teacher been there. Josie, "a thin, homely girl of twenty, with a dark-brown face and full and thick, hard hair . . . herself longed to learn—and thus she ran on, talking fast and loud, with much earnestness and energy." There were ten children in her family who with their parents occupied a four-room, dull frame cottage. The father was "a quiet, simple soul, calmly ignorant, with no touch of vulgarity," while the mother was "strong, bustling, and energetic, with a quick, restless tongue, and an ambition to live "like folks." The mother and Josie scolded the men in their family for "easiness" and "carelessness" but everyone knew the Sisyphean dimensions of the life they lived.[6]

Some thirty children came to the school that Du Bois set up, most of them irregularly. Each weekend the teacher stayed with a different family, rotating among the homes of his students. He learned their ways, their world, and their dreams for escaping poverty, ignorance, and oppression. Josie's mother used the times he was with them to boast about her daughter. Josie had bought a sewing machine; she worked at service in the winter for four dollars a month and longed to go away to school. Du Bois achieved little towards the academic progress of his students during the time he spent with the hill folk, but he learned a

5. Du Bois, *Darkwater*, p. 168.
6. Du Bois, *Souls of Black Folk*, p. 97 [47] and 98 [47].

great deal about race and class. He discovered how "poverty, poor land, and low wages; and above all . . . the Veil . . . hung between [them] . . . and Opportunity." They were "without" and beyond "the World," and the barriers were too high for them to scale without direct external intervention. Ten years later he returned to the site of his "school" for reasons of sentiment. Some things were better: the log schoolhouse was gone and in its place was a board building with glass windows; but much trouble had visited Josie's family in between. Years before, one brother, unjustly accused of stealing, had attacked his white accuser for which he was imprisoned. Josie and another brother walked nine miles each day to see their brother through the bars, until he escaped and the two brothers ran away. Josie worked and worried; the family sold their farm and moved nearer to town. For a year Josie did housework in Nashville and took home money to "furnish the [new] house and change it to a home." Then that spring, a younger sister brought home a "nameless" child. Josie worked harder, with no time for thoughts of school; her face grew more wan and tired, until one day, like a hurt child, she lay down to sleep and never woke again.[7]

Josie's story turns on the effects of race and class on the black underclass in an industrial, technological society, and also on Du Bois's perception of the black woman's determination to transcend these difficulties through work, self reliance, and independence. In his later fiction, the theme of work is even more prominent. He believed that black people would improve their lot only through hard physical and intellectual work. The role of women and work is well defined in Du Bois's writings. Even in this early piece, Josie, the "hope" of her family, has vision as well as the will to work to achieve her goals. Du Bois was also aware that in real life the results do not always meet expectations, and he does not deny the pathos in her failure to succeed. In Josie, he honors the black woman, not for her success, but for her selflessness, for her love of family, for her belief in a better future for black people, and for her strength, willingness, and determination to work for a better life. Important too is the fact that Josie's work and efforts are in and for a narrow world, and that the outcome of her efforts, whether success or failure, would make no immediate impact on the larger world. Du Bois's sensitivity to the pain and anguish as well as to the hopes and dreams of those women whose lives and work appeared to fill only small circles is noteworthy. In actuality, such was the nature of the lives and work of the overwhelming number of black women in America, and the story of Josie acknowledges and pays tribute to them. Although the effects of race and class were less destructive on the women in Du Bois's family, like Josie, their immediate influence was concentrated in

7. Du Bois, *Souls of Black Folk*, pp. 102–04 [50–52].

their families, but the ultimate ends of the struggles and achievements of all black women mark the progress of an entire race of people.

Scholars who admire W. E. B. Du Bois know that he did not make his reputation as a man of belles-lettres, but as Arnold Rampersad points out in "W. E. B. Du Bois as a Man of Literature," his imaginative output, which constitutes more than a respectable corpus, anticipates the writings of many who became the most significant figures in twentieth-century black literature.[8] Rampersad's essay, which focuses on Du Bois's vision, especially on his literary innovations, illuminates the nature of his contributions to the field. Among these, images of women in these writings provide one important index to his general political and philosophical insights and to his personal convictions concerning women's place in life and art. Portraits of women permeate these works, and even when they appear to be no more than background figures they embody and carry forward the ideas of the works in an important way. Unfortunately, readers and critics often overlook the full merits of these characterizations, and in so doing lose valuable insights into the workings of his mind.

"Of the Coming of John," in the *Souls of Black Folk*, is an example of a work in which the black women are completely ignored in the criticism of the story. Emphasis falls on the plight of the young black man whose northern sojourn and education make it impossible for him to stay in his "place" when he returns home. This is the primary thrust of the tale, which has a shadow image in the tale of white John in the same narrative; but the black women, black John's mother and sister, also serve a vital function in the unfolding of the events.

In the story, Du Bois's black hero follows the literary conventions associated with the journey from innocence to experience. As a young man, he leaves the South for the North, in search of education and the dignity of a full human life. Several years later, after a difficult period of growth and development, he returns South. However, because of his changed self-concept, which affects his position on race, the black and white communities find him unacceptable as a teacher for the local black school. In the aftermath of his accidental killing of the white John to protect his sister from rape by the latter, he chooses to die by suicide rather than permit a lynch mob to carry out his execution. It is a story that brings all of the South's problems of race and sex to the forefront of our consciousness.

Only brief mentions of the women in black John's life appear in this story, yet their roles are of primary importance to his journey to self-hood and to his ultimate understanding of the racial issues and conflicts of southern life. Credit for John's stability and his motivation to em-

8. Arnold Rampersad, "W. E. B. Du Bois as a Man of Literature," *American Literature*, 51 (Mar. 1979), 50–68.

brace the hazards of experience goes to his mother and sister. Although unable to escape the patterns of black women's lives in the South, they imbue him with the energy and determination to rise above the conditions of black subservience to the inhumane domination of whites. They are not peripheral to the action, for Du Bois shows that their faith in him is the only factor that takes him through the difficulties between the poles of innocence and experience. Black women as the source that empowers black men to discover their dignity, and by extension, the force that determines the course of their race is an implicit theme in the undertones of "Of the Coming of John."

In addition, Du Bois gives John's sister Jennie an image that makes her a great deal more than the force behind black male achievement and leadership. She foreshadows the new generation of black women who emerge in his novels—the heroines of *The Quest of the Silver Fleece* and *Dark Princess*. While she mourns for the sadness of his life, and for his alienation from old friends and family, Jennie stakes her claims for her own journey on to the knowledge that will make her his intellectual counterpart. " 'John,' she said, 'does it make everyone— unhappy when they study and learn lots of things?' " His affirmative response is her call to discard old ways and to move black women forward into equality with black men in the front lines of the struggle for all black people, and for a full identity for black women. John dies at the moment when he realizes his full dignity as a man, turning to the "Sea" and finding that "the world whistled in his ears."[9] We imagine that his sister leaves the bluff and lives to redeem his dignity and her own.

Not fully the equivalent of the subtext in the narrative, the function of the black women in this story is submerged beneath the immediacy of the racial confrontation between the black male protagonist and white male authority. However, given the date of this story, the prevailing male attitudes toward women as literary characters, and black male political views of women in the racial struggle, Du Bois's fictional women are in advance of their time. What is most important is that the supporting roles of the women, in relationship to their men, are positive, and that his vision goes beyond that to imagine a woman, poor and uneducated, to whom he gives the consciousness that will permit her to make her life a challenge to the status quo.

*   *   *

9. Du Bois, *Souls of Black Folk*, 257–63 [150–54].

SUSAN MIZRUCHI

Neighbors, Strangers, Corpses: Death and Sympathy in the Early Writings of W. E. B. Du Bois†

In the climactic mourning chapter of *The Souls of Black Folk* (1903), W. E. B. Du Bois describes the Atlanta funeral procession for his eighteen-month-old son.

> Blithe was the morning of his burial, with bird and song and sweet-smelling flowers. The trees whispered to the grass, but the children sat with hushed faces. And yet it seemed a ghostly unreal day,— the wraith of Life. We seemed to rumble down an unknown street behind a little white bundle of poesies, with the shadow of a song in our ears. The busy city dinned about us; they did not say much, those pale-faced hurrying men and women; they did not say much,—they only glanced and said, "Niggers!"
>
> We could not lay him in the ground there in Georgia, for the earth there is strangely red; so we bore him away to the northward, with his flowers and his little folded hands. In vain, in vain!—for where, O God! beneath thy broad blue sky shall my dark baby rest in peace,—where Reverence dwells, and Goodness, and a Freedom that is free?[1]

The scene records a stunning lapse of fellow feeling, an inability to see beyond the Black type to acknowledge a universal grammar of suffering. Du Bois's reproof here is muted and indirect: the abrupt cropping of the paragraph expresses typographically what cannot be conveyed by ordinary language. The moment is isolated, set apart; one must turn away from a human action that replicates the inhumanity of death. This figurative recoiling is confirmed by the immediate details of the parents' departure "northward" to bury their son. Du Bois maintains a "hushed" tone throughout, not because he is too numb to feel this slight keenly but in order to avoid responding emotionally to a display that has denigrated sentiment itself. For what is being represented by this scene is not just a lack of identification with Black pain, but the possibility that sympathetic actions have themselves become the pathway of estrangement. Where we expect to find instinctive recognition of another's feeling, we now find race hatred. It is not simply that sympathy is absent; it is that sympathy is supposed to be there. The

---

† Reprinted from *Centuries' Ends, Narrative Means*, edited by Robert Newman, pp. 191–211, with the permission of the publishers, Stanford University Press. © 1996 by the Board of Trustees of the Leland Stanford Junior University.

1. W. E. B. Du Bois, *The Souls of Black Folk*, ed. John Hope Franklin (New York: Avon Books, 1965), 352–53. Subsequent references to this edition will be included parenthetically in the text. Bracketed page numbers refer to this Norton Critical Edition.

encounter derives its dramatic force from the highly structured nature of funeral rites. In all cultures strict rules of etiquette govern expressions of grief and their reception. This denial of sympathy is a violation of custom, obvious to everyone. The air of suppressed violence in the scene arises from the expectation of sympathy, on the part of Black mourners and White bypassers alike. It is at the moment when they are invited to provide the most human of responses that the Whites "discover" their bigotry.

There is a special poignance in Du Bois's decision to locate his insights about sympathy in the funeral of his own son. Du Bois, like Emerson, demonstrates an ability to make personal tragedy resonate with collective and, in this case, political meaning. The scene implies that the act of sympathy may require not only the exclusion but the disappearance of certain groups. While we are meant to read the blood in Du Bois's red earth, the color is also intended as a racial property of the bodies buried there. Du Bois's image recalls a detail from an earlier moment of *Souls*: that the territory around Atlanta was "the ancient land of the Cherokees" (286) [76]. Describing the battles before the Indian retreat, Du Bois's conclusion confirms the theme of succession: "Small wonder the wood is red. Then came the black slaves. Day after day the clank of chained feet" (293) [82]. This is the history behind the theory of Social Darwinism. Arguments for the natural decline of nations, with superior replacing inferior in seasonal progression, are countered by a narrative of force and violence. If the red earth fails to jog our memories, we have the colloquial "pale-faced" to convince us of the parallel. "Observe the fate of the American Indian," Du Bois suggests, "and you will understand current speculation on the destiny of their Black counterparts."

For what is most peculiar about this later moment is its implication that death and "niggers" have become synonymous in White minds. The incident has a disturbing literalness if one takes into account contemporary child mortality statistics for Blacks—56 percent higher, according to demographers, than comparable statistics for White children in the urban north and south.[2] In light of these facts, Du Bois's image

2. See Samuel Preston and Michael Haines, *The Fatal Years: Child Mortality in Late-Nineteenth-Century America* (Princeton: Princeton University Press, 1991), who point out that the key variable in child mortality statistics was rural versus urban life, and cite Du Bois *(The Philadelphia Negro)* in support of their claim for the negative effects of Black "progress" (from farm to city) in the early modern period. Blacks in urban areas, they contend, "were subjected to many of the same mortality hazards as foreign immigrants to cities. But . . . were essentially beyond the pale of the social programs and settlement houses that were designed to ease the transition for immigrants to a new land" (94–95). They attribute the high rates of child mortality among Blacks to their isolation within populated areas: "Race was a caste-like status in 1900, and the degraded social and economic circumstances of blacks, who had virtually no chance of entering the mainstream of American life, is undoubtedly reflected in their exceptionally high mortality" (210). In general, "people furthest from the reach of the modern state—and furthest from one another—enjoyed the best health conditions." The modern state at this point in its history knew how to bring people together to their detriment, but had yet to achieve "the technical and social triumphs" that would reduce the risks of that association. Having neighbors in this period was costly.

of the Georgia soil as an unmarked grave for Blacks and Indians expands to include the unrealized histories of the Black infant thousands. But the scene's metaphorical implications are equally disturbing: for Whites, Blacks cannot possess a ritualized relationship to death because they are identified with death.

This paper will explore the following series of propositions. That Americans at the turn of the century seriously debated the possible extinction of Black culture—a discussion carried out mainly in social scientific journals and books, but extending as well to other aesthetic, juridical, and religious arenas—and this dialogue of death only becomes meaningful, in all of its historical peculiarity, against the backdrop of two emerging forms of inquiry: the social scientific revision of death and social scientific accounts of sympathy as fundamental to sociality. Growing emphasis on the reception of death and on differences in cultural response and interpretation, accompanies increasing attention to the function of sympathy as a means of differentiation and exclusion. Death itself, its social versus universal significance, its reception within different communities, its typological uses in distinguishing the human from the inhuman, provides a critical impetus for Du Bois's interdisciplinary imaginings at the turn of the century. I want to highlight the status of *The Souls of Black Folk* as a "border text," my term for a book that crosses disciplinary boundaries while helping to define them, a designation I discuss in more detail below. His professional investment in the field of sociology led him to empirical confrontations with prevailing claims for Black extinction. His literary aspirations resulted in eloquent meditations on the meaning of death and on the beliefs and rituals surrounding it particular to his people. Du Bois's engagement with the subject of death culminated in reflections on a sacrificial rite whose enactment in this period was approaching "epidemic" proportions: lynching. The final section of my paper will consider the form that these reflections took.

The experience of Du Bois's funeral band suggests how Black identity, funeral rites, the darkness and grief occasioned by death, have come to form a procession of their own in White minds. This conflation of matter and mind, of Black bodies and sorrowful thoughts, recalls a line from one of Emily Dickinson's letters: "I have just seen a funeral procession go by of a negro baby, so if my ideas are rather dark you need not marvel."[3] This is obviously a pun. My interest lies in one consequence of Dickinson's ambiguity (is her mind stained by the ritual or its object?), the idea that race can "dark[en]" thought in the same way as grief, that physical difference—Blackness—is a calamity equivalent to any other misfortune. Yet it might be more accurate, and more in

3. Letter to Abiah Root, January 12, 1846, in *The Collected Letters of Emily Dickinson*, ed. Thomas H. Johnson (Cambridge, Mass.: Harvard University Press, 1958), 1:24.

keeping with Du Bois, to say that physical difference most profoundly affects the reception of misfortune, which becomes apparent in this case when Dickinson's remark is restored to its own epistolary context, framed by the sympathetic expressions that precede and follow it. In the same letter, Dickinson describes with effusiveness her readiness to "sympathize with" her correspondent's "cold." In an earlier letter (to the same correspondent), she expresses great compassion for a friend who has lost her mother and feels it "keenly."[4] These sufferings (small and large) evoke outpourings of sentiment, while the funeral procession of the black baby is neatly confined to a play of words. This is not to deny the conventionality of my contrast (Dickinson is obviously responding to friends in one case, strangers in the other), nor to deny that Dickinson's remark may express genuine sadness over the baby's death. Least of all do I claim to draw any conclusions about Dickinson's "attitudes toward race" from this passing observation. My point is that the Black appears to occupy a representative status of stranger, which is defined against the other representative status of kin by the fact that it elicits emotional distance. It is not the affinity of suffering that elicits sympathy. It is the affinity of those who suffer. Sympathy has less to do with identifying what is universally human about a particular individual, than with universalizing a certain set of human particulars.

Du Bois's meditations on survival and sympathy were part of a wider context, which included novelist Pauline Hopkins's remark that "the dawn of the twentieth century finds the Black race fighting for existence in every part of the globe." She envisioned Africa, "stretching her hands to the American Negro, crying aloud for sympathy in her hour of trial." Hopkins's fears were echoed by the journalist Ida B. Wells, who saw rape charges against Black males as attempts to place them "beyond the pale of human sympathy" in order to justify their elimination through lynching.[5] According to these African-Americans writing at the turn of the century, it had become possible to exclude entire peoples from the claims of sympathy. This is consistent with reports from medical historians that nineteenth-century interpretations of responses to physical suffering were sharply divided along racial, ethnic, and class lines. The notion that certain groups were less susceptible to pain rationalized outrageous cruelties during the slave era and supported the withholding of anesthesia from certain patients (typically, Blacks, immigrants, and the lower classes) later in the century.[6] Such developments help to explain the regularity with which Du Bois laments

4. Ibid., 24, 22.
5. Hopkins and Wells are quoted by Hazel Carby, "On the Threshold of Woman's Era: Lynching, Empire, and Sexuality in Black Feminist Theory," in Race, Writing, and Difference, ed. Henry Louis Gates (Chicago: University of Chicago Press, 1985), 310, 308.
6. See Martin S. Pernick, A Calculus of Suffering: Pain, Professionalism, and Anesthesia in Nineteenth-Century America (New York: Columbia University Press, 1985).

(throughout writings from this period) the tendency to view Blacks as an undifferentiated collectivity—as if thinking in collective terms about humanity necessarily imperiled vulnerable social groups.[7]

Race Traits and Tendencies of the American Negro (1896) by Frederick Hoffman, a Prudential insurance statistician commissioned to assess the group's relative "insurability," seemed designed to confirm Du Bois's fears. This study of Black life expectancy contains a long section on "pauper burials," which Hoffman claims occur with marked frequency among Blacks (his figures for Washington, D.C., from 1888 to 1894, for example, estimate 84.36 percent of pauper burials to be Black, despite their comprising only 32.89 percent of the total population). Exaggerated statistics of this sort appear throughout the book. Less characteristic is the oddly lyrical and gloomy description that accompanies this data. "Whoever has witnessed the pauper funeral of a negro," he writes, "the bare pine box and the common cart, the absence of all that makes less sorrowful the last rites over the dead, has seen a phase of negro life and manners more disheartening perhaps than anything else in the whole range of human misery. Perhaps only the dreary aspect of the negroes' [burial ground], the low sad hills, row after row, partly washed away by the falling rains, unrelieved by a single mark of human kindness, without a flower and without a cross, only the pauper lot itself, may be more sad and gruesome than the display of almost inhuman apathy at the funeral."[8] This scene fulfills a claim advanced on the book's first page, where Hoffman announces that his controversial contribution to the nature-nurture debate will explain the notable lack of "that natural bond of sympathy," which might be expected to exist "between people of the same country, no matter how widely separated by language and nationality." The book is an eccentric blend of social psychology, liberal philosophy, reformism, statistical analysis, ethnological description, and racist dogma. This is unsurprising given an author whose publications over two decades included, in addition to Race Traits, a history of the Prudential Life Insurance company (1900), and a book on pauper burials in large cities (1917).[9] More noteworthy is the possibility that Du Bois had Hoffman's passage somewhere in mind while drafting his own funeral scene. Du Bois knew Race Traits and Tendencies, he reviewed it and refuted it more than once in sociological

---

7. See, for example, the reference in Souls to "a color-prejudice that classes Phyllis Wheatley and Sam Hose in the same despised class" (336) [000] or his observation from The Negro American Family (New York: Arno and the New York Times, 1909), that "few modern groups show greater internal differentiation of social conditions than the Negro American, and the failure to realize this is the cause of much confusion."

8. Frederick Hoffman, Race Traits and Tendencies of the American Negro (New York: Macmillan, 1896), 246–49.

9. Frederick Hoffman, A History of the Prudential Life Insurance Company (Newark, N.J.: Prudential Press, 1900) and Pauper Burials and the Internment of the Dead in Large Cities (Newark, N.J.: Prudential Press, 1917).

writings that appeared between 1896 and the 1903 publication of
Souls.[1] The scenes are curiously compatible, that is if we consider Du
Bois's as the mirror image of Hoffman's. One consequence of opening
a dialogue between them is the exposure of the potent and meaningful
sentimentality of Du Bois's scene. The "blithe" morning, the "bird and
song," the "sweet-smelling flowers," take on an air of aggression when
set against Hoffman's drama of nullification: "falling rains" and "bare
pine box," "unrelieved by a single mark of human kindness," not even
"a flower." Hoffman's scene is typical of the way in which their exclusion from sympathy was projected onto Blacks themselves as a "race
trait" of carelessness and apathy. Charges of primitive insensibility
(Blacks were often compared to the "uncivilized" peoples described by
contemporary ethnographers) were used to excuse White atrocities such
as lynching, castration, and near-cannibalism. It was as if these White
antagonists were caught in some perverse state of sympathetic identification which made them helplessly susceptible to the barbaric atavisms
of their victims. Needless to say, Du Bois recognized the dangerous
subtext of Hoffman's allegations. Hoffman's thesis that Blacks can't
mourn properly—they lack appropriate ritual modes and objects; loss
with them does not translate into grief—is answered by Du Bois's record
of White actions that deliberately destroy the ritual content of Black
burials.

When Whites look at these mourners and mutter "Niggers," they are
defining Blacks through their exclusion from sympathy as outside the
borders of community. This is consistent with Du Bois's color symbolism in this passage. The first three color allusions are "red earth,"
"white poesies," and "niggers"—a term that thwarts the prospects of a
red, white, and blue design. Blue is introduced at the passage's end in
the form of a hope or plea ("where, O God! beneath thy broad blue
sky shall my dark baby rest in peace?"), to remind us of a national
promise unfulfilled. The note of dissonance, however, does not come
from the Blacks who embody this execration. While the white poesies
and red earth are labeled as objective parts of the scene, the color black
is enclosed in quotes, an idiom that degrades its speaker.

To accept the possibility that we are being asked to read the social
exclusion of Blacks here in terms of a foiled national symbol (the American flag) is to accept that the passage has implications for the relationship between sentimental bonds and nationality. The black hole in the
flag (where the blue should be) signifies a potential gap between the
impulse of sympathy and the rites of an American democracy, a gap
that is overlooked in a contemporaneous analysis of race prejudice by
the sociologist W. I. Thomas. Thomas suggests that "the dependence
of cultural groups on signs of solidarity is seen in the enthusiasms

1. Du Bois's review appeared in *Publications of the American Academy of Political Science* (January 1897).

aroused by the display of the flag of our country."[2] The key term here is culture, for America's uniqueness as a nation lies in the fact that it is not a single "cultural group" but a plurality of cultures. As Thomas assumes, sympathy is concrete and possessive, it expresses immediate attachments: to family, religion, ethnicity. In traditionalist nations like Italy, Germany, or France, the rites of citizenship are based on these bonds. A complex cultural affect complements national identity, often serving as an arsenal for aggressive nationalist agendas (as in Nazi Germany). In the United States, sentimental attachments have always existed in tension with the rational principles ("e pluribus unum" "inalienable rights") that are the foundation of national unity.

Du Bois's scene reminds us that in a heterogeneous nation with open borders, sympathy has the opposite of its traditional effect: it threatens rather than supports the collective identification of citizens. From this perspective, the scene stages the dilemma of social bonds in a pluralist democracy. It introduces two of the most obvious sources of human commonality, death and mourning, and the sympathetic response to it, and shows how both function to differentiate and exclude. Indeed, one could argue that the red, white, and black scheme of this passage also invokes (in more universal terms) the three elemental bodily products, but subordinates them to a more dramatically represented politics of color. White is the life source, the color of semen and mother's milk; red is menstrual blood or blood shed in war or hunting; black is feces, the sign of bodily dissolution.[3] It is no coincidence that convictions of the particularity of death (variations in mortuary practices both within and across cultures), and of the limits of sympathy's harmonizing effects are both especially heightened in this period. Du Bois's consistent declarations of distrust in the sentiments, and attraction to social science, are explained in part by his awareness that appeals to the emotion (of the kind on display in nationalist celebrations like parades and fireworks demonstrations, as well as in universal practices like mourning) have so often been vehicles of intolerance.

For Du Bois, there is an interplay between physical, emotional, and social losses: the death of the Black child; the overidentification of Blacks with funeral rites; the distorted response to Black grief are all of a piece. The failure to honor the proprieties of death rites and the disavowal of sympathy's liberalizing role together exemplify the loss of faith in universals that lent a special urgency to the development of the social sciences in this period. Writing in the powerfully moving language that characterizes *The Souls of Black Folk* as a whole, Du Bois captures in one astonishingly brief scene the complicated relationship

2. W. I. Thomas, "The Psychology of Race Prejudice," *The American Journal of Sociology* 9 (March 1904): 599.
3. These are drawn from Victor Turner's work on color symbolism in Ndembu ritual, quoted in *Sacrifice*, ed. M. F. C. Bourdillon and Meyer Fortes (New York: Academic Press, 1980), 21–22.

between death rituals, the problem of the stranger, and the faculty of sympathy.

Let me emphasize how much of what we know about changing views of death at the turn of the century is encompassed by Du Bois's moment of mourning. There is first of all the distinction that had become current between death as a universal versus death as a social particular. As a universal event that "happens" to everyone, it was the great democratizer; as a social event, it expressed prevailing hierarchies and forms of estrangement. In his Durkheimian study, *The Collective Representation of Death* (1907), Robert Hertz notes that in most cultures the death of a stranger or slave will "occasion no ritual," for "their death merely consecrates an exclusion from society which has in fact already been completed."[4] Du Bois's scene reminds us that all cultures define the borders between acceptable and unacceptable peoples by manipulating their associations with death: an association that was increasingly in this era thought to be an arbitrary one. W. I. Thomas cites testimony from a range of explorers (including Marco Polo, Charles Darwin, and David Livingstone) on cultures where death's symbolic hue is white. Thomas's catalog, drawn from places as diverse as Africa, India, and Australia, reflects a growing understanding of death as an event whose interpretation varies from one culture to another, with as great or greater consequences for the people left behind as for the deceased person.[5] Through elaborate discrimination of cultural practices and beliefs, typological classification of funeral rites, and philosophical speculation on the reception of death, social scientific analyses by authors such as W. E. Roth, Emile Durkheim, Robert Hertz, Nathaniel Shaler, and, later, Newbell Niles Puckett sought to submit this fundamentally incoherent event to rational method.[6]

Du Bois too portrays death as a problem of reception: a series of effects and affects, muting trees, silencing children, dimming song, conferring an aura of ghastly unreality overall. But sociologically, the most profound implications of his scene are compressed into the word that transforms a family mourning the loss of their only child into a statistic, the prejudicial magic that turns a group of individuals for whom death is an unexpected trauma into a collectivity for whom death is customary. The Whites play the role of serpent in an Edenic idyll of proper mourning. They represent the fall into a certain social scientific knowledge of humanity as universally insignificant and socially estranged.

---

4. Robert Hertz, *The Collective Representation of Death*, trans. Rodney and Claudia Needham (Aberdeen, U.K.: University Press of Aberdeen), 76, 85.
5. Thomas, "Psychology of Race Prejudice," 600–604.
6. Hertz, *Collective Representation of Death*; W. E. Roth "Burial Customs and Disposal of the Dead," *North Queensland Ethnography Bulletin*, no. 9 (July 1907): 363–403; Nathaniel Shaler, *The Individual: A Study of Life and Death* (New York: D. Appleton, 1900); Newbell Niles Puckett, *Folk Beliefs of the Southern Negro* (1926; Montclair, N.J.: Patterson Smith, 1968).

Death here is at once shrunken and enlarged: it is shrunken from a universal to a contemporary plane of explanation and meaning; it is enlarged as a society-centered rather than personal event. In one sense there is nothing particular to racial politics in the idea that death is routinized when it is viewed as something that is happening to a social group rather than to an individual. Such a difference is the basis for the rise of F. L. Hoffman's life insurance industry, whose redefinition of death, in collective and statistical terms, was its means of investing it with predictability and control. "Nothing is more uncertain than the duration of a single life," wrote Elizur White, a founder of the industry, "nothing is more certain than the duration of a thousand lives."[7] This view prepared the way for the commodification of death, which now possessed a value that could be determined by the laws of probability. In this way and more, death proved beneficial to the living: every death contributed to social progress (in the words of Charles Ellwood, an editor of the *American Journal of Sociology*, "Progress everywhere waits on death—the death of the inferior individual—and nowhere more so than in racial problems"),[8] and fostered the integration of the community. The act of mourning, according to contemporary analysts like Nathaniel Shaler, inspired "greater fellowship between men than any other basis of fellowship can afford," an idea that inevitably implied the reverse—that it exposed differences between them.[9] Because the distinction between the living and the dead is an absolute, arguably the most absolute distinction that can be made, death not only provided a metaphor for defining the status of outsiders but death practices themselves were an important means for differentiating aliens from like kinds or kin.

It is the failure to acknowledge the force of kinship that is at issue in Du Bois's scene: the inability of White pedestrians to identify with the grief of a mother and father. I consider it significant that the paradigm for sympathetic identification in Max Scheler's *The Nature of Sympathy* (1913) is likewise familial, two parents before "the dead body of a beloved child . . . who feel in common the 'same' sorrow, the 'same' anguish . . . they feel it together in the sense that they feel and experience in common not only the self-same value situation, but also the same keenness of emotion in regard to it." For their "friend . . . who joins them and commiserates," such sorrow can only be an " 'external' matter."[1] What is critical about this moment for Scheler, and what makes it acutely representative of the status of sympathy in

7. Quoted in James Farrell, *Inventing the American Way of Death* (Philadelphia: Temple University Press, 1980), 69.
8. Charles Ellwood, review of *The Color Line: A Brief On Behalf of the Unborn*, by William Benjamin Smith, *The American Journal of Sociology* 11 (November 1905): 574.
9. Shaler, *The Individual*, 219.
1. Max Scheler, *The Nature of Sympathy*, trans. Peter Heath, ed. Werner Stark (Hamden, Conn.: Archon Books, 1970), 12–13.

the modern world, is its self-enclosure. The scene is instructive for what it can't reveal about other potential sympathetic circumstances, for how it doesn't pertain, and in this sense it is best understood as an anti-example. Scheler's scene, like Du Bois's, implies that kinship is the final boundary of sympathy: they use mourning (a ritual designed to master the separation of the dead, sometimes by denial as in the idea of ghosts or visitations), in order to show how the sympathetic re-sponse—usually associated with harmony and inclusion, embracing an-other's experience and extending one's own—functions increasingly in the modern era to distinguish aliens from neighbors. Both scenes spin out into a series of impossibilities so far as feeling is concerned: the failure of friend (in Scheler) or stranger (in Du Bois) to empathize with one's pain replicates the distance felt by both sets of parents from their dead offspring. Du Bois's scene dramatizes a double betrayal: their be-trayal by fate (which forges an insuperable border between themselves and their child) is seconded by the passing Whites (who express their separation from the community). It is telling in this regard that the Black parents turn away from their son at the moment of death (351) [132], a fulfillment of a folk decree that anticipates the actions of the Whites.

The question of race remains implicit in Scheler, who offers this scene as exemplary, I believe, to illustrate the reliance of sympathy, in theory and in practice, on notions of similarity and difference. His elusive (and unparalleled) "community" of mourning parents high-lights the extent to which liberal conceptions of sympathy have always invited the identification of affinities and exclusions. Sympathetic states described by writers like Adam Smith are really states of "infection," in Scheler's words, where the individual is overtaken or inhabited by an-other's point of view. The ascription of a kind of porousness to mental life is part of the general tendency of these theories to confuse emo-tional and physical experience. For the ease with which another's per-spective can be internalized is directly related to the other's physical qualities of familiarity or resemblance. On the contrary, Scheler holds, emotional connection to another human being is facilitated, not pre-cluded, by the recognition of difference: authentic sympathy requires a capacity for distance that is balanced by the imaginative access to oth-ers' experiences. The modern world is bereft of "communities of feel-ing," it provides little potential for genuine sympathy not because of its increasing heterogeneity (culturally, ethnically, nationally), but because the inability to confront, either in intellectual or in moral terms, the changing configurations of social relations results in the denial of what is profoundly common in human emotional life.

The very *idea* of sympathy is a problem for Scheler: his effort to chart the concept's history, to explore its sociological basis, is inspired by his belief that the need to construct a theory about sympathy signals its demise as a harmonizing social force. Scheler seems to intuit that theorists of sympathy have been unreflectively motivated by new global tensions arising from interracial, interethnic, and international contact (Scheler critiques Hume's "naive" position on prejudice, for instance, with reference to "the American race problem").[2] These hidden and not so hidden agendas can be traced from Hume's *Human Nature* (where sympathy is "a resonance between people's feelings, made possible by their identical constitution"),[3] to contemporaneous sociological definitions of sympathetic identification as inherent (e.g., F. H. Giddings's citation of interracial marriage taboos as proof of the natural yearning for "like kinds"),[4] to works of pseudosociology like *The Neighbor* by Nathaniel Shaler (Du Bois's geology professor at Harvard), which views sympathy as the highest faculty of human evolution. This last book is an example of what I think is a crucial aspect of interdisciplinary discussions from the turn of the century through our own time. I have called this the "border text," a work that at once defines and bridges divisions among professional disciplines (such as sociology, anthropology, psychology), and in turn, between these disciplines and more popular audiences. Marked by their accessible language and broad appeal, these texts cut across emerging specializations in ways that accentuate the process of specialization itself.[5]

Shaler's "natural history of human contacts" aims at a scientific account of neighborliness, arguing that a psychic resistance to aliens (a term that for Shaler includes Blacks, Jews, the wounded, and the dead) is the most basic of human responses. For illustration, Shaler recalls an apparition during a foggy morning walk in Tuscany: "an unclassifiable creature which looked like a cow walking on its hind legs," a sight that inspires "dread" until the subject is revealed as "a man in a cow costume . . . a fellow of our species," and the "sympathies" are activated. Shaler's apparition provokes a contrast between skins that are removable and skins that are not, between differences that can be dis-

2. Ibid., 263. I draw upon the work of Scheler, the era's foremost theorist of sympathy, because of the importance of this category for Du Bois in this period. Scheler's treatment of sympathy and the emotions represents a German tradition of critical sociology that seems especially compatible with Du Bois's thinking. Like Du Bois, Scheler is alert to the mixed consequences of increased contact among human kinds, as revealed by this sample from his book on sympathy * * * In the course of its history, civilization has given rise to quite new forms of cruelty, brutality, envy, malice, etc. which never previously existed. Closer contacts and increased solidarity of interests have brought new 'vices' as well as new 'virtues,' in their train" (134). Any reader of Scheler must be struck by the work's eclecticism: a blend of Catholicism, socialism, and a critical sociology that anticipated the Frankfurt School. Scheler's own term for it was "the philosophy of the open hand." He was fascinated with the topics of ethnicity, cultural difference, and intolerance, an undercurrent of all his writings, but perhaps most directly evident in his response to the first world war* * *
3. Quoted in Robert Park, *The Crowd and the Public* (1904), ed. Henry Elsner (Chicago: University of Chicago Press, 1972), 32–33.
4. F. H. Giddings, *The Principles of Sociology* (New York: Macmillan, 1896), xiii–xiv.
5. A more recent example of the border text is *The Bell Curve* (New York: Free Press, 1994), by Richard Herrnstein and Charles Murray. As these examples show, part of the border text's appeal is its politically controversial nature.

missed as optical illusions and differences that are magnified by a reduction of physical distance. The man in the cow costume recalls the
ancient Semites described by Robertson Smith in his study of kinship
and sacrifice, who draped themselves in the skins of sacrificial victims
as a means of securing "divine protection." This custom, in which
Smith locates the origins of the "robe of righteousness," gives way to a
practice of offering sacrificial substitutions—sometimes animals, sometimes social strangers—for members of the community. In keeping with
this, one could say that a strange skin which is removable identifies a
beneficiary of the sacrificial rite, while a strange skin that is not, identifies a victim.[6]

Shaler's thoughts on proximity and strangeness invite comparison
with Du Bois's scene, a comparison illuminated by Orlando Patterson's
understanding of slavery as "institutionalized marginality," a system designed to reconcile the contradictory charge of housing aliens within.
Patterson cites, among expressions of this contradiction, the Cherokee
description of slave identity: one possesses "the shape of a human being,
but no human essence."[7] Shaler's man in the cow costume represents
the opposite conundrum—a human being in essence despite his shape,
whose reconciliation as human is signaled by his arousal of sympathy.

Du Bois's Black mourners pose a far greater dilemma for the spectators of his scene. They are neither human shapes without human
essence nor human essences without human shape. To assume their
conformity with the structural position of the slave would imply an
intimacy and connection that is clearly absent here. This accords with
Shaler's conviction that the tragedy of modernity is its terrible capacity
to bring strangeness ever closer, without the formal means of keeping
it within bounds. Whites can only voice their alienation weakly,
through inadequate terms such as "nigger and the like," which are
themselves "barriers to sympathetic advance." Shaler's inability to separate such categories from their subjects leads him to conclude, in a
chapter titled "The Way Out," that a sympathetic humanitarianism will
not reach its highest form until the disappearance of those who fail to

6. Nathaniel Shaler, *The Neighbor: The Natural History of Human Contacts* (Boston: Houghton, Mifflin, 1904), 30–32. By the time he taught Du Bois, Shaler's reputation as a writer on racial topics was well established. They published in many of the same journals (*The Atlantic Monthly* and *The Independent*, for example), sometimes in the same issue. When Du Bois proclaims in his article "Is Race Friction Between Blacks and Whites in the United States Growing and Inevitable?" *The American Journal of Sociology* 13 (March 1908): 834–38, that "the world is shrinking together, it is finding itself neighbor to itself in strange, almost magic degree" it is difficult not to hear an echo of his teacher's book. *The Neighbor* is listed in the bibliography of Du Bois's edited volume, *The Negro American Artisan*, Atlanta University Publications, no. 17 (Atlanta, Ga.: Atlanta University, 1912), 14. And see W. Robertson Smith, *Lectures on the Religion of the Semites* (1889; New York: Ktav Publishing House, 1969), 437 and passim. Smith emphasizes that belief in the "sacred purposes" of the sacrificial skin predominated "at the stage of religious development in which the god, his worshippers, and the victim were all members of one kindred" (435–36).
7. Orlando Patterson, *Slavery and Social Death* (Cambridge, Mass.: Harvard University Press, 1982), 46–47.

inspire it.[8] A reconsideration of Du Bois's White onlookers as serpents in the garden of mourning will help to specify the historical claims of this passage. Shaler's argument marks Blacks with the quality of antique or remnant; they are the collective sacrifice to the development of a broadbased sympathy. Du Bois, in contrast, sees that Blacks in his time have become the special object of a uniquely modern point of view—the sociological imagination. His insight is supported by Ralph Ellison, who observes that sociology became "closely concerned with the Negro after Emancipation gave the slaves the status—on paper at least—of nominal citizens . . . the end of the slave system created for this science the pragmatic problem of adjusting our society to include the new citizens," an obsession that has sometimes caused Blacks to feel like "phantoms that the white mind seeks unceasingly, by means both crude and subtle, to lay."[9]

One might go so far as to classify the era's writers on sympathy along a continuum. Their theories range from confrontations with the vexed and complicated circumstances of sympathy, to a symptomatic registration of these circumstances. At the symptomatic end of the spectrum, we find Nathaniel Shaler, together with sociologists Franklin Giddings, Robert Park, and Albion Small. The critical end includes Max Scheler, whose antagonism toward the category of sympathy becomes more explicable in light of these other sentimentalizations, and Du Bois. Du Bois and Scheler are among sympathy's most powerful modern analysts in judging the faculty to be in crisis. Throughout *Souls* Du Bois tends to capture emotions in color (*awe* over his son's birth is "brown"; *hope* in the future prospects of Black John is "yellow"; *wonderment* on the part of the young Alexander Crummel is "blue and gold"). And there is no image that does more to register the combined material and emotional effects of color than the indeterminate (simultaneously colorful and colorless) color line itself. The book's color symbolism becomes a way of emphasizing that the role of emotions as social forces cannot be fully assessed without reference to the national and international drama of race relations.

The story of sympathy's downfall has a critical epilogue: the deliberate un-neighboring of Blacks. Du Bois notes the tie between sympathy and segregation in an 1899 volume of the *Atlanta University Publications*, speaking here, not incidentally, about the funeral business: "Segregated as a social group there are many semi-social functions in which the prevailing prejudice makes it pleasanter that he should serve himself if possible. Undertakers, for instance, must come in close and sympathetic relations with the family. This has led to Negroes taking up this branch of business, and in no line have they had greater

8. Shaler, *Neighbor*, 196–97; 327–30.
9. Ralph Ellison, review of *The White Dilemma* by Gunnar Myrdal, in *The Death of White Sociology*, ed. Joyce Ladner (New York: Vintage, 1973), 82–83.

success."[1] From the turn of the century to our own time, the policy of segregation has been implemented with increasing efficiency, culminating in a residential segregation so pronounced that some recent analysts have labeled it "American Apartheid."[2] Comparing the post-Emancipation prospects of Blacks to the expectations of European immigrants from the same era, Stanley Lieberson observes that there is an actual "deterioration in the position of blacks over time," a decline that is "hardly to be expected" if this position were mainly attributable to the institution of slavery and its aftereffects.[3] My claim is that we have in Du Bois's America, partly in response to the post-Emancipation gains and challenges of Blacks, an attempt to reinvent their "social death"[4] under slavery in a new, more intensely metaphorical form.

The Souls of Black Folk can be read as a book of the dead. "Herein lie buried many things" (209) [5], Du Bois proclaims in the very first line, and he goes on to characterize Black American existence repeatedly as a "living death" (216, 349, 354, and so on) [133, 140]. The Sorrow Songs are ghostly ("haunting melody" from the "dark past"), the first chapter opens with a staged exchange between an animate White interlocuter and an inanimate Black subject, and the veiled life of the "doubly conscious" Black (not "true self-consciousness, but the revelation of the other world") looks decidedly deadly. Eleven (out of fourteen) chapter epigraphs (both musical and literary) image graves, ashes, corpses, mourners—while two of the three chapters written expressly for the collection ("Of the Passing of the First-Born" and "Of the Coming of John") culminate in death and lynching.

The book's symbolic center is Du Bois's elegiac reflections on his son's death. They reveal how personal loss is at once deflected and sustained by an apprehension of its collective ramifications. Grief in *The Souls of Black Folk* takes on a monumental quality because individual death among certain groups can never be separated from the dilemma of group survival. Du Bois's account of the dread aroused by the infant's mulatto features is a way of acknowledging that all young Black lives are marked from the beginning by uncertainties about the larger group's perpetuation (350) [131]. In this sense, Du Bois's treatise

---

1. W. E. B. Du Bois, *The Negro in Business*, Atlanta University Publications, no. 4 (Atlanta, Ga.: Atlanta University, 1899), 14.
2. See Douglas S. Massey, *American Apartheid* (Cambridge, Mass.: Harvard University Press, 1993).
3. Stanley Lieberson, *A Piece of the Pie: Blacks and White Immigrants Since 1880* (Berkeley: University of California Press, 1980), 365. In a 1911 retrospective on the Emancipation era for a British audience, Du Bois makes plain "the economic core" of the decline in Black status through the period, which he calls, "renewed slavery by force and use of the courts." Black disenfranchisement, the construction of labor laws to facilitate imprisonment for debt and for leaving an employer, the neglect of Black schools, were so many means of ensuring "a backward step in the organization of labor such as no modern nation would dare to take in the broad daylight of present economic thought." W. E. B. Du Bois, "The Economics of Negro Emancipation in the United States," *The Sociological Review* 4 (1911): 310.
4. My use of the term is derived from Patterson's *Slavery and Social Death*.

on mourning offers a significant contrast to its Emersonian analog, "Experience." For Du Bois, it is not the elusiveness of death that appalls, but the ease with which it envelops Black life, destroying an already provisional domesticity. The "fetid Gulf wind" that carries the son's illness, devastating the parental "dreams" and "plans," recalls passages from Du Bois's sociological works describing the perilous exposure of Black homes. Emerson's complaint is that we can never be sufficiently exposed to feel the effects of our exposure. Du Bois complains that there is no way for Blacks to avoid feeling the damage of their experience. Du Bois struggles to reconcile private grief and collective identification, to join Black elite and Black masses. This purpose is complicated by a demographic plot that implies disproportionately lower reproductive rates among the Black elite and distinguishes the relative values of different Black lives.

Du Bois's 1899 sociological work, *The Philadelphia Negro*, commissioned by White leaders convinced that the morbid condition of Philadelphia's Black community was responsible for a more general municipal malaise, provides another perspective on this death talk. Du Bois's assignment was to codify the urban eyesore that was Negro Philadelphia, on behalf of its eventual removal. But Du Bois's revisionary sociology ended up challenging the functionalist theory it was supposed to sustain, by exposing its hypocrisy. Du Bois's ironic retrospect on *The Philadelphia Negro* explains how the science of society was reconceived by his study. It became, in effect, "a Gospel of Sacrifice," with its new gospel text, "the mud sill theory of society: that society must have the poor, the diseased, the wretched, the criminal, upon which to build its temples of light."[5] He also challenged sociological practice by documenting a Black Philadelphia that no one had wanted to see: the thriving institutions of a Black middle class. The book is structured in terms of an immigrant thematics, portraying Philadelphia as a Negro Ellis Island, a racial gateway between feudal South and modern North. It also represents Du Bois's personal quest for professional legitimacy, his immigration ticket, as it were, into the newfound land of sociology. *The Philadelphia Negro* applies sociological theory and method to the circumstances of a stratified and self-identified Black community. To this end, it opens with a Weberian gesture designed to contain Du Bois's bias—Blackness—through an explanation of the decision to capitalize "Negro" throughout. The gesture, more importantly, signifies its author's intent to insert a live and articulate Black body (as opposed to a criminal or morbid one) into the social text of Philadelphia.

Despite Du Bois's revisionary aims, however, the book ends with a capitulation to a more subtle kind of death projection for the Black people. It shows how the Black middle classes had actively cultivated

5. See Du Bois, *Souls*, 267, and *Dusk of Dawn*, in *Du Bois: Writings*, ed. Nathan Huggins (New York: Library of America, 1986), 678.

a certain social invisibility. It reveals them caught, like any ambitious immigrant group, in a dialectic of their own unmaking. The final chapter on Black-White intermarriage offers an assimilationist prophecy consistent with the utopian schemes of liberal sociologists who were predicting the gradual extinction of Blacks through a racial amalgamation that was already underway ("survival of the fittest" elaborated genetically).[6]

To confront *The Souls of Black Folk* in the wake of Du Bois's sociological work is to recognize how it transforms a dialogue of death into living art. This is exemplified by the book's attention to the regenerative aspects of folk ritual, mortuary rites in particular. As I have implied, the image of the Whites turning away from the funeral may indicate their unconscious replication of a Black folk decree (observed previously by the parents), that it is bad luck to look at death. This moment is linked to other chapter references—to omens, crosses, sacrifices, journeys, burial customs—which invoke a vast tradition of Black folk practice, representing an apparently alternative system of value. This alternative perspective is also captured by the musical notes of Sorrow Songs placed at the head of each chapter. As published *adaptations* of the original slave songs, brought into conformity with Euro-American tastes, they confirm the difficulty of preserving authentic oral culture. As oral inscriptions of the sufferings of slavery, whose own preservation seems tenuous, they embody the dilemma of Black cultural survival.[7] Eric Sundquist shows how these songs represent at once an elite language, legible only to those who read music, and a secret ethnic code, audible only to those who know how the songs "really" sound. Finally, the Sorrow Songs harbor the book's evolving prophecy concerning prospects for the unification of colored interests throughout the world. Because they are largely *composites* of various cultural voices, associated especially with the isolated inhabitants of the Sea Islands off the coasts of South Carolina and Georgia, they seem relatively immune to American influences. Songs of diaspora, without geographic bounds, they

6. The sociologist Lester Ward, for example, anticipates a "composite photograph" of "the great united world-race" of the future, with non-Aryan features reduced to a feminized "softening influence," in "Social Differentiation and Integration," *The American Journal of Sociology* 8 (May 1903): 733. Ward's prediction seems eerily fulfilled ninety years later by a *Time* magazine special issue, "The New Face of America" (fall, 1993), which features a computer-generated composite of "the kind of offspring that might result from seven men and seven women of various ethnic and racial backgrounds." Presented, according to its editors, "in the spirit of fun and experiment," the image seems remarkably free of all but the most muted of non-Caucasian attributes.

7. I am indebted here to Eric Sundquist's interpretation of *Souls* in *To Wake the Nations* (Cambridge, Mass.: Harvard University Press, 1993), see especially 490–539. The Songs were published in the following forms, *Hampton and Its Students*, ed. M. F. Armstrong and Helen Ludlow, with songs arranged by Thomas Fenner (New York: Putnam, 1874), and J. B. T. Marsh, *The Story of the Jubilee Singers with Their Songs* (Boston: Houghton Mifflin, 1872). See also Lawrence Levine, *Black Culture and Black Consciousness* (New York: Oxford University Press, 1977), 17–55, 159–70, and Houston Baker's fascinating account of *Souls* as a "singing book," in *Modernism and the Harlem Renaissance* (Chicago: University of Chicago Press, 1987), 58–68.

point to the cross-cultural foundations of African-American culture and to potential international alliances of the future.[8]

The dialogue of death is specific to an era: at this historical moment it was possible, especially in certain social scientific circles, to imagine Black culture in terms of decline and even extinction. But these associations have persisted in the twentieth century, as a variety of echoes in literary, social scientific, and popular-media sources. As a rule, neither historian nor social scientists of the American nineteenth and twentieth centuries have responded conceptually to these traces, in contrast to a contemporaneous African-American literature. African-American authors have read past the exaggerated (and refutable) statistics on the morbidity of Black culture to identify a consistent pattern of thinking. In so doing, they have reached a deeper sociological depth than social scientists themselves. Their work has been especially informed by Du Bois's famous formulation of Black double-consciousness, an intense dialectical condition of self and social awareness, which might be understood as a kind of sociological sixth sense. I think of Ralph Ellison's hero at the end of *Invisible Man* buried alive in a crypt of light; or of Richard Wright's *The Long Dream*, which chronicles the life of an undertaker's son. There may be no writer who captures the sociological implications of modern African-American life with more power than Toni Morrison, whose works are also richly evocative of a Black symbolic, centered in the possibilities of folk belief. Take *The Bluest Eye*, whose metaphor for the peripheral existence of Blacks ("on the hem of life") is death. As a domestic correlative to this condition of social death, Morrison's Black psyche is a permanently empty kitchen. No experience of possession, no amount of objects, no stocked and swollen cupboards and jars, can compensate for the foundational experience and ever-present threat of dispossession. The novel's lead character, a small, dark Hester Prynne, ends her days in "a little house . . . on the edge of town." Now a compulsive wastepicker, in fulfillment of her life as a repository for the waste of the town ("which we dumped on her and which she absorbed"), she is, for Morrison, at least one significant emblem of Black status in America. And consider *Song of Solomon*, which opens with the suicide of a life insurance agent and centers on the devitalized existence of a Black middle-class family called the Deads. Most recently, there is the work of playwright Suzan-Lori Parks,

---

8. One of Du Bois's fullest contemporary prophecies of a worldwide culture of color was his response in the 1908 *AJS* debate on "Race Friction." There he describes the increasing prominence and self-awareness of the world's darker nations and rejects extinctionist and assimilationist arguments, asserting the inevitability of racial cohabitation across the globe. He replaces the vague problematic of the heart with the hard logic of bodies and numbers. Alternately imaged as "the darker two thirds" of the world, or "the mass of dark serfs and slaves," the world's colored populations will neither dwindle away, nor recede into decorative coloration in some world composite photograph of the future. Rather they will be prime contenders in the creation of a "new commerce" and "new humanity." For the full citation of this debate see note 6, page 284.

The Death of the Last Black Man in the Whole Entire World (1992) and *The America Play* (1994), a brilliant portrayal of a Black culture steeped in the rituals of death and mourning.[9] The nonliterary sound-ings of this theme are notably less self-conscious. There is the Moyni-han report on the morbidity of the Black family; Andrew Hacker's *Two Nations*, which Orlando Patterson critiques in his response to the first Rodney King verdict for its "late twentieth-century prototypical Black who wanders on the margins of the White world, overwhelmed by his blackness, a slug on the salt of America's obsessive whiteness"; and media characterizations of Black males as an "endangered species." Finally, consider the label "Death Row Records," favored by rap artists such as Snoop Doggy Dog, which regionalizes the creativity of Black youth as a ghostly limbo, somewhere between deviance and a (possibly compensatory?) land of the dead.[1]

I want to emphasize that this reading of Du Bois's early work explores only one aspect of a rich and complicated endowment. I believe it to be an important one, but of course there are others well worthy of analysis. Let me end by sketching out, briefly, a line of inquiry I develop at greater length in my book-in-progress, "The Science of Sacrifice: American Literature and Modern Social Theory." One of my claims is that sacrifice, as both concept and event, is central to modern social scientific thought. We can recognize it as a fundamental category of exchange: what you have to give up in order to get what you want. In defining sacrifice as the condition of value, Georg Simmel contrasts it with the "naturalness" of aesthetic productions, whose charm derives from the "sacrifices ordinarily required to gain such things." Max We-ber refers repeatedly to the "intellectual sacrifice" required of the reli-gious believers he pities and envies. And Emile Durkheim offers vivid analyses of sacrificial rites at home (altruistic suicide) and abroad (self-mortification in the mourning ceremonies of the Australian aborigi-

9. For those of my readers who remain unpersuaded by what may seem an unduly morbid characterization of attitudes toward Blacks at the turn of the century, let me offer the example of a postmodern drama set in this period, *The America Play* * * * In the isolated, surrealist world of *The America Play*, gravedigging, mourning, and confidence keeping (secreting the final words of the dead) are the sole occupations. Perhaps most striking for my concerns is the portrayal of sympathy, as a stage effect, devoid of instinctive content. Sympathy, like any other human artifact, needs to be invented. The son recalls the day when his father first showed him " 'the Weep,' 'the Sob' and 'the Moan.' How to stand just so with the hands and feet (to capitalize on what we in the business call 'the Mourning Moment')." Like any com-modity, it can be bought and sold: "There's money init" the son is told. Parks's play, which premiered at the Yale Repetory Theatre on January 13, 1994, was published in *American Theatre*, March 1994, 25–39.

1. Orlando Patterson, "White Poor, Black Poor," *New York Times*, May 3, 1992, 17. Also relevant in this regard is the eloquent bestseller by Leon Bing, *Do Or Die* (New York: Harper Collins, 1991), an "insider account" of Los Angeles youth gangs composed mainly of African-American males. In the dead-end world of the Crips and the Bloods, one sacrifices another ("do") so as not to be sacrificed oneself ("die"). But of course this is a contradiction or even negation of sacrifice. What seems most revealing about the highly ritualized nature of gang life is the way it implicates and distorts sacrificial logic.

nes).[2] While sacrifice in theory and in practice plays a significant role in turn-of-the-century social science (and this is as true of its American variant), a contemporaneous literature, I argue, *stages* sacrifice. It offers what might be called a corresponding sacrificial theater. These literary spectacles range from the feasting warriors of Frank Norris's *McTeague*, to the foot soldiers of Stephen Crane's *Red Badge of Courage*, sacrificed to their "bloodswollen God," from the wasted working class of Gertrude Stein's *Three Lives* to the female adolescents of Henry James's *Awkward Age*, imagined as sacrificial lambs. *The Souls of Black Folk*, Du Bois's magnificent fusion of sociological and literary method, includes conceptualizations of sacrifice as well as stagings of sacrificial action.

Du Bois's text is framed by rites of sacrifice. They begin with the Hebrew invocation of kinship in the "Forethought" ("I . . . am bone of the bone and flesh of the flesh," 209 [6]), an allusion to the sacrificial meal where all, human and god, become one substance.[3] They end with the "After-thought," where Du Bois declares his book an offering in the "wilderness" (389) [164]. The chapter on his son recalls two biblical moments of sacrificial substitution. In one, blood drops are substituted for human bodies; in the other, God's body is sacrificed for the sins of the human collectivity. The chapter's title, "Of the Passing of the First-Born," alludes to the Passover story, where the Hebrews are commanded to mark their doorposts with lamb's blood, a sacrificial sign that ensures that the angel of death will "pass over" their homes and spare their firstborn sons.[4] Belief in the protective powers of the color red (persisting to this day in Jewish and Black, among other, folk traditions) can be traced back directly to this passage in Exodus. At the same time, characterizations of the son as a "revelation of the divine . . . his baby voice the voice of the Prophet that was to rise within the Veil" (351) [131] associate his birth and death (as critics have duly noted) with the story of Christ.

The echoing lines near the chapter's beginning—"I saw, as it fell *across* my baby, the shadow of the Veil. . . . I saw the shadow of the Veil as it *passed over* my baby" (my italics, 350) [131], seem to equalize

2. See Georg Simmel, "Exchange," in *Georg Simmel on Individuality and Social Forms*, ed. Donald Levine (Chicago: University of Chicago Press, 1971), 53–54, and 44–50; Max Weber, "Science as Vocation," in *From Max Weber*, ed. H. H. Gerth and C. Wright Mills (New York: Oxford, 1946), 148, 153–56; Emile Durkheim, *Suicide*, trans. John Spaulding and George Simpson (New York: Free Press, 1961), 217–40, and *The Elementary Forms of the Religious Life*, trans. Joseph Ward Swain (New York: Free Press, 1965), 434–61.

3. See Smith, *Lectures*, 313 and passim, and Sigmund Freud, *Totem and Taboo: Some Points of Agreement Between the Mental Lives of Savages and Neurotics*, trans. James Strachey (New York: Norton, 1950), 135.

4. See, in *The Body in Pain* (New York: Oxford University Press, 1984), 238–39 and passim, Elaine Scarry's brilliant reading of the Passover mark's significance throughout the Hebrew Bible. She notes, for example, how it is "elaborated into an intricate blueprint of rescue" through God's instructions on the fine points of housebuilding in the story of Noah, and how it embodies an "explicit" "rhythm of substitution and sparing" in Malachi.

the sacrificial symbols of crucifixion and passover. But of course they are not equivalent. The obstructed first sentence, where the infant's body, enclosed in commas, appears caught by the shadowy Veil (though perhaps also draped, as in royal robes), recalls a New Testament sacrifice that was.[5] The second sentence, a single breath suggesting immunity through unimpeded moment, highlights a Hebrew sacrifice that was not. These two biblical alternatives provide insight into Du Bois's view of Black American experience at this time: as a sacrificial possibility fulfilled or averted. The collective symbolic status glimmering through the death of this young Black hope (Du Bois notes how the entire race was "sacrificed in its swaddling clothes on the altar of national integrity," 238 [32]) is at once the work of an uncommon fate and an all-too-common agency. His uncommon fate is that of a Christian God whose suffering served to justify ever after, as Albert Camus observed, "the endless and universal torture of innocence."[6] The common agency, in Du Bois's words, is the "economic and social exclusion" that might well "succeed in murdering" Blacks "until they disappear from the face of the earth" (*Philadelphia Negro*, 388). Its brutal and extravagant extension is lynch law.

The link between his son's death and Christ's sacrifice evidently resonated for Du Bois with a form of sacrifice that preoccupied him in this period—lynching. I think we are meant to hear the "whistle" in Black John's "ears" at his lynching, as the completion of the "shadow . . . song" in the "ears" of the mourners at Burghardt Du Bois's funeral (377, 353) [154, 133]. Surveying the Atlanta lands of the Cherokees earlier in *Souls*, Du Bois draws our attention to the spot "where Sam Hose was crucified" (285) [75]. The display of Hose's charred knuckles in an Atlanta storefront a month before Burghardt's death (Du Bois heard about it but avoided the spectacle) turned Atlanta, according to Du Bois's biographer, into "a poisoned well, polluted with the remains of Sam Hose and reflecting the drawn image of Burghardt."[7] The proximity of these two Black deaths highlights Du Bois's burden throughout this chapter, to reconcile his own analytical distance from a Black America stigmatized by high mortality with a firsthand experience that tragically confirms his own implication in it.

I hope I have made sufficiently clear that the stigma of excessive Black mortality, especially as it adhered after the turn of the century, was at least in part an expression of the very opposite concern: the surprising vitality of Black population rates. In the same 1908 *American Journal of Sociology* debate where he identified American "race friction" as a problem of international proportions, Du Bois labeled Amer-

5. Scarry, *Body in Pain*, 360, cites the work of the art historian Kenneth Clark on "draped" and "undraped" portraits of Christ on the Cross.
6. Quoted by Peter Berger in *The Sacred Canopy* (New York: Anchor, 1969), 76–77.
7. David Levering Lewis, *W. E. B. Du Bois: The Biography of a Race* (New York: Holt, 1993), 228.

ica's color line the war plan of besieged Whites, who had rightly deduced that the hard logic of bodies and numbers was bound to favor the world's darker peoples.[8] The practice of lynching confirmed the inversion that was taking place. For lynching was invariably imagined as an act of vengeance: a retribution for the White female victims of Black hypersexuality (or hyperfecundity), often exacted quite literally through the accompanying ritual of castration. The suspicion that Black population growth was in fact vigorous was manifested in reactions to the prospect of Black suffrage, a development that "ended a civil war by beginning a race feud" (Souls, 238) [32].

Lynching was a monstrous inversion of the mortality issue, the proof that far from being fated, the elimination of Blacks required aggressive action, extending to the mutilation of their reproductive organs. Lynching also represented a monstrous fulfillment of the sympathy crisis: a frenzied unification of White sentiment, a segregated, incestuous sympathy gone wild. The lynch mob was the logical culmination of sympathy's rewriting as a circumscribed intragroup exchange. Here group identity was founded in the ritual sacrifice of social strangers. This aspect of sympathetic identification was especially apparent to James Elbert Cutler, a disciple of William Graham Sumner and author of the social scientific study Lynch-Law (1905). As a stage for the problems of mob behavior, intolerance, and social integration and a litmus test for the shortcomings of liberalism, it is easy to see why lynching caught the attention of contemporary social scientists. In this light, Du Bois's disclaimer, that lynching made him doubt the value of rational analysis, seems more a matter of personal experience than professional judgment. Still, Cutler's obvious sympathies for lynching, and the fact that his effort to explain lynching scientifically often amounted to explaining it away, serve to substantiate Du Bois's charge. There is no doubt that the resemblances between American lynchings and the violent, cannibalistic rites of uncivilized peoples were deeply disconcerting to the liberal practitioners of social science.[9] But Cutler views lynching as both an expression of social instability, and a critical means for managing social difference. Lynch law could not have escalated, he points out, were the majority of citizens out of "sympathy with the mob." Nor would lynching subside until the American legal system was relieved of its commitment to "abstract principles concerning the rights of all men" and brought into conformity with the "ethnic and societal factors

8. See Du Bois, "Race Friction," 837. For more on the gains of the Black middle-classes in this era, as expressed in efforts to "re-construct" or "re-present" the "American Negro," see Henry Louis Gates, "The Trope of the New Negro and the Reconstruction of the Image of the Black," Representations 24 (fall 1988): 129–55.

9. Orlando Patterson has noted in this regard that American lynchings occurring around the turn of the century sometimes even had cannibalistic overtones. From Patterson's commentary on the San Diego MLA Special Session, "The African-American Author as Sociologist," December 28, 1994.

involved in the race question."[1] Cutler's claim is fully consistent with
the conclusions on sympathy reached by Nathaniel Shaler and F. H.
Giddings. Political ideals were one thing, social facts another. Until
they were reconciled, there would be collective effusions such as
lynchings.

Undoubtedly, the most striking passage in *Lynch-Law* is Abraham
Lincoln's account of those "sacrificed" in an exemplary rash of violence: "First . . . gamblers—a set of men certainly not following for a
livelihood a very useful or very honest occupation. . . . Next, negroes
suspected of conspiring to rise an insurrection . . . then, white men
supposed to be leagued with the negroes; and finally, strangers from
neighboring States . . . till dead men were literally dangling from the
boughs of trees by every roadside, and in numbers almost sufficient to
rival the native Spanish moss of the country as a drapery of the forest."[2]
Lincoln's haunting description transforms lynched strangers into "ri-
vals" even in death, now of the more "native" moss. Despite differences
in content, Lincoln's list anticipates in its apparent oddity a much later
assortment of victims by Rene Girard: "prisoners of war, slaves, small
children, unmarried adolescents . . . [sometimes] the king himself."[3]
These analytical attempts to discriminate the identities of typical victims
can be seen as fragile borders, in their own right, against the chaos that
is supposedly foreclosed by ritual violence. But they help to pinpoint
just what is at stake in sacrificial designs. Sacrifice is always at least in
part motivated by a threatened erasure of social distinctions. The victims are considered expendable because they are casteless, or have
somehow abandoned the bounds of caste. As social strangers, or neighbors without strong allies, their deaths do not entail acts of vengeance.

In biblical Hebrew the generic term for sacrifice is "korban"—"to
bring near"—which implies the effort to bring a God or gods closer to
human experience.[4] It is clear from Du Bois's hopeless apostrophes
throughout the chapter (alternately to Death, Fate, and God), that he
has little faith in the prospects for such intimacy. Du Bois is an unwilling Abraham: he offers up his son with a resentful eye toward "all"
that I have "foregone at thy command, and without complaint . . . save
that fair young form" (354) [134]. Du Bois's resentment raises questions
about resistance, and the place of sacrificial rites within the Black community itself. This is consistent with the sacrificial elements of Black
folk religion as Du Bois portrays it in *Souls*, specifically the Obi worship

---

1. James Elbert Cutler, *Lynch-Law: An Investigation into the History of Lynching in the United States* (New York: Longmans, Green, 1905), 3–4, 279, and passim.
2. Ibid., 111–12.
3. In *Violence and the Sacred* (Baltimore, Md.: Johns Hopkins University Press, 1977), 12–13, 95–98, Rene Girard goes on to note how the second ritual slaughter of the scapegoat often included the flagellation of its genitals, the sign that some sexual transgression, threatening "the violent abolition of distinctions" was being avenged.
4. Bourdillon and Fortes, *Sacrifice*, xvi.

of slavery days. It's unclear from Du Bois's description who the victims were, or how the particular aims of such "blood-sacrifices" were construed (341–43) [124–25]. But he seems intent on confirming the lingering impact of this vengeful spirituality. This theme is brought forth to the book's conclusion where he notes how "fire and blood, prayer and sacrifice, have billowed over this people, and they have found peace only in the altars of the God of Right" (387) [162]. American Blacks have been much sacrificed, he suggests, but they are not without their own forms of sacrificial agency. Du Bois's preoccupations with death and sacrifice form a central part of his legacy: to confront them is to recognize how the identification of a negative cultural typology can be a source of creative inspiration, critique, and ultimately, perhaps, even renewal. There is no stronger evidence of this final possibility than Du Bois's "After-thought," conveyed in the form of a sacrificial offering. "Hear my cry, O God the Reader; vouchsafe that this my book fall not still-born into the world wilderness" (389) [164].

ARNOLD RAMPERSAD

Slavery and the Literary Imagination: Du Bois's *The Souls of Black Folk*†

W. E. B. Du Bois's *The Souls of Black Folk* was a controversial book when it appeared in 1903, but few readers opposed to it could deny its originality and beauty as a portrait of the Afro-American people. In the succeeding years, the collection of essays lost little of its power, so that it remains acknowledged today as a masterpiece of black American writing. In 1918, the literary historian Benjamin Brawley still could feel in Du Bois's book "the passion of a mighty heart" when he hailed it as the most important work "in classic English" published to that time by a black writer.[1] About thirty years after its appearance, the poet, novelist, and NAACP leader James Weldon Johnson judged that Du Bois's work had produced "a greater effect upon and within the Negro race in American than any other single book published in this country since *Uncle Tom's Cabin*."[2] With admiration bordering on reverence for the book, Langston Hughes recalled that "my earliest memories of written words are those of Du Bois and the Bible."[3] In the 1960s, the

† From *Slavery and the Literary Imagination: Du Bois's* The Souls of Black Folk, ed. Arnold Rampersad and Deborah E. McDowell (Baltimore: Johns Hopkins University Press, 1989), pp. 104–24. Bracketed page numbers refer to this Norton Critical Edition.
1. Benjamin Brawley, *The Negro in Literature and Art* (New York: Duffield, 1918), 18.
2. James Weldon Johnson, *Along This Way* (New York: Viking, 1968), 203.
3. John Henrik Clarke, Esther Jackson, Ernest Kaiser, and J. H. O'Dell, eds., *Black Titan: W. E. B. Du Bois: An Anthology by the Editors of Freedomways* (Boston: Beacon Press, 1970), 8.

astute literary critic J. Saunders Redding weighed the impact of *Souls of Black Folk* on a variety of black intellectuals and leaders and pronounced it "more history-making than historical."[4] In 1973, Herbert Aptheker, the leading Du Bois editor and scholar, hailed the text as "one of the classics in the English language."[5]

These are fervent claims for a book of thirteen essays and a short story written by an academic who had been rigidly trained in history and sociology (especially at Harvard and the University of Berlin, where Du Bois did extensive doctoral work), and whose previous books had been an austere dissertation in history, *The Suppression of the African Slave-Trade to the United States*, and an empirical sociological study of urban blacks, *The Philadelphia Negro*. Clearly, however, *The Souls of Black Folk* was something other than academic history and sociology. If white academics and intellectuals mainly ignored its existence (although Henry James called it "the only Southern book of distinction published in many a year"), its impression was marked on the class of black Americans who provided the leadership of their race.[6] Among black intellectuals, above all, *The Souls of Black Folk* became a kind of sacred book, the central text for the interpretation of the Afro-American experience and the most trustworthy guide into the grim future that seemed to loom before their race in America.

The main cause of the controversy surrounding *The Souls of Black Folk* was its devastating attack on Booker T. Washington. The head of the Tuskegee Institute in Alabama was already a famous man when his autobiography *Up from Slavery* was published in 1901. His epochal compromise speech at the Atlanta Exposition in 1895 had catapulted him to the position of leading spokesman for his race before the white world, a friend of rich industrialists like Andrew Carnegie and a dinner guest in the White House of Theodore Roosevelt. Nevertheless, *Up from Slavery* reinforced Washington's authority to a significant extent. Above all, he has used the skeleton of the slave narrative form (that is, the story of a life that progresses from a state of legal bondage to a state of freedom and a substantial degree of self-realization) not only to describe his rise in the world but also to dramatize the heart of the Tuskegee argument that the salvation of Afro-America lay in self-reliance, conciliation of the reactionary white South, a surrender of the right to vote and the right to social equality, dependence on thrift and industriousness, and an emphasis on vocational training rather than the liberal arts in the education of the young. To these ideas, Du Bois and *The Souls of Black Folk* were unalterably opposed.

I wish to suggest here that perhaps the most important element in

4. W. E. B. Du Bois, *The Souls of Black Folk*, ed. J. Saunders Redding (New York: Fawcett, 1961), ix.

5. Herbert Aptheker, *Annotated Bibliography of the Published Writings of W. E. B. Du Bois* (Millwood, N.Y.: Kraus-Thomson, 1973), 551.

6. Henry James, *The American Scene* (Bloomington: Indiana University Press, 1960), 418.

the making of Du Bois's book, which drew on his previously published material but also on fresh work, derived in significant degree from his full awareness of *Up from Slavery*. While this could hardly be an altogether novel suggestion—given Du Bois's attack on Washington in his book—the crucial area of difference between them has not been adequately recognized. I would argue that this crucial element involved Du Bois's acute sensitivity to slavery both as an institution in American history and as an idea, along with his distaste for Washington's treatment of the subject in *Up from Slavery*. To some extent Du Bois's book functions, in spite of its only partial status as an autobiography, as a direct, parodic challenge to certain forms and assumptions of the slave narrative (in all their variety) which had so aided Booker T. Washington's arguments. While it does so mainly to refute the major ideas in Washington's influential text, at the same time its contrariness of form is made obligatory by Du Bois's peculiar attitudes toward slavery.

The resulting book can be seen as marking Du Bois's sense (and that of the many writers and intellectuals influenced by him) of the obsolescence of the slave narrative as a paradigm for Afro-American experience, as well as the beginning of a reflexive paradigm, allied to the slave narrative, that leads the reader—and the race described in the book—into the modern Afro-American world. William L. Andrews has pointed out elsewhere in this book [*Slavery and the Literary Imagination*], in his essay on slavery and the rise of Afro-American literary realism, that postbellum slave narratives de-emphasized the hellishly destructive nature of slavery and offered it instead as a crucible in which future black manhood was formed. Du Bois's approach, I would argue, is in part a revival of the earlier, antebellum spirit of black autobiography and the slave narrative, but in more significant part also differs from that earlier spirit. In both the earlier and the later slave narratives there is progress for the black as he or she moves away from slavery. Du Bois's central point, as we shall see, is different.

For Booker T. Washington in *Up from Slavery*, slavery was not an institution to be defended overtly. Nevertheless, its evils had been much overstated, as he saw them, and its blessings were real. The evils, insofar as they existed, were to be acknowledged briefly and then forgotten. While this approach in some senses is to be expected of an autobiography by a man born only seven years before emancipation, it also underscores Washington's public attitude to American slavery in particular and to history in general. In Washington's considered view, neither slavery nor history is of great consequence—or, at the very least, of daunting consequence to any black man of sound character who properly trains himself for the demands of the modern world. In *Up from Slavery*, Washington writes flatly of "the cruelty and moral wrong of slavery," and he remarks conclusively about the former slaves that "I have never seen one who did not want to be free, or one who would return to slavery."[7] "I condemn it as an institution," he adds (US, 37). Tellingly, however, this condemnation springs from a need to clarify the major message about slavery in his chapter on his slave years, "A Slave among Slaves." The need itself springs from the patent ambiguity of Washington's view of slavery.

Whatever he intends to do, Washington stresses the fundamentally innocuous, almost innocent, nature of the institution. Of his white father (said to be a prosperous neighbor, who refused to acknowledge him) and of his poor, black mother (who sometimes stole chickens in order to feed herself and her children), Washington's judgment is the same. In lacking the courage or generosity to acknowledge his son, his father "was simply another unfortunate victim of the institution which the Nation unhappily had engrafted upon it at the time" (US, 30). In her thievery, his mother "was simply a victim of the system of slavery" (US, 31). Moreover, Washington's lack of hostility to his father allegedly reflected the complacent attitudes of other blacks to whites. There was no "bitter feeling toward the white people on the part of my race" about the fact that many whites were fighting as soldiers in the Confederate army to preserve slavery; where slaves had been treated "with anything like decency," they showed love and tenderness to their masters, even those in the military (US, 35). The chapter "A Slave among Slaves" ends with a striking tableau of the day of emancipation. Whites are sad not because of the loss of valuable property but "because of parting with those whom they had reared and who were in many ways very close to them" (US, 39). Blacks are initially ecstatic, but the older freedmen, "stealthily at first," return later to the "big house" to consult their former masters about their future (US, 40).

Doubtless sincere in his expressions of antipathy to slavery, Washington nevertheless emphasizes the benefits gained by blacks through the institution. "Notwithstanding the cruel wrongs inflicted upon us," he asserts, "the black man got nearly as much out of slavery as the white man did" (US, 37). With Afro-Americans comprising the most advanced community of blacks in the world (as Washington claimed), slavery was indisputably a fortunate act. Indeed, it was further proof of the notion that "Providence so often uses men and institutions to accomplish a purpose" (US, 37). Through all difficulties, Washington continues to derive faith in the future of black Americans by dwelling on "the wilderness through which and out of which, a good Providence has already led us" (US, 37).

For Washington, the acknowledgment of Providence piously marks his negation of the consequences of forces such as those of history, psychology, economics, and philosophy at play in the field of slavery.

7. Booker T. Washington, *Up from Slavery*, in *Three Negro Classics* (New York: Avon, 1965), 37. Subsequent parenthetical references in the text are to this edition; hereafter abbreviated as *US*.

(Providence does not perform a more positive function in his scheme, in which there is little room for religious enthusiasm or spiritual complexity. Of religion and spirituality in *Up from Slavery* he writes: "While a great deal of stress is laid upon the industrial side of the work at Tuskegee, we do not neglect or overlook in any degree the religious and spiritual side. The school is strictly undenominational, but it is thoroughly Christian, and the spiritual training of the students is not neglected" [*US*, 135].) Willing to share in the belief that economic competition and greed had been at the root of slavery, and that slavery itself was ultimately the cause of the Civil War, he pushes no further into causes and effects even as he everywhere, as a champion of pragmatism, lauds the value of "facts" and the "need to look facts in the face" (*US*, 37). In his scheme, the mental legacy of slavery to the black freedman is not conflict, but a blank, a kind of tabula rasa on which is to be inscribed those values and skills that would serve the freedman best in the new age. Although he offers a critical view of the past of his people, "who had spent generations in slavery, and before that generations in the darkest heathenism," Washington in fact invites a vision of the Afro-American as black Adam (*US*, 71). This Adam is, in a way, both prelapsarian and postlapsarian.[8] He is an Adam in the Eden of the South, with the world before him. He is also Adam who has fallen. The fall was slavery itself. Slavery, as seen in this context, is a "fortunate fall"—the fall by which Africans gained the skills and the knowledge needed for the modern world. But who is responsible for the fall? Who has sinned? The answer surely must be the black slave himself, since *Up from Slavery* places no blame on the white world. The failure to investigate the origins, the nature, and the consequences of slavery has led Washington to a subtle and yet far-reaching defamation of the African and Afro-American peoples.

The black American Adam, in his prelapsarian guise, and in the simplicity of his capabilities, must be protected from the fruit that would destroy him—in this case, knowledge in the form of classical learning. Otherwise, the black man may become a kind of Satan, excessively proud. Washington denounces the idea, apparently embraced eagerly by many blacks in the aftermath of the Civil War, "that a knowledge, however little, of the Greek and Latin languages would make one a very superior human being, something bordering almost on the supernatural" (*US*, 71–72). Inveighing against false black pride, he dismisses passionate black claims to the right to vote. The secret of progress appears to be regression. Deploring the mass black migration to the cities, he often wishes "that by some power of magic I might remove the great bulk of these people into the country districts and plant them upon the soil, upon the solid and never deceptive foundation of Mother

8. Prelapsarian refers to the period before the Fall of humankind. In the postlapsarian era, Adam and Eve were expelled from the Garden of Eden [*Editors*].

Nature, where all nations and races that have ever succeeded have gotten their start" (*US*, 77). His garden is a priceless source of resuscitation. There, "I feel that I am coming into contact with something that is giving me strength for the many duties and hard places that await me out in the big world. I pity the man or woman who has never learned to enjoy nature and to get strength and inspiration out of it." (*US*, 173).

This refusal to confront slavery (or even the understandable association in the minds of many blacks of agricultural work with the terms of slavery) and this black variation on the myth of an American Adam make *Up from Slavery* an odd slave narrative according to either the antebellum or the postbellum model. Nevertheless, the hero moves from slavery to freedom and into his future as from darkness to light. Holding the story together is the distinction Washington quietly makes between himself and the other ex-slaves in general. He is the hero of a slave narrative. He sheds the dead skin of slavery, seeks an education, builds on it, and emerges as a powerful, fully realized human being, confident, almost invincible (within the bounds of discretion). This is seen as a possibility also for Washington's disciples, as the graduates of Tuskegee are represented. "Wherever our graduates go," he writes near the end of his book, "the changes which soon begin to appear in the buying of land, improving homes, saving money, in education, and in high moral character are remarkable. Whole communities are fast being revolutionized through the instrumentality of these men and women" (*US*, 202). The same cannot be said of the masses of blacks who have not been to Tuskegee or who have not come under the Tuskegee influence in some other way. In *Up from Slavery*, they remain blanks. This was hardly the first slave narrative in which the central character saw great distance between himself and other blacks. In Du Bois's *The Souls of Black Folk*, however, that distance would shrink dramatically.

When *The Souls of Black Folk* appeared in 1903, slavery had been officially dead in the United States for forty years. Du Bois himself, thirty-five years of age in 1903, had not been born a slave. Indeed, he had been born on free soil, in Great Barrington, Massachusetts, in a family that had lived there for several generations. One ancestor had even been a revolutionary soldier. Nevertheless, the shadow of slavery hangs powerfully over *The Souls of Black Folk*. Thus Du Bois acknowledged the fact that his book is about a people whose number included many who had been born slaves, and a vast majority who were immediately descended from slaves. On this central point, *The Souls of Black Folk* is a stark contrast to *Up from Slavery*.

In July 1901, shortly after the latter appeared, Du Bois reviewed it in *Dial* magazine. This was his first open criticism of Washington. In

1895, he had saluted Washington's compromising Atlanta Exposition speech as "a word fitly spoken."[9] In the following years, however, he had watched with increasing dismay as the head of Tuskegee propagated his doctrine of compromise and silenced much of his opposition through his manipulation of elements of the black press and other sources of power. Du Bois's attack on him in *Dial* was decisive. The *Dial* review, followed by *The Souls of Black Folk* (where the review again appeared, in adapted form), created "a split of the race into two contending camps," as James Weldon Johnson later noted astutely.[1] Cryptically noting that Washington had given "but glimpses of the real struggle which he has had for leadership," Du Bois accused him of peddling a "Lie."[2] Surveying the various modes of black response to white power from the earliest days in America, he concluded that the vaunted Tuskegee philosophy for black self-improvement was little more than "the old [black] attitude of adjustment to environment, emphasizing the economic phase."

In *The Souls of Black Folk*, unable to fashion an autobiography to match Washington's, young Du Bois nevertheless infused a powerful autobiographical spirit and presence into his essays. From about three dozen of his published articles on aspects of black history and sociology, he selected eight for adaptation or reprinting as nine chapters in *The Souls of Black Folk*. The brief fifth chapter, "Of the Wings of Atalanta," about commercialism and the city of Atlanta, was new, as were the last four chapters: "Of the Passing of the First-Born," Du Bois's prose elegy on the death of his only son, Burghardt; "Of Alexander Crummell," his tribute to an exceptional black man; "Of the Coming of John," a short story; and "Of the Sorrow Songs," an essay on spirituals. Holding these various efforts together is the central figure of Du Bois, who presents himself as a scholar and historian but more dramatically as an artist and a visionary who would not only depict the present state of black culture but also try to prophesy something about its future and the future of the nation.

Du Bois understood clearly that the representation of slavery was central to the entire task. Unlike Washington in *Up from Slavery*, he believed that slavery had been a force of extraordinary—and mainly destructive—potency. Destructive as it had been, however, slavery had not destroyed every major aspect of the African character and psychology (topics on which Washington had been silent); the African core had survived. But so had slavery. Where Washington saw opportunity on every hand for the black, if the right course was followed, Du Bois proclaimed that American slavery was not dead. In one guise or an-

9. Herbert Aptheker, ed., *Selections; 1877–1934*; vol. I of *The Correspondence of W. E. B. Du Bois* (Amherst: University of Massachusetts Press, 1973), 39.
1. James Weldon Johnson, *Black Manhattan* (New York: Knopf, 1930), 134.
2. W. E. B. Du Bois, "The Evolution of Negro Leadership," *Dial* 31 (July 16, 1901): 53–55.

other, it still persisted, with its power scarcely diminished. The act of emancipation had been both a fact (such as Washington loved to fasten on) and a mirage: "Years have passed since then—ten, twenty, forty; forty years of national life, forty years of renewal and development, and yet the swarthy spectre sits in its accustomed seat at the Nation's feast. . . . The Nation has not yet found peace from its sins; the freedman has not yet found in freedom his promised land."[3]

Although there were elements of agreement between Washington and Du Bois on the nature of slavery, *The Souls of Black Folk* portrays the institution in terms essentially opposite to those in *Up from Slavery*. Du Bois does not deny that slavery had its benign side, but in almost every instance his conclusion about its effects is radical when compared with Washington's. American slavery had not been the "worst slavery in the world," and had known something of "kindliness, fidelity, and happiness"; nevertheless, it "classed the black man and the ox together" (*SBF*, 231) [27]. Less equivocally, and more typical of Du Bois's view of slavery, black men were "emasculated" by the institution. Emancipation brought them "suddenly, violently . . . into a new birthright" (*SBF*, 227) [23]. The white southern universities had been contaminated by "the foul breath of slavery" (*SBF*, 269) [60]. Instead of the providential view of slavery espoused by Washington, for Du Bois the institution had amounted to "two hundred and fifty years of assiduous education in submission, carelessness, and stealing" (*SBF*, 323) [108].

Du Bois's emphasis on slavery as a social evil is only one part of the scheme by which he measures the Afro-American and American reality. Central to his argument is his belief in the persistence of the power of slavery beyond emancipation. Many current ills had their start in slavery. The widespread tendency of white businessmen and industrialists to see human beings as property, or "among the material resources of a land to be trained with an eye single to future dividend," was "born of slavery" (*SBF*, 274) [65]. The "plague-spot in sexual relations" among blacks—easy marriage and easy separation—"is the plain heritage from slavery" (*SBF*, 306) [93]. Many whites in the South live "haunted by the ghost of an untrue dream" (*SBF*, 262) [55]. "Slavery and race-prejudice are potent if not sufficient causes of the Negro's position" today (*SBF*, 251) [44]. Du Bois does not pretend, in the manner of a demogogue, that slavery and neo-slavery are absolutely identical. He sometimes proposes a new slavery as only a distinct possibility. The power of the ballot, downplayed by Booker T. Washington, is absolutely needed—"else what shall save us from a second slavery?" (*SBF*, 220) [15]. And yet, if the black man is not actually a slave, he is actually not free. "Despite compromise, war, and struggle," Du Bois insists, "the Negro is not free" (*SBF*, 239) [33] and is in danger "of

3. W. E. B. Du Bois, *The Souls of Black Folk*, in *Three Negro Classics*, 216 [12]. Subsequent parenthetical references in the text are to this edition; hereafter abbreviated as *SBF*.

being reduced to semi-slavery" (*SBF*, 250) [44]. Repeatedly he invokes the central symbol of enslavement to portray the status of the modern black. Today, blacks are "shackled men" (*SBF*, 272) [64].

In the final analysis, black Americans live in neo-slavery. The race passed from formal slavery through an interim illusion of emancipation ("after the first flush of freedom wore off") into a new version of slavery that in many respects continues the old (*SBF*, 308–309) [95–96]. The law courts were used by the white South as the first means of "reenslaving the blacks" (*SBF*, 330) [113]. Examining estates that once were slave plantations, Du Bois marvels at how the design and disposition of the black cabins are "the same as in slavery days" (*SBF*, 303) [91]. While for Booker T. Washington the Tuskegee education eradicates the vestiges of slavery from students at the institute, Du Bois sees the legacy of slavery as inescapable: "No people a generation removed from slavery can escape a certain unpleasant rawness and *gaucherie*, despite the best of training" (*SBF*, 280) [70]. Even the Tuskegee philosophy, as has been pointed out, reflects for Du Bois, in its spirit of compromise, the timidity forced on blacks by slavery.

It is vital to recognize that, far from being the result of distorting bitterness or propaganda, Du Bois's position on neo-slavery at the turn of the century, which he amply documents with vivid examples (many drawn from his personal experience), is fully supported by a wide range of leading historians. Central to their analysis were not simply the repressive local laws but the even more confining decisions of the Supreme Court in *Plessy* v. *Ferguson* in 1896, which held that "separate but equal" facilities were constitutionally valid, and in *Williams* v. *Mississippi* in 1898, which endorsed that state's plan to strip blacks of the franchise given them after the Civil War. Rayford W. Logan dubbed the period before the end of the century the "Nadir" of the Afro-American experience.[4] "When complete," C. Vann Woodward wrote of these segregationist laws, "the new codes of White Supremacy were vastly more complex than the ante-bellum slave codes or the Black Codes of 1865–66, and, if anything, they were stronger and more rigidly enforced."[5]

Du Bois's attitude toward slavery, the black present, and the black future is heavily dependent on his attitude toward the preslavery situation of blacks—that is, to Africa. In *The Souls of Black Folk* he does not dwell on the historical evidence of African civilization before slavery that twelve years later would form virtually the main subject of his Pan-Africanist volume, *The Negro* (1915). But where Washington writes only of heathenistic darkness in *Up from Slavery*, Du Bois concedes

---

4. See Rayford W. Logan, *The Negro in American Life and Thought: The Nadir, 1877–1901* (New York: Dial, 1954).
5. C. Vann Woodward, *Origins of the New South, 1877–1913* (Baton Rouge: Louisiana State University Press, 1951), 212.

heathenism but also attributes to the slave a complex, dignified, and usable past. "He was brought from a definite social environment," Du Bois explains,"—the polygamous clan life under the headship of the chief and the potent influence of the priest. His religion was nature-worship, with profound belief in invisible surrounding influences, good and bad, and his worship was through incantation and sacrifice" (*SBF*, 341) [123]. In other words, the African lived in a stable, consistent, complex social order, complemented by strong and formal religious beliefs. Far from being a blank, the mind of the black, both in Africa and as a slave brought to the New World, was a remarkable instrument. And because of this background, the slave's natural reaction to slavery was not passivity—which was learned later—but revolt. "Endowed with a rich tropical imagination," Du Bois asserts, "and a keen, delicate appreciation of Nature, the transplanted African lived in a world animate with gods and devils, elves and witches; full of strange influences,—of Good to be implored, of Evil to be propitiated. Slavery, then, was to him the dark triumph of Evil over him. All the fateful powers of the Underworld were striving against him, and a spirit of revolt and revenge filled his heart" (*SBF*, 343) [124].

In ascribing to the black in Africa and in the New World a mind that in its own way is as powerful as that of any other race in the world, Du Bois does more than merely try to boost his race's reputation. He shifts the terms of the debate toward the question of the black mind and character, and introduces questions of history, psychology, myth, and art. He also introduces into his scheme at least two other elements severely downplayed by Washington in *Up from Slavery*. One is the role of imagination; the other, that of memory. Otherwise derogatory of blacks, many white racial "scientists," including the Count de Gobineau, the author of the influential *Essay on the Inequality of Human Races*, had often credited them with remarkable imaginative and artistic faculties (the "rich tropical imagination" Du Bois ascribed to the transplanted African). Du Bois allows this credit to influence not only what he wrote about blacks but also how he wrote it.

Booker T. Washington, finding little that is useful in the African and the slave past, seems in *Up from Slavery* to harbor a deep suspicion of the black imagination, or even to be unaware that it exists. Indeed, his entire attitude toward the imagination contrasts with Du Bois's. While he reads books, or advocates the reading of books, he mentions no novels or poems. He is proud of the fact that his keenest pleasures are in the practical world. "Few things are more satisfactory to me than a high-grade Berkshire or Poland China pig," he writes. "Games I care little for" (*US*, 174). Du Bois is different. From early in his life, he tells us, he has seen the development of his imagination as one possible key to simultaneous self-realization and the leadership of his race against the whites. "Just how I would do it I could never decide," he writes of his youthful dreams of racial and personal victory; "by reading law, by healing the sick, by telling the wonderful tales that swam in my head,—some way" (SBF, 214) [10].

In fact, Du Bois's greatest cultural claims for blacks are in the areas of art and imagination. In these claims, slaves play the decisive role. He lauds them as musicians, especially when music is blended with spirituality in the "sorrow songs." In a nation where "vigor and ingenuity" are prized, rather than beauty, "the Negro folk-song—the rhythmic cry of the slave—stands to-day not simply as the sole American music, but as the most beautiful expression of human experience born this side the seas" (SBF, 378) [155]. Of the three gifts from blacks to American culture, the first is "a gift of story and song—soft, stirring melody in an ill-harmonized and unmelodious land" (SBF, 386) [162]. (The other gifts are toil and "a gift of the Spirit.")

Recognizing imagination as a source of black strength, and confirming the power of the imagination in Africa, slavery, and thereafter, also freed Du Bois as a thinker and a writer. In his previous book, *The Philadelphia Negro*, he had warned fastidiously that the scholar "must ever tremble lest some personal bias, some moral conviction or some unconscious trend of thought due to previous training, has to a degree distorted the picture in his view."[6] This timidity is abandoned in *The Souls of Black Folk*, which is full of impressionistic writing, including occasionally startling descriptions of people and places, and clearly subjective judgments. Du Bois based the book on his scholarly knowledge of history and sociology, but the eye and mind of the artist are given almost free play.

He was well aware of the possible price of indulging the imagination and even believed that he had paid a part of that price. A year after the book appeared, in a note about it published in the *Independent*, Du Bois conceded that "the style and workmanship" of *The Souls of Black Folk* did not make its meaning "altogether clear."[7] He was sure that the book presented a "clear central message," but also that around this core floated what he called a shadowy "penumbra" of vagueness and partly obscured allusions. Similarly, in his preface, "The Forethought," Du Bois was restrained in outlining his plans. He will sketch, "in vague, uncertain outline," the spiritual world in which the ten million black Americans live (SBF, 209) [5]. In both pieces, Du Bois is acknowledging the "tropic imagination" of blacks, of which he is one. His elite, formal, Western education has curbed this tropic imagination for too long; now it is free.

A crucial factor here is the connection thus proclaimed between the author of *The Souls of Black Folk* and the masses of American blacks, the despised slaves they had been or were descended from, and the

6. W. E. B. Du Bois, *The Philadelphia Negro: A Social Study* (Philadelphia, 1899), 3.
7. W. E. B. Du Bois, "The Souls of Black Folk," *Independent* 57 (November 17, 1904): 1152.

Africans beyond the seas. Du Bois made this connection for all to see when he said of his book, in the note in the *Independent* just cited, that "in its larger aspects the style is tropical—African."[8] In his "Forethought," too, he had linked himself to other blacks, and to slaves: "Need I add that I who speak here am bone of the bone and flesh of the flesh of them that live within the Veil?" (*SBF*, 209) [6].

By indulging his imagination, Du Bois gains for his book much of its distinction. Where Booker T. Washington stresses cold facts, and avoids metaphors and similes, imagination leads Du Bois to the invocation of keen images to represent black reality, and to major insights. Chief among the images is that of "the Veil," which hangs between the black and white races, an apparently harmless fabric but one that the rest of the book shows to be in some respects an almost impregnable wall, and the prime source of misery. In one place he even links his image of the veil to the symbol of an ongoing slavery; at one and the same time, he records "the wail of prisoned souls within the veil, and the mounting fury of shackled men" (*SBF*, 272) [64]. Linked to the image of the veil, but going beyond it, and inscribed in the very title of the book, is the idea of black American "double consciousness" (*SBF*, 215) [11]. Taking the basic idea of double consciousness as a feature or a capability of the human brain from the reflections of leading psychologists of the time, such as his former professor William James, Du Bois applied the notion with telling force to the mental consequences of the social, political, and cultural conflicts that came with being Afro-American. Perhaps no more challenging single statement about the nature of the black American mind, about the psychological consequences of slavery and racism, has ever been offered. Both the notion of black invisibility and of innately conflicted Afro-American consciousness would be reflected powerfully in future black poetry and fiction.

The "souls" of the title is a play on words. It alludes to the "twoness" of the black American that Du Bois initially suggests in his first chapter. America, a predominantly white country, yields the black "no true self-consciousness, but only lets him see himself through the revelation of the other world" (*SBF*, 214–15) [11]. The result is "a peculiar sensation, this double-consciousness, this sense of always looking at one's self through the eyes of others, of measuring one's soul by the tape of a world that looks on in amused contempt and pity. One ever feels his twoness,—an American, a Negro; two souls, two thoughts, two unreconciled strivings; two warring ideals in one dark body, whose dogged strength alone keeps it from being torn asunder" (*SBF*, 215) [11]. "Such a double life," Du Bois writes later, in his chapter on religion, "with double thoughts, double duties, and double social classes, must

8. Ibid.

give rise to double words and double ideals, and tempt the mind to pretence or revolt, to hypocrisy or radicalism" (*SBF*, 346) [127]. Another way of seeing these two souls surely is as a contest between memory and its opposite, amnesia. American culture demands of its blacks amnesia concerning slavery and Africa, just as it encourages amnesia of a different kind in whites. For Du Bois, blacks may not be able to remember Africa but they should remember slavery, since it has hardly ended.

"In the days of bondage," he writes of the slaves, stressing their imagination, "they thought to see in one divine event the end of all doubt and disappointment; few men ever worshipped Freedom with half such unquestioning faith as did the American Negro for two centuries. . . . In song and exhortation swelled one refrain—Liberty; in his tears and curses the God he implored had Freedom in his right hand. At last it came,—suddenly, fearfully, like a dream" (*SBF*, 216) [12]. The first decade after the war "was merely a prolongation of the vain search for freedom, the boon that seemed ever barely to elude their grasp,—like a tantalizing will-o'-the-wisp, maddening and misleading the helpless host" (*SBF*, 217) [13]. Freedom never came, but something else did, very faintly, that "changed the child of Emancipation to the youth with dawning self-consciousness, self-realization, self-respect" (*SBF*, 218) [14].

The fundamental progression of the Afro-American in history, as seen by Du Bois, is from a simple bondage to a more complex bondage slightly ameliorated by this "dawning" of "self-consciousness, self-realization, self-respect." "In those sombre forests of his striving, his own soul rose before him, and he saw himself,—darkly as through a veil; and yet he saw in himself some faint revelation of his power, of his mission" (*SBF*, 218) [14]. This realization, although "faint," facilitates Du Bois's shift toward what one might call cultural nationalism in the black: "He began to have a dim feeling that, to attain his place in the world, he must be himself, and not another." Cultural nationalism does not mean anti-intellectualism: "For the first time he sought to analyze the burden he bore upon his back, that deadweight of social degradation partially masked behind a half-named Negro problem."

The diminution of the myth of freedom, the elevation of the power of slavery, allows Du Bois to establish a continuum of African and Afro-American psychology. Times change and the nature and amount of data change, but the black mind remains more or less constant, for Du Bois sees it as irrevocably linked to its African origins. If that constancy is anywhere observable, it is for Du Bois in black Christian religion, which in the main is a product of slavery. For him, "the frenzy of a Negro revival in the untouched backwoods of the South" re-creates tellingly "the religious feeling of the slave" (*SBF*, 338) [120]. The full meaning of slavery "to the African savage" is unknown to Du Bois, but he believes that the answer is to be found only in "a study of Negro religion as a development" from heathenism to the institutionalized urban churches of the North (SBF, 339) [121]. The black church is the key to knowing "the inner ethical life of the people who compose it" (SBF, 343) [124]. Then follows a venture in analysis that may be taken as the foundation of Du Bois's sense of the Afro-American mind, or soul.

By the 1750s, after the initial impulse to revolt had been crushed by white power, "the black slave had sunk, with hushed murmurs, to his place at the bottom of a new economic system, and was unconsciously ripe for a new philosophy of life" (SBF, 344) [125]. The Christian doctrine of passive submission facilitated this shift in which "courtesy became humility, moral strength degenerated into submission, and the exquisite native appreciation of the beautiful became an infinite capacity for dumb suffering." A century later, black religion had transformed itself once again, this time around the cry for abolition, which became a "religion to the black world. Thus, when Emancipation finally came, it seemed to the freedman a literal Coming of the Lord. His fervid imagination was stirred as never before, by the tramp of armies, the blood and dust of battle, and the wail and whirl of social upheaval" (SBF, 345) [126]. Forty years later, with the world changing swiftly, Du Bois sees "a time of intense ethical ferment, of religious heart-searching and intellectual unrest." This leads him, looking backward and forward, into history and into the future. "From the double life every American Negro must live, as a Negro and as an American, as swept on by the current of the nineteenth while yet struggling in the eddies of the fifteenth century,—from this must arise a painful self-consciousness, an almost morbid sense of personality and a moral hesitancy which is fatal to self-confidence" (SBF, 346) [127]. These are the secondary, but almost equally binding, shackles of neo-slavery.

The authenticity of slavery as metaphor for the black experience is firmly underscored in the most "creative," or imaginative, areas of *The Souls of Black Folk*. These are the autobiographical passages of the book; the biographical chapter, on Alexander Crummell; and the short story, "Of the Coming of John." The sharpest focus of the autobiographical element occurs in "Of the Passing of the First-Born," about the death of Du Bois's son (who died of dysentery in Atlanta). In certain respects this is an almost classical elegy, in impassioned and yet formal language. But it is one in which the central mourner, as a black, can find no consolation. Thus it is in truth anti-Christian, a bitter parody of the Christian elegy such as Milton's *Lycidas*.[9] For Du Bois, unable

9. John Milton (1608–1674), English poet and author of *Lycidas* (1638). Milton is best known for *Paradise Lost* (1667), the story of Satan's rebellion against God and Adam and Eve's expulsion from the Garden of Eden, and generally regarded as the greatest epic written in the English language [Editors].

to believe in Booker T. Washington's Providence, doubt completely infects his vision of his son's future: "If still he be, and he be There, and there be a There, let him be happy, O Fate!" (*SBF*, 352) [133]. Perhaps one day the veil will be lifted and the imprisoned blacks set free, but not in Du Bois's time: "Not for me,—I shall die in my bonds" (*SBF*, 353) [133]. The metaphor of black life as slavery preempts the annealing possibilities of the elegy.

This chapter underscores the memorable autobiographical impressions left by the first few pages of the book, in which Du Bois discusses his first, youthful encounter with racism: "Then it dawned upon me with a certain suddenness that I was different from the others [his white classmates]; or like, mayhap, in heart and life and longing, but shut out from their world by a vast veil" (*SBF*, 214) [10]. Taking refuge in fierce competitiveness, he wins small victories but understands at last that "the worlds I longed for, and all their dazzling opportunities, were theirs, not mine." Many of his black friends deteriorate into sycophancy or into hatred and distrust of whites. Du Bois does not, but "the shades of the prison-house closed round about us all; walls strait and stubborn to the whitest, but relentlessly narrow, tall, and unscalable to sons of night."

Thus, just as the acceptance of the idea of neo-slavery forbids Du Bois the writing of classical elegy, with its formal consolation, so does that acceptance also forbid Du Bois the writing of anything that resembles either the "classical" slave narrative—the account of a life that has passed from bondage to freedom, from darkness to light—or its white American counterpart, the rags-to-riches autobiographical tale built on the materialist base of the American Dream. Indeed, if one isolates Du Bois as the hero of *The Souls of Black Folk*, one sees the reverse pattern. He goes from light into darkness, from the freedom of infancy and childhood into the bondage of maturity. Each modern black American, he argues implicitly, re-creates this regressive journey. So too has the black race, in its New World experience, enacted a historical regression. Preslavery African manhood and womanhood have deteriorated into passivity, moral hesitancy, cynicism, and rage.

Du Bois does not see all blacks as succumbing to pressure, but in any event those who resist have no hope of a lasting triumph. The most honored single figure in *The Souls of Black Folk* is Alexander Crummell (1819–1898), who struggled against tremendous odds but succeeded in being ordained as a priest in the almost entirely white Protestant Episcopal Church, earned a degree from Cambridge University, then went on to years of diligent service in Africa and the United States. Crummell also helped to found the American Negro Academy, in which Du Bois himself was involved. Clearly he stands as Du Bois's idea of the highest achievement among black Americans. Pointedly, Crummell was born when "the slave-ship still groaned across the Atlantic" (*SBF*, 355) [135]. His life is one of trial and tribulation, but also of resistance to doubt, hatred, and despair. He decides early to live for his people: "He heard the hateful clank of their chains; he felt them cringe and grovel, and there rose within him a protest and a prophesy" (*SBF*, 357) [136–37]. But no great triumph followed. For all his service and achievement, Crummell's name is now barely known. "And herein lies the tragedy of the age: not that men are poor,—all men know something of poverty; not that men are wicked,—who is good? not that men are ignorant,—what is Truth? Nay, but that men know so little of men" (*SBF*, 362) [141–42]. Again, the consolation of faith is impossible: "I wonder where he is today?"

The short story "Of the Coming of John" (in a sense, one of "the wonderful tales that swam in my head" to which Du Bois alludes early in the book) further underscores the destructive force of neo-slavery (*SBF*, 214) [142]. Black John, a simple country boy, comes to "Wells Institute" to be educated. But education cannot save him from racism, and his spirit deteriorates: "A tinge of sarcasm crept into his speech, and a vague bitterness into his life" (*SBF*, 367) [146]. Education alienates him from his own people; he returns home only to be struck by the "sordidness and narrowness" of what he had left behind (*SBF*, 370) [148]. Unwittingly he tramples on the religious beliefs of the local blacks, and he preaches democracy in the black school although it is under the control of a reactionary white judge. Dismissed from his job there, he wanders in a daze until he sees his sister tussling with a white man he had known as a boy. He kills the man. John tells his mother he is is going away—"I'm going to be free" (*SBF*, 376) [153]. Not understanding, she asks if he is going north again. "Yes, mammy," John replies, "I'm going,—North." He is soon lynched by revengeful whites. Going north and freedom are meaningless for John and for blacks in America. Freedom does not exist, except in death.

Education is only one of the forces that, subverted by racism and neo-slavery, betray John when he should have been elevated by them. For a person of Du Bois's complicated and elite schooling, this must have been a particularly poignant aspect to the condition he describes. Education should lead to light and truth. Booker T. Washington rearranged the chronology of his life in *Up from Slavery* to end his book close to the dizzying personal height of a Harvard honorary degree awarded in 1896 to the former illiterate slave. With the invitation in hand, "tears came into my eyes" (*US*, 190). But education for John leads to darkness and death. The fate of Alexander Crummell and of the author of *The Souls of Black Folk* is not much more exalted.

The Souls of Black Folk offers no transcendent confidence in the future. Du Bois's essay on religion, "Of the Faith of the Fathers," ends with an assertion of the existence of "the deep religious feeling of the real Negro heart, the stirring, unguided might of powerful human souls who have lost the guiding star of the past and seek in the great night a new religious ideal" (*SBF*, 349) [129]. Only in concluding the book does Du Bois appeal to the longest possible historical view. The assumption of whites that certain races cannot be "saved" is "the arrogance of people irreverent toward Time and ignorant of the deeds of men. A thousand years ago such an assumption, easily possible, would have made it difficult for the Teuton to prove his right to life" (*SBF*, 386) [162]. As powerful as it was, American slavery thus becomes for him, in the end, only an episode in the African people's history, not the history itself.

Before this point, however, he has engaged slavery valiantly in his text. His point of view is clear. Admitting and exploring the reality of slavery is necessarily painful for a black American, but only by doing so can he or she begin to understand himself or herself and American and Afro-American culture in general. The normal price of the evasion of the fact of slavery is intellectual and spiritual death. Only by grappling with the meaning and legacy of slavery can the imagination, recognizing finally the temporality of the institution, begin to transcend it.

ERIC J. SUNDQUIST

From Swing Low: *The Souls of Black Folk*†

First off, he was a whisper, a will to hope, a wish to find something worthy of laughter and song. Then the whisper put on flesh. His footsteps sounded across the world in a low but musical rhythm as if the world he walked on was a singing-drum. . . . The sign of this man was a laugh, and his singing-symbol was a drum-beat. . . .

He had come from Africa. He came walking on the waves of sound. Then he took on flesh after he got here. The sea captains of ships knew that they brought slaves in their ships. They knew about those black bodies huddled down there in the middle passage, being hauled across the waters to helplessness. John de Conquer was walking the very winds that filled the sails of the ships. He followed over them like the albatross.

It is no accident that High John de Conquer has evaded the ears of white people. They were not supposed to know. You can't know what folks won't tell you. If they, the white people, heard some scraps, they could not understand because they had nothing to hear things like that with. . . .

So after a while, freedom came. Therefore High John de Conquer has not walked the winds of America for seventy-five years now. His people had their freedom, their laugh and their song. They have traded it to the other Americans

† Reprinted by permission of the Publisher from *To Wake the Nations* by Eric J. Sundquist, pp. 457–90, Cambridge, Mass.: Harvard University Press, Copyright © 1993 by the President and Fellows of Harvard College. Bracketed page numbers refer to this Norton Critical Edition.

for things they could use like education and property, and acceptance. High John knew that that was the way it would be, so he could retire with his secret smile into the soil of the South and wait.

Zora Neale Hurston, "High John de Conquer"

"In their fondness for eschatology, and the joy with which they antic-ipate the day of judgment and dwell upon its terrific and sublime fea-tures, the hymns are a fair echo and antiphone of the preaching which they accompany."[1] William Barton's portrait of African American spir-ituals selects only one of the many complex levels of allegory of which they, like the performative sermonic texts of the black church, are con-stituted. Not thoughts of Judgment Day alone but rather of earthly liberation and escape north, of a return to Africa or a revitalization of African beliefs, and the instilling of race consciousness—these are the forces that variously animate the spirituals' message of the freedom that will be found in a world beyond the veil of antebellum chattel slavery or, at a later historical moment, beyond the neo-slavery of post-Reconstruction peonage, legislated ignorance, and race violence. Bar-ton's 1899 assessment was characteristic of his day in its subordination of the political dimension of the spirituals, but his recognition that they formed an antiphonal construct in which the preacher's voice could be a contrapuntal or harmonic accompaniment provides a useful vantage point from which to see their function as literature. What is more, it offers a fresh means to evaluate the strategy and structure of *The Souls of Black Folk*, the preeminent modern text of African American cultural consciousness. Du Bois's masterwork is a text of many dimensions—a first-rate, if unorthodox, history of post—Civil War race relations in the South; a trenchant essay in sociological and economic analysis; a brief for black education; and a study in comparative European American and African American cultures. Yet what is perhaps the most powerful feature of Du Bois's text has also been its least carefully regarded: his commentary on the transforming power, from slave culture through post-Reconstruction modernity, of the central expressive form of African America, the "sorrow songs."

In arguing for the centrality of the sorrow songs to *The Souls of Black Folk*, I mean to remedy a deficiency in critical evaluations of Du Bois without losing sight of the many modes of discourse that operate throughout the work. My emphasis will fall neither on the literary or musicological character of the spirituals as such, nor on Du bois's rel-atively brief commentary on various elements of slave religion, but rather on the way in which he appropriated their core expression of African American culture, their *soul*, in order to create a foundation for modern African American culture as an extension of slave culture. His own comparative indifference to black churches and religious lead-

1. William E. Barton, *Old Plantation Hymns* (Boston: Lamson, Wolffe, 1899), p. 20.

ership during his maturity makes Du Bois's comments on the preacher in "Of the Faith of Our Fathers" seem rather isolated from his career's vast social and political argumentation. It would be a mistake, moreover, to confuse Du Bois's formal rhetorical style and narrative structure in *The Souls of Black Folk*, whatever its unusual generic accomplishment, with the cadences of the black preacher. If black religion did not provide him a language, however, it did provide the central matrix of his reconstruction of African American culture.[2]

In the sorrow songs, which both frame and carry forward the most resonant arguments of *The Souls of Black Folk*, Du Bois discovered a deep spiritual intonation for his cultural voice, one that would vivify his writing for at least three decades and make his work unique in its blending of poetics and politics, what he would eventually refer to as the necessary union of art and propaganda. If I concentrate on what initially seems a rather narrow topic within the available approaches to Du Bois's multivalent work, my purpose is to accomplish several things at once: to estimate the centrality of song to African American culture, both its extension of the folk traditions of slavery into a later era and its incorporation of the tonal semantics of vernacular culture into modern literary form; to trace Du Bois's own remarkably comprehensive theorizing about African American economic labor, political rights, and aesthetic endeavor in its continual reference to the grounding principles of survival and salvation articulated in the communal art of the spirituals; and, by extension, to argue that in the history of early twentieth-century American culture, traditional interpretations notwithstanding, few intellectual figures hold such a commanding presence as Du Bois. *The Souls of Black Folk* is one of the indispensable works of the early modern period, in literature and intellectual history alike; and yet, like Du Bois's work as a whole, it is not often carefully read and even less appreciated.

In the Kingdom of Culture

All of the key words in Du Bois's title ("souls," "black," "folk") retain a charged ambiguity. As Arnold Rampersad has remarked, "folk" verges on "nation" to such a degree in *The Souls of Black Folk* that it must be seen as an elaboration upon the idea of a racial nation as Du Bois had defined it in his landmark essay "The Conservation of Races" in 1897.[3] At the same time, however, "folk" moves toward a more specific geography, a stronger sense of soil and place not encompassed by "nation"—the geography of the black folk of the South, which could

2. Arnold Rampersad, *The Art and Imagination of W. E. B. Du Bois* (Cambridge, Mass.: Harvard University Press, 1976), pp. 36–38, 76; Manning Marable, "The Black Faith of W. E. B. Du Bois: Sociocultural and Political Dimensions of Black Religion," *Southern Quarterly* 23 (Spring 1985), 15–33.
3. Rampersad, *The Art and Imagination of W. E. B. Du Bois*, p. 74.

be the cradle of a black American nation (even, as would ultimately be the case in *Darkwater* and *Dark Princess*, the cradle of a Pan-African, diasporic, multicolored "nation") but could not be synonymous with it. The dividing line between "folk" and "nation" was one of many such liminal states upon which Du Bois rested his greatest and most characteristic arguments, not because his art was one of compromise but rather because it was one of constant encroachments and tensions. Like the line between colors (as in his famous aphorism "The problem of the twentieth century is the problem of the color-line") or the line between "American" and "Negro" cultures (as in his equally famous theory of "two-ness," of African American double consciousness) or the line between a post-Reconstruction Victorian world of imperial rule and scientific racism on the one hand, and the modern era of anticolonial revolt and the escalation of civil rights activism on the other, the line between "folk" and "nation" shifted and blurred in usage. "Folk" diminished and gave way to "nation" as Du Bois's Pan-African thought, latent in *The Souls of Black Folk*, came to the fore; but the voice of the folk rang with clarity in his early masterpiece, where it was grounded in "the Negro folksong—the rhythmic cry of the slave," which he, among others, considered "the sole American music" as well as "the singular spiritual heritage of the nation and the greatest gift of the Negro people."[4]

Nevertheless, when Du Bois, invited to collect some of his sociological essays into a book, "stepped within the Veil" of black America to compose his concluding chapters, he connected himself for the first substantial time to a folk with whom he did not have a great deal in common. His preface to *The Souls of Black Folk* is instructive in this regard. After the usual acknowledgment to publishers for permission to reprint previous essays that appeared in the *Atlantic Monthly*, the *Dial*, *Annals of the American Academy of Political and Social Science*, and elsewhere, Du Bois writes: "Before each chapter, as now printed, stands a bar of the Sorrow Songs,—some echo of haunting melody from the only American music which welled up from the black souls in the dark past. And, finally, need I add that I who speak here am bone of the bone and flesh of the flesh of them that live within the Veil?"[5] Du Bois forecasts the antiphonal relationship that would exist between music and text in the succeeding essays, a relationship in which the two forms gradually coalesce, as the volume unfolds, into an inseparable articulation of the tonal and the semantic dimensions of African American cultural expression. He also indicates his own peculiar relationship to that culture. His rhetorical question ("need I add . . .") already contains the famous theory of double consciousness that would mark Du Bois's

4. W. E. B. Du Bois, *The Souls of Black Folk* (New York: Viking Penguin, 1989), pp. 13, 35, 205 [11, 17, 155].
5. Ibid., p. 2.

place within the Veil. But the question, surely, was addressed as much to himself as to his reader. His New England birth; his Harvard and Berlin graduate education; his love of European culture; his mixed-race identity, which was sometimes perversely charged against him by Garvey's[6] circle as a sign of his disloyalty to black nationalist concerns; his reputation for a stiff, impersonal demeanor—in short, the range of characteristics that would remain a vague counterweight to the certain fact that he had to ride the Jim Crow car in America just like every other black person—all these things kept Du Bois from any sort of comfortable unification with the folk consciousness epitomized by the black spirituals.[7] Yet it was precisely that ambivalence, one that echoed the larger state of African-American culture, that allowed Du Bois to write so effectively in his volume and to do so primarily through the matrix of the sorrow songs.

The liminal, syncretic character of Du Bois's vision, although it was grounded in the circumstances of his birth and upbringing, should not be misconstrued as a simple dichotomy between "American" and "American Negro" of the sort Frederick Douglass continually expressed and which has typically been identified as the heart of Du Bois's sociological definition of black identity. Rather, the dichotomy embraced the broader cultural rift between "African" (or "Negro") and "American," and it was this tension, as much as his theoretical musings, that led Du Bois to an amorphous interpretation of the category of race that would have significant implications for his nationalist aesthetic. The unstable nature of race and nationality in Du Bois's thought appears as early as "The Conservation of Races," an extraordinarily elusive performance prepared for the American Negro Academy, which he founded with Alexander Crummell. Defining "race" and "nation" as virtually synonymous without fully collapsing the distinction between the two, Du Bois in this essay was unable to discard all traces of "race" as a phenomenon of color with biological roots and tie it resolutely to

6. Marcus Garvey (1887–1940), Jamaican-born advocate of black nationalism. While living in the United States, he founded the Universal Negro Improvement Association, which promoted international black unity. Garvey's brilliant oratory in proposing his "back to Africa" movement made him the most influential African American leader in the 1920s. He also published a popular newspaper, *Negro World*. Following a mail fraud scandal, Garvey was jailed in 1925, and in 1927 he was deported to Jamaica [*Editors*].

7. A stronger statement of this problem in Du Bois's perspective—one that, despite its kernel of truth, suffers from its own prejudice and loses sight of Du Bois's achievement—was made in 1935 by E. Franklin Frazier, who spoke of Du Bois as a "cultural hybrid" and a classic case of the "marginal man": "Once back in America and Atlanta [after his education abroad], he was just a 'nigger.' Fine flower of western culture, he had here the same status as the crudest semi-barbarous Negro in the South. In the *Souls of Black Folk* [*sic*] we have a classic statement of the 'marginal man' with this double consciousness: on the one hand sensitive to every slight concerning the Negro, and feeling on the other hand little kinship or real sympathy for the great mass of crude, uncouth black peasants with whom he was identified. . . . The *Souls of Black Folk* is a masterly portrayal of Du Bois's soul . . . [but] when he takes his pen to write of the black masses we are sure to get a dazzling romantic picture." Quoted in Tony Martin, *Race First: The Ideological and Organizational Struggles of Marcus Garvey and the Universal Negro Improvement Association* (Westport, Conn.: Greenwood Press, 1976), p. 298.

shifting environmental parameters. Race instead corresponds to a "vast family of human beings" infused with a common purpose or idea—a world-spirit or *Volksgeist*, to cite the German formulation that Du Bois had clearly appropriated. That "Negro" included a familial link to Africa is evident in Du Bois's optimistic challenge that black Americans are to take their "just place in the van of Pan-Negroism." The dichotomy, that is to say, is dynamic, and the choice as Du Bois represents it even here is between realizing a "distinct mission as a race" and "self-obliteration [as] the highest end to which Negro blood dare aspire."[8]

At times Du Bois's double consciousness left him open to accusations of Eurocentrism and blinded him to important elements of African life and the colonial situation. By the same token, however, it was just the reverse of debilitating: it made him acutely aware of the democratic implications of race theory. Finding neither a sound basis for a scientific definition of race nor a cultural-historical explanation that was not virtually open-ended, Du Bois returned again and again to quasi-mystic notions such as "genius," "strivings," and "common memory." Although he drew a far more romanticized picture of his double ancestry in *Darkwater*, in the later volume *Dusk of Dawn* he admitted that his speech, cultural patterns, and family customs were derived from New England. "My African racial feeling," as he calls it, "was then purely a matter of my own learning and reaction." Race, therefore, was not given to one but was to be acquired, absorbed, invented in a specific cultural circumstance that would be marked, yet not adequately defined, by color or other physical features. What Du Bois means by "reaction," however, is not far to seek. When he applied in 1908 for membership in the Massachusetts Society of the Sons of the American Revolution on the basis of his great-great-grandfather's war record, his application was denied because he could not produce a birth certificate of the man who had, of course, been a slave stolen from Africa. As Du Bois remarks, with a simplicity that overflows any theoretical barriers to his definition of race: "I felt myself African by 'race' and by that token was African and an integral member of the group of dark Americans who were called Negroes."[9]

The problem of where race was to be located, as much as the rise of invidious sciences of race, led to Du Bois's volksgeistian definitions. When he turned his attention to "real history" in "The Conservation of Races," however, one can see how little, in the end, it mattered to him that his central concern was so slippery. At first glance Du Bois seems aligned with his contemporaries who argued, for example, that

8. W. E. B. Du Bois, "The Conservation of Races," in *W. E. B. Du Bois: Writings* (New York: Library of America, 1986), pp. 815–26; Anthony Appiah, "The Uncompleted Argument: Du Bois and the Illusion of Race," in Henry Louis Gates, Jr., *"Race," Writing, and Difference* (Chicago: University of Chicago Press, 1986), pp. 21–37.
9. W. E. B. Du Bois, *Dusk of Dawn: An Essay toward an Autobiography of a Race Concept* (New York: Schocken Books, 1968), p. 115.

"race is deeper than culture," that it is an "indwelling spirit" or "Will which is the force behind culture" and cannot be changed by environment or successfully copied (only deceptively "imitated") by other races.[1] On occasion Du Bois's definitions move in this direction, but increasingly over the course of his essays it becomes evident that what mattered to him was not race as such but "the race idea, the race spirit, the race ideal." The location—indeed, the incarnation—of such spirit was not in the liberal ego of the individual but in his representative nature: "We see the Pharaohs, Caesars, Toussaints, and Napoleons of history and forget the vast races of which they were but epitomized expressions." One can argue that this is the most revealing passage in Du Bois's essay, for it not only puts the question of race in more strictly nationalist terms and anticipates, in a grander form, Du Bois's notion of the "talented tenth" who would lead the race forward, but it also outlines Du Bois's own messianic conception of himself. To be the "epitomized expression" of African Americans would not override but would rather contain in vital tension the conflict between nation and race, and between American and Negro. The messianic leader was thus an Emersonian representative man like Toussaint in Haiti, Jefferson Davis in the South (on whom Du Bois spoke in his graduation speech at Fisk), Bismarck[2] in Germany (on whom he spoke in a valedictory address at Harvard), or the black nationalist leaders of Africa who began their rise to power in the early twentieth-century independence movements. Joel Williamson has suggested that Du Bois's thought was Hegelian[3] in that it epitomized the view that consciousness is achieved not individually but through a people's rising to awareness of its collective spirit or soul. Appropriating theories of race nationalism available to him as a student at Fisk, Harvard, and Berlin, Du Bois thus struggled to institutionalize the world-spirit of Africa and made himself, in Williamson's curious but apt phrase, "the Christ of the soul movement."[4]

The messianic dimensions of Du Bois's intellectual efforts and public leadership would not be fully evident for a number of years. Yet one

1. Maurice S. Evans, *Black and White in the Southern States: A Study of the Race Problem in the United States from a South African Point of View* (New York: Longmans, 1915), pp. 13–15.
2. Otto von Bismark (1815–1898), German statesman, premier of Prussia (1862–90), and chancellor of Germany (1871–90). Known as the "Iron Chancellor," he provoked the Franco-Prussian War (1870–71) and defeated France. Bismark initiated numerous social reforms, and his economic policies both strengthened Germany's position in Europe and assured the acquisition of overseas territories [*Editors*].
3. Georg Wilhelm Friedrich Hegel (1770–1831), German philosopher who wrote on ethics, aesthetics, history, politics, and religion. Hegel believed that an absolute spirit guides both the universe and human reason. The Hegelian dialectic posits a process of change in which a thesis generates its opposite, the antithesis, which eventually leads to a new concept (synthesis) that will become the thesis of a new triad [*Editors*].
4. Du Bois, "The Conservation of Races," p. 817; Joel Williamson, *The Crucible of Race: Black-White Relations in the American South since Emancipation* (New York: Oxford University Press, 1984), p. 411.

can find the prophecy of that achievement in *The Souls of Black Folk*, not simply because generations of black readers would remember their encounter with it as a stunning experience (James Weldon Johnson, for example, maintained that it "had a greater effect upon and within the Negro race in America than any other single book published in this country since *Uncle Tom's Cabin*," while Claude McKay recalled that "the book shook me like an earthquake. Dr. Du Bois stands on a pedestal illuminated in my mind. And the light that shines there comes from my first reading of *The Souls of Black Folk*"),[5] but rather because the book is so completely saturated with the simultaneously bardic and polemical spirit of the great documents of nationalist consciousness. To what degree Du Bois, at different points in his career, may be considered a "nationalist" is, of course, worth careful scrutiny. It is possible, indeed, to locate Du Bois entirely outside of a black nationalist tradition and to place him, for example, in the tradition of American pragmatism.[6] I want to argue, however, that because the concept of African American "nationalism," like the concept of race itself, was utterly fluid for Du Bois—was, in effect, a kind of matrix against which he could measure fluctuating images of what it meant to be a black American as well as a race leader—it must be taken as instrumental to his transformation of the role of priest and the "text" of the spirituals into the defining elements of modern African American leadership.[7] The racial consciousness that is a cornerstone of Du Bois's philosophy was most of all a means for him to harness those national "powers of body and mind" that have "in the past been strangely wasted, dispersed, or forgotten" and fashion them toward the purpose of the African American's historical "striving: to be a co-worker in the kingdom of culture, to escape both death and isolation, to husband and use his best powers and his latent genius."[8]

To the extent that *The Souls of Black Folk* advanced what would today be recognized as a moderate Afrocentric argument—that African social and historical customs, however fragmentary, and to some degree the spiritual framework of African belief systems are retained in African American culture—it is logically succeeded by *Darkwater*. The latter, a

5. James Weldon Johnson, *Along This Way: The Autobiography of James Weldon Johnson* (1933; rpt. New York: Viking, 1968), p. 203; Claude McKay, *A Long Way from Home: An Autobiography* (1937; rpt. New York: Harcourt, Brace and World, 1970), p. 110.
6. See Cornel West, *The American Evasion of Philosophy: A Genealogy of Pragmatism* (Madison: University of Wisconsin Press, 1989), pp. 138–50.
7. I have in mind a definition of nationalism as glossed by Clifford Geertz: "The images, metaphors, and rhetorical turns from which nationalist ideologies are built are essentially devices, cultural devices designed to render one or another aspect of the broad process of collective self-redefinition explicit, to cast essentialist pride or epochalist hope into specific symbolic forms, where more than dimly felt, they can be described, developed, celebrated, and used. To formulate an ideological doctrine is to make (or to try to make—there are more failures than successes) what was a generalized mood into a practical force." See Clifford Geertz, *The Interpretation of Cultures: Selected Essays* (New York: Basic Books, 1973), p. 252.
8. Du Bois, *The Souls of Black Folk*, pp. 5–6 [11].

post–World War I messianic text that culminated the first long stage of Du Bois's evolution of Pan-African philosophy, tied the labor and language of the black American South, in slave culture and after, to that of Africa and the greater colonial world abroad. From the very beginning of his career, however, nationalist tendencies were poised to become paradigms for Pan-Africanism, and Du Bois, as one of the first Third World writers, must always be judged with such an imaginative horizon in view. If that fact makes Du Bois seem a less "American" writer, however, it is only because our definitions of American modernism (not to say American authorship) have been inadequate. My two chapters on Du Bois, organized respectively around *The Souls of Black Folk* and *Darkwater*, create something of an artificial division within roughly two decades of his career, in part because the former text so stands out in its general argument and, as I will contend, in its particular use of the spirituals, and in part because a proper interpretation of the latter has to be constructed from diverse sources. It will be nonetheless clear, I hope, to what an extent Du Bois's thought and literary efforts were driven by a consistent, evolving philosophy of racial consciousness from the very outset.

Du Bois's celebration of the folk world represented by the spirituals tempered his own commitment to a progressivist ideal that was too easily identified with elite European American culture and with his own proclaimed belief in the elevating leadership of a black talented tenth whose achievements, he argued throughout his early career, would raise up the masses below them. Indeed, because Du Bois refused to accept as necessary the contradiction between elite and folk culture, his use of the spirituals was itself an example of this belief in action. When he put the spirituals at the center of *The Souls of Black Folk* and identified their slave creators as the foundational voice of black culture, Du Bois responded on the one hand to the white cultural critics and ethnographers who misconstrued, or at the least dominated the interpretations of, the value of African American culture, and on the other to what he took to be the inadequate assertiveness of black cultural leadership. In addition, his radical positioning of the black spirituals offered him a further way to subvert the authority of Booker T. Washington, the man whom he made his foremost antagonist in the early years of his career and the notorious centerpiece of his critique of African American leadership in *The Souls of Black Folk*. Washington had paid tribute to the spirituals as a coded language of liberation in *Up from Slavery*, where he noted that with the coming of the Civil War the slaves "gradually threw off the mask, and were not afraid to let it be known that the 'freedom' in their songs meant freedom of the body in this world." Moreover, in 1905, perhaps under the influence of Du Bois, Washington's preface to Samuel Coleridge-Taylor's *Twenty-Four Negro Melodies Transcribed for the Piano* (a work by a British

black composer who answered contemporary calls for a classical treatment of the spirituals) announced that the black spiritual "reminds the
race of the 'rock whence it was hewn,' it fosters race pride, and in the
days of slavery it furnished an outlet for the anguish of smitten hearts."[9]
For the most part, however, Washington's Franklinesque programs of
domestic and industrial education had little place for reminders of slavery or celebrations of race consciousness. What would become Du
Bois's best-known chapter in The Souls of Black Folk was devoted to
his attack on Washington, and other chapters, most notably "Of the
Wings of Atalanta," were also extended rebuttals of Washington's accommodationist policies. Not just the music he chose to associate with
Washington—"A Great Camp-Meeting in the Promised Land," which
heads the Washington chapter, turns out to be a most ambiguous salute
to Washington's career—but the infusion of music itself into his text
was a mode of resistance launched upon Washington's more familiar
ground. Whereas Washington was a son of the South, born in slavery
and resolutely tied to black southerners, Du Bois was a folk parvenu,
as it were. His years at Fisk University and his summer of teaching in
rural Tennessee constituted no more than an apprenticeship (in this
he was an avatar of Jean Toomer's character Ralph Kabnis in Cane),
and yet in one great rhetorical gesture he destroyed Washington's ascendancy. His superior intellectual training and taking of the higher
moral ground might alone have been enough to defeat Washington on
the issues of education, suffrage, and civil rights. But it was his seizure
and celebration of indigenous African American culture that allowed
Du Bois rebelliously to sweep away Washington's populist advantage,
replacing his philosophy of the toothbrush with a philosophy of black
soul and transfiguring the narrow conception of labor and nation building in Washington's program into a broad, exhilarating call for the labor necessary to construct a black American wing in the "kingdom of
culture."[1]

Although his two signal decisions about the published form of the
essay collection are related, the addition of the chapters on life within
the Veil (that is, the last five chapters of The Souls of Black Folk, only
one of which, "Of the Faith of Our Fathers," had been previously
published) was not so provocative a cultural act as was the featuring of
the spirituals at the head of each chapter. This act was itself complex
in ways that have scarcely been examined. Previous readers have studied

9. Booker T. Washington, Up from Slavery (New York: Viking Penguin, 1986), p. 20; Samuel
Coleridge-Taylor, Twenty-Four Melodies Transcribed for the Piano (Boston: Oliver Ditson,
1905), p. viii.
1. Du Bois, The Souls of Black Folk, p. 5 [11]. Cf. Arnold Rampersad, "Slavery and the Literary
Imagination: Du Bois's The Souls of Black Folk," in Arnold Rampersad and Deborah Mc-
Dowell, eds., Slavery and the Literary Imagination (Baltimore: Johns Hopkins University Press,
1989), pp. 104–24.

the role of the chapter devoted to the sorrow songs in the overall structure of *The Souls of Black Folk* or have commented generally on the
contribution made by the musical epigraphs to Du Bois's notion of
double consciousness. But there has been little attempt to chart the
significance of the individual selections or to develop a theory of the
music's function within the larger text. In his concluding chapter Du
Bois identifies most but not all of the spirituals he has employed in the
text, but he does not match the titles to the chapters in all cases; at best
his documentation is haphazard, although I will suggest that it is of a
piece with the central epistemological challenge posed by the spirituals
themselves. For their part, critics and editors of *The Souls of Black Folk*
have seldom used Du Bois's own clues to much purpose, let alone
adduced the lyrics of the relevant spirituals or identified those musical
epigraphs not named by him. In doing so, I leave somewhat open to
question the exact nature of Du Bois's intentions in choosing the individual sorrow songs. The meaning of his choices must arise from
inference and implication in the case of individual chapters and their
epigraphic bars of music; while in the case of the text as a whole that
meaning resides in its unique choral construction. First I offer a pre-
liminary sketch of these issues before turning to a chapter-by-chapter
interpretation of the spirituals and, finally, to a more speculative theory
of the function of the songs in African American culture as Du Bois
constructs it in *The Souls of Black Folk*.

"This Wonderful Music of Bondage"

All that was left were a few names of what they called nations which they
could no longer even pronounce properly, the fragments of a dozen or so
songs, the shadowy forms of long-ago dances and rum kegs for drums. The
bares bones. The burnt-out ends. And they clung to them with a tenacity she
suddenly loved in them and longed for in herself. . . .

Hands flashing, he spurred the drumming on. Yet every so often in the midst
of the joyousness and speed he would pause, and placing his left elbow on the
drumhead he would draw his right thumb across the top. . . .

And the single, dark, plangent note this produced, like that from the deep
bowing of a cello, sounded like the distillation of a thousand sorrow songs. For
an instant the power of it brought the singing and the dancing to a halt—or
so it appeared. The theme of separation and loss the note embodied, the
unacknowledged longing it conveyed summed up feelings that were beyond
words, feelings and a host of subliminal memories that over the years had
proven more durable and trustworthy than the history with its trauma and its
pain out of which they had come. After centuries of forgetfulness and even
denial, they refused to go away. The note was a lamentation that could hardly
have come from the rum keg of a drum. Its source had to be the heart, the
bruised still-bleeding innermost chamber of the collective heart.

For a fraction of a second the note hung in the yard, knifing through the revelry to speak to everyone there. To remind them of the true and solemn business of the fete. Then it was gone.

Paule Marshall, *Praisesong for the Widow*

To begin with, the spirituals allowed Du Bois to offer commentary on all the essays, for the texts and titles that are deleted but nonetheless silently accompany each strand of music can be read as quite deliberate editorial selections. The musical bars thus function, as I have already implied, as epigraphs of a sort, and yet these "African" songs remain functionally at odds with the "Western" belletristic epigraphs with which each is matched, coiled in a kind of anarchic symbiosis until the sorrow songs finally prevail in the last chapter. Without question, Du Bois sought an ideal of culture beyond the color line, where, "wed with Truth," he could "dwell above the Veil," where he could "sit with Shakespeare . . . move arm in arm with Balzac and Dumas," and "summon Aristotle and Aurelius[2] and what soul I will," all to meet him "graciously with no scorn or condescension."[3] His well-known passage defined a world in which the alternating epigraphs would be in communion, not in conflict, in which the Western and African traditions might harmoniously coexist. To the extent that *The Souls of Black Folk* achieves such a communion, however, it does so only hypothetically. Writing at a historical moment of bleak social and political prospects for African Americans, Du Bois marked the gulf between black and white America in many ways, not least in the blunt dialectical challenge of his epigraphs. At the interpretive level the paired epigraphs most often act as a joint dialectical commentary on the individual chapters; in this respect they might (to cite Boas[4] again) be styled "alternating sounds" in the simple sense that they provide a double gloss on Du Bois's various essays in sociological and cultural analysis. Yet such a dialectic is clear only after the music has been recognized and the lyrics "transcribed"—only, one could say, after the musical epigraphs have been coded in a discourse that corresponds more closely to the poetic epigraphs.

Du Bois, of course, meant to gain for the spirituals (and black art

2. Lucius Domitius Aurelianus (c. 212–275), one of Rome's great emperors. He defended his empire against numerous invasions and regained Britain, Gaul, Spain, Egypt, and Syria. Honoré de Balzac (1799–1850), French writer and great master of the novel. Over a twenty-year period he wrote *The Human Comedy*, a collection of novels and stories representing a wide band of social classes. Most famous are *Père Goriot* (1835) and *Cousin Bette* (1847). Alexandre Dumas (1802–1870), French author of the highly romantic novels *The Three Musketeers* (1844) and *The Count of Monte Cristo* (1845). Aristotle (384–322 B.C.E.), Greek philosopher who studied under Plato. His influential writings include *De Anima*, *Metaphysics*, *Nicomachean Ethics*, *De Poetica*, and *Politics* [*Editors*].
3. Du Bois, *The Souls of Black Folk*, p. 90 [74].
4. Franz Boas (1858–1942), German-American anthropologist who revolutionized the world of anthropology by pioneering the use of statistical methods. His studies include field work with the Central Eskimos, indigenous British Columbians, and Native Americans. Among his books are *The Mind of Primitive Man* (1911) and *Race, Language and Culture* (1940) [*Editors*].

generally) recognition as part of world culture; but to do so he risked the paradox that their "language" would remain alien or be dismissed by white (or black) readers, and he pursued the recuperation of a culture seemingly at odds with his own elite education and erudite tastes. The spirituals are thus one measure among others of the way in which the revisions Du Bois made when he gathered his essays into a book extended his identification with, and his commitment to, black American culture and to its nebulous African roots. By incorporating the spirituals into the fabric of his text, Du Bois turned sociological commentary into a sensate, vocalized text—radically crossing generic boundaries, employing the languages of silence and implication to carry significant communicative burdens, and dwelling in the most profound autobiographical way in the spiritual resources of his texts. William Ferris would later complain in *The African Abroad* that Du Bois wrote too much as an individual, "crying out in righteous indignation and piteous wail" rather than speaking in "a prophetic voice, freighted with a message of the eternal."[5] In fact, however, the personal and the prophetic were embedded within each other for Du Bois, as the remainder of his career would prove time and again. The subtitle of his third book that could be called an autobiography, *Dusk of Dawn: The Autobiography of a Race Concept* (1940), reflected this peculiar conjunction of the subjective and the transhistorical in more stark terms than had *Darkwater* in 1920 or *The Souls of Black Folk* before it. In a 1904 review of his own book, moreover, Du Bois spoke of the style of *The Souls of Black Folk* as "tropical—African," and explained the "intimate tone of self-revelation" that runs through the book, in contrast to a more traditional impersonality and judiciousness, as a function of the fact that "the blood of my fathers spoke through me and cast off the English restraint of my training and surroundings."[6] Such a self-conceptualization, yoked to his prefatory assertion that the folk spirituals of slavery were "of me and mine" and his appropriation of their prophetic structure, is the clearest evidence that Du Bois identified early on with a "race concept" (as he would conceive himself according to

5. Ferris's rather self-serving remarks chided Du Bois for not having written a book (more like his own) that swept dramatically through history to prove that the entirety of Western religious and political thought could be marshaled against the injustices of American racism. By the same token, however, Ferris recognized that the personal element and what he considered Du Bois's thorough pessimism were perhaps necessary to rouse the American conscience and had made *The Souls of Black Folk* what it appeared by 1913 to have become—"the political Bible of the Negro race," with Du Bois "the long-looked-for political Messiah, the Moses that will lead them out of the Egypt of peonage, across the Red Sea of Jim Crow legislation, through the wilderness of disfranchisement and restricted opportunity and into the promised land of liberty of opportunity and equality of rights." See William H. Ferris, *The African Abroad, Or His Evolution in Western Civilization*, 2 vols. (New Haven: Tuttle, Morehouse, and Taylor, 1913), I, 274–76.
6. William H. Ferris, *The African Abroad, Or His Evolution in Western Civilization*, 2 vols. (New Haven: Tuttle, Morehouse, and Taylor, 1913), I, 275. W. E. B. Du Bois, *Book Reviews of W. E. B. Du Bois*, ed. Herbert Aptheker (Millwood, N.Y.: Kraus-Thomson, 1977), p. 9.

the subtitle of *Dusk of Dawn*) that was partly willed into being, adopted like a messianic mantle, and partly delivered from spiritual resources within.

The musical epigraphs are therefore "alternating sounds" in the other sense that I have outlined already in the example of Chesnutt[7]—an example of a cultural "language" (in this case black) that cannot be properly interpreted, or even "heard" at all, since it fails to correspond to the customary mapping of sounds and signs that make up the languages of the dominant (in this case white) culture. The spirituals represented Du Bois's pointed assertion that African American culture could be codified, that it was worthy of preservation, and, whatever the degree of its assimilation by the dominant European American culture, that it spoke identifiably in a language of its own. But it was also a language at the very least open to misconstruction, and more likely to remain opaque to the dominant culture, a fact scarcely less true today than when Du Bois wrote. To the uninformed reader the musical texts are but printed notes; whereas to the initiated listener not only do they constitute the language of song, but the unarticulated text (the unprinted words) is heard as well. The bars of music posed a pointed challenge to their contemporary audience, for they demanded a familiarity with a cultural language that most whites did not have and that an increasing number of middle-class blacks renounced as an unhealthy reminder of slavery (in 1909, for example, black students at Howard University refused to sing spirituals, though similar resistance had arisen ever since the conclusion of the Civil War).[8] And they did so, I will suggest as well, by incorporating and rearticulating the trope of silence—one of the central tropes, as we have seen in the case of Chesnutt's folktales, of African American cultural expression. Hidden within the veil of black life, the music and words of the sorrow songs form a hidden, coded language in *The Souls of Black Folk*, one that recapitulates the original cultural function of the spirituals themselves. In a more comprehensive sense, therefore, the music functions antiphonally with respect to Du Bois's written text, such that one must "hear" sounds that are not on the page.

Du Bois's text in this way amplified the traditional remarks by folk music collectors that no common annotations were adequate to capture the slides, blue notes, and shouts of black song. A full discussion of the theoretical dimensions of this issue can be postponed for the moment,

7. Charles Wadell Chesnutt (1858–1932), lawyer and author. Chesnutt was the dominant African American fiction writer for over thirty years—from the publication of his "The Goophered Grapevine" in the *Atlantic Monthly* (1887) until the beginnings of the Harlem Renaissance (ca. 1920). Between 1899 and 1905 he published six books, beginning with a collection of short stories (*The Conjure Woman*). Most scholars agree that his greatest literary achievement was *The Marrow of the Tradition*, a novel based on the 1898 race riot in Wilmington, North Carolina [Editors].

8. Newman I. White, *American Negro Folk-Songs* (Cambridge, Mass.: Harvard University Press, 1928), p. 3.

but the long-standing recognition that black spirituals defied accurate transcription bears directly on Du Bois's act of cultural preservation. Of paramount importance here are the remarks by James Miller McKim and his daughter Lucy (who together transcribed and published a group of songs by blacks in Port Royal, South Carolina, in 1862), by William Allen in *Slave Songs of the United States* (1867), by Theodore Seward, the musical arranger for J. B. T. Marsh's *Story of the Jubilee Singers with Their Songs* (1872), and by Thomas Fenner in his contribution of arrangements and commentary to *Hampton and Its Students* (1874), all of whom it appears Du Bois read. In addition to Du Bois's firsthand experience in northern and southern churches, he also had before him the repeated comments of these song collectors and numerous ethnographers that black music was difficult to annotate according to European standards. Three representative remarks may be excerpted. William Allen felt that "the best that we can do . . . with paper and types, or even with voices, will convey but a faint shadow of the original. The voices of the colored people have a peculiar quality that nothing can imitate; and the intonations and delicate variations of even one singer cannot be reproduced on paper. And I despair of conveying any notion of the effect of a number singing together, especially in a complicated shout." Lucy McKim offered a poetic description that would often be quoted: "It is difficult to express the entire character of these negro ballads by mere musical notes and signs. The odd turns made in the throat; and that curious rhythmic effect produced by single voices chiming in at different irregular intervals, seem almost as impossible to place on score, as the singing of birds, or the tones of an Aeolian Harp." Writing in the *Journal of American Folklore* in 1903, the year *The Souls of Black Folk* was published, Charles Peabody gave the example of a black Mississippi man's work song periodically "intoned" as he plowed behind a mule for fifteen hours a day, a song that "melted into strains of apparently genuine African music, sometimes with words, sometimes without. Long phrases there were without apparent measured rhythms, singularly hard to copy in notes." Likewise, Peabody found a black woman's lullaby "quite impossible to copy, weird in interval and strange in rhythm; peculiarly beautiful."[9]

As I noted when citing Peabody's fieldwork in the discussion of dialect in chapter 4, the difficulty of transcription was common in the case of music and oral narrative alike, and was frequently noted by white folklorists in the 1890s. The same could be said for some other folk songs or tales in ethnic dialect, of course, but African Americans

9. William Francis Allen, Charles Pickard Ware, and Lucy McKim, *Slave Songs of the United States* (1867; rpt. New York: Arno Press, 1971), pp. iv–v; Lucy McKim, "Songs of the Port Royal Contrabands," *Dwight's Journal of Music* 21 (November 8, 1862); rpt. in Bruce Jackson, ed., *The Negro and His Folklore in Nineteenth-Century Periodicals* (Austin: University of Texas Press, 1967), p. 62; Charles S. Peabody, "Notes on Negro Music," *Journal of American Folklore* 16 (1903), 148–52.

presented the greater complexity of generations of isolating enslavement and a cultural inheritance in which the tonal semantics of oral African culture were pronounced. The more common interpretation even among schooled theoreticians of socialization, as one can note in the case of Robert Park, was that blacks brought very little culture with them from Africa, losing what they did in the vicissitudes of slavery, and produced seemingly incomprehensible or fragmentary songs solely because of their inadequate grasp of the English language.[1] As Boas might have argued on the basis of the thesis brought forward in "On Alternating Sounds," however, the white American (European) ear simply did not "hear" black sound and had but imperfect instruments to transcribe and preserve it. A comparable problem faces the reader of Du Bois's text. His theory of black culture, imparted indirectly and embedded in conventionally transcribed texts that replicated these very problems, must be deduced from a context, as well as a text, filled with barriers to common European American epistemological models. In its very structure and modality, however, Du Bois located *The Souls of Black Folk* on a critical dividing line between two worlds schematically epitomized by the distinction between word and music, organically vocalizing his text at a moment of political and cultural crisis in the African American world.

One sign of the crisis lay in the fact that black spiritual music was under siege. True, spirituals were being collected and published in great quantities by the turn of the century (a fact from which Du Bois benefited since the transcriptions he used were not his own). This was accompanied, however, by an overwhelming sense that black music was about to be lost as the older generations died and the middle class sought to distance itself from all reminders of slavery. Older African Americans, particularly those who had known the spirituals under the regime of southern slavery, frequently remarked that "new" versions of the songs, performed or collected in volumes, were but pale imitations of the "originals." As on the black musical stage in its evolution out of minstrelsy in the late nineteenth century, so in modern choral presentation of the spirituals the issues of originality and authenticity were unavoidably complex. In the arts as in social and political life, cultural preservation and memory itself, the very roots of a people's being, were set in contest with demanding notions of progress and assimilation to white cultural models.

Toward the end of the century, an elderly Kentucky woman delivered a superb description of the folk view of the "origin" of the spirituals as well as a vivid jeremiad against the declension of black faith in the younger generations. Recalling the form of worship and the relationship

---

1. Robert E. Park, *Race and Culture* (1918; rpt. Glencoe, Ill.: Free Press, 1950), pp. 267–79.

between the preacher's scripture and the evolution of African American music under slavery, she said:

> And, honey, de Lord would come a-shinin' thoo dem pages and revive dis ole nigger's heart, and I'd jump up dar and den and holler and shout and sing and pat, and dey would all cotch de words and I'd sing it to some ole shout song I'd heard 'em sing from Africa, and dey'd all take it up and keep at it, and keep a-addin' to it, and den it would be a spiritual. Dese spirituals am de best moanin' music in de world, case dey is de whole Bible sung out and out. Notes is good enough for you people, but us likes a mixtery. Dese young heads ain't wuth killin', fur dey don't keer bout de Bible nor de ole hymns. Dey's completely spiled wid too much white blood in 'em, and de big organ and de eddication has done took all de Holy Spirit out en 'em, till dey ain't no better wid der dances and cuttin' up dan de white folks.

Or, as Sterling Brown would later write in "Children's Children":

> When they hear
> These songs, born of the travail of their sires,
> Diamonds of song, deep buried beneath the weight
> Of dark and heavy years;
> They laugh. . . .
>
> They have forgotten, they have never known
> Long days beneath the torrid Dixie sun,
> In miasma'd rice swamps;
> The chopping of dried grass, on the third go round
> In strangling cotton;
> Wintry nights in mud-daubed makeshift huts,
> With these songs, sole comfort. . . .[2]

However metaphorically the Kentucky woman intended her remark about the infusion of "white blood" to be taken, it summed up the generational change from "Old" to "New" Negro that Du Bois would dramatize most effectively in "Of the Coming of John" and illustrated an essential component of the paradox of double consciousness. Such a declension of ancestral traditions, a vexing issue in black cultural and intellectual history from the Civil War on through the early decades of the twentieth century, had stringent political implications insofar as

---

2. Anonymous woman quoted in Jeanette Robinson Murphy, "The Survival of African Music in America," *Popular Science Monthly* 55 (1899); rpt. in Jackson, *The Negro and His Folklore in Nineteenth-Century Periodicals*, pp. 328–29; Lawrence Levine, *Black Culture and Black Consciousness: Afro-American Folk Thought from Slavery to Freedom* (New York: Oxford University Press, 1977), pp. 163–64; Sterling Brown, *Collected Poems of Sterling A. Brown*, ed. Michael S. Harper (Chicago: Triquarterly Books, 1989), p. 104. See also Alain Locke, "Sterling Brown: The New Negro Folk Poet," in Nancy Cunard, ed. *Negro: An Anthology*, abridged ed. Hugh Ford (1934; rpt. New York: Frederick Ungar, 1970), pp. 88–92.

plantation mythology required a perpetuation of the Christian submissiveness associated with the faith of "old-time darkies." But to remember and honor slave culture, even to continue its central communal traditions, was not, Du Bois and others set out to prove, necessarily at odds with the New Negro's fight for justice and rights. Indeed, the remembrance of the slave past was continuous with social struggle, as the important place of the freedom songs within the civil rights movement a half century later would prove. Du Bois could easily have taken to heart the remarks of Howard Odum and Guy Johnson in their 1925 study *The Negro and His Songs*, a book he was to review favorably: "Posterity has often judged peoples without having so much as a passing knowledge of their inner life, while treasures of folklore and song, the psychic, religious, and social expression of the race, have been permitted to remain in complete obscurity."[3]

In the particular case of the spirituals there was the additional question of how best to preserve them. As Du Bois argued, numerous more or less authentic groups seeking to emulate the famous Fisk Jubilee Singers "filled the air with debased melodies which vulgar ears scarce know from the real." What constituted a "real" spiritual, however, was a serious question. Well before the end of the century the difficulty of properly transcribing and annotating the spirituals was compounded by the obverse difficulty introduced by concert and published versions that inevitably simplified the songs, forcing them into a regularized tempo and the more rigid mold of the European tempered scale. In the view of Thomas Fenner, musical director at Hampton Institute and arranger of one of the two collections from which Du Bois evidently drew most of his sorrow songs, so little of the spirit that created black music—"the overpowering chorus . . . the swaying of the body; the rhythmical stamping of the feet; and all the wild enthusiasm of the negro campmeeting"—could be "transported to the boards of a public performance" that it became a fine point whether or not one could "develop" the music (that is, transcribe and arrange it for choral presentation) "without destroying its original characteristics." Writing in the *Southern Workman*, F. G. Rathbun reiterated Fenner's arguments in claiming that education itself was causing the decay of the original music at Hampton: "Corrected punctuation and singing make the difference. It is very difficult to teach an educated colored youth to render these songs in the old time way. White people, however well trained musically, make absolute failures of them. How to sing them cannot be explained

3. Howard W. Odum and Guy B. Johnson, *The Negro and His Songs: A Study of Typical Negro Songs in the South* (Chapel Hill: University of North Carolina Press, 1925), p. 8; Du Bois, *Book Reviews*, pp. 84–85. On the spirituals sung as freedom songs in the modern civil rights movement, see Pete Seeger and Bob Reiser, eds., *Everybody Says Freedom: A History of the Civil Rights Movement in Songs and Pictures* (New York: Norton, 1989), and Guy Carawan and Candie Carawan, eds., *Sing for Freedom: The Story of the Civil Rights Movement through Its Songs* (Bethlehem, Penn.: Sing Out, 1990).

in words. Study all the rules you please and then go listen to a native."
Within one or two more generations the problem was more acute. In
his new edition of the Hampton spirituals, published in 1927, Nathaniel
Dett (who was African American) apparently attempted to elide the
differences between the slave generations and the early twentieth century when he remarked that "the harmonizations and tunes in this book
are as they are sung at Hampton Institute where the singing of these
songs has been traditional since 1868." But in an appendix which included several of the spirituals that were most radically different from
their earlier published forms, Dett admitted that a comparison of his
new edition of the Hampton songs with previous editions would "show
that the way many of the Negro folk-songs are sung at present is quite
different from that recorded nearly a half-century ago." (Among those
included so that "nothing may be lost" is Dett's most notable example
of "Roll, Jordan, Roll," in which the blue tonality characteristic of
much African American performance is transcribed although it is missing from the modern, concertized version.) At extremity, any theory of
the spirituals would have to confront directly Zora Neale Hurston's
claim, to which I will return, that no "real" spirituals had ever been
recorded or transcribed since to do so entailed a necessary violation of
the essential improvisatory freedom of African American song. Whether
or not one agrees with Hurston, it is beyond doubt that concert per-
formances modified the spirituals to make them more acceptable to a
wide (and often white) audience in the North and in Europe, and that
their publication typically in standardized English and regularized
musical transcriptions exacerbated the process of simplification and
debasement.[4]

In his revised commentary Dett indicated further consequences of
publication that bear on Du Bois's cultural history. Although he deplored the musical deracination of the spirituals on the minstrel stage
and in much modern concert performance, Dett himself always referred to the songs as "hymns" and grouped them under various headings ("Hymns of Consolation," "Hymns of Deliverance," "Hymns of
Judgment," and so on), deliberately subordinating their unique musical
and ideological character to a prescribed conformity to white Protestant
practice. "While it is true that the songs of themselves offer much that
is novel in the way of poetry, melody, harmony, and rhythm," he noted,
"fundamentally it will be discovered that they correspond in sentiment

4. Du Bois, *The Souls of Black Folk*, p. 206 [156]; M. F. Armstrong and Helen W. Ludlow,
Hampton and Its Students, with Fifty Cabin and Plantation Songs, arranged by Thomas P.
Fenner (New York: Putnam's, 1874), p. 172; F. G. Rathbun, "The Negro Music of the South,"
Southern Workman 22 (November 1893), 174; R. Nathaniel Dett, ed., *Religious Folk-Songs
of the Negro as Sung at Hampton Institute* (Hampton, Va.: Hampton Institute Press, 1927),
preface p. xviii; appendix p. i. Because it is Fenner's commentary that I will cite in the case
of the Hampton volume, subsequent notes will refer to Fenner as author rather than Armstrong and Ludlow.

with all the basic ideas of orthodox religious dogma." Dett's judgment here is correct in outline, of course, but it entirely obscures the multiple political-cultural meanings—of escape from slavery, of resistance to the regime's brutality, of both actual and spiritual journeys to the North or to the motherland of Africa—that had become semantically encoded in the language of the sorrow songs. Whatever the motive for Dett's editorial procedure (one is inclined to think he was driven by the necessity of patronage for Hampton Institute), he concluded his preface with an admission that "the younger Negro student of today is not quite the slave of yesterday," that contemporary spirituals and their singers have suffered not just by their distance from antebellum slavery but more particularly from "the influence of the white man's education, of the concert-hall, the phonograph, and the radio." The best that can be hoped for is a slight recovery of "the depth, sincerity, and pathos which marked [the singing] of the other days." In this losing battle Dett's admonition was itself but a dim echo of the argument already made by his predecessor, Fenner, more than a generation earlier and well in advance of *The Souls of Black Folk*. As Fenner recognized, publication of the spirituals, whatever its cost to "originality," was imperative if the songs were to be saved: "The freedmen have an unfortunate inclination to despise [the music], as a vestige of slavery; those who learned it in the old time, when it was the natural outpouring of their sorrows and longings, are dying off, and if efforts are not made for its preservation, the country will soon have lost this wonderful music of bondage."[5]

Fenner's arresting last phrase (like most of Hampton's early staff, he was white) captures the ratio between oppression and cultural creativity that would remain a hallmark of black music long after slavery. The rhetorical meaning of the "lost" music varied between plantation mythology for many whites and something akin to conscious cultural nationalism for some blacks. It is inevitably one of the pointed ironies of the African American cultural record that many of the more than one hundred collections of spirituals published in various formats by 1930, the majority by whites, were wrapped in the memorial shroud of plantation mythology or perpetuated offensive stereotypes. The burlesque of the spirituals by blackface minstrelsy was only an overt sign of the pervasively racist evaluation that African American music would continually face in a Jim Crow culture.[6] In their sympathy for the fading world of the Old South, historiography and memoirs dominated by neo-Confederate nostalgia could, in fact, blithely reinscribe racist norms within the crucial work of cultural preservation. A fairly late text by a southern woman, Lily Young Cohen's *Lost Spirituals*, was one of many

5. Dett, *Religious Folk-Songs of the Negro*, pp. x, xviii; Fenner, *Hampton and Its Students*, p. 172.
6. Robert C. Toll, *Blacking Up: The Minstrel Show in Nineteenth-Century America* (New York: Oxford University Press, 1974), pp. 236–37.

written overtly in the tradition of Uncle Remus. Cohen touchingly recalled the love of her family's faithful post–Civil War servants, especially
her mammy, but she also interspersed her maudlin memories with valuable transcriptions of lullabies, work songs, spirituals, and shouts. As her
publisher pointed out in an introductory note: "Here the Negro himself
is treated as a spiritual; so is his prose; so is his verse. And all are *lost*." The
spirituals, of course, were no more about submission to bondage and acceptance of racial hierarchy (even if those elements were present in the
language) than were the folktales that formed the basis for the work of
Harris[7] and Chesnutt. A number were straightforward testaments of faith
in Christian salvation, and in this they corresponded to the assertion of
Henry Burleigh in the preface to his popular arrangement of spirituals for
solo voice—that they were "spontaneous outbursts of intense religious
fervor" that bespoke a deep "faith in the ultimate justice and brotherhood
of man." But the majority were also infused with the coded language of
protest, escape, and liberation. As Sterling Brown would later write,
echoing Du Bois, Douglass, and others, the spirituals' allegories of freedom spoke with finality *against* the legend of the contented slave—"this
world was not their home," Brown remarks—but too few white listeners
were ready by the turn of the century to hear more than reanimated
strains of the Old South.[8] The enervating influence of plantation mythology throughout American culture made it difficult for blacks or
whites to write sincerely about the legitimate value of black music, let
alone deploy it as an instrument of racial consciousness for a skeptical
(black) or hostile (white) audience.

The collective record of white and black America's joint preservation
of the spirituals therefore makes for a unique, complex case of ethnography in which *The Souls of Black Folk* has a central role. The relationship of the spirituals to prevailing notions of "progress" was marked
by continual tension. In an article appearing in *Century Magazine* in
1899, for example, Marion Haskell transcribed a number of spirituals
in careful dialect. Noting in conclusion the increasing aversion of black
colleges to the singing of spirituals, however, he relegated their social

7. Joel Chandler Harris (1848–1908), American regionalist writer from Georgia. A white author,
he narrated his tales in the voice of a fictional former slave, Uncle Remus. Popular in part
because of their use of African American folklore and dialect, Harris's books include *Uncle
Remus: His Songs and His Sayings* (1881) and *Tar Baby* (1904) [Editors].

8. Lily Young Cohen, *Lost Spirituals* (New York: Walter Neale, 1928), p. ix; H. T. Burleigh,
Negro Spirituals (New York: G. Ricordi, 1917), unpaginated; Sterling Brown, "Negro Folk
Expression: Spirituals, Seculars, Ballads and Work Songs," *Phylon* 14 (Winter 1953), 47–49.
See also Levine, *Black Culture and Black Consciousness*, pp. 19–42; Albert J. Raboteau, *Slave
Religion: The "Invisible Institution" in the Antebellum South* (New York: Oxford University
Press, 1978), pp. 243–66; John W. Blassingame, *The Slave Community: Plantation Life in the
Antebellum South*, rev. ed. (New York: Oxford University Press, 1979), pp. 137–48; Miles
Mark Fisher, *Negro Slave Songs in the United States* (1953; rpt. Secaucus, N.J.: Citadel Press,
1978), pp. 66–146; James H. Cone, *The Spirituals and the Blues: An Interpretation* (New
York: Seabury Press, 1972), pp. 34–57; and Wyatt Tee Walker, *"Somebody's Calling My
Name": Black Sacred Music and Social Change* (Valley Forge, Pa.: Judson Press, 1979),
pp. 15–96.

message and artistic value to a receding historical moment. "While rejoicing in the progress of the race," he added, "one cannot but feel that these quaint old spirituals, with their peculiar melodies, having served their time with effectiveness, deserve a better fate than to sink into oblivion as unvalued and unrecorded examples of a bygone civilization." The turn-of-the-century view of the spirituals as "quaint" (Du Bois himself used the word) drained them of immediacy and power while reflecting the common assumption that the spirituals not only represented a passing stage in black American "thought" but occupied a distinctly lower rung on the evolutionary ladder of culture. For example, the black essayist Kelly Miller, writing soon after Du Bois, reiterated the widespread argument that the sorrow songs were the spontaneous "folk-genius" of the race, a "blind, half-conscious poetry" that rose from the "imprisoned soul" of slaves and could now be seen to have served as a kind of cultural prelude to more advanced forms of thought: "Music is the easiest outlet of the soul. The pent-up energy within breaks through the aperture of sound while the slower and more accurate deliberations of the intellect are yet in the process of formulation." Miller's provocative metaphor of the aperture of sound, a most useful figure for the release into the flow of historical expression of African American music, nearly occludes his troubling reliance on a developmental schema that subordinates the "childlike" phase of oral folk culture to the "maturity" of intellect and writing. Unmediated by "cumbersome intellectual machinery," the spirituals were a plaintive "cry," in Miller's definition a beautiful, compelling, but necessarily primitive articulation of black aspirations.[9]

In this view Miller and others echoed the standard interpretation of professional musicologists. In the opinion of Richard Wallaschek, the spirituals, at best imitations of European compositions as he saw it, were "not musical songs at all, but merely simple poems." And in the same year, 1893, Frederick Root's address to the International Folk-Lore Congress at the World's Columbian Exposition asserted that "the utterances of the savage peoples" could be omitted from a concert of folk songs and national music because they were "hardly developed to the point at which they might be called music." Foreshadowing Dvořák's famous call for a national music founded upon the "primitive" melodies of black and American Indian music, Thomas Fenner two decades earlier had hoped, somewhat more charitably, that "this people which has developed such a wonderful musical sense in its degradation will, in its maturity, produce a composer who could bring a music of the future out of this music of the past." The fact that James Weldon Johnson

---

9. Marion Alexander Haskell, "Negro 'Spirituals,'" *Century Magazine* 36 (August 1899), 581; Kelly Miller, "The Artistic Gifts of the Negro," in *Radicals and Conservatives, and Other Essays on the Negro in America* (originally published as *Race Adjustment*, 1908; rpt. New York: Schocken Books, 1968), p. 248.

would say much the same thing half a century later in *The Book of American Negro Spirituals* (1925) is a measure of the compelling ideology of progressivism and the stifling cultural climate with which black vernacular art in particular had to contend. In 1934 V. F. Calverton's provocative view that blacks had created in their spirituals and folktales "a form of expression, a mood, a literary *genre*, a folk-tradition, that are distinctly and undeniably American," while whites had been satisfied to continue their inferior imitation of European culture, was certainly a minority opinion and was destined to remain so for years to come.[1]

At the heart of the doubts voiced by whites and blacks alike about the value of the original spirituals lay the prevailing conceptions of African history, and hence of African cultural inheritances, as primitive and debased, a belief that in turn substantially informed contemporary ethnographic contentions, in the case of the spirituals as well as that of folktales, over the joint questions of African retentions and African American creativity. Du Bois would not begin to argue vigorously for the African roots of black American culture for another ten years. Nonetheless, he put himself decisively on the Africanist side in the debate over retentions; more important, he discovered a formal means by which he could foreground the creation of an original culture, whatever its exact borrowings, by black Americans in slavery and after.

The best known of the spirituals tended to be ones that had no demonstrable white models, while even those that did were greatly transmuted. From the 1890s forward, as I indicated in my earlier discussion of Harris and Chesnutt, a minority of folklorists who were simply misinformed or who resisted the notion that blacks could have been responsible for creating such a great body of musical work either denied that there were any African elements in the spirituals or, by focusing on the Protestant origins of the spirituals, belittled the creation that took place in the crucible of black enslavement. This was less true of early commentators but became more frequently the case as analysis was undertaken after the turn of the century by professional folklorists, a group, it is fair to say, that was not always immune to the racism of the day. In this case, too, the problem of transcription contributed to, rather than revealed, forms of cultural blindness. Because transcriptions could not get very close to the hearts of the people and, as published, constituted a rather small body of the available material, they were also responsible for misleading opponents of the African retentions theory into believing that virtually all black spirituals were simply crude derivations from white hymns. There is little question that, although black slaves (or free persons) in some cases borrowed generously from Prot-

---

1. Richard Wallaschek, *Primitive Music* (London: Longmans, Green, 1893), p. 60; Frederick Root quoted in Levine, *Black Culture and Black Consciousness*, p. 20; Fenner, *Hampton and Its Students*, p. 172. See also Levine, *Black Culture and Black Consciousness*, pp. 166–69, and V. F. Calverton, "The Growth of Negro Literature," in Cunard, *Negro: An Anthology*, p. 79.

estant hymns or other Anglo-American materials (as did black preachers), and that some of the elements characteristic of black musical tonality and rhythm can also be found in other ethnic folksongs, the spirituals were an African American creation in which syncretism played a strong role but in which the foremost voice was that of the heterogeneous African peoples carried into slavery and there fused into one diverse but recognizable "nation." Even Newman White, who argued vigorously in favor of the theory that the spirituals were derived almost exclusively from white Protestant models, nonetheless allowed that they had been "thoroughly naturalized as vehicles of the Negro imagination," and he bluntly pointed out that "the white man would be both stupid and prejudiced if he failed to see that the Negro has long since made [the spirituals] his own." White's theories of origins are demonstrably problematic, yet whatever the degree of syncretism, borrowed Anglo-American materials appearing in the spirituals tended to be thoroughly "reassembled"—to use the term put forward by John Work, a scholar at Fisk University whose studies Du Bois would later praise—almost always given a more powerful tonality and a more intricate rhythm in which the scalar and rhythmic roots in African music are often strong. Most important, the message of the spirituals—deliverance from bondage, the return to a lost homeland, reward for extreme persecution and suffering—added an ideological dimension to the music that was seldom present in any white models.[2]

On the face of it, *The Souls of Black Folk* belongs only in limited ways to the debate over African retentions, Du Bois's contribution appearing to be occasionally insightful but relatively minor. Indeed, he writes at times with a quizzical detachment. Of the "characteristics of Negro religious life," for example, he says: "Numerous are the attractive lines of inquiry that here group themselves. What did slavery mean to the African savage? What was his attitude toward the World and Life?

---

2. Dena Epstein, *Sinful Tunes and Spirituals: Black Folk Music to the Civil War* (Urbana: University of Illinois Press, 1977), p. 344; White, *American Negro Folk-Songs*, pp. 25, 57; John W. Work, *American Negro Songs and Spirituals* (New York: Bonanza Books, 1940), p. 8; W. E. B. Du Bois, "John Work: Martyr and Singer," *Crisis* 32 (May 1926), 32–34. The most extensive argument for the black borrowing from white models was made by George Pullen Jackson in *White Spirituals in the Southern Uplands* (Chapel Hill: University of North Carolina Press, 1933), pp. 242–302, and *White and Negro Spirituals: Their Life Span and Kinship* (New York: J. J. Augustin, 1943), pp. 145–233, and White, *American Negro Folk-Songs*, passim. For countering views, see especially Marshall W. Stearns, *The Story of Jazz* (New York: Oxford University Press, 1956), pp. 79–89, 125–26; Rudi Blesh, *Shining Trumpets: A History of Jazz*, rev. ed. (1958; rpt. New York: Da Capo, 1976), pp. 25–148; John Lovell, Jr., *Black Song: The Forge and the Flame: The Story of How the Afro-American Spiritual Was Hammered Out* (New York: Macmillan, 1972), pp. 63–126; Gunther Schuller, *Early Jazz: Its Roots and Musical Development* (New York: Oxford University Press, 1968), pp. 3–62; and Portia K. Maultsby, "Africanisms in African-American Music," in *Africanisms in American Culture*, ed. Joseph E. Holloway (Bloomington: Indiana University Press, 1990), pp. 185–210. Useful summaries of and commentary on the debate are available in D. K. Wilgus, "The Negro-White Spiritual," in Alan Dundes, *Mother Wit from the Laughing Barrel: Readings in the Interpretation of Afro-American Folklore* (1973; rpt. New York: Garland, 1981), pp. 81–94, and Paul Oliver, *Savannah Syncopators: African Retentions in the Blues* (New York: Stein and Day, 1970), passim.

What seemed to him good and evil,—God and Devil? Whither went his longings and his strivings, and wherefore were his heart-burnings and disappointments? Answers to such questions can come only from a study of Negro religion as a development, through its gradual changes from the heathenism of the Gold Coast to the institutional Negro church of Chicago." Du Bois goes on to offer an extremely truncated analysis of the transformation of the "heathen rites" of African "Voodooism" into the Negro Christian church; and although it is far from insignificant that he posits a followable line of development from West Africa to urban America, he adds little to existing ethnographic arguments. Even his more forthright claims about the sources of black spirituals are sometimes marked by borrowed generalizations: "The Music of Negro religion is that plaintive rhythmic melody, with its touching minor cadences, which, despite caricature and defilement, still remains the most original and beautiful expression of human life and longing yet born on American soil. Sprung from the African forests, where its counterpart can still be heard, it was adapted, changed, and intensified by the tragic soul-life of the slave, until, under the stress of law and whip, it became the one true expression of a people's sorrow, despair, and hope." Du Bois's location of the source of the spirituals in the "African forests" coincided with his argument that the slave preacher derived his leadership from the central role of the African priest (a view he would repeat and extend in his 1903 study *The Negro Church*), and together these claims made up a substantial early argument in favor of African retentions. Still, Du Bois's characterization of the spirituals' melodic line echoes a number of earlier commentators, and from the point of view of content this is a far less rigorous analysis than that found, for instance, in Jeanette Robinson Murphy's 1899 article in *Popular Science Monthly*, one of the first to make a strong case for African sources of the spirituals and one of the first to detail ably some of the technical features of African American vocalization. Employing recognizably archetypal terms of civilization and savagism (just one index of her own rather reactionary views on southern race issues), Murphy argued that "the stock is African, the ideas are African, the patting and dancing are African. The veneer of civilization and religious fervor and Bible truth is entirely superficial. The African is under it all, and those who study him and his weird music at short range have no difficulty in recalling the savage conditions that gave it birth."[3] Although the

3. Du Bois, *The Souls of Black Folk*, pp. 155–56 [121]; Murphy, "The Survival of African Music in America," p. 328. When it was included in her later collection *Southern Thoughts for Northern Thinkers* (New York: Bandanna Publishing, 1904), Murphy's important essay was further diminished by being surrounded by stereotypical portraits of southern mammies; defenses of southern handling of the "Negro problem"; black sermons in a minstrel mold; Murphy's own musical compositions (e.g., "Dat's What de Mammy Good For"); and indulgences in plantation mythology (e.g., "I have interviewed all of my life great numbers of ex-slaves, and I have yet to find one old slave who will say that he or she was cruelly treated" [p. 11]).

degree of their belief in African retentions might vary, a growing number of folklorists and commentators in the 1890s had begun to reach similar conclusions. In that context Du Bois's elegantly concise description of the American transmutation—or "tragic intensification," as he puts it—of original African song into black American sorrow song was a description in small of *The Souls of Black Folk* itself, an act of cultural transfiguration that melded African and white American traditions into a distinctly African American cultural form, as had the spirituals themselves.

Du Bois admitted that he did not write from a technical standpoint; he knew only that "these songs are the articulate message of the slave to the world," that although the songs "came out of the South unknown to me, one by one . . . yet at once I knew them as of me and mine."[4] He wrote, that is to say, not as a musicologist (not even as an ethnographer in any particular sense) but rather as a cultural historian and racial advocate. Even though he made significant local additions to the analytic literature on spirituals (his remarks on the relative absence of the themes of fatherhood, of successful love, courtship, or wedding, and of home were striking), Du Bois's most telling contribution was conceptual. His commitment to a cultural ideal of double consciousness kept him from outright racial chauvinism, and he argued, for instance, that the pathos of "Poor Rosy" (a black folk song that he probably took either from the 1862 studies of James Miller McKim or from William Allen's collection) was comparable to that of a familiar German folk song. From the perspective of scholarship, his chapters on black religion and the sorrow songs extended a tradition of commentary initiated among black writers by Frederick Douglass in his remarks on slave music. At the same time, Du Bois did so with an eye to the fact that the explication of black music had been largely taken over in the post–Civil War years by sympathetic white commentators such as Allen, Higginson, McKim, Barton, and Murphy. Without question, he relied on the work done by these writers; but *The Souls of Black Folk*, which William Stanley Braithwaite would later call "a book of tortured dreams woven into the fabric of the sociologist's document," constructed for the spirituals and the eviscerating experience of slavery on which they were based a rich impressionistic history from "within the Veil" of blackness that no white critic could entirely inhabit. In stark contrast to the untenable claim by Newman White that New Negro pride in the spirituals was taught *to* blacks by the many whites who published collections in the early twentieth century—revealingly, White does not mention Du Bois—*The Souls of Black Folk* was the most vital essay in African American historical and artistic reconstruction.[5] Du Bois's own

4. Du Bois, *The Souls of Black Folk*, pp. 206, 204, 212 [156, 155].
5. William Stanley Braithwaite, "The Negro in American Literature," in Alain Locke, ed., *The New Negro* (1925; rpt. New York: Atheneum, 1974), p. 40; White, *American Negro Folk-Songs*, p. 18.

critical act was thus one of reappropriation, a critically syncretic gesture that mimicked the history of the spirituals as Du Bois simultaneously put black music at the center of black history; preserved it from loss in an age devoted to extreme racism on the one hand and blithe dismissals of the Negro past on the other; and retrieved it from the cultural stewardship of white ethnographers and cultural critics, insisting that the memory of African dispossession and life under slavery belonged first of all to those still living out its legacy.

In designating the African American preacher the "most unique personality developed by the Negro on American soil," at once "a leader, a politician, an orator, a 'boss,' an intriguer, [and] an idealist," Du Bois was therefore very close to painting his ideal self-portrait in *The Souls of Black Folk*. Foremost among the duties of the black minister, he said in an essay of 1905, was to raise "life to a plane above pay and mere pleasure" in order to generate "the sort of spiritual rebirth which the black millions of America are consciously or unconsciously looking for." More telling in his assessment of such spiritual leadership, perhaps, was James Weldon Johnson, who wrote of the preacher in *God's Trombones* (1927) that "it was through him that the people of diverse languages and customs who were brought here from diverse parts of Africa and thrown into slavery were given their first sense of unity and solidarity," a point that might be debated but that corresponds to Du Bois's own view and is not a bad characterization of Du Bois's intentions in *The Souls of Black Folk*. Du Bois's provisional identification with the preacher was even more pronounced in one aspect of the role that he drew directly from the "Priest or Medicine-man" (conjurer) of Africa, namely, his capacity as "the interpreter of the Unknown, the comforter of the sorrowing, the supernatural avenger of wrong, and the one who rudely but picturesquely expressed the longing, the disappointment, and resentment of a stolen and oppressed people." Du Bois could take on the conjurer's roles of judge and physician only in figurative terms, yet he was preeminently a "bard," perhaps the most revealing name that he used to describe the black preacher and one that accorded with the function of the itinerant minister, often also a fine singer, who traveled among plantations in the role of a bard.[6] Indeed, it is perhaps the bardic function that most distinguishes *The Souls of Black Folk* from the narrower genres of autobiography, political history, or social essay. All of those elements are present, to be sure; but the addition of the sorrow songs and Du Bois's self-conscious identification with the

6. Du Bois, *The Souls of Black Folk*, pp. 155, 159 [123]; W. E. B. Du Bois, "The Minister" (1906), in *Writings by W. E. B. Du Bois in Periodicals Edited by Others*, ed. Herbert Aptheker, 3 vols. (Millwood, N.Y.: Kraus-Thomson, 1982), I, 328; James Weldon Johnson, *God's Trombones: Seven Negro Sermons in Verse* (New York: Viking, 1927), p. 2. See also A. M. Chirgwin, "The Vogue of the Negro Spiritual," *Edinburgh Review* 247 (January 1928), 65, and Sterling Stuckey, *Slave Culture: Nationalist Theory and the Foundations of Black America* (New York: Oxford University Press, 1987), pp. 254–58.

preacher as a kind of cultural priest, fused here to the bardic function of epic and Romantic poetry which Du Bois borrowed equally from a Western cultural tradition, are the key elements that make the book the first properly theoretical document of African American culture.

Within a few years Johnson would celebrate the anonymous collective composers of the slave spirituals in his famous poem "O Black and Unknown Bards" (which first appeared in *Century Magazine* in 1908). Likewise, in his portrait of "Singing Johnson," a traveling black singer from Johnson's childhood, he found the means to fix metonymically the unknown bards—preachers, collective worshippers, laboring men and women in slave cabins and cotton or cane fields—who together created the primary reservoir of African American vocal culture. Singing Johnson was remembered by his namesake as a man of great vocal and improvisatory skill, but also a man "with a delicate sense of when to come to the preacher's support after the climax in the sermon had been reached by breaking in with a line or two of a song that expressed a certain sentiment, often just a single line." The singer appeared barely fictionalized in *The Autobiography of an Ex-Coloured Man* (begun in 1905 but not published until 1912) and again in *The Book of American Negro Spirituals*, and he provided the reservoir of experience on which Johnson drew directly for his own contribution to the literary stylization of black folk culture, *God's Trombones*, where he outlined his conception of the proper mode of "intoning" the sung sermonic verse. The black bards epitomized by Singing Johnson were "makers of songs and leaders of singing. They had to possess certain qualifications: a gift of melody, a talent for poetry, a strong voice, and a good memory."[7] The communal singer's role was antiphonal; his music answered or extended the preacher's text—a text that, in the predominant African American form, was already highly vocalized, largely improvised, and filled with the sonoral features that characterize much black (and some white) folk preaching—and thus existed in the liminal modality between word and music that defined the essence of spirituals as they shaded into shouts and sermons. Like the freely improvised spiritual, the black sermonic performance moves between song and chant. In its recourse to polyrhythmic structure and the inflections of blue tonality, the folk preacher's style moves in and out of the domain of the spiritual—to such an extent, as Winthrop Sargeant remarked in his classic study of the origins of jazz and blues, that "just where the song begins and speech leaves off . . . is a difficult point to establish." Metrical patterns and dramatic tension created out of the possibilities of sound itself shape the semantic content of the black sermonic style, and the audience participates through its own cries and shouts in the nar-

7. James Weldon Johnson and J. Rosamond Johnson, *The Books of American Negro Spirituals*, 2 vols. in I (1925, 1926; rpt. New York: Da Capo, 1969), I, 21–23; Johnson, *God's Trombones*, pp. 5–10.

rative creation of a lived scriptural story that has sources in the African chants of tribal law, historical narrative, and folk story.[8]

Needless to say, there is no literal equivalent for such a folk performance in *The Souls of Black Folk*. Whatever his experiments in genre and composition, Du Bois for the most part hewed to a formal, academic style of writing. Even so, his role as bard continually pressed him toward such theorizing, most notably in the concluding chapter of the volume, where the problem of "anonymity" laid bare in each of the musical epigraphs—the problem, in effect, of basing a cultural theory on a set of ceaselessly shifting texts composed, singly or communally, by "unknown bards" and preserved in widely disparate and insufficient transcriptions—is most fully set forth and the relationship between music and language revealed to be rife with hidden messages. Like James Weldon Johnson (or, for that matter, like Singing Johnson), Du Bois had before him no less a task than the creation of a black national culture—or rather, not so much its creation as the proof of its existence. The bardic function of his task went beyond the elucidation of American slave culture or its origins as a conglomeration of many distinct languages and traditions during the middle passage. It entailed developing Frederick Douglass's central insight: "I have sometimes thought, that the mere hearing of those songs would do more to impress truly spiritual-minded men and women with the soul-crushing and death-dealing character of slavery, than the reading of whole volumes of its mere physical cruelties." As James Miller McKim remarked in one of the first interpretations of the spirituals: "They tell the whole story of these people's life and character. There is no need after hearing them, to inquire into the history of the slave's treatment."[9] But more than that, the task demanded the location of an African ground, even one that remained mythic in scope; and it entailed, therefore, tying the prophetic dimension of the spirituals to an African past. The establishment of an African American cultural poetics had to demonstrate the continued presence in America of an African culture where speech and song more closely approached each other on the continuum of cultural sound, where the vocalized "talk" of drums and rhythmic instruments was paramount, and where *nommo*, the power of the word in its oral

8. Winthrop Sargeant, *Jazz: Hot and Hybrid*, 3rd ed. (New York: Da Capo, 1975), p. 185. See also Stearns, *The Story of Jazz*, pp. 130–33; Gerald L. Davis, *I Got the Word in Me and I Can Sing It You Know: A Study of the Performed African-American Sermon* (Philadelphia: University of Pennsylvania Press, 1985), pp. 24–66; Jon Michael Spencer, *Sacred Symphony: The Chanted Sermon of the Black Preacher* (New York: Greenwood Press, 1987), pp. 2–16; Bruce A. Rosenberg, *Can These Bones Live? The Art of the American Folk Preacher*, rev. ed. (1970; rpt. Urbana: University of Illinois Press, 1988), pp. 11–12, 50–54, 72–81; and C. Eric Lincoln and Lawrence H. Mamiya, *The Black Church in the African American Experience* (Durham, N.C.: Duke University Press, 1990), p. 349.

9. Frederick Douglass, *My Bondage and My Freedom*, ed. William L. Andrews (Urbana: University of Illinois Press, 1987), p. 65; James Miller McKim, "Negro Songs," *Dwight's Journal of Music* 19 (August 9, 1862), rpt. in Jackson, *The Negro and His Folklore in Nineteenth-Century Periodicals*, p. 59.

dimension, governed human interaction to a far greater degree than in the Western tradition. Du Bois sought not to erase the Western, European American tradition but to balance it through a black ethnography capable of establishing the lyrical code lying within African American culture.[1]

It is this dimension of "double-consciousness"—one allied to his more open-ended remarks about the conflict between "American" and "Negro"—that Du Bois most brilliantly exploited in composing *The Souls of Black Folk*. A brief look at the changes Du Bois made in his description of double consciousness—the most famous idea advanced by Du Bois, perhaps the most famous advanced by any African American—will clarify this point. As Robert Stepto has shown, all of the revisions Du Bois made in his already published essays when he prepared them for inclusion in *The Souls of Black Folk* showed a pronounced philosophical and poetic deepening of his analytic vision. Among them was one revision concerning his theory of double consciousness that can be said to have shaped his thought for the remainder of his long life. The passage reads: "One ever feels his twoness,—an American, a Negro; two souls, two thoughts, two unreconciled strivings; two warring ideals in one dark body." In its most basic sense the passage is a definition of the social, psychological, and spiritual effects of America's harsh segregation, which yields the African American "no true self-consciousness, but only lets him see himself through the revelation of the other world." More, however, is at stake. The passage goes on to proclaim Du Bois's desire to derive from this double self one that transcends such strife, a "better and truer self" according to which he would neither "Africanize America, for America has too much to teach the world and Africa," nor "bleach his Negro soul in a flood of Americanism, for he knows that Negro blood has a message for the world." The last phrase is a revision of "for he believes—foolishly, perhaps, but fervently—that Negro blood has yet a message for the world." Du Bois thus turns his theory much more decidedly in the direction of the racial essentialism he had announced a few years earlier in "The Conservation of Races." Wanting to avoid the imputation of biological racialism, and yet uncomfortable with the environmentalist reduction of race to "culture," Du Bois had placed his emphasis on the quasi-mystical notion of "strivings," which now recurs with new weight in the title of the chapter, "Of Our Spiritual Strivings," in which the theory of double consciousness appears. The message of "Negro blood" is further underlined by a more significant addition to the ensuing passage. Elaborating on his view that the racist denial of opportunity to blacks in

1. Janheinz Jahn, Muntu: *An Outline of Neo-African Culture*, trans. Marjorie Grene (London: Faber and Faber, 1961), pp. 132–40, 185–90; Molefi Kete Asante, *The Afrocentric Idea* (Philadelphia: Temple University Press, 1987), pp. 43–48, 85–93; Clyde Taylor, " 'Salt Peanuts': Sound and Sense in African/American Oral/Musical Creativity," *Callaloo* 5 (October 1982), 3.

America has allowed the "powers of body and mind" to be "wasted and dispersed," Du Bois now adds the crucial verb "forgotten" and immediately inserts a telling idea: "The shadow of a mighty Negro past flits through the tale of Ethiopia the Shadowy and of Egypt the Sphinx. Throughout history, the powers of single black men flash here and there like falling stars, and die sometimes before the world has rightly gauged their brightness." This focus on what has been forgotten, on a great African–African American past and great heroes (evoked in the beautiful metaphor of the falling stars as souls, itself possibly derived from African belief, which would reappear in the spirituals, for instance in "Stars in the Elements") would become ever more important to Du Bois.[2] Yet even at this point he recognizes its strong implications for him as an artist and for the founding of an African American cultural theory: "The innate love of harmony and beauty that set the ruder souls of his people a-dancing and a-singing raised but confusion and doubt in the soul of the black artist; for the beauty revealed to him was the soul-beauty of a race which his larger audience despised, and he could not articulate the message of another people."[3]

Such a war of "two unreconciled ideals," a stock subject in African American writing from Phillis Wheatley and Frederick Douglass on through the Harlem Renaissance[4] (most notably in James Weldon Johnson's 1928 essay "The Dilemma of the Negro Author") and beyond,

2. Like "My Lord, What a Mourning," Du Bois's musical epigraph to chapter 2 of *The Souls of Black Folk*, "Stars in the Elements," which he later quotes in "The Sorrow Songs," is one of several spirituals with comparable symbolism in the narrative line:

> Oh, the stars in the elements are falling,
> And the moon drips away into blood,
> And the ransomed of the Lord are returning unto God.
> Blessed be the name of the Lord.

Other versions read "returning home to God." As Du Bois notes, "Stars in the Elements" is a spiritual of "the Last Judgment," but "with some traces of outside influence." To extend the decidedly less Christianized, more African resonance of Du Bois's passage in a cosmological direction, one might also suggest that he sought to revitalize an African notion that had been easily submerged in the analogous teachings of Christianity, namely, the belief in the true self as a "little man" or soul within that was waiting not so much to be reborn, as in the Christian cosmos, as to be discovered as always existing and already engaged, during life, in its journey back to the world of spirit. See W. E. B. Du Bois, *The Souls of Black Folk* (New York: Viking Penguin, 1989), p. 213; Mechal Sobel, *Trabelin' On: The Slave Journey to an Afro-Baptist Faith* (1979; rpt. Princeton: Princeton University Press, 1988), pp. 14, 71, 109–16.

3. Du Bois, *The Souls of Black Folk*, pp. 5–6 [12]; Robert B. Stepto, *From behind the Veil: A Study of Afro-American Narrative* (Urbana: University of Illinois Press, 1979), pp. 54–55.

4. Term describing the emergence of African American literature, music, and art in the 1920s, which flourished until the depth of the Great Depression in 1932. In literature, the concentration of a number of talented writers living in Harlem gave rise to increased publication of works about African American life. In his magazine *The Crisis*, W. E. B. Du Bois encouraged creative writing by reviewing and publishing authors. Major figures associated with the Harlem Renaissance included Arna Bontemps, Langston Hughes, Alain Locke, Claude McKay, Countee Cullen, James Weldon Johnson, Zora Neale Hurston, and Jean Toomer. In both *The Book of American Negro Poetry* (1922), edited by James Weldon Johnson, and Alain Locke's *The New Negro* (1925), an effort was made to present this new literary achievement to both white and black audiences [*Editors*].

seems hardly surprising now, so completely has Du Bois's observation entered our thinking. Although the theory of double consciousness, as I will note in chapter 6, had already been elaborated by William James and others as a psychological theory of personality, with which Du Bois was likely familiar, few had seen so clearly as he its special application to race, most of all the degree to which the core of African American identity not only had been shaped but likely would remain shaped for years to come by a series of paradoxical doublings at once painful and empowering. Few had seen so clearly, as Thomas Holt writes, that "alienation—raised to a conscious level, cultivated, and directed—has revolutionary potential." Even so, it is the less obvious aspect of double consciousness that is worth more attention. As Du Bois's revisions of his famous passage indicate, the doubling at issue is not simply that of "Negro" and "American"—that is, black American versus a universalized, colorless American—but rather African versus American. The second doubling is contained within the first (doubles it, as it were) and bears directly upon the artist, for example, who would display the beauty of black song and dance to an audience who despises it—a white audience in the first place, but also that portion of the black middle-class audience that sought to deny its heritage, to "bleach [its] Negro soul in a flood of Americanism." The question of double consciousness seen within this set of terms is open to a variety of constructions, including Arnold Rampersad's suggestion that it be understood as a contest in African American consciousness between "memory" and "amnesia" about the slave past and Africa, and Sterling Stuckey's argument that Du Bois had to call forth a theory of Africanity from behind the veil of his own initial skepticism that it could be traced through the chronology of the diaspora. Those things that are "hidden" and "buried," which Du Bois in his "Forethought" to the volume sets out to recover, would therefore have to include the amorphous elements of black consciousness derived concretely or figuratively from an African heritage that would eventually mature into a Pan-African philosophy.[5]

Over the course of Du Bois's literary work, the recurrent notion of "soul-beauty" becomes more and more charged with political, separatist significance, but even in the revisions of *The Souls of Black Folk* the African dimension is clearly marked, as his first major foray into African history and culture, *The Negro* (1915), would prove. "Negro" is thus not equivalent to "black American" but is already a term of the diaspora for Du Bois, pointing to a "nation," or, as the earlier text has it, a "folk," whose double consciousness is grounded in the soil of

5. Thomas Holt, "The Political Uses of Alienation: W. E. B. Du Bois on Politics, Race, and Culture, 1903–1940," *American Quarterly* 42 (June 1990), 306; Du Bois, *The Souls of Black Folk*, p. 5 [11]; Rampersad, "Slavery and the Literary Imagination: Du Bois's *The Souls of Black Folk*," p. 118; Stuckey, *Slave Culture*, pp. 258–73.

slavery but may ultimately be traced to an African home. He was already driving toward the recognition that would come in 1923 when the Christmas singing he heard in Monrovia, a transfiguration of mission revival hymns in an "unknown tongue—liquid and sonorous . . . tricked out and expounded with cadence and rhythm," seemed to Du Bois the "same rhythm I heard first in Tennessee forty years ago: the air is raised and carried by men's strong voices, while floating above in obbligato, come the high mellow voices of women—it is the ancient African art of part singing, so curiously and insistently different."[6] The germ of *The Negro* and its fundamental cultural premise lay in *The Souls of Black Folk*. Du Bois had the voice but not yet the historical knowledge to tell his Pan-African story; the two would finally join forces in *Darkwater*.

These revisions to what would come to be the most dramatic and often-cited passage of *The Souls of Black Folk*, which point to a crucial intensification in Du Bois's consciousness of African culture as a source of black soul, also bear closely on the theory of the sorrow songs adumbrated in the book's last chapter. Important though the discovery and preservation of identifiable retentions might be, the incorporation of African elements into black American literary art—in a process that might both pay tribute to and augment the example of black music— was equally important. Whereas Chesnutt did so in his folktales and Johnson, Hurston, Brown and others in their poetry and fiction, Du Bois initially connected himself to Africa through the role of the bard, or *griot*, as a communal singer and historian. The spirituals themselves constitute a profound panoramic chronicle of early black America— one of grand epic scope, as commentators such as Hiram Moderwell and Alain Locke argued, for which the best historical analogy is the spiritual account of the Jews' deliverance from bondage and the best analogue the scripture and psalms devoted to it.[7] In his fusion of them with his own text, Du Bois accentuated his role as the epic singer of the New Negro nation—and of a nation, the United States itself, that was Negro in critical ways. Along with Chesnutt, Twain, Harris, Johnson, and coming writers of the New Negro Renaissance and the Southern Renaissance[8] alike, he redirected American culture into a channel that was decidedly southern, decidedly black.

---

6. Du Bois, *Dusk of Dawn*, p. 119.
7. Hiram Kelly Moderwell, "The Epic of the Black Man," *New Republic* 12 (September 8, 1917), 154–55; Alain Locke, "The Negro Spirituals," in Locke, *The New Negro*, p. 200.
8. Term referring to the explosion of writing between World War I and World War II about the American South. The authors tried to come to terms with the pre-Civil War South as well as voicing their anxieties about the future of the New South. Major figures included William Faulkner, Thomas Wolfe, Zora Neale Hurston, Eudora Welty, and Jean Toomer. The New Negro Renaissance refers to the Harlem Renaissance. With the publication of *Survey Graphic*'s "Harlem" number in 1925, it seemed that a "New Negro" had arrived on the cultural scene. Alain Locke, Harvard Ph.D. and Rhodes scholar, edited the *Survey Graphic* issue and later revised and published it in book form as *The New Negro* [Editors].

At the same time, the interaction between music and prose argument in *The Souls of Black Folk* carried forward into an American setting a role whose origins lay in African communal life. In West African traditions that had already been detailed by eighteenth- and nineteenth-century travelers, the *griot* performed on a number of ritual occasions —during preparations for hunting or war, for example, at religious services or rites of birth, marriage, and death, or in praise of individuals, where such songs were on occasion infused with satire or the spirit of subversive signifying. The archetypal ancestors of Singing Johnson, the African *griots* were communal genealogists and historians who sang of their people's historical events and their kings and rulers in a repertoire of song that was constantly subject to innovation. Singly or in groups, sometimes employing the accompaniment of drums and other instruments, such bards preserved the national memory—if one may use "national" in the loose sense of peoples unified by culture, custom, and "race" that Du Bois seemed to prefer. As Maurice Delafosse wrote of African oral culture in the early twentieth century: "It is curious to note that peoples reputed to be ignorant and barbarous have found a means to take the place of libraries by supporting amongst themselves successive generations of living books, each one of which adds to the heritage it has received from the precedent. These so-called savages have at their call, historical compendiums and codes just as we have, only it is in the cerebral convolutions of their traditionalist griots, and not on paper, that their annals and theirs laws are imprinted."[9] The figure of the "living book" contains within it a classic erasure of the line between oral and written; of more concentrated significance, the figure contains an erasure of the line between language (speech) and music that defines much African expressivity. The praise songs of *griots* in traditional as well as contemporary African practice dwell within the assumption that sound is tangible, that it has epistemological "force" that is carried in the aural dimension. The performance of the bard elides the distinction between word and music, sermon and song, and their reciprocal relationship—what Ben Sidran refers to as the "galvanization of

9. Eileen Southern, *The Music of Black Americans: A History* (New York: Norton, 1971), pp. 5–8, 14–15; Oliver, *Savannah Syncopators*, pp. 44–48; Maurice Delafosse, *The Negroes of Africa*, trans. F. Fligleman (c. 1931), quoted in Fisher, *Negro Slave Songs in the United States*, p. 2. The "living book," it might be added, is thus a trope related by inversion to that of the "talking book" (the slave, mystified by writing, assumes that the book speaks to its master), which Henry Louis Gates, Jr., has analyzed as the central trope by which black writers beginning in the eighteenth century confronted the problem of literacy, initiating "a motivated, and political, engagement with and condemnation of Europe's fundamental figure of domination, the Great Chain of Being." Refigured in the trope of the mastery of letters which constituted the essence of liberation in the slave narratives—the most exemplary case was that of Frederick Douglass—the talking book, according to Gates, became an ironic trap in which the registers of vocality and blackness were inevitably emptied of semantic power: "How can the black subject posit a full and sufficient self in language in which blackness is a sign of absence?" See Henry Louis Gates, Jr., *The Signifying Monkey: A Theory of Afro-American Literary Criticism* (New York: Oxford University Press, 1988), pp. 167–69.

meaning and pitch into a single vocalization"—constitutes the foundation of African American artistic culture.[1]

Du Bois's style itself could not achieve such a unification of force; but his deliberate merger of poetic and sociological discourses, of the musicological and the historiographic, was itself a radical acquisition of power that was simultaneously political and performative. Simply the formal relationship between music and language in *The Souls of Black Folk* alerts us to the fact that Du Bois, as Houston Baker has remarked, was composing a "singing book" (in contrast to Washington's "speaking manual," *Up from Slavery*). His representations of musical language were a means to conflate African and American selves and "invoke ancestral spirits and ancient formulas that move toward an act of cultural triumph," building, like the Fisk Jubilee Singers, a new edifice of culture out of "melodies of ancient spiritual song." Du Bois's "singing book" was an extension of the "living book" of the African bard. Indeed, a closer examination of the spirituals that Du Bois chose, of his evocation of important African survivals, whether deliberate or accidental, and of the remarkable vocalizations that his revision and extension of published material entailed substantiates the fact that the musicocultural and historical functions of Du Bois's text were inseparably fused into a single vocalized unit. If one follows out the logic of Sidran's claim that blue tonality and vocalization were "a means of bringing out the individualism in an otherwise destroyed personality"—destroyed, that is, by slavery's ravaging of an African consciousness—Du Bois opened to view the theoretical underpinnings of a cultural poetics capable of both recovering and magnifying the language of African America.[2]

* * *

1. Paul Stoller, "Sound in Songhay Cultural Experience," *American Ethnologist* 3 (1984), 559–70; Ben Sidran, *Black Talk* (1971; rpt. New York: Da Capo, 1983), pp. 6–19, quote at p. 13. See also Blesh, *Shining Trumpets*, pp. 32–33, 42–46; Schuller, *Early Jazz*, pp. 5–6, 54–56; and Ernest Borneman, "The Roots of Jazz," in *Jazz: New Perspectives on the History of Jazz*, ed. Nat Hentoff and Albert J. McCarthy (1959; rpt. New York: Da Capo, n.d.), pp. 6, 14–16.
2. Houston A. Baker, Jr., *Modernism and the Harlem Renaissance* (Chicago: University of Chicago Press, 1987), pp. 58–68; Sidran, *Black Talk*, p. 13.

SHAMOON ZAMIR

"The Sorrow Songs"/"Song of Myself": Du Bois, the Crisis of Leadership, and Prophetic Imagination†

Much of the critical discussion of *The Souls of Black Folk* (1903) has focused on the debate between W. E. B. Du Bois and Booker T. Washington regarding the aims and forms of Afro-American education and the nature of Afro-American cultural leadership. Du Bois's well-known humanist critique of Washington's emphasis on the primary importance of technical training is mapped out in "Of Mr. Booker T. Washington and Others," the third chapter of *Souls*, first published in 1901, and in his essay "The Talented Tenth" (1903), published the same year as *Souls*.[1] Most commentators have accepted that *Souls* and "The Talented Tenth" outline a consistent and fundamentally identical program for educational reform and cultural leadership. But such a view can be sustained only if the third chapter of *Souls* is read in isolation from the rest of the book. The fourteen chapters that make up *Souls* constitute more than a collection of disparate essays. They are organized into a complex literary structure that interweaves a series of historical, sociological, political, and cultural commentaries with autobiographical reflections and dramatizations. This structure can best be described as a *Bildungsbiographie*. The interplay of the various elements of this *Bildungsbiographie* does not so much affirm the programmatic optimism of "The Talented Tenth" as open this confidence to critical investigation.

The very first chapter of *Souls* acknowledges that "the contradiction of double aims" that is a result of Afro-American "double-consciousness" afflicts not only "the black artisan" and "the Negro minister" but also "the black *savant*" and "black artist."[2] The crisis of the Afro-American intellectual and artist is more fully dramatized in the last five chapters of *Souls*. In this essay I argue that in *Souls* the program of "The Talented Tenth" is confronted with the history of racism and violence that constantly thwarts this program. The confrontation leads to a rupture of the prophetic model of leadership derived from the Afro-American church and represented for Du Bois by Alexander Crummell,

---

† From *The Black Columbiad: Defining Moments in African American Literature and Culture* (Cambridge, MA: Harvard University Press, 1994), pp. 145–66. Bracketed page numbers refer to this Norton Critical Edition.

1. The third chapter of W. E. B. Du Bois, *The Souls of Black Folk*, was first published in the *Dial* (1901). "The Talented Tenth" first appeared in *The Negro Problem: A Series of Articles by Representative Negroes of To-Day* (New York: James Pott & Co., 1903); contributors included Booker T. Washington, Du Bois, and others.
2. W. E. B. Du Bois, *The Souls of Black Folk*, in Du Bois, *Writings*, ed. Nathan Huggins (New York: The Library of America, 1986), p. 363 [11]; hereafter cited in the text as *SBF*.

the founder of the American Negro Academy. In place of this model there emerges in *Souls* a poetic understanding of the prophetic imagination, represented by Du Bois himself as he attempts to describe and analyze Afro-American culture. This emergence is most clearly dramatized in "Of the Sorrow Songs," the celebrated final chapter of *Souls*, in which Du Bois reflects on the meaning of the great Afro-American spirituals. The structure of the prophetic imagination in *Souls* is, however, quite distinct from the forms that dominate the American transcendentalism of Emerson or Whitman. The structure of *Souls* embodies a very different relationship of consciousness to history and of self to *communitas*.

In his poem "W. E. B. Du Bois at Harvard," Jay Wright understands that "the prosody of those dark voices" that sing the "old songs" is Du Bois's "connection" to his "fledgling history,"[3] but it is a connection that cannot be taken for granted. Du Bois's dramatization of his relationship to the "sorrow songs" is marked by a representational hesitancy. His commentary is not based in an exactly shared history between his post-Emancipation northern self and the roots of the songs in a long history of southern violence and slavery. These differences, determined by factors of geography, class, and education, emerge only very allusively and elliptically in the final chapter of *Souls* because Du Bois appears to be caught between wanting, on the one hand, to disguise them in order to strengthen the political challenge to the white reader and, on the other, to acknowledge them within a non-dogmatic art. An immediate and concrete sense of the differences and the strategic hesitancies can be given by comparing Du Bois's accounts of his encounters with the sorrow songs in the chapter with his quite different accounts of these same encounters in his later autobiographical writings and also, in one instance, in an earlier part of *Souls*.

"Of the Sorrow Songs" opens with Du Bois's earliest recollection of hearing the spirituals and describes the powerful sense of recognition they evoked:

> Ever since I was a child these songs have stirred me strangely. They came out of the South unknown to me, one by one, and yet at once I knew them as of me and of mine. Then in after years when I came to Nashville I saw the great temple builded of these songs towering over the pale city. To me Jubilee Hall seemed ever made of the songs themselves, and its bricks were red with the blood and dust of toil. Out of them rose for me morning, noon and night, bursts of wonderful melody, full of the voices of my brothers and sisters, full of the voices of the past. (*SBF* 536 [155])

3. Jay Wright, *The Homecoming Singer* (New York: Corinth, 1971), p. 37.

Although there is just glimpse enough of the distance and difference between North and South, as the shadow of strangeness and the "unknown" momentarily passes across the transparent meaning of the songs, the overwhelming sense of the passage is one of an intensely felt cultural identity experienced as an almost familial bond.

When Du Bois returns to the memories of his earliest encounters with the spirituals at the end of his life, there is a much more inflected sense of cultural difference in his account. He remembers in his *Autobiography* (1968) that he "heard the Negro folksong first in Great Barrington, sung by the Hampton Singers. But that was *second-hand, sung by youth who never knew slavery.*"[4] The songs were, then, an importation into the (predominantly white) New England culture of Du Bois's hometown of Great Barrington, Massachusetts—and an importation weakened for Du Bois by divorce from its historic and geographic roots, a divorce that reflects the situation of Du Bois as listener as much as that of the singers. Du Bois goes on to describe how he "heard the Negro songs by those who made them and in the land of their American birth" (A 120) when he first went south as an undergraduate and taught school in rural Tennessee. There he attended his first revival meeting. As Du Bois details his curiosity and excitement at the novelty of the situation, his posture is very much that of an ethnographic participant-observer reporting from the field. After the "quiet and subdued" church meetings in the Berkshires, Du Bois finds himself in the midst of "a pythian madness, a demoniac possession" that reveals "a scene of human passion such as I had never conceived before" (A 120). This same passage occurs in Chapter 10 of *Souls* (493 [120]). The feelings of the young Du Bois reproduce the same exoticism that led the white middle-class reading public at the turn of the century to seek out works that revealed how "the other half" lived.

There is similar variation between Du Bois's recollections in *Souls* of an African song that had been handed down in his own family and his tracing of the genealogy of the song in later autobiographical writing. In the middle part of the final chapter of *Souls* he writes:

> My grandfather's grandmother was seized by an evil Dutch trader two centuries ago; and coming to the valleys of the Hudson and Housatonic, black, little, and lithe, she shivered and shrank in the harsh north winds, looked longingly at the hills, and often crooned a heathen melody to the child between her knees, thus:
>
> > Do bana coba, gene me, gene me!
> > Do bana coba, gene me, gene me!
> > Ben d' nuli, nuli, nuli, nuli, ben d' le.

4. W. E. B. Du Bois, *The Autobiography of W. E. B. Du Bois* (New York: International Publishers, 1968), p. 120 (emphasis added); hereafter cited in the text as A.

The child sang it to his children and they to their children's children, and so two hundred years it has travelled down to us and we sing it to our children, *knowing as little as our fathers what its words may mean, but knowing well the meaning of its music.* (SBF 538 [157], emphasis added)[5]

Again, the overriding sense here is of a transcendent bond, though at the same time the ambivalent wavering between not knowing the meaning of the words to the song and fundamentally understanding the meaning of the music hints at the fact that although the historical continuity of black culture in America is hardly in doubt, it is nevertheless fractured enough to require a sympathetic leap.

Du Bois's later autobiographical writing presents a less transcendent vision. In *Dusk of Dawn* (1940) Du Bois writes that he is, in fact, not sure if his great-great-grandmother was born in Africa or in America and does not know where she learned the song.[6] This acknowledgment comes at the close of a long section of the autobiography in which Du Bois traces his very mixed and complicated family genealogy back to its French Huguenot, Dutch, African, and even Native American roots (*DD* 630–637). The song sung by his great-great-grandmother then becomes his "only one direct cultural connection" with Africa (*DD* 636). After quoting the passage on the African song from *Souls* at length, Du Bois adds that "living with my mother's people I absorbed their culture patterns and these were not African so much as Dutch and New England" (*DD* 638). His "African racial feeling was then purely a matter of . . . later learning and reaction," of Du Bois's "recoil from the assumptions of the whites" and his "experience in the South at Fisk," though "it was none the less real and a large determinant of [his] life and character" (*DD* 638).

The passages from the final chapter of *Souls* which I have quoted signal certain hesitancies, but these hesitancies are more than securely contained within Du Bois's impassioned acceptance of a common history of oppression. But his dramatization of his own relationship to the songs in *Souls* is more subtle than this. It manages finally to suggests the extent of both separation and identity and so resists the alibi of an essentialized idea of *communitas*. The scene that closes *Souls*, the climax of the final chapter, presents a tableau in which Du Bois's relationship to the songs is represented with greater self-reflexivity and complexity:

If somewhere in this whirl and chaos of things there dwells Eternal Good, pitiful yet masterful, then anon in His good time America shall rend the Veil and the prisoned shall go free. Free, free as

5. Du Bois provides musical notation along with the lyrics in *Souls*.
6. W. E. B. Du Bois, *Dusk of Dawn: An Essay toward an Autobiography of a Race Concept*, in Du Bois, *Writings*, pp. 636–637; hereafter cited in the text as *DD*.

the sunshine trickling down the morning into these high windows of mine, free as yonder fresh young voices welling up from the caverns of brick and mortar below—swelling with song, instinct with life, tremulous treble and darkening bass. My children, my little children, are singing to the sunshine, and thus they sing:

> Let us cheer the weary traveller,
> Cheer the weary traveller,
> Let us cheer the weary traveller,
> Along the heavenly way

And the traveller girds himself, and sets his face toward the Morning, and goes his way. (*SBF* 545 [163–64])[7]

This curious scene is a careful revision of both Du Bois's own description of hearing the spirituals at Nashville's Jubilee Hall, which opens the chapter on the sorrow songs, and of Plato's well-known allegory of the cave in his *Republic*, with Du Bois as Plato's enlightened man caught between the light of the sun and the darkness of the caverns. This double revision embodies a plural intentionality on Du Bois's part. Du Bois tries to dramatize simultaneously the independence and artistic integrity of the collective voice that sings through the songs and his own relationship to this voice as a bourgeois intellectual. Such a representational strategy comes as no surprise within the framework of Herderian organic history which dominates the final chapter of *Souls*,[8] and to some extent Du Bois is inevitably trapped within this historical model's paradox of desired immersion and identity and the distance of interpretive authority. Nevertheless, it would be to misrepresent Du Bois's writing if his own openness to displacement by the songs were ignored.

Du Bois's treatment of the spirituals seems at first to be marked by a pronounced sense of cultural elitism or hierarchization that reinforces pastoral nostalgia. Nashville's Jubilee Hall, "towering over the pale city" at the opening of the chapter on the spirituals, has, by the end, become the academic tower of Atlanta University, where Du Bois taught from 1897 to 1910, and where he sits listening to the songs drifting up from below through the "high windows" of the university building. Whereas the young Du Bois, as an undergraduate in his late teens, had been overwhelmed by his first hearing of the songs and an initial sense of community promised by "the voices of my brothers and sisters," the older professor sits alone in his office, a little more removed and re-

---

7. Du Bois provides musical notation along with the lyrics in *Souls*.
8. For more on Herderian elements of Du Bois's commentary on the spirituals, particularly on the links between Du Bois's work and that of the Harvard communalists, see Bernard Bell, *The Folk Roots of Contemporary Afro-American Poetry* (Detroit: Broadside Press, 1974), pp. 20–24. [Herderian refers to the ideas of Johann Gottfried von Herder (1744–1803), a German philosopher who developed an evolutionary approach to history that emphasized the uniqueness of each historical age—*Editors*.]

flective in his attention to the singing of "my children, my little children." This "older" Du Bois was, in fact, only in his mid-thirties at the time he wrote the last chapter of *Souls*,[9] but the kindly (and grating) paternalism of the closing scene belies this fact and offers the reader a self-image that artificially stresses a sense of advanced age and therefore a more pronounced sense of distanced contemplation. There is here, in fact, also a reversal of the genealogy that marks the transmission across the generations of the African song handed down in Du Bois's family. That song was sung by the parents of each generation to their children but with its meaning obscure to "the children" and their "fathers" alike; here the children sing to their father, who struggles to read the meaning of their songs.

There is, then, submerged beneath the sociological and aesthetic meditations on black music in the final chapter, an authorial self-fashioning and an autobiographical narrative of Du Bois's development from infancy (when the African song is first heard) to youthful immersion (in Tennessee) and to mature self-consciousness (at Atlanta University). This narrative is told as an ongoing dialectical engagement between Du Bois and the sorrow songs which unfolds primarily across the historically charged landscape of the South, from Nashville to Atlanta. Du Bois's commentary on the songs is itself a product of the older self and represents a discourse of a different, more self-conscious nature than the songs themselves, the organicism of the latter being, within Du Bois's Herderian communalism, by definition unself-reflexive. Du Bois's particular interpretive access to the content at the heart of the songs is therefore guaranteed not simply by his fraternal or paternal bonds with the culture and history of the songs but also by those perspectives available to him as a trained academic, intellectual, and writer (these positions being in no sense identical). The unveiling of the songs appears to be dependent on their mediation by and incorporation into the different order of reflection and art represented by Du Bois's writing. This seems to shift the axis of articulation away from the songs themselves toward Du Bois's written synthesizing.[1]

This self-fashioning on Du Bois's part pushes his dramatization of

9. *Souls* was published in 1903, and the chapter on the sorrow songs was written expressly for the book. This would make the setting of the final scene contemporaneous with the date of publication and would put Du Bois's age at thirty-five.

1. There are similar contradictory tensions in Frederick Douglass's commentary on the slave songs in *Narrative of the Life of Frederick Douglass* (1845; rpt. New York: Penguin, 1982), p. 57. Douglass notes that the words to some of the songs "would to many seem unmeaning jargon"; they were nevertheless "full of meaning" to the slaves themselves. But he then goes on to state that he himself "did not, when a slave, understand the deep meaning of those rude and apparently incoherent songs." The reason for this was that the slave Douglass was himself "within the circle; so that I neither saw nor heard as those without might see and hear." The songs "told a tale of woe which was then altogether beyond my feeble comprehension." This lack of comprehension seems curious, given Douglass's detailed and gruesome description of life as a slave. But Douglass is in fact, like Du Bois, suggesting a difference between orders of understanding, between "meaning" and "*deep* meaning," between immediate response and retrospective reflection and analysis.

his relationship to the songs toward what James Clifford has described as the allegorical structure of "salvage, or redemptive, ethnography," where "the recorder and interpreter . . . is custodian of an essence, unimpeachable witness to an authenticity." As Clifford accurately notes, this structure "is appropriately located within a long Western tradition of pastoral."[2] Within such an allegoric narrative "the self, cut loose from viable collective ties, is an identity in search of wholeness, having internalized loss and embarked on an endless search for authenticity. Wholeness by definition becomes a thing of the past (rural, primitive, childlike) accessible only as a fiction, grasped from a stance of incomplete involvement."[3] Clifford's ethnographic commentary helps describe the radical desire that is the content of both Du Bois's critical nostalgias and his problematic stance of "historical and cultural aestheticism"[4] in the final chapter of Souls.

The ambivalences of Du Bois's relationship to black American folk culture, signaled by what I have referred to as the representational hesitancies of "Of the Sorrow Songs" and further highlighted by the comparison of this chapter with later autobiographical writings, are much more fully dramatized in Du Bois's rewriting of Plato's allegory of the cave.[5] Du Bois's revision of the opening scene of this chapter (his encounter with the songs at Nashville) at the chapter's end (with Du Bois hearing the songs at Atlanta) unfolds within this other revision and must be read through it.

Plato's allegory is designed "to illustrate the degrees in which our nature may be enlightened or unenlightened."[6] In a cave there are prisoners, chained and immobile since birth, who know nothing of reality other than the shadows cast on the cave wall by a fire behind them. These simulacra they take to be real. One prisoner becomes free and finds true enlightenment when he leaves the cave and walks out into the sunshine. The allegory is concerned with the dilemma facing this one individual who is fully aware of a higher, transcendent reality but is derided as a fool and rejected by the unenlightened prisoners. Du Bois's location within the academic tower at the end of Souls ap-

---

2. James Clifford, "On Ethnographic Allegory," in Writing Culture: The Poetics and Politics of Ethnography, ed. James Clifford and George E. Marcus (Berkeley: University of California Press, 1986), p. 113.

3. Ibid., p. 114.

4. I have taken this phrase from Fredric Jameson's description of "existential historicism," a kind of relativist position, in his "Marxism and Historicism," New Literary History, 11, no. 1 (1979): 51. Jameson argues that "existential historicism" replaced geneticist and evolutionary models of explanations with "something like a transhistorical event: the experience . . . by which historicity as such is manifested by means of the contact between the historian's mind in the present and a given synchronic cultural complex from the past" (51). This helps highlight the politics of the allegorical structure of relativist ethnography delineated by Clifford.

5. See Plato, Republic, 7. 514A–521B.

6. The Republic of Plato, trans. Francis MacDonald Cornford (1941; rpt. Oxford: Oxford University Press, 1945), p. 227.

pears at first simply to reproduce this dilemma. He is caught between the vision of freedom promised by the transcendental "Eternal Good" and the "free . . . sunshine trickling down the morning into these high windows" on the one hand and the "prisoned" blacks, the "voices welling up . . . from the caverns of brick and mortar below," on the other. Du Bois's implied self-identification with Alexander Crummell, and the theories of education and progress that undergird that identification, briefly mentioned earlier, suggests the obvious appropriateness of the allusion to the Platonic parable. Plato too is advocating the leadership of a cultured elite as a guarantee of "the welfare of the commonwealth."[7]

In Atlanta, however, not only are the voices from below singing "to the sunshine" and urging on "the weary traveller" in his quest (whereas in Plato the prisoners have no conception of freedom), but also the voices from the caverns are themselves "instinct with life" and as "free" as the sunshine that represents higher enlightenment.[8] Du Bois is not trapped between enlightenment and ignorance but poised between different forms of insight and understanding. "Beneath the conventional theology and unmeaning rhapsody" (*SBF* 541 [000]) of the sorrow songs there is a hard and bitter knowledge of historical experience which challenges the transcendental cultural universalism championed in the progressive reformism of "The Talented Tenth." Unlike Plato's prisoners, the slaves who created the sorrow songs and the voices that sing at the end of *Souls* have suffered actual, not metaphorical, enslavement and oppression, and their music give voice to a poetry of experiential truths, not unwitting falsehood. The poised tableau at the end of *Souls*, then, is not so much an allegorical rewriting of Plato as a momentary breaking of the allegorical spell because it acknowledges that the "prisoned" cannot be turned into symbols in support of an idealist political program. In opening himself up in sympathetic understanding to "the souls of black folk," Du Bois, like his projected white reader, finds a mirror behind the veil. The image at the close of *Souls* of the "weary traveller" who "girds himself" and "goes his way," cheered on by his "children," is not an image of a false collectivity parasitically recuperated into the promise of messianic leadership but a genuinely tragic and political vision that returns Du Bois for strength to the grounds of solitude.

The Platonic revisions through which Du Bois dramatizes an ambivalence of cultural authority between himself as interpreter and the songs comes as the conclusion to a series of chapters that are meditations on

---

7. Ibid., p. 234.
8. If the University of Atlanta is supposed to represent the institutional embodiment of the program of educational reform outlined in "The Talented Tenth," then it is also important to note that Du Bois spends some time in "The Sorrow Songs" explaining that Fisk University, where he himself had studied, was founded on $150,000 raised by the Fisk Singers on their national and international tour begun in 1871 (*SBF* 266–267 [155–56]).

the role of religious leadership among Afro-Americans. After the survey in the first nine chapters of the political, economic, and educational issues that affect black American life, the last five chapters of *Souls* are concerned primarily with religious culture—particularly with the political and social function of the religious leader and with the jeremiad of the preacher-prophet as the dominant model of leadership rhetoric available to Afro-Americans. As in "The Sorrow Songs," Du Bois manages to establish both a historical and a contemporary understanding of Afro-American religious culture by combining anthropological and sociopolitical commentaries. Nonetheless, acute assessments of the centrality of religion in Afro-American culture are juxtaposed with dramatizations of the fracture of faith. It is this fracture that underlies Du Bois's distinction between the political and historical content of the songs and the "conventional theology" of their lyrics. The redemptive biblical typologies of religious prophecy are repeatedly qualified by personal experiences of loss and violence. Du Bois inverts the prophetic models of ascent and uplift. It is within the space cleared by these qualifications that Du Bois's model of his own solitary insight and understanding can be properly described.

The terms in which Du Bois describes himself listening to the sorrow songs at the close of *Souls* refigure the description of Alexander Crummell's growth into enlightenment and leadership earlier in the book. In Chapter 12 Du Bois argues that the education of Crummell at the hands of white abolitionists proved to be a process of mutual transformation. The white schoolboys discovered a realm "of thought and longing beneath one black skin, of which they had not dreamed before. And to the lonely boy came a new dawn of sympathy and inspiration" (*SBF* 514 [136]). It is through the sympathy awakened by education that Crummell is able to overcome his hatred for the white world and to see for the first time "the sun-swept road that ran 'twixt heaven and earth" (*SBF* 514 [136]), a vision of higher cultural ideals offered by the white world. But it is also because of this newly inspired sympathy that Crummell himself can hear "the bronzed hosts of a nation calling" and "the hateful clank of their chains" from "behind the forests," and can respond with a career of "protest" and "prophecy" as "a priest—a seer to lead the uncalled out of the house of bondage" (*SBF* 514 [137]). Educational training and the revelation of higher goals necessarily entail a distancing from the repeated cycles of despair in the dark forest, and though sympathy promises a return to roots, it is a return in which both identity and difference must be acknowledged. Crummell answers the call of his fellow blacks but as the priestly head of "the headless host" (*SBF* 514 [137]).

The scene where Du Bois listens to the spirituals "welling up from the caverns of brick and mortar below" as the "free . . . sunshine," the enlightening embodiment of the "Eternal Good," trickles through the "high windows" refigures the dialectic of Crummell's sympathetic imagination moving between "the sun-swept road" and the "forest." Just as Crummell "girded himself to walk down the world" (SBF 514 [137]), so too Du Bois as "the weary traveller" at the very end of the book "girds himself, and sets his face toward the Morning, and goes his way." Du Bois's placing of this allusive self-fashioning at the end of Souls seems at first to suggest that the autobiographical narrative of the book should be read as a teleological[9] ascent. In a way the double ontogenic and phylogenic narrative seems to suggest an optimistic reading as the most appropriate one for the book. The narrative seems, after all, to move from racist alienation to personal enlightenment, from continued social discrimination and exclusion to the fulfillment of educational ideals at the universities of Fisk and Atlanta as "the advanced guard" toils "slowly, heavily, doggedly" up "the mountain path to Canaan" (SBF 367 [13]). This would align Souls with the redemptive biblical typologies and rhetoric of the "American jeremiad" inherited by the slave narratives and the message of uplift in Washington's autobiography Up From Slavery (1901), a contemporary version of the slave narrative combined with the Horatio Alger myth.[1] Frederick Douglass's earlier (1845) Narrative of the Life of Frederick Douglass had itself produced a version of American individualistic self-genesis.[2] But, as Arnold Rampersad has suggested, Souls can also be read as an inverted slave narrative, one that reverses the plot of enlightenment and attained freedom.[3] From this perspective the narrative of Souls moves from Emancipation (in "Of the Dawn of Freedom") to the slave songs and their reassertion of continued oppression and violence, from a prelapsarian infancy (in the opening scene of the first chapter) to a repeated return to the condition of the divided self.

There is little in the chapter on Crummell to suggest that Du Bois is in any way critical of or ambivalent about Crummell's political and cultural programs. Crummell was, in fact, the direct inspiration for Du Bois's own proposal for a vanguard of Afro-American leaders. In 1897 Crummell had established the American Negro Academy, whose aim was to promote an interest in literature, science, and art among Afro-Americans as a way of developing a scholarly and refined elite. This

---

9. Teleology explains events in terms of ends, goals, or purposes [Editors].
1. On the importance of biblical jeremiad rhetoric in American culture, see Sacvan Bercovitch, The American Jeremiad (Madison: University of Wisconsin Press, 1978). For the impact of this typological tradition on American minority writing, see Werner Sollors, Beyond Ethnicity: Consent and Descent in American Culture (New York: Oxford University Press, 1986), pp. 40–65.
2. See the comparison of Douglass and Emerson and the location of Douglass's text in the American Renaissance of the mid-nineteenth century in the conclusion of Russell Reising, The Unusable Past: Theory and the Study of American Literature (New York: Methuen, 1986), pp. 256–272.
3. Arnold Rampersad, "Slavery and the Literary Imagination: Du Bois's The Souls of Black Folk," in Slavery and the Literary Imagination, ed. Deborah E. McDowell and Arnold Rampersad (Baltimore: The Johns Hopkins University Press, 1989), pp. 106, 121.

program was adopted with almost no modification by Du Bois in "The Talented Tenth."[4] But the unqualified eulogy to Crummell is carefully placed between the threnody for the loss of Du Bois's infant son in "Of the Passing of the First-Born" and the fictionalized dramatization of the negation of his own adult ideals by racist violence and prejudice in "Of the Coming of John." The closing moments of the latter, where the educated John, having returned to work in the South, faces the sea as the lynch mob thunders toward him, refer the reader to the closing moments of the chapter on Crummell, where, on the morning before his death and at the end of a life of solitary struggle and hardship, he sits "gazing towards the sea" (SBF 520 [142]). If the tragic end of "Of the Coming of John" cuts short the visionary projections of the eulogy for Crummell, these projected trajectories are already threatened by the gothic omen of the death of "the first-born" in the previous chapter.

"Of the Passing of the First-Born" opens with biblical resonance: "Unto you a child is born" (SBF 506 [130]). Du Bois sees "the strength of [his] own arm stretched onward through the ages through the newer strength" of the child's, and hears in "the baby voice" of his son "the voice of the Prophet that was to rise within the Veil." But the "hot winds" that roll into Atlanta from "the fetid Gulf" strangle this redemptive hope almost at birth (SBF 508 [131]). The sense of loss and personal grief is, however, mixed with a sense of relief:

> All that day and all that night there sat an awful gladness in my heart—nay, blame me not if I see the world thus darkly through the Veil—and my soul whispers ever to me, saying, "Not dead, not dead, but escaped; not bond, but free." No bitter meanness now shall sicken his baby heart till it die a living death, no taunt shall madden his happy boyhood. Fool that I was to think or wish that this little soul should grow choked and deformed within the Veil! (SBF 510 [133])

This is perhaps Du Bois's most ironic and bitter condemnation of American racism. As Arnold Rampersad notes, "Of the Passing of the First-Born" is in certain respects "an almost classical elegy, in impassioned yet formal language. But it is one in which the central mourner, as a black, can find no consolation. Thus it is in truth anti-Christian, a bitter parody of the Christian elegy."[5] Du Bois only reinforces the anticonsolatory thrust of his mourning by placing its antireligious reversals after the chapter "On the Faith of the Fathers."

For the most part Du Bois keeps his personal life out of Souls. The autobiographical narrative is always woven along the edges of the cul-

---

4. For further information on Crummell and an assessment of his influence on Du Bois, see Manning Marable, W. E. B. Du Bois: Black Radical Democrat (Boston: Twayne, 1986), pp. 32–40.
5. Rampersad, "Slavery and the Literary Imagination," p. 120.

tural and political commentaries of the book. It reinforces or counterpoints but is never the primary or sole site of exploration. Those denunciations of racism that draw on autobiographical experience penetrate because their articulation is always so overly restrained. This is precisely why the impassioned grief of the elegy for the dead son is so unexpected and overwhelming. Suddenly a personal loss that has little to do with the history or politics of racism occupies center stage, and stoic reticence gives way to public mourning. Throughout *Souls* Du Bois has struggled to build a refuge of reason against both racism and the irrationality of "the vein of vague superstition" among Afro-Americans themselves. But the death of his son seems to unhouse the faith in rationality and providence alike, even if only for a moment. It is as if the seat of arbitrary violence and irrationality were discovered at the very heart of nature itself.

John, the educated black hero who returns to the South to teach in Chapter 13 of *Souls*, is the embodiment of what Du Bois's infant son might have become. But John's death at the hands of a lynch mob also represents the life that the son has escaped through his untimely death. The eulogy on Crummell is placed precariously between the deaths of the son and of John. But prophetic progressivism is threatened by more than white racism or personal tragedy. Crummell's brand of uplift acknowledges the political and economic handicaps that defeat Afro-American struggle, but it also assumes the legitimacy of a dichotomy of civilization and barbarism across the color line. For Crummell, Afro-American folk and proletarian culture must be purged of its rudeness and heathen retentions. At moments Du Bois shares this Victorian moralistic valuation of Afro-American culture. But his commentary on the spirituals also describes a transcendent musical embodiment of the historical consciousness that destabilizes such dichotomizations. The aesthetic relativism that marks the final chapter of *Souls* pushes prophetic cultural self-confidence toward insecurity because it brings this confidence face to face with a collective consciousness of terror and suffering.

At a time when most Afro-Americans were Baptists or Methodists, Crummell was an Episcopalian. The Episcopal church was associated with the black bourgeoisie and the upper classes:

> The church had dignified rituals and was far removed from the plantation culture that [Crummell] identified with barbarism, depravity, and weakness. Episcopalianism, with its principles of "submission to authority, respect for rules, quietness and order," was congenial to Crummell's conservative temperament. The American Episcopal church brought him into contact with Anglicanism and nurtured his sense of participating in the literary and intellectual traditions of England. The Anglican music and architecture

appealed to him, as did the Anglican liturgy. His religious sentiments were closely linked to aesthetic preferences that were uncommon among black Americans.[6]

Du Bois's own self-fashioning in his first description in *Souls* of his
earliest encounter with plantation culture is very much in the image
of Crummell's Episcopalianism. The young Du Bois, "fresh from the
East," is overwhelmed by "a pythian madness, a demonic possession."
As he notes with restrained humor, "To be sure, we in Berkshire were
not perhaps as stiff and formal as they in Suffolk of olden time; yet we
were very quiet and subdued, and I know not what would have happened those clear Sabbath mornings had some one punctuated the
sermon with a wild scream, or interrupted the long prayer with a loud
Amen!" (*SBF* 493 [119–20]).

Throughout the chapter titled "Of the Faith of the Fathers," Du
Bois's Victorian unease persists as he traces the development of Afro-
American religion "through its gradual changes from the heathenism
of the Gold Coast to the institutional Negro church of Chicago" (*SBF*
495 [121]). But at the same time the moralism that denigrates the
African origins of Afro-American religion as "Voodooism" (*SBF* 498
[123]) is balanced by a political consciousness that sees the transition
from "Obi worship" to Christianity as a transformation of the spirit of
revolt into "passive submission" (*SBF* 499 [125]), though Du Bois also
notes that, with the growth of the abolition movement and freedom,
religion for the Afro-American "became darker and more intense, and
into his ethics crept a note of revenge, into his songs a day of reckoning
close at hand" (*SBF* 501 [126]).

To summarize the argument so far, Victorian moralism and Herderian romanticism are not the only stances that characterize Du Bois's
commentaries on Afro-American religion or religious music. There is
also an awareness of social and political function and content. The
historical memory that marks the spirituals is the collective resource on
which the messianic ardor of a Crummell draws. But at the same time
that Du Bois's dramatizations recognize that the tragic sensibility and
redemptive longings of the songs must be lifted into the activism of the
preacher-prophet's salvationary historicism, they also tether the latter to
the historical realism that resonates in the performance and lyrics of
the former.

In the end, the literary imagination of *Souls* is not able to propose a
model of political leadership that will answer the doubts of the book's
deeply negative historical consciousness. The late nineteenth and early

6. Wilson Jeremiah Moses, *Alexander Crummell: A Study of Civilization and Discontent* (New
York: Oxford University Press, 1989), p. 281. For a brief history of the place of the Episcopal
church in Afro-American culture and history, see the entry "Episcopalians" in the *Encyclopedia of Black America*, ed. W. Augustus Low and Virgil A. Clift (New York: McGraw-Hill,
1981), pp. 372–377.

twentieth centuries are, for the Afro-American, "a time of intense ethical ferment, of religious heart-searching and intellectual unrest." Such a time of radical doubt "must give rise to double worlds and double ideals, and tempt the mind to pretence or to revolt, to hypocrisy or to radicalism" (*SBF* 502 [127]), a division that Du Bois charts along the North-South axis (*SBF* 503 [128]). But if the polarization of dangerous "anarchy" (*SBF* 504 [127]) and "hypocritical compromise" (*SBF* 505 [128]) suggests a defense of the liberal center, Du Bois reveals a middle ground occupied by assimilation or fatalistic acquiescence:

> Between the two extreme types of ethical attitude which I have thus sought to make clear wavers the mass of the millions of Negroes, North and South; and their religious life and activity partake of this social conflict within their ranks. Their churches are differentiating—now into groups of cold, fashionable devotees, in no way distinguishable from similar white groups save in color of skin; now into large social and business institutions catering to the desire for information and amusement of their members, warily avoiding unpleasant questions both within and without the black world, and preaching in effect if not in word: *Dum vivimus, vivamus.* (*SBF* 504–505 [129])

Du Bois adds that "back of this still broods silently the deep religious feeling of the real Negro heart, the stirring, unguided might of powerful human souls who have lost the guiding star of the past and are seeking in the great night a new religious ideal" (*SBF* 505 [129]). Crummell is the "guiding star" that promises the incarnation of this ideal, and it is an ideal fully endorsed by Du Bois in "The Talented Tenth." But it is also an ideal whose horizon of possibility perpetually recedes in the face of the political and cultural history charted by *Souls*.

The refusal to give unqualified endorsement to a message of uplift in *Souls* is, of course, no failure at all. It is the very ground on which the book's challenge to American political and cultural idealism is built. By concluding *Souls* with a chapter on the spirituals, Du Bois focuses on an art that embodies a sense of history and memory. The way that "The Sorrow Songs" rounds off the autobiographical narrative trajectory of *Souls* also reveals the poetic conceptualization of the historical consciousness that underlies Du Bois's own literary structure.

In the brief "Afterthought" which concludes *Souls*, Du Bois asks the reader to "vouchsafe that this my book fall not still-born into the world-wilderness," and hopes that from it will "spring . . . vigor of *thought* and *thoughtful deed*" (*SBF* 547 [164], emphasis added). Du Bois as "the weary traveller" is not a reincarnated priest-prophet. He is the companion of Blake's "Mental Traveller."[7] In "The Mental Traveller"

---

7. No direct influence is suggested here, only a certain affinity.

"the Babe" liberty is "begotten in woe" and "born in joy." But the child
is "given to a Woman Old," society, "who nails him down upon a
rock."[8] As Foster Damon explains, Blake's poem "is the formula of the
history of the idea of Liberty, showing how it is born, how it triumphs,
how in its age its opposite is born, how it is cast out, how it then
rejuvenates, until it becomes a babe again, and the cycle recurs."[9] Souls
also dramatizes the recurring struggles of the consciousness of freedom
and of bondage. As in Blake, it is from a knowledge of this struggle
that prophetic vision is created in Souls.

Prophecy is understood here not in a predictive or futuristic sense
but as Northrop Frye describes it (though without his religiosity) in his
study of Blake:

> An honest man is not quite the noblest work of God until the faith
> by which the just live develops into full imaginative vision. The
> fully imaginative man is therefore a visionary whose imaginative
> activity is prophecy and whose perception produces art. These two
> are the same thing, perception being an act . . . It is the superior
> clarity and accuracy of the prophet's vision that makes him an
> artist, and that makes the great artist prophetic.[1]

In American transcendentalism, as in European romanticism, poetic
prophecy is preoccupied with the dialectics of passivity and activity. On
the American side, the primary mode of transcending passivity is
through a voluntaristic act of *seeing*. A brief examination of Emerson
and Whitman, particularly of the triumph in their work of sight over
the other senses and of a self defined by seeing, will provide a context
in which the poetics of Souls's structuring can be clearly understood.

In *Nature* (1836), his first major work, Ralph Waldo Emerson seeks
to reverse the Pauline[2] relegation of prophetic vision to a future world
in which the fall is recovered. For Saint Paul, "now we see in a mirror,
darkly," but "when that which is perfect is come," then we shall see
"face to face" (1 Cor. 13:12, 10). Emerson, however, argues that "the
foregoing generations beheld God and nature face to face; we through
their eyes," and asks, "Why should not we also enjoy an original relation
to the universe?"[3] The prophet of the New World restores his vision by

8. "The Mental Traveller," in *The Complete Poetry and Prose of William Blake*, ed. David V.
Erdman, rev. ed. (New York: Doubleday, 1988), pp. 483–484.
9. S. Foster Damon, *A Blake Dictionary: The Ideas and Symbols of William Blake*, rev. ed.
(Hanover, N.H.: University Press of New England, 1988), p. 288.
1. Northrop Frye, *Fearful Symmetry: A Study of William Blake* (1947; rpt. Princeton: Princeton
University Press, 1969), p. 59.
2. Term applied to the branch of Christian theology that is heavily influenced by the New
Testament writings of St. Paul (d. A.D. 64? or 67?). As early as Paul's first letter to the Corinthians, Paul emphasized causal relations in which God is represented as the first and final
cause. Paul warns against turning away from the Creator to honor his creation. [Editors]
3. *Nature*, in *Selections from Ralph Waldo Emerson*, ed. Stephen E. Whicher (Boston: Houghton
Mifflin, 1957), p. 21.

becoming "a transparent eyeball" whose Platonic insight transcends society:

> I am nothing; I see all; the currents of the Universal Being circulate through me; I am part or parcel of God. The name of the nearest friend sounds then foreign and accidental: to be brothers, to be acquaintances, master or servant, is then a trifle and a disturbance. I am the lover of uncontained and immortal beauty. In the wilderness, I find something more dear and connate than in the streets or villages. In the tranquil landscape, and especially in the distant line of the horizon, man beholds somewhat as beautiful as his own nature.[4]

By contrast with *Nature*, *Souls* opens not with a seeing subject but with a moment of being seen. Whereas Emerson seeks solitude in nature, the boy Du Bois is seeking the company of his white and black playmates when he is repulsed by the "glance [of] one girl, a tall newcomer" (*SBF* 364 [10]). The black body and not "the tranquil landscape" becomes the field of the "Not Me" in which the white subject unfolds its freedom. The moment when the gaze penetrates is the moment when the biblical veil, Du Bois's favorite conceit for the color line, descends and obscures vision in *Souls*. But if the penetrative gaze sets off a process of objectification and the division of consciousness, it also endows the Afro-American with a "second-sight in this American world" (*SBF* 364 [10]). The look of Du Bois's new playmate is like that "certain Slant of light" that is both "an imperial affliction" and a source of tragic understanding in Emily Dickinson:

> Heavenly Hurt, it gives us—
> We can find no scar,
> But internal difference,
> Where the Meanings, are—[5]

Not only does *Souls* open with being seen, but it closes with Du Bois *listening* to the voices singing the spirituals, a more social act than seeing, and sending out into the world his *written* work. This presents a very different ratio of the senses than the one that dominates in Emerson, or even the more "amative" Whitman, and also a very different conceptualization of visionary action. Emerson's attempts to defend the mind as active in "The American Scholar" (1837) and Walt Whitman's poetic self-fashioning in "Song of Myself" (1855) can help illustrate the differences between Du Bois's formulations and American transcendentalism.

4. Ibid., p. 24.
5. Emily Dickinson, *The Complete Poems*, ed. Thomas H. Johnson (London: Faber and Faber, 1975), no. 258, p. 118.

"The American Scholar" is a program for the cultivation of the life of the mind in the new nation. Emerson writes that "the so-called 'practical men' sneer at speculative men, as if, because they speculate or *see*, they could do nothing." Emerson takes this to be a false accusation:

> Action is with the scholar subordinate, but it is essential. Without it he is not yet man. Without it thought can never ripen into truth . . . The preamble of thought, the transition through which it passes from the unconscious to the conscious, is action. Only so much do I know, as I have lived. Instantly we know whose words are loaded with life, and whose not.
>
> The world—this shadow of the soul, or *other* me—lies wide around. Its attractions are the keys which unlock my thoughts and make me acquainted with myself. I run eagerly into this tumult. I grasp the hands of those next me, and take my place in the ring to suffer and to work, taught by an instinct that so shall the dumb abyss be vocal with speech.[6]

Despite this last image of collective toiling, Emerson's formulations of the activity of visionary understanding and cultural leadership describe, for the most part, a solitary and passive process. The sense of self-reliance and mastery in the face of the "Not Me" is, after all, dependent on the passivity of seeing.[7] In the passage from "The American Scholar" the transition from seeing to saying involves no process of hearing. Notwithstanding the image of the ring of grasped hands, the scholar does not work from a social location. What is vocalized is in fact not a social or historical knowledge but the passive emergence of preexisting Platonic forms autonomous of consciousness. In Du Bois's revision of Plato, however, the bright revelation of pure and transcendent forms in the light outside the cave is eschewed in favor of the knowledge embodied in the voices of the prisoned inside the cave. As Denis Donoghue observes:

> The site of [Emerson's] poetry and his sageness is the history of voluntarism. The more we read *Nature*, the more clearly it appears that the whole essay is predicated upon the capacity of Will. Not knowledge but power is its aim; not truth but command . . . So if we go back to the transparent eyeball passage and read it as a voluntaristic act rather than an instance of the Sublime, we find that the eyeball becomes transparent because a light higher than its own sensory light is made to shine through it . . . We have

6. Ralph Waldo Emerson, "The American Scholar" (1837), in *Selections*, p. 70.
7. See Kenneth Marc Harris, *Carlyle and Emerson: Their Long Debate* (Cambridge, Mass.: Harvard University Press, 1978), p. 69.

access to [Emerson's work] only by recourse to the vocabulary of Will and to its social form, a pragmatics of the future.[8]

The interaction of the senses and the social politics in Whitman's "Song of Myself" from *Leaves of Grass* are closer to Du Bois than is Emerson, but they are still marked by a fundamental difference that is useful in describing *Souls*. Whitman, like the author of *Souls*, is "attesting sympathy."[9] The poet of the "Song of Myself" touches and feels in his democratic openness in a way Emerson never does (and with a corporeal candor that is also alien to the Victorian Du Bois): "I believe in the flesh and the appetites, / Seeing, hearing, feeling" (*LG* 53). And the poet's "voice goes after what [his] eyes cannot reach" (*LG* 55). In his social openness Whitman is led to make vocal not just "the threads that connect the stars" but political outrage on behalf of the oppressed and socially excluded:

> Through me many long dumb voices,
> Voices of the interminable generations of prisoners and slaves,
> Voices of the diseas'd and despairing and of thieves and dwarfs,
> . . .
> Through me forbidden voices
> Voices of sexes and lusts, voices veil'd and I remove the veil,
> Voices indecent by me clarified and transfigured. (*LG* 52–53)

It is the poet's transfiguration of the voices that lifts the veil. This is closer to Du Bois, but the transfiguration dramatized in the last chapter of *Souls* is somewhat different.

As Larzer Ziff demonstrates, sight ultimately triumphs over the other senses even in Whitman because the other senses are a threat to prophetic stability and self-confidence. With the appearance of the other senses Whitman's prophetic power of digesting good and evil, ugliness and beauty, into the incorporative self on equal terms "becomes entangled in self-doubt":

> The doubtings, of course, are plotted. It is through a marvelous series of sights that Whitman arrives at the middle point of *Song of Myself*, where he can stand up and, after naming so much else, name himself: "Walt Whitman, an American, one of the roughs, a kosmos." As he compiles those sights he brushes aside the opposition to his gathering strength that comes from sound and touch: "Trippers and askers surround me." But they are not the

8. Denis Donoghue, "Emerson at First: A Commentary on *Nature*," in *Emerson and His Legacy: Essays in Honor of Quentin Anderson*, ed. Stephen Donadio et. al. (Carbondale: Southern Illinois University Press, 1986), pp. 44–45.
9. Walt Whitman, *Leaves of Grass*, ed. Sculley Bradley and Harold W. Blodgett (New York: W. W. Norton, 1973), p. 50; hereafter cited in the text as *LG*.

"Me myself," and when he affirms, "Apart from the pulling and hauling stands what I am," he does so by showing that he "looks."[1]

Unlike Whitman, Du Bois does not attempt to recuperate a threatened self-confidence or a stable self and its powers of incorporation. In the final moments of "The Sorrow Songs" Du Bois is left listening. He does not master the songs but is sent out into the world by them. Tragedy and evil are not assimilated. It is true that, like Whitman, Du Bois transfigures the voices he hears. But he does not incorporate them into the imperial command of his own voice. Through his "Afterthought" he foregrounds the *writtenness* of his transfiguration and the separation between the spirituals and the "book" that is *Souls*.

In "The Mental Traveller" liberty, crucified by society, is born again, though only to undergo perpetually the cycle of defeat and renewal. Du Bois's fear in his "Afterthought" that his book might fall "still born" into the world metaphorically gathers up the dialogues of fathers and sons, of parents and children, which dominate the last five chapters of *Souls*, from the faith of the fathers and the death of the newborn son, to Crummell as father and John as defeated son, and finally to Du Bois as the father listening to the singing of his children. *Souls*, like Blake's "frowning Babe," is created out of a memory and knowledge of the sacrifice of freedom. The same intertwining of memory and transcendence marks the closing moments of Du Bois's *Autobiography*. There, too, as in *Souls*, there is no surrender of hope; there is only an un-American recognition that democratic idealism must remember the past and that this memory sustains the true human purpose of active knowledge:

> This is a wonderful America, which the founding fathers dreamed until their sons drowned it in the blood of slavery and devoured it in greed. Our children must rebuild it. Let then the Dreams of the Dead rebuke the Blind who think that what is will be forever and teach them that what was worth living for must live again and that which merited death must stay dead. Teach us, Forever Dead, there is no Dream but Deed, there is no Deed but Memory. (A 422–243)

The sense of the last sentence is that not only is the dream an activity in its own right but also there can be no meaningful action unless it is also an act of remembering feeding the dream.

---

1. Larzer Ziff, *Literary Democracy: The Declaration of Cultural Independence in America* (New York: Penguin, 1982), pp. 235–236.

William Edward Burghardt Du Bois: A Chronology

1868	Born William Edward Burghardt Du Bois, February 23, in Great Barrington, Massachusetts. Only child of Alfred Du Bois and Mary Silvina Burghardt. Mother and child move to family farm owned by Othello Burghardt, Mary Silvina's father, in South Egremont Plain.
1872	Grandfather Othello Burghardt dies September 19. Family moves back to Great Barrington, where Mary Sylvina works as domestic servant.
1879	Moves with mother to rooms on Railroad Street. Mother suffers stroke, which partially paralyzes her, but must continue to work despite disability.
1883–85	Writes occasionally for *Springfield Republican*, the most influential regional newspaper. Reports on local events for the *New York Globe*, a black weekly, and its successor, the *Freeman*.
1884	Graduates from Great Barrington High School. Works as timekeeper on a construction site.
1885	Mother dies March 23 at age 54. Scholarship arranged by local Congregational churches for Du Bois to attend Fisk University in Nashville. Enters Fisk with sophomore standing. Gravely ill with typhoid fever in October; recovers to resume studies and to edit *Fisk Herald*, the school newspaper.
1886–87	Teaches at black school near Alexandria, Tennessee, for two summers. Begins singing with Mozart Society (Fisk).
1888	Receives B.A. from Fisk. Enters Harvard College as a junior after receiving a Price-Greenleaf grant.
1890	Awarded second prize in Boylston oratorical competition. Receives B.A. *cum laude* in philosophy on June 25. Delivers commencement oration on Jefferson Davis, which receives national press attention. Enters Harvard Graduate School in social science.

1891   Awarded M.A. in history from Harvard. Begins work on doctorate. Presents paper on suppression of African slave trade at meeting of American Historical Association, Washington, D.C.

1892   Awarded grant by Slater Fund to study in Germany at Friedrich Wilhelm University, Berlin.

1893   Grant extended for one more year.

1894   Denied doctoral degree at Friedrich Wilhelm University due to residency requirements. Denied further aid from Slater Fund; returns to Great Barrington. Receives teaching chair in classics at Wilberforce University, Xenia, Ohio.

1895   Awarded Ph.D. in history, first black to receive a Ph.D. from Harvard.

1896   Marries Nina Gomer, student at Wilberforce. Doctoral thesis, *The Suppression of the African Slave-Trade to United States of America, 1638–1870*, published as first volume of Harvard Historical Monograph Series. Hired by University of Pennsylvania to conduct a sociological study on the black population of Philadelphia's Seventh Ward.

1897   Joins Alexander Crummell and other black intellectuals to found the American Negro Academy, an association dedicated to black scholarly achievement. Appointed professor of history and economics, Atlanta University. Edits series of sociological studies on black life, *Atlanta University Studies* (1898–1914). First child, Burghardt Gomer Du Bois, born in Great Barrington on October 2.

1899   *The Philadelphia Negro* published by University of Pennsylvania. Burghardt Gomer Du Bois dies on May 24 in Atlanta; buried in Great Barrington. Articles published in *Atlantic Monthly* and *The Independent*.

1900   In July attends first Pan-African Congress in London; elected secretary and, in his address, declares that "the problem of the twentieth century is the problem of the color line." Enters exhibit at Paris Exposition; wins grand prize for display on black economic development. October 21, daughter Nina Yolande born in Great Barrington.

1901   Publishes "The Freedman's Bureau" in *Atlantic Monthly*.

1902   Booker T. Washington offers him teaching position at Tuskegee Institute; Du Bois declines.

1903   *The Souls of Black Folk* published in April. "The Talented Tenth" published in *The Negro Problem*.

1904   Resigns from Washington's Committee of Twelve for the Advancement of the Negro Race due to ideological differences. Publishes *Credo* in *The Independent*.

1905   Holds first conference of the Niagara Movement; elected general secretary. Founds and edits *The Moon Illustrated Weekly*.

1906   Second meeting of the Niagara Movement. *The Moon* ceases publication. Atlanta riots, with white mobs targeting blacks, occur in September, prompting Du Bois to compose his most famous poem, *A Litany of Atlanta*. After riots Du Bois's wife and daughter move to Great Barrington.

1907   Niagara Movement in disarray due to debt and dissension. Founds and edits *Horizon*, monthly paper that folds in 1910.

1908   Fourth conference of Niagara Movement; few attend.

1909   National Negro Committee, dominated by white liberals, formed (will become NAACP); Du Bois joins. Fifth and last Niagara Conference. *John Brown*, a biography, published.

1910   Appointed director of publications and research for NAACP; also elected to board of directors as only black member. Moves to New York City to found and edit *The Crisis*, official publication of NAACP.

1911   Attends Universal Races Conference in London. *The Quest of the Silver Fleece*, first novel, published. Joins Socialist Party.

1912   Endorses Woodrow Wilson in *The Crisis*; resigns from Socialist Party.

1913   Writes and presents *The Star of Ethiopia*, a pageant staged to commemorate the fiftieth anniversary of emancipation.

1914   Supports women's suffrage in *The Crisis*. Supports Allied effort in World War I despite calling imperialist rivalries a cause of war.

1915   Booker T. Washington dies November 14. *The Negro* published. Protests D. W. Griffith's film *The Birth of a Nation*.

1917   Ill at beginning of year, undergoes kidney operations. Supports establishment of separate training camps for black officers as only alternative to insure black participation in combat.

1918   July editorial for *The Crisis*, "Close Ranks," urging cooperation with white citizens. War Department offers Du Bois commission as army captain to address racial issues, but offer withdrawn after controversy. Goes to Europe in December to evaluate conditions of black troops for NAACP.

1919   Organizes first Pan-African Conference in Paris, elected executive secretary. Returns to U.S. in April and writes "Returning Soldiers" editorial, which U.S. postmaster Burleson tries to suppress; issue sells 106,000 copies, the most ever for *The Crisis*.

1920   Founds and edits *The Brownies' Book*, monthly magazine for children. Publishes *Darkwater: Voices from within the Veil*, a collection of essays.

1921   Second Pan-African Conference held in London, Brussels, and Paris. Signs group protest against Henry Ford's support of the anti-Semitic forgery, *Protocols of the Elders of Zion*.

1922   Works for passage of the Dyer Anti-Lynching Bill, which is blocked by Senate.

1923   Writes "Back to Africa," article attacking Garvey for encouraging racial division. Organizes Pan-African Conference in London, Paris, and Lisbon; declines to attend Paris session due to disproval of French assimilationists. Receives Spingarn Medal from NAACP. Travels to Liberia to represent U.S. at inauguration of president.

1924   Publishes *The Gift of Black Folk: The Negroes in the Making of America*.

1925   Contributes "The Negro Mind Reaches Out" to Alain Locke's *The New Negro: An Interpretation*, one of the most influential works of the Harlem Renaissance.

1926   Founds Krigwa Players, a Harlem theater group. Travels to the Soviet Union to examine life after the Bolshevik Revolution. Praises Soviet achievements in *The Crisis*.

1927   Fourth (and last) Pan-African Conference held in New York.

1928   Daughter Yolande weds poet Countee Cullen in Harlem; marriage ends within a year. Novel *Dark Princess, A Romance*, published.

1929   *The Crisis* faces financial collapse.

1930   Awarded honorary Doctor of Laws degree from Howard University.

1932   Granddaughter, Du Bois Williams, born to Yolande and her second husband, Arnett Williams.

1933   Losing faith in the possibilities of integration; begins to question publicly his position on segregation. Accepts one-year visiting professorship at Atlanta University. Relinquishes editorship of *The Crisis* but retains general control of magazine.

1934   Writes editorials encouraging voluntary segregation and criticizing integrationist policies of NAACP. Resigns as editor of *The Crisis* and from the NAACP. Accepts chairmanship in sociology at Atlanta University. Named editor-in-chief of *Encyclopedia of the Negro*.

1935   Publishes historical study, *Black Reconstruction*.

1936   Spends five months in Germany on grant to study industrial education. Travels through Poland, Soviet Union, Manchuria, China, and Japan.

1938   Receives honorary Doctor of Laws degree from Atlanta University and honorary Doctor of Letters degree from Fisk.

1939   *Black Folk, Then and Now*, revised edition of *The Negro*, published.

1940   Publishes autobiography, *Dusk of Dawn*. Founds and edits *Phylon*, a quarterly magazine examining black issues. Awarded honorary Doctorate of Humane Letters at Wilberforce.

1941–42   Proposes and then coordinates study of southern blacks for black land-grant colleges.

1943   Organizes First Conference of Negro Land-Grant Colleges, Atlanta University. Informed by Atlanta University that he must retire by 1944. Attempts to have decision reversed.

1944   Named first black member of the National Institute of Arts and Letters. Despite his protests, retired from Atlanta University. Although hesitant to work with Walter White, accepts position as director of special research. Moves back to New York; "My Evolving Program for Negro Freedom" published in Rayford Logan's collection *What the Negro Wants*.

1945   Writes weekly column for the Chicago *Defender*. Serves as consultant, with Mary McLeod Bethune and Walter White, at San Francisco conference that drafts the United Nations charter; criticizes charter for failing to oppose colonialism. Presides at Fifth Pan-African Conference, Manchester, England, in October. Nina Du Bois suffers a stroke, which paralyzes her left side. Publishes the first volume of *Encyclopedia of the Negro* with co-author Guy B. Johnson. Publishes an anti-imperialist analysis of the post-war era, *Color and Democracy: Colonies and Peace*. Resigns from American Association of University Professors in protest of conferences held in segregated hotels.

1946   Invites leaders of 20 organizations to New York to draft petition to United Nations on behalf of African Americans; appeal becomes NAACP project.

1947   Edits and writes introduction to *An Appeal to the World*, collection of essays sponsored by the NAACP to enlist international support for the fight against racial discrimination in America. In the United Nations, the appeal is supported by the Soviet Union but opposed by the United States. Publishes *The World and Africa*.

1948   Fired from NAACP after his memorandum critical of Wal-
               ter White and the NAACP board of directors appears in
               The New York Times. Supports Henry Wallace, the Pro-
               gressive Party candidate for president. Takes unpaid position
               as vice-chairman (with Paul Robeson) of the Council of
               African Affairs, an organization listed as "subversive" by the
               United States attorney general. Begins writing for the *Na-
               tional Guardian*.

1949   Helps sponsor and addresses Cultural and Scientific Con-
               ference for World Peace in New York. Attends First World
               Congress of the Defenders of Peace in Paris. Travels to the
               All-Union Conference of Peace Proponents in Moscow.

1950   Nina Gomer Du Bois dies in Baltimore in July; buried in
               Great Barrington. Elected chairman of the Peace Informa-
               tion Center, an organization dedicated to the international
               peace movement and the banning of nuclear weapons. Or-
               ganization disbands under pressure from the Department of
               Justice. Du Bois nominated by American Labor Party as
               U.S. senator from New York. Receives 4 percent of the vote
               statewide, 15 percent in Harlem.

1951   Secretly marries Shirley Graham, aged 45, a writer, teacher,
               and civil rights activist, on Valentine's Day. Indicted earlier
               that month as "unregistered foreign agent" under the Mc-
               Cormick Act. Du Bois, along with 4 other officers of the
               Peace Information Center, alleged to be agents of foreign
               interests. Fingerprinted, searched, and handcuffed before
               released on bail in Washington, D.C. National lecture tours
               and fundraising campaign for defense expenses total over
               $35,000. Five-day trial in Washington ends in acquittal.

1952   Publishes *In Battle for Peace*, an account of his trial. State
               Department refuses Du Bois a passport on grounds that his
               foreign travel is not in the national interest. Later, State
               Department demands a statement declaring that he is not
               a Communist Party member; Du Bois refuses. Advocacy of
               left-wing political positions widens distance between Du
               Bois and black mainstream.

1953   Prints eulogy for Stalin in *National Guardian*. Reads 23rd
               Psalm at the funeral of Julius and Ethel Rosenberg, exe-
               cuted as Soviet spies. Awarded International Peace Prize by
               World Peace Council.

1954   Surprised reaction to the Supreme Court Brown decision,
               which outlawed public school segregation: "I have seen the
               impossible happen."

1955   Refused passport to attend World Youth Festival in Warsaw.

1956   Supports Reverend Martin Luther King, Jr., during the Montgomery bus boycott. Refused passport to lecture in the People's Republic of China.

1957   Publishes *The Ordeal of Mansart*, first volume *The Black Flame*, a planned trilogy of historical novels chronicling black life from Reconstruction to mid-twentieth century. Bust of Du Bois unveiled at the Schomburg Collection of the New York Public Library. Refused passport to attend independence ceremonies in Ghana. Great-grandson Arthur Edward McFarlane II born.

1958   Ninetieth birthday celebration at Roosevelt Hotel, New York; 2,000 people attend. Begins *The Autobiography of W. E. B. Du Bois*, drawn largely from other works. Ruling of Supreme Court allows Du Bois to obtain passport. World tour includes England, France, Belgium, Holland, Czechoslovakia, East Germany, and the Soviet Union. Receives honorary doctorate from Humbolt University in East Berlin, known as Friedrich Wilhelm University when Du Bois attended in 1892–94.

1959   Meets with Nikita Khrushchev. In Beijing, makes broadcast to Africa over Radio Beijing and meets with Mao Zedong and Zhou Enlai. Awarded the International Lenin Prize. Publishes the second volume of *The Black Flame* trilogy, *Mansart Builds a School*.

1960   Participates in the celebration of Ghana's establishment as a republic. Travels to Nigeria for inauguration of its first African governor-general.

1961   Daughter Yolande dies of heart attack in March. *Worlds of Color*, final book in *The Black Flame* trilogy, published. Accepts invitation of Kwame Nkrumah to move to Ghana and direct revival of the *Encyclopedia Africana* project. Before leaving for Africa, applies for membership in the Communist party.

1962   Travels to China. Autobiography published in Soviet Union.

1963   Becomes citizen of Ghana. Turns 95 in February. Dies in Accra, Ghana, August 27, the eve of civil rights march on Washington. Buried in state funeral in Accra on August 29.

1968   *The Autobiography of W. E. B. Du Bois* published in the United States.

Selected Bibliography

•Indicates works included or excerpted in this Norton Critical Edition.

Works of W. E. B. Du Bois

The Suppression of the African Slave-Trade to the United States of America, 1638–1870. New York: Longmans, Green, 1896.

Atlanta University Publications on the Study of Negro Problems. Publications of the Atlanta University Conferences, ed. Du Bois (1898–1913).

The Philadelphia Negro: A Social Study. Boston: Ginn and Company, 1899.

The Souls of Black Folk: Essays and Sketches. Chicago: A. C. McClurg, 1903.

John Brown. Philadelphia: George W. Jacobs, 1909.

The Quest of the Silver Fleece: A Novel. Chicago: A. C. McClurg, 1911.

The Negro. New York: Henry Holt, 1915.

Darkwater: Voices from within the Veil. New York: Harcourt, Brace & Howe, 1920.

The Gift of Black Folk: Negroes in the Making of America. Boston: Stratford, 1924.

Dark Princess: A Romance. New York: Harcourt, Brace, 1928.

Africa—Its Place in Modern History. Girard, Kansas: Haldeman-Julius, 1930.

Africa—Its Geography, People and Products. Girard, Kansas: Haldeman-Julius, 1930.

Black Reconstruction: An Essay toward a History of the Part Which Black Folk Played in the Attempt to Reconstruct Democracy in America, 1860–1880. New York: Harcourt, Brace, 1935.

Black Folk Then and Now: An Essay in the History and Sociology of the Negro Race. New York: Henry Holt, 1939.

Dusk of Dawn: An Essay toward an Autobiography of a Race Concept. New York: Harcourt, Brace, 1940.

Color and Democracy: Colonies and Peace. New York: Harcourt, Brace, 1945.

The World and Africa: An Inquiry into the Part Which Africa Has Played in World History. New York: Viking, 1947.

In Battle for Peace: The Story of My 83rd Birthday. With Comment by Shirley Graham. New York: Masses & Mainstream, 1959.

Mansart Builds a School. New York: Mainstream, 1959.

Worlds of Color. New York: Mainstream, 1959.

An ABC of Color: Selections from over a Half Century of the Writings of W. E. B. Du Bois. Berlin: Seven Seas, 1963.

The Autobiography of W. E. B. Du Bois: A Soliloquy on Viewing My Life from the Last Decade of Its First Century. Herbert Aptheker, ed. New York: International Publishers, 1968.

Collections

Aptheker, Herbert, ed. *Against Racism: Unpublished Essays, Papers, Addresses, 1887–1961. W. E. B. Du Bois.* Amherst: University of Massachusetts Press, 1985.

——, ed. *The Complete Published Works of W. E. B. Du Bois.* 35 vols. Millwood, NY: Kraus-Thomson, 1973.

——, ed. *The Correspondence of* W. E. B. Du Bois. 3 vols. Amherst: University of Massachusetts Press, 1973–78.
——, ed. *Writings by* W. E. B. Du Bois in Periodicals Edited by Others. 4 vols. Millwood, NY: Kraus-Thomson, 1982.
Foner, Philip S., ed. W. E. B. Du Bois Speaks: Speeches and Addresses 1890–1919. New York: Pathfinder, 1970.
Huggins, Nathan I., ed. W. E. B. Du Bois: Writings. New York: Library of America, 1986.
Lewis, David Levering, ed. W. E. B. Du Bois: A Reader. New York: Henry Holt, 1985.
Sundquist, Eric J., ed. *The Oxford* W. E. B. Du Bois Reader. New York: Oxford University Press, 1996.

Bibliographies

Aptheker, Herbert. *Annotated Bibliography of the Published Writings of* W. E. B. Du Bois. Millwood, NY: Kraus-Thomson, 1973.
McDonnell, Robert W., and Paul C. Partington. W. E. B. Du Bois: A Bibliography of Writings About Him. Whittier, CA.: Paul C. Partington Book Publisher, 1989.
Partington, Paul C. W. E. B. Du Bois: A Bibliography of His Published Writings. Whittier, CA: Paul C. Partington Book Publisher, 1977.

Biographies

Broderick, Francis L. W. E. B. Du Bois: A Negro Leader in Time of Crisis. Stanford: Stanford University Press, 1959.
Du Bois, Shirley Graham. *His Day Is Marching On: A Memoir of* W. E. B. Du Bois. Philadelphia: Lippincott, 1971.
•Lewis, David Levering. W. E. B. Du Bois: Biography of a Race, 1868–1919. New York: Henry Holt, 1993.
Marable, Manning. W. E. B. Du Bois: Black Radical Democrat. Boston: Twayne, 1986.
Rudwick, Elliot M. W. E. B. Du Bois: Propagandist of the Negro Protest. 1960; rpt. New York: Atheneum, 1968.

Critical Works

Appiah, Anthony. "The Uncompleted Argument: Du Bois and the Illusion of Race." *Critical Inquiry* 12 (Autumn 1985): 21–37.
Aptheker, Herbert. *The Literary Legacy of* W. E. B. Du Bois. White Plains, NY: Kraus International, 1989.
Baker, Houston A. Jr. "The Black Man of Culture: W. E. B. Du Bois and *The Souls of Black Folk*." In *Long Black Song*. Charlottesville: University of Virginia Press, 1972.
Bell, Bernard, Emily Grosholz, and James Stewart, eds. W. E. B. Du Bois on Race and Culture: Philosophy, Politics, and Poetics. New York: Routledge, Chapman, and Hall, 1996.
Blight, David W. "W. E. B. Du Bois and the Struggle for American Historical Memory." In *History and Memory in African-American Culture*, ed. Genevieve Fabre and Robert O'Meally. New York: Oxford University Press, 1994.
Bremen, Brian A. "Du Bois, Emerson, and the 'Fate' of Black Folk." *American Literary Realism* 24 (Spring 1992): 80–88.
•Bruce, Dickson D., Jr. "W. E. B. Du Bois and the Idea of Double Consciousness." *American Literature: A Journal of Literary History, Criticism, and Bibliography* 64.2 (June 1992): 299–309.

Byerman, Keith. *Seizing the Word: History, Art, and the Self in the Work of W. E. B. Du Bois*. Athens: University of Georgia Press, 1994.

Early, Gerald, ed. *Lure and Loathing: Essays on Race, Identity, and the Ambivalence of Assimilation*. New York: Allen Lane, 1993.

Frederickson, George M. *The Black Image in the White Mind: The Debate on Afro-American Character and Destiny, 1817–1914*. New York: Harper and Row, 1971.

•Gooding-Williams, Robert. "Du Bois's Counter-Sublime." *The Massachusetts Review: A Quarterly of Literature, the Arts and Public Affairs* 35.2 (Summer 1994): 202–24.

Herring, Scott. "Du Bois and the Minstrels." *MELUS* 22 (Summer 1997): 3–18.

Jones, Gavin. "'Whose Line Is It Anyway?' W. E. B. Du Bois and the Language of the Color-Line." In *Race Consciousness: African-American Studies for the New Century*, ed. Judith Jackson Fossett and Jeffrey A. Tucker. New York: New York University Press, 1997.

•McKay, Nellie. "W. E. B. Du Bois: The Black Women in His Writings—Selected Fictional and Autobiographical Portraits." In *Critical Essays on W. E. B. Du Bois*, ed. William L. Andrews. Boston: G. K. Hall, 1985.

Meier, August. "The Paradox of W. E. B. Du Bois." In *Negro Thought in America, 1880–1915; Racial Ideologies in the Age of Booker T. Washington*. Ann Arbor: University of Michigan Press, 1963.

•Mizruchi, Susan. "Neighbors, Strangers, Corpses: Death and Sympathy in the Early Writings of W. E. B. Du Bois." In *Centuries' Ends, Narrative Means*, ed. Robert Newman. Stanford, CA: Stanford University Press, 1996.

Peterson, Dale. "Notes from the Underworld: Dostoyevsky, Du Bois, and the Discovery of the Ethnic Soul." *Massachusetts Review* 35 (Summer 1994): 225–47.

Posnock, Ross. "The Distinction of Du Bois: Aesthetics, Pragmatism, Politics." *American Literary History* 7 (Fall 1995): 500–524.

Rampersad, Arnold. *The Art and Imagination of W. E. B. Du Bois*. Cambridge: Harvard University Press, 1976.

•Rampersad, Arnold, and Deborah E. McDowell, eds. *Slavery and the Literary Imagination: Du Bois's The Souls of Black Folk*. Baltimore: Johns Hopkins University Press, 1989.

Schrager, Cynthia D. "Both Sides of the Veil: Race, Science, and Mysticism in W. E. B. Du Bois." *American Quarterly* 48 (December 1996): 551–87.

•Sundquist, Eric J. "Swing Low: *The Souls of Black Folk*. In *To Wake the Nations*. Cambridge, MA: Harvard University Press, 1993.

Warren, Kenneth W. "Troubled Black Humanity in *The Souls of Black Folk* and *The Autobiography of an Ex-Colored Man*." In *The Cambridge Companion to American Realism and Naturalism: Howells to London*, ed. Donald Pizer. Cambridge: Cambridge University Press, 1995.

West, Cornel. "W. E. B. Du Bois: The Jamesian Organic Intellectual." In *The American Evasion of Philosophy: A Genealogy of Pragmatism*. Madison: University of Wisconsin Press, 1989.

Williamson, Joel. *The Crucible of Race: Black-White Relations in the American South Since Emancipation*. New York: Oxford University Press, 1984.

Zamir, Shamoon, *Dark Voices: W. E. B. Du Bois and American Thought, 1888–1903*. Chicago: University of Chicago Press, 1995.

•———. "'The Sorrow Songs' / 'Song of Myself': Du Bois, the Crisis of Leadership, and Prophetic Imagination." In *The Black Columbiad: Defining Moments in African American Literature and Culture*. Cambridge, MA: Harvard University Press, 1994.